DATE DUE

DEMCO 38-296

The Philosophy of Legal Reasoning

*A Collection of Essays by Philosophers
and Legal Scholars*

Series Editor

Scott Brewer
Harvard Law School

A GARLAND SERIES
READINGS IN PHILOSOPHY
ROBERT NOZICK, *ADVISOR*
HARVARD UNIVERSITY

Contents of the Series

Moral Theory and Legal Reasoning

Edited with an introduction by

Scott Brewer
Harvard University

GARLAND PUBLISHING, INC.
A MEMBER OF THE TAYLOR & FRANCIS GROUP
New York & London
1998

Library of Congress Cataloging-in-Publication Data

Moral theory and legal reasoning / edited with an introduction by
  Scott Brewer.
        p.   cm. — (The philosophy of legal reasoning ; 3)
     Includes bibliographical references.
     ISBN 0-8153-2657-2 (v. 3 : alk. paper). — ISBN 0-8153-2654-8
     (set : alk. paper)
       1. Law—Methodology. 2. Law—Interpretation and construction.
     3. Judicial process. 4. Law and ethics. 5. Reasoning. I. Brewer,
     Scott. II. Series.
     K213.P494 1998 vol. 3
     340'.1 s—dc21   98-5171
     [340'.1]   CIP

Printed on acid-free, 250-year-life paper
Manufactured in the United States of America

Contents

Introduction

This five-volume set contains some of this century's most influential or thought-provoking articles on the subject of legal argument that have appeared in Anglo-American philosophy journals and law reviews. Legal decisions have long been a deeply significant part of the history and life of societies that aspire to satisfy some version of the "rule of law" ideal. These decisions—at least those rendered by a jurisdiction's most prominent courts—are also often accompanied by detailed publicly available statements of the arguments supporting those decisions. For these reasons, among many others, understanding the dynamics of legal argument is of vital interest not only to legal academics, judges, lawyers, and law students, but also to citizens who are subject to law and who vote, directly or indirectly, for the legislators, regulators, and judges who write and interpret laws.

Because of the importance to civil societies of legal decisons and the legal arguments offered to justify them, the subject of legal argument has long been closely studied by scholars and other analysts. These theorists have explicated and criticized the dynamics of legal argument from vastly different perspectives. It is thus not surprising that these theorists have reached strikingly different conclusions, with equally distinct concerns and emphases. Theorists of legal argument have, for example, maintained that legal argument is principally driven by *a priori* legal-cum-moral truths applied to individual cases by formal logical inferences, or that the driving force of legal argument is a more or less thinly veiled imposition of a judge's preferred social or economic policy, or that legal argument is or should be (theorists sometimes blur the line between the descriptive and the prescriptive in their analyses) the incessantly self-critical and self-correcting reasoned elaboration of legal rules and standards that transcend immediate partisan results, or that legal arguments offered by judges are little more than a mystificatory and would-be legitimating veneer covering such darker motives as race, class, or gender bias, or that legal argument is the interpretive effort by judges in the forum of principle to make the law the best it can be from a moral point of view, or is the decision of those legal officials who hold authoritative power by virtue of socially adopted rules.

This set of volumes represents all of the theories just encapsulated, and others as well. As the brief, and certainly incomplete, list in the foregoing paragraph suggests, theorists of legal argument produce what can seem a whelming welter of diverse explanations. Even so, the vast majority of theories of legal argument revolve around two central focal points—rather, perhaps, like the oval-shaped ellipse, which orbits around two fixed foci.

One focus is the role of different *modes of logical inference* in legal argument. There are four basic logical structures that operate in legal argument (indeed, it can be argued plausibly that these are the four that organize all arguments, in all intellectual domains): *deduction, induction, abduction,* and *analogy.* It may help the reader to have a few basic definitions of these terms at the outset—even though by no means all the theorists whose articles are included will use these terms in their analyses. First, the basic term 'argument.' The defining characteristic of *argument,* including legal argument, is the inference of a conclusion from one or more premises. As just noted, all arguments, including legal argument, deploy one or more of four principal and irreducible (though analogical inference is tricky in this regard) modes of logical inference: (i) *deductive inference,* in which the truth of the premises guarantees the truth of the conclusion as long as the conclusion is arrived at by an acceptable deductive inference rule; (ii) *inductive inference,* in which the truth of the premises cannot guarantee the truth of the conclusion, but when the premises are carefully chosen, their truth can warrant belief in the truth of the conclusion to greater or lesser degrees of probability; (iii) *abductive inference,* in which an explanatory hypothesis is inferred as the conclusion of an argument with two distinct types of premise: first, a proposition that describes some event or phenomenon that the abductive reasoner believes stands in need of *explanation,* and second, a proposition to the effect that, *if* the explanatory hypothesis that is inferred ("abducted") were in fact *true* or otherwise warranted, then the explanandum would be sufficiently explained for the reasoner's purposes; and (iv) *analogical inference,* in which a reasoner relies on particular examples to discover (indeed, to "abduce") a rule that states what are the relevant similarities or differences between a less well-known item (the "target" of the analogical inference) and a better known item (the "source" of the analogical inference). The other focal point of theories of legal argument is the role of various types of *norms* in legal argument, including *legal norms* (norms issued by proper legal authorities or endorsed by other social norms—the proper account of legal norms divides "legal positivists" and "natural law" theorists), *moral norms* (norms concerned with right and wrong), *epistemic norms* (norms concerned with true or otherwise warranted beliefs), *linguistic norms* (norms concerned with understanding the meaning of texts), and "instrumental" or "prudential" norms (those nonmoral norms that are "instrumental" to helping a reasoner achieve a goal he or she has chosen to pursue).

Even when they do not explicitly use this exact terminology of "logical inference," "deduction," "induction," "norm," and the like, in one way or another all of the articles in these volumes are within the intellectual gravitational orbit of these two focal points. One hastens to add that, far from being dry and remote "academic" exercises, the inquiries pursued by these articles touch on many of the most pressing and contentious issues in contemporary legal, moral, and political debate—as the list of conclusions of various theories of legal argument in the second paragraph of this introduction clearly indicates.

Several criteria have guided the selection of articles in this set. The broad impact of an article among scholars, judges, and lawyers was certainly a leading criterion, and a great many of the articles satisfy it. But that criterion was by no means the only one. Some of the articles in these volumes are fairly recent, and more time will be needed to assess their enduring impact on the worlds of legal thought and practice. It can be said fairly that even these more recent articles present fresh and thought-provoking claims and insights, worthy of being considered even if only to be ultimately rejected. The criterion of intellectually fertile provocation guided the selection of some of the older articles in the volumes (for example, some of those in volume one), which were chosen neither for fame nor influence but rather because they present an important perspective on an issue that—in this editor's opinion—has received far too little attention in twentieth-century American jurisprudence and legal education: the role of *deductive* inference in legal argument. Even though the role of one or more of the four basic logical inferences is a focus of theories of legal argument, generations of legal academics, judges, and lawyers have tended to ignore or understate the role of deductive inference, largely without understanding enough about what deductive inference is or the many very important ways in which it does guide legal argument. They have been led to this point largely because of the influentially expressed and often parroted sentiment of Justice Oliver Wendell Holmes Jr. and several of his followers, that "[t]he life of the law has not been logic: it has been experience."[1] By 'logic' Holmes meant deductive logic, and his maxim-al hyperbole has done much to encumber the proper understanding of the rational dynamics of legal argument. Several of the articles in these volumes were chosen to help readers rediscover and revivify this important issue and to see its importance for broader political and moral questions.

All in all, I am confident that the articles in these volumes will well repay the attentiveness of readers who wish to think seriously about the nature of significance of legal argument as a vital part of broader legal and political processes, as long as they bring reading minds that are fairly "braced with labor and invention."

Notes

[1] Oliver W. Holmes, *The Common Law*, ed. Mark DeWolfe Howe (Boston: Little, Brown, 1963) p.5.

[1] Oliver W. Holmes, *The Common Law* 1 ed. Mark DeWolfe Howe (?: ?, 1963).

DAVID O. BRINK

Legal Theory,
Legal Interpretation,
and Judicial Review

Though constitutional theory has often acknowledged its connections with political philosophy, it has rarely noticed any interesting connections with that part of legal philosophy concerned with the nature of law (legal theory). There are, however, connections between constitutional theory and legal theory which are worth noticing and developing. In particular, familiar disputes within constitutional theory about whether recent Supreme Court decisions exceed the legitimate scope of judicial review depend in a rather complicated way on familiar disputes within legal theory about the nature and determinacy of law. This connection can be located within the theory of interpretation, for the disputes both within legal theory and within constitutional theory are best seen and assessed as disputes over the nature of legal interpretation.

i. LEGAL THEORY

Two issues of concern within recent legal theory are the nature of law and the extent to which law is complete or determinate. What features must a social system have in order to be a legal system? When is a standard or norm within a social system a legal standard? How is law related to morality? These are familiar questions about the nature of law. Different theories of the nature of law have different implications for the completeness of law. We might call cases *hard* cases if they raise legal issues which are highly controversial, issues about which reasonable people with legal

I would like to thank Paul Brest, Ted Everett, Dagfinn Føllesdal, Thomas Grey, David Lyons, Alan Sidelle, Bonny Sweeney, the Editors of *Philosophy & Public Affairs*, and an audience at Case Western Reserve Law School for helpful comments on earlier versions of this article.

training disagree. The completeness issue is usually understood to concern the extent to which hard cases are legally determinate. If there are cases which are genuinely legally indeterminate, courts can decide such cases only by exercising discretion (that is, by exercising at least a limited legislative capacity).

2. THE STANDARD THEORY OF LAW AND HARD CASES

It is a common view, especially among lawyers in jurisprudential discussions of hard cases (as opposed to their view in the briefs they write in hard cases), that in such cases the law is indeterminate and that judges must exercise discretion if they are to decide these cases. Philosophers of law such as Ronald Dworkin and Rolf Sartorius have challenged this view in recent years,[1] but it must still be regarded as the standard view of hard cases. H.L.A. Hart's *Concept of Law* is still the clearest and most persuasive statement of both the standard theory of hard cases and the standard theory of law on which it rests. Hart argues as follows.[2]

(1) The law consists of legal rules formulated in general terms.
(2) All general terms are "open textured": they contain a "core" of settled meaning and a "penumbra" or "periphery" where their meaning is not determinate.[3]
(3) There will always be cases not covered by the core meaning of legal terms within existing legal rules.
(4) Hence these cases are legally indeterminate.
(5) Hence courts cannot decide such cases on legal grounds.

1. Ronald Dworkin, *Taking Rights Seriously*, 2d ed. (London: Duckworth, 1978) (hereafter TRS), esp. chaps. 2, 4, 13, and *A Matter of Principle* (Cambridge: Harvard University Press, 1985) (hereafter MP), chap. 5; Rolf Sartorius, "Social Policy and Judicial Legislation," *American Philosophical Quarterly* 8 (1971): 151–60, *Individual Conduct and Social Norms* (Encino, Calif.: Dickenson, 1975), pp. 181–210, and "Bayes' Theorem, Hard Cases, and Judicial Discretion," *Georgia Law Review* 11 (1977): 1269–75.

2. See H.L.A. Hart, *The Concept of Law* (New York: Oxford University Press, 1961) (hereafter CL), pp. 121–32. See also H.L.A. Hart, *Essays in Jurisprudence and Philosophy* (New York: Oxford University Press, 1983), pp. 7–8, 107–8, 136, 157. I understand from conversation with Joseph Raz that he intends his "sources thesis" in *The Authority of Law* (New York: Oxford University Press, 1979), chap. 3, to rest on a semantic argument very similar to the kind of semantic argument which, we will see, Hart makes in CL.

3. Legal terms are also open textured for the related reason that lawmakers suffer from limited knowledge and limited determinacy of aim. They cannot anticipate all possible situations that may arise under a rule and do not have well-formed aims about such situations (CL, p. 125).

(6) Hence courts must decide such cases, if at all, on nonlegal (for example, moral and political) grounds; that is, the courts must exercise judicial discretion and make, rather than apply, law.

Hart gives a simple illustration of his claim: the legislature enacts a law which prohibits the introduction of vehicles into a park. Hart claims that "vehicle" has in this context a core of settled meaning which includes citizens' cars and motorcycles, so the rule prohibits these vehicles from being in the park. But, Hart claims, other vehicles, such as police cars and bicycles, fall within the peripheral meaning of "vehicle," so there is no fact of the matter as to whether the rule prohibits these vehicles. A judge deciding cases on the periphery must make a *nonarbitrary choice.* Hart also mentions the more interesting example of civil (tort) laws which hold manufacturers liable for damages resulting from injuries caused to others by the negligent manufacture of their products. Under such laws manufacturers are expected to exercise *due care* in the manufacture of their goods. Certain conduct clearly meets, and other conduct clearly fails to meet, the standard of due care. The laws specifying manufacturers' liability cover these cases. But reasonable people will dispute about whether other cases meet or fail to meet the standard of due care. Parties to these disputes cannot be convicted of failing to understand the meaning of "due care"; its meaning is indeterminate in these applications. Consequently, the rules of manufacturers' liability do not cover these cases. Courts must decide such cases by exercising discretion.

3. RULES AND PRINCIPLES

As is well known, Dworkin disagrees with Hart's claims about hard cases. Instead, Dworkin claims, in virtually every case, including the hardest of hard cases, one litigant is entitled—as a matter of legal right—to a decision in his favor. Dworkin's disagreement with Hart over hard cases is usually understood to depend upon their disagreement over the nature of law. Dworkin thinks the law is richer than Hart does: the law consists of principles as well as rules. We shall see below why this disagreement with Hart over the question of whether law consists only of rules is rather superficial and so is, among other things, inadequate to explain the depth of their disagreement over the nature of law and hard cases. In order to see this, however, we must examine the usual understanding of the disagreement between Dworkin and Hart.

3

Though there are various ways in which Dworkin wants to disagree with Hart, it is clear that an important part of his disagreement is with premise (1) in Hart's argument about hard cases. Dworkin denies that the law consists solely of rules which have been explicitly enacted: the law also consists of principles and policies which do not depend for their legal status upon any kind of prior official, social recognition or enactment. Dworkin uses two examples to illustrate this claim: *Riggs* v. *Palmer*[4] and *Henningsen* v. *Bloomfield Motors, Inc.*[5]

In *Riggs*, the court declared, contrary to the "plain meaning" of the relevant probate statutes, that an heir could not inherit under the provisions of an otherwise valid will if he or she murdered the testator. While conceding that the statute did not bar inheritance under such conditions, the court held that it is a fundamental principle of the common law that "no one shall be permitted to profit from his own fraud, or to take advantage of his own wrong, or to found any claim upon his own iniquity, or to acquire property by his own crime."[6]

In *Henningsen* there was a contract to buy an automobile, signed by both parties, which expressly limited the manufacturer's liability to "making good defective parts." The contract was properly executed, and there seemed no other established legal rule which could expand the manufacturer's liability. Henningsen's wife was injured as the result of defects in the manufacture of his car. Henningsen sued to collect compensatory damages, and the court found for Henningsen despite the express limitations in the contract. The court cited various general principles of law. Despite its recognition of principles requiring the enforcement of freely made contracts, the court based its decision on the following principles: (i) manufacturers who produce potentially dangerous products such as automobiles have special responsibilities which require courts to ensure that the terms of contracts involving such manufacturers are fair to both public and consumer interests; (ii) courts will not be used as instruments of injustice; and (iii) courts will not enforce contracts in which one party takes unfair advantage of the other's economic necessities.

Dworkin claims that these (and many other) cases illustrate the existence of legal principles which are different from legal rules and which Hart's "model of rules" cannot accommodate. But what exactly is the dif-

4. 115 N.Y. 506, 22 N.E. 188 (1889).
5. 32 N.J. 358, 161 A.2d 69 (1960).
6. 115 N.Y. at 511, 22 N.E. at 190.

ference between rules and principles? If these common law principles are to differ from legal rules, they cannot be simply holdings in previous case law, for Hart's model of rules can surely explain the legal status of precedent. At points Dworkin suggests that the difference between principles and rules is primarily formal; rules and principles function in different ways. Rules apply in an all-or-nothing fashion, whereas principles do not (TRS, p. 24). And principles have weight, while rules do not (TRS, pp. 26–27). Though I cannot argue the claim here, I think that these formal distinctions are dubious. Fortunately, Dworkin also provides an informal account of the nature of principles and their relation to rules:

> True, if we were challenged to back up our claim that some principle is a principle of law, we would mention any prior cases in which that principle was cited, or figured in the argument. We would also mention any statute that seemed to exemplify that principle (even better if the principle was cited in the preamble of the statute, or in the committee reports or other legislative documents that accompanied it). Unless we could find some such institutional support, we would probably fail to make out our case, and the more support we found, the more weight we could claim for the principle. (TRS, p. 40)

The suggestion here seems to be that principles provide the *rationale* for legal rules. We might develop this suggestion as follows. According to Hart, (the primary) legal rules are law by virtue of having the sort of pedigree specified in the legal system's rule of recognition (CL, pp. 77–107). These legal rules—call them *first-order legal standards*—are typically, though not necessarily, the result of authoritative enactment. Now, legal principles of the sort exemplified in *Riggs* and *Henningsen*, though not authoritatively enacted, may be understood as part of the law because they underlie or provide the rationale for legal rules. Call these legal principles *second-order legal standards.*

Dworkin's own view of legal principles is somewhat more complex than this.[7] But this is a good first approximation to his views and represents a

---

7. Dworkin, of course, does not use the terms "first-order" and "second-order legal standards." These are my technical terms intended to suggest that the latter (Dworkin's principles) are to be identified largely by their relation to the former (particular statutes, constitutional provisions, precedents, legal institutions, etc.). I do not mean to suggest that second-order legal standards are in any interesting sense "second-class" legal standards. Moreover, these technical terms allow me to remain neutral in the debate between Dworkin and some of his critics over whether (to use my terminology) second-order standards include

5

plausible understanding of the nature of the legal principles exemplified in *Riggs* and *Henningsen* and their difference from legal rules.

It is Dworkin's view that the law consists of both rules and principles. But why is this? Why regard these second-order standards (principles) as legal standards? Dworkin says that what he means by calling these standards legal standards is that they are considerations which judges "must take into account" when deciding cases (TRS, pp. 26, 35). But how are we to understand this explanation? Does Dworkin mean to make the normative claim that judges would be making a moral or political mistake by failing to consult these principles, or perhaps the descriptive, sociological claim that they would be likely to trigger critical attitudes from other legal principals if they failed to consult these principles? There are problems with either interpretation of Dworkin's explanation. The normative claim, even if true, would seem to run together the issues of what judges have an obligation to do and what the law is or requires. Without further argument, this would simply beg the question against Hart and other legal positivists. The descriptive, sociological claim would seem to establish that there are legal principles which differ from legal rules, but it makes it difficult to see Dworkin's complaint about Hart. For Hart would presumably claim that in systems where failure to appeal to underlying principles would trigger critical attitudes among members of the legal community, the rule of recognition will recognize this relationship between principles and rules as a source of law and so recognize these second-order standards as legal standards.

For these reasons, Dworkin must mean something different from either the normative or the sociological claim. But what? The answer which I think we can and should give and which Dworkin's more recent claims suggest is that these principles are part of the law because failure to appeal to them would involve an *interpretive* mistake.[8] This brings us to ques-

---

policies as well as principles. In fact, the account of legal interpretation developed below (Sec. 11) suggests that this dispute cannot be answered in the abstract but only in the process of constructing theories of law for particular legal systems and particular bodies of law within such systems.

8. See Ronald Dworkin, *Law's Empire* (Cambridge: Harvard University Press, 1986) (hereafter LE). Dworkin himself does not explicitly make the connection between his interpretive conception of law and his earlier criticism of Hart's "model of rules." Also, we should notice a difference between Dworkin's and my interpretive explanation of the legal status of second-order standards. As we shall see below, I distinguish this interpretive construal of the claim that judges "must take into account" second-order standards from the

tions about the nature of interpretation and allied issues about the nature of meaning.

4. INTERPRETATION AND SEMANTICS

It is in part because Dworkin thinks there is law in addition to legal rules that he thinks that legal indeterminacy and the need for judicial discretion do not follow from the existence of open texture in legal rules.[9] It would be a mistake, though, to dispute Hart's theory of hard cases on this basis alone. If Hart's semantic claim in premise (2) of his argument is true, then we should expect to find legal indeterminacies even if the law consists of principles in addition to rules. Legal principles, as well as legal rules, contain general terms which have open texture. And it would be absurd to suppose that wherever the meaning of a legal rule is unclear, there is a legal principle whose meaning is. Most interesting and controversial cases will occur in the penumbra of rules and principles (in *Henningsen*, for example, whether Henningsen's contract was too unjust to enforce could not be construed as settled by the core meaning of "injustice").

Any serious criticism of Hart's theory of hard cases, therefore, must address his semantic assumptions. Nor should the need to think about the semantics of legal interpretation be surprising. Judges, lawyers, and other legal principals must interpret the *language* of various legal standards such as constitutional provisions, statutes, and precedents. Different theories of legal interpretation will rest, implicitly or explicitly, at least in part upon different semantic theories (that is, different theories about the meaning and reference of language). The relevance of semantic theory to legal interpretation is often overlooked,[10] but semantic theory has impor-

---

normative interpretation of that same claim discussed above. It is much less clear that Dworkin makes any such distinction, either in his earlier writings or in LE. In my "Legal Positivism and Natural Law Reconsidered," *The Monist* 63 (1985): 364–87, I argue, among other things, that this is a defect in Dworkin's earlier work, and I think similar criticisms apply to Dworkin's claims about legal interpretation in LE. This disagreement will not, however, be a focus of the present article (indeed, I think Dworkin should find quite a bit to agree with here). In the notes below I point out places where this disagreement might be relevant.

9. *Riggs* and *Henningsen* both illustrate the importance of legal principles not only for cases where the legal rules are unclear but also for cases where the legal rules are clear.

10. But see, e.g., Reed Dickerson, *The Interpretation and Application of Statutes* (Boston: Little, Brown, 1975); Michael Moore, "The Semantics of Judging," *Southern California Law Review* 54 (1981): 151–294; and Frederick Schauer, "An Essay on Constitutional Language," *UCLA Law Review* 29 (1982): 797–832.

tant lessons to teach us about the appropriate structure of legal interpretation.

It is useful to approach these issues about the semantics of legal interpretation by examining some of Dworkin's claims about judicial discretion. Dworkin distinguishes three senses of "discretion" (TRS, pp. 32–33):

(a) Weak sense (a): A judge has discretion in this sense just in case she must exercise judgment in making her decision.
(b) Weak sense (b): A judge has discretion in this sense just in case her decision is final and authoritative.
(c) Strong sense: A judge has discretion in this sense just in case her decision is not controlled by standards set by the authority in question.

Only (c) is relevant to whether judges must exercise a (perhaps limited) legislative function in hard cases. The usual arguments for judicial discretion (in the strong sense) seem to depend upon equivocations between these different senses of discretion. The Legal Realists (at least the "rule skeptics" among them) equivocate between (b) and (c), because they fail to distinguish between finality and infallibility of judicial decisions (compare CL, pp. 138–44). And Hart seems to equivocate between (a) and (c).

5. The Traditional Theory of Law and the Traditional Semantic Theory

I think Hart's argument for the need for discretion does involve something like the inference from (a) to (c), but it would be a mistake to think that this is mere confusion or equivocation on his part. Hart's claims about the open texture of language allow him both to infer (a) from reasonable disagreement about the law and to infer (c) from (a). When reasonable people with legal training disagree about the extension of a term, we are in the penumbra of the term's meaning, and its application is, therefore, indeterminate.

The claim that general terms are open textured is a fairly familiar one. But what is its justification? It is explained most naturally, I think, as relying on a traditional empiricist semantic theory of the sort held by Locke, Frege, C. I. Lewis, and Rudolph Carnap.[11] My discussion of these seman-

11. John Locke, *An Essay concerning Human Understanding*, ed. P. H. Nidditch (New

tic issues will, of necessity, ride roughshod over many interesting details; however, I do not believe that the schematic nature of my discussion will produce any significant or relevant distortion.

Simplifying a bit, the traditional empiricist semantic theory makes two basic claims:

(i) the meaning of a word or phrase is the set of (identifying) properties or descriptions which speakers associate with it, and

(ii) the meaning of a word determines its reference.

So, according to this semantic theory, the meaning of a term is the set of criteria which speakers use to apply the word, and the extension of that term includes all and only those things which satisfy these criteria. Thus the meaning of the term "bachelor" is given by the description "unmarried man" which people associate with the term, and the reference or extension of the term is all and only those things which satisfy this description (that is, all and only unmarried men).

We can distinguish *conventionalistic* and *individualistic* versions of the traditional semantic theory corresponding to different ways of construing the kind of association required in (i). An individualistic theory makes the meaning of a word depend upon the criteria which *the speaker* associates with the word, while a conventionalistic theory makes the meaning of a word depend upon the criteria with which the word is *conventionally* associated or with which it is associated by a *majority of speakers*.

Hart would seem to accept a conventionalistic version of the traditional semantic theory. Legal terms have determinate meaning so long, and only so long, as speakers by and large agree in the properties or descriptions which they associate with particular legal terms. The meaning of these legal terms, according to (i), is the set of criteria conventionally associated with them. And, according to (ii), the law is a function of what satisfies those criteria.

An easy case is a case which possesses those features (properties) or satisfies those descriptions which are conventionally associated with the legal term in question; we can tell this by the fact that reasonable people

York: Oxford University Press, 1975), bk. III (e.g., III, iii, 12ff.); Gottlob Frege, "Sense and Reference," in *Translations from the Philosophical Writings of Gottlob Frege*, trans. M. Black and P. Geach (Oxford: Blackwell, 1980), pp. 57–58; C. I. Lewis, *An Analysis of Knowledge and Valuation* (La Salle: Open Court, 1946), pp. 65, 133, 150–51, 168; Rudolph Carnap, *Meaning and Necessity*, 2d ed. (Chicago: University of Chicago Press, 1956), pp. 1, 16, 19, 233–34, 242–43, 246.

agree about the application of the legal term to this case or by the fact that they agree in their beliefs about the extension of the legal term. But in hard cases people disagree about whether the legal terms apply; the features of these cases are not *conventionally* associated with any legal terms. Legal language has no determinate meaning in such cases, and so, according to (ii), the cases are legally indeterminate. So, on this semantic theory, judges in hard cases are not bound by determinate legal standards; if they are to decide such cases, they must exercise discretion in the strong sense.

6. Problems for the Traditional Semantic Theory: How to Represent Disagreement

Any adequate assessment of Hart's theory of legal interpretation, therefore, must address the traditional semantic theory. We should resist Hart's theory of legal reasoning, I shall argue, because we should resist the traditional semantic theory. Criticisms of Hart's theory and claims similar to those Dworkin makes can be defended as resting on a more plausible semantics for legal interpretation.

It will be easier to criticize the semantic theory underlying Hart's claims by looking at its implications in nonlegal areas; if its implications in nonlegal areas are implausible, then our criticisms of its legal implications cannot be dismissed as question begging.

Consider the implications of the traditional semantic theory for nonlegal discourse, say, the discourse of a scientific community at a particular time or over a fairly short period of time. How does such a theory explain what we would normally describe as disagreement among scientists about the properties of some physical unit or magnitude, say, mass? If there is a prevailing theory about mass, disputed only by a minority, then a conventionalistic version of the traditional semantic theory must claim that the minority contradicts itself when it denies that mass has the properties conventionally associated with it. But this is an absurd consequence: we may think the minority wrong, but their claims need not be incoherent.

At this point, a defender of the traditional semantic theory might shift from a conventionalistic to an individualistic version of this theory. On the individualistic theory, the majority means one thing by a term, the minority something else. And because meaning determines reference, as long as different things satisfy the different associated descriptions which constitute these different meanings, the referents of their use of "mass" will be different. But this consequence is also absurd, for it now identifies two different idiolects within the scientific community. It is now impossible to represent the disagreement between the majority and the minority as a disagreement over the nature of mass; there is no disagreement, because they mean quite different things by "mass" and (assuming that different things satisfy these different descriptions) so refer to quite different things. Their "disagreement" is like the one between the person who says "the bank [= savings institution] is a safe place for one's money" and the person who says "the bank [= river embankment] is not a safe place for one's money."

Or suppose that there is synchronic agreement within a scientific community but diachronic disagreement between successive scientific communities. Consider the apparent disagreement between Newtonian and Einsteinian conceptions of mass.[12] Newtonians and Einsteinians conventionally associate different sets of properties with the term "mass." The traditional semantic theory implies that these two communities mean different things by the term "mass" and, as a result (again on the assumption that different things possess these properties), refer to different things when they use the term. The apparent disagreement between the two communities is only an apparent disagreement of the sort described in the previous paragraph; Newtonians and Einsteinians are really talking past each other. But this consequence is also absurd: it implies that there can be no such thing as *disagreement* between successive scientific traditions; there can only be scientific *change*.[13]

There are, of course, legal analogues to these counterintuitive scientific implications of the traditional semantic theory. If we are conventionalists,

12. I am no expert on the history of physics, but I understand that Newton made at least two claims about mass which Einstein denied: (1) that the mass of a particle equals twice its kinetic molecular energy divided by the square of its velocity, and (2) that mass is conserved in all interactions.

13. There are some who have been willing (and perhaps eager) to embrace these implications of the traditional semantic theory for scientific disagreement. For instance, some have understood Thomas Kuhn's *Structure of Scientific Revolutions*, 2d ed. (Chicago: University of Chicago Press, 1970), to have these and other relativistic implications and have embraced Kuhn's work for that reason. I am not interested in defending my semantic claims against all *possible* challenges; the sort of scientific relativism whose falsity I am assuming is sufficiently peculiar and counterintuitive for my dialectical purposes. Those who wish to see this kind of semantic scientific relativism addressed seriously might consult Israel Scheffler, *Science and Subjectivity*, 2d ed. (Indianapolis: Hackett, 1982).

we must regard a legal claim held by a minority as incoherent. The minority must simply be conceptually confused; they "haven't grasped the meaning" of the relevant legal terms. If we are individualists, we must regard the "dispute" between the majority and the minority as illusory; the "disputants" mean and refer to different things when they speak of, say, "due care," "equal protection," or "cruel and unusual punishment," and so there is really nothing about which they disagree. When, over time, people change their beliefs about what constitutes, say, due care, equal protection, or cruel and unusual punishment, the meaning of the corresponding terms changes, and so the referent or subject matter changes. The traditional semantic theory does not distinguish *change in belief* and *change in subject matter*.[14] It is impossible, therefore, to represent, say, the disagreement of Chief Justice Warren in *Brown* v. *Board of Education of Topeka*[15] with Justice Brown in *Plessy* v. *Ferguson*[16] about the meaning or reference of "equal protection."

In general, we want to be able to explain how there can be genuine disagreement, how people who have different beliefs about a thing can nonetheless be talking about the same thing. The traditional semantic theory does not allow us to explain such disagreement, and that is reason to reject it.

7. Outlines of an Alternative Semantic Theory

If we reject the traditional semantic theory, what do we replace it with? A more plausible semantic theory must reject (i) or (ii) (or both) in the traditional semantic theory. We must give up either the claim that the mean-

14. Of course, the traditional semantic theory can allow that some beliefs do not fix meaning or reference. On a conventionalist view, as I have noted, minority beliefs do not determine meaning or reference. And any version of the traditional theory may want to distinguish between *identifying* descriptions associated with a term, which do (and must) determine its meaning and reference, and other descriptions which are in some way *nonessentially* associated with the term. Thus the traditional theory can allow that changes in beliefs corresponding to these nonessential descriptions will not force changes in meaning or subject matter. I admit all this, though I leave it to friends of the traditional theory to explain how this distinction is to be drawn. My only point is that the traditional theory cannot distinguish between changes in belief corresponding to identifying descriptions and changes in subject matter.

15. 347 U.S. 483 (1954) (declaring that racially segregated educational facilities violate the equal protection clause of the Fourteenth Amendment).

16. 163 U.S. 537 (1896) (upholding racial segregation in public transportation under the equal protection clause of the Fourteenth Amendment).

ing of a term is the set of properties associated with it or the claim that meaning determines reference.

One possibility is this: assume, for the moment, that we accept something like the traditional theory of meaning (i), according to which the meaning of a term is the set of properties or descriptions associated with it. If so, then our criticisms of the traditional semantic theory show us that we must reject (ii), the claim that meaning determines reference. According to (i), the meaning of a term depends upon the speaker's (or the linguistic community's) beliefs about the referent of that term. If we reject (ii) while maintaining (i), we reject the claim that a speaker's (or a linguistic community's) beliefs determine the things which his (or their) words refer to. Instead, we might claim that the reference of our words is determined by the way the world is and not by our beliefs about the world. The referent of the term "water," say, is just the substance in the world, whatever it is, with which we and those who taught us about water actually interact and have interacted in the appropriate way. What explains the fact that our use of the term "water" refers to this substance is that there is a causal-historical path of the appropriate sort connecting our use of the term, via various intermediaries, with the substance itself. This implies that we can use a word to refer even if there is a great deal we do not know about its referent. Thus, for example, I can use the expression "beech tree" and succeed in referring to beech trees, as when I order my workers to cut down the beech trees, even if I cannot tell a beech from an elm.

If we want to know what the referent of a term is or at least find out more about it we must engage in the relevant kind of theorizing. Thus if I want to know about the referent of "beech" I must study botany or consult someone who has—a botanist. Beliefs do not determine reference: our theories could be mistaken about the real referents of our terms (the history of science shows us this). But our best theories do provide us with our best evidence about what the nature of these referents is. In trying to discover the nature of the referents of our terms, we can at any time do no better than the best available evidence.

These suggestions about reference are drawn from the work of philosophers of language such as Saul Kripke and Hilary Putnam.[17] Kripke and

17. Saul Kripke, *Naming and Necessity* (Cambridge: Harvard University Press, 1980); Hilary Putnam, "Meaning and Reference," repr. in *Naming, Necessity, and Natural Kinds*, ed. S. Schwartz (Ithaca: Cornell University Press, 1977), and "The Meaning of 'Meaning,'"

Putnam have defended these claims for the semantics of both proper names and general terms, such as natural kind terms. Putnam, as I understand him, actually offers a somewhat different response to the problems with the traditional semantic theory; he suggests that we preserve the traditional semantic theory's connection between meaning and reference and use these considerations about reference to revise its theory of meaning. The meaning of a term, on his view, is not given by the set of properties which any individual or group associates with that term. The meaning of our words depends, instead, at least in part upon the facts about the nature of things in the world which we use our words to try to describe and with which we and others have interacted.[18]

There are many ways one might respond to the problems with the traditional semantic theory, but any response must, as the two suggestions I have discussed do, distinguish appropriately between changes in our beliefs and changes in the meaning or reference of our terms and recognize the role of theoretical considerations in ascertaining the meaning or reference of natural kind terms.[19] If we accept either of these suggestions, we can avoid the absurd consequences to which the traditional semantic theory leads. Though the best available relevant theories will provide us with our best access to the real nature of what our words refer to, the meaning or reference of our terms is not determined by anyone's beliefs. This explains how people with radically different theories (beliefs) about a subject matter can disagree. Though they make different claims about x, "x"

---

repr. in Hilary Putnam, *Mind, Language, and Reality* (New York: Cambridge University Press, 1975).

18. Putnam's actual theory of meaning, though rather sketchy, is much more complex than this. Putnam's full proposal is that meaning is a "vector" consisting of (i) syntactic markers, (ii) semantic markers, (iii) stereotypes (which do not determine extension), and (iv) (modal) extension. Thus the vector for "water" would be (i) mass noun; (ii) natural kind, liquid; (iii) transparent, colorless, odorless, potable; (iv) H_2O. See "The Meaning of 'Meaning.'" I ignore these additional features of Putnam's alternative account as nonessential to my present purposes.

19. As some of my more empiricist friends have reminded me, other responses to these problems with the traditional empiricist semantic theory's account of the meaning and reference of *particular* terms try harder to retain the general spirit of empiricist semantics. Cf. Alan Sidelle, *Necessity, Essence, and Individuation: A Defense of Conventionalism* (Ithaca: Cornell University Press, forthcoming), and Dagfinn Føllesdal, "Essentialism and Reference," in *The Philosophy of W.V.O. Quine*, ed. P. A. Schilpp (La Salle: Open Court, 1986). I have no quarrel here with such alternative responses provided that they do distinguish appropriately between changes in belief and changes in meaning and reference and that they recognize the role of theoretical considerations in ascertaining meaning and reference.

can mean or refer to the same thing in both of their mouths. Newtonians and Einsteinians have different beliefs about the nature of mass, but this does not prevent them from referring to the same property of objects, since the fact that they refer to the property mass is determined by their inter-action with a real physical magnitude (mass) and not by their beliefs about it.

8. THE SEMANTICS OF LEGAL INTERPRETATION

What do these semantic claims imply about legal interpretation? The in-terpretive claims I will consider and those I will advance are all general claims about legal interpretation per se; they do not discriminate among the objects of legal interpretation. So I will not address questions about, say, how statutory and constitutional interpretation might differ.[20]

I will follow Putnam and preserve the traditional semantic theory's claim that meaning determines reference by revising the traditional the-ory of meaning. (Those who prefer to preserve the traditional theory of meaning and sever the connection between meaning and reference can recast my claims *mutatis mutandis*.) There are a number of important consequences of this semantics for legal interpretation.

First, this semantics allows us to represent legal disagreement: lawyers can mean the same thing by, say, "cruel and unusual" punishment, namely, whatever properties of a punishment which make it cruel and un-usual, and so can be referring to the same thing even though they disagree in their theories or beliefs about the nature of justifiable punishment.

Second, disagreement about the disposition of hard cases establishes in-determinacy in neither the meaning of legal standards nor the law. Our legal standards have determinate reference insofar as the law is determi-nate. For instance, if we abstract momentarily from the complexities in-troduced by the doctrine of precedent, cases arising under the Eighth

20. I have found that many lawyers think it absurd to make global interpretive claims, be-cause they believe that constitutional, statutory, and common law interpretation are quite different. But the assertion that there are important global interpretive claims to make in no way implies that there can be no significant differences among these three kinds of legal interpretation. If, as I shall argue (Sec. 11), interpretation of a body of law requires a descrip-tive moral and political theory of that body of law and its institutions, then it is quite possible that interpretation of different kinds of law (having different political sources) will be subject to some different constraints. But these interpretive differences will obtain (if they do) *in vir-tue of*, among other things, the truth of these global interpretive claims.

Amendment are legally determinate, no matter how hotly contested, as long as the punishment in question is either cruel and unusual or not; cases arising under the due process clauses of the Fifth and Fourteenth Amendments are legally determinate so long as the procedures in question are fair or not; statutes imposing strict liability upon companies for injuries caused by their manufacture or disposal of toxic substances are legally determinate in their application insofar as the substances are toxic or not.

Of course, some people will want to claim that legal provisions, such as many constitutional amendments, which incorporate moral or political language will be less semantically determinate than legal provisions which incorporate, say, scientific language, precisely because political morality is (metaphysically) less determinate than science. This view would have important implications for the nature and determinacy of legal (and especially constitutional) interpretation. But it rests on a kind of moral skepticism which requires *separate* argument and is not established merely by appeal to disagreement among legal principals over the scope of legal provisions containing moral or political language.[21] Nor, if the alternative semantic theory I have adopted is correct, can this skepticism about the determinacy of political morality be established merely by appeal to general moral disagreement.

Also, some may want to dispute the application of this semantic theory to legal interpretation. Putnam and Kripke, they will say, are not offering general semantic theories. But although this is true, it does not block application of their theories to legal interpretation. Interpretive disputes occur in the law primarily over the interpretation of the law's use of general terms, and Kripke and Putnam have defended these semantic claims for the semantics of general terms, such as natural kind terms. "Fair" and "cruel" are natural kind terms just as much as "toxic" is; they are general terms which refer to properties, and they "do explanatory work" or "pull

---

21. I argue at length against antirealist metaethical views in my *Moral Realism and the Foundations of Ethics* (New York: Cambridge University Press, forthcoming); "Externalist Moral Realism," in *Moral Realism: Proceedings of the 1985 Spindel Conference*, ed. N. Gillespie (*Southern Journal of Philosophy*, Supplement 24 [1986]); and "Moral Realism and the Sceptical Arguments from Disagreement and Queerness," *Australasian Journal of Philosophy* 62 (1984): 111–25. See also Peter Railton, "Moral Realism," *Philosophical Review* 95 (1986): 163–207, and Nicholas Sturgeon, "Moral Explanations," in *Morality, Reason, and Truth*, ed. D. Copp and D. Zimmerman (Totowa, N.J.: Rowman and Allanheld, 1984), and "What Difference Does It Make Whether Moral Realism Is True?" in *Moral Realism*, ed. Gillespie.

their weight" in certain kinds of thinking, reasoning, and theorizing. "Cruel" and "fair" denote moral kinds, as "toxic" denotes a chemical kind.[22]

Third, this semantic theory gives us reason to reject certain interpretations of the "plain meaning rule."[23] Though the plain meaning rule is usually formulated as a principle or canon of statutory construction, it has analogues in constitutional and common law interpretation. On one interpretation, the plain meaning rule says only that legal interpretation must respect the meaning of the language of the provision being interpreted. Though this claim is not quite tautological (see Section 9), its plausibility is due largely to how little it tells us. In particular, it does not tell us how to ascertain a legal provision's meaning. On another reading, though, the plain meaning rule says that a legal provision's meaning is exhausted by its "plain" or "conventional" meaning. So construed, the plain meaning rule incorporates a particular semantic claim or assumption: it asserts that a legal provision's meaning is a function of the descriptions which are conventionally associated with the words and phrases in which the provision is expressed. This would be a reasonable interpretive claim if the traditional semantic theory were true. But it is not, and, in particular, meaning is not to be identified with, and reference is not determined by, the descriptions which people associate with, or their beliefs about the extension of, their words. Determination of the meaning and reference of legal standards will often require reliance on theoretical considerations about the real nature of the referents of language in the law, considerations which may well outstrip conventional wisdom on the subject.

Fourth, this semantic theory gives us reason to discount the semantic importance of framers' intent in interpreting statutes and constitutional provisions. To see this, we need to distinguish between *specific* and *abstract intent*.[24] This is a distinction of degree, not kind, but nonetheless it

22. Here a comparison of moral kind terms, such as "cruel" or "fair," with chemical or biological kind terms, such as "toxic," may be more revealing than a comparison with the kind term "water." Moral kinds, like toxins, are less unitary than water. Just as there are many different stuffs which are toxins and which poison the body in different ways, so too moral kinds, such as cruelty, can be realized in a large variety of ways (e.g., in quite different kinds of behaviors), and may, in fact, admit of subkinds (e.g., psychological cruelty and physical cruelty). These claims are, of course, all perfectly consistent with the alternative semantic picture I am sketching.

23. My discussion of the plain meaning rule draws on, but does not follow, that of Dickerson, *The Interpretation and Application of Statutes*, pp. 229–33.

24. After writing an earlier version of this article, I discovered Dworkin's similar distinction

is an important distinction. We can identify a spectrum of abstractness along which different characterizations of the framers' intent or purpose might fall. A highly abstract intention of the framers of many laws is the desire or intention to do the right thing. But this abstract intent will be common to a great many legal standards. An abstract intent, which is specific to the specific legal provisions of which it is an intent, will be the *kind* of principle, policy, or value which the framers of the provision were trying to realize. For instance, the abstract intent (or one of the abstract intentions) of the framers of a particular tax law might be to enact a moderately progressive or fair income tax scheme. A specific intent, by contrast, is to regulate certain actions and not others and is determined by the framers' beliefs about the extension of their abstract intent. Thus, given their collateral beliefs about, among other things, economic theory, the framers of a particular tax law have specific intentions to tax certain levels of income at certain rates and to allow particular deductions and credits to certain groups.

It is often claimed that specific intent is a very important constraint upon legal interpretation; determination of a legal provision's meaning must be guided by the specific intentions of the framers of that provision. Proponents of this claim can admit that it may sometimes be quite difficult to identify framers' intent, but they insist that the correct interpretation of any legal provision must be guided by, or at least must not violate, the framers' (specific) intentions.[25]

Consider a law imposing strict standards of due care in the handling of toxic substances enacted in, say, 1945. Relying perhaps on (then) current scientific evidence, the legislators in 1945 had beliefs about what substances are toxic, and this determined their (specific) intentions in enacting the statute. We now have different and better theories about toxins. Should we place much weight on the (specific) legislative intent underlying this statute? Should we continue to impose strict liability only on the

---

between abstract and concrete intent in "The Forum of Principle," repr. in MP, pp. 48–49. My discussion of the semantic and nonsemantic treatment of framers' intentions or purposes might be usefully compared with Dworkin's. In both "The Forum of Principle" and LE Dworkin seems to argue that it is primarily *on normative grounds* that we should discount the concrete intentions of the framers. Though there may be a good normative argument that we should discount the framers' specific or concrete intentions in deciding cases, I shall argue on nonnormative grounds that specific intent is (at least typically) no constraint upon legal interpretation.

25. See notes 39 and 40 below.

handling of those substances which the enacting legislators intended to
regulate? We might if we accepted the traditional semantic theory: failure
to appeal to legislative intent would result, according to that theory, in a
change in the meaning of the statute. But appealing to (specific) legislative intent in this way means failing to impose strict standards of due care
on the handling of substances which we have every reason to believe are
toxic. (Indeed, we might now have good reason to believe that substances
not regarded as toxic in 1945 are actually *more* toxic than the substances
then regarded as toxic.)

Our alternative semantic theory gives the right interpretive results here.
The 1945 statute imposes legal regulations on the handling of those
things which are, in fact, toxic. A given legal community can do no better
than rely on the best available chemical evidence in trying to determine
the reference of "toxic substance." The intentions or beliefs of the enacting legislature concerning toxic substances and their handling are at most
starting points in our own inquiry into the meaning of the statute, and
where we have reason to believe that the beliefs of the legislature were
badly mistaken, legislative intent is no constraint at all.

These claims may seem innocent enough when applied to the interpretation of our 1945 strict liability statute, but their import for the interpretation of constitutional provisions is more startling. Many people think
that when interpreting the meaning of important constitutional provisions
containing moral or political language, such as the First, Fifth, Sixth,
Eighth, Ninth, Tenth, and Fourteenth Amendments, we must pay close
attention to what the framers of these provisions intended in enacting
them (their specific intentions) and that their intentions place constraints
upon constitutional interpretation independently of the plausibility of the
framers' moral and political beliefs. But, again, this would be an important
semantic constraint only if the traditional semantic theory were true. In
that case, the framers' beliefs about the provisions would fix the original
meaning and reference of those provisions. Failure to respect the framers'
(specific) intentions would imply failure to respect the meaning of those
provisions. But, as we have seen, we should reject the traditional semantic
theory. The meaning and reference of our terms is given by the way the
world is—in the case of the moral and political terms found in many constitutional provisions, by certain kinds of social and political factors. We
discover the meaning of these constitutional amendments, therefore, by
relying on substantive moral and political theory and argument. Thus, in

interpreting the Eighth Amendment's prohibition of cruel and unusual punishment, we must make judgments about the morality of certain forms of punishment. We should heed the (specific) intentions of the framers only so far as we have reason to believe that their theories about the morality of punishment are plausible. The framers' beliefs about punishment are at most a starting point for our interpretation of the Eighth Amendment; the constraints which they impose are entirely dependent upon their plausibility. (I will return to some of these issues of constitutional interpretation in Section 13.)

9. INTERPRETATION AND PURPOSE

Any general theory about the nature of legal interpretation must make clear the role of semantics in interpretation. It is tempting to think that semantics exhausts interpretation. Isn't interpreting a phrase or text just the attempt to determine its meaning or reference? If it is, then interpretation just is the determination of semantic content, and our sketch of the semantics of legal interpretation provides a complete (if sketchy) picture of legal interpretation.

But there is room to doubt that semantics exhausts interpretation. Determination of a legal provision's meaning and reference may not exhaust the task of interpreting that provision. Consider Hart's statute forbidding vehicles in the park. On almost any semantic theory, including both the traditional theory and our alternative theory, "vehicles" clearly includes police cars within its extension. Thus, if semantics exhausted interpretation, the correct interpretation of this statute would clearly imply that police cars are forbidden in the park. This claim about the interpretation of the statute should be puzzling; even if we agree that the statute, properly interpreted, prohibits police cars from the park, we are unlikely to think that this interpretation is obviously or uncontroversially correct. Or consider the First Amendment: "Congress shall make *no* law respecting an establishment of religion . . . or abridging the freedom of speech or of the press; or the right of the people peaceably to assemble . . ." (emphasis added). Here too, at least part of the *meaning* of the amendment is clear; it provides an absolute guarantee of freedom of speech, press, religion, and so forth. Though, on our theory of meaning, there can be controversy over what counts as an infringement of one of these rights, there can be no controversy over whether the amendment's meaning is that these rights are absolute.[26] But this has not been the traditional *interpretation* of the First Amendment,[27] and even if it were the correct interpretation, its superiority as an interpretation would not be as clear as it would have to be if semantics exhausted interpretation.

Suppose we agree that these cases give us reason to doubt the claim that interpretation is exhausted by determining meaning. What else is involved in interpretation? It is important to remember that the primary objects of legal interpretation—statutes, constitutional provisions, and precedents—like most objects of interpretation, are human artifacts, the products of purposeful activity. In interpreting the products of purposeful activity, we must appeal to the purposes which prompted and guided the activity whose product we are trying to understand. This suggests that legal interpretation should involve appeal to the reasons, purposes, and intentions of those who enacted the law. This should sound familiar from our discussion of legal principles, and it supplies our real reason (and perhaps Dworkin's) for regarding underlying principles or second-order standards as legal standards; these principles play an essential role in the interpretation of first-order legal standards.

10. WHICH PURPOSE?

I have suggested that legal interpretation of legal standards involves appeal to underlying principles as well as to the meaning of the words in which the standards are expressed. But this proposal leaves unanswered many important questions about the determination of purpose or intent and the relation between meaning and purpose. These questions cannot be satisfactorily answered, or even all addressed, here. Something must be said, however, about the determination of intent or purpose, and this will have important implications for the resolution of the other questions (about the relation between meaning and purpose, for example).

Neither the interpretive need to appeal to underlying purposes nor our discussion of legal principles explains how we are to determine which

---

26. This, of course, is the sort of interpretation of the First Amendment usually attributed to Justice Black.

27. Obscene and libelous speech have been excluded from First Amendment protection; see, e.g., *Chaplinsky v. New Hampshire*, 315 U.S. 568 (1942). Subversive advocacy can be restricted if it poses a "clear and present danger"; see *Schenck v. United States*, 249 U.S. 47 (1919), and *Brandenburg v. Ohio*, 395 U.S. 444 (1969).

principles express the purposes underlying the legal standard which we are trying to interpret. As our discussion of the semantics of legal interpretation revealed, we can characterize the purposes or intentions of the framers of a legal standard at various levels of abstraction. This fact presses on us the following question: Are the purposes which legal interpretation requires us to identify and which legal principles express abstract or specific?

It might be tempting to think that we have already answered this question in arguing against reliance on specific intent in Section 8. But that was an argument against *semantic* reliance on specific intent. The present issue is how to select the appropriate description—in particular, the appropriate level of abstraction—of the framers' intentions or purposes.

The choice between abstract and specific intent arises because we can identify the purposes of the legal standard we are interpreting either with the kind of goal or value which the framers sought to realize (abstract intent) or with the regulation of particular things and activities which they sought (specific intent). Typically both kinds of intentions or purposes exist. But which is dominant? Which intention should guide interpretation? We can, I think, rule out the most abstract intention—the desire to do the right thing—since this intention will underlie a great many otherwise quite diverse legal standards and so will not allow us to distinguish one legal standard from another. But how do we decide between less abstract, but still abstract, intention and specific intention?

Meaning itself is often a good guide as to the level of abstraction of the intention we are looking for. One situation in which we face a choice among intentions at different levels of abstraction involves legal standards couched in general or abstract terms, as the amendments in the Bill of Rights are. Here the more abstract language supports the dominance of the more abstract intention. Though the framers' moral beliefs about punishment may have led them to expect the Eighth Amendment's prohibition of cruel and unusual punishment to prohibit only, say, certain forms of torture, the fact that they chose the general language of "cruel and unusual punishment" is evidence that their dominant intention was to prohibit punishments which are in fact cruel and unusual, not to prohibit certain specific forms of torture. For it was certainly within their power to adopt a much more restricted amendment, explicitly prohibiting only certain forms of torture. So when the language of the legal provision is abstract, this tends to show that the dominant intention was abstract.

22

But, of course, attention to language is not going to reveal any tension between meaning and purpose which might help explain our belief that meaning does not exhaust interpretation. In particular, attention to the language of the First Amendment or Hart's traffic regulation will not explain why the meaning of these legal provisions fails to exhaust their proper interpretation. We need some independent evidence of purpose and its level of abstraction.

The appropriate kind of evidence must be counterfactual. Consider a different, but related, interpretive problem. Agents often possess many motives from which they might have acted or which their actions might be taken to express. In interpreting and assessing an agent's behavior in such circumstances, we often want to know what the agent's dominant motive was. The usual way we go about determining this is by trying to answer various counterfactual questions about what the agent would have done if certain of her beliefs or desires had been different in certain ways. If I want to know whether it was Bonny's conception of her own interest or her concern for Barney which made her keep her promise to Barney, I will try to decide, among other things, whether she would have kept a similar promise to Barney had it required somewhat greater sacrifice on her part. It is not always easy to answer such counterfactual questions, but plausible answers to such questions seem to be our best guide to dominant motive. Given the similarities among motives, purposes, and intentions, we might rely on a similar sort of counterfactual test to determine which purpose or intention underlying a legal standard is dominant: Would the framers still have enacted the legal provision in question, in its current form, even if their beliefs about the extension of their abstract intent had been different? It can be difficult to answer this question if one accepts the framers' collateral beliefs oneself, since in some cases it can be very difficult to imagine that one's collateral beliefs are false. But this does not affect the theoretical importance of the test to determining dominant intention.

The fact that framers' specific intent is determined by their beliefs about the extension of values which their abstract intent expresses provides general reason to believe that this test, properly performed, will typically establish the dominance of abstract intent. Since specific intent results from abstract intent plus collateral beliefs about the extension of abstract intent, the appropriate change in one's collateral beliefs would change one's specific intentions.

23

Consider an abstractly worded legal provision. Would I, a framer of the Eighth Amendment who is also a proponent of capital punishment (let us say), have voted for the amendment if I had believed (as I then did not) that capital punishment is cruel and morally indefensible? Presumably yes. This shows that my dominant intention in enacting this abstractly worded constitutional provision was the abstract intention to prohibit punishments which are extremely inappropriate morally—whichever punishments these turn out to be—not the particular kinds of punishment which I then believed to be cruel and unusual.

Moreover, this test should establish that dominant intent is typically abstract even where the language of the legal provisions being interpreted is not abstract but highly specific. Here the meaning (we might say) will be specific. But the dominant purpose will typically still be abstract. Interpretation of specifically worded legal provisions will still require appeal to underlying purposes or intentions, and there will still exist both specific and abstract intentions. If language were our only guide as to the appropriate description of purpose, this might suggest that we should be guided by specific intent in these circumstances. But the counterfactual test points in a more abstract direction. Would I, a framer of a highly specific and complex tax plan, have supported it if I had believed (as I then did not) that this plan would in the long run impose disproportionate financial burdens on a particular class of people? Presumably not. This shows that my dominant intention in enacting this specifically worded legal provision was an abstract intention to implement a tax plan which is, among other things, at least minimally fair.

Properly applied, the counterfactual test should show that the dominant purposes underlying first-order legal standards are typically abstract intentions, that is, the kinds of values, policies, and principles which the framers of the law were trying to realize. Legal principles express these abstract intentions and must guide legal interpretation.[28] But meaning

28. Dworkin considers and rejects the use of such a counterfactual test to support the dominance of concrete intent; see "The Forum of Principle," in MP, pp. 50–51. I agree with Dworkin but go further and maintain (a) that this test is the appropriate way to determine dominant purpose or intent and (b) that this test will support the dominance of abstract intent.

I have defended the dominance of abstract, rather than specific, intent on both semantic and nonsemantic grounds. This provides (additional) justification for Dworkin's claims that legal standards formulated in general or abstract moral or political language, as many constitutional provisions are, express moral or political "concepts," rather than specific "concep-

and purpose can conflict, and this gives rise to certain interpretive difficulties. Since the dominant purpose will usually be abstract intent, such conflicts will arise when the legal provision's meaning is specific *and* the framers' collateral beliefs are false or questionable. But conflict can also arise between meaning and purpose when the language of a provision is general and the dominant intent is abstract. Thus we have a conflict between meaning and purpose if a traffic regulation prohibits vehicles in the park and its abstract intent is to facilitate safe park recreation, since police cars are vehicles but facilitate safe park recreation. Similarly, we have a conflict between meaning and purpose if the abstract intent behind the absolutist language of the First Amendment is protection of political or civic freedom,[29] since restrictions on obscene speech (as opposed to sexually explicit speech which expresses social or intellectual ideas or attitudes) arguably do not restrict political freedom. Since meaning and purpose are both essential to interpretation, neither source of such conflicts can be dismissed. A proper theory of legal interpretation should, among other things, address the treatment, if not the resolution, of such interpretive conflicts.

11. The General Structure of Legal Interpretation

Recall Dworkin's disagreement with Hart's "model of rules." Dworkin claims that the law consists of legal principles as well as legal rules. Our discussion of legal interpretation allows us to explain clearly the difference between legal rules and principles and the legal status of these principles.[30]

According to Hart, every legal system has a rule (or rules) of recogni-

---

tions" of those concepts, and that interpretation of such standards must identify the best conception of those concepts (TRS, pp. 134–37; LE, pp. 70–72). For concepts just are the kinds of values and principles which form the abstract intent of a standard's framers, and conceptions just are the beliefs or theories about the extension of these concepts which form the specific intent of the standard's framers. The dominance of abstract intent, therefore, supports Dworkin's claim that constitutional interpretation must seek to identify the best conception of the framers' concepts, rather than reproduce the framers' conceptions.

29. I offer this only as a *possible* First Amendment purpose which would help explain why First Amendment interpretation does not extend First Amendment protection to obscene speech. I do not claim that this reading of First Amendment purpose is better than alternative readings or even that it is a very plausible reading; I use it for illustrative purposes only.

30. My discussion of the general nature of legal interpretation builds upon arguments and claims in my "Legal Positivism and Natural Law Reconsidered."

tion. That rule states the criteria which legal principals and political officials must employ (even if only implicitly) in identifying standards of appropriate legal behavior. In the United States legal system, for example, there is a rule of recognition which recognizes (roughly) three main sources of law: constitutional provision, legislative enactment, and judicial decision. Legal rules or first-order legal standards are standards having a source specified by the legal system's rule of recognition.

But first-order legal standards require interpretation. Determination of their meaning is part of this interpretive task. Determination of the meaning of first-order legal standards will often be difficult and controversial and require complex theoretical reasoning of various kinds. We might identify first-order legal standards with their meaning.

But first-order legal standards are also the products of purposeful activity; their interpretation, therefore, also requires appeal to their underlying purposes. First-order legal standards do not exist in a vacuum; they are introduced for certain reasons, perform certain social and political functions, and realize certain principles of political morality. These principles express the framers' abstract intent. Since these principles play a role in the interpretation of first-order legal standards, they too are legal standards; I have called them second-order legal standards.

Because first-order legal standards are typically enacted to secure moral and political values and because they typically serve moral or political functions, second-order legal standards are typically moral and political standards. Of course, identification of second-order standards will be controversial and will not be settled by appeal to the moral and political beliefs conventionally associated with the first-order legal standards in question. Identification of second-order legal standards will often require a good deal of theoretical reasoning concerning the structure of the moral and political values underlying particular first-order legal standards. Reasonably uncontroversial examples of second-order legal standards within the United States legal system are the common law principle that no one should profit from his own wrong, the criminal law principle that there should be no liability without fault, the contract law principle that plaintiffs should mitigate damages, the constitutional law principle of the priority of moral and political rights over economic rights, and the structural principle of the separation of powers.

This sketch of a theory of law makes legal interpretation out to be a more complex and theoretical affair than the standard theory of law would lead us to believe. A standard is a legal standard within a legal system, on this alternative theory, just in case it is (a) a rule of recognition, (b) a first-order legal standard, or (c) a second-order legal standard. First-order legal standards are standards having a source specified in the system's rule of recognition; their content is their semantic content. Second-order legal standards are standards which underlie or provide the rationale for the system's first-order legal standards or its rule of recognition; they are the abstract intent of the system's first-order legal standards.

So far, our theory of legal interpretation provides us with an account of how to identify *particular laws*; this does not itself explain how we interpret *the law* on a particular issue. Determination of what the law requires could *turn* on the interpretation of some one legal standard, but typically a variety of legal rules and especially principles will bear on the correct answer to a legal question. Conflicts can arise both among first-order legal standards and (as we saw in Section 10) between first- and second-order legal standards. (*Riggs* and *Henningsen* illustrate these sorts of conflicts; *Riggs* involves a conflict between first- and second-order standards, and *Henningsen* involves a conflict among second-order standards.) The legal system's rule of recognition may resolve some conflicts among first-order legal standards—for instance, by giving priority to certain kinds of law (for example, constitutional over legislative) or, in the case of precedent, by recognizing higher and lower courts within a jurisdiction. But the rule of recognition cannot be counted on to resolve all conflicts within or between levels of legal standards. To decide such conflicts we must assign weight to competing legal standards. The natural way to construe the weight of legal standards is *functionally*. Second-order standards underlie or provide the rationale for first-order legal standards. We might assign weight to second-order standards, then, by determining both the number *and* the importance of the first-order legal standards which they support. This will require us to determine which first-order legal standards are most important to the operation and functioning of our legal system. Sometimes this will be easy. The doctrine of the separation of powers is more fundamental than the requirement that there be two witnesses to the execution of a will. Sometimes this will be hard. Is the First Amendment guarantee of freedom of the press more important than the Sixth Amendment right to a fair trial? In order to decide these hard cases, we would have to reconstruct the moral and political foundations of our legal system.

This requires the legal interpreter to engage in (or at least rely upon) moral and political theory. We might call this *descriptive* moral and political theory and contrast it with *normative* moral and political theory. That is, the legal interpreter must try to identify the moral and political values underlying our laws and legal institutions and practices and organize them into a coherent theory of political morality (or at least as coherent a theory as possible). This descriptive task is different from the normative task of trying to construct, from a clean slate, the standards of true or sound political morality. In legal systems whose laws and legal institutions and practices exemplify true or sound political morality to a significant extent, the descriptive moral and political theory required in legal interpretation will approximate normative political theory. But descriptive and normative moral and political theory are distinct, and in most legal systems the descriptive moral and political theory required in legal interpretation will diverge more or less from normative political theory.[31] Thus, racial equality is not a political value which an accurate descriptive moral and political theory of the South African legal system might recognize, while it is a value which normative moral and political theory will recognize. It is in some sense an open question within normative moral and political theory whether some form of liberalism is correct; it cannot be in any comparable way an open question whether the descriptive moral and political theory of the United States legal system is or includes some form of liberalism.

This gives us a better conception of legal weight; the more firmly entrenched within the legal system a principle is, the more legal weight it has. The way in which we determine what the law requires in some controversy, then, is to see which decision coheres best with the total body of legal standards duly weighted. In a legal system such as ours, what the law requires in any given case is that decision which coheres best with existing legal principles, constitutional provisions, statutes, and precedents. Clearly these coherence calculations will be complex and controversial and will call for the exercise of a good deal of judgment, but neither of these facts shows that one decision will not provide the best fit with the background body of existing law. Good judges and lawyers can approximate the process necessary to identify what the law requires on some is-

31. On this issue about the nature of interpretation, Dworkin and I appear to part company. Compare TRS, p. 340, and LE, pp. 101–2, 110, 231, 239, 255, with my "Legal Positivism and Natural Law Reconsidered," pp. 371ff.

Legal Theory,
Legal Interpretation,
and Judicial Review

sue, but, as Dworkin suggests, carrying out this theoretical work thoroughly and perfectly is a Herculean task (TRS, pp. 105–6).

Both Dworkin's superhuman judge, Hercules, and mere mortals might try to shorten the interpretive process in a certain way. Rather than attempt full coherence calculations in an attempt to find the decision which is in equilibrium for each separate case, they might try to set out an elaborate theory of law which articulates the structure of our legal system, the values on which it rests, and the relative weight of various legal rules and principles. Given what we have said, constructing such a theory of law would involve determination of the moral and political foundations of civil, criminal, and constitutional law and of the sort of moral and political theory or scheme of which these fundamental values could be a part. Once they had such a theory of law, Hercules and lesser judges could decide cases, especially hard cases, by reference to it.

If my argument has been correct, familiar positions and disputes within legal theory rest on claims or assumptions about the nature of interpretation—in particular, assumptions about semantics and underlying purpose and their respective roles within interpretation. I have tried to show how standard views about law and legal interpretation rest on mistaken or implausible assumptions about these elements of interpretation. Our alternative semantic theory and the dominance of abstract intent support a different, more theoretical account of law and legal interpretation. I now want to explore the implications of these claims about legal interpretation for some familiar disputes within constitutional theory.

12. JUDICIAL REVIEW AND ITS RATIONALE

A traditional issue in constitutional theory is the legitimacy of judicial review. Are courts entitled to review the constitutionality of democratically enacted (federal or state) legislation? There have been various ways of understanding this question. Some of these are:

(1) Does the Constitution authorize judicial review?
(2) Did the framers of the Constitution intend courts to exercise judicial review?
(3) Is judicial review compatible with democratic theory?
(4) Is judicial review compatible with our political scheme?
(5) If the exercise of a certain sort of judicial review is legitimate, have

courts restricted themselves to the legitimate forms of judicial review in the process of invalidating legislation?

These and other questions about judicial review have not always been clearly distinguished, and this failure to separate distinct issues has, I think, produced a good deal of confusion. A proper theory of judicial review should address each of these issues. I cannot, of course, resolve any of these issues here; much less can I provide a proper theory of judicial review. But (5) turns crucially on assumptions about the nature of constitutional interpretation, and the account of legal interpretation developed above has important implications for its resolution. In particular, our account of legal interpretation undermines familiar arguments that many of the Supreme Court's decisions over the last few decades, especially in civil rights cases, exceed the legitimate scope of judicial review.

Since (5) assumes the theoretical legitimacy of some kind of judicial review, it may be worth explaining first how this assumption might be justified.

Judicial review is the power of the judiciary to declare federal and state legislation unconstitutional. Like most writers on this subject, I shall focus on the power of the federal judiciary, and in particular the Supreme Court, to exercise judicial review. But what is the source of this power? Judges and scholars have offered and criticized various answers to this question.[32] The strongest rationale, and the rationale most relevant to our present purposes, is the argument from *institutional role* advanced by Alexander Hamilton in *Federalist* 78[33] and by Chief Justice Marshall in *Marbury* v. *Madison*:[34] (1) it is the institutional role of the judiciary to interpret and apply the law; (2) the Constitution is the supreme law of our legal system; (3) hence the Court must interpret and apply the Constitution; (4) hence if the Court determines that some statute conflicts with the Constitution, it must declare the statute unconstitutional. According to

32. See, e.g., and compare *Marbury* v. *Madison*, 1 Cranch 137 (1803); *Eakin* v. *Raub*, 12 Seargent & Rawle 330 (Pa. 1825) (Gibson, J., dissenting); Alexander Bickel, *The Least Dangerous Branch* (New Haven: Yale University Press, 1962), pp. 1–16; and William van Alstyne, "A Critical Guide to Marbury v. Madison," *Duke Law Journal* 1969 (1969): 16–29.

33. Alexander Hamilton, John Jay, and James Madison, *The Federalist*, ed. E. M. Earle (New York: Random House, 1937). References to *The Federalist* will be by number and paragraph.

34. 1 Cranch 137 (1803).

Legal Theory,
Legal Interpretation,
and Judicial Review

this rationale, it is the institutional role of the judiciary as interpreter of the law which grounds the power of judicial review.[35]

The Federalist is often taken to defend the doctrine of the separation of powers thought to underlie the Constitution, and some have thought that judicial review is inconsistent with this doctrine because, they claim, judicial review substitutes the will of the judiciary for the will of the legislature. Here the separation of powers is understood to stand for the *separation of governmental functions*.[36] This separation of function is understood (roughly) as follows: the legislature is supposed to make law; the judiciary is supposed to interpret and apply the law; and the executive is supposed to enforce the law as interpreted by the judiciary. The division of labor between the legislature and the judiciary has a democratic rationale: it is thought that those who make our laws should be democratically accountable, as legislators are and as (federal and some state) judges are not.[37] Judicial review may seem to violate the doctrine of the separation of powers, so understood, by substituting the will of the judiciary for the will of the legislature and so violating the requirement that only democratically accountable legislatures make law.

But it should already be clear—and the rest of *Federalist* 78 makes it

35. This is only one of Marshall's justifications of judicial review in *Marbury*. Justice Gibson's dissent in *Eakin*, Bickel (*The Least Dangerous Branch*, pp. 1–16), and van Alstyne ("A Critical Guide to Marbury v. Madison") challenge Marshall's arguments for judicial review. While I agree with a number of their challenges to Marshall's other justifications of judicial review, this justification, I would maintain, holds up under examination.

36. See *Federalist* 78:7. The separation of powers also stands for two types of *balance of power*: the balance of power (a) between the ruler and the ruled (51:4, 9–10) and (b) among the rulers (51:1, 6, 9). The relationship between the separation of governmental functions and the balance of powers seems to be this: the balance of power between ruler and ruled is to be secured by a balance of power among the rulers, which is to be secured by the separation of governmental functions.

37. There are reasons to question the accuracy of this rationale. Recent empirical studies of democracy often claim that legislators are less accountable than this rationale suggests; and features of the judicial appointment process and problems of the enforceability of, and compliance with, judicial orders may make the judiciary look more accountable than this rationale suggests. See, e.g., Robert Dahl, *A Preface to Democratic Theory* (Chicago: University of Chicago Press, 1956), and *Pluralist Democracy in the United States: Conflict and Consent* (Chicago: Rand McNally, 1967), and Peter Railton, "Judicial Review, Elites, and Liberal Democracy," *Nomos* 25 (1983): 158–59. Though these claims make the contrast between the accountability of legislators and that of judges less sharp, it would be difficult to claim that there is no significant contrast here which might underwrite the separation of functions.

still clearer—how this claim misunderstands the doctrine of judicial review. The power which the institutional rationale discussed above gives the Court is the power to interpret the Constitution and measure legislation against this interpretation; call this *interpretive* judicial review. It is not the power for the Court to decide whether it thinks legislation is wise (78:7); this would be a kind of *noninterpretive* judicial review.[38] While the doctrine of the separation of powers (or functions) offers no support to noninterpretive review, it supports interpretive judicial review. It is the function of the courts to apply the law, and it is the function of the legislature to make law—subject to certain constitutional limits. Since the Constitution is a law, it is the job of the courts to decide whether the legislature has heeded its constitutional limits.

Moreover, it should be clear that *The Federalist* anticipated the need to exercise (interpretive) judicial review. The doctrine of the separation of powers and the doctrine of federalism are based on the recognition of political factions. The authors of *The Federalist* were well aware that political factions could form coalitions and attempt to advance their interests legislatively by systematically disadvantaging political minorities. The framers were familiar with the phenomenon of the "tyranny of the majority" (51:10). It was in large part to protect certain interests of political minorities from legislative encroachment by the majority that certain features of the Constitution and many of its amendments were adopted (78:9). So, parts of the Constitution were intended as constraints on democratic legislation, and the framers expected the courts—as appliers of the law—to see that legislative action did not violate these constraints.

13. CONSTITUTIONAL INTERPRETATION AND THE SCOPE OF JUDICIAL REVIEW

Critics of judicial review often worry, not that interpretive judicial review is improper, but rather that the courts have frequently not confined themselves to this legitimate exercise of judicial review but have instead inval-

38. Readers familiar with recent discussions among constitutional scholars of "interpretive" and "noninterpretive" review (see note 46 for some references) should be aware that my use of these labels departs from conventional use in at least one important way. The labels are usually associated with particular assumptions about the nature and limits of constitutional interpretation—assumptions I shall reject in Section 13. The labels do no harm and are, in fact, useful if we do not prejudge the issue of what counts as interpretation and what does not.

idated legislation merely because they have thought it unwise policy, and so exercised noninterpretive review. If so, in such cases the courts have not applied preexisting law—the Constitution—but have legislated or created law. And *this* would seem to constitute a breach of the separation of powers. These critics claim that the courts have abused the power of judicial review in a fairly systematic way.

The critics' complaint is quite general; it is directed against a variety of Supreme Court decisions over the last several decades concerning civil rights issues, such as the "incorporation" of key provisions of the Bill of Rights (applicable against the federal government) into the Fourteenth Amendment (making them applicable against state governments) and many of the so-called substantive due process and equal protection cases (concerning, for example, rights of the accused in criminal proceedings, the right to privacy, legislative districting, and school desegregation). Though the complaint is made and debated in scholarly circles,[39] it is not a merely theoretical or academic concern. The complaint is made and debated in popular forums as well and has adherents in both the current administration and the federal judiciary.[40]

In order to assess this complaint, we need to distinguish two possibilities. The complaint alleges that the Court has not applied the Constitution but instead made decisions based on nonlegal, "policy" (that is, extraconstitutional) grounds. But even if this claim is true, it could be true in two different ways. The Court could have consciously disregarded the limits of legitimate judicial review and invalidated legislation, not because it thought it unconstitutional, but because it thought the legislation unwise. Alternatively, the Court might have created law, rather than applied the Constitution, not because it set out to create law or revise policy, but because it interpreted the Constitution mistakenly.

Both critics and friends of the Court often act as if the issue were fidelity

---

39. See, for example, Robert Bork, "Neutral Principles and Some First Amendment Problems," *Indiana Law Journal* 47 (1971): 1–35; Raoul Berger, *Government by the Judiciary* (Cambridge: Harvard University Press, 1977); and Henry Monaghan, "Our Perfect Constitution," *New York University Law Review* 56 (1981): 353–96. As we shall see, many other scholars, while not themselves endorsing this complaint, nonetheless share important interpretive assumptions with its proponents.

40. Edwin Meese, "Construing the Constitution," *University of California Davis Law Review* 19 (1985): 22–30; William Rehnquist, "The Notion of a Living Constitution," *Texas Law Review* 54 (1976): 693–706; and Bork, "Neutral Principles and Some First Amendment Problems."

to the Constitution, as it would be if the first possibility were realized. But the real issue typically is not whether to apply the Constitution, but *how to interpret the Constitution*.[41] And, of course, there is no guarantee that judges will not make legal mistakes or legal misinterpretations. This can happen just as easily when courts are trying to apply statutes or resolve apparent conflicts among statutes as when they try to resolve possible conflicts between the Constitution and statutes (compare *Federalist* 78:16). So if the Court has systematically legislated and so exceeded the bounds of legitimate, interpretive judicial review, it is because it has sincerely employed a mistaken theory of constitutional interpretation. The real issue, then, is whether the Court's civil rights decisions reflect a systematically mistaken theory of constitutional interpretation.

   The critics' complaints about judicial review typically rest on one of two assumptions about constitutional interpretation. First, it is claimed that in the troublesome cases the Court has exceeded the scope of legitimate judicial review because it has invalidated legislation on grounds not explicitly provided for "within the four corners" of the document of the Constitution. This claim assumes that constitutional interpretation must be guided by, and cannot exceed, the "plain meaning" of language which actually occurs in the text of the Constitution.[42] Second, it is claimed that in the troublesome cases the Court has exceeded the scope of legitimate judicial review because it has invalidated legislation on the basis of reasoning which is not faithful to the (specific) intentions of the framers of the Constitution.[43] Though these two grounds for the critics' complaint are

   41. It would be a mistake, though, to suppose that the issue never is or could be fidelity to the Constitution. On some issues there may be legislative barriers to the enactment of genuinely popular legislation. These are issues on which minority views are entrenched in such a way as to block the passage of legislation with fairly wide popular appeal (e.g., the Equal Rights Amendment). It might be that in some such cases a politically independent judiciary would be in a position to, and should, implement desirable social policy. (These remarks should not be taken to imply that the Constitution, properly interpreted, does not already recognize the equal rights of women.) Or, alternatively, clearly tyrannical majorities which violate minority moral or political interests not protected by the Constitution may present a case for justifiable intentional judicial legislation. (Though friends of the Ninth Amendment may wonder whether there are any significant moral or political rights not protected by the Constitution.) Not every case of (conscious) judicial legislation can be justified in this way. But this sort of justification of judicial legislation is further reason for caution in condemning the actual history of the judicial invalidation of democratic legislation.
   42. See, e.g., Bork, "Neutral Principles and Some First Amendment Problems," pp. 8, 10.
   43. See, e.g., Bork, ibid., pp. 13, 17; Berger, *Government by the Judiciary*, pp. 3, 6, 45, 80, 89, 106, 115, 133, 286, 314, 363, 407; Monaghan, "Our Perfect Constitution," pp. 374ff. Cf.

Legal Theory,
Legal Interpretation,
and Judicial Review

not always distinguished,[44] they are distinct; the plain meaning of a document need not match the specific intentions of the framers of that document. This is especially likely where the language of the document is very general or abstract, as it is in the constitutional provisions whose interpretation is in question here.[45]

The two grounds of the critics' complaint share two assumptions about many important decisions of the Court: (a) the Court is no longer interpreting and applying the Constitution, but is instead applying extraconstitutional values, and (b) judicial review is legitimate only if it represents interpretation and application of the Constitution. What they differ over are the reasons for asserting (a); they make different assumptions about the nature of constitutional interpretation.

Moreover, these assumptions about the nature of constitutional interpretation are extremely pervasive; they are accepted by friends, as well as critics, of judicial review. A number of friends of judicial review concede (a), because they assume that constitutional interpretation must respect either the plain meaning of explicit constitutional provisions or the (specific) intentions of the framers. Thus these two grounds for asserting (a) are designated as two different versions of "interpretivism" and other

---

Chief Justice Taney in *Dred Scott v. Sandford*: "[The Constitution] speaks not only with the same words, but with the same meaning and intent with which it spoke when it came from the hands of the framers, and was voted on and adopted by the people of the United States. Any other rule of construction would abrogate the judicial character of this court and make it the mere reflex of popular opinion or passion of the day" (19 Howard at 426 [1857]); "The duty of the court is, to interpret the instrument they [the drafters of the Constitution] have framed, with the best lights we can obtain on the subject, and to administer it as we find it, according to its true intent and meaning when it was adopted" (id. at 405). In looking only at particular passages appealing to framers' intent it can be difficult to determine whether the writer is appealing to specific or abstract intent. But the purposes to which these writers put this appeal show that it is specific intent which they must have in mind. For only appeal to specific intent could underwrite the sort of quick, a priori objection to large bodies of the record of judicial review which these writers make. If we accept the appeal to abstract intent in the interpretation of the relevant constitutional provisions, we can go on to reject the Court's decisions only after sustained moral, political, and social argument about the proper extension of the values which these provisions express.

44. See Bork, "Neutral Principles and Some First Amendment Problems."

45. One good example of the way plain meaning and specific intent can diverge comes from the "free and equal clauses" to be found in the bills of rights in many southern state constitutions in the nineteenth century. While the plain meaning of these clauses would make slavery unconstitutional, this was clearly not an effect which the drafters of these clauses took them to have. See Robert Cover, *Justice Accused: Antislavery and the Judicial Process* (New Haven: Yale University Press, 1975), pp. 42ff., esp. 50–51.

methods of adjudication are referred to as forms of "noninterpretivism."[46] These friends concede that the Court has in many of these cases exceeded its function of interpreting and applying the Constitution and made decisions based on extraconstitutional moral and political grounds. Thus we find Michael Perry, a friend of the Court's record of judicial review, claiming that "there is no point belaboring what today few if any constitutional scholars would deny: that precious few twentieth-century constitutional decisions striking down governmental action in the name of the rights of individuals—the decisions featured in the 'individual rights' section of any contemporary constitutional law casebook—are the product of interpretive review."[47] The friends display their friendship with judicial review by rejecting (b); they claim that the Court should exercise certain forms of noninterpretive review and implement certain extraconstitutional values.[48]

I am sympathetic with skepticism about (b) and with the claim that judges have moral and political obligations besides the obligation to interpret and apply the law.[49] Thus I am sympathetic with the claim that we might be able to give a normative justification for certain exercises of judicial review even if that review could not be represented as good constitutional interpretation. But such a defense of judicial review must face the objection from democracy and the separation of powers; it must explain how this kind of judicial legislation can be justified. Such a defense might argue either that the extraconstitutional values which the Court should enforce are themselves democratic values or that democratic values are not always the most important values.[50] I think that both of these defenses

46. See Thomas Grey, "Do We Have an Unwritten Constitution?" *Stanford Law Review* 28 (1975): 703–18 (but see his more recent "The Constitution as Scripture," *Stanford Law Review* 37 [1984]: 1–25); Paul Brest, "The Misconceived Quest for the Original Understanding," *Boston University Law Review* 60 (1980): pp. 204–38; John Ely, *Democracy and Distrust* (Cambridge: Harvard University Press, 1980), chap. 1; and Michael Perry, *The Constitution, the Courts, and Human Rights* (New Haven: Yale University Press, 1982). Brest uses the labels "originalism" and "nonoriginalism," but he seems to make the same assumptions about what counts as interpretation.

47. Perry, *The Constitution, the Courts, and Human Rights*, p. 92. Though I am confident that this quotation gives a misleading impression of the extent of consensus on these issues among constitutional scholars, it expresses well Perry's own view and the view of *many* constitutional scholars.

48. Of course, not all of the friends of judicial review are equally good friends. Ely's friendship, for instance, is more selective than that of the other friends of judicial review.

49. See my "Legal Positivism and Natural Law Reconsidered," pp. 376ff.

50. See note 41 above. Railton, "Judicial Review, Elites, and Liberal Democracy," offers

are promising and should be explored in any proper theory of judicial review, but they require sustained normative argument which may not be necessary to defend large parts of the record of judicial review if, as I believe, we should reject the interpretive assumptions underlying (a).

Whether the Court is interpreting the Constitution or, instead, appealing to extraconstitutional values depends, of course, on what counts as legal, and in particular constitutional, interpretation. And the critics' (and friends') assumptions about the nature of constitutional interpretation are not only unargued for but, in fact, implausible.

The first assumption is that constitutional interpretation must respect the plain meaning of explicit constitutional language; let us call this the *plain meaning theory* of constitutional interpretation. As its name suggests, this theory of interpretation is a theory about how to determine the meaning or reference of constitutional provisions and might be defended by appeal to traditional semantic assumptions. There are two problems with the plain meaning theory. First, it seems incomplete. As our discussion here has suggested, semantics does not exhaust interpretation; interpretation must also appeal to underlying purpose. So even if the semantic assumptions of the plain meaning theory were correct, the plain meaning theory would at most be part of the correct theory of constitutional interpretation; it would have to be supplemented by an account of how to determine underlying purpose.

Incompleteness is not a fatal problem. But the second problem which the plain meaning theory faces is fatal. The plain meaning theory would be a reasonable way to determine the meaning and reference of constitutional provisions if, as the traditional semantic theory claims, the meaning of a word or phrase consisted in the descriptions conventionally associated with it and meaning determined reference. Then constitutional decisions which went beyond the conventional associations of explicit constitutional language could not be defended as constitutional interpretation. But this semantic theory is wrong. Meaning is not to be identified with, nor is reference determined by, the descriptions which any person or group associates with the language in question. Beliefs about the meaning and reference of constitutional language must be justified by appeal to the best available conceptions and theories about the real nature of the institu-

critical discussion of the former suggestion; Thomas Nagel, "The Supreme Court and Political Philosophy," *New York University Law Review* 56 (1981): 519–24, develops the latter suggestion.

tions, relations, and considerations which that language talks about. In the case of constitutional provisions which incorporate moral and political language, determination of the meaning and reference of these provisions will require the interpreter to engage in or rely on substantive moral and political theory.[51]

The second interpretive assumption underlying the views of both critics and friends of judicial review is that constitutional interpretation must respect what I have called the specific intentions of the framers; let us call this the *specific intent theory* of constitutional interpretation. The specific intent theory might be put forward as a theory about the semantics of constitutional interpretation, as a theory about how to determine underlying purpose, or both. However, it can be defended on none of these grounds.

Recent constitutional literature has raised a number of methodological and philosophical problems for specific intent theory.[52] What sort of historical evidence should be used to determine the specific intent of framers who are no longer alive? How reliable is this information? Can framers be said to have intentions about situations which they did not foresee or could not have envisaged? Whose intentions should we be concerned with—those of the members of the Constitutional Convention, those of the participants in state ratification, or those of the people whom these participants were supposed to represent? How do we aggregate conflicting intentions? These are all interesting and serious problems *within* specific intent theory. But the problems for that theory run deeper. Specific intent theory would be an implausible theory of constitutional interpretation even if it had satisfactory answers to these problems.

As an account of the semantics of constitutional interpretation, specific intent theory assumes that in determining the meaning of constitutional provisions we should be interested in what the language of the provisions meant at the time of enactment. If the traditional semantic theory were

---

51. Good examples of the kind of interpretation required here are Thomas Scanlon, "A Theory of Freedom of Expression," *Philosophy & Public Affairs* 1, no. 2 (Winter 1972): 204–26, and David Richards, *The Moral Criticism of Law* (Belmont, Calif.: Wadsworth, 1977), esp. chaps. 3 and 4.

52. See, e.g., Walter Murphy, "Constitutional Interpretation: The Art of the Historian, the Magician, or the Statesman?" *Yale Law Journal* 87 (1978): 1764–65; Brest, "The Misconceived Quest for the Original Understanding," pp. 209–10; Ely, *Democracy and Distrust*, chap. 2; and Dworkin, "The Forum of Principle," in MP, pp. 38–39. Not surprisingly, similar problems afflict specific intent theories of statutory interpretation; see, e.g., Max Radin, "Statutory Interpretation," *Harvard Law Review* 43 (1930): 863–85, and Gerald MacCallum, "Legislative Intent," *Yale Law Journal* 75 (1966): 754–82.

correct, the specific intentions of the framers of a constitutional provision (if we could identify them) would be a fairly reliable guide to the (original) meaning of the provision. Decisions based on moral and political reasoning whose conclusions the framers would not have endorsed could not be defended as constitutional interpretation. But, of course, we have found good reason to reject the traditional semantic theory on which this defense of the specific intent theory rests and to accept a semantic theory which often requires appeal to moral and political theory whose conclusions the framers would not have endorsed.

If our account of legal interpretation is approximately correct, constitutional interpretation must ascertain not only the meaning of constitutional provisions but their underlying purpose or rationale as well. Specific intent theory might be defended, not as an account of the semantics of constitutional interpretation, but as an account of how to determine underlying purpose. But in legal interpretation in general, and constitutional interpretation in particular, it is more plausible to identify a constitutional provision's underlying rationale with abstract, rather than specific, intent. The abstract character of the language used in the constitutional provisions whose interpretation is in question and the counterfactual test of dominant intent conspire to establish abstract intent as the appropriate kind of intent or purpose on which to focus in constitutional interpretation. Constitutional interpretation should try to identify the kind of moral and political values underlying various constitutional provisions and must then rely on substantive moral and political theory in determining the extension of these values.

The critics' complaint about the record of judicial review, therefore, is not compelling. Their complaint concerns the style, rather than the particular details, of a series of cases in which the Court has relied on substantive moral and political claims to declare state and federal legislation unconstitutional. Though this complaint rests on common assumptions about the nature and limits of constitutional interpretation which can be given philosophical motivation, these assumptions reflect unexamined and ultimately implausible claims about the nature and limits of legal, and in particular constitutional, interpretation. The Court can and must rely on substantive moral and political theory in interpreting and applying the Constitution.[53]

53. My discussion of the received assumptions about constitutional interpretation and my own alternative theory of constitutional interpretation might profitably be compared with

A complaint which relies on general, theoretical assumptions calls for a general, theoretical response. An adequate reply to this complaint about the record of judicial review, therefore, does not require detailed analyses of cases. Our claims about interpretation vindicate the style, if not the content, of the Court's decisions against these common complaints. Thus this defense of the Court does not show that every exercise of judicial review has been legitimate, much less that the Court's constitutional interpretation has been irreproachable. But then we would not expect a theory about the nature of constitutional interpretation to establish this. Individual judges and particular Courts can make both local and global interpretive mistakes. It is on this assumption that constitutional doctrine evolves.

For all this, it might still be helpful to examine briefly two cases to see the possible implications of our discussion of constitutional interpretation. The first case is *Brown*. *Brown* invalidated segregated educational facilities as violations of the equal protection clause of the Fourteenth Amendment; in so doing, it overruled *Plessy* by claiming that separate facilities were inherently unequal. But *Brown* is difficult to defend as a case of interpretive review on either the specific intent or the plain meaning theory of constitutional interpretation. For present purposes, we might think of the equal protection clause as prohibiting unjustified or invidious governmental discrimination or as requiring, as Dworkin suggests (TRS, pp. 226–27), that governmental action treat citizens with equal concern and respect. Though separate educational facilities would *now* conventionally be regarded as (invidiously) discriminatory or as inconsistent with equal concern and respect, this was not true at the time *Brown* was decided. (Perhaps more importantly, whether *Brown* was correctly decided should not turn on whether separate facilities were conventionally regarded as discriminatory or as inconsistent with equal concern and respect.) So even if a decision today similar to *Brown* could be justified on interpretive grounds by appeal to the plain meaning theory, *Brown* cannot be so justified. Nor, it seems, can *Brown* be justified by appeal to specific intent theory, for it seems fairly certain that the specific intentions of (at least the majority of) the framers of the Fourteenth Amendment did not include the

---

three recent discussions which I regard as defending largely complementary claims: David Richards, "Constitutional Interpretation, History, and the Death Penalty," *California Law Review* 71 (1983): 1372–98; Dworkin, LE, esp. chaps. 2, 7, 10; and David Lyons, "Constitutional Interpretation and Original Meaning," *Social Philosophy and Policy* 4 (1986): 75–101.

regulation of segregated educational facilities.[54] We may think that the framers of the Fourteenth Amendment had the abstract intent to prohibit governmental discrimination or governmental action inconsistent with equal concern and respect and that the correct conception of the extension of this value shows that segregated facilities violate the equal protection clause. But this would be to rely on abstract intent and our collateral beliefs about the extension of the values expressed in that abstract intent. It seems clear that the framers of the Fourteenth Amendment held different collateral beliefs and so different specific intentions. If so, *Brown* cannot be defended by appeal to specific intent.

If we accept these assumptions about the nature and limits of constitutional interpretation, we must conclude that *Brown* cannot be defended as interpretive review; it can be defended, if at all, only as a legitimate exercise of noninterpretive review. Critics of judicial review have in general been reluctant to focus on *Brown.* They have either failed to see that *Brown* cannot be squared with their insistence on interpretive review and their assumptions about interpretation,[55] regarded *Brown* as illegitimate but too well entrenched to oppose,[56] or concluded that *Brown* is a legitimate instance of noninterpretive review.

But there are no such problems in accepting the legitimacy of *Brown* if our claims about the semantics of constitutional interpretation are correct. Part of interpreting the equal protection clause and applying it to *Brown* is ascertaining the meaning and extension of "equal protection." Assuming that part of its meaning is to prohibit (invidious) discrimination and to ensure that governmental action treats citizens with equal concern and respect (showing this may itself require appeal to abstract intent), the interpreter must rely on moral, political, and social claims in ascertaining the semantic content of the equal protection clause. Reasonable moral and political claims about the nature of discrimination and equal concern and respect together with reasonable social claims about the nature and effects

---

54. See Berger, *Government by the Judiciary*, chap. 7.
55. This seems to be the explanation of Bork's acceptance of *Brown*; see Bork, "Neutral Principles and Some First Amendment Problems," pp. 14–15. With *Brown* he seems willing to rely on a version of abstract intent theory together with his own collateral beliefs about discrimination. If he were willing to apply these interpretive assumptions elsewhere (and if he applied the counterfactual test of dominant intent correctly and attempted to justify his collateral moral and political views), he might take a rather different view of the Court's record than he does.
56. See Berger, *Government by the Judiciary*, pp. 412–13.

of segregated education imply that segregated educational facilities do not fall within the extension of "equal protection." Appeal to the abstract intent underlying the equal protection clause of the Fourteenth Amendment would seem to point in exactly the same interpretive direction. A very good case can be made, therefore, for regarding *Brown* as a paradigmatic exercise of legitimate, interpretive judicial review.

Our second case is more controversial. One case typically cited to illustrate the critics' position is *Griswold* v. *Connecticut*,[57] in which the Court invalidated a Connecticut statute prohibiting the sale and use of contraceptives on the ground that this statute violated a married couple's constitutional right of privacy.[58] Douglas, who wrote the majority opinion, admitted that the Constitution did not explicitly grant a right of privacy but claimed that the right to privacy could be found in "the penumbra" of the First Amendment (freedom of speech and association), the Third Amendment (the right not to have one's house invaded in peacetime without one's consent), the Fourth Amendment (freedom from unreasonable search and seizure), the Fifth Amendment (guarantee of due process), and the Ninth Amendment (nonenumerated rights retained by people) and applied to state legislation through the Fourteenth Amendment. *Griswold* is a favorite of the critics both because Douglas's opinion is thought to represent a strained interpretation and because its recognition of a constitutional right to privacy is thought to have laid the groundwork for such "excesses" as *Eisenstadt* v. *Baird*[59] and *Roe* v. *Wade*.[60]

But does *Griswold* represent a strained interpretation of the Constitution? Of course, a right to privacy is, as Douglas concedes, nowhere enumerated in the Constitution, so *Griswold* cannot be defended by appeal to the plain meaning of explicit constitutional language. Equally clearly, the framers did not intend the Bill of Rights to preclude birth control legislation, so *Griswold* cannot be defended by appeal to the framers' specific intent. But, as we have seen, there is no compelling motivation for these constraints upon constitutional interpretation. Determination of the

57. 381 U.S. 479 (1965).
58. See, e.g., Bork, "Neutral Principles and Some First Amendment Problems," pp. 7–8; Monaghan, "Our Perfect Constitution," pp. 381–82. Cf. Grey, "Do We Have an Unwritten Constitution?" pp. 709, 713n; Ely, *Democracy and Distrust*, p. 2; and Perry, *The Constitution, the Courts, and Human Rights*, pp. 1–2, 11, 117–18.
59. 405 U.S. 438 (1972) (invalidating a statute prohibiting the sale of contraceptives to *unmarried* people as a violation of their constitutional right of privacy).
60. 410 U.S. 113 (1973) (invalidating a Texas statute prohibiting abortions before as well as after the viability of the fetus).

meaning and extension of the provisions of the Bill of Rights and the Fourteenth Amendment protecting moral or political values will require a good
deal of moral and political reasoning about the nature and scope of the political rights recognized in those amendments. And in providing interpretations of constitutional provisions, we must appeal, as we have seen, to
underlying purpose as well as meaning. Both the language of these constitutional provisions and our counterfactual test establish that the appropriate description of underlying purpose will be abstract. So we need to
identify the kind of moral and political values which the relevant constitutional amendments are supposed to protect. This interpretive task requires that we engage in descriptive moral and political theory; we must
see what moral and political principles underlie our constitutional provisions. To see what the Constitution as a whole, properly interpreted, implies about *Griswold* we would have to identify these moral and political
principles and their place in a coherent moral and political theory of the
Constitution.

Now this is just the sort of reasoning which Douglas's opinion in *Griswold* contains. Of course, we might like to see Douglas's claims worked
out more systematically. In particular, it would be nice to know something
more about the scope of a right to privacy. Is it a general right to privacy?
Or is it a right to privacy only in certain matters, and if so, which? (Answers to these questions are important, since the scope of this right will
certainly affect whether we think *Griswold* is a good precedent for *Roe.*)
But the form of his argument is clear enough. Douglas argues, not implau-
sibly, that at least part of the rationale for the First, Third, Fourth, Fifth,
and Ninth Amendments is a principle of privacy or personal autonomy
which protects certain of an individual's interests from governmental interference. And it is difficult to imagine a plausible political theory of the
Constitution which would not include a strong principle of privacy or personal autonomy. And, whatever its exact scope, it is not implausible to
think that any such right of privacy which really served as part of the rationale for all of these otherwise disparate amendments would protect the
sexual and reproductive privacy of a married couple. *Griswold*, therefore,
establishes no clear abuse of judicial review.

14. Conclusion

Though my argument has been somewhat programmatic, it has, I think,
established the importance and plausibility of both a general program

43

linking constitutional theory and legal theory via their common interest in legal interpretation and the particular interpretive theory developed here. Important debates in constitutional theory and legal theory have too long failed to address underlying interpretive issues. Common positions in constitutional and legal theory rely on unexamined and, in fact, implausible assumptions about these issues. I have defended a particular theory of legal interpretation incorporating particular views about the semantics of legal interpretation and the nature of underlying purpose. This theory undermines common views in legal theory about the nature and determinacy of law and common views in constitutional theory about the nature of constitutional interpretation and the legitimacy of judicial review. These are reasons for legal theory and constitutional theory to pursue jointly this general program and to take seriously the particular account developed here of how this general program should be worked out.

THE ETHICAL BASIS OF LEGAL CRITICISM

FELIX COHEN*

THAT all valuations of law are moral judgments, that the major part of legal philosophy is a branch of ethics, that the problem which the judge faces is, in the strictest sense, a moral problem, and that the law has no valid end or purpose other than the maintenance of the good life are propositions which jurists are apt to resent with some acerbity. In the orthodox juristic tradition there is some sort of boundary between the realm of law and the realm of morality or ethics; legal philosophy deals with justice ·rather than with goodness; morality is at most an emergency consideration in the problem before a judge, and his decision of that problem will be right or wrong in some non-ethical sense; finally it is not the business of the law to make men good provided only it makes them act justly. It is submitted that these tenets of current juristic faith spring from an indefensible view of the nature and scope of ethics and tinge current legal criticism with a peculiar confusion.

Before examining the relation of law to ethics, it may be well to point out that those who deny the ethical responsibilities of law and legal science do not refrain from passing what we should ordinarily call ethical judgments upon the law. A historical school of law vehemently disclaims concern with ethics or natural law,[1] but repeatedly invokes a *Volksgeist* or a *Zeitgeist* to decide what the law ought to be.[2] An analytical school of jurisprudence

---

* Book Review and Current Legislation Editor of Columbia Law Review for 1930-1931; contributor to Encyclopedia of the Social Sciences; now research assistant to Bernard L. Shientag, Justice of the Supreme Court of the State of New York, and lecturer at the Rand School of Social Science and the New School of Social Research.

This article forms an introductory chapter in a study of "Ethical Systems and Legal Ideals" to be published by the Vanguard Press.

[1] See MAINE, EARLY HISTORY OF INSTITUTIONS (7th ed. 1914) 370 and lectures 12 and 13 *passim;* Savigny, *Ueber den Zweck dieser Zeitschrift* (1815) 1 ZEITSCHRIFT FÜR GESCHICHT. RECHTSWISSENSCHAFT 4-5.

[2] See CARTER, THE PROPOSED CODIFICATION OF OUR COMMON LAW (1884) 86 *et seq.* (a paper prepared at the request of the committee of the Bar Association of the City of New York, appointed to oppose the measure). This pamphlet is largely based upon Savigny's essay, VOM BERUF UNSRER ZEIT FÜR GESETZGEBUNG UND RECHTSWISSENSCHAFT (1814), translated by Hayward as THE VOCATION OF OUR AGE FOR LEGISLATION AND JURISPRUDENCE (1831), which was written under somewhat similar circumstances in answer to the demand for codification of German law (See THIBAUT, UEBER

again dismisses questions of morality,[3] and again decides what the law ought to be by reference to a so-called logical ideal.[4] Those who derive the law from the will of the sovereign usually introduce without further justification the implication that it is good to obey that will.[5] And those who define law in terms of prevailing social demands or interests frequently make use of an undisclosed principle to the effect that these demands ought to be satisfied.[6]

The objection, then, is not that jurists have renounced ethical judgment, but that they have renounced ethical science. Ethical science involves an analysis of ethical judgments, a clarification of ethical premises. Among the current legal crypto-idealisms there can be no edifying controversy since there is no recognition of the moral issues to which their differences reduce. One looks in vain in legal treatises and law review articles for legal criticism conscious of its moral presuppositions. The vocabularies of logic and aesthetics are freely drawn upon in the attempt to avoid the disagreeable assertion that something or other is intrinsically better than something else. Particular decisions or legal rules are "anomalous" or "illogical", "incorrect" or "impractical", "reactionary" or "liberal", and unarguable ethical innuendo takes the place of critical analysis.[7] Little wonder then

---

DIE NOTHWENDIGKEIT EINES ALLGEMEINEN BÜRGERLICHEN RECHTS FÜR DEUTSCHLAND, reprinted in THIBAUT, CIVILISTISCHE ABHANDLUNGEN (1814) 404).

It was characteristic that Maine's famous generalization "status to contract" (MAINE, ANCIENT LAW (1861) c. 5) was proposed and generally received as an indication of the desirability of free contract.

[3] See AMOS, SCIENCE OF JURISPRUDENCE (1872) 18; POLLOCK, ESSAYS IN JURISPRUDENCE AND ETHICS (1882) c. 1 (*The Nature of Jurisprudence*) 18-32.

[4] A good example of this ethical use of analysis is found in the development of the *prima facie* theory of torts (see POLLOCK, LAW OF TORTS (1st ed. 1887) c. 1) which purports to be merely an analysis of what has always been the law but actually gives the old law of conspiracy a new impetus (see Note (1930) 30 COL. L. REV. 510) and threatens to extend its vagaries over the individual life.

[5] "Legislatures and courts formulate or seek to formulate the will of all of us as to the conduct of each of us in our relations with each other and with all. That will ought to be wholly effective. That it fails of effect in any degree is a misfortune." Pound, *Enforcement of Law* (1908) 20 GREEN BAG 401.

[6] See Pound, *Jurisprudence*, in HISTORY AND PROSPECTS OF THE SOCIAL SCIENCES (1925) 472, and Pound, INTRODUCTION TO THE PHILOSOPHY OF LAW (1922) 95-99.

[7] One might expect to find in the American Law Institute's attempted "Restatements" of various branches of the common law some attempt to work out the meaning of controversial rules of law in terms of social consequences and some indication of the moral standards which make the rule laid down in Mississippi preferable to the rule laid down in Ohio. Instead, one meets the pious fiction, implicit in the very title of the enterprise, that

that on a more abstract plane of thought the classification of ideas has taken the place of legal philosophy,[8] while Hegelian pictures of inevitable trends are offered as substitutes for the delineation of the desirable.[9]

It is probable that the dependence of jurisprudence upon ethics is partly obscured by the habit of smuggling ethical notions into one's definition of law. Blackstone could define law as "a rule of civil conduct prescribed by the supreme power in a state, commanding what is right and prohibiting what is wrong." [10] This is very much like the benevolent definition of a sou as a small coin to be given to the poor. Upon such a definition the question of whether law is good cannot be significant, and ethical questions

---

the common law is a system within which intellectual inspection reveals a definite answer for every legal question. Decisions are hailed as "correct" or "incorrect" rather than "good" or "bad", and truth is obtained either in accordance with the mathematical precepts of the Valentinian Law of Citations (426 A. D.), or by projecting evolutionary "tendencies" found in the past decisions of courts, or by reacting aesthetically to the harmony or discord between a questioned rule and the rest of the legal "system." *Cf.* the strictures of Kantorowicz upon the German civil code, RECHTSWISSENSCHAFT UND SOZIOLOGIE (1911) 8.

[8] All who appreciate Dean Pound's unparalleled equipment in legal philosophy must hope that such taxonomic studies as LAW AND MORALS (1924); *The Scope and Purpose of Sociological Jurisprudence* (1911) 24 HARV. L. REV. 591, (1911-12) 25 HARV. L. REV. 140, 489; *The End of Law as Developed in Legal Rules and Doctrines* (1914) 27 HARV. L. REV. 195; *The End of Law as Developed in Juristic Thought* (1914) 27 HARV. L. REV. 605, (1917) 30 HARV. L. REV. 201 are preludes to some affirmative statement of valid legal standards or ideals.

[9] Courts frequently rely or purport to rely not on actual decisions but on tendencies in series of past decisions. The fact that two earlier cases have each stretched a rule a little further than existing precedents in each case warranted is taken to indicate the desirability of stretching the rule still further in a third case. The assumption seems to be that all change is for the better and is infinitely capable of extension. The philosophical generalization of this type of argument is, of course, evolutionism. Dean Pound has frequently followed Hegel, Marx, and Spencer in putting forward evolutionary schemes of legal history in answer to strictly ethical questions. See INTRODUCTION TO THE PHILOSOPHY OF LAW (1922) 95-99; *Justice According to Law* (1913) 13 COL. L. REV. 696, (1914) 14 COL. L. REV. 1, 103, especially at 117-21; *The Theory of Judicial Decision* (1923) 36 HARV. L. REV. 641, 802, 940, especially at 954-8. But this identification of the inevitable and the desirable under the banner of Progress is, as Huxley, Sidgwick, G. E. Moore, and M. R. Cohen have demonstrated, intellectually indefensible,—however gratifying emotionally it may be to feel that cheering for the winning side is the substance of morality.

[10] BLACKSTONE, COMMENTARIES *44. That "right" and "wrong" in this definition are ethical rather than strictly legal terms is made clear in Blackstone's own exegesis upon his definition. *54-55. Much confusion in the reading and, it may be suspected, in the writing of continental legal philosophy arises from the fact that *Recht, droit, diritto,* etc. denote at the same time the positive concept of law and the normative notion of right, justice or ideal law.

are either evaded by denying the appellation *law* to certain en-
actments and courses of judicial decision or else settled by the
complacent and preposterous assumption that whatever sover-
eigns have commanded is good. Law is law, whether it be good
or bad, and only upon the admission of this truism can a meaningful discussion of the goodness and badness of law rest.

Upon any of the current positive definitions of law, *e. g.*, "the
body of rules according to which courts decide controversies",[11]
the indispensability of ethics in legal criticism is immediately
obvious.[12] Ethics involves all final applications of the terms *good*,

---

[11] This definition (see Keyser, *On the Study of Legal Science* (1929)
38 YALE L. J. 413) seems to me to avoid an unfortunate ambiguity in
Gray's definition of law as "composed of the rules which the courts . . .
lay down for the determination of legal rights and duties." GRAY, NATURE
AND SOURCES OF THE LAW (1909) § 191. I do not think that Gray meant to
equate law with rules *enunciated* by courts, but if he did Mr. Frank's
criticism that such rules are often merely verbal and in any case subject
to interpretation, with the result that they must be considered sources of
law (like statutes) rather than law, is irrefutable. See FRANK, LAW AND
THE MODERN MIND (1930) 121-32. In any case, Gray failed to recognize
with sufficient clarity that judges make law only in the way that electrons
make physics and amoebae make biology. What is law, as that term is
most commonly used by lawyers, is the way or pattern in which judges
decide cases, and this way or pattern may be as remote from the mind of
the judge as is the Gestalt psychology from Köhler's anthropoid subjects.
As a matter of fact a lawyer looking for "the law" on a point will generally
pay more attention to a wholly unofficial schematization of decided cases
found in a legal treatise than to a judicial opinion which "lays down" the
law. Where this is not the case, it is because of the scholarship of the
particular judge rather than his authority.

[12] In a recent article Professor Dickinson has attacked the realistic or
positive definition of law on the ground that it does not fit the problem of
the judge himself, who does not want to know what he is about to do.
(*Legal Rules: Their Function in the Process of Decision* (1931) 79 U. OF P.
L. REV. 833, 843-844). But this is to assume that a judge's duty is to *find*
the law rather than to *mold* it, an assumption which no realist makes. In
a similar vein Dickinson argues that if we should call judicial responsive-
ness to unworthy motives law, it would become "difficult . . . to find any
proper standard for criticizing the behavior of the judge." (*ibid.* 838) Again
by assuming without question the traditional premises which realists have
been attacking, Dickinson arrives at an absurdity which he ascribes to his
opponents. Unless one assumes that law is above ethical criticism, there
is no difficulty in criticizing a judge for making or perpetuating bad law.
The confusion becomes evident when Dickinson asserts that "a legal rule,
even though derived by generalization from what has been done, is not a
rule of isness because it either may or may not be applied in the next case,
i. e., the case for which the rule is sought, depending on the volition of the
judge." (*ibid.* 860, note 51) Obviously if a legal rule is a general formulation of judicial behavior, it must explain the next case as well as the last
case. The existence of legal rules is not disturbed by judicial volition, since
rules are simply descriptions of the way judicial volition works. And a description of judicial volition is a rule of *isness*. Dickinson has confused
normative and descriptive science by failing to recognize that a description

bad, better, best, right, ought, and *their derivatives.*[13] We may decide whether law is *good for* strengthening social bonds or *bad for* the peace of mind of criminals, without any appeal to ethics, but when we come to the question of whether the strengthening of social bonds or the peace of mind of criminals is good, and whether law which has the described effects is good, we are in the realm of ethics. Thus every valuation of law, every formulation of the ideal object or end of law, must be either categorical and ethical, or conditional, in terms of some ulterior aim which can itself be valued ethically. In either case, there is no way of escaping the final responsibility of law to ethics, and, since the legal order is a complex of human activities, to morality.

Although the criticism of elements of the legal order is ethical, it does not exhaust the realm of ethics, for ethical judgments can certainly be passed upon other things than law, and even upon things which law can in no wise affect. To delimit the realm of ethics which is relevant to law is merely to outline the body of ethically justiciable facts which law can comprehend or affect. And that body of facts, of course, is something which will vary with the level of commercial, industrial, and military development reached in a given society, with the temper of a people and their political-ethical beliefs, and with all other factors that go to determine the balance of powers and desires upon which law enforcement rests. To neglect, for instance, the influence of the machine gun in strengthening the forces behind law against rebellious populations and thus making it possible for the state to legislate in fields once closed to it is simply to make legal *ideals* of ancient *facts.* There is no realm of human conduct that we can hold eternally absolved from the possibility of judicial con-

---

of purposive behavior is not itself purposive. He has said nothing which reveals the impossibility or undesirability of a descriptive science of judicial conduct. He has offered no reason for believing that *law* as the realists understand the term is not a more precise concept (his own criterion of definition) than the amorphous Something which is neither a description of what courts actually do nor a formulation of what they ought to do (*ibid.* 861-862) but a jumble of the two notions whose only merit is faithfulness to the fundamental confusions in modern juristic thought.

[13] I follow G. E. Moore in this use of the word *ethics* to cover all problems of goodness and its related concepts, whether or not concerned with human conduct, leaving the term *morality* to designate the narrower field of value judgments of voluntary human acts. This use of the term *ethics* is, I think, too well substantiated historically to require apology. "Axiology" or "theory of values" may be more accurate appellations for our subject from a philological point of view, since they avoid the suggestion of a particular reference to human conduct. But both names are much too clumsy for consistent usage, and the latter at least carries its own aura of ambiguity, being extended in application to values other than goodness (*e. g.*, truth and beauty), while frequently restricted, from the viewpoint of method, to a particular naturalistic philosophy.

trol and the need of juristic attention. The only permanent restriction that we can fix upon the realm of ethical goods in terms
of which law must be judged is found in the proposition that law
can affect only human activities and such other happenings as
depend upon human activities.[14] The good life [15] is the final and
indispensable standard of legal criticism.[16]

This proposition is commonly attacked on two grounds. In the
first place, it is claimed, we do not know what the effects of law
will be. And in the second place, we do not know what the good
life is.

Both of these objections are true in a certain sensé, but in that
sense they do not contradict our conclusion. It is certainly true
that we cannot calculate all the effects of law or of anything
else. And it is equally obvious that our knowledge of ethics and
of human nature is not great enough to permit us to describe
completely and in detail what constitutes the good life for each
person or even for the abstract man. But if there is any such
thing as human knowledge, we certainly have a fair degree of it
upon both these subjects. And, as a great French jurist, M. Pierre
Tourtoulon, has said, "There is no need to throw to the dogs
everything that is not fit for the altars of the gods." A recognition of the inadequacy of our knowledge in these fields can
bring a sweet scepticism into our political beliefs, but it cannot
deny them. To quote again from Tourtoulon, "The greatest jurist
has only very vague ideas concerning the services that the laws
which he expounds and explains render to society . . . The first
step toward wisdom is the knowledge that we are ignorant of
nearly all the functions of our laws, or of the evil or the good
which they may bring us." [17]

The inadequacy of human knowledge, we may conclude, does
not destroy the usefulness of our form of evaluation. In fact, a
judgment of ethical values whose truth is recognized to be partially dependent upon the accuracy of human scientific knowledge
seems to be far more useful than the sort of judgment which assumes that however uncertain the physical results of an act may

---

[14] Possible intrinsic goods in the legal order, *e. g.*, the happiness of judges
and the aesthetic satisfactions of lawyers, are themselves elements in lives
affected by law. Non-human goods achievable by law, *e. g.*, the well-being
of domestic animals, may be accounted for in the instrumental valuation
of the human lives through which they are attained.

[15] In speaking of the good life I do not, of course, mean to imply that
different sorts of living may not be equally valuable. The *good life* is
simply a concept common, though applying in varying degrees, to all lives
worth living.

[16] See ARISTOTLE, POLITICS, Bk. 7, c. 1; NICHOMACHAEN ETHICS, Bk. 1,
c. 2; RUSSELL, POLITICAL IDEALS (1917) 4.

[17] TOURTOULON, LES PRINCIPES PHILOSOPHIQUES DE L'HISTOIRE DU DROIT
(1908) translated in 13 MODERN LEGAL PHILOSOPHY SERIES (1922) 24.

be, we can know clearly in advance whether they will be good or bad.

Suppose, however, that this is erroneous, and that our actual judgments of law in terms of the good life are wholly unreliable and useless. Still it does not follow that the theory which makes legal values dependent upon such causal efficacy is false. Great confusion has been caused in ethical controversy by the belief that knowing and publishing the truth is always good, and that it is therefore unnecessary to distinguish between the goodness or usefulness of an ethical theory and its truth.[18] The judgment that the value of law depends upon the law's efficacy in promoting the good life would be true even if it were wholly useless in legal criticism. But I believe that this judgment is far from useless, for although it offers no material measure of legal values, it provides a logical base upon which all significant discussion of the subject can rest.[19] In this field of the valuation of law, as in most other domains of thought, confusion is a more potent source of evil than is error. A formal principle of this sort cannot insure against error, but it can bring light to the foundations of our thinking. It can bring our traditional legal controversies into the fertilizing context of ethical science. It can free legal criticism from blind deduction from obsolete moral postulates. It can illumine "social engineering" by inducing a critical attitude towards the social interests that the law is asked to protect.[20] It

---

[18] An interesting example of the attempt to prove propositions by showing the disastrous effects of disbelief is provided in a recent volume by Professor Brumbaugh which bears the promising title LEGAL REASONING AND BRIEFING: "Thus all things made legal are at the same time made legally ethical because it is law, and the law must be deemed ethical, or the system itself must perish." (p. 7).

[19] The responsibility of law and juristic science to pure ethics, which is analysed in this article, does not exhaust the significance of this principle. The relevance of sociological data to law, which is the converse aspect of this formula (What *are* the effects of law upon human life?), is developed in Pound, *The Scope and Purpose of Sociological Jurisprudence, supra* note 8, especially at 512.

[20] The current notion that the function of the jurist is simply to secure adequate enforcement for the expressed demands of society (see L. K. Frank, *Institutional Analysis of the Law* (1924) 24 COL. L. REV. 480, 497-8 for an interesting *reductio ad absurdum* of this view) derives from a dangerous metaphor. Society is not vocal. The expressed demands of society are the demands of vocally organized groups, and a discreet deference to the power of such groups should not lead us to confuse their demands with "social welfare." *Cf.* Judge Hough's criticism of this confusion in his review of Dean Pound's SPIRIT OF THE COMMON LAW (1922), in (1922) 22 COL. L. REV. 385: "The present lecturer can and does sum up the judicial duty of decision by saying that the jurists of today (and judges are presumable jurists) are content to seek the jural postulates of the civilization of the time—a phrase extremely easy of translation into keeping one's ear to the ground to hear the tramp of insistent crowds."

can bring legal scholarship into a more intimate contact with
practical legal problems by reminding jurists that logical, historical, and sociological analyses of law are merely necessary intro-
ductions to the argument: This decision or statute is desirable
because in some way it promotes the good life.

II

That the valuation of law is thus dependent upon our concept of
the good life is perhaps a truism, but it is certainly not a commonplace. The ignoring or tacit rejection of this dependence is
extremely general in juristic literature, although few legal writers have made their disavowal explicit. To M. Leon Duguit we
may profitably appeal for a statement of the typical position
that the field of law is independent of ethics and morality. To
show the inadequacy of this doctrine is to point to the error upon
which a vast amount of legal philosophizing is based.

Law, according to Duguit, has for its sole purpose, social solidarity. Solidarity, he insists, is a fact, not a rule of conduct. "It
is not an imperative." [21] Duguit shows inductively that law
makes for social solidarity and that such solidarity is a feature
of all societies. But, as with so many other jurists, this inductive generalization suffers a gradual metamorphosis [22] and is
finally used as the sole basis for such commands or ethical judgments as the following: "Respect every act of individual will determined by an end of social solidarity;" [23] "every individual
ought to abstain from any act that would be determined by an
end contrary to social solidarity;" [24] "it is a crime to preach
the struggle of classes." [25] Since it is impossible to derive the
goodness of an act from its frequency or universality, Duguit's
judgments can be true only if the doctrine of solidarity is, in

---

[21] DUGUIT, L'ETAT: LE DROIT OBJECTIF ET LA LOI POSITIVE, translated in
7 MODERN LEGAL PHILOSOPHY SERIES (1916) 259.

[22] Professor Husik, in a review of TOURTOULON'S PHILOSOPHY IN THE
DEVELOPMENT OF LAW in (1923) 71 U. OF P. LAW REV. 416 thus sum-
marizes the procedure: " . . . one starts with the proposition, 'Men live
in society', which is perfectly true, and ends up with the statement, 'The
aim of the life of the individual is to contribute to the development of
the social body', which is far from being a scientific statement and may
easily be denied. Moreover if the last proposition is intended as imposing
an obligation, it can never be logically derived from the statement of a
fact. Most, if not all, of the books dealing with natural law by advocates
of that doctrine, such as Thomas Aquinas, Grotius, Lorimer, are guilty of
this fallacy." (pp. 418, 419).

[23] DUGUIT, *op. cit. supra* note 21, at 290.

[24] *Ibid.* 292.

[25] DUGUIT, LES TRANSFORMATIONS GENERALES DU DROIT PRIVÉ DEPUIS LE
CODE NAPOLEON (1920) § 48. Translated in 11 CONTINENTAL LEGAL HIS-
TORY SERIES, 135.

contradiction to his own claims, an ethical imperative. It seems fair to characterize such a position as crypto-idealism. Duguit has not gotten rid of ethics at all, as he proposes to do, but he has agreed not to use the *word* "ethics" lest his extremely shaky ethical system be challenged.[26]

Although Duguit's aversion to the concepts of ethics is not very widely shared outside the realm of jurisprudence, he can claim the support of many philosophers for the faulty method by which he actually builds up his ethical system. Bertrand Russell thus analyzes the method:

"It may be laid down that every ethical system is based upon a certain *non sequitur*. The philosopher first invents a false theory as to the nature of things, and then deduces that wicked actions are those which show that his theory is false. To begin with the traditional Christian: he argues that, since everything always obeys the will of God, wickedness consists in disobedience to the will of God. We then come on to the Hegelian, who argues that the universe consists of parts which harmonize in a perfect organism, and therefore wickedness consists of behavior which deminishes the harmony—though it is difficult to see how such behavior is possible, since complete harmony is metaphysically necessary. Bergson . . . shows that human beings never behave mechanically, and then, in his book on *Laughter*, he argues that what makes us laugh is to see a person behaving mechanically— *i. e.*, you are ridiculous when you do something that shows Bergson's philosophy to be false, and only then. These examples have, I hope, made it plain that a metaphysic can never have ethical consequences except in virtue of its falsehood; if it were true, the acts which it defines as sin would be impossible." [27]

The application of this analysis has been modestly under-estimated by Mr. Russell. For all ethical theories which are extracted from positive thought, scientific as well as metaphysical, show a similar weakness. Everything obeys the law of evolution. Therefore those societies that do not obey the law of evolution are inferior. All men act instinctively. Therefore those who repress their instincts are bad. All commercial transactions take place in accordance with the laws of supply and demand. Therefore every interference with the laws of supply and demand is undesirable. All law springs from the national spirit. Therefore law which does not spring from this spirit (code law, etc.) is bad.[28]

---

[26] M. Duguit naively confesses to having experienced some disquietude with his ultimate appeal to social fact when Germany was destroying Belgium. But the final punishment of Germany apparently convinced him that social force is its own justification. Duguit, *Objective Law* (1921) 20 Col. L. Rev. 817, (1921) 21 Col. L. Rev. 17, 126, 242, especially 254-56.

[27] Russell, Sceptical Essays (1928) c. 7 (*Behaviorism and Values*) 94.

[28] It is only with the aid of this fallacy that the historical, analytical,

It is unnecessary to multiply examples.

The abduction of law from the domain of morality is defended by Professor E. M. Morgan in a slightly different manner. He writes:

"It must be remembered that the law does not have the same purpose as religion or ethics or morals. It is not concerned with developing the spiritual or moral character of the individual but with regulating his objective conduct toward his fellows. Consequently courts will have to formulate and apply some rules which have no relation at all to morals, some which have to place a loss upon one of two equally blameless persons, some which impose liability regardless of fault and some which refuse to penalize conduct denounced by even the morally blind. It must be apparent that the moral law has no mandate upon the content of the rules of the road. . . " [29]

This passage is so clearly typical of a view widely maintained (particularly in our American law schools) that we may profitably subject it to a closer criticism than its position in a student's handbook might otherwise warrant. In the first sentence we are told that law does not have the same *purpose* as religion or ethics or morals. It is upon the ambiguity of this word that the specious force of the rest of the argument depends. If the word refers to the state of mind of judges or legislators, the assertion that this differs from the state of mind of moralists, ethical philosophers, and religious leaders is perhaps true but is completely irrelevant to Professor Morgan's ethical conclusions as to what the law ought to do. If by the "purpose" of law is meant that at which law *ought* to aim, the statement is relevant, indeed basic, to his further conclusions, but obviously false. For the law ought to secure the good life, which is the ideal purpose of moral and religious rules as well.

In the second sentence of this excerpt we are told that law is not concerned with certain noble ends. Again the same basic ambiguity. If the law is not actually concerned with man's spiritual

---

metaphysical, and sociological schools of jurisprudence are able to wage civil war. Were the interests of these schools properly confined to the history, the internal analysis, the metaphysical status, and the sociological functioning of law, repectively, conflict would be impossible and we should see, instead, simply a salutary division of labor. But each school has smuggled an ethics into its positive studies. To the argument of the historicists that since law is a product of national custom, the *Rechtsgefühl*, or the *Volksgeist*, it ought to follow these lines, the analytical school replies that since law is the command of the sovereign or the ruling of the courts, it *ought* to obey these latter masters. Jurists of metaphysical and sociological persuasion add to the heat of the fray with equally invalid brands of crypto-idealism.

[29] Morgan, Introduction to the Study of Law (1926) 32-33.

or moral character, that is an unfortunate fact which we ought to remedy. But if this assertion means that the law ought not to be determined with reference to such factors, it is simply false. Man's moral life is fundamentally molded by rules of property law, family law, etc., and the refusal to follow the meaning of such legal rules into their ultimate moral or spiritual implications is the essence of legalistic obscurantism.

In the third sentence we are told that *consequently* courts *have to* formulate rules which have no relation at all to morals, and here the confusion between the *is* and the *ought* bears its first fruits. Thus far Professor Morgan's statements can be justified if given a non-ethical interpretation, but if such an interpretation be given, the inference of *have to* (apparently ethical) from *does* and *is* is clearly fallacious. Here an ethical interpretation of the preceding sentences is required, and that, we have seen, results in error.

Thus Professor Morgan's conclusions are, if valid, based upon false premises, and, if based upon true premises, invalid. Their truth, as distinguished from the validity of their inference, can be defended, but only upon the assumption that the word *morality* is severed from reference to objective conduct and even to such problems of "inner belief" as are involved in the distribution of liabilities apart from fault, etc. Of course, if any one wishes to use the words *morality* and *ethics* in this milk-and-watery significance, no logical objection can be raised. But when such a use of terms results in, or springs from, the belief that judgments of good and evil can legitimately be applied only to man's secret intentions, we are called upon to point out that this is an indefensible theory of morality.

A great many other jurists have attempted in one way or another to discover an "end of law" independent of ethics or morality. Korkunov writes, "Morality furnishes the criterion for the proper evaluation of our interests; law marks out the limits within which they ought to be confined." [30] But it is obvious that the law does not actually do this, and if the reply is made that at least law ought to do this, then we must turn to morality for the basis and significance of this *ought*. Vinogradoff writes, "Law is clearly distinguishable from morality. The object of law is the submission of the individual to the will of organized society, while the tendency of morality is to subject the individual to the dictates of his own conscience." [31] Berolzheimer supplies the following argument, based, it seems, upon the unpleasant connotations of the idea of *expediency:* "If all law has

---

[30] KORKUNOV, GENERAL THEORY OF LAW (1909), translated from the Russian in 4 MODERN LEGAL PHILOSOPHY SERIES (1909) 52.
[31] VINOGRADOFF, COMMON SENSE IN LAW (1914) 58.

in view the welfare of society, then law abdicates in favor of administration; the ideal of political expediency displaces the · idea of right." [32] But it is impossible to exhaust the instances of this juristic attempt to abduct law from the domain of ethics and morality. Suffice it to say that the writers who make the ideal end of law independent of morality never refrain from passing ethical or moral judgments upon law. They have simply rejected particular moral theories, such as that of the infallibility of conscience (Vinogradoff), believing, correctly for the most part, that these doctrines are useless for jurisprudence, and incorrectly assuming that they are the whole of morality. A more or less unconscious moral standard is made the basis of their valuations of law, and while such a morality has frequently been more correct than the current ethical theory which was rejected, the resulting confusions of thought have been atrocious.

III

But there are further objections to our fundamental principle. Even those who admit, in general, the ultimate responsibility of law to morality sometimes suggest that there is at least a large body of law in the criticism of which ethics must be quite irrelevant. The boundaries of this non-moral realm may be variously drawn and may be either of a substantive character or of an adjectival or functional significance. In either view, such a claim is fatal to the soundness of our theory, which denies the ultimate validity of all legal criticism which is not ethical. It is our task, then, to examine and, if possible, to refute these objections.

There is, in the first place, a comparatively trivial interpretation which may be given them, in terms of which no incompatibility with our basic contentions can arise. By non-moral domains in the law we may mean sets of equally valuable alternatives. In this sense of the term, law, like every other aspect of human life, may be non-moral, but in these domains there can be no appeal from morality to a non-moral principle (precedent, custom, etc.) to decide which alternative is better than the other. By the very formulation of our problem we have denied that any alternative is better than the others. It is only the claim that in certain domains of law valid problems of what ought to be done may be solved without any appeal to the concept of the good life that we are concerned to refute.

Such a claim is presented by the theory that a large part of civil law, especially commercial law, constitutes a domain in which some principles other than those of morality must be our

---

[32] BEROLZHEIMER, RECHTSPHILOSOPHISCHE STUDIEN (1903) c. 6, § 22, at 143.

guide.[33] What jurists frequently mean, I suppose, when they
speak of the existence and necessity of non-moral law, is that
there are many questions of conduct which would be morally indifferent if there were no law, but which become morally significant under the reign of law, and in regard to which it is morally
imperative that the law take some definite stand. While the application of this proposition is often greatly exaggerated,[34] its
truth cannot be denied. The fact that something is affected by
legal sanctions adds certain moral considerations to any problem
of conduct. The possibility of being punished and of causing
consequent harm to friends and dependents, the possibility of
harming those who rely upon the law, the possibility of destroying social order, which in some degree is a necessary condition of
the good life, all these are pertinent facts in a moral judgment,
which may appear only after law is created. All this, however,
offers no ground for supposing that a rule of law which sanctions
or condemns a previously indifferent act is itself a non-moral
rule in the sense of being immune to moral appraisal. The demand that I save a friend's life and the act by which this is accomplished do not cease to be moral if there are a number of
slightly different ways of attaining this result, among some of
which my choice is morally indifferent. So when a legislature
chooses between a rule keeping traffic to the left and one keeping
it to the right, if it is ever the case that physiological peculiarities or social habits do not make one of the contemplated rules
less dangerous than the other, the demand that the law enact
one of the two possible rules is no less a moral demand because
of the indeterminateness of the alternative. It is upon such a
moral demand that the justification of so-called non-moral law
must rest, and such a demand may easily so outweigh all the
other factors in the situation that it would be good, say, to keep
to the right, that being the law, even though the law ought to
have been made, originally, the other way.

A second claim of exemption from the domain of morality is
commonly advanced on behalf of the judicial function. The question which a judge faces in coming to a decision, it is argued,
is purely legal, not moral. Legislatures may endeavor to decide
what the law ought to be, but it is for the judge to decide what,
in any particular case, the law is. It is apparently in this vein
that Maine, distinguishing the philosophy of law from the philosophy of legislation, says, "The jurist, properly so called, has noth-

---

[33] The argument is particularly directed to such rules as those determining the age of majority, the interpretation of standard phrases in deeds
and wills, etc.

[34] For example as in Hobbes' doctrine that morality first arises under the
reign of law.

ing to do with any ideal standard of law or morals."[35] And in the same vein Dean Pound has said, "The utilitarian theory of Bentham was a theory of legislation. The social theory of the present is a theory of legal science."[36] So, in the general philosophy of the Anglo-American bench and bar, "public policy" (the legal equivalent for "morality") seems to be relevant to the decision of a case only when precedents and statutes fail and the function of the judge becomes "legislative."

Now it is clearly true that the nature of the good does not determine the decisions of judges. Such a determination, as Santayana remarks, is the essence of magic. It is also true that judges generally come to decisions without thinking about moral principles.[37] But it is not true that the goodness or rightness of a decision can be measured except in moral terms.

It may be the case, again, that the professional disavowal of "moral" considerations refers only to the "conscience" theory of morality exemplified in Professor Morgan's dichotomy between "moral character" and "objective conduct." As such it is a valuable defense against the sentimental theory of justice, now increasingly fashionable,[38] which abstracts from the elements of a case everything but the interests of the two parties, and weighs these by an intuitive application of the judge's code of "fairness." But in its actual use, the theory we are attacking goes far beyond this repudiation of sentimentalism. Its actual effect is to exclude the conscious consideration of ethical issues from the judicial mind and to lend weight to the unconscious and uncriticized value standards by which judges decide what they *ought* to do. Fundamentally it attempts to set up as a standard of legal criticism truth or consistency rather than goodness. But neither truth nor consistency can be rivals to goodness, in legal criticism or anywhere else. Truth and consistency are categories which apply to propositions or to sets of propositions, not to

---

[35] MAINE, EARLY HISTORY OF INSTITUTIONS (7th ed. 1914) 370 and lectures 12 and 13 *passim.*

[36] Pound, *Mechanical Jurisprudence* (1908) 8 COL. L. REV. 605, 613; and see Pound, *The Scope and Purpose of Sociological Jurisprudence, op. cit. supra* note 8, at 140 n. 4.

[37] The judge, of course, makes all sorts of moral assumptions, not only in choosing among competing doctrines but as well in the supposedly logical processes of generalization, classification, and construction by which respectable "rules" are drawn from precedent and statute. In difficult cases such moral assumptions frequently become explicit and may even invite analysis. But the question to which the judge's critical faculties are regularly restricted is: "What decision would an intelligent lawyer familiar with statutes and past decisions expect in this situation?" or, more politely, "What *is* the law?"

[38] See Hutcheson, *The Judgment Intuitive: the Function of the "Hunch" in Judicial Decision* (1929) 14 CORN. L. Q. 274; FRANK, LAW AND THE MODERN MIND (1930) *passim.*

actions or events. A judicial decision is a command, not an assertion. Even if any sense could be found in the characterization of a decision as true or false (or, in the non-ethical sense of the terms, right or wrong, correct or erroneous), such truth or falsity could not determine what decision, in any case, ought to be given. That is a question of conduct and only the categories of ethics can apply to it. In answering such a question, the ethical value of certainty and predictability in law may outweigh more immediate ethical values, but this is no denial of the ethical nature of the problem. *Consistency*, like *truth*, is relevant to such a problem only as an indication of the interest in legal certainty, and its value and significance are ethical rather than logical. The question, then, of how far one ought to consider precedent and statute in coming to a legal decision is purely ethical. The proposition that courts ought always to decide "in accordance with precedent or statute" is an ethical proposition the truth of which can be demonstrated only by showing that in every case the following of precedent or statute does less harm than any possible alternative.

The ethical responsibilities of the judge have so often been obscured by the supposed duty to be logically consistent in the decision of different cases that it may be pertinent to ask whether any legal decision can ever be logically inconsistent with any other decision. In order to find such an inconsistency we must have two judgments, one for the plaintiff and one for the defendant. But this means that we must have two cases, since a second judgment in the same case would supersede the first judgment. And between the facts of any two cases there must be some difference, so that it will always be logically possible to frame a single legal rule requiring both decisions, given the facts of the two cases. Of course such a rule will seem absurd if the difference between the two cases is unimportant (*e. g.*, in the names or heights of the two defendants). But whether the difference is important or unimportant is a problem not of logic but of ethics, and one to which the opposing counsel in the later case may propose opposite answers without becoming involved in self-contradiction.

The confusion arises when we think of a judicial decision as implying a rule from which, given the facts of the case, the decision may be derived (the logical fallacy of affirming the consequent).[39] That logically startling deduction of the "law of

---

[39] The periodic attempts of students of the common law to put forward logical formulae for discovering "the rule of a case" all betray an elementary ignorance of the logical fact that no particular proposition can imply a general proposition. Wambaugh, Salmond, Gray, Black, Morgan, and Goodhart agree that the rule of a case (the *ratio decidendi*, the proposition for which a case is a precedent) is a general proposition necessary to the

precedents" from judicial precedents, Black's *Handbook of the Law of Judicial Precedents,* thus sums up the matter:

"Even if the opinion of the court should be concerned with unnecessary considerations, or should state the proposition of law imperfectly or incorrectly, yet there is a proposition necessarily involved in the decision and without which the judgment in the case could not have been given; and it is this proposition which is established by the decision (so far as it goes) and for which alone the case may be cited as an authority." [40]

But elementary logic teaches us that every legal decision and every finite set of decisions can be subsumed under an infinite number of different general rules, just as an infinite number of different curves may be traced through any point or finite collection of points. Every decision is a choice between different rules which logically fit all past decisions but logically dictate conflicting results in the instant case. Logic provides the springboard but it does not guarantee the success of any particular dive.

If the doctrine of *stare decisis* means anything, and one can hardly maintain the contrary despite the infelicitous formulations which have been given to the doctrine, the consistency which it demands cannot be a logical consistency. The consistency in question is more akin to that quality of dough which is necessary for the fixing of a durable shape. Decisions are fluid

---

particular decision. See WAMBAUGH, STUDY OF CASES (2d ed. 1894) c. 2; Salmond, *Theory of Judicial Precedents* (1900) 16 L. Q. REV. 376; GRAY, *op. cit. supra* note 11, at § 555; BLACK, JUDICIAL PRECEDENTS (1912) 40; MORGAN, *op. cit. supra* note 29, at 109-10; Goodhart, *Determining the Ratio Decidendi of a Case* (1930) 40 YALE L. J. 161. Logical objections to this conception are dismissed by Professor Morgan as "hypercritical" and "too refined for practical purposes." But Professor Oliphant, who refuses to be deterred by such warnings (see his reply in *Mutuality of Obligation in Bilateral Contracts at Law* (1928) 28 COL. L. REV. 997 n. 2 to Professor Williston's charges of scholasticism, *The Effect of One Void Promise in a Bilateral Agreement* (1925) 25 COL. L. REV. 857, 869) has suggested an alternative conception that is logically sound and practically far more useful. Rules of increasing generality, each of them linking the given result to the given facts, spread pyramid-wise from a decision. The possibility of alternative modes of anaylsis makes a decision the apex not of one but many such pyramids. No one of these rules has any logical priority; courts and lawyers choose among competing propositions on extralogical grounds. Oliphant, *A Return to Stare Decisis* (1928) 6 AM. LAW SCHOOL REV. 215, 217-18; and *cf.* LLEWELLYN, BRAMBLE BUSH (1930) 61-66; Bingham, *What is the Law?* (1912) 11 MICH. L. REV. 1, 109, 111 n. 31. The picture clearly suggests that the decision bears to the rules the same relation that Professor Whitehead has traced between a point and the surfaces that would ordinarily be said to include the point. See THE PRINCIPLES OF NATURAL KNOWLEDGE (1919) c. 8; THE CONCEPT OF NATURE (1919) c. 4.

[40] *Loc. cit. supra* note 39.

until they are given "morals." It is often important to conserve with new obeisance the morals which lawyers and laymen have read into past decisions and in reliance upon which they have acted. We do not deny that importance when we recognize that with equal logical justification lawyers and laymen might have attached other morals to the old cases had their habits of legal classification or their general social premises been different. But we do shift the focus of our vision from a stage where social and professional prejudices wear the terrible armor of Pure Reason to an arena where human hopes and expectations wrestle naked for supremacy.

No doubt the doctrine of *stare decisis* and the argument for consistency have a significance which is not exhausted by the social usefulness of predictable law. Even in fields where past court decisions play a negligible role in molding expectations, courts may be justified in looking to former rulings for guidance. The time of judges is more limited than the boundaries of injustice. At some risk the results of past deliberation in a case similar to the case at bar must be accepted. But again we invite fatal confusion if we think of this similarity as a logical rather than an ethical relation. To the cold eyes of logic the difference between the names of the parties in the two decisions bulks as large as the difference between care and negligence. The question before the judge is, "Granted that there are differences between the cited precedent and the case at bar, and assuming that the decision in the earlier case was a desirable one, is it desirable to attach legal weight to any of the factual differences between the instant case and the earlier case?" Obviously this is an ethical question. Should a rich woman accused of larceny receive the same treatment as a poor woman? Should a rich man who has accidentally injured another come under the same obligations as a poor man? Should a group of persons, *e. g.*, an unincorporated labor union, be privileged to make all statements that an individual may lawfully make? Neither the ringing hexameters of *Barbara Celarent* nor the logic machine of Jevons nor the true-false patterns of Wittgenstein will produce answers to these questions.

What then shall we think of attempts to frame practical legal issues as conflicts between morality, common sense, history or sociology, and logic (logic playing regularly the Satanic role)? One hesitates to convict the foremost jurists on the American bench of elementary logical error. It is more likely that they have simply used the word "logic" in peculiar ways, as to which they may find many precedents in the current logic textbooks.[41]

---

[41] See M. R. Cohen, *The Subject Matter of Formal Logic* (1918) 15 JOUR. OF PHIL. 673.

Bertrand Russell has warned us:

"When it is said, for example, that the French are 'logical', what is meant is that, when they accept a premise, they also accept everything that a person totally devoid of logical subtlety would erroneously suppose to follow from that premise. . . . Logic was, formerly, the art of drawing inferences; it has now become the art of abstaining from inferences, since it has appeared that the inferences we feel naturally inclined to make are hardly ever valid." [42]

If we construe the word "logic" in the light of this warning, we may readily agree with Mr. Justice Holmes when he asserts that "the whole outline of the law is the resultant of a conflict at every point between logic [*viz.* hasty generalization] and good sense",[43] and find some meaning in the statement of Judge Cardozo that "the logic of one principle" prevails over the logic of another [44] or in his pride that "We in the United States have been readier to subordinate logic to utility." [45]

---

[42] RUSSELL, SKEPTICAL ESSAYS (1928) c. 7 *(Behaviorism and Values)* 99.

[43] HOLMES, COLLECTED LEGAL PAPERS (1920) *(Agency)* 49, 50.

[44] CARDOZO, NATURE OF THE JUDICIAL PROCESS, (1921) c. 1 *(Introduction. The Method of Philosophy)* 41. Judge Cardozo illustrates (*op. cit.* 38-39) the method of logic or philosophy, which is distinguished from the methods of history or evolution, of custom or tradition, and of sociology, with the rule that one who contracts to purchase real property must pay for it even though, before the sale is actually completed, the property is substantially destroyed. This, he maintains, is the projection to its logical outcome of the principle that "equity treats that as done which ought to be done," a principle which does not apply to the sale of chattels which did not come under the jurisdiction of Chancery. But what sort of principle is this? It is certainly not a logical principle, *i.e.*, a proposition certifiable on logical grounds alone, since it is obviously false. If it were true no plaintiff in equity could ever obtain a judgment since he could never in the face of such a rule show that the defendant had *not* done what he ought to have done. Would it not be quite as logical for a court to say "equity does not treat that as done which has not been done"? If a rule is undesirable we do not make it less undesirable by deducing it from another rule too vague to be liked or disliked and then concentrating our attention on the process of inference rather than the premise. What is in question in the case proposed is not a logical problem or a choice of judicial methods but a conflict of social interests, and there is much that may be said in favor of throwing upon the party who contemplates future enjoyment of a definite piece of real property the risk of its destruction and the necessity of insurance. But what may thus be said bears no peculiar *imprimatur* of logic. See also CARDOZO, THE GROWTH OF THE LAW (1924) 79-80.

[45] CARDOZO, THE GROWTH OF THE LAW (1924) 77. This is said with regard to the tendency in recent decisions (of which Judge Cardozo's opinion in MacPherson v. Buick Mfg. Co., 217 N. Y. 382, 111 N. E. 1050 (1916) is a noteworthy landmark) to extend the scope of a manufacturer's obligations to the ultimate consumer with regard to the quality of the product.

We may have to interpret the word "logical" as synonymous with "aesthetically satisfying" in order to understand the statement of Mr. Justice Brandeis and Mr. Warren that a distinction between cases where "substantial mental suffering would be the natural and probable result" of an act and cases "where no mental suffering would ordinarily result" is not logical though very practical.[46] Such an identification of the rules of logic with those of intellectual aesthetics seems to be assumed at times by Judge Cardozo as well.[47]

No verbal definition is intrinsically objectionable. But it seems fair to suggest that the use of the word "logic" in the senses exemplified in these typical passages seriously lowers the probability of clear thinking on the relation between law and ethics. Most of us think of logic as the most general and formal of the sciences.[48] Upon that basis we may say, paraphrasing a remark of Mr. Justice Holmes, that conformity with logic is only a necessity and not a duty. The bad judge is no more able to violate the laws of logic than he is to violate the laws of gravitation. He may, of course, ignore both. It is not our purpose to deny that there would be less judicial stumbling were courts more constantly aware of the logical relations between particular and universal, between premise and conclusion, between form and content.

IV

The theory which denies ethical justiciability to law, in whole or in part, cannot be maintained. Its superficial plausibility

---

Again the rejected "privity" analysis of the situation seems to be peculiarly "logical" because it permits the deduction of an undesirable rule from another undesirable rule which is too vague to arouse the resentment which the deduced rule arouses.

See also *ibid*. 83, where "adherence to logical and advancement of utility" are balanced in terms of "the social interest which each is capable of promoting."

[46] Warren and Brandeis, *The Right of Privacy* (1890) 4 HARV. L. REV. 193, reprinted in SELECTED ESSAYS IN THE LAW OF TORTS (1924) 122, 126.

[47] "If I am seeking logical consistency, the symmetry of the legal structure, how far shall I seek it?" CARDOZO, NATURE OF THE JUDICIAL PROCESS 10, and *cf. ibid*. 33-34.

[48] "If it was so, it might be; and if it were so, it would be, but as it isn't, it ain't. That's logic." CARROLL, THROUGH THE LOOKING GLASS c. 4. And see WITTGENSTEIN, TRACTATUS LOGICO-PHILOSOPHICUS (1922)(§§ 6.1, 6.1262; M. R. Cohen, *op. cit. supra* note 41; Hoernlé, Review of SCIENCE OF LEGAL METHOD (1918) 31 HARV. L. REV. 807; Russell, PRINCIPLES OF MATHEMATICS, (1903) c. 1; Adler, *Law and the Modern Mind: A Symposium* (1931) 31 COL. L. REV. 99-101; Keyser, *On the Study of Legal Science* (1929) 38 YALE L. J. 413.

arises from the narrow connotation given to the terms *ethics* and *morality* when they are extruded from the field of legal criticism. The falsity of the theory arises from the fact that, along with the promptings of "conscience", the principal values of life are banished from the juristic consciousness and an inadequate "practical" ethics substituted. The invalidity of the inference by which this theory is established arises from the fallacy *(quaternio terminorum)* by which the extrusion from legal criticism of "ethics" in its broadest sense is inferred from a denial of its legal importance in its narrower connotation. Finally, the confusion of the theory lies in the indeterminate character of the system of values substituted by our jurists for what they call "ethics" and "morality."

Law is just as much a part of the domain of morality as any other phase of human custom and conduct. It has no special purpose, end, or function, no restriction of moral scope, other than that variable restriction which its positive and practical nature may impose in the way of limitations of efficacy and applicability. We may, if we like, call *the good which law can achieve* "justice." But if "justice" means anything less than that total, it is not a valid basis of legal criticism. To say that something or other is beyond the "proper scope" of law is either to say that law on that subject will bring about more harm than good or it is to indulge in meaningless verbiage. The evaluation of law must be made in terms of the good life, and to demonstrate the nature of this standard is the task of ethics, and more particularly, of morality. Difficult as that task is and uncertain as its conclusions have been, it is a vicious illusion to suppose that the task of statesman or judge is less difficult, or that his conclusions can be more certain.

Law as Interpretation†

Ronald Dworkin*

In this essay I shall argue that legal practice is an exercise in interpretation not only when lawyers interpret particular documents or statutes, but generally. Law so conceived is deeply and thoroughly political. Lawyers and judges cannot avoid politics in the broad sense of political theory. But law is not a matter of personal or partisan politics, and a critique of law that does not understand this difference will provide poor understanding and even poorer guidance. I propose that we can improve our understanding of law by comparing legal interpretation with interpretation in other fields of knowledge, particularly literature. I also expect that law, when better understood, will provide a better grasp of what interpretation is in general.

I. Law

The central problem of analytical jurisprudence is this: What sense should be given to propositions of law? By propositions I mean the various statements lawyers make reporting what the law is on some question or other. Propositions of law can be very abstract and general, like the proposition that states of the United States may not discriminate on racial grounds in supplying basic services to citizens, or they can be relatively concrete, like the proposition that someone who accepts a check in the normal course of business without notice of any infirmities in its title is entitled to collect against the maker, or very concrete, like the proposition that Mrs. X is liable in damages to Mr. Y in the amount of $1150 because he slipped on her icy sidewalk and broke his hip. In each case a puzzle arises. What are propositions of law really about? What in the world could make them true or false?

The puzzle arises because propositions of law seem to be descriptive—they are about how things are in the law, not about how they should be—and yet it has proved extremely difficult to say exactly what

† © 1982 by Ronald Dworkin. All rights reserved. Permission to reprint may be obtained only from the author. A version of this essay was published in the Fall 1982 issue of *Critical Inquiry*. 9 CRITICAL INQUIRY 179 (1982). This paper was presented in a symposium on politics and interpretation held at the University of Chicago in the fall of 1981.
* Professor of Jurisprudence and Fellow of University College, Oxford; Professor of Law, New York University. A.B. 1953, Harvard University; B.A. 1955, Oxford; LL.B. 1957, Harvard University.

527

it is that they describe. Legal positivists believe that propositions of law are indeed wholly descriptive: they are in fact pieces of history. A proposition of law, in their view, is true if some event of a designated law-making kind has taken place, and otherwise not. This seems to work reasonably well in very simple cases. If the Illinois Legislature enacts the words, "No will shall be valid without three witnesses," then the proposition of law, that an Illinois will needs three witnesses, seems to be true only in virtue of that historical event.

But in more difficult cases the analysis fails. Consider the proposition that a particular affirmative action scheme (not yet tested in the courts) is constitutionally valid. If that is true, it cannot be so just in virtue of the text of the Constitution and the fact of prior court decisions, because reasonable lawyers who know exactly what the Constitution says and what the courts have done may yet disagree whether it is true. (I am doubtful that the positivists' analysis holds even in the simple case of the will; but that is a different matter I shall not argue here.)

What are the other possibilities? One is to suppose that controversial propositions of law, like the affirmative action statement, are not descriptive at all, but are rather expressions of what the speaker wants the law to be. Another is more ambitious: controversial statements are attempts to describe some pure objective or natural law, which exists in virtue of objective moral truth rather than historical decision. Both these projects take some legal statements, at least, to be purely evaluative as distinct from descriptive: they express either what the speaker prefers—his personal politics—or what he believes is objectively required by the principles of an ideal political morality. Neither of these projects is plausible, because someone who says that a particular untested affirmative action plan is constitutional does mean to describe the law as it is rather than as he wants it to be or thinks that, by the best moral theory, it should be. He might, indeed, say that he regrets that the plan is constitutional and thinks that according to the best moral theory, it ought not to be.

There is a better alternative: propositions of law are not simply descriptive of legal history in a straightforward way, nor are they simply evaluative in some way divorced from legal history. They are interpretive of legal history, which combines elements of both description and evaluation but is different from both. This suggestion will be congenial, at least at first blush, to many lawyers and legal philosophers. They are used to saying that law is a matter of interpretation; but only, perhaps, because they understand interpretation in a certain way. When a statute (or the Constitution) is unclear on some point, because

528

some crucial term is vague or because a sentence is ambiguous, lawyers say that the statute must be interpreted, and they apply what they call "techniques of statutory construction." Most of the literature assumes that interpretation of a particular document is a matter of discovering what its authors (the legislators, or the delegates to the Constitutional Convention) meant to say in using the words they did. But lawyers recognize that on many issues the author had no intention either way and that on others his intention cannot be discovered. Some lawyers take a more skeptical position. They say that whenever judges pretend they are discovering the intention behind some piece of legislation, this is simply a smoke screen behind which the judges impose their own view of what the statute should have been.

Interpretation as a technique of legal analysis is less familiar in the case of the common law, but not unfamiliar. Suppose the Supreme Court of Illinois decided, several years ago, that a negligent driver who ran down a child was liable for the emotional damage suffered by the child's mother, who was standing next to the child on the road. Now an aunt sues another careless driver for emotional damage suffered when she heard, on the telephone many miles from the accident, that her niece had been hit. Does the aunt have a right to recover for that damage? Lawyers often say that this is a matter of interpreting the earlier decision correctly. Does the legal theory on which the earlier judge actually relied, in making his decision about the mother on the road, cover the aunt on the telephone? Once again skeptics point out that it is unlikely that the earlier judge had in mind any theory sufficiently developed so as to decide the aunt's case either way, so that a judge "interpreting" the earlier decision is actually making new law in the way he or she thinks best.

The idea of interpretation cannot serve as a general account of the nature or truth of propositions of law, however, unless it is cut loose from these associations with the speaker's meaning or intention. Otherwise it becomes simply one version of the positivist's thesis that propositions of law describe decisions made by people or institutions in the past. If interpretation is to form the basis of a different and more plausible theory about propositions of law, then we must develop a more inclusive account of what interpretation is. But that means that lawyers must not treat legal interpretation as an activity *sui generis*. We must study interpretation as a general activity, as a mode of knowledge, by attending to other contexts of that activity.

Lawyers would do well to study literary and other forms of artistic interpretation. That might seem bad advice (choosing the fire over the

529

frying pan) because critics themselves are thoroughly divided about what literary interpretation is, and the situation is hardly better in the other arts. But that is exactly why lawyers should study these debates. Not all of the battles within literary criticism are edifying or even comprehensible, but many more theories of interpretation have been defended in literature than in law, and these include theories that challenge the flat distinction between description and evaluation that has enfeebled legal theory.

II. Literature

A. *The Aesthetic Hypothesis*

If lawyers are to benefit from a comparison between legal and literary interpretation, however, they must see the latter in a certain light, and in this section I shall try to say what that is. (I would prefer the following remarks about literature to be uncontroversial among literary scholars, of course, but I am afraid they will not be.) Students of literature do many things under the titles of "interpretation" and "hermeneutics," and most of them are also called "discovering the meaning of a text." I shall not be interested, except incidentally, in one thing these students do, which is trying to discover the sense in which some author used a particular word or phrase. I am interested instead in arguments that offer some sort of interpretation of the meaning of a work as a whole. These sometimes take the form of assertions about characters: that Hamlet really loved his mother, for example, or that he really hated her, or that there really was no ghost but only Hamlet himself in a schizophrenic manifestation. Or about events in the story behind the story: that Hamlet and Ophelia were lovers before the play begins (or were not). More usually they offer hypotheses directly about the "point" or "theme" or "meaning" or "sense" or "tone" of the play as a whole: that *Hamlet* is a play about death, for example, or about generations, or about politics. These interpretive claims may have a practical point. They may, for example, guide a director staging a new performance of the play. But they may also be of more general importance, helping us to an improved understanding of important parts of our cultural environment. Of course, difficulties about the speaker's meaning of a particular word in the text (a "crux" of interpretation) may bear upon these larger matters. But the latter are about the point or meaning of the work as a whole, rather than the sense of a particular phrase.

Critics much disagree about how to answer such questions. I want, so far as is possible, not to take sides but to try to capture the disagreements in some sufficiently general description of what they are

530

disagreeing about. My apparently banal suggestion (which I shall call the "aesthetic hypothesis") is this: an interpretation of a piece of literature attempts to show which way of reading (or speaking or directing or acting) the text reveals it as the best work of art. Different theories or schools or traditions of interpretation disagree on this hypothesis, because they assume significantly different normative theories about what literature is and what it is for and about what makes one work of literature better than another.

I expect that this suggestion, in spite of its apparent weakness, will be rejected by many scholars as confusing interpretation with criticism or, in any case, as hopelessly relativistic, and therefore as a piece of skepticism that really denies the possibility of interpretation altogether. Indeed the aesthetic hypothesis might seem simply another formulation of a theory now popular, which is that since interpretation creates a work of art, and represents only the fiat of a particular critical community, there are only interpretations and no best interpretation of any particular poem or novel or play. But the aesthetic hypothesis is neither so wild nor so weak nor so inevitably relativistic as might first appear.

Interpretation of a text attempts to show *it* as the best work of art *it* can be, and the pronoun insists on the difference between explaining a work of art and changing it into a different one. Perhaps Shakespeare could have written a better play based on the sources he used for *Hamlet* than he did, and in that better play the hero would have been a more forceful man of action. It does not follow that *Hamlet*, the play he wrote, really is like that after all. Of course, a theory of interpretation must contain a subtheory about identity of a work of art in order to be able to tell the difference between interpreting and changing a work. (Any useful theory of identity will be controversial, so this is one obvious way in which disagreements in interpretation will depend on more general disagreements in aesthetic theory.)

Contemporary theories of interpretation all seem to use, as part of their response to that requirement, the idea of a canonical text (or score, in the case of music, or unique physical object in the case of most art). The text provides one severe constraint in the name of identity: all the words must be taken account of and none may be changed to make "it" a putatively better work of art. (This constraint, however familiar, is not inevitable. A joke, for example, may be the same joke though told in a variety of forms, none of them canonical; an interpretation of a joke will choose a particular way in which to put it, and this may be wholly original, in order to bring out its "real" point or why it

531

is "really" funny.) So any literary critic's style of interpretation will be sensitive to his theoretical beliefs about the nature of and evidence for a canonical text.

An interpretive style will also be sensitive to the interpreter's opinions about coherence or integrity in art. An interpretation cannot make a work of art more distinguished if it makes a large part of the text irrelevant, or much of the incident accidental, or a great part of the trope or style unintegrated and answering only to independent standards of fine writing. So it does not follow, from the aesthetic hypothesis, that because a philosophical novel is aesthetically more valuable than a mystery story, an Agatha Christie novel is really a treatise on the meaning of death. This interpretation fails, not only because an Agatha Christie novel, taken to be a treatise on death, is a poor treatise less valuable than a good mystery, but because the interpretation makes the novel a shambles. All but one or two sentences would be irrelevant to the supposed theme; and the organization, style, and figures would be appropriate not to a philosophical novel but to an entirely different genre. Of course some books originally offered to the public as mysteries or thrillers (and perhaps thought of by their authors that way) have indeed been "reinterpreted" as something more ambitious. The present critical interest in Raymond Chandler is an example. But the fact that this reinterpretation can be successful in the case of Chandler, but not Christie, illustrates the constraint of integrity.

There is nevertheless room for much disagreement among critics about what counts as integration, about which sort of unity is desirable and which irrelevant or undesirable. Is it really an advantage that the tongue of the reader, in reading a poem aloud, must "mime" motions or directions that figure in the tropes or narrative of the poem? Does this improve integrity by adding yet another dimension of coordination? Is it an advantage when conjunctions and line endings are arranged so that the reader "negotiating" a poem develops contradictory assumptions and readings as he goes on, so that his understanding at the end is very different from what it was at discrete points along the way? Does this add another dimension of complexity to unity, or does it rather compromise unity because a work of literature should be capable of having the same meaning or import when read a second time? Schools of interpretation will rise or fall in response to these questions of aesthetic theory, which is what the aesthetic hypothesis suggests.

The major differences among schools of interpretation are less subtle, however, because they touch not these quasi-formal aspects of art but the function or point of art more broadly conceived. Does literature have (primarily or substantially) a cognitive point? Is art better when it is in some way instructive, when we learn something from it about how people are or what the world is like? If so, and if psychoanalysis is true (please forgive that crude way of putting it), then a psychoanalytic interpretation of a piece of literature will show why it is successful art. Is art good insofar as it is successful communication in the ordinary sense? If so, then a good interpretation will focus on what the author intended, because communication is not successful unless it expresses what a speaker wants it to express. Or is art good when it is expressive in a different sense, insofar as it has the capacity to stimulate or inform the lives of those who experience it? If so, then interpretation will place the reader (or listener or viewer) in the foreground. It will point out the reading of the work that makes it most valuable—best as a work of art—in that way.

Of course theories of art do not exist in isolation from philosophy, psychology, sociology, and cosmology. Someone who accepts a religious point of view will probably have a different theory of art from someone who does not, and recent critical theories have made us see how far interpretive style is sensitive to beliefs about meaning, reference, and other technical issues in the philosophy of language. But the aesthetic hypothesis does not assume that anyone who interprets literature will have a fully developed and self-conscious aesthetic theory. Nor that everyone who interprets must subscribe entirely to one or another of the schools I crudely described. The best critics, I think, deny that there is one unique function or point of literature. A novel or a play may be valuable in any number of ways, some of which we learn by reading or looking or listening, rather than by abstract reflection about what good art must be like or for.

Nevertheless anyone who interprets a work of art relies on beliefs of a theoretical character about identity and other formal properties of art, as well as more explicitly normative beliefs about what is good in art. *Both* sorts of beliefs figure in the judgment that one way of reading a text makes it a better text than another way. These beliefs may be inarticulate (or "tacit"). They are still genuine beliefs (and not merely "reactions") because their force for any critic or reader can be seen at work not just on one isolated occasion of interpretation, but in any number of other occasions, and because they figure in and are amenable to argument.[1] (These weak claims do not, of course, take sides in the running debate on whether there are any necessary or sufficient

---

1. *See* Evans, *Semantic Theory and Tacit Knowledge*, in L. WITTGENSTEIN, TO FOLLOW A RULE (S. Holtzman & C. Leich eds.) (1981).

533

"principles of value" in art, or whether a theory of art could ever justify an interpretation in the absence of direct experience of the work being interpreted.)[2]

None of this touches the major complaint I anticipated against the aesthetic hypothesis: that it is trivial. Obviously (you might say) different interpretive styles are grounded in different theories of what art is and what it is for and what makes art good art. The point is so banal that it might as well be put the other way around: different theories of art are generated by different theories of interpretation. If someone thinks stylistics are important to interpretation, he will think a work of art better because it integrates pronunciation and trope; if someone is attracted by deconstruction, he will dismiss reference in its familiar sense from any prominent place in an account of language. Nor does my elaboration of the hypothesis in any way help to adjudicate amongst theories of interpretation or to rebut the charge of nihilism or relativism. On the contrary, since people's views about what makes art good art are inherently subjective, the aesthetic hypothesis abandons hope of rescuing objectivity in interpretation except, perhaps, among those who hold very much the same theory of art, which is hardly very helpful.

No doubt the aesthetic hypothesis is in important ways banal—it must be abstract if it is to provide an account of what a wide variety of theories disagree about—but it is perhaps not so weak as all that. The hypothesis has the consequence that academic theories of interpretation are no longer seen as what they often claim to be—analyses of the very idea of interpretation—but rather as candidates for the best answer to the substantive question posed by interpretation. Interpretation becomes a concept of which different theories are competing conceptions. (It follows that there is no radical difference but only a difference in the level of abstraction between offering a theory of interpretation and offering an interpretation of a particular work of art.) The hypothesis denies, moreover, the sharp distinctions some scholars have cultivated. There is no longer a flat distinction between interpretation, conceived as discovering the real meaning of a work of art, and criticism, conceived as evaluating its success or importance. Of course some distinction remains because there is always a difference between saying how

2. It may be one of the many important differences between interpretation in art and law, which I do not examine in this essay, that nothing in law corresponds to the direct experience of a work of art, though some lawyers of the romantic tradition do speak of a good judge's "sixth sense," which enables him to grasp which aspects of a chain of legal decisions reveal the "immanent" principle of law even though he cannot fully explain why.

534

good a particular work can be made to be and saying how good that is. But evaluative beliefs about art figure in both these judgments.

Objectivity is another matter. It is an open question, I think, whether the main judgments we make about art can properly be said to be true or false, valid or invalid. This question is part of the more general philosophical issue of objectivity, presently much discussed in both ethics and the philosophy of language, and no one is entitled to a position who studies the case of aesthetic judgment alone. Of course no important aesthetic claim can be "demonstrated" to be true or false; no argument can be produced for any interpretation that we can be sure will commend itself to everyone, or even everyone with experience and training in the appropriate form of art. If this is what it means to say that aesthetic judgments are subjective—that they are not demonstrable—then of course they are subjective. But it does not follow that no normative theory about art is better than any other, nor that one theory cannot be the best that has so far been produced.

The aesthetic hypothesis reverses (I think to its credit) a familiar strategy. E.D. Hirsch, for example, argues that only a theory like his can make interpretation objective and particular interpretations valid.[3] This seems to me a mistake on two connected grounds. Interpretation is an enterprise, a public institution, and it is wrong to assume, a priori, that the propositions central to any public enterprise must be capable of validity. It is also wrong to assume much about what validity in such enterprises must be like—whether validity requires the possibility of demonstrability, for example. It seems better to proceed more empirically here. We should first study a variety of activities in which people assume that they have good reasons for what they say, which they assume hold generally and not just from one or another individual point of view. We can then judge what standards people accept in practice for thinking that they have reasons of that kind.

Nor is the point about reversibility—that a theory of art may depend upon a theory of interpretation as much as vice versa—an argument against the aesthetic hypothesis. I am not defending any particular explanation of how people come to have either theories of interpretation or theories of art, but only a claim about the argumentative connections that hold between these theories however come by. Of course, even at the level of argument, these two kinds of theories are mutually reinforcing. It is plainly a reason for doubting any theory of what an object of art is, for example, that the theory generates an obvi-

3. E. HIRSCH, VALIDITY IN INTERPRETATION (1967).

ously silly theory of interpretation. My point is exactly that the connection is reciprocal, so that anyone called upon to defend a particular approach to interpretation would be forced to rely on more general aspects of a theory of art, whether he realizes it or not. And this may be true even though the opposite is, to some extent, true as well. It would be a mistake, I should add, to count this fact of mutual dependence as offering, in itself, any reason for skepticism or relativism about interpretation. This seems to be the burden of slogans like "interpretation creates the text," but there is no more immediate skeptical consequence in the idea that what we take to be a work of art must comport with what we take interpreting a work of art to be than in the analogous idea that what we take a physical object to be must sit well with our theories of knowledge; so long as we add, in both cases, that the connection holds the other way around as well.

B. Author's Intention

The chief test of the aesthetic hypothesis lies, however, not in its resistance to these various charges, but in its explanatory and particularly its critical power. If we accept that theories of interpretation are not independent analyses of what it means to interpret something but are rather based in and dependent upon normative theories of art, then we must accept that they are vulnerable to complaints against the normative theory in which they are based. It does seem to me, for example, that the more doctrinaire author's intention theories are vulnerable in this way. These theories must suppose, on the present hypothesis, that what is valuable in a work of art, what should lead us to value one work of art more than another, is limited to what the author in some narrow and constrained sense intended to put there. This claim presupposes, as I suggested earlier, a more general thesis that art must be understood as a form of speaker-audience communication; but even that doubtful thesis turns out, on further inspection, not to support it.

Of course the "intentionalists" would object to these remarks. They would insist that their theory of interpretation is not an account of what is valuable in a book or poem or play but only an account of what any particular book or poem or play means and that we must understand what something means before we can decide whether it is valuable and where its value lies. And they would object that they do not say that only intentions of the author "in some narrow and constrained sense" count in fixing the meaning of his work.

In the first of these objections, the author's intention theory presents itself not as the upshot of the aesthetic hypothesis—not as the best theory of interpretation within the design stipulated by that hypothesis—but rather as a rival to it, a better theory about what kind of thing an interpretation is. But it is very difficult to understand the author's intention theory as any sort of rival to the present hypothesis. What question does it propose to answer better? Not, certainly, some question about the ordinary language or even technical meaning of the words "meaning" or "interpretation." An intentionalist cannot suppose that all his critics and those he criticizes mean, when they say "interpretation," the discovery of the author's intention. Nor can he think that his claims accurately describe what every member of the critical fraternity in fact does under the title "interpretation." If that were so, then his strictures and polemics would be unnecessary. But if his theory is not semantic or empirical in these ways, what sort of a theory is it?

Suppose an intentionalist replies:

It points out an important issue about works of literature, namely: What did the author of the work intend it to be? This is plainly an important question, even if its importance is preliminary to other equally or more important questions about significance or value. It is, in fact, what most people for a long time have called "interpretation." But the name does not matter, so long as the activity is recognized as important and so long as it is understood that scholars are in principle capable of supplying objectively correct answers to the question it poses.

This reply comes to this: we can discover what an author intended (or at least come to probabilistic conclusions about this) and it is important to do so for other literary purposes. But why is it important? What other purposes? Any answer will assume that value or significance in art attaches primarily to what the author intended, just because it is what the author intended. Otherwise, why should we evaluate what this style of interpretation declares to be the work of art? But then the claim that interpretation in this style is important depends on a highly controversial, normative theory of art, not a neutral observation preliminary to any coherent evaluation. Of course no plausible theory of interpretation holds that the intention of the author is always irrelevant. Sometimes it is plainly the heart of the matter, as when some issue turns on what Shakespeare meant by "hawk" as distinguished from "handsaw." But it is nevertheless controversial that we must know whether Shakespeare thought Hamlet was mad or sane pretending to be mad in order to decide how good a play he wrote. The intentionalist thinks that we do, and that is exactly why his theory of interpretation is not a rival to the aesthetic hypothesis but rather a suitor for the crown that hypothesis holds out.

537

The second objection to my charge against author's intention theories may prove to be more interesting. Intentionalists make the author's state of mind central to interpretation. But they misunderstand, so far as I can tell, certain complexities in that state of mind; in particular they fail to appreciate how intentions *for* a work and beliefs *about* it interact. I have in mind an experience familiar to anyone who creates anything, of suddenly seeing something "in" it that he did not previously know was there. This is sometimes (though I think not very well) expressed in the author's cliché, that his characters seem to have minds of their own. John Fowles provides an example from popular fiction.

> When Charles left Sarah on her cliff edge, I ordered him to walk straight back to Lyme Regis. But he did not; he gratuitously turned and went down to the Dairy.
>   Oh, but you say, come on—what I really mean is that the idea crossed my mind as I wrote that it might be more clever to have him stop and drink milk . . . and meet Sarah again. That is certainly one explanation of what happened; but I can only report—and I am the most reliable witness—that the idea seemed to me to come clearly from Charles, not myself. It is not only that he has begun to gain an autonomy; I must respect it, and disrespect all my quasi-divine plans for him, if I wish him to be real.[4]

Fowles changed his mind about how the story in *The French Lieutenant's Woman* "really" goes in the midst of writing it, if we are to credit this description. But he might also have changed his mind about some aspect of the novel's "point" years later, as he is rumored to have done after seeing the film made from his book. He might have come to see Sarah's motives very differently after reading Harold Pinter's screenplay or watching Meryl Streep play her; Pinter and Streep were interpreting the novel, and one or both of their interpretations might have led Fowles to change *his* interpretation once again. Perhaps I am wrong in supposing that this sort of thing happens often. But it happens often enough, and it is important to be clear about what it is that happens.

The intentionalist wants us to choose between two possibilities. Either the author suddenly realizes that he had a "subconscious intention" earlier, which he only now discovers, or he has simply changed his intention later. Neither of these explanations is at all satisfactory. The subconscious is in danger of becoming phlogiston here, unless we suppose some independent evidence, apart from the author's new view of his work, to suggest that he had an earlier subconscious intention. I

---

4. J. FOWLES, THE FRENCH LIEUTENANT'S WOMAN 96-97 (1969).

do not mean that features of a work of art of which an author is unaware must be random accidents. On the contrary, if a novel is both more interesting and more coherent if we assume the characters have motives different from those the novelist thought of when he wrote (or if a poet's tropes and style tend to reinforce his theme in ways he did not appreciate at the time), the cause of this must in some way lie in the artist's talent. Of course there are unsolved mysteries in the psychology of creation, but the supposition of subconscious *intentions*, unsupported by other evidence of the sort a psychoanalyst would insist on, solves no mysteries and provides no explanation. This is not crucial to the point, however, because whether or not Fowles had a subconscious intention to make Charles or Sarah different characters from the "quasi-divine plan" he thought he had, his later decisions and beliefs neither consist in nor are based on any discovery of that earlier intention. They are produced by confronting not his earlier self but the work he has produced.

Nor is any new belief Fowles forms about his characters properly called (as in the intentionalist's second suggestion) a new and discrete intention. It is not an intention about what sort of characters to create because it is a belief about what sort of characters he has created; and it is not an intention about how others should understand the book, though it may or may not include an expectation of that sort. Fowles changed his view in the course of writing his book, but he changed it, as he insists, by confronting the text he had already written, by treating its characters as real in the sense of detachable from his own antecedent designs, in short by interpreting it, and not by exploring the subconscious depths of some previous plan or finding that he had a new plan. If it is true that he changed his mind again, after seeing the film, then this was, once again, not a retrospective new intention or a rediscovered old one. It was another interpretation.

An author is capable of detaching what he has written from his earlier intentions and beliefs, of treating it as an object in itself. He is capable of reaching fresh conclusions about his work grounded in aesthetic judgments: that his book is both more coherent and a better analysis of more important themes read in a somewhat different way from what he thought when he was writing it. This is, I think, a very important fact for a number of reasons; but I want, for my present purpose, only to emphasize one. Any full description of what Fowles "intended" when he set out to write *The French Lieutenant's Woman* must include the intention to produce something capable of being treated that way, by himself and therefore by others, and so must include the

539

intention to create something independent of his intentions. I quote Fowles once again, and again as a witness rather than for his metaphysics: "Only one reason is shared by all of us [novelists]: *we wish to create worlds as real as, but other than, the world that is.* Or was. That is why we cannot plan . . . . We also know that a genuinely created world must be independent of its creator . . . ."[5]

I suspect that regarding something one has produced as a novel or poem or painting, rather than a set of propositions or marks, *depends* on regarding it as something that can be detached and interpreted in the sense I described. In any case, this is characteristically how authors themselves regard what they have done. The intentions of authors are not simply conjunctive, like the intentions of someone who goes to market with a shopping list, but structured, so that the more concrete of these intentions, like intentions about the motives of a particular character in a novel, are contingent on interpretive beliefs whose soundness varies with what is produced and which might be radically altered from time to time.

We can, perhaps, isolate the full set of interpretive beliefs an author has at a particular moment (say at the moment he sends final galleys to the printer) and solemnly declare that these beliefs, in their full concreteness, fix what the novel is or means. (Of course, these beliefs would inevitably be incomplete, but that is another matter.) But even if we (wrongly) call this particular set of beliefs "intentions," we are, in choosing them, ignoring another kind or level of intention, which is the intention to create a work whose nature or meaning is not fixed in this way, because it is a work of art. That is why the author's intention school, as I understand it, makes the value of a work of art turn on a narrow and constrained view of the intentions of the author.

III. Law and Literature

A. The Chain of Law

These sketchy remarks about literary interpretation may have suggested too sharp a split between the role of the artist in creating a work of art and that of the critic in interpreting it later. The artist can create nothing without interpreting as he creates; since he intends to produce art, he must have at least a tacit theory of why what he produces is art and why it is a better work of art through this stroke of the pen or the brush or the chisel rather than that. The critic, for his part, creates as he interprets; for though he is bound by the fact of the work, defined in

5. *Id.* at 96 (emphasis in original).

the more formal and academic parts of his theory of art, his more practical artistic sense is engaged by his responsibility to decide which way of seeing or reading or understanding that work shows it as better art. Nevertheless there is a difference between interpreting while creating and creating while interpreting, and therefore a recognizable difference between the artist and the critic.

I want to use literary interpretation as a model for the central method of legal analysis, and I therefore need to show how even this distinction between artist and critic might be eroded in certain circumstances. Suppose that a group of novelists is engaged for a particular project and that they draw lots to determine the order of play. The lowest number writes the opening chapter of a novel, which he or she then sends to the next number who adds a chapter, with the understanding that he is adding a chapter to that novel rather than beginning a new one, and then sends the two chapters to the next number, and so on. Now every novelist but the first has the dual responsibilities of interpreting and creating, because each must read all that has gone before in order to establish, in the interpretivist sense, what the novel so far created is.[6] He or she must decide what the characters are "really"

---

6. Even the first novelist has the responsibility of interpreting to the extent any writer must, which includes not only interpreting as he writes but interpreting the genre in which he sets out to write. Will novelists with higher numbers have less creative "freedom" than those with lower? In one sense, no novelist has any freedom at all, because each is constrained to choose that interpretation which (he believes) makes the continuing work of art the best it can be. But we have already seen (and the discussion of law below will elaborate) two different dimensions along which any interpretation can be tested: the "formal" dimension, which asks how far the interpretation fits and integrates the text so far completed, and the "substantive" dimension, which considers the soundness of the view about what makes a novel good on which the interpretation relies. It seems reasonable to suppose that later novelists will normally—but certainly not inevitably—believe that fewer interpretations can survive the first of these tests than would have survived had they received fewer chapters. Most interpreters would think that a certain interpretation of *A Christmas Carol*—that Scrooge was inherently evil, for example—would pass the test of integrity just after the opening pages, but not towards the end of the novel. Our sense that later novelists are less "free" may reflect just that fact. This does not mean, of course, that there is more likely to be consensus about the correct interpretation later rather than earlier in the chain, or that a later novelist is more likely to find an argument that "proves" his interpretation right beyond rational challenge. Reasonable disagreement is available on the formal as well as the substantive side, and even when most novelists would think only a particular interpretation could fit the novel to a certain point, some novelist of imagination might find some dramatic change in plot that (in his opinion) unexpectedly unifies what had seemed disparate and unnecessary, and redeems what had seemed wrong or trivial. Once again, we should be careful not to confuse the fact that consensus would rarely be reached, at any point in the process, with the claim that any particular novelist's interpretation must be "merely subjective." No novelist, at any point, will be able simply to read in a mechanical way the correct interpretation off the text he receives, but it does not follow from that fact alone that one interpretation is not superior to others overall. In any case, it will nevertheless be true, for all novelists beyond the first, that the assignment to find (what they believe to be) the correct interpretation of the text so far is a different assignment from the assignment to begin a new novel of their own. For a fuller discussion, see Dworkin, *"Natural" Law Revisited*, 34 U. Fla L. Rev. 165 (1982).

like; what motives in fact guide them; what the point or theme of the developing novel is; how far some literary device or figure, consciously or unconsciously used, contributes to these, and whether it should be extended or refined or trimmed or dropped in order to send the novel further in one direction rather than another. This must be interpretation in a non-intention-bound style because, at least for all novelists after the second, there is no single author whose intentions any interpreter can, by the rules of the project, regard as decisive.

Some novels have in fact been written in this way (including the soft-core pornographic novel *Naked Came the Stranger*[7]), though for a debunking purpose, and certain parlor games for rainy weekends in English country houses have something of the same structure. But in my imaginary exercise the novelists are expected to take their responsibilities seriously and to recognize the duty to create, so far as they can, a single, unified novel rather than, for example, a series of independent short stories with characters bearing the same names. Perhaps this is an impossible assignment; perhaps the project is doomed to produce not simply a bad novel but no novel at all, because the best theory of art requires a single creator or, if more than one, that each have some control over the whole. (But what about legends and jokes?) I need not push that question further because I am interested only in the fact that the assignment makes sense, that each of the novelists in the chain can have some idea of what he or she is asked to do, whatever misgivings each might have about the value or character of what will then be produced.

Deciding hard cases at law is rather like this strange literary exercise. The similarity is most evident when judges consider and decide "common-law" cases; that is, when no statute figures centrally in the legal issue, and the argument turns on which rules or principles of law "underlie" the related decisions of other judges in the past. Each judge is then like a novelist in the chain. He or she must read through what other judges in the past have written not simply to discover what these judges have said, or their state of mind when they said it, but to reach an opinion about what these judges have collectively *done*, in the way that each of our novelists formed an opinion about the collective novel so far written. Any judge forced to decide a law suit will find, if he looks in the appropriate books, records of many arguably similar cases decided over decades or even centuries past by many other judges of different styles and judicial and political philosophies, in periods of dif-

---

7. P. ASHE, NAKED CAME THE STRANGER (1969).

ferent orthodoxies of procedure and judicial convention. Each judge must regard himself, in deciding the new case before him, as a partner in a complex chain enterprise of which these innumerable decisions, structures, conventions, and practices are the history; it is his job to continue that history into the future through what he does on the day. He *must* interpret what has gone before because he has a responsibility to advance the enterprise in hand rather than strike out in some new direction of his own. So he must determine, according to his own judgment, what the earlier decisions come to, what the point or theme of the practice so far, taken as a whole, really is.

The judge in the hypothetical case I mentioned earlier, about an aunt's emotional shock, must decide what the theme is, not only of the particular precedent of the mother in the road, but of accident cases, including that precedent, as a whole. He might be forced to choose, for example, between these two theories about the "meaning" of that chain of decisions. According to the first, negligent drivers are responsible to those whom their behavior is likely to cause physical harm, but they are responsible to these people for whatever injury—physical or emotional—they in fact cause. If this is the correct principle, then the decisive difference between that case and the aunt's case is just that the aunt was not within the physical risk, and therefore she cannot recover. On the second theory, however, negligent drivers are responsible for any damage they can reasonably be expected to foresee if they think about their behavior in advance. If that is the right principle, then the aunt may yet recover. Everything turns on whether it is sufficiently foreseeable that a child will have relatives, beyond his or her immediate parents, who may suffer emotional shock when they learn of the child's injury. The judge trying the aunt's case must decide which of these two principles represents the better "reading" of the chain of decisions he must continue.

Can we say, in some general way, what those who disagree about the best interpretation of legal precedent are disagreeing about? I said that a literary interpretation aims to show how the work in question can be seen as the most valuable work of art, and so must attend to formal features of identity, coherence, and integrity as well as more substantive considerations of artistic value. A plausible interpretation of legal practice must also, in a parallel way, satisfy a test with two dimensions: it must both fit that practice and show its point or value. But point or value here cannot mean artistic value because law, unlike literature, is not an artistic enterprise. Law is a political enterprise, whose general point, if it has one, lies in coordinating social and indi-

543

vidual effort, or resolving social and individual disputes, or securing justice between citizens and between them and their government, or some combination of these. (This characterization is itself an interpretation, of course, but allowable now because relatively neutral.) So an interpretation of any body or division of law, like the law of accidents, must show the value of that body of law in political terms by demonstrating the best principle or policy it can be taken to serve.

We know from the parallel argument in literature that this general description of interpretation in law is not license for each judge to find in doctrinal history whatever he thinks should have been there. The same distinction holds between interpretation and ideal. A judge's duty is to interpret the legal history he finds, not to invent a better history. The dimension of fit will provide some boundaries. There is, of course, no algorithm for deciding whether a particular interpretation sufficiently fits that history not to be ruled out. When a statute or constitution or other legal document is part of the doctrinal history, the speaker's meaning will play a role. But the choice of which of several crucially different senses of speaker's or legislator's intention is the appropriate one cannot itself be referred to anyone's intention but must be decided, by whoever must make the decision, as a question of political theory.[8] In the common-law cases the question of fit is more complex. Any particular hypothesis about the point of a string of decisions ("These decisions establish the principle that no one can recover for emotional damage who did not lie within the area of physical danger himself.") is likely to encounter, if not flat counter-examples in some earlier case, at least language or argument that seems to suggest the contrary. So any useful conception of interpretation must contain a doctrine of mistake—as must any novelist's theory of interpretation for the chain novel. Sometimes a legal argument will explicitly recognize such mistakes: "Insofar as the cases of *A v. B* and *C v. D* may have held to the contrary, they were, we believe, wrongly decided and need not be followed here." Sometimes the doctrine of precedent forbids this crude approach and requires something like: "We held, in *E v. F*, that such-and-such, but that case raised special issues and must, we think, be confined to its own facts" (which is not quite so disingenuous as it might seem).

This flexibility may seem to erode the difference on which I insist, between interpretation and a fresh, clean-slate decision about what the law ought to be. But there is nevertheless this overriding constraint.

---

8. See Dworkin, *The Forum of Principle*, 56 N.Y.U. L. Rev. 469 (1981).

544

Any judge's sense of the point or function of law, on which every aspect of his approach to interpretation will depend, will include or imply some conception of the integrity and coherence of law as an institution, and this conception will both tutor and constrain his working theory of fit—that is, his convictions about how much of the prior law an interpretation must fit, and which of it, and how. (The parallel with literary interpretation holds here as well.)

It should be apparent, however, that any particular judge's theory of fit will often fail to produce a unique interpretation. (The distinction between hard and easy cases at law is perhaps just the distinction between cases in which they do and do not.) Just as two readings of a poem may each find sufficient support in the text to show its unity and coherence, so two principles may each find enough support in the various decisions of the past to satisfy any plausible theory of fit. In that case substantive political theory (like substantive considerations of artistic merit) will play a decisive role. Put bluntly, the interpretation of accident law, that a careless driver is liable to those whose damage is both substantial and foreseeable, is probably a better interpretation, if it is, only because it states a sounder principle of justice than any principle that distinguishes between physical and emotional damage or that makes recovery for emotional damage depend on whether the plaintiff was in danger of physical damage. (I should add that this issue, as an issue of political morality, is in fact very complex, and many distinguished judges and lawyers have taken each side.)

We might summarize these points this way. Judges develop a particular approach to legal interpretation by forming and refining a political theory sensitive to those issues on which interpretation in particular cases will depend; they call this their legal philosophy. It will include both structural features, elaborating the general requirement that an interpretation must fit doctrinal history, and substantive claims about social goals and principles of justice. Any judge's opinion about the best interpretation will therefore be the consequence of beliefs other judges need not share. If a judge believes that the dominant purpose of a legal system, the main goal it ought to serve, is economic, then he will see in past accident decisions some strategy for reducing the economic costs of accidents overall. Other judges, who find any such picture of the law's function distasteful, will discover no such strategy in history but only, perhaps, an attempt to reinforce conventional morality of fault and responsibility. If we insist on a high order of neutrality in our description of legal interpretation, therefore, we cannot make our

545

description of the nature of legal interpretation much more concrete than I have.

B. Author's Intention in Law

I want instead to consider various objections that might be made not to the detail of my argument but to the main thesis, that interpretation in law is essentially political. I shall not spend further time on the general objection already noted: that this view of law makes it irreducibly and irredeemably subjective, just a matter of what particular judges think best or what they had for breakfast. Of course, for some lawyers and legal scholars this is not an objection at all, but only the beginnings of skeptical wisdom about law. But it is the nerve of my argument that the flat distinction between description and evaluation on which this skepticism relies—the distinction between finding the law just "there" in history and making it up wholesale—is misplaced here because interpretation is something different from both.

I shall want, therefore, to repeat the various observations I made about subjectivity and objectivity in literary interpretation. There is no obvious reason in the account I gave of legal interpretation to doubt that one interpretation of law can be better than another and that one can be best of all. Whether this is so depends on general issues of philosophy not peculiar to law any more than to literature; and we would do well, in considering these general issues, not to begin with any fixed ideas about the necessary and sufficient conditions of objectivity (for example, that no theory of law can be sound unless it is demonstrably sound, unless it would wring assent from a stone). In the meantime we can sensibly aim to develop various levels of a conception of law for ourselves, to find the interpretation of a complex and dramatically important practice which seems to us at once the right kind of interpretation for law and right as that kind of interpretation.

I shall consider one further, and rather different, objection in more detail: that my political hypothesis about legal interpretation, like the aesthetic hypothesis about artistic interpretation, fails to give an adequate place to author's intention. It fails to see that interpretation in law is simply a matter of discovering what various actors in the legal process—constitutional delegates, members of Congress and state legislatures, judges, and executive officials—intended. Once again it is important to see what is at stake here. The political hypothesis makes room for the author's intention argument as a conception of interpretation, a conception which claims that the best political theory gives the intentions of legislators and past judges a decisive role in interpreta-

546

tion. Seen this way, the author's intention theory does not challenge the political hypothesis but contests for its authority. If the present objection is really an objection to the argument so far, therefore, its claim must be understood differently, as proposing, for example, that the very "meaning" of interpretation in law requires that only these officials' intentions should count or that at least there is a firm consensus among lawyers to that effect. Both of these claims are as silly as the parallel claims about the idea or the practice of interpretation in art.

Suppose, therefore, that we do take the author's intention theory, more sensibly, as a conception rather than an explication of the concept of legal interpretation. The theory seems on firmest ground, as I suggested earlier, when interpretation is interpretation of a canonical legal text, like a clause of the Constitution, or a section of a statute, or a provision of a contract or will. But just as we noticed that a novelist's intention is complex and structured in ways that embarrass any simple author's intention theory in literature, we must now notice that a legislator's intention is complex in similar ways. Suppose a delegate to a constitutional convention votes for a clause guaranteeing equality of treatment without regard to race in matters touching peoples' fundamental interests; but he thinks that education is not a matter of fundamental interest and so does not believe that the clause makes racially segregated schools unconstitutional. We may sensibly distinguish an abstract and a concrete intention here: the delegate intends to prohibit discrimination in whatever in fact is of fundamental interest and also intends not to prohibit segregated schools. These are not isolated, discrete intentions; our descriptions, we might say, describe the same intention in different ways. But it matters very much which description a theory of legislative intention accepts as canonical. If we accept the first description, then a judge who wishes to follow the delegate's intentions, but who believes that education is a matter of fundamental interest, will hold segregation unconstitutional. If we accept the second, he will not. The choice between the two descriptions cannot be made by any further reflection about what an intention really is. It must be made by deciding that one rather than the other description is more appropriate in virtue of the best theory of representative democracy or on some other openly political ground. (I might add that no compelling argument has yet been produced, so far as I am aware, in favor of deferring to a delegate's more concrete intentions, and that this is of major importance in arguments about whether the "original intention" of the Framers requires, for example, abolishing racial discrimination, or capital punishment.)

547

When we consider the common-law problems of interpretation, the author's intention theory shows in an even poorer light. The problems are not simply evidentiary. Perhaps we can discover what was "in the mind" of all the judges who decided cases about accidents at one time or another in our legal history. We might also discover (or speculate) about the psychodynamic or economic or social explanations of why each judge thought what he or she did. No doubt the result of all this research (or speculation) would be a mass of psychological data essentially different for each of the past judges included in the study, and order could be brought into the mass, if at all, only through statistical summaries about which proportion of judges in which historical period probably held which opinion and was more or less subject to which influence. But this mass, even tamed by statistical summary, would be of no more help to the judge trying to answer the question of what the prior decisions, taken as a whole, really come to than the parallel information would be to one of our chain novelists trying to decide what novel the novelists earlier in the chain had collectively written. That judgment, in each case, requires a fresh exercise of interpretation which is neither brute historical research nor a clean-slate expression of how things ideally ought to be.

A judge who believed in the importance of discerning an author's intention might try to escape these problems by selecting one particular judge or a small group of judges in the past (say, the judges who decided the most recent case something like his or the case he thinks closest to his) and asking what rule that judge or group intended to lay down for the future. This would treat the particular earlier judges as legislators and so invite all the problems of statutory interpretation including the very serious problem we just noticed. Even so, it would not even escape the special problems of common-law adjudication after all, because the judge who applied this theory of interpretation would have to suppose himself entitled to look only to the intentions of the particular earlier judge or judges he had selected, and he could not suppose this unless he thought that it was the upshot of judicial practice as a whole (and not just the intentions of some *other* selected earlier judge) that this is what judges in his position should do.

IV. Politics in Interpretation

If my claims about the role of politics in legal interpretation are sound, then we should expect to find distinctly liberal or radical or conservative opinions not only about what the Constitution and laws of our nation should be but also about what they are. And this is exactly

548

what we do find. Interpretation of the equal protection clause of the Constitution provides especially vivid examples. There can be no useful interpretation of what that clause means independent of some theory about what political equality is and how far equality is required by justice, and the history of the last half-century of constitutional law is largely an exploration of exactly these issues of political morality. Conservative lawyers argued steadily (though not consistently) in favor of an author's intentions style of interpreting this clause, and they accused others, who used a different style with more egalitarian results, of inventing rather than interpreting law. But this was bluster meant to hide the role their own political convictions played in their choice of interpretive style, and the great legal debates over the equal protection clause would have been more illuminating if it had been more widely recognized that reliance on political theory is not a corruption of interpretation but part of what interpretation means.

Should politics play any comparable role in literary and other artistic interpretation? We have become used to the idea of the politics of interpretation. Stanley Fish, particularly, has promoted a theory of interpretation which supposes that contests between rival schools of literary interpretation are more political than argumentative: rival professoriates in search of dominion. And of course it is a truism of the sociology of literature, and not merely of the Marxist contribution to that discipline, that fashion in interpretation is sensitive to and expresses more general political and economic structures. These important claims are external: they touch the causes of the rise of this or that approach to literature and interpretation.

We are now concerned with the internal question, about politics in rather than the politics of interpretation.[9] How far can principles of political morality actually count as arguments for a particular interpretation of a particular work or for a general approach to artistic interpretation? There are many possibilities and many of them are parasitic on claims developed or in these essays. It was said that our commitment to feminism, or our fidelity to nation, or our dissatisfaction with the rise of the New Right, ought to influence our evaluation and appreciation of literature. Indeed it was the general (though not unanimous) sense of the conference that professional criticism must be faulted for its inattention to such political issues. But if our convictions about these particular political issues count in deciding how good some novel or play or poem is, then they must also count in deciding, among particular

---

9. See *Politics of Interpretation*, 9 CRITICAL INQUIRY 1 (1982).

549

interpretations of these works, which is the best interpretation. Or so they must if my argument is sound.

We might also explore a more indirect connection between aesthetic and political theory. Any comprehensive theory of art is likely to have, at its center, some epistemological thesis, some set of views about the relations that hold among experience, self-consciousness, and the perception or formation of values. If it assigns self-discovery any role in art, it will need a theory of personal identity adequate to mark off the boundaries of a person from his or her circumstances, and from other persons, or at least to deny the reality of any such boundaries. It seems likely that any comprehensive theory of social justice will also have roots in convictions about these or very closely related issues. Liberalism, for example, which assigns great importance to autonomy, may depend upon a particular picture of the role that judgments of value play in people's lives; it may depend on the thesis that people's convictions about value are beliefs, open to argument and review, rather than simply the givens of personality, fixed by genetic and social causes. And any political theory that gives an important place to equality also requires assumptions about the boundaries of persons, because it must distinguish between treating people as equals and changing them into different people.

It may be a sensible project, at least, to inquire whether there are not particular philosophical bases shared by particular aesthetic and particular political theories so that we can properly speak of a liberal or Marxist or perfectionist or totalitarian aesthetics, for example, in that sense. Common questions and problems hardly guarantee this, of course. It would be necessary to see, for example, whether liberalism can indeed be traced, as many philosophers have supposed, back into a discrete epistemological base, different from that of other political theories, and then ask whether that discrete base could be carried forward into aesthetic theory and there yield a distinctive interpretive style. I have no good idea that this project could be successful, and I end simply by acknowledging my sense that politics, art, and law are united, somehow, in philosophy.

550

NATURAL LAW AND LEGAL REASONING*

JOHN FINNIS**

I

Legal reasoning is, broadly speaking, practical reasoning. Practical reasoning moves from reasons for action to choices (and actions) guided by those reasons.[1] A natural law theory is nothing other than a theory of good reasons for choice (and action).

"Reasons", "choices" and "action" are words afflicted with a fundamental ambiguity. Its principal source is that we are animals, but intelligent. All our actions have an emotional motivation, involve our feelings and imagination and other aspects of our bodiliness; and all can be observed (if only, in some cases, by introspection) as pieces of behaviour. But rationally motivated actions also have an intelligent motivation, and seek to realize (protect, promote) an intelligible good. So our purposes, the states of affairs which we seek to bring about, have a double aspect: the goal which we imagine and which engages our feelings, and the intelligible benefit which appeals to our rationality by promising to instantiate, either immediately or instrumentally, some basic human good. The word "reason" is often used loosely to refer to one's purposes, without distinguishing between a purpose motivated ultimately by nothing more than feeling and a purpose motivated by one's understanding of a basic human good. I shall be using the word "reason", except where the context shows otherwise, to refer only to reason in the latter sense.[2]

An account of basic reasons for action should not be exclusively rationalistic. It should not portray human flourishing in terms only of the exercise of our capacities to reason. We are organic substances, animals, and part of our genuine well-being is our bodily life, maintained in health,

---

* The text of Professor Finnis's article has been retained in the form in which it was circulated to other contributors to this symposium. The author has subsequently added seven new footnotes, explaining or qualifying the text. These additional notes are signalled by being enclosed in square brackets.

**Professor of Law and Legal Philosophy, University of Oxford.

[1] [This statement about practical reasoning takes as the paradigmatic locus of practical reasoning the third of the four orders identified in part III below. And it takes only the central case; not all practical reasoning issues in choice, and choice (in the strong sense of "choice") is not characteristically guided by all the reasons considered in deliberation, for choice is characteristically between rationally (even if not reasonably) open alternative options, and so the reasons for the option(s) rejected in choice do not "guide the choice."]

[2] For my use here of "purpose," "goal," "feeling," "benefit," "motivated" and "basic human good," *see* Grisez, Boyle, & Finnis, *Practical Principles, Moral Truth, and Ultimate Ends*, 32 AM. J. JURIS. 99-151 (1987) [hereinafter Grisez, Boyle and Finnis].

vigour and safety, and transmitted to new human beings. To regard human life as a basic reason for action is to understand it as a good in which indefinitely many beings can participate in indefinitely many occasions and ways, going far beyond any goal or purpose which anyone could envisage and pursue, but making sense of indefinitely many goals.[3] And this sense of "reason for action" is common to all the other basic goods: knowledge of reality (including aesthetic appreciations of it); excellence in work and play whereby one transforms natural realities to express meanings and serve purposes; harmony between and amongst individuals and groups of persons (peace, neighbourliness and friendship); harmony between one's own feelings and one's judgments and choices (inner peace); harmony between one's choices and one's judgments and behaviour (peace of conscience and authenticity in the sense of consistency between one's self and its expression); and harmony between oneself and the wider reaches of reality including the reality that the world has some more-than-human source of meaning and value.

To state the basic human goods is of course to propose an account of human nature.[4] But it is not an attempt to deduce reasons for action from some pre-existing theoretical account of human nature in defiance of the logical truth (well known to the ancients) that you cannot deduce an "ought" from an "is"—since you cannot find in the conclusion to a syllogism what is not in the premises. Rather, a full account of human nature can only be given by one who understands the human goods practically, i.e., *as* reasons for choice and action, making full sense of feelings, spontaneities and behaviour. (So Aristotle's principal treatise on human nature is his *Ethics* which is from beginning to end an attempt to identify the human good, and is, according to Aristotle himself, from beginning to end an effort of *practical* understanding; the *Ethics* is not derivative from some prior treatise on human nature.)

So one begins to see the sense of the term "natural law": reasons for actions which will instantiate and express human nature precisely because they participate in and realize human goods.

II.

Just here a sound theory of practical reasoning, and therefore of legal reasoning, will part company from many theories on the market. It parts company, for example, from the denial that there are any objective human goods save, perhaps, freedom of choice—a denial which lies at the heart of Critical Legal Studies, as its foundational texts make plain. Of the four (bad) reasons offered by Roberto Unger for denying that there are objective human goods, the one most dear to his heart, I think, is that to affirm that there are such goods "denies any significance to choice other than

---

[3] *See* J. FINNIS, J. BOYLE & G. GRISEZ, NUCLEAR DETERRENCE, MORALITY AND REALISM 277-8 (1987); J. FINNIS, NATURAL LAW AND NATURAL RIGHTS 84-5, 100 (1980) [hereinafter NATURAL LAW].

[4] *See* J. FINNIS, FUNDAMENTALS OF ETHICS 20-22 (1983).

the passive acceptance or rejection of independent truths . . . [and] disregards the significance of choice as an expression of personality."[5]

On the contrary, it is the diversity of *rationally* appealing human goods which makes free choice both possible and frequently necessary—the choice between rationally appealing and incompatible alternative options, such that nothing but the choosing itself settles which option is chosen and pursued.[6] I shall be arguing that many aspects of individual and social life—and many individual and social obligations—are structured by choice between rationally appealing options whose rational appeal can be explained only in terms, ultimately, of basic human opportunities understood to be objectively good.

But if the basic human goods open up so much to rational choice, where are we to find the concept of choices which, though rational, ought to be rejected—are unreasonable, wrongful, immoral?

Moral thought is simply practically rational thought at full stretch, integrating emotions and feelings but *undeflected* by them. The fundamental principle of practical rationality is: Take as a premise at least one of the basic reasons for action and follow through to the point at which you somehow instantiate that good in action—do not act pointlessly. The fundamental principle of *moral* thought is simply the demand to be fully rational: In so far as it is in your power, allow nothing but the basic reasons for action to shape your practical thinking as you find, develop, and use your opportunities to pursue human flourishing through your chosen actions—be entirely reasonable.[7] Aristotle's phrase *orthos logos*, and his later followers' *recta ratio*, right reason, should simply be understood as "unfettered reason", reason undeflected by emotions and feelings. Undeflected reason will be guided by the ideal of integral human fulfillment, i.e. by the ideal of the instantiation of all the basic human goods in all human persons and communities.

Emotion may make one wish to destroy or damage the good of life in someone one hates, or the good of knowledge; so one kills or injures, or deceives that person, just out of feelings of aversion. That is a simple, paradigmatic form of immorality. We can say that hereabouts there is a general, so to speak methodological moral principle, intermediate between the basic principles of practical reason (the basic goods or reasons for action) and particular moral norms against killing or lying: this intermediate moral principle, which some call a mode of responsibility,[8] will exclude meeting injury with injury, or responding to one's own weakness or setbacks with self-destructiveness.

---

[5] R. Unger, Knowledge and Politics 77 (1975). On this and the other bad reasons see Finnis, *The Critical Legal Studies Movement* in J. Eekelaar and J. Bell, Oxford Essays in Jurisprudence: Third Series 144-165 at 16-35 (1987) [hereinafter *Critical Legal Studies*]; or in 30 Am. J. Juris. 21-42 at 40-42 (1985).

[6] On free choice and its conditions, *see, e.g.*, Grisez, Boyle and Finnis, *supra* note 2, at 256-60; J. Boyle, G. Grisez & O. Tollefsen, Free Choice: A Self-Referential argument (1976).

[7] *See* Grisez, Boyle and Finnis, *supra* note 2, at 119-25.

[8] Thus Grisez, Boyle and Finnis, *supra* note 2, at 284-7; in Natural Law and Natural Rights, I call them "basic requirements of practical reasonableness" Natural Law, *supra* note 3, at 100-33, and in Fundamentals of Ethics, I call them "intermediate moral principles", *supra* note 4, at 69-70, 74-6.

More immediately relevant to political and legal theory is the mode of responsibility, or intermediate moral principle, requiring that one act fairly: that one not limit one's concern for basic human goods simply by one's feelings of self-preference or preference for those who are near and dear. Fairness does not exclude treating different persons differently; it requires only that the differential treatment be justified either by *inevitable* limits on one's action or by intelligible requirements of the basic human goods themselves. I shall have more to say about the legitimate role of feelings in making fair choices in which one prioritizes goods by one's feelings without prioritizing persons simply by feelings.

There are other intermediate moral principles. Very important to the structuring of legal thought is the principle which excludes acting against a basic reason by choosing to destroy or damage any basic human good in any of its instantiations in any human person. The basic reasons for action, as the phrase suggests, present one with many reasons *for* choice and action, and since one is finite, one's choice of any purpose, however far-reaching, will inevitably have as side-effect the non-realisation of other possible instantiations of that and of other basic human goods. In *that* sense, every choice is "against some basic reason". But only as a side-effect. The choices which are excluded by the present mode of responsibility are those in which the damaging or destruction of an instantiation of a basic human good is chosen, as a means. The mode of responsibility which I first mentioned excludes making such damage or destruction one's end; the present mode excludes making it one's means. The concepts of ends and means come together in the conception so fundamental to our law: intention.[9]

III.

At this point, one begins to notice how a theory of natural law cannot be a theory only of human goods as principles of practical reasoning. Practical reasoning must take into account, and a theory of practical reason must accommodate within its account certain features of our world. world.

---

[9] On the analysis of human action here sketched, see Grisez, Boyle and Finnis, *supra* note 2, at 288-90; on the mode of responsibility which excludes choosing to destroy, damage or impede a basic human good, *see id.* at 286-7. The ultimate intelligibility of this mode—the mode which is the principal source of the *absolute* specific moral norms identified in Judaeo-Christian tradition—is this (stated very summarily, and without the further clarifications which readers may well desire): A basic human good always is a reason for action and always gives a reason *not* to do what would destroy, damage or impede some instantiation of that good; but since the instantiations of human good at stake in any morally significant choice are not rationally commensurable, there can never be a sufficient reason not to act on the first-mentioned reason—only emotional factors such as desire or aversion could motivate a choice to reject the first-mentioned reason by choosing to destroy, damage or impede that instantiation of a basic human good.

The distinction between what is chosen as end or means, i.e. intended, and what is foreseen and accepted as a side-effect (i.e. an unintended effect) is a feature of the human situation which is more or less spontaneously and more or less clearly understood in unreflective practical reasoning, but which must be brought to full clarity in a reflective ethical, political or legal theory. The reality of freedom of choice, and the significance of choices as lasting in the character of the chooser beyond the time of the behavior which executes the choice—this too is a reality which ethical and political theory must attend to and accommodate.

Other similarly significant features of our situation include such basic facts as that which Robert Nozick overlooked when he declared that everything, or virtually everything comes into the world already attached to someone having an entitlement over it—the reality being, on the contrary, that the natural resources from which everything made has been made pre-exist all entitlements and came into the world attached to nobody in particular, so that the resources of the world are fundamentally *common* and no theory of entitlements can rightly appropriate any resource to one person so absolutely as to negate that original communality of the world's stock.[10] (Here one will think of the principle of eminent domain, or of the way in which laws of insolvency, while quite reasonably varying from country to country, are all structured around some principle of equality amongst creditors or within ranks of creditors.[11])

One further feature of the world to be accommodated by a sound theory of natural law is the distinction between the orders of reality with which human reason is concerned. There is the order which we can understand but which is in no way established by human understanding—the order of nature as investigated by the natural sciences, and reflected upon by metaphysicians. There is the order which one can bring into one's own inquiries, understanding and reasoning—the order studied by logic, methodology and epistemology. There is the order which one can bring into one's own dispositions, choices and actions—one's *praxis*, one's doing—the order studied by some parts of psychology, by biography and the history of human affairs, and by moral and political philosophy. And there is the order one can bring into matter which is subject to our power so as to make objects such as phonemes, words, poems, boats, computer programmes, ballistic missiles and their inbuilt trajectories—the order of *poiesis*, of making—studied in the arts and technologies, and in linguistics and rhetoric.[12]

The four orders are simply illustrated in any interesting human state of affairs. Consider, for example, a seminar: You hear the *sounds* produced by my vocal chords: first order; you hear my *expositions, arguments and explanations*, and bring your understanding into line with mine (if only to judge my propositions mistaken): second order; you hear *me*, each of

---

[10] R. Nozick, Anarchy, State and Utopia 160 (1974); Natural Law, *supra* note 3, at 187.

[11] See Natural Law, *supra* note 3, at 188-93.

[12] On the four orders, see *id.* at 136-8, 157.

us sitting here disposed to speak and listen by our free choices to engage in this human activity and relationship of participation in a seminar: third order; and finally you hear the *English language* and statements ordered by an expository technique, each of us making and decoding the formalized symbols of a language and the less formalized but still conventional symbols, signs and expressions of a cultural form: fourth order. Thus, four irreducibly distinct senses of "hearing."

Legal rationality, I suggest, has its distinctiveness, and its peculiar elusiveness, because, in the service of a third-order purpose—the chosen purpose of living together in a just order of fair and right relationships— there has been and is being constructed a fourth order object, "the law" as in "the law of Ohio," a vastly complex cultural object, comprising a vocabulary with artfully assigned meanings, rules identifying permitted and excluded arguments and decisions, and correspondingly very many series of processes (such as pleading, trial, conveyance of property, etc.) constituted and regulated according to those formulae, their assigned meanings, and the rules of argument and decision.

This cultural object, constructed or posited by creative human decision, is an instrument which we adopt for a moral purpose, and which we adopt because we have no other way of agreeing amongst ourselves over significant spans of time about precisely *how* to pursue our moral project *well*. Political authority in all its manifestations, including legal institutions, is a technique for doing without unanimity in making social choices—where unanimity would almost always be unattainable or temporary—in order to secure practical unanimity about how to coordinate our actions with each other, which, given authority, we do simply by conforming to the patterns authoritatively chosen.[13]

Legal reasoning, indeed, is technical reasoning, at least in large part— not moral reasoning. Like all technical reasoning, it is concerned to achieve a particular purpose, a definite state of affairs which can be achieved by efficient disposition of means to end. The particular end here is the resolution of disputes by the provision of a directive sufficiently definite and specific to identify one party to the dispute as right (in-the-right) and the other as wrong (not-in-the-right).

Hence the law's distinctive devices: defining terms, and specifying rules, with sufficient and necessarily artificial clarity and definiteness to establish the "bright lines" which make so many real-life legal questions *easy questions*. Legal definitions and rules are designed to provide the citizen, the legal adviser and the judge with an algorithm for deciding as many questions as possible—in principle every question—Yes (or No), this course of action would (or would not) be lawful; this arrangement is valid; this contract is at an end; these losses are compensable in damages and those are not; and so forth. As far as it can, the law seeks to provide sources of reasoning—statutes and statute-based rules, common law

---

[13] *See also id.* at 231-7; Finnis, *The Authority of Law in the Predicament of Contemporary Social Theory,* 1 J. LAW AND PUB. POL. 115-37 (1984).

rules, and customs—capable of ranking (commensurating) alternative dispute resolutions as right or wrong, and *thus* better and worse.

Lawyers' tools of trade—their ability to find and use the authoritative sources—are means in the service of a purpose sufficiently definite to constitute a technique, a mode of technical reasoning: the purpose, again, is the unequivocal resolution of every dispute that can in some way be foreseen and provided for. Still, this quest for certainty, for a complete set of uniquely correct answers, is itself in the service of a wider good which like all basic human goods is not reducible to a definite goal but is rather an open-ended good in which persons and their communities can participate without ever capturing or exhausting it: the good of just harmony. This good is a moral good just insofar as it is itself promoted and respected as one aspect of the ideal of integral human fulfillment. As a moral good its implications are specified by *all* the moral principles that could bear upon it.

IV.

Thus there emerges the tension which Ronald Dworkin's work on legal reasoning has done so much to clarify—even though his own attempt to overcome the tension is, I believe, most instructive precisely by its own failure to grasp the real nature and implications of the tension.[14]

Dworkin tries to show that a *uniquely* correct ("the right") answer is available in "most" hard cases. But his efforts, I shall argue, provide an even better dialectical case for the contrary and classical view. In the classical view, while there are many ways of going and doing wrong, there are in most situations of personal and social life a variety of incompatible *right* (i.e. not wrong) options. And, while personal choice or authoritative social decision-making can greatly reduce this variety of options for the person who has made that commitment or the community which accepts that authority, still those choices and decisions were themselves not required by reason, i.e., were not preceded by any rational judgment that *this* option is the right answer or the best solution. On the view which I am calling "classical", and which I believe to be correct, we approach cases which have not been simply settled by prior choice or an applicable social rule—hard cases—with a view to finding good answers, and rejecting bad ones, but we should not dream of finding a *best* answer.

My denial that uniquely correct, or best, answers are available to most non-technical questions of praxis has nothing to do with any sort of skepticism. Nor is it related to a popular argument which Dworkin is rightly concerned to scorn and demolish—the argument that disagreement is endemic and inevitable, and therefore justified. For disagreement is a mere fact about people, and is logically irrelevant to the merits of any practical or other interpretative claim.

---

[14] In what follows, I focus on R. DWORKIN, LAW'S EMPIRE (1986); *see also* Finnis, *On Reason and Authority in Law's Empire*, 6 LAW AND PHILOSOPHY 357-80 (1987).

Nor does my denial rest on the observation that none of us has the "superhuman" powers of Dworkin's imaginary ideal judge. An ideal human judge, no matter how "superhuman" his powers, could not sensibly search for a uniquely correct legal answer to a hard case (as lawyers in sophisticated legal systems use that term). For in such a case, the search for the one right answer is particularly incoherent and senseless, in much the same way as a search for the American novel which meets the two criteria "most romantic and shortest" (or "best and funniest"; or "most American and most profound").

In judicial reasoning as portrayed by Dworkin, two incommensurable criteria of judgment are in use—and these two criteria or dimensions of judgment correspond to the third (moral) and fourth (technical) orders of rationality. The first of these dimensions Dworkin calls "fit": coherence with the existing legal "materials"—note the appropriately "technological" term—created by past political decisions, i.e., with legislation and authoritative judicial decision (precedent). The second Dworkin calls "justifiability" (confusingly, since both dimensions are necessary to justifying a judicial decision; his previous name was better: inherent substantive moral "soundness").[15]

Given these two dimensions of assessment, we can say that a hard case is hard (not merely novel) when not only is there more than one answer which violates no applicable rule, but also the available answers can be ranked in different orders along each of the relevant criteria of evaluation: for novels, their brevity, their American character, humour, profundity, etc.; for judicial judgments, or theories of law, their fit, their *inherent* moral soundness, etc. Thus there emerges what theorists of rational choice call "intransitivity", a phenomenon which theories of rational choice (such as a game and decision theory) confessedly cannot handle: solution A is better than solution B on the scale of legal fit, and B than C, but C is better than A on the scale of moral soundness; so there is no sufficient reason to declare A overall "legally better" than C, or C than A, or B than either. If the rank order was the same on both scales, of course, the case was never a hard one, and the legal system already had what one always *desires* of it: a uniquely correct answer.

In earlier works, Dworkin tried to deflect the problem of incommensurability of criteria by proposing a kind of lexical ordering: candidates for "best account" of the law of Ohio in 1988 must fit the existing Ohio legal materials *adequately*, and of those which satisfy this "threshold" criterion, that which ranks highest in intrinsic moral soundness is overall, absolutely, "the best" even though it fits less well than (an)other(s).[16] But

---

[15] [Throughout this discussion of Dworkin's dimensions of assessment, I shall take for granted his assumption that "morality" and "moral soundness" refer to a "dimension of assessment" which can sometimes be rightly (in some sense of "right" relevant to judicial duty) subordinated to some other criterion or criteria (such as "fit"). But the truth here is different, though not simple: morality always trumps every other criterion of choice, though not in such a way as to make immoral choice irrational; but the truth conditions of any moral truth(s) relevant to a judge include facts about fit; if the facts about fit cannot (on moral standards of judgment) be reconciled with morality, one is in a *lex injusta* situation, as to which see NATURAL LAW, *supra* note 3, ch. 12.]

[16] *See, e.g.,* R. DWORKIN, TAKING RIGHTS SERIOUSLY 340-42 (1978).

this solution was empty, for he identified no criteria, however sketchy or "in principle," for specifying when fit is "adequate," i.e. for locating the threshold of fit beyond which the criterion of soundness would prevail. (It is like searching for the funniest novel among those that are short "enough.") Presumably, candidates for "the right answer" to the question "When is fit adequate?" would themselves be ranked in terms both of fit and of soundness. An infinite regress, of the vicious sort which nullify purported rational explanations, was well under way.

In his book, *Law's Empire*, Dworkin abandons the simple picture of a lexical ordering between the criteria of fit and soundness—between legal-technical and moral considerations. We are left with little more than a metaphor: "balance"—as in "the general balance of political virtues" embodied in competing interpretations or accounts of the law. But in the absence of any metric which could commensurate the different criteria, the instruction to balance (or, earlier, to weigh) can legitimately mean no more than: bear in mind, conscientiously, all the relevant factors, and *choose*; or, in the legal sphere, hear the arguments in the highest court, and then: *vote*.

In understanding practical rationality in all its forms, it is important to take account of a feature of the phenomenology of choice. *After* one has chosen, the factors favoring the chosen alternative will usually seem to outweigh, overbalance, those favoring the rejected alternatives. The chosen option—to do X, to adopt rule Y—will seem (to the person who chose, if not to onlookers) to have a supremacy, a unique rightness. But the truth is that the choice was not rationally determined, i.e., was not guided by "the right answer." (And this does not mean it was *irrational*: it was between rationally appealing options.) Rather, the choice established the "right" answer—i.e., established it in, and by reference ultimately to, the dispositions and sentiments of the chooser.[17] When the choice is that of the majority in the highest relevant appeal court (a mere brute fact), the unique rightness of the answer is established not only by and for the attitude of those who have chosen it, but also for the legal system or community for which it has thus been authoritatively decided upon, and laid down as or in a *rule*.

V.

I have been discussing, in a special context, something of much wider importance: the incommensurability of goods and reasons at stake in morally significant choice (such as the choice before the judge in a genuine hard case).[18] The phenomenon of incommensurability is central to an understanding of the moral and political rationality which underpins (though not exhausts) legal rationality.

The problem of incommensurability—the problem that there is no *rationally* calibrated scale for "weighing" the goods and bads at stake in

---

[17] *See* G. Grisez, *Against Consequentialism*, 23 AM. J. JURIS. 21, 46-7 (1978).

[18] [This is inexact. The incommensurability of reasons is not an instantiation of the incommensurability of goods, and differs from the latter incommensurability, except where all the reasons (e.g. aesthetic considerations) at stake are non-moral.]

moral and political choice—is in reality much more intense than in the simple Dworkinian picture of legal reasoning along the two dimensions of legal fit and moral soundness. Everyone confronts that incommensurability when having to choose between coming to a lecture, reading a good book, going to the cinema, and talking to friends. At the other extreme, so to speak, is the incommensurability of the relevant goods and bads in relation to such a fundamental social choice as to have or to reject or renounce a nuclear deterrent. An exploration of such a choice amply illustrates and explains the impotence of all forms of aggregative reasoning towards morally significant choice—choice outside the purely technical or technological task of identifying the most efficient means to a single limited goal.[19]

For *morally significant choice* would be impossible if one of the options could be shown to be *the best* on a single scale which, as all aggregative reasoning does, ranked all options in a single transitive order.[20] If there were a reason (for doing X) which some rational method of comparison (e.g., aggregation of goods) identified as preferable, the alternative reason (against doing X) thus identified as rationally inferior would cease to be rationally appealing in respect to that situation of choice. The reason thus identified as preferable, and the option favored by that reason, would be rationally unopposed. There would remain *no choice*, in the morally significant sense of choice, between the alternative options.[21] For one has a morally significant choice just where one really does have reasons for alternative options; for then the choice can be *free*, no factor but the choosing itself *settling* which alternative is chosen. So the reason why there are morally significant choices is precisely that there is no rational method of identifying the reasons *for* alternative options, *prior to moral judgment*, as rationally simply superior and inferior. That is to say, the instantiations of basic human goods, instantiations considered precisely as reasons for moral judgment and for action, are incommensurable with one another. And this is not surprising, for these instantiations are nothing other than aspects of human persons, present and future, and human persons cannot be weighed and balanced.[22]

---

[19] *See* Grisez, Boyle and Finnis, *supra* note 2, at 177-272. Joseph Raz has explored the problem, with some similar conclusions, in the important chapter on incommensurability in his THE MORALITY OF FREEDOM 321-66 (1986).

[20] [This is stated too strongly. It is sufficient if one option "dominates" all the others; there will then be no morally significant, rationally guided *choice*, even if the remaining, dominated alternatives cannot themselves be ranked in a single transitive order.]

[21] [This sentence, like each of the two sentences following it, is stated too strongly. There remains the possibility that in choosing, a person follows a non-rational motive (e.g. fear of pain) against reason(s). But this possibility is irrelevant to the present discussion, which is an examination of aggregative *reasoning* towards morally significant choice.]

[22] [Again, this is a little too blunt. The good or harm done to a human person by a choice cannot be weighed and balanced against e.g. the good or harm done to the chooser in and as a result of that choice. But there can be situations in which an option concerning persons is "dominant".]

But one *can* identify reasons *against* an option, wherever (for example) that option involves *choosing* (intending) to destroy, damage or impede a basic human good, or imposing on persons, even as a side-effect, harms or burdens which one would not impose on oneself or one's friends and which one imposes for no motive other than differential feelings. Such reasons against a certain option must be respected unless some reason *for* that action is rationally preferable.[23] But what the argument about incommensurability shows is that *no* reason can be identified as rationally preferable to the reason not to choose to destroy or damage a basic good in a human person, or to the reason not to act unfairly.

VI.

The results of this reflection on incommensurability are of great importance for legal reasoning.

The first result is that there are moral absolutes, excluding intentional killing, intentional injury to the person, deliberate deception for the sake of securing desired results, enslavement which treats a human person as an object or a lower rank of being than the autonomous human subject. These moral absolutes, which *are* rationally determined and essentially determinate, are the backbone of the important human rights, and of the criminal law and the law of intentional torts, not to mention all the rules and principles which penalize intentional deception, withdraw from it all direct legal support, and exclude it from the legal process.

A second result concerns the implications of fairness. The core of the moral norm of fairness is the Golden Rule: "Do to others as you would have them do to you; Do not impose on others what you would not want to be obliged by them to accept". Although this too is a requirement of practical rationality, a rational norm of impartiality, its concrete application in personal life presupposes a commensuration of benefits and burdens *which reason is impotent to commensurate*. For, to apply to Golden Rule, one must know what burdens one considers *too great* to accept. And this knowledge, constituting a pre-moral commensuration, can only be one's intuitive awareness of one's own differentiated *feelings* towards various goods and bads as concretely remembered, experienced or imagined. This, I repeat, is not a rational and objective commensuration of goods and bads; but once established in one's feelings and identified in one's self-awareness, it enables one to measure one's options by a rational and objective standard of inter-personal impartiality: fairness.

Similarly, in the life of a community, the preliminary commensuration of rationally incommensurable factors is accomplished not by rationally determined judgments, but by *decisions*. Is it fair to impose on others the

---

[23] [This sentence, taken in isolation from the following sentences, is misleading. In a situation in which the reasons *against* an option are of the sort referred to in the previous sentence, there cannot be a rationally preferable reason *for* the action; the class of exceptions referred to by the "unless . . ." clause is a null class.]

risks inherent in driving at more than 10 miles per hour? Yes, in our community, since our community has by custom and law *decided* to treat those risks and harms as *not too great*. Have we a rational critique of a community which decided to limit road traffic to 10 m.p.h. and to accept all the economic and other costs of that decision? No, we have no rational critique of such a community. But we do have a rational critique of someone who drives at 60 m.p.h. but who, when struck by another, complains and alleges that the mere fact that the other's speed exceeded 10 m.p.h. proved that other's negligence. And we have a rational critique of one who accepts the benefits of the road traffic law and of other communal decisions but who rejects the burdens as they bear on him and those in whom he feels interested; and so forth. In short, the decision to permit road traffic to proceed faster than 10 m.p.h. was *rationally under-determined.*[24] But *once the decision has been made*, it provides an often *fully determinate* rational standard for treating those accused of wrongful conduct or wrongfully inflicting injury.

In the working of the legal process, much turns on the principle—a principle of fairness—that litigants (and others involved in the process) should be treated by judges (and others with power to decide) *impartially*, in the sense that they are as nearly as possible to be treated by each judge as they would be treated by every other judge. It is this above all, I believe, that drives the law towards the artificial, the *techne* rationality of laying down and following a set of positive norms identifiable as far as possible simply by their "sources" (i.e., by the fact of their enactment or other constitutive event) and applied so far as possible according to their publicly stipulated meaning, itself elucidated with as little as possible appeal to considerations which, because not controlled by facts about sources (constitutive events), are inherently likely to be appealed to differently by different judges. This drive to insulate legal reasoning from moral reasoning can never, however, be complete, as Dworkin's work reminds us.

The two principal results of the phenomenon of incommensurability are implications which rule out the technique of legal reasoning known as Economic Analysis of Law. For it is central to that technique that every serious question of social order can be resolved by aggregating the overall net good promised by alternative options, in terms of a simple commensurating factor (or maximand), viz. wealth measured in terms of the money which relevant social actors would be willing and able to pay to secure their preferred option. Equally central to Economic Analysis is the assumption, or thesis, that there is no difference of principle between buying the right to inflict injury intentionally and buying the right not to take precautions which would eliminate an equivalent number and type of injuries caused accidentally. A root and branch critique of Eco-

---

[24] Of course, this does not mean that it was "indeterminate" in the strong sense of the word which the Critical Legal Studies Movement uses so vaguely and uncritically, i.e., indeterminate in the sense of being wholly unguided by reason.

nomic Analysis of Law will focus on these two features of it. Less fundamental critiques, such as Ronald Dworkin's (helpful and worthwhile though it is), leave those features untouched. Indeed, Dworkin's own distinction between rights and collective goals, the latter being proposed by Dworkin as the legitimate province of legislatures, is a distinction which uncritically assumes that collective goals can rationally be identified and preferred to alternatives by aggregation of value without regard to principles of distributive fairness and other aspects of justice—principles which themselves constitute rights, and which cannot be rationally traded off against measurable quantities of value.[25]

VII.

In sum: Much academic theory about legal reasoning greatly exaggerates the extent to which reason can settle what is greater good or lesser evil, and minimizes the need for authoritative sources which, so far as they are clear and respect the few absolute moral rights and duties, are to be respected as the only rational basis for judicial reasoning and decision, in relation to the countless issues which do not directly involve those absolute rights and duties. A natural law theory in the classical tradition makes no pretence that natural reason can determine the one right answer to those countless questions which arise for the judge who finds the sources unclear.

(*See Critical Legal Studies, supra* note 5, at 147, 157-61.) For the good of human bodily life and integrity is a genuine reason always practically relevant; and some further rational criteria for decision are provided by facts about human reaction times and susceptibility to impact, and by the rational demand for consistency with our individual and communal tolerance or intolerance of other—non-traffic—threats to that good.

[25] *See* Finnis, *A Bill of Rights for Britain? The Moral of Contemporary Jurisprudence,* 71 PROC. BRIT. ACAD. 303, 318-22 (1985).

PRINCIPLED DECISION-MAKING AND THE SUPREME COURT

M. P. GOLDING*

Times change and with them the fashions, even fashions in legal thinking. In the not too distant past, some of the most respected voices among our legal theorists called for a less "legalistic" law and minimized the role of "logic" and "reason" in the judicial process. It is not clear how representative of the legal community the proponents of such views were; they seemed to have regarded themselves as voices crying in the wilderness. Nor is it always clear, to me at least, what it was that was being attacked and what it was that was being advanced. Yet it is not uncommon for these views to be taken as the typical American contribution to jurisprudence. Although no American can fail to be influenced in some measure by these conceptions, it is interesting to notice that some of our most distinguished writers have called for a return to reason in law, especially in high places, *i.e.*, the Supreme Court.

Perhaps this is the "inevitable reaction, long overdue."[1] Even Judge Arnold, whose hard-boiled realism and rapier-like style have suffered no decline, seems to accept "reason" as an "ideal." He has, nevertheless, severe reservations that "reason would replace the conflicting views now present on the Court if the Court had more time for the 'maturing of collective thought.'"[2] Whether the Court is overworked is a question that probably can best be answered by the demigods who inhabit our Mt. Olympus, and whether diminishing its workload will result in opinions grounded more in reason and principle is certainly problematical. Few would deny that such a result is desirable; however, it is no easy task to formulate the nature of such opinions or the criteria whereby we could determine whether such a result had been achieved.

A notable undertaking along these lines is the Holmes Lecture of Professor Herbert Wechsler.[3] This lecture has already occasioned a minor literature, in part focusing on matters of interest to constitutional lawyers[4] and in

---

* Assistant Professor of Philosophy, Columbia University.
1. Henkin, *Some Reflections on Current Constitutional Controversy*, 109 U. PA. L. REV. 637, 654 (1961).
2. Arnold, *Professor Hart's Theology*, 73 HARV. L. REV. 1298, 1312 (1960). See also Griswold, *The Supreme Court, 1959 Term—Foreword: Of Time and Attitudes—Professor Hart and Judge Arnold*, 74 HARV. L. REV. 81 (1960); Hart, *The Supreme Court, 1958 Term—Foreword: The Time Chart of the Justices*, 73 HARV. L. REV. 84 (1959).
3. Wechsler, *Toward Neutral Principles of Constitutional Law*, 73 HARV. L. REV. 1 (1959), reprinted, with some introductory remarks, in WECHSLER, PRINCIPLES, POLITICS, AND FUNDAMENTAL LAW 3-48 (1961) [hereinafter cited to the book as WECHSLER].
4. Black, *The Lawfulness of the Segregation Decisions*, 69 YALE L.J. 421 (1960); Heyman, *The Chief Justice, Racial Segregation and the Friendly Critics*, 49 CALIF. L. REV. 104 (1961); Pollak, *Racial Discrimination and Judicial Integrity: A Reply to Professor Wechsler*, 108 U. PA. L. REV. 1 (1959).

part focusing on matters of a more theoretical nature.[5] Although its main thrust may be of a more practical scope, no one can deny that Professor Wechsler's lecture raises important issues of jurisprudence and legal philosophy.[6] In what follows I shall attempt to deal with some of these issues. Notwithstanding their broad scope, I shall in general confine myself to the Supreme Court, partly because Professor Wechsler so restricts himself, but mainly because it occupies a special position in our legal system—a position which, I shall try to show, makes it particularly susceptible to the demands he makes of it.

I. Neutrality and Principled Decision-Making

If I do not misinterpret Professor Wechsler's lecture, my approach to these issues differs somewhat from his. Nevertheless, I believe that without overstretching Professor Wechsler's language what I have to say can be fairly found in it; therefore, I shall follow the main lines of his exposition. The differences between our approaches to these great issues of legal philosophy—if there really are any differences—arise from my difficulty in comprehending the meaning of the expression "general and neutral principles of law." In one place, Professor Wechsler speaks of "generality" and "neutrality" as "surely the main qualities of law."[7] Surely Professor Wechsler is not here endorsing Austin's exclusion of particular commands from the realm of law.[8] Although it may be that generality and neutrality are in *some* sense

---

5. Miller & Howell, *The Myth of Neutrality in Constitutional Adjudication*, 27 U. Chi. L. Rev. 661 (1960); Mueller & Schwartz, *The Principle of Neutral Principles*, 7 U.C.L.A.L. Rev. 571 (1960).

6. I do not think that the full significance of Professor Wechsler's ideas has been exhausted by the critical articles I have seen. The article by Mueller & Schwartz, *supra* note 5, is a helpful one. I cannot feel the same about the article by Miller & Howell, *supra* note 5. My paper was completed before the publication of Dean Rostow's Coen Lecture in which Professor Wechsler is subjected to severe criticism. See Rostow, *American Legal Realism and the Sense of the Profession*, 34 Rocky Mt. L. Rev. 123 (1962). I think that my paper goes some way toward clarifying if not all of the issues that he raises. Admittedly, the nature of principled judicial decision is a complex topic; many of its facets are hardly touched here. Regarding Dean Rostow's article, I shall make only a few remarks. First, I do not think that the model of principled decision that I outline—and which I think is the nub of Professor Wechsler's view—is at all identical with "mechanical jurisprudence." Secondly, even Dean Rostow implies, but does not make explicit, various standards that ought to control the *procedures* of his "result-oriented" jurisprudence. It would seem that the explication of those standards would follow the lines that I present here. Thirdly, it is "results" that we expect from the courts; not mere results, however, but *just* results. We cannot understand this except in terms of "principle."

7. Wechsler 23.

8. See Austin, The Province of Jurisprudence Determined and Uses of the Study of Jurisprudence 24 (Berlin, Hampshire & Wollheim ed. 1954) :

A law is a command which obliges a person or persons.

But, as contradistinguished or opposed to an occasional or particular command, a law is a command which obliges a person or persons, and obliges *generally* to acts of forebearances of a *class.*

In language more popular but less distinct and precise, a law is a command which obliges a person or persons to a *course* of conduct.

Ibid. Austin gives the following example :

inherent in the very concept of law, whereby we distinguish a legal order from a lawless tyranny, not each and every rule of law need be "general" and "neutral." It is, in fact, impossible to tell by inspection of a given legal rule or principle,[9] in isolation from the context of its application, whether it is "neutral" or "general" in any significant sense. Trivially, almost every legal rule is "general" and there are also levels of generality.[10] Scores of legal rules, purposely designed to favor one party or group over another, are "un-neutral" with respect to social advantage. Since mere inspection does not reveal whether a rule or principle is "general" or "neutral" in the sense required by Professor Wechsler's argument, the key to neutrality and generality must be found elsewhere.[11]

This key is to be found in the *process* or *procedure* of judicial decision-making. The question that uncovers these qualities is: what are the distinguishing characteristics of principled decision-making?[12] I shall attempt to answer this question in outline and, in so doing, indicate how generality and neutrality are built into the very concept of "principled decision-making." I do not think that this is so remote from what Professor Wechsler intends, for in a number of places he speaks of "principled decision" as embodying his notion of neutral principles of law. That he has in mind also the process or procedure of judicial decision-making may be seen from his contrast between "courts of law" and a "naked power organ."[13]

If Parliament prohibited simply the exportation of corn, either for a given period or indefinitely, it would establish a law or rule: a *kind* or *sort* of acts being determined by the command, and acts of that kind or sort being *generally* forbidden. But an order issued by Parliament to meet an impending scarcity, and stopping the exportation of corn *then shipped and in port*, would not be a law or rule, though issued by the sovereign legislature.
Id. at 20. Compare Kelsen's remarks:
But there is no doubt that law does not consist of general norms only. Law includes individual norms, i.e., norms which determine the behavior of one individual in one non-recurring situation and which therefore are valid only for one particular case and may be obeyed or applied only once. Such norms are "law" because they are parts of the legal order as a whole in exactly the same sense as those general norms on the basis of which they have been created.
KELSEN, GENERAL THEORY OF LAW AND THE STATE 38 (1946); see Golding, *Kelsen and the Concept of "Legal System," 57 Archiv für Rechts-und Sozial-Philosophie* 355 (1961).
    9. "Rules" and "principles" are often distinguished, but I shall not overcomplicate my exposition by doing so here.
    10. Mueller & Schwartz, *supra* note 5, at 577, quite correctly drives home the question, "how general is general?"
    11. Professor Wechsler quite rightly rejects "impartial," "disinterested," and "impersonal" as substitutes for his adjective "neutral." WECHSLER xiii. What is of crucial interest to the community is not what the judge *feels* about the parties or the case before him, although this is not uninfluential, but rather how he administers the law. There are standards of judicial impartiality.
    12. The specific question which Professor Wechsler poses is: "what, if any, are the standards to be followed in interpretation [?] Are there, indeed, any criteria that both the Supreme Court and those who undertake to praise or condemn its judgments are morally and intellectually obligated to support?" *Id.* at 15-16. The *kind* of answer which he gives is interesting. He does not say what these standards or criteria are, but rather tells us something *about* them, namely, they must be "general" and "neutral." The approach, then, is "formalistic," although he assumes a background of democratic values.
    13. *Id.* at 27.

A. *The Analogue in Moral Philosophy*

The above question has its analogue in the history of moral philosophy. To be sure, there are differences between moral and legal reasoning; however, the similarities, especially in regard to Professor Wechsler's treatment of judicial neutrality, are sufficient to justify a brief discussion here. One can not disregard the fact that Professor Wechsler elaborates his ideal of the judicial process within the scope of the broad ethical conceptions of political theory.

In no analysis of moral notions does principle play a greater role than in Immanuel Kant's. He rejected the view that the rightness or wrongness of an act is determinable by a straightforward reference to its consequences. The "moral value" of an act, says Kant, "does not depend on the reality of the object of the action but merely on the principle of volition by which the action is done without any regard to the objects of the faculty of desire."[14] Rather, two of the necessary constituents of a morally right action are: (1) that it be done on principle; and (2) in conformity with a principle.[15] Not every putative principle, however, is a genuine moral principle. It is the function of the various formulations of the Categorical Imperative to serve as a test of putative principles.

It would be out of place to give here an extended account of Kant's ethical theory, a theory not without its serious difficulties. For my present concerns we need consider only a few points. In developing his conception of a genuine moral principle Kant appeals to a very simple consideration. Every moral decision makes a universal claim: if an act is right for me, it must be right for every similarly situated person. For me arbitrarily to make an exception of myself is clearly the very negation of principle.[16] So also, to distinguish some individual, or class of individuals, arbitrarily and thus claim that it is right for me to treat him, or them, differently from the way I treat others, is the very *negation* of principle. To act in such ways is not to act on principle or in conformity with a principle, and to decide to act in such ways is not to make a principled decision. What Kant is doing in developing his notion of a genuine moral principle is to build into it—or rather show how there are built into it—the notions of generality and neutrality in one of their modes.

The obvious question elicited by Kant's view is: what are reasonable grounds for difference of treatment? This question raises a tremendously difficult problem for Kant. Most people would say that in determining

---

14. KANT, *Foundations of the Metaphysics of Morals,* in CRITIQUE OF PRACTICAL REASON 61 (Beck ed. 1949).

15. Kant also requires that it be done for the sake of principle, *i.e.,* out of a sense of duty. But this is not relevant here.

16. How this statement is related to the idea expressed in the previous sentence need not concern us here. See generally Edgley, *Impartiality and Consistency,* 37 PHILOSOPHY 158 (1962) ; Monro, *Impartiality and Consistency,* 36 *id.* at 161 (1961).

whether I am permitted to make an exception of myself or some other individual in a given case it is legitimate to appeal to the consequences that my action would have; but this way is barred to Kant. Nevertheless, Kant's notion is not without its practical importance, for it throws a "definite *onus probandi* on the man who applies to another a treatment of which he would complain if applied to himself . . . ."[17] It is important, also, to recognize the scope of Kant's notion: it is not restricted to differences made in respect of *persons*. Rather, it applies equally to *circumstances* or situations. Thus, moral action, or principled moral decision-making, must not only be "impartial" with respect to persons, but also must be "impartial" with respect to similar circumstances. No putative principle of action can be a genuine moral principle if it allows me to act differently in similar circumstances, unless a significant distinction between the circumstances can be shown to exist. Here again, the *onus probandi* falls on the person who would make such a distinction. As a consequence, consistency, in one of its modes, is built into the concept of principled moral decision-making.

It is evident that, for Kant, one's mere likes and dislikes cannot be the ground of moral action or principled moral decision-making. But insofar as Kant pretends to be analyzing our common moral notions, I think that he goes wrong in believing that our likes and dislikes, or as we should say now, our values, are irrelevant to moral action and principled decision-making.[18] Nevertheless, he is correct in his rejection of *mere* likes and dislikes as the basis of morality.

The same rejection is found in Bentham, whose utilitarian moral philosophy is quite different from Kant's. The principle of sympathy and antipathy, namely, "that principle which approves of certain actions . . . merely because a man finds himself disposed to approve or disapprove of them" is

> a principle in name [rather] than in reality: it is not a positive principle of itself, so much as a term employed to signify the negation of all principle. What one expects to find in a principle is something that points out some external consideration, as a means of warranting and guiding the internal sentiments of approbation and disapprobation: this expectation is but ill fulfilled by a proposition, which does neither more nor less than hold up each of those sentiments as a ground and standard for itself.[19]

Thus, Bentham, whose universalistic ethical hedonism assigns to likes and

---

17. SIDGWICK, THE METHODS OF ETHICS 380 (6th ed. 1907); *cf.* WECHSLER 155 (remarks on the issues of the Nuremberg Trial).

18. There certainly are occasions when it would be silly to say that one ought not take one's likes and dislikes into account. As has often been pointed out, it would generally be foolish for a man to ignore his likes and dislikes in deciding whether to marry a certain woman. Kant might hold, however, that such a decision is morally neither right nor wrong; but it is not difficult to think of situations in which a couple might have an obligation to marry, according to Kant.

19. BENTHAM, AN INTRODUCTION TO THE PRINCIPLES OF MORALS AND LEGISLATION 15-16 (1823 ed.).

dislikes a central role in moral judgment, is at one with Kant in rejecting the method of *ad hoc* evaluation.

In operating the hedonic calculus, Bentham tells us that we must "take an account of the *number* of persons whose interests appear to be concerned . . . ."[20] In so doing, each person is to be considered impartially. "Each is to count for one, and no one for more than one." Bentham nowhere justifies this impartiality. Clearly, it is not deducible from the Principle of Utility (the greatest happiness principle). Rather, he assumes it, because without it the Principle of Utility would not be a principle at all. Part of the meaning of principled decision-making is that persons or similar circumstances are to be treated in the same manner, unless a relevant distinction is shown to exist.

B. *The Characteristics of Principled Decision-Making*

In what follows I shall develop more fully the nature of principled decision, but it may be useful to summarize a few of its salient features at this juncture. A decision or judgment is principled only when it is guided by some "external consideration," *i.e.*, a guiding principle that contributes to the deliberation on the case. Such a principle is a *reason* (or part of the reasons) for the decision. It cannot be a reason for the decision unless it determines, at least to some extent, the outcome of the process of deliberation. This means that a principle cannot be so flexible as to allow for free-wheeling discretion. Furthermore, in applying a principle, the instant case must be treated as an instance of a more inclusive class of cases, *i.e.*, the case at hand is treated in a certain manner because it is held to be proper to treat cases of its type in that manner. In this way every principled judgment makes, or rests upon, a universal, or general, claim. When the given case is treated differently from the way in which it is held to be proper to treat cases of its type the decision-maker is required to distinguish it from these cases. Here, too, such distinctions must be drawn in a principled way : it is not sufficient to justify the different treatment of persons or circumstances simply on the ground that one is dealing with one person or circumstance rather than another. That is to say, in principled decision-making one is permitted to make exceptions of this sort only insofar as they fall within a class of cases considered appropriate for the different treatment.

Although the nature of distinction-making in principled decision-making is a complex topic deserving separate, detailed treatment, brief discussion about it is in order here. First, it is obvious that in many cases people disagree on whether there exist significant enough differences between apparently similar persons or circumstances to permit their being treated in disparate ways. But this fact in no way affects the account of principled decision I am

---

20. *Id.* at 31.

presenting. This account does not assume or require that people agree in their judgments. It is quite consistent with it that two parties should be opposed in their judgments and yet both be principled. Second, when such distinctions are made, the criteria for determining which differences are significant or relevant must be drawn in a principled way.[21] Not just *any* distinction—which can always be found—will do.

Briefly put, the requirements for principled decision are: (1) that a reason for the disposition of the case be given; and (2) that the case be so decided because it is held to be proper to decide cases of its type in this way. It is in the meeting of the requirements for principled decision that the qualities of neutrality and generality are achieved. Naturally, I have presented them only in their barest outline. To do more would be to broach the most intricate problems in the analysis of moral reasoning. I have also formulated these requirements in a most general and broad way, so as to be acceptable to a wide variety of moral theories. It is worth mentioning that these requirements are part of a minimal analysis of the concept of "distributive justice."

It is important to recognize the fact that the above requirements constitute necessary conditions of a principled decision. I do not doubt that more is required in order to explicate the notion of a *justified* decision. It is especially important to recognize that I have been discussing the way one ought to go about justifying a judgment, and not the psychological process of reaching a judgment.[22] One's decision is principled if one supports it by reasons or reasoning of this kind. Of course, in situations in which people are expected to make principled decisions it is expected that the psychological process will accord with the above procedures. (It is what we expect of a principled man.) And it seems to me that this does happen at least sometimes. On the other hand, even when a decision is a so-called "guts reaction" it might be a mistake to underrate the role of these procedures, for they may have been "internalized."

From the above delineation of principled decision-making it follows that the typical kind of argument that will be employed in both deliberation and criticism is that of *reductio ad absurdum*. One's judgment is "tested not only by the instant application but by others that the principles imply."[23] When a principle is advanced in support of a decision and this principle would necessarily permit some given case to be treated in a manner different from the way in which by hypothesis it must be treated, one is forced either to distinguish the cases or, failing this, to reject the principle. Rationality, of which principled decision is an element, requires pragmatic consistency of this sort.[24]

---

21. See Mueller & Schwartz, *supra* note 5, at 578-80.
22. See generally WASSERSTROM, THE JUDICIAL DECISION 26-38 (1961).
23. WECHSLER 21.
24. Another way of attacking the reasoning behind a judgment is to call into question the alleged facts that it supposes; but I am not concerned with this here.

Obviously, one's decisions lose their moral force when we indulge in inconsistency. Professor Wechsler quite correctly characterizes the criteria of principled decision as ones which we are "morally and intellectually obligated to support."[25]

In contrast with principled decision-making is the method of *ad hoc* evaluation. Professor Wechsler gives numerous examples from our constitutional politics, past and present, of the *ad hoc* type of evaluation. Whether, and in what circumstances, this method is to be deplored is beyond the scope of this paper. The analysis of principled political decision-making is, of course, a complex topic. The factor of *compromise*, which plays such an important part, would seem to add another dimension to the treatment that has been given so far. I recognize that compromise may also be an element in judicial decision in a number of ways, but this would require separate consideration beyond the scope of this article.

II. Principled Judicial Decision-Making

Previously, I alluded to the fact that principled judicial decision-making is both similar to and different from principled moral decision-making. The truth of the matter as I see it is that with two provisos principled judicial decision is formally congruent with principled moral decision. The two provisos are, first, that a legal system is able to stipulate in a large measure the principles that must be employed in deliberation and, second, a legal system may stipulate what grounds are and what grounds are not legitimate grounds for the different treatment of persons or circumstances. So, for example, a legal system may stipulate that mere racial difference is (or is not) an acceptable ground for the different treatment of individuals in certain types of cases.

Within the scope of these limitations it still remains possible to speak of principled judicial decision-making. Our legal system has no privileged status. Not only are systems possible that differ from ours in content, but so also can principled decisions occur within the framework of such systems. For in such systems courts can function as "courts of law" and may embody in their procedures "the main constituent of the judicial process . . . ."[26] Thus, when a legal system does make racial (or other) differences relevant, it is still possible for principled judicial decision to exist, so long as the requirements for principled decision are met within the terms of the law that the system lays down. Principled legal judgment is not so much a matter of content as it is of form. Neutrality and generality are to be found not in the content of the law but in its application or administration. Prin-

---

25. Wechsler 16.
26. *Id.* at 21.

cipled judicial decision-making is possible in a tyranny. This is worth stressing, if only because Professor Wechsler's ideas move within a liberal democratic context. But I should also suppose that if we range states along a scale—"ideal" democracy at one end and "ideal" tyranny at the other—there is a point of no return, a point at which the form and content of the tyranny become inseparable, making it impossible to speak of principled judicial judgment.[27]

A legal system, then, may broadly fix the starting-points of deliberation and the criteria of relevant distinctions. It is the lesson of American jurisprudence that this fixity has its limits and that a degree of discretion is inevitable. But we still demand that, so far as possible, courts be principled in their exercises of this discretion. This applies with greatest force to the Supreme Court when it has constitutional questions before it. Lower courts often have no choice once the higher courts have spoken. (One need only think of the different results in cases after *Brown v. Board of Educ.* had the Court affirmed the separate-but-equal doctrine in regard to public education.) But the Supreme Court, when ruling on constitutional issues, has no higher guide than the Constitution itself. Of course, there are times when "the relative compulsion of the language of the Constitution, of history and precedent" do combine to make the answer clear; but frequently they do not. Professor Wechsler maintains, and I agree, that the due process clauses ought to be read as "a compendious affirmation of the basic values of a free society . . . ."[28] Furthermore, it is possible to overstate the specificity of other provisions of the Bill of Rights addressed to more specific problems. They, too, must be read as "an affirmation of the special values they embody rather than as statements of a finite rule of law . . . ."[29] Constitutional interpretation by the Supreme Court, then, most closely approximates moral decision-making, and when it is principled it will rest "on reasons with respect to all the issues in the case, reasons that in their generality and neutrality transcend any immediate result that is involved"[30] in the way outlined above.

I should now like to consider in detail some further points in connection with Professor Wechsler's exposition. But before I turn to Professor Wechsler's allusion to some opinions of Holmes as possible exemplars of principled judicial decision and examine some aspects of Professor Wechsler's appraisals of review, I think it important to make clear why the question that forms the subject of his paper is the same for the critics as it is for the Court.

---

27. It seems, again, that by contrast democratic states are the most moral, for not only must they adhere to the requirements of principled decision-making in the courts but also in the legislature. I shall not develop this point here, however, but simply point out that even in such case it is plain that there may be "partial" or "un-neutral" laws.
28. Wechsler 24, 26.
29. *Ibid.* It is obvious that Professor Wechsler is no "strict constructionist."
30. *Id.* at 27.

The reason is quite simple. The ground rules for the *intelligent* discussion of any issue—and, as Professor Wechsler correctly indicates, what he says is true not only of a critique of the Court, but "applies whenever a determination is in question, a determination that it is essential to make either way"[31]—are exactly the same as the general requirements for principled decision-making. Consider for a moment what distinguishes *constructive* criticism from useless criticism, what distinguishes a discussion that is worthy of one's participation from a discussion that is not, and the truth of this will be apparent. No criticism is worth listening to unless it is constructive to some degree. The contrast with this is criticism of the mere "I like it" or "I don't like it" variety. Autobiographical remarks such as these are of interest only when it is important to know what someone's preferences are. But they mark the end of discussion, not its beginning; they function as "conversation stoppers." Discussion ends when we come to the bedrock of differences in preference, but it cannot begin there.[32] Constructive criticism and useful discussion can proceed only when reasons for a judgment are advanced that not only include but go beyond the case at hand.[33] If these reasons, or principles, are not ruled out *ab initio* as unacceptable (*e.g.*, in law when contrary principles are stipulated), then debate typically continues in the *reductio ad absurdum* manner. Would the critic treat such and such similar cases in the same way as he treats the instant case? If not, how does he distinguish them? Failing this, must he not reject the reason or principle on which his judgment rests? Just as a factual proposition is shown to be false if it implies a false statement, so also is a practical principle shown to be unacceptable if it leads to pragmatic inconsistencies, or when it would require treating some given case in a way in which *ex hypothesi* it may not be treated. Nothing that I have said in this paragraph is incompatible with the view that all our judgments rest ultimately on our preferences, and that differences in judgment rest on fundamental and perhaps ineradicable differences in preference.[34]

The utilization of the above type of *reductio* argument is well-illustrated by Mr. Justice Holmes's dissent (his first as a member of the Court) in

---

31. *Id.* at 16.

32. See BENTHAM, *op. cit. supra* note 19, at 6. Of course, even when this point is reached, the argument may continue over the *facts* of the issue. See note 24 *supra*.

33. I think that Professor Wechsler goes too far when he says that an attack upon a judgment of the Court involves the assertion that the reasons which prevailed with the tribunal are *irrelevant*. WECHSLER 16. The reasons may have been relevant but inconclusive.

34. It is often incorrectly thought that aesthetic evaluation, which seems most intimately and immediately bound up with our likes and dislikes, is an exception to the kind of principled decision which ought to apply to the courts and their critics. But that this is not so may be seen from the distinction we draw between good and bad art critics. The evaluations of the bad critic are always *ad hoc*, a mere expression of likes and dislikes. The evaluations of the good critic are constructive. He gives reasons for his judgement and in so doing shows how the work of art may be improved, even though he might not have the talent to do it better himself.

Northern Sec. Co. v. United States,[35] to which Professor Wechsler refers.[36] The question in this case was whether, under the Sherman Act, "it is unlawful, at any stage of the process, if several men unite to form a corporation for the purpose of buying more than half the stock of each of two competing interstate railroad companies [Northern Pacific and Great Northern], if they form the corporation, and the corporation buys the stock."[37] A majority of the Court, emphasizing the power of Congress to regulate interstate commerce, held that such activity is unlawful, given the effect that such an arrangement is bound to have upon competition between the railroads. Holmes, in his brilliant way, proceeded to give the Court a lesson in statutory construction, in how "to read English intelligently."[38] His language sparkles with "neutrality." In this case, involving J. Pierpont Morgan and James J. Hill, Holmes wrote that "we must read the words before us [the Sherman Act] as if the question were whether two small exporting grocers should go to jail."[39] He rejected the argument of counsel for the Government as leading to the unacceptable conclusion that there is "no part of the conduct of life with which, on similar principles, Congress might not interfere. . . . Commerce depends upon population, but Congress could not, on that ground, undertake to regulate marriage and divorce."[40] The Government's principle must be rejected, for it would lead to treating a case in a way in which it may not be *ex hypothesi*. Driving home this point, he continues:

> This act is construed by the government to affect the purchasers of shares in two railroad companies because of the effect it may have, or, if you like, is certain to have, upon the competition of these roads. If such a remote result of the exercise of an ordinary incident of property and personal freedom is enough to make that exercise unlawful, there is hardly any transaction concerning commerce between the States that may not be made a crime by the finding of a jury or a court.[41]

Again, an unacceptable conclusion. Furthermore, Holmes writes: "If I am [wrong], then a partnership between two stage drivers who had been competitors in driving across a state line, or two merchants once engaged in rival commerce among the states, whether made after or before the act, if now continued, is a crime."[42] This also is too hard for Holmes to swallow, and when a principle leads to constitutionally impermissible conclusions it must be rejected. We see Holmes in this dissent playing the part of the critic, rejecting the argument of the Government and the judgment of the

---

35. 193 U.S. 197, 400 (1904).
36. WECHSLER 33.
37. 193 U.S. at 401.
38. *Ibid.*
39. *Id.* at 402.
40. *Id.* at 403 & 402.
41. *Id.* at 403.
42. *Id.* at 410.

majority because in part they fail to adhere to the requirements for principled decision. It should be mentioned that it is one thing for the critic to show that some given decision is not principled and another to show that it is wrong. The superficial reader of Professor Wechsler's article is liable to get the impression that there is no difference between the two.

Perhaps one of the most difficult theoretical points in Professor Wechsler's paper concerns the place of values in principled judicial decision-making. I am not sure that I have understood his position on this or, if I follow it, that I agree with what he has to say. Before attacking this issue head-on, it is useful to consider an example provided by Holmes's dissent in the *Abrams* case,[43] to which, together with his dissent in *Gitlow*,[44] Professor Wechsler invidiously compares[45] the main opinion in *Sweezy v. New Hampshire*.[46]

It seems that for Holmes the crucial point in *Abrams* was that of intent. It is, he says,

> too plain to be denied that [the leaflet urges] . . . curtailment of production of things necessary to the prosecution of the war . . . . But to make the conduct criminal, that statute requires that it should be 'with intent by such curtailment to cripple or hinder the United States in the prosecution of the war.' It seems to me that no such intent is proved.[47]

Passing on to the question of the freedom of speech, Holmes argues that

> it is only the present danger of immediate evil or an intent to bring it about that warrants Congress in setting a limit to the expression of opinion where private rights are not concerned. . . . [B]y the same reasoning that would justify punishing persuasion to murder, the United States constitutionally may punish speech that produces or is intended to produce a clear and imminent danger that it will bring about forthwith certain substantive evils that the United States constitutionally may seek to prevent.[48]

Professor Wechsler, apparently conceding that Holmes's position is framed in terms of "neutral and general principles," queries in a footnote: "Is it possible, however, that persuasion to murder is only punishable constitutionally if the design is that the murder be committed 'forthwith'?"[49] This is instructive (aside from the common law point being made), for it shows that even what Professor Wechsler takes to be a "neutral principle" may be objectionable. It is important to keep in mind that Holmes regarded *Abrams* as dealing with the expression of political opinion, and, although stating that

---

43. Abrams v. United States, 250 U.S. 616, 624 (1919).
44. Gitlow v. New York, 268 U.S. 652, 672 (1925).
45. WECHSLER 35-36.
46. 354 U.S. 234 (1957).
47. 250 U.S. at 626.
48. *Id.* at 628 & 627.
49. WECHSLER 35-36 n.83.

"persecution for the expression of opinions seems to me perfectly logical,"[50] he believed that our Constitution opts for a particular value. This is the "theory of our Constitution," which is "an experiment, as all life is an experiment."[51] This "theory" is that "the ultimate good desired is better reached by free trade in ideas—that the best test of truth is the power of the thought to get itself accepted in the competition of the market . . . ."[52] This is the root of the "clear and present danger" restriction.[53] Holmes, therefore, asserts that "while that experiment is part of our system I think that we should be eternally vigilant against attempts to check the expression of opinions that we loathe and believe to be fraught with death, unless they so imminently threaten . . . ."[54] To this should be added Holmes's dissenting remark in *Gitlow*: "If, in the long run, the beliefs expressed in proletarian dictatorship are destined to be accepted by the dominant forces of the community, the only meaning of free speech is that they should be given their chance and have their way."[55]

The *Abrams* dissent illustrates at least one way in which values enter into constitutional interpretation. It is important not to press too far his analogy between expression of opinion and persuasion to murder. Aside from the matter of intent, the essential problem *Abrams* poses is that of putting two values in the balance for the purpose of deciding the case. On the one side we have national security, which it is the legitimate function of government to protect, and on the other the "theory of our Constitution." It is not a question of Holmes's "choosing" these values. (I think that the use of the phrase "choosing a value" in legal writing is unfortunate.) The Constitution, so to speak, has chosen them, in Holmes's understanding. And he further takes it that the Constitution chooses to risk the "experiment" which the "theory of our Constitution" involves. He sees that risk as going as far as a "clear and present danger" to national security. It is not, as Judge Learned Hand implies, that these opinions "may prove innocuous." They may, in fact, be "destined to be accepted by the dominant forces of the community." It is, moreover, "perfectly logical" to suppress them. But this is not the "theory of our Constitution"; one can not maintain this "theory" *with all its attendant risks* and at the same time permit the suppression of opinion in the name of national security. Of course, there is a limit—that of "clear and present

---

50. 250 U.S. at 630.
51. *Ibid.*
52. *Ibid.*
53. See Hand, The Bill of Rights 58-59 (1958) : "The only ground for this exception which I have ever heard is that during the interval between the provocation and its realization correctives may arise, and that it is better to accept the risk that they may not be sufficient than to suppress what, however guilty in itself, may prove innocuous." Did Homer nod in *Abrams*?
54. 250 U.S. at 630.
55. 268 U.S. at 673.

danger." To breach this limit, however, is to subvert the "theory," the value of freedom of expression, which the Constitution has chosen.

I am not here concerned with whether Holmes's reading of the "theory of our Constitution" is correct; I am sure that many constitutional lawyers would find it disputable. I am concerned, rather, with what it illustrates, namely, that constitutional interpretation does not occur within a vacuum of values. By this I do not simply mean that judges bring with them a personal set of values or that the determination of constitutional or other questions frequently reflects a "choice of values"; my meaning is, rather, that affirmations of various values are written into the Constitution, "values that must be given weight in legislation and administration at the risk of courting trouble in the courts."[56] The Court, then, cannot avoid taking these values into account in constitutional adjudication. To do otherwise would be to fail to adhere to the requirements for principled decision-making. These values supply *substantive* criteria of principled judgment. We are entitled to reject any principle of decision that, if acted upon, would lead to the frustrating of accepted values. But this is workable only when values are not in competition.

Is it possible to speak of principled judicial decision-making when more than one value is at stake, when it is impossible for a plurality of values to be fulfilled in equal measure? Certainly one would like to emphasize together with Professor Wechsler "the role of reason and of principle in the judicial, as distinguished from the legislative or executive, appraisal of conflicting values . . . ."[57] But what is that role? Certainly one would like to agree with him that the virtue or demerit in a judgment turns "entirely on the reasons that support it and their adequacy to maintain any choice of values it decrees . . . ."[58] But what is the test of adequacy? I cannot see much in the way of an answer to these questions in Professor Wechsler's lecture.

The above questions raise the most complicated problems in the analysis of legal reasoning. I fail to grasp Professor Wechsler's position if it consists in the statement that one ought to, or even can, supply "neutral principles" for "choosing" between competing values. I can, of course, choose between two competing values by reference to a third value which is more comprehensive or supreme, that is, when there is already an ordering of values. Assuming such an ordering, it seems to make sense to speak of "reasoned choice between competing values." Although I doubt it, perhaps this is precisely what Professor Wechsler is implying in his comment on the "preferred position" controversy when he says that it has virtue "insofar as it recognizes that some ordering of social values is essential; that all cannot be given equal weight, if the Bill of Rights is to be maintained."[59] But it is

56. WECHSLER 26.
57. *Id.* at 23.
58. *Id.* at 27.
59. *Id.* at 35.

difficult to see how the ordering itself is to be made on "neutral principles."

Perhaps, however, even lacking such an ordering of values, all is not lost for principled decision-making. Another brief glance at Holmes's dissent in *Abrams* will illustrate what I have in mind. Two values were involved in the deciding of this case—national security and freedom of expression—neither of which could be ignored. What Holmes did was to make his best judgment as to the point beyond which one cannot go if the value of national security is to be maintained, as he believed it must, when it competes with the value of free expression, which on his understanding of the Constitution ordinarily has precedence. That point is "clear and imminent danger," which now functions as a standard or criterion to be applied in situations when these two values are in competition. This standard, though clearly and eminently vague, will now function for him as a principle of decision in this and other cases of its type. We may apply to this principle the type of critical evaluation that I have heretofore adumbrated.

Thus, when, in deciding a case, a tribunal is faced with two competing values and there is no good reason to be advanced for preferring one value over another, so that the preference given to one value is entirely arbitrary, if you please, we may still require that the tribunal formulate a standard or criterion that shall function as a principle of decision in this and other cases of its type. This principle is general in the sense that it covers but also transcends the instant case. It is not, of course, inherently "neutral" in any sense, except that there may be neutrality in its application, *i.e.*, it may be applied in a principled way. Would the decision-maker apply this principle in such-and-such similar cases? It not, how does he distinguish the cases? Failing this, must he not reject the principle? What I have just said obtains not only in cases in which there are two competing values, but also, more broadly, in cases in which there are two (or more) countervailing considerations, *e.g.*, two conflicting principles, which must both be taken into account such that the presence of one of them does not in all cases rule out the applicability of the other. Granted that both such countervailing considerations have weight, the decision-maker is required to draw a line fixing their limits.

It seems to me that the aspect of principled decision I have just described is not so remote from what Professor Wechsler demands of the Court in his appraisal of judicial review. To this extent his position seems perfectly intelligible, although I confess my inability to understand him if he requires that the "choice of values" itself be made on "general and neutral principles." I am also uncertain that I understand how Professor Wechsler can demand that courts decide "on grounds of adequate neutrality and generality" and at the same time maintain that courts should decide "only the case they have before them."[60] There is, of course, an obvious sense in which a court *does*

---

60. *Id.* at 21.

decide *only* the case that is before it. But if a tribunal is to be principled, what it must do in essence is to anticipate the kinds of criticism that might be made of its decision. It must attempt to explain away at least the more apparent inconsistencies. In doing this the tribunal, in effect, "decides" cases which are not before it. I think that we will see that this is precisely what Professor Wechsler is demanding in some of his appraisals of judicial review. Before turning to some phases of these appraisals, I should like to raise a question that I think is of importance for the subsequent discussion. I have argued that, in a case the resolution of which depends upon taking into account countervailing considerations, principled judgment requires that the decision-maker formulate a general criterion that shall serve as a principle of decision in cases of its type. Will this procedure always be wise? Are there not areas of the law, such as those involving problems of procedural due process, in which it may plausibly be argued that it is better to have each case come up for decision in its own right than to have the Court lay down in advance general principles of judgment? I shall come to this in a moment.

There is hardly any need to show in detail how Professor Wechsler's comments on some older cases illustrate the requirements of principled decision thus far presented. Were not, he asks, the principles which the Court affirmed "strikingly deficient in neutrality, sustaining, for example, national authority when it impinged adversely upon labor, as in the application of the Sherman Act, but not when it was sought to be employed in labor's aid?"[61] The deficiency in neutrality here must be that the Court failed to articulate a significant ground for such disparity of treatment. So also must we understand his remark that some decisions are now read "with eyes that disbelieve" in part because "the Court could not articulate an adequate analysis of the restrictions it imposed on Congress in favor of the states . . . ."[62] Professor Wechsler further speculates "whether there are any neutral principles that might have been employed to mark the limits of the commerce power of the Congress in terms more circumscribed than the virtual abandonment of limits in the principle that has prevailed."[63] I think it obvious that any such principles could be no more or less "neutral" than Holmes's criterion of "clear and present danger." The commerce power of Congress poses problems of federalism and cases involving the reach of the commerce power necessarily bring into play countervailing considerations. The neutrality of such limiting principles would not inhere *in* the principles, just as it does not inhere in the limiting principle of "clear and present danger," but rather, if at all, in the manner of applying them, *i.e.*, in principled application.

---

61. *Id.* at 32.
62. *Ibid.*
63. *Id.* at 33.

III. PRINCIPLED DECISION-MAKING AND CIVIL RIGHTS

We come finally to those cases that pose for Professor Wechsler the hardest test of his belief in principled adjudication, namely, those involving the white primary, racially restrictive covenants, and segregation in the public schools. The decisions in these cases, be believes, "have the best chance of making an enduring contribution to the quality of our society of any that I know in recent years."[64] Yet he questions how far they rest on "neutral principles" and are, thus, entitled to approval in the only terms which he acknowledges to be relevant to a judicial decision.

The problems in the first two categories of cases arise under the prohibitions of the fourteenth or fifteenth amendments which have been held to reach not only explicit deprivation by statute but also action of the courts and of subordinate officials purporting to exert authority deriving from public office.[65] Although I do not find all of his ingenious solutions compelling, Professor Pollak has admirably discussed[66] the issues involved in such detail that it would be unprofitable to retrace this ground here. I propose, therefore, to limit myself to one point, and then conclude with a defense of the desegregation decision, arguing that it does exhibit characteristics of principled judgment, although the Court's opinion in *Brown v. Board of Educ.*[67] is not entirely satisfying.

The main issue presented by the primary and covenant cases concerns the notion of "state action." One supposes that the paradigm of "state action" in these areas would be a statute that explicitly discriminates on racial grounds. But as soon as we move away from this everything becomes less clear. May the Democratic Party of Texas, which is a "private" organization, exclude Negroes from its primaries? If a "private" party is free to enter into a restrictive covenant, may a state be charged with infringing the fourteenth amendment if its courts give effect to such an agreement? Professor Wechsler asks: "What is the principle involved? Is the state forbidden to effectuate a will that draws a racial line, a will that can accomplish any disposition only through the aid of law, or is it a sufficient answer there that the discrimination was the testator's and not the state's?"[68] If I understand Professor Wechsler's complaint, it is that the Court has failed to lay down, in the cases dealing with these issues,[69] a criterion of "state action," or of "unconstitutional state action," or of "discriminatory state action."[70] In these cases one is forced to

---

64. *Id.* at 37.
65. *Id.* at 37-38, citing, *inter alia, Ex parte* Virginia, 100 U.S. 339, 347 (1880).
66. Pollak, *Racial Discrimination and Judicial Integrity: A Reply to Professor Wechsler*, 108 U. PA. L. REV. 1 (1959).
67. 347 U.S. 483 (1954).
68. WECHSLER 40.
69. Principally, Smith v. Allwright, 321 U.S. 649 (1944), and Shelley v. Kraemer, 334 U.S. 1 (1948).
70. See the suggestive article of Horowitz, *The Misleading Search for "State Action" Under the Fourteenth Amendment*, 30 So. CAL. L. REV. 208 (1957).

take account of the countervailing considerations of "state" and "private" action. If a "private" party is by hypothesis free to discriminate, except when prohibited by law, at what point does such discrimination become invalid when it is enabled, permitted, or enforced by an organ of a state? As Professor Wechsler asks, what is the principle involved?

I suggested above that there might be areas of the law, such as procedural due process, in which it is inadvisable to lay down criteria or standards of the type under consideration here. There is an almost immeasurable variety of cases which could conceivably involve the notions of "state" and "private" action. In *Smith v. Allwright* the Court maintained that the discrimination practiced by a party entrusted by Texas law with the determination of the qualifications of participants in the primary was "endorsed," "adopted," and "enforced" by the state. This conclusion was reached only after close attention to the *role* played by such primaries in the electoral process, rather than by an application of a general criterion.[71] Perhaps this, too, is an area in which it is best to proceed on a case-by-case basis, and the Court, in refusing to lay down a criterion, has chosen wisely.

But if it is proper for the Court to approach the problems of "state" and "private" action in this way, it is, nevertheless, not unfair to ask the Court to give some explanation for the apparent inconsistencies among the cases it has decided. If it is true that not every instance of judicial cognition of private discrimination is state action prohibited by the fourteenth amendment, can we distinguish those classes of cases in which it obtains from those in which it does not?[72] The requirements of principled decision impose such a task on the Court. In other words, the question whether the Court should refrain from laying down a criterion in cases of the sort I have mentioned really goes to the knotty issue of the *scope* of the criterion that the Court ought to give: how broadly, or how narrowly, should the principle be framed? This question is of great practical significance, for principles enunciated by higher courts inevitably affect decisions of lower courts. Moreover, an articulated principle stands as a commitment by the higher court itself with respect to future cases in which the fact situation may be slightly different. On the one hand, principles seem to have a way of fixating themselves in the mind of the decision-maker and impel him, in the next case, to go farther than he may really want. On the other hand, a narrowly formulated principle

---

71. Smith v. Allwright, 321 U.S. 649 (1944) ; *cf.* Terry v. Adams, 345 U.S. 461 (1953). Professor Wechsler inquires whether the decisions in *Smith* and *Terry* mean that religious parties are proscribed, and whether such a proscription would not infringe rights protected by the first amendment. WECHSLER 40. My answer is that the first topic of consideration would be the role of such a party in the electoral process. If it plays the role of the Democratic Party or Jaybirds in Texas or the Democratic Party in a Louisiana locality, there is good reason for proscribing it. Are not the rights of members of other religious groups infringed in such a situation?
72. See Pollak, *supra* note 66, at 12-16.

might supply no guidance to a lower court. Of course, no one supposes that principled decision is an easy task. (Perhaps it is to just these issues that Professor Wechsler's remark that courts should decide "only the case they have before them"[73] is addressed.) The complexity of this problem is increased when we consider its relation to the doctrine of precedent; but I am not prepared to deal with these matters at this time.

The question of school desegregation hardly seems susceptible of judicial neutrality. It stirs even in Professor Wechsler the "deepest conflict" in testing his thesis.[74] Fortunately, the decision in *Brown* does not hinge on the slippery notions of "state" and "private" action, although they may become relevant in cases arising from devices adopted by states seeking to avoid the consequences of that decision. In order to determine whether and in what respects this case departs from the model of principled decision-making, which I take to be what is most comprehensible in Professor Wechsler's conception of "neutral principles," it will be useful to have before us the heart of the Court's opinion:

> We must consider public education in the light of its full development and its present place in American life throughout the Nation. Only in this way can it be determined if segregation in public schools deprives these plaintiffs of the equal protection of the laws. . . . Such an opportunity [education], where the state has undertaken to provide it, is a right which must be made available to all on equal terms.
>
> We come then to the question presented: Does segregation of children in public schools solely on the basis of race, even though the physical facilities and other "tangible" factors may be equal, deprive the children of the minority group of equal educational opportunities? We believe that it does. . . . To separate them from others of similar age and qualification solely because of their race generates a feeling of inferiority as to their status in the community that may affect their hearts and minds in a way unlikely ever to be undone. . . .
>
> We conclude that in the field of public education the doctrine of "separate but equal" has no place. Separate educational facilities are inherently unequal. Therefore, we hold that the plaintiffs and others similarly situated . . . are, by reason of the segregation complained of, deprived of the equal protection of the laws guaranteed by the Fourteenth Amendment. This disposition makes unnecessary any discussion whether such segregation also violates the Due Process Clause of the Fourteenth Amendment.[75]

There are in the Court's argument five points to be noticed: (1) the focus is solely upon education—it is "in the field of public education" that "the 'separate but equal' doctrine has no place"; (2) it is taken as axiomatic, and there is no disputing it, that when a state undertakes a program of public

---

73. WECHSLER 21.
74. *Id.* at 43.
75. 347 U.S. at 492-95.

education it must be available to all on equal terms; (What this means is the crucial point.) (3) segregation in education is constitutionally bad because it "generates a feeling of inferiority"; (4) "separate educational facilities are inherently unequal"; and (5) the issue is disposed of entirely on equal protection grounds.

Considering the focus of the opinion, Professor Wechsler seems entirely justified in his criticism of the Court's per curiam extension of the ruling to other public facilities in later cases.[76] But I think that one can explain this focus and that one may infer from the Court's actions that *Plessy v. Ferguson*[77] is in effect overruled "in form."[78]

The effects of segregation on Negro children and, in particular, whether segregation "generates a feeling of inferiority" are topics that have been widely discussed. The testimony of "modern authority" has been raked over the coals. Professor Black thinks that this testimony did no more than to demonstrate what is obvious to every sane man.[79] Professor Cahn believes that the Court made no more than a passing reference, "alluding to them graciously as 'modern authority.' "[80] He thinks that the belief that the Court's judgment was a result, either entirely or in major part, of the opinions of the social scientists is both erroneous and dangerous. Nor is Professor Wechsler without his doubts. "Much depended," he says, "on the question that the witness had in mind, which rarely was explicit." And this is not all. "[I]f the harm that segregation worked was relevant, what of the benefits that it entailed: sense of security, the absence of hostility? Were they irrelevant?"[81]

To me, what is least satisfying about the opinion in *Brown* is the unclarity of the relationship between the Court's judgment that segregated schools generate a feeling of inferiority and its judgment that separate educational facilities are "inherently unequal." Is the second meant to follow from the first? What then is the force of the word "inherently"? Although I agree that segregation does stigmatize Negroes with a badge of inferiority, and although I also tend to accept the argument of some that as a matter of fact "separate but equal" facilities are rarely equal, I find it hard, together with Professor Wechsler, to think that the decision really turned upon the facts.[82] But I would phrase this in a slightly different way: I do not think that the decision turned *merely* upon the Court's understanding of the facts; the element of principle plays a crucial role in the Court's reasoning.

Throughout one's reading of the opinion one must keep in mind the legal

---

76. WECHSLER 31.
77. 163 U.S. 537 (1896).
78. *Contra*, HAND, *op. cit. supra* note 53, at 54.
79. Black, *The Lawfulness of the Segregation Decisions*, 69 YALE L.J. 421 (1960).
80. Cahn, *Jurisprudence*, 30 N.Y.U.L. REV. 150, 160 (1955).
81. WECHSLER 44-45.
82. *Id.* at 45.

position of segregated schools before the *Brown* decision, the import of the "separate but equal" doctrine. Under the fourteenth amendment, the pre-*Brown* doctrine was that the *only* requirement regarding public schools was that Negroes and whites may be treated in a separate manner so long as the schools in any given state were equal in facilities, etc., in that state. In other words, with *no need of any touch of a justification* it was permissible for a state to single out a group of individuals and educate them separately from other groups so long as there was equality of facilities, etc., apparently on the theory that no showing of injury, necessary to successfully challenging legislation on equal protection grounds, could be made. It is this *at the very least* which is no longer the legal position after *Brown*.

As I see it, the decision in *Brown* turns upon two separate points. First, that segregation in public schools is invalid because it is in principle a denial of equality: such schools are "inherently unequal." Second, that it is constitutionally bad because it generates a feeling of inferiority in the minority group, *i.e.*, the group not politically dominant.[83] The first point is directed toward the item mentioned above. It holds, no matter what the feelings are which are generated. Segregation, with or without equal facilities, taken by itself and without some justification for meting out a *different* treatment to equals under the law, is constitutionally bad. What is affirmed here is the prima facie *right* of Negroes to attend the same schools as whites; a right which they can be prevented from exercising only if some adequate justification can be given for so preventing them. Clearly, their race alone, under the fourteenth amendment, is certainly not sufficient as an adequate justification.

On the first point, then, I do not see how the Court could have validated segregated public schools, even granting equal facilities. The major premise of the decision is that when a state undertakes a program of public education it must be made available to all on equal terms. This proposition is really the individualization, for this case, of a more general one about state programs: they all must be made available to all on equal terms. So, if a state undertakes a program of home nursing care to poor, disabled persons, it, too, must be available to all on equal terms. (This is to be distinguished from another "more general" proposition that home nursing care must be made available to all irrespective of their economic status.) *Disparity of treatment* of equals must be justified by the discriminator if *he* is to be principled. Could the Court here have acknowledged such disparity of treatment—and enforced separation, even if "separate but equal," is just that—granted that Negroes have a legitimate claim to equal treatment under the fourteenth amendment?

As I reconstruct this aspect of the Court's reasoning, the equal protection and due process clauses of the fourteenth amendment are intimately

---

83. Professor Wechsler's gloss. See *id.* at 45.

related—and are they so separate anyway? It is interesting to note that in *Bolling v. Sharpe*,[84] dealing with segregated schools in the District of Columbia, the Court arrived at the same result as *Brown* on fifth amendment due process grounds. Finally, in *Cooper v. Aaron* the Court makes its stand clear: "the right of a student not to be segregated *on racial grounds* in schools so maintained is indeed so fundamental and pervasive that it is embraced in the concept of due process of law."[85] In sum, principled decision requires sameness of treatment in public education—unless some justification can be offered for the different treatment, and distinction of race *alone* is not an acceptable ground for permitting separate school facilities. This is implicit in the Court's opinion in *Brown*, although that opinion leaves much to be desired.

The *onus probandi* of providing a justification for racially segregated public schools fell on the states that maintained such schools. There are, of course, justifications for racially segregated schools that could conceivably be offered. It could be argued that Negroes and whites differ significantly in native intellectual capacity, so that the purposes of education would be frustrated by integration. Such ploys ring a familiar bell, having been used by European countries to justify the domination of their colonies. But even if it were granted that this is true—which it is not—the measure of the sincerity of the discriminator would be whether he is prepared to maintain classes of Negroes and whites who possess a low-level of intelligence. It is fairly evident that this ploy amounts to little more than dodging the issue. It could, again, be argued that although Negroes *do* have the right to attend integrated schools, because under the fourteenth amendment race is not an acceptable ground of distinction, the very attempt to integrate the schools is so fraught with danger to peace that Negroes ought to be prevented from exercising their right. But the weight of this argument would vary from community to community, and at best it only goes to the issue of how quickly integration ought to be instituted. I think that although the Court required (in the second *Brown* decision)[86] that it be done with all "deliberate speed," the Court did, nevertheless, partially acknowledge some merit in this argument in recognizing that the variations in local conditions did affect the rate of integration. It is true that in *Cooper*, in its instructions to the district

---

84. 347 U.S. 497 (1953). The permissibility of the separation of children by "normal geographic school districting" is implied in the Court's order handed down when the segregation cases were assigned in 1953 for reargument. Brown v. Board of Educ., 345 U.S. 972, 973 (1953). Interestingly, this is not mentioned in the subsequent opinions. I am not certain as to how this really does affect those cases in which a *de facto* segregation (as distinct from an "enforced separation") results.

85. 358 U.S. 1, 19 (1958). (Emphasis added.) See generally the hindsight opinion of Professor Pollak in which he refers to the "comprehensive standards which the Fourteenth Amendment imposes on all state activity." Pollak, *supra* note 66, at 24-30.

86. 349 U.S. 294 (1955).

courts,[87] the Court excluded "hostility to racial desegregation" as a relevant factor from a district court's consideration regarding the rate of desegregation. But this, I believe, wisely reflected the Court's realistic view that to recognize hostility to desegregation as a ground for delay could only result in a permanent deprivation of the right of Negro children in this context.

It is worth noting that the two examples given above as possible justifications for retaining segregated schools differ in a significant respect. The first makes reference to something within the sphere of education itself, while the second refers to some governmental objective outside of education as such. These represent two different forms of justification of exceptions to principle, but I shall not attempt to explore this any further here.

This brings us to the second aspect of the *Brown* decision. Not only was the Court convinced as a matter of principle that Negroes have a prima facie right to sameness of treatment in public education, but the Court was also convinced that Negroes are positively harmed by such discrimination. This bodes ill for any conceivable justification for retaining enforced segregation. Obviously this fact weighed heavily in the minds of the members of the Court as they listened to and read the arguments put forth by counsel of states that practiced racial segregation. Even without it only the weightiest considerations could have overridden the right of Negroes to attend integrated schools; how much more so with it! Thus, even if one grants the benefits that Professor Wechsler alleges segregation might have entailed (sense of security and absence of hostility),[88] granting also the harms, the Court would have been hard put to see much merit in the purported justifications for segregation. Segregated schools are at best a mixed blessing to Negroes, and it is not clear that their virtues overbalance the vices to such an extent that, excluding other considerations, the right which Negroes have in principle ought to be denied them.[89]

---

87. "[A] District Court, after analysis of the relevant factors (which of course, excludes hostility to racial desegregation), might conclude that justification existed for not requiring the present nonsegregated admission of all qualified Negro children." 358 U.S. at 7. It would naturally be self-defeating, in ordinary situations, to allow opposition to a principle to be a ground for making an exception to the principle.
88. WECHSLER 45.
89. I am not sure where this leaves the enforced separation of the sexes. Can some justification for it be found? An interesting area in which race and sex may be compared is that relating to juries. The Supreme Court has reversed the convictions of some Negroes when it was shown that the given state practiced a discriminatory racial policy in the selection of jurors. Eubanks v. Louisiana, 356 U.S. 584 (1958). In a recent case, Hoyt v. Florida, 368 U.S. 57 (1961), a woman who was convicted by an all-male jury of the baseball bat murder of her husband appealed on the ground that "such jury was the product of a state jury statute which works an unconstitutional exclusion of women from jury service." *Id.* at 58. Under that statute women are not required to serve on juries; they are permitted, however, to volunteer for service. But this was held not to be a purposeful or arbitrary discrimination. Writing for the Court, Mr. Justice Harlan said:
> Despite the enlightened emancipation of women from the restrictions and protections of bygone years, and their entry into many parts of community life formerly considered to be reserved to men, woman is still regarded as the center of home

Professor Wechsler suggests another approach to the issue of segregation, and I shall conclude my remarks with a comment upon it.

> For me [he says], assuming equal facilities, the question posed by state-enforced segregation is not one of discrimination at all. Its human and its constitutional dimensions lie entirely elsewhere, in the denial by the state of freedom to associate, a denial that impinges in the same way on any groups or races that may be involved. . . . But if the freedom of association is denied by segregation, integration forces an association upon those for whom it is unpleasant or repugnant. Is this not the heart of the issue involved, a conflict in human claims of high dimension . . . . Given a situation where the state must practically choose between denying the association to those individuals who wish it or imposing it on those who would avoid it, is there a basis in neutral principles for holding that the Constitution demands that the claims for association should prevail? I should like to think there is, but I confess that I have not yet written the opinion. To write it is for me the challenge of the school-segregation cases.[90]

With all respect to Professor Wechsler, I do not see how one can say that the question "is not one of discrimination *at all.*" Discrimination is certainly no less relevant than the freedom of association. Principled decision-making requires that the different treatment of equals be justified, and the *onus probandi* falls on the discriminator. As I see it, Professor Wechsler's question really comes down to this: is the "evil" of the imposition of association on those who wish to avoid it sufficient to justify the different, and hence unequal, treatment of equals? Put this way, I suggest that a better constitutional case can be made for the negative answer. But in any event I should like to have more instruction on what kind of constitutionally protected right the freedom of association is. As far as I am aware it is no more than the right of individuals to combine for a common (legal) end,[91] which seems irrelevant to the question of segregated use of public facilities, assuming them to be equal. Moreover, how far can we extend the claim of those who wish to avoid an association that is unpleasant to them? Could this not lead to the invalidation of any form of compulsory education?

These remarks are the words of a friendly critic. I accept, in the only way I can understand it, Professor Wechsler's ideal of judicial decision-making. And it is important to recognize that it is an ideal that, as an ideal, is no less valid for its being so rarely realized in practice—if such be the case.

---

and family life. We cannot say that it is constitutionally impermissible for a State, acting in pursuit of the general welfare, to conclude that a woman should be relieved of the civic duty of jury service unless she herself determines that such service is consistent with her own special responsibilities. *Id.* at 60-61. Perhaps this suggests the line of reasoning that would justify (for it clearly needs justification) the permissibility of the *enforced* separation of the sexes in schools.

90. WECHSLER 46-47.
91. See NAACP v. Alabama, 357 U.S. 449 (1958).

THE ENDURING SIGNIFICANCE OF
NEUTRAL PRINCIPLES

KENT GREENAWALT*

INTRODUCTION

Almost twenty years have passed since Herbert Wechsler delivered his Oliver Wendell Holmes lecture, *Toward Neutral Principles of Constitutional Law*.[1] Although no one piece fully conveys the richness and rigor of Professor Wechsler's conception of constitutional law and the role of the judiciary,[2] *Neutral Principles* sets out starkly, eloquently, and courageously some of his fundamental beliefs about constitutional decisionmaking. Shifts in jurisprudential fashion, as well as marked changes in constitutional doctrine and the composition of the Supreme Court, would make this an apt time to review what is almost certainly the most cited and most controversial discussion of constitutional issues since World War II, even if this were not an occasion to honor the incomparable contributions to American law and legal thought of its distinguished author.

Although *Neutral Principles* bears Herbert Wechsler's unmistakable stamp, the lecture was also representative of what my colleague Louis Henkin has felicitously called the "inevitable reaction long overdue"[3] to the more radical versions of legal realism. Stressing the nonrational aspects of judicial decision, some realists had talked as if judicial decisions were essentially indistinguishable from other decisions, as if all one could reasonably hope for was a "mature" decisionmaker, as if the process of "reasoned justification" merely conceals the emperor's nakedness.[4] The realist portrayal of judges as essentially unrestrained conflicted disturbingly with democratic ideals which place legislative authority in popularly elected and politically responsible bodies. The portrayal was particularly troublesome

---

* Professor of Law, Columbia University. B.A. 1958, Swarthmore; B.Phil. 1960, Oxford; LL.B. 1963, Columbia University.

1. 73 HARV. L. REV. 1 (1959), *reprinted in* H. WECHSLER, PRINCIPLES, POLITICS, AND FUNDAMENTAL LAW 3 (1961) [hereinafter cited as PRINCIPLES, POLITICS, AND FUNDAMENTAL LAW]. Subsequent citations are to pages in the book. The lecture will hereinafter be referred to as *Neutral Principles*.

2. For a sample of his other writings on the subject, see THE NATIONALIZATION OF CIVIL LIBERTIES AND CIVIL RIGHTS (1968); *The Courts and the Constitution*, 65 COLUM. L. REV. 1001 (1965); *The Political Safeguards of Federalism: The Role of the States in the Composition and Selection of the National Government*, 54 COLUM. L. REV. 543 (1954), *reprinted in* PRINCIPLES, POLITICS, AND FUNDAMENTAL LAW, *supra* note 1, at 49; *Stone and the Constitution*, 46 COLUM. L. REV. 764 (1946), *reprinted in* PRINCIPLES, POLITICS, AND FUNDAMENTAL LAW, *supra* note 1, at 83; *The Clear and Present Danger Test*, 9 AM. L. SCH. REV. 881 (1941) [all works hereinafter cited by title].

3. Henkin, *Some Reflections on Current Constitutional Controversy*, 109 U. PA. L. REV. 637, 654 (1961).

4. *See* T. ARNOLD, THE SYMBOLS OF GOVERNMENT (1935); J. FRANK, LAW AND THE MODERN MIND (1949); F. RODELL, WOE UNTO YOU, LAWYERS! (2d ed. 1957). Arnold uses the metaphor of the emperor's clothing in Arnold, *Professor Hart's Theology*, 73 HARV. L. REV. 1298 (1960). For a discussion of legal realism as a variety of decisionism, see Shklar, *Decisionism*, in NOMOS VII: RATIONAL DECISION 1 (C. Friedrich ed. 1964).

in the context of constitutional law, given the direct clash between the judicial and political branches that constitutional invalidation involves and the then still vivid recollections of the misadventures of the 1930's Supreme Court. If judges in constitutional cases were really no different from legislators, one of two obvious lessons could be drawn: either Justice McReynolds and his brethren had made no fundamental mistakes about judicial authority and constitutional interpretation but had erred, if at all, only in their "legislative" wisdom, or judicial "legislators" should defer to elected legislators when the latter have expressed themselves. As Wechsler's predecessor in the Holmes lectureship, Judge Learned Hand had drawn the second lesson in the strongest terms, despairing not only of judicial development of open-ended phrases like "equal protection" and "due process of law," but also of judicial reliance on the first amendment and other relatively specific protections of individual rights in overriding decisions of the "political" branches.[5]

In his call for neutral principles of law, Wechsler joined others who had emphasized the centrality of reasoned justification for judicial decisions,[6] a position labelled by one legal historian as the belief in "reasoned elaboration."[7] Among Wechsler's special contributions were his development of the tantalizing concept of neutral principles, his employment of the idea of reasoned justification as a basis for greater judicial review of the political branches than Judge Hand and other proponents of extreme restraint supported, and his fearless application of his standards to criticize civil rights decisions of the Supreme Court. Wechsler wrote at a time when the Court's "activism" was largely limited to claims of equality of black Americans; he preceded Justice Goldberg's accession to the bench and the formation of a majority that displayed a more pervasive unwillingness to defer to decisions of the political branches when cases involved claims of individual rights. It was left to later commentators, such as Alexander Bickel and Philip Kurland, to deliver widesweeping indictments of the Warren Court's performance, claiming that the Court had constitutionally enshrined its own egalitarian sentiments without adequate justification.[8]

---

5. L. HAND, THE BILL OF RIGHTS (1958).
6. *See, e.g.,* H.M. HART & A.M. SACKS, THE LEGAL PROCESS (tent. ed. 1958) [hereinafter cited as HART & SACKS]; Bickel & Wellington, *Legislative Purpose and the Judicial Process: The Lincoln Mills Case,* 71 HARV. L. REV. 1 (1957); Griswold, *The Supreme Court, 1959 Term—Foreword: Of Time and Attitudes—Professor Hart and Judge Arnold,* 74 HARV. L. REV. 81 (1960); Hart, *The Supreme Court, 1958 Term—Foreword: The Time Chart of the Justices,* 73 HARV. L. REV. 84 (1959); Jaffe, *Foreword to The Supreme Court, 1950 Term,* 65 HARV. L. REV. 107 (1951); Sacks, *Foreword to The Supreme Court, 1953 Term,* 68 HARV. L. REV. 96 (1954).
7. White, *The Evolution of Reasoned Elaboration: Jurisprudential Criticism and Social Change,* 59 VA. L. REV. 279 (1973). The phrase "Reasoned Elaboration" was borrowed from HART & SACKS, *supra* note 6, at 161 ff.
8. In A. BICKEL, THE SUPREME COURT AND THE IDEA OF PROGRESS (1970), Bickel says that the Warren Court "relied on events for vindication more than on the method of reason for contemporary validation," *id.* at 12, and he argues that the charges against the Warren Court of subjectivity of judgment, analytical laxness, intellectual incoherence, and imagining of history, *id.* at 45, "can be made out, irrefutably and amply," *id.* at 47. Kurland concludes in P. KURLAND, POLITICS, THE CONSTITUTION, AND THE WARREN COURT (1970) that opinions of the Warren Court "have tended toward fiat rather than reason," *id.* at xxii, and that the Court "has failed abysmally to persuade the people that its judgments have been made for sound reasons," *id.* at 205.

Nor has the passing of the Warren Court abated concern over the adequacy of justifications of Supreme Court decisions. The Burger Court has been criticized for failing to provide sufficient reasons for its results, both when it has matched the Warren Court's activism, as in Roe v. Wade,[9] and when it has drawn back from the import of earlier decisions. Clearly, the problems discussed in Neutral Principles are of more than historical interest. Indeed, they reach to the very core of the process of judicial decision and will retain importance as long as judges sit in this country.

Neutral Principles has always held a special fascination for me, partly because I was a student of Herbert Wechsler's shortly after its publication. Like others, I was troubled that cases like Shelley v. Kraemer[10] and Brown v. Board of Education,[11] which seemed obvious victories for truth and right, were under sharp attack by someone whose intellectual power and integrity claimed such great respect; and I spent some hours puzzling over the opinions and his article, trying to fathom how the decisions might be saved from his critique. My interest continued when I served as a law clerk to John M. Harlan. I knew that he and Wechsler greatly admired each other, and, as I compared my perceptions of the Court's activities with the model set up in Neutral Principles, I concluded that no modern Justice had striven harder or more successfully than Justice Harlan to perform his responsibilities in the manner suggested by the model. The themes of Neutral Principles have since then been a continuing subject of discussion in the classroom and with colleagues but this invitation to pay tribute to Herbert Wechsler presents an opportunity to attend to those themes in a more systematic way.

In the first part of this Article I state what I believe to be the crucial jurisprudential concepts in Neutral Principles. I not only outline Wechsler's major theses but also discuss some theses mistakenly attributed to him by critics. In the second part, I elaborate on why the effort to formulate neutral principles is so important. The third part concerns the attainability of "neutral principles." It also discusses some responsibilities of judges which were not treated by Wechsler in his article but which sometimes conflict with the aspiration of achieving neutral principles. I do not believe definitive guidance is available for how judges should resolve such conflicts. In the fourth part, I address summarily some more encompassing theories for describing the constraints under which judges should operate in deciding constitutional cases, asserting that each is conceptionally inadequate and that the more plausible theories, even if accepted, are of little practical usefulness. Finally, I conclude that the search for neutral principles is, as Wechsler contends, fundamental in the process of constitutional decision-making.

---

9. 410 U.S. 113 (1973).
10. 334 U.S. 1 (1948).
11. 349 U.S. 294 (1954).

I. The Meaning of Neutral Principles

A. *The Elements of Wechsler's Theses*

Addressing the question of how determinations of courts reviewing the actions of other branches of government can have legal quality even though they inevitably involve choices of value, Professor Wechsler states: "The answer . . . inheres primarily in that they are—or are obliged to be—entirely principled. A principled decision . . . is one that rests on reasons with respect to all the issues in the case, reasons that in their generality and their neutrality transcend any immediate result that is involved." [12]

This is the heart of the jurisprudential aspect of *Neutral Principles.* Although Wechsler concerns himself with constitutional decisions, it is clear that he thinks courts should act on the basis of neutral principles in other areas of decision as well, for he says "the main constitutent of the judicial process is precisely that it must be genuinely principled." [13]

1. *The Basic Meaning of Neutrality.* What does Wechsler mean by the phrase "reasons that in their generality and their neutrality transcend any immediate result . . ."? [14] In his lecture, he attacks summary dispositions that fail to offer any reasoned justification for their results, but he also criticizes some decisions supported by substantial opinions, on the ground that the principles offered are not ones that can be neutrally applied. Understanding what Wechsler means by neutrality is crucial to understanding his thesis and is an indispensable safeguard against misinterpretation.

A person gives a neutral reason, in Wechsler's sense, if he states a basis for a decision that he would be willing to follow in other situations to which it applies. Suppose, for example, *A* says, "Communists should be allowed to preach Marxist doctrine because everyone has a right to say what he believes as long as he does not encourage imminent criminal acts." If *A* would deny a person urging that whites are innately superior to the members of other races the right to speak, then the reason he asserts in defense of the Communist is not one which *A* subscribes to as a neutral principle. When Wechsler says that "principles are largely instrumental as they are employed in politics" he means that political actors often employ arguments in defense of particular results that they would be unwilling to give similar weight to in other situations to which the arguments apply. Sometimes when a person like *A* offers a reason in defense of a position the observer will not know whether the stated principle is a neutral one for *A* or is being used only instrumentally, but *A*'s real view will be tested when the issue arises in connection with the speech of white supremacists. However, it is often possible to know immediately whether a decision is urged or justified on the basis of neutral principles. No reason may be offered at all, or the reason

---

12. Principles, Politics, and Fundamental Law, *supra* note 1, at 27.
13. *Id.* at 21.
14. *Id.* at 27.

offered may be one we are confident *A* would reject in other contexts, either because he has already done so or because its application in those contexts appears obviously unacceptable.

The issue of neutral principles and the Supreme Court is best illustrated in connection with *Shelley v. Kraemer.* In that case, the Court dealt with a private covenant to discriminate against blacks in the sale of property and held that judicial enforcement of the covenant constituted impermissible state action under the fourteenth amendment. In his original lecture, Wechsler doubted strongly that the Court would hold it to be impermissible state action to enforce a will that discriminates on racial grounds or to treat as a trespasser one who is asked to leave private premises because of his race.[15] A few years later he put the criticism this way:

> The Court's opinion rested the decision on the simple ground that the covenant embodied a discrimination and that the enforcement order of the court is action of the state. Both of these propositions are correct. Yet I submit that it is clear that they do not suffice to uphold the judgment, unless it is affirmed that a private discrimination becomes a discrimination by the state whenever it is legally enforced. But such a proposition is absurd and would destroy the law of wills and a good portion of the law of property, which is concerned precisely with supporting owners' rights to make discriminations that the state would not be free to make on the initiative of officials. Hence, I suggest that this was not a principled decision in the sense that is demanded of the courts.[16]

Wechsler's critique of *Shelley, Brown v. Board of Education,* and some of the "white primary" decisions, assumes a large common ground between Supreme Court Justices and thoughtful students of constitutional law as to what results are acceptable,[17] but it is important to distinguish some different perspectives from which the test of neutrality might be applied to a decision. One question is whether the reasons offered are ones the decisionmaker would be willing to apply neutrally to the other situations that they cover. A second and different question is whether the critic believes the reasons offered are ones that can defensibly be applied to those other situations. Still different inquiries are whether reasons might be supplied other than those found in the opinion which the decisionmaker or his critic or both would be willing to have applied consistently.

When Wechsler criticizes grounds of decisions, he suggests that the reasons offered are ones that neither the judges nor their critics would be willing to apply broadly. His main concern is with judicial craftsmanship and its relation to judicial decision. His primary argument is that the Court has not actually offered grounds for decision that pass the test of neutrality.

---

15. *Id.* at 40-43.
16. Wechsler, *The Nature of Judicial Reasoning,* in Law and Philosophy 290, 295 (S. Hook ed. 1964).
17. *See* Principles, Politics, and Fundamental Law, *supra* note 1, at 36-47.

He may express skepticism that such grounds could be found, but his criticisms of the Supreme Court's work stand even if others are able to offer support in neutral principles for the results the Supreme Court has actually reached.

The point can again be illustrated with reference to *Shelley v. Kraemer*. Louis Pollak has urged that the result in *Shelley* was correct because it should be unconstitutional for the state to assist "a private person in seeing to it that others behave in a fashion which the state could not itself have ordained."[18] Louis Henkin has suggested that whenever the state supports private discrimination it should be said to be responsible for it and that the determinative constitutional inquiry in such cases should be whether there are countervailing constitutional values that make state support of the discrimination permissible.[19]

Let us suppose each of these theories could be neutrally applied and that, contrary to what Wechsler himself apparently believes,[20] one or both represent sound constitutional positions. The Supreme Court's opinion in *Shelley* is still faulty, because it fails to provide an adequate justification for the decision. And, if the opinion reflects the Justices' perceived justification for the decision, the process by which the Court arrived at the decision was also flawed, because the Justices did not work through the question of whether principles that would support the decision and that could be neutrally applied to the other cases they would cover did actually represent a more appropriate constitutional standard than principles that would lead to a contrary outcome. Nevertheless, if we accept Pollak's or Henkin's approach, the result in *Shelley* is defensible or supportable in terms of neutral principles and, further, is to be preferred to a contrary outcome that might also be defensible in terms of neutral principles.

2. *Generality and Guidance.* The principles that support a decision must be, according to Wechsler, adequately general as well as neutral. They must reach out beyond the narrow circumstances of the case. As Martin Golding has put it, the "instant case must be treated as an instance of a more inclusive class of cases, *i.e.,* the case at hand is treated in a certain manner because it is held to be proper to treat cases of its type in that manner."[21] If an opinion is so limited to the facts that the reasoning gives

---

18. Pollak, *Racial Discrimination and Judicial Integrity: A Reply to Professor Wechsler,* 108 U. PA. L. REV. 1, 13 (1959). Under this approach, a will provision that encouraged a survivor to discriminate—$100,000 to *X* but only if she marries a Presbyterian—would not be enforceable, but a will provision that reflected only the testator's discrimination—$100,000 to *X* who did marry a Presbyterian, nothing to *Y* who married a Baptist—would be enforceable. Also enforceable would be a private person's wish to eject someone from his property on discriminatory grounds.

19. Henkin, Shelley v. Kraemer: *Notes for a Revised Opinion,* 110 U. PA. L. REV. 473 (1962).

20. In an introduction to PRINCIPLES, POLITICS, AND FUNDAMENTAL LAW, *supra* note 1, at xv, he indicated his inability to accept Professor Pollak's rationale; and his discussion of *Shelley v. Kraemer* at a 1963 conference made no reference to the line of analysis proposed by Professor Henkin. Wechsler, *supra* note 16, at 295-96.

21. Golding, *Principled Decision-Making and the Supreme Court,* 63 COLUM. L. REV. 35, 40 (1963).

little or no guidance as to how related situations would be treated, then the opinion fails the criterion of generality, even if it be assumed that the court is willing to apply its exceedingly narrow principles neutrally to the (very rare) other cases that they cover. In *Burton v. Wilmington Parking Authority*,[22] for example, the Supreme Court's opinion enumerates a number of contacts between state government and a coffee shop, concluding that in sum they implicate the state in the shop's racial discrimination. But the opinion provides scant indication as to what other patterns of state involvement will lead to the same conclusion.

The typical formulation of a general principle, at least if it states the basic legal principle underlying the holding,[23] will indicate with considerable clarity how the court thinks some class of related cases should be treated. For example, if a court says that a Marxist must be allowed to express his socialist ideas because they do not encourage imminent harm, it implies that other persons expressing other controversial ideas that do not encourage imminent harm will also be protected. But some formulations, though in general form, may not give such clear guidance. The formulation may be so open-ended that it leaves uncertainty as to how any, or most, other cases will be decided. Ordinarily a highly particularistic decision, like *Burton*, can be said at least to imply some general open-ended standard, such as: When various involvements between the state and private business create a close nexus between the two, the discrimination of the business will be attributed to the state. The standard, plus the decision, may tell us how some very close connections of the state and private business would be treated and how some highly tenuous connections would be treated, but as to a large range of moderately close connections it provides no clear guidance. Moreover, if the Court had informed us of its general standard of decision prior to *Burton*, we might not have been able confidently to have predicted the result in that case.

In areas as diverse as state action, coerced confessions,[24] and burdens on interstate commerce, the Supreme Court has employed open-ended standards that indicate some kind of weighing of factors or balancing but that do not unambiguously yield results in many of the cases to which they apply. Wechsler leaves some doubt as to whether he believes such standards qualify as general principles.[25] Perhaps we should consider the broad

---

22. 365 U.S. 715 (1961); *see* Lewis, Burton v. Wilmington Parking Authority—*A Case Without Precedent*, 61 COLUM. L. REV. 1458 (1961).

23. As I suggest below, *see* notes 66-78 and accompanying text *infra*, when we consider some underlying principles of interpretation, these may not produce clear answers to many particular cases.

24. I refer to the old voluntariness standard, *see, e.g.,* Culombe v. Connecticut, 367 U.S. 568 (1961), not the *Miranda* rules.

25. The point is not addressed explicitly in his original lecture, but Wechsler does indicate that Holmes's clear and present danger test is a position framed in terms of neutral and general principles. PRINCIPLES, POLITICS, AND FUNDAMENTAL LAW, *supra* note 1, at 35-36. He had much earlier characterized that test as doing nothing more than requiring "an extended judicial review in the fullest legislative sense of the competing values which the particular situation presents." *The Clear and Present Danger Test, supra* note 2, at 887. Four years after the *Neutral Principles* lecture, he commented that no one had improved on Thomas Reed Powell's

standard to be a general principle, but one that demands ad hoc evaluations to resolve particular cases. However they are labelled, such constitutional standards fail to distinguish with much precision the protected from the unprotected among the situations they cover.

3. *Principles of Law.* In the body of Wechsler's essay, there is no direct discussion of the distinction between principles of law and other general principles that might be advanced in support of a decision, but the pervasive assumption is that judges are limited to principles that have legal relevance.[26] Not every principled moral argument for a position is one that a court is free to adopt.[27] As I shall indicate below, I think some confusion has been caused by critics who have taken some of Wechsler's implicit premises about American constitutional law and mistakenly built them into his concepts of neutrality and generality. It is critical that Wechsler has never regarded "neutral principles" as a comprehensive guide to proper constitutional decision; it is, in his view, merely a "negative requirement," a "minimal criterion."[28] A judge must still decide what possible principles of decision have legal relevance and which among possible competing principles carry more power in the legal order.

4. *Principles as to Every Step in the Decision.* Professor Wechsler says, "A principled decision . . . is one that rests on reasons with respect to all the issues in the case,"[29] and he suggests that the relative compulsion of the language of the Constitution, of history, and of precedent is "a matter to be judged, so far as possible, by neutral principles. . . ."[30] If his thesis is modest in the sense of setting only minimum criteria for decision, it is ambitious in reaching every step of the interpretive process. A court has not met Wechsler's standard simply by stating a principled and neutral holding, that is, a rule of law of some generality which the court is prepared to apply to other cases that it covers. The court must also justify its holding on a principled basis, that is, the court must make principled determinations on such questions as how much significance to accord the expressed views of the framers and whether to give weight to sociological evidence.[31]

---

suggestion that the Court's basic test for burdens on interstate commerce is that "[t]he States may burden interstate commerce but not too much." Wechsler, *supra* note 16, at 298-99. He continued, "How much is too much is, perhaps, beyond the possibility of principled decision," and characterized determinations in such cases as "a special case of free decision." *Id.* at 299.

    26. Wechsler speaks, for example, of the province of the courts reviewing legislation as the principled appraisal of "values that can reasonably be asserted to have constitutional dimension." PRINCIPLES, POLITICS, AND FUNDAMENTAL LAW, *supra* note 1, at 22.

    27. Particular legal standards may, of course, refer judges to open-ended assessments of morality or social desirability, and it may well be that such assessments should also influence a judge who is deciding among possible legal standards. *See* Greenawalt, *Policy, Rights, and Judicial Decision*, 11 GA. L. REV. 991 (1977). All I mean to assert here is the obvious proposition that the legal materials may preclude altogether or greatly affect the weight of a principled argument of considerable moral force. For example, when prohibition was actually enshrined in the American Constitution, a principled defense of the right to use liquor along the lines of John Stuart Mill's *On Liberty* would have been obviously unavailing as a piece of constitutional argumentation.

    28. Wechsler, *supra* note 16, at 299.

    29. PRINCIPLES, POLITICS, AND FUNDAMENTAL LAW, *supra* note 1, at 27. *See also id.* at 21.

    30. *Id.* at 24.

    31. See Wechsler's criticism of the way the Court treated the sociological evidence in *Brown v. Board of Education, id.* at 44-45.

5. *Reasoning that is Reflected in the Opinion.*   It is strongly implicit in the Holmes lecture that in order to satisfy its responsibilities the Supreme Court must in its opinion explicate its real grounds of decision.   Wechsler is critical of brief per curiam opinions for cases of genuine difficulty.   In areas where that has become the Court's practice, he says "the Court has been decreeing value choices in a way that makes it quite impossible to speak of principled determinations or the statement and evaluation of judicial reasons, since the Court has not disclosed the grounds on which its judgments rest." [32]   If the Court fails when it gives no reasons for its decisions, it follows that it must also fail if it gives false reasons, even if the false reasons are not themselves demonstrably inconsistent with neutral principles. It may be possible for a judge to make the rule of the case one that he would adhere to in other situations it covers, even if he misleads as to the reasons for his decision.   Suppose a judge states a broad principle of first amendment protection in a Communist case, not for the reasons he offers, but because he thinks the cause of white supremacy, dear to his heart, will be served by that principle.   The rule itself satisfies the test of neutral principles. But whatever purported methods of interpretation the judge uses in the opinion to yield that broad rule would not be followed by him when they would disserve his real purposes in deciding this case the way he does.   Thus an opinion that conceals the true grounds of decision must surely be judged deficient against the standard of neutral principles.

This completes my summary of what I take to be Herbert Wechsler's thesis.   Judges must decide all the issues in a case on the basis of general principles that have legal relevance; the principles must be ones the judges would be willing to apply to the other situations that they reach; and the opinion justifying the decision should contain a full statement of those principles.

B.   *The Limits of Wechsler's Thesis*

If one is to come to grips with what Wechsler does assert, it is vital not to misconstrue those assertions.   Many critics have read him to say much more than can plausibly be found in the lecture, perhaps in part because of their dismay with his application of his thesis to some of the Supreme Court's civil rights decisions, perhaps in part because they simply assume that he takes positions to be found in the work of some other advocate of "reasoned elaboration."   Other mistaken interpretations do claim some support in the text but do not survive careful scrutiny of its entirety.   In indicating the limits of Wechsler's critical criteria, my concern is with his position; I do not consider whether other authors of generally similar views make arguments erroneously attributed to him.

---

32. *Id.* at 28.

1. *Mechanical Jurisprudence and Correct Decision.* Most obviously, Professor Wechsler does not mean to revive mechanical jurisprudence.[33] Nothing in the lecture suggests that correct answers to difficult constitutional questions can be readily derived from the materials at hand. Nor does he mean to equate principled decision with correct decision. Indeed, he cites the clear and present danger test as formulated by Holmes as an example of a principle that does meet his criteria, but which he thinks incorrect in some of its potential applications.[34] An opinion can be principled but unsound in its interpretation of the Constitution. And a result can be "correct" even though the opinion fails Wechsler's test, though presumably if the result is correct an opinion defending it could be written that would comply with the test.

2. *Mental Processes of Decision and Justification.* Wechsler does not purport to describe the mental processes by which judges do or should reach decisions.[35] A judge who initially relies on intuition to reach a tentative result can act consistently with Wechsler's thesis so long as he does not reach a final decision until he has determined that his intuitive judgment is supported by "neutral principles" to which he subscribes.

3. *Conflicting Values and Uniformity of Treatment.* Wechsler does not contend that judges can decide constitutional cases without weighing conflicting values. He explicitly recognizes that judges must often make difficult choices among values[36] and he does not suggest that the judge can somehow be neutral among those values.[37]

Some scholars believe that in a deeper sense judges are supposed to be neutral among constitutional values, neutral in giving the weight to each value that is determined by the Constitution itself or some broader set of legal materials.[38] Most constitutional scholars, including Professor Wechsler, would acknowledge that the materials largely determine the weight to be given conflicting values and would agree that a conscientious judge should not freely substitute the values he believes are right for those to be found in the Constitution itself and other relevant legal materials. To this extent, the proposition that a good judge should try to be neutral in approaching value conflicts in constitutional cases would win wide acceptance. But most modern scholars would be skeptical of the claim that the ideal judge could

---

33. Arthur S. Miller and Alan W. Scheflin claim that those arguing for principled decisionmaking "are calling for a return to mechanical jurisprudence, however sophisticated its current version may be." Miller & Scheflin, *The Power of the Supreme Court in the Age of the Positive State: A Preliminary Excursus Part One: On Candor and the Court, Or, Why Bamboozle the Natives?*, 1967 DUKE L.J. 273, 281 n.27.

34. PRINCIPLES, POLITICS, AND FUNDAMENTAL LAW, *supra* note 1, at 35-36.

35. The point is developed more fully in Golding, *supra* note 21, at 40-42.

36. PRINCIPLES, POLITICS, AND FUNDAMENTAL LAW, *supra* note 1, at 22.

37. The criticism of his position on the ground that judges cannot be neutral in the sense of finding "ascertainable objective standards," Miller & Howell, *The Myth of Neutrality in Constitutional Adjudication*, 27 U. CHI. L. REV. 661, 663 (1960), misses the point of his thesis.

38. *See* R. SARTORIUS, INDIVIDUAL CONDUCT AND SOCIAL NORMS 175, 196-97 (1975); Bork, *Neutral Principles and Some First Amendment Problems*, 47 IND. L.J. 1, 7-8 (1971).

always manage without relying on his own value judgments about right social behavior, and Wechsler advances no such thesis for sitting judges.[39]

The term "neutral" is frequently used to mean substantive neutrality. Thus, when the Supreme Court writes of neutrality in connection with the state and religion, it means that the state must be neutral between different religions and that it must neither advance nor discourage the exercise of religion.[40] That is certainly one proper sense of neutral, but it is not Wechsler's. Suppose a Supreme Court Justice read the equal protection clause to bar all classifications that disadvantaged blacks and to bar no other classifications, asserting that to be the historical intent behind the clause. If the Justice applies this reading of the clause consistently and is consistent in other circumstances in his method for determining historical intent and in the weight he assigns that intent, his principle of decision, though starkly favoring one group in comparison with others, would still meet Wechsler's test, since the Justice would be willing to apply his principle and the interpretive standards that underlie it to the cases that they cover. Thus, Wechsler does not mean by neutral principles to assert that judges can be neutral among values, either in the obviously wrong sense that they can avoid value choices, or in the debatable sense that they should strive "neutrally" to draw all their value judgments from the legal materials, nor does he mean that their choices must necessarily treat all relevant groups similarly.

4. *Deference, Historical Intent, and Other Interpretive Guides.* Wechsler's basic position does not answer many fundamental questions about constitutional decision: whether judges should defer greatly to the decisions of other branches of government or more freely implement their own views, whether they should stick to the intent of the framers or develop constitutional guarantees in accord with changing social conceptions, whether they should decide all cases under standards that are non-instrumentalist or can sometimes properly engage in a balancing of social harms and advantages. The general principles which a judge is willing consistently to apply might or might not include deference to other branches,[41] reliance on historical intent, a demand for noninstrumental standards.

But it may be thought that in some more subtle sense Wechsler must necessarily imply positions on these issues. Because principles of deference

---

39. Nothing Wechsler says is, for example, inconsistent with Louis Pollak's statement that the kind of neutrality he [Pollak] "espouses does not preclude the disciplined exercise by a Supreme Court Justice of that Justice's individual and strongly held philosophy." Pollak, *supra* note 18, at 33.

40. *See, e.g.,* Walz v. Tax Comm'n, 397 U.S. 664 (1970).

41. Wechsler does say at one point that courts should impose a choice of values on other branches only when "persuaded, on an adequate and principled analysis, that the choice is clear." PRINCIPLES, POLITICS, AND FUNDAMENTAL LAW, *supra* note 1, at 34. I do not interpret this isolated comment as intended to mean that a judge must refrain from voting for invalidation unless he thinks the principles that persuade him will appear clearly persuasive to most other observers, and thus do not take Wechsler to be here endorsing a strongly deferential position resembling James B. Thayer's classic statement. *See* Thayer, *The Origin and Scope of the American Doctrine of Constitutional Law*, 7 HARV. L. REV. 129 (1893). *Cf.* E.V. ROSTOW, THE SOVEREIGN PREROGATIVE—THE SUPREME COURT AND THE QUEST FOR LAW 30 (1962) (strongly criticizing the demand for clarity).

and reliance on historical intent may be easier to state and less controversial than more "activist" grounds of decision, it is possible that rigorous insistence on neutral principles would incline most judges toward the less activist end of the judicial spectrum. That is a possibility I discuss below, but I wish now to consider an analysis advanced by Alexander Bickel, which suggests a closer connection between adherence to neutral principles and the proper position of the courts vis-à-vis the other branches. For Bickel, principles must be very general in their scope, and the ambit of compromise and expedience is sharply demarked from that of principle.[42] Courts should avoid getting involved in areas where expedience has an important role to play. They should also avoid "line-drawing, judgment of and by degree," since "the judgment of degree may be impossible to make save by sheer arbitrariness . . . ."[43] The principles on which courts rely in constitutional cases need not claim general assent at the time but they must be ones that will gain such assent "in a rather immediate foreseeable future."[44] A Supreme Court wedded to Professor Bickel's philosophy would leave to the political branches many areas in which the Warren Court became involved, and it would refrain from constitutional invalidation unless it could ascertain some very broad principle that could rather quickly win wide acceptance.

Bickel's richly developed position goes considerably further than anything Wechsler says, and indeed includes elements that cannot be squared with Wechsler's stated views. Wechsler does not demand that principles be widely accepted at the time they are announced or even be likely soon to command wide acceptance, and one has the sense that Wechsler is much less sympathetic than Bickel to the notion of a court sharply attentive to prevailing opinion. The fact that Wechsler does not dwell on generality a great deal is a strong indication that he does not think acceptable principles must be very broad. As Ernest Brown wrote on the republication of Wechsler's lecture, " 'Principles' is a[n] . . . elusive, or multi-faceted, word, but neither context, definition, or common usage appears to require that it suggest unyielding universals, or absolutes, as Professor Bickel has apparently understood."[45] It is in fact hard to see how Wechsler could take Bickel's position. Even relatively absolute constitutional principles have been assumed to have exceptions. For example, restraints on publication of troop movements may be justified in wartime and classification in terms of race or national origin may occur if the need for them is extraordinarily pressing.[46] Such limits on

---

42. A. BICKEL, THE LEAST DANGEROUS BRANCH 58-64 (1962).
43. A. BICKEL, *supra* note 8, at 60.
44. A. BICKEL, *supra* note 42, at 239.
45. Brown, Book Review, 62 COLUM. L. REV. 386, 387 (1962) (reviewing PRINCIPLES, POLITICS, AND FUNDAMENTAL LAW).
46. A curfew for Japanese-Americans was supported by a unanimous vote in Hirabayashi v. United States, 320 U.S. 81 (1943).
Four out of the five members of the Court who discussed the constitutional issue in Regents of the Univ. of Cal. v. Bakke, 98 S. Ct. 2733, 2766 (1978) (Brennan, White, Marshall & Blackmun, JJ.), asserted that when racial criteria are employed to benefit previously disadvantaged groups, the standard for review is less strict.

governmental behavior may give way if the social need is very, very great. In Bickel's terms, these are compromises with expediency. How is the Supreme Court to eschew such compromises? Only by avoiding decision on the merits, and that is precisely Bickel's recommendation. Without specifying what lower courts are to do with such cases, Bickel allows the Supreme Court to be unprincipled in avoiding decision on the merits.[47] Wechsler will not admit that way out of the dilemma; he asserts that on matters of justiciability the Court must be principled as elsewhere and thus must not avoid decision on the merits of properly presented cases. Thus, only by precluding exceptions demanded by reason could Wechsler endorse Bickel's notion of absolute principles. We may confidently assume that he has some more flexible, less absolute requirement in mind.

5. *Following Precedent.* Finally, Wechsler does not assert that the court in a second case must actually adhere to what is implied by the principles of a first case. He is writing about methods of justification, not the weight to be accorded precedent. Suppose in case *A*, the court announces a principle that would dictate a similar result in case *B*. The principle, and the like result in case *B*, are plausible interpretations of the Constitution. Some years later case *B* comes along. When the facts are actually before it, the court recognizes, say on the basis of new evidence of historical intent, either that case *A* was wrongly decided or that there is an important distinction between the two cases that should lead to the contrary result in *B*. It then decides *B* differently from *A*, either replacing the rule of *A* with a contrary rule or substantially qualifying the rule of *A*. In neither case has the court necessarily done anything inconsistent with the "neutral principles" thesis; both opinions might well be written in a manner that corresponds fully with its test.

II. THE IMPORTANCE OF NEUTRAL PRINCIPLES

Are neutral principles so important? Wechsler assumes a positive answer rather than attempting to demonstrate one, but it is not difficult to elaborate the essentials of his position. If judges hold themselves to the discipline of neutral principles, they are more likely to render appropriate decisions in particular cases, those decisions are more likely to be perceived as appropriate by others who are interested in the process, and the decision and the opinion supporting it will better promote the development of the law. These points are interrelated, but they are also separable and it is valuable to focus on them discretely.

A. Neutral Principles and Appropriate Decisions

1. *Non-legal decisions.* It may be well to start by inquiring into the relationship between neutral principles and rational decisions. All of us make

---

47. *See* A. BICKEL, *supra* note 42, at 111-98.

countless choices each day that we could justify as being rational. Most of these are so routine that we do not consciously reason about them; it may even be questionable whether the word "decision" is properly applied to such mundane choices as having breakfast, going to work, etc. But if we were challenged we could provide a reasoned justification for them. We could say that for reasons of health, energy, and pleasure it is desirable to eat when one has not eaten for a long time. We could state a general principle, applicable at least to ourselves, that eating breakfast is a desirable practice, and we could formulate broader principles, such that that one should maintain his health and vigor, that would support our breakfast principle. Eating breakfast and going to work on ordinary days are "easy cases." [48] The choice presented on a particular day is a typical instance of situations covered by a broad standard we have come to accept and do not bother to reexamine each time. We could write a principled "opinion" defending the choice, but we would see little point in doing so.[49]

With some frequency, we face choices that do not fit so conveniently under already developed standards. This may be because the whole issue is simply one that does not arise very many times in our lives, for example, choice of career. It may also be because the factual situation does not fit comfortably within our developed standards, for example, we are ill enough so we would ordinarily stay home from work but the work to be done that day is especially significant. One method of making decisions in such situations is to try somehow to add up the considerations for and against a particular decision and to see how the scales tip. If we justify our decision in that way we may, because we have elaborated the kinds of factors to which we give considerable weight, indicate implicitly a good deal about how we would make other decisions.[50] But we have not pursued the course of formulating a general principle for that decision that reaches other situations. Now, it might be suggested that whether we are aware of it or not, at least two principles of decision are implied. One is that if all the factors were repeated in precisely the same way in a future situation and no new relevant factors were present, we would decide the same way. Surely such consistency is a minimal criterion of a "rational" decision. But, so formulated, the principle is of little use, for life never repeats itself exactly. The broader principle of decision is that when similar issues arise, a weighing of relevant factors is the proper way to resolve them. This principle is one of general application but it gives little guidance as to what the actual outcome of a variant factual situation would have been or will be.

---

48. This is assuming, of course, that one is not ill or desperately trying to lose weight, in which event he might worry about whether to have breakfast or go to work.
49. R.M. Hare has written, in THE LANGUAGE OF MORALS 129 (1952), "[A]ll value judgments are covertly universal in character, which is the same as to say that they refer to, and express acceptance of, a standard which has an application to other similar instances."
50. For example, if a person decides not to become a deep sea diver because he rates physical comfort and safety very high, it would be expected that he would not decide to become a fireman.

A second method of reaching decision in those situations where accepted standards do not dictate an outcome is to try to imagine a more general class of instances and consider how we believe they should be treated. Suppose, for example, a young lawyer who is ill is told by his doctor that if he does not rest himself immediately, he risks serious long-term consequences to his health. He and his senior partner are involved in the consummation of an important business transaction to take place the following day, and, since he has done the most extensive work on the matter, he is aware that the client will inevitably have less effective representation if he is absent. Like many young lawyers he is somewhat compulsive about his work and is concerned with his advancement in the firm, and, like most younger people, finds it hard to take too seriously his own mortality and physical vulnerability. So he is initially inclined to go to the office. But then he reflects on what advice he would give a friend in a similar situation, what he thinks he would expect if he desperately needed his personal secretary to do some work and she reported the same risk, what he thinks he would expect of a young lawyer if he were the senior partner. He discovers that in each hypothetical setting, despite the disadvantage to the client, he would advise the ill person to stay home. This leads to deeper examination of his own values and he finds that he believes that one should not risk serious injury to one's long-term health unless one's failure to work is likely to risk someone else's life or health. He concludes that his initial inclination to go to work was not really consistent with fundamental principles to which he subscribes.

If the lawyer sought to justify a decision to stay home along these lines, he would be able to state a principle of decision of considerable generality and definiteness, one that despite its uncertainty at the edges, would yield clear answers to many related situations.

There is no sharp dichotomy between the approach of balancing factors and the approach of imagining related situations and formulating principles to cover them. They may be employed together; the "principles" approach itself usually reflects and relies on weighing of factors; and the factor-weighing approach will sometimes yield at least implicitly principles of clarity and definiteness. Yet, there remains a significant difference in method, and it is interesting to inquire why one would choose to emphasize one method rather than the other if one's only concern were to reach the best decision in the particular instance. Two of the crucial variables are the number of importantly relevant factors and one's confidence in his ability to weigh appropriately.

If there are a great number of important factors to take into account, it is more difficult to imagine what are different yet sufficiently similar situations and it is much harder to formulate a principle of decision that does not suffer from acute narrowness (because it replicates the whole congeries of relevant factors) or unhelpful open-endedness. When the crucial factors are few, such as danger to one's health and the importance of one's work, definite principles are easier to conceive.

There is, regrettably, no exact scale for weighing competing considerations as one weighs oranges. An explicit weighing process may itself be something of a corrective to the bias reflected in an intuitive decision, but bias may infect the way in which one weighs as well. Imagining similar settings, especially settings in which one's own position is altered, can be an important further corrective. Thus, the ill lawyer's reflection on advice he would give to a friend may more accurately indicate his considered judgment about the values of health and work than his attempt to weigh their importance while focusing only on his own situation.

The effort to conceive similar settings and develop principles is particularly important when people make moral choices. It may be wrong to suppose that the proper moral decision for a person has nothing at all to do with his own special characteristics,[51] but those characteristics are ordinarily much less central than they would be for choice of career or spouse or how to spend one's leisure time. Thus the external factors loom much larger in comparison with subjective characteristics than for many other decisions people make. This reduces the number of importantly relevant factors and makes it easier to conceive of similar situations involving other people or involving oneself in a different role.

Serious moral choices typically involve some conflict between an action that would serve one's narrow self-interest and an action that would satisfy responsibilities toward others.[52] The dangers of bias are extreme; either we value too highly our own interest or over-compensate and undervalue it. The discipline of imagining similar situations in which we are not involved or play a different role more nearly enables us to place appropriate values on competing considerations.

The search for general principles can also affect our judgment in another way. We may discover that some of our intuitive moral views are not consistent with other intuitive views or with generalized principles to which we subscribe. As we test our intuitive reactions to particular situations against our accepted principles, both may give a little, until we arrive at what John Rawls calls a "reflective equilibrium," in which our sense of right for particular issues matches our principles.[53]

2. *Legal decisions.* The reasons why attention to related situations and the attempt to formulate general principles can be valuable for making moral and other non-legal decisions apply to the legal decisions of a judge. A judge only rarely has a tangible personal stake in the outcome of a case, but biases of all sorts may incline him in favor of one party or result rather than

---

51. One's own capacity to deal psychologically with various possible choices may, for example, affect what is the morally right decision for oneself, and so perhaps may the kind of character one is trying to develop.
52. Sometimes, of course, the question is which of competing claims on behalf of other persons shall be satisfied, *e.g.*, shall I leave my money after death to my children or to "worthy" causes?
53. J. RAWLS, A THEORY OF JUSTICE 48-50 (1971).

another.[54] The discipline of neutral principles as a method of reasoned decision can make him as disinterested as is possible and can signal the reflective evaluation that will more nearly bring congruence of particular outcomes and broad principles. And, as Alexander Bickel has put it, "[t]he restraints of reason tend to ensure also the independence of the judge, to liberate him from the demands and fears—dogmatic, arbitrary, irrational, self- or group-centered—that so often enchain other public officials." [55]

There are some peculiar features of law and a judge's role that make neutral principles especially important to him when he is trying to reach an appropriate decision. The main stuff of the law is rules cast in general form— rules found in the Constitution, created by legislatures, or developed in earlier judicial decisions. More amorphous guides to decision, such as standards of interpretation, are similarly general. One legal ideal is that similar cases should be decided similarly; the outcome of legal disputes should not depend on the personal characteristics of particular litigants or particular judges. There are few, if any, unique situations from a legal perspective. When judges decide a case one way, they do so because they believe there are reasons for the result that would, or at least should, win support among other judges of similar cases if those reasons were understood.

Because of these characteristics of law, a judge naturally compares the result to which he is initially inclined with the outcomes of cases that are clear under existing rules, and he considers what other sorts of cases would be reached by a general principle that would embrace the case at hand. By this process of deliberation, he tests the appropriateness of his initial inclination. Moreover, insofar as decisions of tribunals represent the maturing of collective thought,[56] the technique of posing cases and suggesting principles orally and in draft opinions is a crucial method of communication among judges, one that often precedes final agreement on a result.

The limits of a judge's role provide an additional reason for following the discipline of neutral principles. Some of the most difficult cases for judges are those in which they believe the law should yield one result, but statutes or precedents point toward a contrary result. How far the judge should follow his considered sense of what would make good law in contrast to the apparent judgment of his predecessors or the legislature is a pervasive problem, but the issue of his role is particularly acute in constitutional adjudication, because a decision of unconstitutionality explicitly overrides a determination by another branch of government. If the judge reflects on his

---

54. See Erwin Griswold's eloquent discussion of the attributes of a conscientious judge in Griswold, *supra* note 6.

55. A. BICKEL, *supra* note 8, at 82. He also says, "[N]o formal method of reasoning from axioms will answer questions of moral philosophy and political theory plainly and definitively, but it will help answer them differently than a process open to trials of strength, and to the free play of interest, predilection, and prejudice." *Id.* at 87.

56. *See* Hart, *supra* note 6, at 100. Thurman Arnold has ridiculed the notion that among strong minded judges there is such a thing as the maturing of collective thought in Arnold, *Professor Hart's Theology,* 73 HARV. L. REV. 1298, 1312 (1960). But Erwin N. Griswold has convincingly argued for its reality, especially in connection with the large majority of cases that do not reduce to some ultimate value judgment. Griswold, *supra* note 6, at 93-94.

general views about the proper conditions for a judgment of unconstitutionality, he is less likely to let his displeasure with a particular statutory rule or administrative practice lead him to the acceptance of an inappropriate role in that case.

Even more fundamentally, part of the definition of a judge's appropriate role in a constitutional case may, as Wechsler indicates,[57] relate to reasoned justification. Legislatures are representative and politically responsible and the legitimacy of statutes derives largely from these characteristics.[58] Courts are not representative and responsible in the same senses. Courts dealing with typical constitutional issues represent a sober second thought of the community, comparing contemporary actions with enduring fundamental values. These values are already embodied or can be embodied in some principled form.[59] If judges are unable to discover a principled justification for invalidation of a legislative decision, that is very strong evidence that the appropriate disposition is to accept that decision.

B. *Neutral Principles and the Perceptions of Others*

For any well functioning governance, it is as important that decisions seem appropriate as well as that they are appropriate. This is especially true for the courts, which are supposed to dispense even-handed justice. John Ladd has suggested that an aspect of treating a rational being rationally is to explain "to him through reasons why a decision that adversely affects his interest has been reached." [60] The litigants in a legal case, especially the losing one, have an important stake in reasoned justification. So also do the participants in other branches of government and the community at large. The disquiet that accompanies a widespread sense that power is not being legitimately exercised is itself an unfortunate social consequence; it may be followed by active steps to curb that power. Thus, it is vital that courts assure not only litigants but all those concerned with the integrity of the judicial process that decisions are grounded on sound bases. As Edward Levi has put it, "the function of articulated judicial reasoning is to help protect the court's

---

57. PRINCIPLES, POLITICS, AND FUNDAMENTAL LAW, *supra* note 1, at 21-23.

58. That is not to say that it is a matter of indifference whether legislative decisions are defensible in terms of neutral principles. Wechsler has spoken, for example, of legislative codification:

> I submit that larger legislative management is necessary and desirable, that, indeed, there is no other way to prevent the anarchical proliferation of a system of case law . . . . [I]t is only by unhurried canvassing of all the issues in a field, the systematic rooting out of inconsistencies, the time-consuming search for information that can shape and inform policy, that the entire corpus of a field of law can be evaluated and reframed.

Wechsler, *Comment on American Legal Institutions,* in LEGAL INSTITUTIONS TODAY AND TOMORROW 303, 307 (M. Paulsen ed. 1959).

59. *But see* Chayes, *The Role of the Judge in Public Law Litigation,* 89 HARV. L. REV. 1281 (1976), suggesting the important policymaking and administrative role of courts in public law litigation in which courts devise and administer very complex and far-reaching remedies. *See also Special Project—The Remedial Process in Institutional Reform Litigation,* 78 COLUM. L. REV. 784 (1978).

60. Ladd, *The Place of Practical Reason in Judicial Decision,* in NOMOS VII: RATIONAL DECISION 126, 144 (C. Friedrich ed. 1964).

moral power by giving some assurance that private views are not masquerading behind public views." [61] Open interest weighing alone may provide some reassurance, but observers unsympathetic with the result may believe that the judge's finger is on the scales. A justification in terms of neutral principles is more likely to persuade that the decision is based on enduring values and not the judge's predisposition to reach a particular result in that case.

C. Neutral Principles and the Development of Law

If the holding of a case is formulated in terms of a neutral principle, other courts will be able to perceive what the court rendering the decision regarded as similar cases to be treated the same way. That guidance will be necessary for a lower court attempting to understand the law laid down by its superior court; it will also be significant when the deciding court subsequently looks to its own precedents in its examination of related legal problems. The principle of decision in the first case may then be regarded as adequate to determine the result in the second case, or as the base on which to build a more expansive principle, or as the starting point for a reformulation that will narrow the principle's compass. The law develops by analogy to earlier cases [62] and principles of decision make up what Edward Levi has aptly called a moving classification system.[63]

In statutory and common-law cases the principle of decision signals to the legislature the court's interpretation of the law, and helps to inform it as to whether some response is needed. Even in constitutional cases, judicial decision is not the end of the line. As Alexander Bickel stressed,[64] the initial decision commences a dialogue with the political branches that will affect the final scope and practical power of announced constitutional standards.

Scholarly critics of the courts who contribute indirectly to the development of law also usually start with announced principles when they evaluate decisions. If decisions were always rendered without opinions or opinions were consistently murky and unenlightening as to the true basis for decision, the job of other courts, legislative bodies, and critics would be much more difficult.

Neutral principles are important not only for the growth of the law but also for public understanding. Narrowly, a principled decision informs po-

---

61. Levi, *The Nature of Judicial Reasoning*, in LAW AND PHILOSOPHY 263, 281 (S. Hook ed. 1964).
62. David Richards has written:
[T]he principle of reasoning by analogy preserves the values of uniformity and stability of legal doctrine in a manner compatible with the flexible development of legal doctrine. In the absence of binding precedents, courts may develop legal doctrine, but they must do so by a publicly articulated process of reasoning that shows how this development is compatible with the reasons underlying existing precedent.
Richards, *Rules, Policies, and Neutral Principles: The Search for Legitimacy in Common Law and Constitutional Adjudication*, 11 GA. L. REV. 1069, 1078 (1977).
63. E. LEVI, AN INTRODUCTION TO LEGAL REASONING (1949).
64. A. BICKEL, *supra* note 8, at 90.

tential litigants of likely subsequent decisions. More broadly, the principled statement of enduring values educates citizens about the accepted premises of shared social life.

III. THE ATTAINABILITY OF NEUTRAL PRINCIPLES AND CONFLICTING GOALS OF JUDICIAL ACTION

The discussion thus far suggests that Herbert Wechsler's model of decisions based on neutral principles is one whose attainment is generally desirable. Indeed, I do not believe any critic denies that at least one thing for which courts should strive is principled justification in the sense that I understand it.[65] Disagreements arise over how attainable such principles are and whether they should give way to other ends of judicial decision. Wechsler writes as if competent courts should be able consistently to formulate such principles and as if their presence is a minimal condition of an acceptable decision in a case that calls for an opinion. It is time to examine those assumptions. For the sake of clarity I shall distinguish two questions. The first is whether in an opinion written by a single judge, in which he has no reason to conceal the true bases of decision and in which he follows ordinary practices in opinion-writing, we should expect him to be able to produce a decision grounded in neutral principles. For simplicity's sake I call this "inherent attainability." The second and more complex question is whether, and when, judges legitimately decide to refrain from explicating the actual principles on which their decision rests. I call this "possible conflicts with other goals."

A. *Inherent Attainability*

Wechsler has been criticized for being unrealistic about the powers of courts to generalize their holdings when they decide difficult cases, especially cases presenting novel questions. I shall discuss this critique first and then turn to what is a much more substantial problem for Wechsler's thesis, its application to underlying issues of interpretation.

1. *Insight and Foresight and the Principle of the Holding.* The question of limited powers of generalization has been put elegantly by Eugene Rostow and Paul Freund. Rostow writes that even "our greatest and most insightful judges"

> grapple with a new problem, deal with it over and over again, as its dimensions change. They settle one case and find themselves tormented by its unanticipated progeny. They back and fill, zig and

---

65. Eugene Rostow, for example, one of Wechsler's sharper critics, has written: The art of generalization, we know, has an indispensable role in the legal process and is an indispensable feature of law as an institution of order. This generalizing aspect of law derives from the basic moral principle, acknowledged by every legal system we know anything about, that similar cases should be decided alike. E.V. ROSTOW, *supra* note 41, at 8.

zag, groping through the mist for a line of thought which will in the end satisfy their standards of craft and their vision of the policy of the community they must try to interpret. The opinions written at the end of such a cycle rarely resemble those composed at the beginning. Exceptions emerge, and new formulations of what once looked like clear principle. If we take advantage of hindsight, we can see in any line of cases and statutes a pattern of growth and of response to changing conditions and changing ideas. There are cases that lead nowhere, stunted branches and healthy ones. Often the judges who participated in the process could not have described the tree that was growing. Yet the felt necessities of society have their impact, and the law emerges, gnarled, asymmetrical, but very much alive—the product of a forest, not of a nursery garden nor of the gardener's art.[66]

Freund discusses the uncertainty at the time *Rylands v. Fletcher* was decided over the ambit of its rule of recovery, and the generations of subsequent cases it took to resolve unanswered questions.[67] He quotes Holmes's comment that "lawyers, like other men, frequently see well enough how they ought to decide on a given state of facts without being very clear as to the *ratio decidendi.*" He continues:

> This is not to exalt blind groping or mystical intuition as marks of a creative judge, but to suggest that insight may outrun foresight, that there may be a time for sowing and a time for winnowing, that the advancement of doctrine need not await an exposition of its full reach, so long as judges are reasonably satisfied that it will not prove to be intractable. These are metaphors which could be annotated extensively from the law of the past.[68]

It is obviously true that judges cannot foresee how they would decide every variant fact situation that resembles in some way the case that is before them. And it would be a prodigious waste of judicial resources for them to attempt to do so. When Edward Levi urged that it would be a mistake to demand "a fully satisfying theory that projects a line to the future and steers a safe course for future conflicts," [69] Wechsler responded that

> it is one thing to anticipate such future cases that perhaps may be distinguishable, without now deciding the sufficiency of the distinction. It is quite another thing to judge the instant case in terms that are quite plainly unacceptable in light of other cases that it is now clear are covered by the principle affirmed in reaching judgment and indistinguishable upon valid grounds.[70]

---

66. *Id.* at 33.
67. Freund, *Rationality in Judicial Decisions*, in NOMOS VII: RATIONAL DECISION 109, 111, 119-20 (C. Friedrich ed. 1964).
68. *Id.* at 120-21.
69. Levi, *supra* note 61, at 274.
70. Wechsler, *supra* note 16, at 297-98.

He said, "the principle of the decision must be viable in reference to applications that are now foreseeable; and . . . viability implies a similar decision or the existence of a possibly acceptable distinction." [71]

Let us suppose, that faced with school segregation, a Supreme Court Justice considers the principle that racial classifications by a state are forbidden by the fourteenth amendment. He perceives that stated baldly, that principle would bar preferential treatment for blacks, "benign" housing quotas, segregation of jails after race riots, and any public records that indicate one's race. On further review, the Justice is persuaded that the principle of *Hirabayashi* [72] and *Korematsu* [73] that extraordinarily grave needs may justify even racial classifications that disadvantage and stigmatize minority group members[74] is sound. He is also persuaded that no constitutional violation occurs if a classification does no significant harm to anyone. He is uncertain what should be done when special benefits are unambiguously given to blacks, but believes that there is a strong argument that since the fourteenth amendment was designed to protect blacks, benefits for blacks (and perhaps other disadvantaged minority racial groups) should be permitted. His hardest problem is the "benign" housing quota, which in immediate effect does disadvantage black applicants; but he thinks the quota may be distinguishable on the basis of its immediate promotion of integration, the motives of its sponsors, or the likelihood that its long-term effect will be to improve the social position of blacks. He can see that each of the possible distinguishing grounds for the housing quota has serious pitfalls, but does not think they are obviously insupportable under the Constitution. His principle of decision now looks something like this:

Racial classifications that disadvantage or stigmatize members of minority racial groups are unconstitutional unless they are necessitated by a very grave public need or, perhaps, unless they promote integration and the long-term advantage of those groups.

Now it may be argued whether the distinctions suggested by this principle are "possibly acceptable" under the Constitution,[75] but if they are, this principle would satisfy Wechsler's demand, though it leaves many important issues unresolved.

Thus, the theoretical question is reduced to whether there are ever situations in which a judge is confident that a result is correct but for which he can discover no principle of significant generality he would be willing to apply to the other cases that it covers. In ordinary life situations, there are occasions when our reason tells us to behave one way and our intuition

71. *Id.* at 298.
72. Hirabayashi v. United States, 320 U.S. 81 (1943).
73. Korematsu v. United States, 323 U.S. 214 (1944).
74. Compare the opinion of Justices Brennan, White, Marshall, and Blackmun in Regents of the Univ. of Cal. v. Bakke, 98 S. Ct. 2733, 2783 (1978), suggesting that any racial classification that stigmatizes is invalid.
75. My own views on this perplexing topic are developed in Greenawalt, *Judicial Scrutiny of "Benign" Racial Preference in Law School Admissions*, 75 COLUM. L. REV. 559 (1975).

another, and our intuition may represent a deeper reason that takes account of needs that have not reached a conscious level. But the law is largely a set of external standards that guide the judge, and it is doubtful if his role is ever to give sway to subconscious feelings he is incapable of articulating.

Undoubtedly there is some tension between the search for general principles and the notion that the court decides only the case before it. The latter notion expresses more confidence in the judge's ability to reach an appropriate decision on the facts than to make general formulations.[76] Nevertheless, it would seem very rare that a conscientious judge would be unable to come up with some principle of decision that would test his intuitions of a proper result against similar hypothetical facts. He might, of course, decide that for a particular area of law, say nuisance or coerced confessions, factor-weighing is the appropriate approach, but that at least would be a general principle of sorts.

Levi has asserted, "Shocking as it may be, even the case that has no articulated theory to support it, but seems right and is treated as a kind of unique incident, has a place in our jurisprudence." [77] Levi himself leaves doubt whether such cases have a place in constitutional jurisprudence, since he says "the articulation of reasons in the opinion is of greater or at least different importance in constitutional cases to the extent that the court's overriding authority has to be justified." [78] If there is a place in our jurisprudence, constitutional or other, for the cases Levi suggests, it is mainly because judges occasionally rely on reasons that are not generally thought to be legally relevant, not because they can find no principles at all they would apply to other situations. This problem is discussed below.

The conclusion is that the complete inability to articulate a principle of decision of some generality is rare. Undoubtedly judges, like others, are not always precise in stating principles of decision, but after adequate time for reflection, they should be able to come close. Given lower court decisions, extensive briefing, the help of law clerks, and interaction with able colleagues, members of the Supreme Court have advantages over many other judges in their efforts to arrive at a principle of decision.

2. *Underlying Methods of Interpretation.* Wechsler asserts the applicability of his thesis to "every step that is involved in reaching judgment . . .," [79] including the relative compulsion of constitutional language, history, and precedent.[80] By naming these three guides to decision, Wechsler did not mean to exclude others,[81] and we might add to his list new social facts—

---

76. My colleague Benno Schmidt has pointed out in conversation that a confused opinion whose underlying principles cannot be confidently ascertained may have much the same effect of limiting the scope of the decision to the immediate facts as would a very narrowly drawn opinion.
77. Levi, *supra* note 61, at 276.
78. *Id.*
79. PRINCIPLES, POLITICS, AND FUNDAMENTAL LAW, *supra* note 1, at 21.
80. *Id.* at 24.
81. Subsequently he spoke of "the weight to be accorded to the text, to history, to precedent, and to the case for a reformulation of the operative norm." Wechsler, *supra* note 16, at 299.

such as the development of electronic eavesdropping—and changing social values—such as greater equalitarianism and increased acceptance of public regulation of economic matters. Whatever Wechsler believes about particular decisions, he does not deny that judges may properly take changing social facts and values into account, so long as they do so consistently.

In any event, the point to be made here would be applicable even for one who adhered to his original list as the exclusive sources of constitutional interpretation. The point is simply this: our hopes for "neutral principles" in respect to basic techniques of interpretation must be more modest than our hopes in respect to the "principle of law" announced in the holding. The latter may be somewhat open-ended, but we can understand reasonably well the main scope of its application and we can ask whether the court that announces it would be willing to apply it to the cases that it covers.

We must expect less in respect to basic techniques of interpretation. Since opinions are written partly to persuade, judges rarely indicate exactly how close they think a case is. Their opinions give more weight to arguments for the result reached than is actually warranted and less weight to contrary arguments. Let us suppose, to simplify, that the competing arguments are ones from precedent and original intent of the framers, and that the latter barely wins out. An opinion which justifies the result in strong terms will appear to give precedent less weight than the judges actually do and original intent more. It will, to this extent, be an unreliable guide for future cases. So long as judges do not typically try to reflect precisely how close a case is or to indicate candidly the exact weight given to each argument, we cannot expect from their opinions an indication of "comparative weight" that can consistently be applied to other cases involving similar issues of interpretation. Since Wechsler meant his lecture to be a call to traditional standards of judicial performance, not a request for a revolution in styles of opinion writing, we may ask what is a realistic expectation in respect to "neutral principles" on methods of interpretation, absent a radical change in opinions. First, judges should be honest about the interpretive guides on which they rely. They should not say a result is determined by historical intent when they realize that intent is wholly inconclusive and in fact are deciding on grounds of policy. Second, they should not make broad statements about interpretation that they do not believe, or that would not receive their adherence upon reflection. They should not say in one case that historical intent is always controlling if it can be ascertained, and turn around in another case and disregard a clear historical intent. Third, they should explicate the special features of interpretation for particular cases. If they believe some constitutional phrases are particularly open to evolution in terms of changing social facts and values they should say so. Fourth, they should try to act consistently. Even if their opinions do not indicate the precise weight of precedent and original intent, they should aim for a consistent pattern in their decisions, due regard being given to the possibility that among different clauses and different constitutional problems the precise interpretive mix may properly vary.

Even if Wechsler's position were taken as a call for candid indication of comparative weight, judicial heeding of that advice would not wholly eliminate the problem. How much weight is given a factor like original intent in a particular case depends on how heavily that factor suggests one result or another as well as the general significance of the factor. Suppose precedent points moderately in one direction but historical research has produced a very clear indication that the historical intent was contrary. The justices decide to follow historical intent. In the next case calling for similar interpretive techniques, precedent points more strongly for a result and the historical materials, while suggesting a contrary result, do not do so very clearly. The court decides to follow precedent. The court has acted consistently but it would be very difficult to verbalize with precision principles that delineate the difference between the two cases. Pointers there can be, and should be, but it is hard to express exactly how strong evidence of historical intent must be before it overcomes precedential weight of varying force. The difficulties are multiplied when the relevant factors of interpretation are increased and when relevant differences among constitutional provisions and problems are taken into account. Interpreting the equal protection clause is not the same as deciding which federal judges must have life tenure. Even when the same clause is interpreted, interpretive weight may vary depending on the issue that is put. Perhaps, for example, an historical intent to grant an individual right against the government (say against being drawn and quartered) should be treated as more conclusive than an historical intent not to grant a right (say against capital punishment), though both concerns involve the cruel and unusual punishment clause.

We must conclude that whatever changes were made in opinions, judges would often not be able to give us verbal formulas of interpretative weight whose application to other cases could be clearly perceived. Because of the absence of such formulations and because of the complexity of weighing competing arguments, it would remain difficult for an observer to evaluate the consistency of a judge from case to case, and difficult even for the judge who aims for consistency to be sure that he was not being swayed by nonrelevant factors in particular cases. In this respect, the use of interpretive guides is similar to the factor weighing approach to particular areas of law like nuisance.

B.   *Conflicts With Other Goals of Judicial Action*

We have seen that generally there is a positive correlation between neutral principles and appropriate decisions that will appear legitimate to nonparticipants in the judicial process and will promote the positive future development of the law. But occasionally compromises with the aim of neutral principles may actually further some of these goals better than would a judge's candid statement of all the reasons for his decision. In this section, we shall examine some circumstances in which judges may self-consciously choose opinions that are defective from Wechsler's point of view. Judges may sacrifice neutral principles in order to achieve a majority opinion, to obscure legally relevant grounds for decision, and to conceal actual grounds of decision whose legal relevance or power is suspect.

1. *Majority Opinions.* As some noteworthy cases have shown,[82] when each Justice in the majority of the Supreme Court writes his own opinion explaining his vote, and does so without joining a common opinion, the result is not likely to be very effective guidance for the lower courts. And given the widespread presupposition that the law that judges interpret is comprehensible, it is doubtful if separate opinions pursuing different lines, however principled, convey the sense of legitimacy to the American public as effectively as does a majority opinion. The English practice of separate opinions may suggest that the American preference for majority opinions is partly a matter of tradition. Nonetheless, majority opinions appear to carry genuine benefits. Indeed, the uneasiness and uncertainty that are introduced when Justices voting together adopt highly disparate approaches to some controversial topic, as occurred for many years in regard to obscenity, lead one to wonder whether that alternative is to be preferred to the practice of unenlightening per curiam dispositions that Professor Wechsler criticized in his Holmes lecture.[83] Yet another reason for majority opinions is judicial economy. Given the caseload of the Supreme Court and the importance of many of its cases, a Justice who felt constrained to spell out in detail his minor complaints concerning the analysis of each majority opinion to which he did not subscribe *in toto* would seriously waste energies better spent on more fundamental issues.

Understandably, therefore, American judges generally think majority opinions are desirable and occasionally they regard it as important that their court not be too closely divided, an attitude most common when an issue is politically controversial. As a consequence, judges often compromise their own views. Each of two judges may have a principled basis for reaching a result, but neither may accept all the reasoning of the other. Since no two judges will have precisely the same views on deep issues of judicial role and legal interpretation, the likelihood of some difference is particularly great in respect to those matters. The result of mutual concessions may necessarily be an opinion that does not stand Wechsler's test very well. The difficulties can be even greater when unanimity or near unanimity is sought, and it is probably not coincidence that the much criticized opinions in *Shelley* and *Brown* were both unanimous. If the members of the Supreme Court badly want to speak with one voice, the pulling and hauling necessary to produce a single opinion may not yield an intellectually satisfying expression.

Supreme Court Justices, and other judges, vary considerably in their willingness to join opinions they do not find intellectually persuasive. To say that compromise is sometimes appropriate is not of course to endorse

---

82. *See, e.g.,* Furman v. Georgia, 408 U.S. 238 (1972); New York Times Co. v. United States, 403 U.S. 713 (1971) (the Pentagon Papers case).
83. PRINCIPLES, POLITICS, AND FUNDAMENTAL LAW, *supra* note 1, at 28-30.

it in every instance. Profound realist that he is, Wechsler has readily acknowledged in conversation the possible conflict between achieving majority opinions and stating in principled form the reasons for one's vote and has advanced no simple method of resolving that dilemma.

2. *Obscuring Legally Relevant Grounds of Decision.* In ordinary cases, judges will have no reason to obscure agreed upon grounds of decision, but sensitive cases may present special problems. Eugene Rostow has spoken of the high sense of strategy and tactics the Supreme Court requires:

> Its influence on our public life depends in large part on the Court's skill in advocacy and its sensitivity to the powerful forces which from time to time, in different combinations, must resist its will. When the Court decides to accept or reject cases, to decide them on this ground or that, to issue warning dicta which are then not made the basis for decision, it is necessarily performing a function far more complex than Professor Wechsler's call for candor in meeting *every* issue in *every* case on the basis of neutral principles of adequate generality. If the Court had in fact lived by Professor Wechsler's rule, it would have disappeared long ago from the stage of American life.[84]

Let us imagine again a Justice faced with school segregation along racial lines. After careful reflection, he is persuaded that the soundest constitutional position is that racial classifications stigmatizing blacks are unconstitutional unless required by urgent necessity. He recognizes that under that principle the laws against interracial marriages are condemned to invalidity. He views the sociological evidence about the harmful effects of segregated schools upon black children as inconclusive and of doubtful relevance. But, aware that a decision requiring desegregation of schools will itself cause tremendous resentment and considerable resistance, he fears that an opinion making it apparent that interracial marriages are constitutionally protected will seriously amplify those problems. He wonders, quite apart from the need to achieve a unanimous opinion, whether it is not socially preferable to cast the prohibition of segregated schools on the narrowest conceivable ground, even if that ground implies possible distinctions among practices of segregation that he does not think relevant. Open development of the legally relevant similarities and differences can perhaps be postponed until the public has swallowed the first step and is in a more accepting mood for subsequent steps. To follow this course would plainly breach Wechsler's model. Discussion of whether such manipulation of grounds of decision is ever warranted is postponed until the next subsection.

3. *Grounds of Decision Whose Legal Relevance or Power is Suspect.* The problem raised here, like that just treated, involves the suppression of true grounds of decision in favor of ones that appear more acceptable.

---

84. E.V. Rostow, *supra* note 41, at 34.

Here, however, the judge's concern is whether his actual bases for decision will be accepted as ones on which it is proper for him to rely as a judge. It is simplest to illustrate the point starkly in connection with a situation in which if he follows his accepted appellate role the judge believes he will effectively sanction injustice in the particular case. Imagine an appellate court reviewing a determination by a trial judge, sitting without a jury, in favor of *W,* the rich white defendant in a negligence case. There are no procedural defects or mistaken decisions on legal issues in the trial judge's treatment of the case. Since the trial judge was acting without a jury, the appellate court is "supposed" to reverse his ruling only if *B,* the poor black plaintiff, was entitled to a directed verdict, that is, if the appellate court can ascertain that *B* should have won even if all disputed evidence is resolved favorably to *W.* The appellate judges carefully review all the documentary and oral evidence and conclude that the undisputed evidence comes very, very close to establishing *W*'s negligence, but that if all disputed evidence were resolved in *W*'s favor, a decision for him would be warranted. The testimony of *B*'s witnesses is much more plausible than that of *W*'s witnesses and on the basis of the transcript they appear more truthful. The judges find it hard to believe that an objective trier of fact could possibly have decided for *W,* but they recognize that such a decision is not demonstrably wrong. They happen to know from personal acquaintance that the trial judge is virulently prejudiced against poor blacks and believe that his bias has carried over in other cases to his judicial behavior, and they attribute his decision to this bias. They are almost sure that *B* should have won the case. What should they do? They can follow the ordinary practice and simply affirm. They can reveal their assumption of the judge's bias and reverse, presumably ordering a new trial. They can write the opinion in such a way that *W*'s undisputed conduct is treated as negligent, so narrowing their description of the conduct that their decision will have no consequences for future negligence cases. The third approach is obviously not consistent with neutral principles but there are serious problems with the other two approaches. The first sustains a result that is almost certainly unjust in the particular case. The second produces as a ground of decision the fact that the trial judge's decision was probably due to bias, a fact that is not apparent from the record of the case and has not been independently established. The judges may fear that if they announce their personal knowledge of the trial judge as a ground for decision, they will not only violate accepted "canons" but also introduce a potentially chaotic element into appellate review. If such grounds were generally accepted, litigants would outdo themselves trying to demonstrate bad qualities of judges who have decided against them, and personal relations among judges would be rendered tense, to say the least. The temptation to follow the third course, to write a disingenous opinion producing a just result and having no ill consequences for the future would be very great.

Even when judges do not consciously manipulate the facts, their personal knowledge may view how they look at a case. One has the feeling that in the 1960's, when the Supreme Court was reviewing convictions of civil rights demonstrators in the South, the Justices were sympathetic to the demonstrators and distrustful of many southern police officials and state trial judges and juries. They may have viewed the records differently from how they would have if the demonstrators had had less worthy causes and there was less reason to suppose official bias, yet this does not appear to be crucial, or even relevant, if the opinions are parsed.[85]

Supreme Court Justices may sometimes face a dilemma that relates to the broad social implications of a case. They may believe that a decision one way will have a great positive effect on society, but their reasons may not be in the traditional catalogue of legal justifications. Many observers approved the Supreme Court's involvement in the reapportionment area because the state legislatures had failed so miserably to apply corrective measures to gross malapportionments. And the one man-one vote rule may be defended as preferable to a test that would require courts to judge the political effect and fairness of particular malapportionments, an immense and potentially treacherous undertaking.[86] Yet these rationales are not reflected in the majority opinion in *Reynolds v. Sims*,[87] which is cast as if equal protection obviously requires one man-one vote, quite apart from the sad history of malapportionment and quite apart from problems of administering alternative standards. Let us suppose a Justice did not buy the rather simplistic approach of the majority opinion, but believed there was a great need for judicial involvement in apportionment and that one man-one vote was the only feasible standard to administer. Should he write an opinion making the existence of a constitutional right turn on the general failures of state legislatures to deal with malapportionments? And should he defend the one man-one vote rule solely in terms of administrability—thereby acknowledging that malapportionments, themselves defensible in terms of constitutional values, will be struck down because courts are not equipped to draw the necessary distinctions? If not, should he resist judicial involvement in apportionment altogether; or should he accept grounding the one man-one vote rule in an apparently more solid base that he regards as overly simple. The Justice in question regards reapportionment as sufficiently unique to bar untoward effects in other equal protection cases if the "simplistic" rationale is advanced, and further, he is confident that the result will win wide popular acceptance. Surely the Justice faces a real dilemma, for the price of intellectual honesty, if he could command a majority vote, might be to render the Court more vulnerable to attack.

There is a more subtle and pervasive problem than the total suppression of the true grounds of decision. I have already mentioned the typical practice of overstating the value of arguments in favor of the result reached. But

---

85. *See, e.g.,* Edwards v. South Carolina, 372 U.S. 229 (1963); Deutsch, *Neutrality, Legitimacy, and the Supreme Court: Some Intersections Between Law and Political Science,* 20 STAN. L. REV. 169, 202 (1968).
86. A fuller discussion is in Greenawalt, Book Review, 19 STAN. L. REV. 1151 (1967).
87. 377 U.S. 533 (1964).

the matter is often more complex. Some arguments for the result are over-stated at the expense not only of contrary arguments but also at the expense of other supportive arguments. When they can do so plausibly, courts often understate the degree of their own creativity, and emphasize arguments of textual language, historical intent, and precedent in comparison with argu-ments of justice and social welfare that may actually carry more weight. It is in such instances that vigorous adherence to Wechsler's model might curb innovation. Judges would either have to confess to the degree of their own power or they would have to bridle its exercise.

One way to look at this subject is to perceive judges as covertly manipu-lating concepts in order to assert power they are not willing to recognize openly. On such a view, one can take the position that since courts, of all organs of government, are least subject to political checks, their power must be exposed clearly to public scrutiny and judges must not engage in covert expansion of it. This is the view Wechsler's thesis suggests. This position does not necessarily imply restraint; it may be thought that public acceptance of great judicial creativity would be forthcoming,[88] but the position would lead to judicial restraint if judges were too cautious to try the experiment. A view fundamentally opposed to Wechsler's is that since judges, at least modern Supreme Court Justices, generally exercise power in beneficent ways and since limitation is the likely unfortunate consequence of complete open-ness, intelligent observers should accept and approve (though perhaps not talk too much about) manipulations of concepts that preserve that power.

There is another somewhat more mystical and less tidy way of looking at the problem. It may be thought that judges who cite as compelling precedents and historical intent that plainly are not dispositive often do not really intend to mislead. Their invocations of past sources may be seen not as purportedly candid explanations of the grounds of decision, but as sym-bolic assurance of truths about judicial disinterestedness and legal continuity that are too complex to express literally in opinions. On this view, it would be mistaken to apply the neutral principles thesis rigorously to matters of interpretation, for the thesis fails to acknowledge the proper allegorical func-tion of that aspect of opinions. If one believes, as Wechsler does and I do, that honest explanation of one's actions is a vital safeguard against irre-sponsible exercise of power,[89] he will not feel very comfortable with the view that opinions are not always to be taken literally. Yet it is hard to deny the grain of truth in that view and the support it has in past judicial action.[90]

If it is the fact that frequently in a court's marshalling of reasons for decision and occasionally even as to the principle of decision or holding, the

---

88. *See* Miller & Scheflin, *supra* note 33.
89. Lon Fuller's suggestion that governments are more likely to act morally when officials must explain their actions to themselves and others is appropriate here. *See* L. FULLER, THE MORALITY OF LAW 158-59 (1964).
90. It may be countered that unsophisticated earlier judges really believed the process of interpretation was as simple as their opinions implied, and that their delusions or limited under-standing provide no warrant for conscious misstatements by modern judges.

counsel of neutral principles can run into conflict with other judicial goals, such as doing justice in the particular case, developing the law in a socially desirable way, and winning acceptance of judicial action, how should judges resolve the conflict? Wechsler's answer in his published work is clear. In his Holmes lecture he said, "The virtue or demerit of a judgment turns . . . entirely on the reasons that support it and their adequacy to maintain any choice of values it decrees . . . ."[91] As he subsequently made clear, he did not mean this literally,[92] since of two principled results one can be more sound than another,[93] and, one might add, of two unprincipled results one can be socially less desirable than another.[94] Nevertheless, he still maintains that principled support is a negative criterion, a minimal requirement,[95] essential if a decision is to possess, in the words of the original lecture, "legal quality."[96] A judge is, therefore, not acting properly as a judge if he consciously sacrifices neutral principles to achieve other goals.

At the other end of the spectrum is the position that "neutral principles" are essentially a tactical device by which judges sustain their power.[97] Judges are perceived, like other political actors, as wishing to maintain or increase their power,[98] and "neutral principles" are a "maxim of prudence" for winning acceptance of its exercise. Martin Shapiro, a political scientist, has developed this view forcefully.[99] Since Shapiro is more interested in describing judicial reality than counseling judges, he does not consider what an individual judge should do when he believes neutral principles will disserve the maintenance of power, but one who starts from Shapiro's premises might well conclude that principles should be dispensed with when not efficacious. Thus, the Justice who thinks the "simplistic" theory in support of one man-one vote will win easier acceptance than the theory that actually persuades him to embrace that standard should suffer no qualms about joining or authoring an opinion written on simplistic lines.[100]

It is possible to view neutral principles as something more than a maxim of prudence and something less than an absolute requirement. What-

---

91. Principles, Politics, and Fundamental Law, *supra* note 1, at 27.
92. In correspondence Wechsler has written, "By no possible reading did I say that the Supreme Court should have cast out of its reckoning the likelihood that a decision one way or another would effect 'an enduring contribution to the quality of our society.'" Shapiro, *The Supreme Court and Constitutional Adjudication: Of Politics and Neutral Principles,* 31 Geo. Wash. L. Rev. 587, 592 (1963).
93. Recall that Wechsler regards the clear and present danger test as principled though defective.
94. For example, the Dred Scott decision is attacked not only for being unprincipled but also for being socially catastrophic.
95. Wechsler, *supra* note 16, at 299.
96. Principles, Politics, and Fundamental Law, *supra* note 1, at 27.
97. *See* Shapiro, *supra* note 92, at 601-04.
98. One wonders why political scientists so rarely discuss humans who are anxious about the exercise of power and are actually pleased when their authority is carefully limited. Perhaps, because such people tend not to be politically active.
99. Shapiro, *supra* note 92, at 601-04.
100. One might thus analogize judicial opinions to legal arguments by private counsel who make principled arguments to courts only because, and insofar as, these arguments are likely to persuade the courts to decide in the favor of their clients and to develop the law in directions sought by the interests they represent. In my view, government lawyers have a responsibility not to make intellectually untenable arguments even if they promise success.

ever may be the importance of neutral principles from the perspective of grand political theory, it may be desirable for individual judges to regard their attainment, or at least the struggle for their attainment, as a crucial aspect of their role. This position will seem particularly appealing if one doubts the astuteness of judges in the arts of political prognostication and propaganda.[101] But to say that the search for neutral principles is an aspect of the judicial role is not to guarantee that there will never be conflicts between their attainment and other aspects of that role or the social purposes that the role ordinarily serves. As Mortimer and Sanford Kadish have so persuasively suggested, judges like other officials face occasions on which their performance of a role in the usual manner will defeat important social ends that role is designed to further.[102] It is too simple to say that on every occasion they must simply adhere to the prescribed role and damn the consequences.

What I am suggesting is an intermediate position toward neutral principles, one that permits their occasional sacrifice but regards them as an important aspect of the judicial role, to be taken as intrinsically worthy of attainment by individual judges.[103] Some further refinement is necessary. Are neutral principles to be taken merely as one aspect among others of the judicial role, to be freely balanced against other considerations? A crucial feature of our social system is a distribution of governmental powers. Courts make decisions when there is a need for reflective and disinterested evaluation of focused issues; they are supposed to accept political choices made in the Constitution and by other branches of government. Neutral principles are critically linked to the limitations on their power; principled justification is both the appropriate basis for decisions and the external evidence of their legitimacy. It is, thus, not one feature of the judicial role but a fundamental and central feature, one that should be knowingly abandoned in a significant way by a conscientious judge only for the most compelling reasons and after agonizing examination of the alternatives.

IV. BROADER THEORIES OF JUDICIAL RESPONSIBILITY
IN CONSTITUTIONAL CASES

As intended by Wechsler the neutral principles thesis is a comparatively modest one, not resolving all the intricate problems of interpretation that confront a judge in constitutional, or other, cases. If some overriding theory

---

101. See the forceful discussion in Linde, *Judges, Critics, and the Realist Tradition*, 82 YALE L.J. 227 (1972).
102. M. KADISH & S. KADISH, DISCRETION TO DISOBEY (1973).
103. Another sort of intermediate position is Bickel's: that judges must be principled on the "merits" but need not be so in avoiding decision. A. BICKEL, *supra* note 42; A. BICKEL, THE SUPREME COURT AT THE BAR OF POLITICS (1962). Because the arguments for and against neutral principles apply to both kinds of determinations, his thesis in its pure form is not maintainable. *See* Deutsch, *supra* note 85, at 217; Gunther, *The Subtle Vices of the "Passive Virtues"—A Comment on Principle and Expediency in Judicial Review*, 64 COLUM. L. REV. 1 (1964). The most that can plausibly be argued is that deviation from principle is more often acceptable on matters of "justiciability."

of constitutional decision could guide judges toward correct decisions, the search for neutral principles might play a role, but one that would be subsidiary and dependent. If, however, clearcut interpretative guides are not forthcoming, the aspiration for neutral principles is an even more important feature of what informed society can ask of its judges.

In this section I examine some actual and possible theories of interpretation that purport to formulate what a Supreme Court Justice's responsibilities are in constitutional cases.[104] My conclusion is that each is theoretically defective, and that insofar as any of them are cast in ways that make them plausible, they would not, even if accepted, be of much assistance for actual Justices. That does not mean it is impossible to say a great deal about the responsibilities of constitutional interpretation, only that those responsibilities are too complex to yield to capsulization.

The treatment in this section is necessarily summary.

A. The Intent of the Framers

It has been suggested in Supreme Court opinions and by scholars that the Court's duty in a constitutional case is to ascertain and effectuate the intent of the draftsmen.[105] In a narrow sense of intent—that is, investigation whether the specific practice was deemed unconstitutional by the framers—such an approach is plainly mistaken, for it forecloses attention to relevant changes of social facts. The framers had no view on wiretapping and electronic eavesdropping, but these practices constitute an evil of the sort covered by the fourth amendment and it is appropriate to treat them as searches. Similarly, the Court properly took account of the modern urban environment in deciding whether a stop and a frisk could be carried out on a probability less than probable cause. Known social facts may affect constitutional decisions because of new perceptions as well as new conditions. Suppose it could be established conclusively that capital punishment served no deterrent purpose, and it could also be established that the framers accepted that penalty on the premise that it did deter. This new perception of fact might alter the constitutional assessment.

Once it is acknowledged that the Constitution is hard to amend and that piecemeal amendment to deal with many small problems would undercut much of the symbolic majesty of the present document, it follows, at a minimum, that courts should take a broad view of the language and intent of the framers, looking at their underlying spirit rather than inquiring only whether a particular practice was meant to be barred. A more plausible framers'

---

104. I have intentionally narrowed the focus here to Supreme Court Justices to avoid discussion of the duty that other courts have to follow authoritative Supreme Court interpretations on constitutional as well as other questions of federal law.

105. *See, e.g.,* Home Building & Loan Ass'n v. Blaisdell, 290 U.S. 398 (1934); R. Berger, Government by Judiciary 363-96 (1977). For a helpful summary and analysis, see Munzer & Nickel, *Does the Constitution Mean What It Always Meant?,* 77 Colum. L. Rev. 1029, 1030-33 (1977).

intent approach would require Justices to apply to the legal issues before them the basic values implicit in the framers' work.

One problem with this approach as the sole guide to interpretation is that it would exclude individual precedents and judicial lines of development except insofar as they shed light on the framers' purposes by convincing analysis and by evidence of the assessment of previous judges. But suppose the sitting judge examines all the arguments and exercises all the humility of which he is capable, and still believes that the previous decisions are wrong. At some point a line of decisions is so firmly embedded in the life of the society that something more than a judgment of imperfect origin is needed before it is overthrown. For example, the basic desegregation decisions are now such an accepted part of our law, whatever may be thought about busing and reverse discrimination, that the Court would be ill-advised to overturn *Brown* even if it thought the decision was wrong.[106] It would take a strong sense that its effects are deleterious and unjust before a Justice should vote to overrule it. Thus, the intent of the framers' approach does not adequately account for precedent and established social institutions.

Nor in theory would it allow adjustment to changing social values, since the Constitution would settle the respective weight values are to be given. Needless to say, a modern judge is hard put to weigh values as he thinks a framer who lived in a different society would have, even if he could get over the problem of finding a representative framer when in fact there were different framers with different values who accepted the same legal language. Some values, of course, cannot be ascribed to the framers; they were not Communists or vegetarians. But within a wide range, the judge is left with little to go on other than the social values he now finds widely accepted and in which he believes. Thus, this broad version of the "intent of the framers" is likely to let in present values inadvertently through the back door. But insofar as it does not do so, insofar as it excludes present values, it excludes something that should be of significance in many cases. Because of the difficulty and undesirability of frequent amendment, a judge properly interprets the Constitution, and particularly its more open-ended phrases, in light of the stable value premises of the society in which he lives. We now live, for example, in a society that is much more equalitarian and more accepting of public regulation of economic matters than was the society of the authors of the original Constitution and the Bill of Rights and the society of the authors of the fourteenth amendment. It is appropriate that the contracts clause and the rights against government takings of property have been somewhat eroded and the content of the equal protection right markedly expanded.

The framers' intent approach might accommodate this need to refer to contemporary values by suggesting that the framers invited the development

---

106. Compare the interesting opinion of Justice Stevens in Runyon v. McCrary, 427 U.S. 160, 189 (1976) (concurring opinion), taking this approach to the issue of statutory interpretation resolved in Jones v. Alfred H. Mayer Co., 392 U.S. 409 (1968).

of constitutional law as social values, or the moral insight of judges,[107] developed. Beyond the obvious fact that the framers often meant to state broad principles rather than precisely defined legal rules, I am not aware of historical evidence that they adverted to the possibility that later values would supplant their own or that they regarded it as a positively desirable feature of the Constitution that their own views about specific practices might be overridden. And even if that view is plausible in respect to some provisions of the Constitution,[108] Justices appropriately give a degree of weight to present social values when interpreting other provisions, such as the privilege against self-incrimination, whose formulation was almost certainly meant to be a shorthand for an existing body of law.

Whatever its theoretical merits, an "intent of the framers" approach supplemented in this way would leave a Justice little guidance on how heavily to count modern values in comparison with those of the framers. Rendering the theory more plausible would virtually eliminate its utility.

B. *The Result That Is Socially Most Desirable*

Though many legal theorists have emphasized that judges in deciding cases must often consider whether their decisions will cause socially desirable consequences,[109] and though social desirability is appropriately given weight in many constitutional cases,[110] no one has proposed social desirability as the single ultimate standard for Justices in constitutional cases. It is easy to see why a simple reference to social desirability is inadequate. Judges are not supposed generally to decide what outcome to a particular constitutional dispute will produce the most social good. The stupidity of legislation is not in itself sufficient warrant for invalidation.

But the standard of social desirability might be made more sophisticated. The judge might be told: Reach the decision that is socially most desirable, taking into account the relative responsibilities and competences of courts and other institutions of government and also the expectations created by past judicial decisions. Under this approach the harmful effects of disregarding constitutional language and legislative judgment could outweigh a socially desirable outcome to the particular dispute. Any plausible approach to

---

107. *See* R. DWORKIN, TAKING RIGHTS SERIOUSLY 131-49 (1977).

108. Wechsler himself has suggested that the text and history of the fourteenth amendment "give the Court broad freedom of decision but its work is ultimately measured by the soundness of its judgment in the circumstances of our time." H. WECHSLER, THE NATIONALIZATION OF CIVIL LIBERTIES AND CIVIL RIGHTS 20 (1968).

109. *See* B. CARDOZO, THE NATURE OF THE JUDICIAL PROCESS 73-97 (1921); R. WASSERSTROM, THE JUDICIAL DECISION (1961); Deutsch, *Precedent and Adjudication,* 83 YALE L.J. 1553 (1974).

110. Open-ended standards like "reasonable search" imply some balancing of social harms and benefits; reference to social desirability is also appropriate when the relevant legal materials are inconclusive; and if it appears clear that a result would cause great social harm, perhaps a judge is warranted in declining to reach that result though persuaded the legal materials point in that direction. *See generally* Greenawalt, *supra* note 27.

constitutional decision must give weight to institutional needs and competence,[111] and "neutral principles" is itself partly based on that assumption. Nevertheless the social desirability test, as modified, is not a comprehensive and adequate guide. First, in some situations in which a Justice might be convinced that one result is socially desirable and that an opinion could be written that would do no general damage, he should still refrain from acting without genuine constitutional authorization. Decision is at least partly backward looking, and in a way that cannot be explained by saying that looking backward is simply the most desirable way to decide how to go forward. Second, even in cases in which a Justice could after-the-fact say "my decision is socially desirable because legislative authority is preserved," usually that is not the basis on which he makes his decisions. He is part of a system in which legislative supremacy, within limits, is presumed, and it is his legal duty to accept it, without calculating its social desirability in particular cases.[112] Thus, the "social desirability" test would strangely use as a criterion of decision a consideration which a Justice is not supposed to focus upon in most constitutional cases. Finally, if a Justice did use the test in a suitably sophisticated form it would not be a great deal of help because it would not indicate what comparative weight to give to language, history, precedent, changing facts, and changing values.

C. *The Result That Is Fairest or Morally Best*

Obviously it is not appropriate in every constitutional case for a Justice to try to decide which outcome is fairest or otherwise morally best.[113] Some constitutional issues, such as the power of states to affect interstate commerce, do not raise issues of morality. And it is also clear that legislatures are constitutionally free to do some things that are less fair or appropriate morally than their alternatives.[114]

If all constitutional cases cannot be reduced to moral evaluation, perhaps at least some can. Ronald Dworkin, for example, has urged that judges are supposed to develop the moral concepts implicit in various open-ended phrases of the Constitution, such as the cruel and unusual punishment clause.[115] Since he concedes some relevance to matters such as precedent, he does not say a judge should be exclusively concerned with the morally

---

111. *See, e.g.,* United States v. Carolene Products Co., 304 U.S. 144, 154 n.4 (1938). My colleague Louis Lusky has developed an elaborate critique of the Supreme Court's performance grounded on the premises of the famous footnote. L. LUSKY, BY WHAT RIGHT? (1975).

112. *See* R. SARTORIUS, *supra* note 38, at 181-210 (1975).

113. I have mentioned the moral value of fairness because so many legal issues involve it, but other moral values are also often at stake. I assume that the inquiry whether a result is morally best is not always synonymous with the inquiry whether a result is most desirable socially, but I do not develop that assumption and the analysis does not depend upon it.

114. It might be answered that fairness is what the parties reasonably expect; but that is only one kind, or aspect, of fairness, and, in any event, courts sometimes justifiably reach decisions that are unexpected even by the best counselled parties.

115. R. DWORKIN, *supra* note 107, at 131-49. For a fuller critical account than is provided here, see Munzer & Nickel, *supra* note 105, at 1037-41.

right outcome, but that is the judge's major inquiry. There is, however, little indication that the framers meant to authorize judges simply to give effect to moral notions they believe correct, substantially unconstrained by previous legal judgments or prevailing social morality. Nor, apart from the framers' design, would such an authorization seem appropriate for our constitutional scheme. Suppose, to take an extreme example, a judge was persuaded that all imprisonment was grossly immoral, that amputation of limbs, exile, and release back into the community after moral condemnation were far more humane and preferable forms of disposition.[116] Surely given the history, general acceptance, and uniform use of imprisonment, he could not properly declare all imprisonment to be unconstitutional. The reason why, in contrast, constitutional abolition of capital punishment is a plausible position is because many states do not have it, many people do not accept it, and the arguments against it (*e.g.,* that it does not deter) are cast in terms of principles of morality that are widely approved. It would be more accurate to say that in interpreting these open-ended provisions, Justices should give great weight to the stable underlying moral sentiments of the community, though this would permit them to reach rational conclusions that might differ from particular moral judgments of the majority of society,[117] would allow them to rely on their own moral judgment when community sentiment was unclear, and might even permit some independent weight to be given to their own judgment on "ultimate" questions.

David Richards has suggested a different connection between moral norms and constitutional adjudication.[118] He urges that the Constitution embodies moral principles corresponding with those of John Rawls's theory of justice,[119] namely the priority of liberty, equality of opportunity, and the difference principle. Professor Richards does not claim these principles can be the basis for interpretation of all constitutional provisions, but they are crucial for issues of individual rights. The underlying premises of Richards's position are that the Constitution reflects a social contract theory in which the framers believed, that the stated principles reflect the most adequate version of social contract theory, and that therefore the Constitution should be interpreted in light of the theory that incorporates those principles.

There is a flaw in this analysis, which is most apparent in connection with the difference principle. According to the difference principle, inequalities can be justified only if they benefit the most disadvantaged groups in society. Thus, differences in income are warranted insofar as they increase production and allow even poor people a higher income than would be possible if all incomes were equal. Richards does not maintain that courts

---

116. I say the example is extreme because the constitutional argument seems so implausible; I do not take the moral position of the hypothetical judge to be indisputably fallacious.

117. As, for example, if the evidence indicated clearly that capital punishment did not serve values most members of the community believed it did serve.

118. *See* D. RICHARDS, THE MORAL CRITICISM OF LAW 44-56 (1977).

119. J. RAWLS, *supra* note 53. Richards develops a theory close to Rawls's in D. RICHARDS, A THEORY OF REASONS FOR ACTION (1971).

should try to apply the difference principle in constitutional cases, sensibly recognizing that courts are ill-equipped for the task. But surely there is a more fundamental objection. The social contract theory in which the framers believed did not include anything like the difference principle. The Lockean natural rights in which they believed are indeed in severe tension with the difference principle. Even if Rawls's and Richards's theory is the best social contract theory, it is not part of the theory of our Constitution.

It can be more plausibly argued that the priority of liberty and equality of opportunity are implicit in our Constitution, and it is these that do the real work in Richards's analysis. Nonetheless the same problem lingers in less obvious form. Though by the time of the fourteenth amendment some notion of equality of opportunity may have existed, it was much less rigorous than that subscribed to by Rawls and Richards to the extent their theory would require organized societal efforts to overcome disadvantages of birth. And priority of liberty as the framers understood it did not extend to many matters of "private morals," such as sexual behavior. If the Court considers criminal penalties for homosexual acts or techniques for financing public schools that permit rich neighborhoods to have better schools than poor ones,[120] the question remains why the Court should apply Rawls's principles, even assuming them to be morally right, in preference to the version of social contract in which the framers believed. One could continue to try to read the Rawlsian analysis back into the framers by saying that it represents a more developed version of what they accepted; but it is more satisfactory to argue that a correct moral outcome is itself deserving of considerable weight and to urge that as the reason why these principles should have some influence even if they go beyond the framers' notions. But, once that point is conceded, priority of liberty and equality of opportunity must take their place with other interpretive guides; and it cannot be argued that every constitutional decision that violates those canons of moral justice is necessarily wrong.

D. *Legal Materials and Discovery of Law*

Recently theories have been advanced that dispute the previously accepted positivist notion that in very hard cases judges no longer discover the law but make the law. The gist of these new theories is that the legal materials themselves are rich enough so that they truly provide an answer in every, or almost every, case.[121] That is not to say a relevant rule of law will always be ready at hand, but that existing materials, including institutional structures, indicate the weight appropriately given to various values and that an accurate weighing of these values will produce a correct result. As Rolf

---

120. Richards's analysis of particular constitutional issues is extraordinarily illuminating and highly relevant, even if one does not accept all of his more general theory of constitutional interpretation.

121. *See* R. DWORKIN, *supra* note 107, at 81-130; Dworkin, *No Right Answer?*, in LAW, MORALITY AND SOCIETY 58 (P.M.S. Hacker & J. Raz eds. 1977); Dworkin, *Seven Critics*, 11 GA. L. REV. 1201, 1241-50, 1264-67 (1977). *See also* R. SARTORIUS, *supra* note 38, at 181-210 (1975).

Sartorius puts it, the decision should be the one that coheres best with all authoritative legal standards.[122]

One obvious question about constitutional law under this theory is how far that law can properly be affected by changes in statutory and common law. Presumably these changes may be given some effect, perhaps more with some constitutional provisions than others, but they cannot be permitted to override fundamental constitutional values. Assuming this problem can be handled, serious and more general difficulties confront any theory of this sort. To some legal theorists, including myself, it seems implausible to suppose that even with their expanding content, legal materials will yield an answer to all the novel questions that are raised.[123] And it is uncertain whether any such theory can deal adequately with the problem of "mistakes," legal norms that point in contrary directions. Moreover, since judges in constitutional, and other, cases are sometimes required to make assessments of social desirability and morality, using their own perspectives or those of the community, clearly the legal materials alone cannot provide a correct answer to those cases, as Sartorius explicitly recognizes.[124] Finally, in cases that are very close, a judge should be recognized as an instrument for incremental legal change, and even if he believes the legal materials tip slightly in one direction, a firm conviction that his own and community views on morality and social desirability push strongly in the other should be sufficient to lead him to decide in that way.[125]

Apart from these theoretical difficulties, such a standard, though suggestive of how judges continue to look for guidance when clear answers are not forthcoming, is not really much help for the judge trying to decide between different modes of interpretation. It is cast at such a general level that a judge who accepted it would still have to resolve questions of comparative weight as best he could.

CONCLUSION: THE ENDURING SIGNIFICANCE OF NEUTRAL PRINCIPLES

Some relatively simple standards that try to encompass all of a judge's duty in constitutional decision are obviously wrong. More plausible standards can still be perceived to have serious theoretical flaws. And, quite apart from these difficulties, they provide little practical guidance for judges or critics. Finally, all these theories say little about the art of opinion writing,

---

122. R. SARTORIUS, *supra* note 38, at 197.
123. *See* Munzer, *Right Answers, Preexisting Rights, and Fairness*, 11 GA. L. REV. 1055 (1977). Both Dworkin and Sartorius do recognize the possibility that in some cases the arguments for a decision each way might be of precisely equal strength. *See* R. SARTORIUS, *supra* note 38, at 201; Dworkin, *Seven Critics*, *supra* note 121, at 1241-50. Sartorius seems to regard that possibility as more likely in practice than does Dworkin, but believes judges will still do best if they proceed as if there is a uniquely correct decision. *Cf.* Greenawalt, *supra* note 27, at 1043-44 (developing the distinction between acting as if there is always a right answer and believing there is always such an answer).
124. R. SARTORIUS, *supra* note 38, at 190-91.
125. A complete account of my views is found in Greenawalt, *supra* note 27, at 1035-53 (1977).

one of the crucial aspects of the judge's craft. It is a great strength of "neutral principles" that it relates to opinions as well as decisions, and forces a judge to confront the relationship between the two. It is also a standard of both theoretical integrity and practical significance. Judges can examine what they do to see how far they are stating principles to which they are willing to adhere and to reexamine tentative judgments when the reasoning supporting them falls short. Not least, neutral principles concern that aspect of legal craft which law professors can best convey to law students. The merciless examination of legal reasoning is, after all, the law professor's profession.

Certainly "neutral principles" alone does not provide a comprehensive guide to constitutional adjudication. Judges must make extraordinarily subtle choices between modes of interpretation, any of which might be defended on principled grounds. The judge's task is not easy, especially when he must resolve the sorts of troubling constitutional issues that make their way to the Supreme Court. Perhaps critics should not be too harsh when Supreme Court opinions fail to state fully reasoned justifications in some of these cases. The faculty of precise generalization is not a simple one to acquire and employ, even for able and experienced lawyers, and as the long history of criticism by other judges and academics evidences, no court escapes unscathed when its opinions are carefully dissected.[126] Some departures from neutral principles are, as we have seen, actually justifiable, since judges need often to compromise in order to agree on majority opinions and, on rarer occasions, may have adequate reasons for intentionally obscuring the grounds of decision. Nonetheless, "neutral principles" does state a standard of which judges should always be conscious and to which, in the absence of very strong countervailing reasons, they should always aspire.

The attention Herbert Wechsler's lecture has commanded over the years is partially to be explained by its elegance and the vital interest in the cases he discussed. But the larger explanation is its eloquent reassertion of some of the deepest values of the law. As a call for integrity and reason in legal processes, it is representative of the whole professional life of its author.

---

126. Bickel wrote of the Warren Court that
    we have not yet—I guess happily—undertaken enough of [content analysis] on a systematic basis to have produced a quantitative, let alone qualitative, yardstick with which to determine whether this Court was substantially weaker analytically, less craftsmanlike, more manipulative of its materials, and more subjective than prior Courts that are now held in high esteem.
A. BICKEL, *supra* note 8, at 45.

Coherence, Hypothetical Cases, and Precedent

S. L. HURLEY*

Coherence accounts of practical reasoning in general, of which legal reasoning is a particular case, postulate the existence of a theory, sought in deliberation, which best displays as coherent the relationships among specific reasons for action which conflict in application to the case to be decided. These relationships are discovered in part by consideration of the way in which the same conflicting reasons apply in other cases, the resolution of which is settled. Ronald Dworkin's account of legal reasoning in *Law's Empire* is an example of a coherence account. Coherence accounts provide elements of various familiar conceptions of practical reasoning, such as the Rawlsian conception of reflective equilibrium as the outcome of a process of mutual adjustment between theory and intuition, and the decision-theoretic conception of rationality in terms of adjustment between data about preferences, criteria of choice, and principles of consistency.[1] I have elsewhere discussed the general rationale and motivation for coherence accounts of practical reasoning, illustrated the process of seeking coherence through deliberation with both legal and ethical examples, abstractly characterized the search for coherence, and considered various problems to which the abstract characterization gives rise.[2] In this paper I shall:

First, briefly set out my abstract characterization of deliberation as a search for coherence;

Second, consider various further examples of legal and ethical reasoning and indicate briefly the way in which they provide instances of my general coherentist characterization of deliberation;

Third, point out the generally similar roles within coherentist accounts of practical reasoning of settled actual cases and settled hypothetical cases as data to be accounted for by the sought-after theory or principles;

Fourth, present an objection to coherence accounts of legal reasoning in particular discussed by Kenneth Kress, who argues that they may give rise to

* Fellow in Philosophy and University Lecturer, St. Edmund Hall, Oxford. For helpful suggestions and comments on earlier drafts that saved me from various errors and unclarities, I am grateful to Ronald Dworkin, Mark Greenberg, and Joseph Raz; needless to say, responsibility for all remaining errors is entirely my own.

[1] See John Rawls, *A Theory of Justice* (Cambridge, Mass, Belknap Press of Harvard University Press, 1971); and Ralph L. Keeney and Howard Raiffa, *Decisions with Multiple Objectives: Preferences and Value Tradeoffs* (New York, Wiley & Sons, 1976).

[2] See my *Natural Reasons* (New York, Oxford University Press, 1989), chapters 4, 10, 11, 12, etc. Many background issues about the nature and objectivity of coherentist practical reasoning are raised by the argument of this article which I cannot here address but do address at length in *Natural Reasons*. They include: the need for substantive constraints on the description of the problem in terms of conflicting reasons, the relationships of these constraints to the structure and process of coherentist deliberation and the explanatory character of the resulting theories, the nature and limitations of the authority of theories about conflicting reasons, and many others.

© Oxford University Press 1990   Oxford Journal of Legal Studies Vol. **10**, No. 2

retroactive application of legal principles when new cases are decided between the occurrence of the events litigated and the litigation of them (the problem of intervening cases); and

Finally, consider various possible responses to Kress's argument. I shall briefly evaluate and put aside the possible responses of giving intervening cases prospective effect only, and of accepting intervening case retroactivity as not so bad. I shall then go on to diagnose the source of the problem by evaluating the relationships among concept of coherence, hypothetical cases, and the doctrine of precedent. I will show that the weaker coherentist requirement of treating like cases alike within practical reasoning in general is not sufficient to give rise to the problem of intervening cases, but that the stronger requirement imposed by the doctrine of precedent within legal reasoning in particular is necessary for the problem to arise. The distinction between the weaker and stronger requirements turns on the asymmetrical treatment of actual and hypothetical cases by the doctrine of precedent, by contrast with their symmetrical treatment in coherentist practical reasoning in general. However, I shall then argue that, when this asymmetry is properly understood, neither is the doctrine of precedent by itself sufficient to give rise to the problem of intervening cases, but only does so when the intervening legal decision is not *ex ante* correct, and that the role of hypothetical cases in coherentist practical reasoning in fact limits the problem of intervening case retroactivity. I shall conclude, following suggestions made by Dworkin, that intervening case retroactivity does not present a problem for coherence accounts such as his in particular.

1. An Abstract Characterization of Deliberation, and Coherence Functions

Our subject matter is deliberation about what to do when the reasons that apply to the alternatives conflict. The alternatives may be possible individual actions (eg, keeping one's promise and risking someone's life, or breaking it and avoiding risk to life), or possible judicial actions (eg, holding that a statute violates the Equal Protection Clause, or that it does not). The reasons that apply to the alternatives may be of various kinds, depending on the context of deliberation. An individual may deliberate about his own conflicting self-interested reasons, when no one else is significantly affected by the alternatives, or about a conflict involving the interests of others; the applicable reasons may be ethical, aesthetic, etc. A judge deliberates about conflicting legal reasons: legal doctrines, precedents, rights, principles, policies, as expressed within various legal practices and institutions, by cases, statutes, a constitution, legal scholarship, etc.

Coherence accounts claim that to say a certain alternative ought to be done is to say that it is favoured by the theory, whichever it may be, that gives the best account of the relationships among the various specific reasons that apply to the alternatives in question. Which theory is in fact the best theory, which best displays the applicable reasons as coherently related, is not specified by a coherence account *per se*. Rather, it is left to deliberation to discover what the best theory is. A coherence account merely claims that what ought to be done is whatever alternative the best theory, whatever that is, favours. Thus the deliberator's task is to discover the theory that best displays coherence. Deliberation involves a process of constructing hypotheses about the content of what I call a 'coherence function', which represents the theory sought and which takes us from alternatives ranked by specific reasons to all-things-considered rankings of alternatives. Of course the coherence function must meet certain conditions, and the all-things-considered ranking must meet certain conditions. For example, the latter ranking should not be intransitive. However, I shall not be considering the full range of these conditions in this article, but only those embodied in the requirements of treating like cases alike and of the doctrine of precedent.[3]

The process of deliberation can be analysed into five stages. At the *first* stage, we specify the problem. We try to arrive at a characterization of the alternatives at issue, and to determine what various specific reasons apply and how they rank the alternatives. We here exercise our abilities to perceive the world in terms of ethical, or legal, or other reason-giving concepts. (This is the issue spotting stage familiar to law students; however, there is much more to legal deliberation than issue spotting.) Assuming the reasons that apply conflict, that is, rank the alternatives at issue differently, we proceed to the *second* stage, and examine more carefully the various specific reasons that apply. Perhaps when we consider the purpose of one reason, it will turn out to have a rather different import than we originally thought in this particular case. At any rate, at this stage we develop and firm up our local conceptions of the various specific reasons that apply, without yet trying to arrive at a global conception of their relations to one another.

At the *third* stage we begin gathering data, by looking for other issues to which the conflicting reasons examined at stage two apply. In particular we are looking for settled cases. They may have actually been decided, or may be posed as hypothetical issues, the resolution of which can be taken as evident. By a 'settled' case, I mean a case which, if actual, is such that its resolution is clear to the relevant decision-maker or decision-makers, and which, if hypothetical, is such that its resolution would be clear to the relevant decision-maker or decision-makers were the case to be considered. (That a resolution of a particular case is or would be clear does not mean that it cannot be mistaken; settledness in particular cases is a matter of what is or would be believed to be correct, not necessarily of what is correct. However, it is of the nature of a coherentist account of what should be done, in terms of coherence with settled cases in general, that not all settled cases can be mistaken. I will return to this point below.) Thus, at least as a conceptual matter, not all actually decided cases are settled, and some settled cases are hypothetical, not actual (see section 8 below for more on this use of 'settled'). We may give settled actual cases more weight than settled hypothetical cases, or we may give them equal weight. The doctrine of precedent in law gives settled actual cases more weight than settled hypothetical cases, though usually only when the settled cases

---

[3] For discussion of such conditions, see my *Natural Reasons*, ibid, ch 12.

are those of the same court or higher courts of the same jurisdiction; actual cases of lower courts or courts of other jurisdictions may be treated on a par with settled hypothetical cases. However, as we shall see, this difference in weight may only be significant under certain circumstances.

The *fourth* stage is the heart of the deliberative process. At this stage we engage in all-out theorizing, looking for hypotheses which account for the resolutions of issues we found at stage three. That is, we are trying to formulate hypotheses about the relationships between the conflicting reasons under various different circumstances present in the stage three cases, which account for those resolutions. To this end we examine the stage three cases for distinctive circumstances or dimensions which seem to enhance or diminish the weight of one of the conflicting reasons in relation to the other. When we have formulated such an hypothesis, we try to test it, by going back to stage three and looking for further settled cases in which the same reasons apply and in which the circumstances identified by the hypothesis are present. We thus go back and forth between stages three and four, looking for settled actual and hypothetical cases that help us to refine our hypotheses about the relationships between the conflicting reasons in various circumstances.

Finally, at the *fifth* stage, we work out the consequences of the best hypothesis we have arrived at for the original case at issue. That is, we apply that hypothesis about the relationships between the applicable reasons to the circumstances present in the case at issue. This hypothesis is a partial specification of a coherence function, which takes us from the rankings of alternatives involving various circumstances or dimensions by the conflicting reasons to an all-things-considered ranking.

This characterization of deliberation can be pictured in terms of a *deliberative matrix*. The data gathered at stage three can be represented as follows, where in each row, alternatives are ranked above or below one another by the applicable reasons.

	Reason X	Reason Y	Resolution, all-things-considered
case at	alt a	alt b	?
issue:	alt b	alt a	
settled	alt d	alt c	alt c
actual	alt c	alt d	alt d
cases:	alt e	alt f	alt e
	alt f	alt e	alt f
settled	alt g	alt h	alt h
hypothetical	alt h	alt g	alt g
cases:	alt j	alt i	alt j
	alt i	alt j	alt i
	etc		

I present the matrix with only two conflicting reasons, X and Y, merely for convenience; there is no restriction on the number of reasons that may be represented. (Indeed, multi-dimensional conflicts give rise to interesting theoretical questions.[4]) During stage four the alternatives are analysed and more fully characterized in terms of various circumstances and dimensions of the cases which may help to explain their resolution. These circumstances may be represented by adding propositions, p, q, etc, to the alternatives in each row. The content of such a proposition may be quantitative or non-quantitative. A hypothesis would then take the form: 'Reason X tends to outweigh Reason Y when it is the case that p, while Reason Y tends to outweigh Reason X when it is the case that q; when it is the case that both p and q, but not r, Reason X has more weight, but when r is present as well, Reason Y has more weight', and so on.[5]

Two points of clarification may be helpful. First, I do not in this article aim to give a full account of what is distinctive about legal reasoning in particular, but rather to consider what follows about legal reasoning from the fact that it has the general features of practical reasoning, understood along coherentist lines. My examples in the next section are intended to illustrate the application of the coherentist account of practical reasoning in general to legal problems, rather than to illuminate what is distinctive about legal reasoning in particular. I will go on to consider the distinctively legal doctrine of precedent in the context set by a view of legal reasoning as having the general features of coherentist practical reasoning. This is important to understand for purposes of my discussion below of the problem of intervening cases, since my eventual response to Kress in sections 7 and 8 turns on the features that legal reasoning shares with practical reason in general, on a coherentist view of it, with respect to the role of hypothetical cases. Such general features of coherentist practical reasoning limit the effects of the distinctively legal doctrine of precedent in giving rise to intervening case retroactivity,

---

[4] Which I pursue in *Natural Reasons*, ibid, chs 12 and 13.

[5] This schematization, applied to legal deliberation, may be compared to that employed by the programme HYPO, developed by Edwina Rissland and her student Kevin Ashley, and discussed in a Harvard Law School seminar conducted by Rissland on artificial intelligence and legal reasoning, Autumn Term 1987. See Kevin D. Ashley, *Modelling Legal Argument: Reasoning with Cases and Hypotheticals*, PhD dissertation, 1987, University of Massachussetts, Dept of Computer and Information Science. While there are many differences in detail between the two approaches, I do not believe there is any incompatibility in principle between them. The role of HYPO's 'dimensions' is similar to the role of my propositions p, q, etc in the analysis of actual and hypothetical settled cases at stage four. Perhaps I try to say a bit more than Rissland and Ashley do about the role of hypotheticals in reaching legal conclusions, in that the answers to hypothetical questions feed back into the resolution of the case at issue via the coherence function, but again I do not believe that what I say is incompatible with their approach. Perhaps the most striking difference is that over whether to use favourableness to conflicting legal doctrines or favourableness to plaintiff as opposed to defendant, as the basic means of organizing the data. Often, within a narrowly limited area of the law, such as trade secrets law, plaintiffs will typically represent one legal doctrine, and defendants another, so that the two approaches are in principle quite similar. However, the doctrine-oriented rather than party-oriented method of organization may have advantages when one comes to generalize beyond a narrowly limited area of the law, so that plaintiff and defendant no longer typically represent particular legal doctrines. By organizing the cases according to legal doctrines directly rather than by plaintiffs' and defendants' positions, one may hope to keep theoretical score as one moves from one area of law to another in which the same doctrines apply, and to bring insights about the relationships between legal doctrines from one area to the next.

Of course, different ways of perceiving what legal doctrines apply will yield different analyses, but that is the way the law is, and an analysis which reflects this relativity of conclusion to starting point may be illuminating. Moreover, we can in principle start with as many different legal doctrines as we think may be relevant; again, there is no need to restrict the number of reasons weighed against one another by the coherence function to two.

and thus illuminate the source of the problem. But I would certainly not claim that the generally coherentist character of legal reasoning as a kind of practical reasoning plus the features of precedent I consider provide a full account of what is distinctive about legal reasoning in particular; this is not my purpose. Second, I would expect the account and illustrations of practical reasoning to be controversial to the extent they represent a kind of deliberative rationality with respect to conflicting ends, values or reasons, the possibility of which has often been denied, for example, in favour of a view of practical reasoning as exclusively instrumental, or in favour of more radically sceptical or nihilistic views about practical rationality (in the legal context, consider certain views associated with the critical legal studies movement, or parodies thereof). However, I cannot join these issues here.

2. Some Examples of Legal and Ethical Deliberation Analysed

I have elsewhere considered in detail and at length a legal illustration of this general account of practical reasoning, the stages of deliberation, and the deliberative matrix. That discussion involved deliberation about the relationships between the conflicting legal doctrines of estoppel and of consideration in cases now usually covered by the doctrine of promissory estoppel.[6] I will not here give another lengthy and detailed illustration, but rather will give several sketchy illustrations. I hope in the former discussion to have persuaded readers that my account can be made to work in detail. In this discussion I rather aim to persuade readers that the account applies readily and intuitively in a wide range of cases. Accordingly I shall not work out the details of my applications here, but shall merely briefly indicate how the framework of my account would fit the examples.

Let us begin with the case of *California* v *Carney*.[7] In *Carney*, Fourth Amendment issues were raised by a warrantless police search of a motor home, parked in a downtown San Diego parking lot. The police had reason to believe that Carney, the owner of the motor home, was exchanging marijuana for sex acts. They observed a young boy enter the motor home and leave again an hour and a quarter later. On questioning by the police, the boy said that such an exchange had just occurred. The police then knocked on the door, and when Carney came out they entered the motor home without a warrant and found marijuana. A further search of the vehicle at the police station revealed more marijuana, in cupboards and in the refrigerator. The parking lot where the warrantless search occurred was a short distance from a courthouse where a warrant could easily have been obtained.

The case and its oral argument, rich in hypothetical cases, have been analysed by Edwina Rissland to illustrate the idea of a 'dimension', which is used by the case-based reasoning programme HYPO to generate hypothetical cases.[8] My treatment of the case essentially adapts her analysis to my framework, and illustrates, I believe, the compatibility of my framework and the notions of a deliberative matrix

---

[6] See *Natural Reasons*, op cit, ch 11.
[7] *California* v *Carney*, 105 SCt 2066 (1985).
[8] Op cit n 3.

and a coherence function, with Rissland's dimension-based analysis. As she points out, *Carney* is a case in which there is a conflict between a citizen's expectations of privacy, protected by the Fourth Amendment's prohibition of unreasonable searches and seizures, and the responsibilities and desires of the police to investigate and control drug use and other prohibited activities. Thus, the first row of our matrix for the case at issue involves at least two kinds of legal reasons: I shall refer to them as reasons of Privacy, and reasons of the Police Power. The alternatives in the case at issue are to allow or to disallow the warrantless search of the motor home in *Carney* under the Fourth Amendment. Reasons of Privacy would favour disallowing the search, while reasons of the Police Power would favour allowing it. We want to discover how reasons of Privacy and reasons of the Police Power are related to one another with respect to warrantless searches. Settled actual cases at the next several rows of the matrix tell us that reasons of Privacy are augmented relative to those of the Police Power in circumstances in which the warrantless search at issue is of someone's home; if we sum up these circumstances in proposition p, we can hypothesize that Privacy is augmented relative to the Police Power when it is the case that p. By contrast, settled cases tell us, the Police Power is augmented relative to Privacy when the warrantless search at issue is of a vehicle; if we sum up the latter circumstances in proposition q, we can hypothesize that Privacy is diminished relative to the Police Power when it is the case that q. We have thus begun to specify a coherence function which weighs Privacy against the Police Power in various circumstances.

While these hypotheses about the relations between Privacy and the Police Power are well supported by settled cases, they really only set the stage for the *Carney* problem, since the motor home in *Carney* is both a home and a vehicle. We need a finer analysis of relevant circumstances in order to resolve the conflict in this case. Thus we look for other settled cases, actual or hypothetical, in which these two reasons come into conflict, in circumstances in which the home–vehicle distinction is difficult to draw. On the basis of such cases, we try to arrive at a hypothesis that will help police to draw the home–vehicle distinction in a reliable and straightforward way in cases in which aspects of both home and vehicle are present; that is, we would like to find a 'bright-line' distinction, which will not require police officers to make excessively subtle or difficult determinations. We will try various hypotheses about the relevant circumstances, or dimensions of cases, and will test them against various actual and hypothetical cases.

The fact that the thing to be searched is a vehicle seems to augment the Police Power reasons relative to those of Privacy in part because it is inherently mobile, such that requiring a warrant would leave it time to 'get away' and would greatly frustrate legitimate exercises of the Police Power, and also because vehicles are not usually used as homes, and thus not the objects of normal expectations of privacy. These hypotheses are developed and tested in oral argument by reference to hypothetical cases in which vehicles are also homes, but some of which are more inherently mobile, or more home-like than others, owing to varying circumstances and dimensions. The presence of wheels is obviously dispensable to inherent mobility in the case of most boats, with respect to which presumably reasons of the Police Power predominate. Nor is the presence of wheels decisive in the case of motor homes with wheels but which are not self-propelling and which are permanently connected to utilities supplies, with respect to which presumably reasons of Privacy predominate. Location in a temporary parking lot as opposed to a permanent motor home park strengthens the case with respect to inherent mobility and hence with respect to the weight of Police Power reasons. But a counter-example to that hypothesis would seem to be the case of someone very poor who cannot afford a permanent spot for his vehicle but lives in it behind curtains, on the move from day to day. The presence of the normal accoutrements of a home, such as a refrigerator, in a vehicle, may strengthen reasons of Privacy; but again we would seem to have a counter-example when the refrigerator is used solely to store marijuana, as seemed to be the case in *Carney*, and not for home-like purposes.

From among these various circumstances and dimensions of hypothetical cases, the best hypothesis will focus on objective factors that are straightforward for the police to ascertain before deciding whether to search without a warrant or not (as the contents of a refrigerator are not), so as to provide police with 'bright-line' guidance. This is because the investigation needed to apply an excessively subtle distinction will make for a prior, unprincipled defeat of reasons of Privacy, while a strong presumption in favour of home-likeness to accommodate all unusual uses of vehicles as homes would in effect eliminate the vehicle exception to the warrant requirement and would thus excessively compromise the Police Power. Thus the need for bright-line guidance in effect provides a way for the theory to get around the apparent counter-example to inherent mobility hypothesis provided by the poor person who lives in his car. The case does not really provide a counter-example, after all, since the police cannot tell that such unusual vehicles are homes without privacy-infringing investigation; and it is already settled by the vehicle exception that the alternative of disallowing searches of *any* vehicles which might possibly be homes has been ruled out. The majority opinion in *Carney* indicates in effect that the best hypothesis makes the relation between reasons of Privacy and those of the Police Power in cases involving vehicles that may be homes turn on objective indications of mobility and use for transportation, rather than on the more difficult-to-ascertain home-like uses of the vehicle. If the presence of the former characteristics is expressed by proposition r, the majority's hypothesis, which they implicitly regard as supported by the hypothetical cases considered, in light of the need for bright-line guidance, is that when it is the case that r, as it was in *Carney*, reasons of the Police Power outweigh reasons of Privacy, and thus support the warrantless search at issue. By contrast, the dissenting opinions seem to prefer a hypothesis which gives more of a role to the home-like character of the place in strengthening reasons of Privacy.

Equal Protection cases raised under the US Constitution are a fertile source of illustrations of the coherentist framework, as the jurisprudence of varying degrees of relationship to various state interests served by challenged classifications lends itself immediately to representation within a deliberative matrix. In discussing several such cases I shall not stop to assign labels, p, q, etc, to the propositions employed in hypotheses about the relationships among the conflicting reasons in various circumstances. I shall merely identify the general categories of reasons in play, and try to draw out the hypotheses about the relations between the reasons in play that are implicitly tested by appeal to various settled cases. It should be evident, however, how labels could be assigned and hypotheses located within a deliberative matrix. In Equal Protection cases one category of legal reasons is provided by the Equal Protection Clause itself: reasons of Nondiscrimination, which oppose legal classifications which fail to treat similarly situated citizens in similar ways. Further categories of reasons are provided by whatever state interests are supposed to be served by the challenged classification.

In *Parham* v *Hughes*[9], for example, the father of an illegitimate child challenged a law which prevented him from recovering for the wrongful death of his child, where an unmarried father who had filed papers to legitimate the child, or the mother of the illegitimate child, would have been allowed to recover. If he could be regarded as similarly situated with other parents of illegitimate children who were allowed to recover for wrongful death, then reasons of Nondiscrimination would favour striking the statute down. However, the state considered that it had an interest in promoting the integrity of the legitimate family unit, and that reasons of Legitimacy favoured restricting recovery for wrongful death to unmarried fathers who had filed to legitimate their children and unmarried mothers. The implication seems to be that such a restriction would provide incentives to unmarried fathers to file to legitimate their children. Moreover, the state also claimed to have an interest in avoiding difficult problems of proof of paternity, and that reasons of Provability favoured the restriction of wrongful death suits for the death of children born illegitimate to fathers who had filed to legitimate and mothers, whose identity would rarely be in doubt. Thus we seem to have a conflict between reasons of Nondiscrimination, on the one hand, and reasons of Legitimacy and of Provability, on the other.

The court held that this state scheme did not violate Equal Protection or Due Process by discriminating against unmarried fathers relative to unmarried mothers, because fathers and mothers of illegitimate children are not similarly situated since, under Georgia law, only fathers *can* by voluntary unilateral action make an illegitimate child legitimate. That is, the plurality opinion seems implicitly to support the hypothesis that when it is the case that men and women are not similarly situated *owing to a difference in their legally imposed abilities and status*, that difference may provide a basis for a statutory classification which does not constitute invidious discrimination, such that, when such a classification is related in the right way to the right kinds of state interests, the latter outweigh reasons of Nondiscrimination.

---

[9] 441 US 347, 99 SCt 1742 (1979).

The dissent appeals to a hypothetical case to refute the plurality's hypothesis. Justice White writes:

> There is a startling circularity in this argument. The issue before the Court is whether Georgia may require unmarried fathers, but not unmarried mothers, to have pursued the statutory legitimization procedure in order to bring suit for the wrongful death of their children. Seemingly, it is irrelevant that as a matter of state law mothers may not legitimate their children, for they are not required to do so in order to maintain a wrongful-death action. That only fathers *may* resort to the legitimization process cannot dissolve the sex-discrimination in *requiring* them to. Under the plurality's bootstrap rationale, a State could require that women, but not men, pass a course in order to receive a taxi license, simply by limiting admission to the course to women.

In the taxi licence hypothetical, men and women would not be similarly situated, owing to their differing legally imposed abilities, ie their differing abilities to enroll in the course. But here it is clearly absurd to suppose that this prior discrimination, unscrutinized, could provide a justification for further discrimination in the form of a statutory classification requiring only women to pass the course in order to get a licence. Thus the hypothetical case provides a counter-example to the plurality's hypothesis. The implication of the dissenting opinion is that the embedded distinction must itself be scrutinized, and not merely taken as given. In *Parham*, the embedded distinction was one with respect to the ability to file papers to legitimate: only men were able to do so. It is hard to see how a rule making it impossible for women to file papers to legitimate children serves either the state interest in promoting the legitimate family unit or in avoiding proof of paternity issues. Permitting women to file as well as men would have no adverse effects whatsoever on either of these state interests.

The dissent goes on to appeal to another counter-example, this time a type of actual rather than hypothetical case, to the hypothesis that reasons of Legitimacy outweigh those of Nondiscrimination if allowing members of one class but not another to sue for wrongful death serves the state interest in promoting the integrity of the legitimate family unit. The dissent points out that unmarried mothers and fathers who file to legitimate but remain unmarried defy the integrity of the legitimate family unit, just as do fathers who fail to file, but the former are allowed to sue for wrongful death while the latter are not.

In *Craig v Boren*, the question was whether a statute prohibiting the sale of weakly alcoholic beer to males under 21 and females under 18 constituted denial to males aged 18 to 21 of equal protection of the law. On behalf of the statute it was urged that statistical evidence about the relative tendencies of males and females aged 18 to 21 to drink and drive supported the gender line. Thus we have a conflict between reasons of Nondiscrimination and the state interest in Preventing Drunk Driving. The Court rejects the hypothesis that reasons of Nondiscrimination can be overcome by the interest in Preventing Drunk Driving when the latter is served by 'statistically measured but loose-fitting generalities concerning the drinking tendencies of aggregate groups'. In doing so it appeals to hypothetical variations on the *Craig* v *Boren* statute involving statistically supported ethnic or racial lines instead of gender lines aimed at alcohol regulation. The assumption made is that such ethnic or racial lines would not be acceptable, despite statistical support, and that reasons of Nondiscrimination would predominate in such cases: 'In fact, social science studies that have uncovered quantifiable differences in drinking tendencies dividing along both racial and ethnic lines strongly suggest the need for application of the Equal Protection Clause in preventing discriminatory treatment that almost certainly would be perceived as invidious.' The Court illustrates its comments with reference to statistical evidence to the effect that Jews, Italian Catholics, and black teenagers tend not to be problem drinkers, in contrast to whites and North American Indians.

Finally, consider the uses of hypothetical and actual cases in ethical argument, as illustrated by the debate between Stephen Pepper and David Luban over whether lawyers in an adversary system should help their clients to do legal but unethical acts. Pepper argues that under many circumstances the answer is 'yes'. He argues roughly as follows. We hold the value of individual autonomy to be more important than getting people to do the ethically right act in a wide range of cases; for example, we allow that people should have the legal power to disinherit a child for marrying outside the faith, even though we may agree that it would be wrong to do so. Individual autonomy in our complex society requires, in many cases, legal assistance; only with the help of lawyers can people, in many circumstances, be 'first class citizens'. Therefore lawyers should give their clients the legal help required for individual autonomy even when it permits them to do unethical acts.

Luban replies by arguing that, while it is true that, since exercising autonomy is good, helping people exercise autonomy is good, this is only half the story. 'The other half is that since doing bad things is bad, helping people do bad things is bad. The two factors must be weighed against each other, and this Pepper does not do'. That is, Pepper's general hypothesis that when helping someone to do a legal but unethical act is favoured by reasons of autonomy, reasons of autonomy prevail, is too crude. Luban appeals to an analogous hypothetical case to defeat the unqualified hypothesis:

Compare this case: The automobile, by making it easier to get around, increases human autonomy; hence, other things equal, it is morally good to repair the car of someone who is unable by himself to get it to run. But such considerations can hardly be invoked to defend the morality of fixing the getaway car of an armed robber, assuming that you know in advance what the purpose of the car is. The moral wrong of assisting the robber outweighs the abstract moral goodness of augmenting the robber's autonomy.[10]

Not only may reasons of autonomy sometimes be outweighed by the wrongness of the act in question, but even if the balance of reasons favours allowing the agent to do the unethical act himself, it does not necessarily follow that it will also favour helping him to do it. The balance between autonomy and conflicting reasons may

[10] David Luban, 'The Lysistratian Prerogative: A Response to Stephen Pepper', [1986] *American Bar Foundation Research Journal*, at 639.

be struck differently in different circumstances, ie with respect to omitting to prevent as opposed to positively aiding.

Another argument Pepper makes is that allowing lawyers to weigh the wrongness of acts and thus act as screens to filter out certain legally permissible acts is to submit individuals to 'rule by an oligarchy of lawyers'.[11] The implication of the term 'oligarchy' is that such weighing and screening by lawyers would constitute an elitist centralization of ethical decision-making highly threatening to the value of individual autonomy, and that, when this would be the result, reasons of autonomy should prevail. Luban offers a counter-example to this implied hypothesis:

> . . . there is no oligarchy of lawyers, actual or potential, to worry about. An oligarchy is a group of people ruling *in concert*, whereas lawyers who refuse to execute projects to which they object on moral grounds will do so as individuals, without deliberating collectively with other lawyers. The worry about a hidden Central Committee of lawyers evaporates when we realize that the committee will never hold a meeting, and that its members don't even know they are on it. An analogy will clarify this. No doubt throughout history people have often been dissuaded from undertaking immoral projects by the anger, threats, and uncooperativeness of their spouses. It would scarcely make sense, however, to worry that this amounts to subjecting autonomous action 'to rule by an oligarchy of spouses'. There *is* no oligarchy of spouses.

Luban seems to accept for the sake of argument that screening by a true Central Committee might well be intolerable. But if weighing and screening by spouses does not constitute an elitist centralization of ethical decision-making highly threatening to the value of individual autonomy, it is not clear how this can be regarded as the result when we substitute 'lawyers' for 'spouses'. Indeed, Luban suggests that informal social pressures are an essential complement to legal rules in regulating harmful behaviour. (Note that I am not here endorsing Luban's conclusions, but only using his arguments to illustrate certain characteristic features of deliberation.)

3. Hypothetical Cases as Thought Experiments

The role of the settled cases appealed to in the above examples of deliberation is analogous in some respects to the role of data in scientific theorizing. In both areas, that is, one looks both for relevant data, or clear cases, and for generalizations that account for what seems to be clearly the case (though of course such apparent clarity is not infallible in either area), and uses the latter generalizations to make determinations about further cases. In neither area is the best account of the data deductively entailed by the data. Nevertheless, in both areas the data in some sense determines the best theory (or theories, in the case of a tie or moderate degree of underdetermination of theory by data). The best theory (or theories—I will hereafter omit the qualification, but it continues to apply) is some function of the

---

[11] Stephen Pepper, 'The Lawyer's Amoral Ethical Role: A Defense, A Problem, and Some Possibilities', [1986] *American Bar Foundation Research Journal*, at 617.

data, in the sense that if the best theory were other than what it is, the data would have to be different in some way. This is just another way of saying that situations that are relevantly similar in respect of data must be treated consistently in theoretical respects, or, more briefly, that like cases should be treated alike. With respect to legal deliberation, this general consistency requirement is that cases relevantly similar, in respect of applicable legal doctrines and distinguishing circumstances, should be similarly resolved.

Of course, the analogy should not be strained; some of the general roles of ethical and legal deliberation and theorizing are very different from those of scientific theorizing. Scientific theories are used to predict what will happen on the basis of causal theories that account for what has happened in well-designed experiments, and sometimes also for what it is thought would have happened under significant counterfactual circumstances. The basis for scientific hypotheses are thus experimental data and sometimes intuitions gathered in 'thought experiments', such as Einstein's famous thought experiments about flashlights emitting beams of light in trains travelling at close to the speed of light. Scientific hypotheses generate predictions which are then tested against the results of further experiments.

By contrast, ethical and legal deliberation can hardly be described as having the role of predicting what will be done on the basis of causal theories. Rather, it has a normative role: to give guidance in extending consistently to the case at issue a series of settled ethical or legal judgments about what should be done when the applicable ethical or legal reasons conflict. Its normative hypotheses thus aim to account for clear resolutions of past cases in which the relevant reasons stood in conflict, and also for clear resolutions of significant hypothetical cases, designed to test the relationships between the conflicting reasons. Deliberative hypotheses are used to generate not mere predictions of decisions and actions, but decisions and actions themselves; hypotheses cannot be tested against the very decisions and actions they generate. Rather, they are tested against cases, both actual and hypothetical, in which the right answer about how a conflict of reasons should be resolved is settled.[12]

Despite the differences between scientific, causal theorizing, and deliberative, normative theorizing, it is important to recognize the way in which both kinds of theorizing are responsible to the data to be explained. The requirement that the sought-after hypothesis explains the data can be seen as the source of the deliberative requirement of consistency, the general requirement that like cases be treated alike. Some philosophers have regarded it as puzzling how one could hold that both:

---

[12] I do not suggest that scientific, ethical or legal deliberation are to be understood instrumentally rather than realistically; it is common ground between instrumentalism and realism that theoretical propositions should be able to be used in practical roles, eg to predict, explain or guide. I am concerned here to avoid overstating the analogy between the practical roles of scientific and deliberative theorizing rather than to take a position on the further issues that divide instrumental and realistic views of theories.

(1) the right answer about which alternative should be done is not entailed by the nonevaluative facts about the alternatives (*nonreductionism*: what should be done does not reduce to nonevaluative facts about the alternatives)

and:

(2) one must treat cases alike in respect of nonevaluative facts alike, so that if there is a difference between two cases in respect of what should be done, there must be some difference between them with respect to the nonevaluative facts about the alternatives as well (*supervenience*: what should be done supervenes on nonevaluative facts about the alternatives).

While there is no logical incompatibility between (1) and (2), the puzzlement about how they can both hold can be expressed by asking: If the right answer is not entailed by the nonevaluative facts, then what is the source of the requirement that cases alike in nonevaluative respects be treated alike?[13] However, recognition of the way in which right answers to questions about what should be done reflects hypotheses that are required to explain the data about settled cases provides a response to this puzzlement. The best theory about the data is not entailed by—cannot be deduced from—the data. Nevertheless, it is essential to the notion of a theory responsible to data that the best theory, whatever it may be, treats like cases alike. The source of this requirement is the essential explanatory aspirations of theories: a theory the content of which varies independently of the data it purports to account for to that extent does no explanatory work. This remains true even though the best theory is not entailed by the data.[14]

Thus, the requirement that like cases be treated alike has its source in the theoretical nature of judgments about what should be done when reasons conflict, which is highlighted by coherence accounts. Moreover, the data to which theories about what should be done are responsible are settled cases, both actual and hypothetical. If in general the role of settled cases in deliberation is somewhat analogous to that of experimental data in scientific theorizing, then the role of hypothetical cases in particular may be regarded as somewhat analogous to that of thought experiments.[15] It is important for our understanding of the requirement that like cases be treated alike that we include settled hypothetical cases, cases the answer to which would be clear were they to arise, as well as settled actual cases among the data to be explained. For reasons that will emerge in what follows, this is particularly important in the case of legal deliberation, where the general requirement that like cases be treated alike must be distinguished from the further specific requirement imposed by the doctrine of precedent. My examples in the previous section make clear that, since legal deliberation and argument often turn not merely on settled actual cases but also on settled hypothetical cases, effective legal reasoning often requires one to discover or construct revealing hypothetical

---

[13] See, for example, Simon Blackburn, *Spreading the Word* (Oxford, Clarendon Press, 1984), ch 6.
[14] For further discussion of supervenience, irreducibility and explanation, see my *Natural Reasons*, op cit, ch 14.
[15] The effective postulation of hypothetical cases thus has something in common with effective experimental design.

cases[16]; a coherence account provides a framework for understanding the function of hypothetical cases in legal reasoning. Hypothetical cases are not merely *posed* by lawyers and judges, but *answers* to questions about how they should be resolved are often taken for granted in a way which the argument of the case at issue depends on. The answers to hypothetical cases may be implicitly assumed rather than explicitly stated, but nevertheless they are often depended on in the reasoning of opinions, in a way that may be explicitly represented within a deliberative matrix. This is to say that legal hypotheses are responsible to data about settled hypothetical cases as well as settled actual cases; both are among the cases with respect to which the requirement that like cases be treated alike must be understood. Nevertheless, as we shall see, the doctrine of precedent imposes a further constraint on legal deliberation in giving actual settled cases *more weight* than that of hypothetical settled cases for purposes of determining what counts as treating like cases alike.

4. Kress on Coherence Accounts and Retroactivity: the Problem of Intervening Cases

In an interesting article entitled 'Legal Reasoning and Coherence Theories: Dworkin's Rights Thesis, Retroactivity, and the Linear Order of Decision', Kenneth Kress argues that the role within coherence theories such as Dworkin's of coherence with past decisions and deference to precedent makes for retroactive applications of the law. In Kress's view, retroactivity may occur if settled law changes between the occurrence of the events being litigated and the adjudication of them, since at adjudication the most coherent account of settled cases will be responsible to actual cases decided after the occurrence of the events litigated. What Kress calls the 'ripple effect'

> . . . depends upon legal rights being a function of settled law and upon the temporal gap between events being litigated and their eventual adjudication. Judicial decisions often change the settled law. Often, if not always, the settled law will be changed between the occurrence of events being litigated and their eventual adjudication. In consequence, a litigant's rights will sometimes also be changed. If changes in the settled law change the dispositive legal right, a litigant who would have prevailed given the legal rights existing at the time of the occurrence will lose because he no longer has that right at the time of adjudication. The opposite is true of the opposing litigant. This is retroactive application of the law.[17]

I shall refer to the problem Kress identifies as *the problem of intervening cases*. Kress regards this as a particularly serious problem for Dworkin's rights-oriented version of a coherence account of legal reasoning, since Dworkin works his account

---

[16] I do not suggest the existence of a positive professional obligation imposed on court or counsel to discover or construct hypothetical cases, but of a normative requirement that arises from characteristic features of legal reasoning as a species of practical reasoning. It may be that my account of the latter is particularly influenced by characteristic features of the legal system in the United States, such as the prominent role of the posing of 'hypos' in Supreme Court oral argument, in legal education, etc.

[17] (1984) 72 *Cal LR* 369, at 380.

up in the course of criticizing Hart's account for the scope it gives to judicial discretion and for the retroactive applications of the law which judicial discretion involves.

However, Kress regards the problem as generalizable: it applies to any coherence account which is conservative in the sense that it adheres to the dominant conception of precedent. According to the latter, legal truths depend in part on prior legal decisions. The general form of the problem is that the best theory about settled law may change between the time the events occurred and the time they are litigated, owing to intervening legal decisions. 'The mere historical fact of a prior decision influences the decisions in later cases, and thus the law, because it enlarges the settled law with which later decisions must cohere.'[18] This is in effect just to say that the prevalent conception of precedent gives more weight to settled actual cases than to settled hypothetical cases for purposes of determining what counts as treating like cases alike.

5. A First Response: Prospective Application

What is the correct response to or diagnosis of the problem of intervening cases? Let us first briefly consider and dismiss, with Kress, the possibility that present legal practice should be changed so as to base legal decisions on law settled at the time the events adjudicated occurred rather than at the time of adjudication. Kress suggests that to give decisions only prospective effect in this way is particularly appropriate when decisions are legislative in character; as he puts it: 'The doctrine of prospective overruling is the legacy of legal realism, the doctrine that maintains that judges legislate'. However, Kress considers and rejects this possible response to his problem, on theoretical grounds and on pragmatic grounds (such as the difficulties of determining which events are relevant for purposes of dating the law to be applied). I find his pragmatic arguments against this line of response fairly persuasive.[19]

---

[18] Kress, ibid, at 400.

[19] At 386–7: 'It is unlikely that the revised . . . theory could be developed in detail, or utilized by judges if it could, for several reasons. First, the possibility of temporally extended events and transactions raises difficult problems in determining the date of the law to be applied. These problems are compounded if several related but separable transactions are being litigated and there are multiple issues. The prospect of applying the law at different times to different but related aspects of a complicated transaction raises unappealing complexity. Further and perhaps insuperable complexity arises if it is possible to analyze the overall transaction in multiple ways into different temporal components. Unless we can be sure that one temporal analysis will be superior to all others, we will need rules to choose among the various analyses. More important, it is unclear what precedential effect should be given to a decision that applies law from many time periods, law that by definition differs from the law that would be applied to an event that occurred at the time of adjudication if litigated at that time.'

See especially Kress's note 77, commenting on the line of criminal procedure cases involving prospective-only application. Kress distinguishes the 'more common form' of prospective-only application, which nevertheless applies intervening decisions to pending cases, from the more extreme form that would be necessary to avoid ripple effect retroactivity, which would deny the 'new' rule to pending cases as well. For the 'more common form', see *Linkletter* v *Walker*, 381 US 618 (1965), which did apply the intervening decision to pending cases.

It may be objected to Kress that he has not addressed the line of criminal procedure cases subsequent to *Linkletter* which explicitly discuss the application of intervening decisions to pending cases. See *Stovall* v *Denno*, 388 US 293 (1967); *Desist* v *US*, 394 US 244 (1969), especially Justice Harlan's dissent; *Shea* v *Lousianna*, 470 US 51 (1985), especially Justice White's dissent. The Court divides over the problem of intervening cases, and moreover, seems to change its own position. *Stovall* and *Desist* come down in favour of nonretroactivity by refusing to apply the

continued on page 237

However, if Kress's own objections to giving intervening cases prospective effect only are persuasive, his problem is not just a problem for coherentists; it cannot be avoided by 'frank' assimilation of adjudication to legislation. Moreover, even if we assume for the sake of argument that the correct response to the problem of intervening cases is to give them prospective effect only, I am not persuaded that this response would be inconsistent with a coherence account. To the extent that retroactivity is the concomitant of a conception of precedent that gives more weight to actual than hypothetical cases, a coherentist could argue that it is the fact that actual decisions may change the law, through the operation of precedent, that makes prospective application appropriate. But this law-changing effect of precedent should not be confused with 'legislative' discretion to make law for the case at hand; these are two logically distinct issues. That is, the occurrence of a judicial decision may change what the law requires from that point on, through the operation of precedent, even though the judge had no antecedent discretion as to how that case should be decided.[20] Even if only mistaken intervening decisions can change the law, as Dworkin urges (see section 8) below, nevertheless a mistaken decision that changes the law through the operation of precedent is logically distinct from quasi-legislative discretion to make new law.

So, if the correct response to the problem of intervening cases is prospective-only application, a coherence account is not thereby defeated, since there is no inconsistency between a coherence account and this response. On the other hand, Kress's pragmatic reasons against this response to the problem are equally valid given legislative accounts of judicial reasoning. So if this response is ruled out, it is not only coherence accounts that are left with a problem. Let us thus suppose, for the sake of argument, that the prospective-only response to the problem of intervening cases is to be ruled out (but for a qualification relating to changes in settled cases with extra-judicial sources, see the end of section 7 below).

6. A Second Response: It Is Not So Bad

Consider a second possible response envisaged by Kress to the problem of intervening cases, namely, that of accepting the retroactivity in question as, for one reason or another, not all that bad. And at any rate, a coherentist might add, the

continued from page 236
intervening decisions to pending cases in which the relevant events of police conduct occurred prior to the intervening decisions. However, Justice Harlan's dissent in *Desist*, favouring precedent over nonretroactivity, becomes the Court's position in *Shea*, where Justice White dissents, arguing on nonretroactivity grounds. A nice self-referential problem of intervening cases about the problem of intervening cases, the logic of which I will not even attempt to untangle!

In reply, it should be kept in mind that the degree to which the Court is willing to consider and countenance intervening case retroactivity in the criminal procedure context, where police reliance on earlier cases is in question, may well not generalize. That is, an acceptable degree of retroactivity with respect to police reliance, which cuts in *favour* of criminal defendants, may not be acceptable in general, that is, where the intervening case might cut *against* criminal defendants and undermine *their* reliance rather than police reliance, or where it might change the positions of civil litigants. It would be interesting to develop an integrated view of retroactivity doctrine within and without the criminal procedure context, and to try to isolate the special effects of the criminal procedure context on retroactivity doctrine, but I cannot do so here.

[20] Kress does allow for this type of view, at 386; he does, at 382, distinguish judicial discretion from judicial creation of law.

problem of intervening cases is not a problem for coherence accounts in particular, since they will still involve less retroactivity than accounts of adjudication as *ex ante* discretionary do.[21]

Just how objectionable would intervening case retroactivity be? Perhaps coherentists should not regard it as a matter for particular concern. Kress offers Dworkin something like this possible position in a footnote (though in fact this is not Dworkin's response to the problem):

> Dworkin believes that the unfairness of retroactive application of law is not fully explained by the rule of law requirements to give prior notice, satisfy justified expectations, and the like. . . . Dworkin must take this position because the controversial nature of right answers even when they exist means, as Dworkin admits, that right answers often cannot be demonstrated and therefore often are not known in advance. . . . Dworkin's objection to retroactivity appears to focus on the importance of giving a principled justification for enforcing judicial decisions. Dworkin's concern with retroactivity derives from the belief that creating and applying new rights at the time of adjudication cannot be given a principled justification. . . . Arguably, therefore, ripple effect retroactivity with its consequential disruption of expectations and failure to provide notice is not the kind of retroactivity that would concern Dworkin.[22]

Though Kress's article was published before *Law's Empire*, this suggestion seems reasonably consistent with Dworkin's views in *Law's Empire* about respect for precedent and coherence as expressing the integrity and personification of the community. On the above suggestion, people would simply be on notice that their claims were subject to requirements of coherence with possible intervening precedents. Perhaps one could justify the retroactivity to people on the grounds of their membership in a community with the virtues of integrity, which unfortunately entail such retroactivity. People could of course try, perhaps through their lawyers, to anticipate intervening precedents as best they could, by identifying any relevant settled hypothetical cases. But the possibility would remain that an unsettled hypothetical case might become a decided actual case and thus create an unanticipated intervening precedent.

We might fill out this possible line of response further. I claimed there is no inconsistency between admitting that the mere fact that a judge has decided a case may change the law and claiming that in deciding it he has no discretion. Perhaps the mere fact that the judge has decided the case changes the law, not through an exercise of discretion, but as a result of his efforts to discover the right answer. The retroactivity problem may arise because in law, as is not the case in science, the mere fact of theorizing by a judge itself counts as a further piece of data for later theorizing. But perhaps so long as the judge can give a principled justification for his decision, even if it was not reliably predictable, the change to the law represented by his decision is not arbitrary. Recognizing such changes, it might be argued, is itself supported by the considerations of coherence and community

---

[21] This *tu quoque* on behalf of coherence accounts seems to be borne out by the Court's oscillation between precedent and nonretroactivity in *Stovall*, *Desist* and *Shea*, op cit, where the issues do not arise as a consequence of any particular theory of adjudication.
[22] Kress, op cit, at 384.

integrity that support respect for precedent. People know that the legal system gives weight, in this timeless sense, to intervening precedents, even if they do not know that they are ahead of time. Is this really any more objectionable than not knowing the right answer itself ahead of time?

Of course, we accept that it may be hard to determine what the best account of settled cases would say about the case at issue, before it is decided. What the best theory really is, and how it bears on the case at issue, may be quite controversial.[23] But these are epistemological problems, not problems of true retroactivity; changes in our knowledge of the law should be distinguished from changes in the law. It simply is often extremely difficult to know what the law requires; perhaps only the best lawyers know for sure, and we cannot afford them. But nevertheless we are held to the law, and we must do the best we can to understand what it is. It is unfortunate, and gives rise to unfairness, that the law is so complex and difficult, and that access to it so expensive and restricted; but again these are not problems of true retroactivity. It might be objected that if from a litigant's practical point of view the effects of the 'mere' epistemological problem and those of 'true' retroactivity are much the same, and we can live with the former, then the latter cannot be so bad. But the stubborn intuition remains that true retroactivity is somehow more profoundly unfair than are the effects of the epistemological problem. Let us therefore, for the sake of argument, also put the 'not-so-bad' response aside.

7. The Source of the Problem: Coherentism vs Precedent

Consider what features of a system of decision-making are necessary or sufficient to give rise to the problem of intervening cases. As we have seen, coherence accounts of practical reasoning give settled cases an important role as the data, so to speak, to which the theories or principles sought in deliberation are responsible. Moreover, coherence accounts impose a general requirement with respect to settled law of treating like cases alike (which I will sometimes refer to as 'the weaker requirement'). That is, legal truths are a function of, among other things, settled law;[24] resolution of the actual case at hand must be consistent with the resolution of comparable settled cases. While, concerning any particular settled case, it is possible that the best theory of settled cases may show that it is mistaken, if theoretical coherence overall with settled cases is the standard, then it is not possible for all settled cases to be mistaken; hence coherentist consistency involves a certain element of conservatism. However, while these elements are present in coherence accounts of legal reasoning in particular, they are not sufficient to give rise to the problem of intervening cases or any distinctive issues about retroactivity. The latter only arise in virtue of a further requirement (that I will sometimes refer to as 'the stronger requirement', since it is not entailed by the weaker requirement),

---

[23] This paper is not intended to address the problem of whether systematically wicked law is really law; on this see, for example, Ronald Dworkin, *Law's Empire* (London, Fontana Press, 1986), at 102–8.

[24] Kress, op cit, at 380.

imposed by the doctrine of precedent in the legal context in particular, namely, that actual settled cases are to be given more weight, in virtue of having actually been decided by a court, than hypothetical settled cases, or, in Kress's words, that 'prior decisions are to be accorded weight which may influence the outcomes in later cases merely by virtue of the fact that the decisions have occurred'.[25] Since the stronger requirement imposed by the doctrine of precedent is not a necessary feature of all coherence theories, Kress is wrong to the extent that he suggests that the prospect of intervening case retroactivity arises for all coherence theories.[26]

Decision theory provides one illustration of coherentist reasoning minus the stronger requirement of precedent; within decision theory, coherence with settled preferences provides a standard for the determination of problematic preferences, but settled preferences about actual alternatives that have issued in actual decisions are not given greater weight in principle than settled preferences about hypothetical cases. Consideration of decision theory, in which no problem of intervening cases arises, will thus help to bring into focus the way in which the problem depends on the stronger requirement of precedent.

Suppose a decision theorist is trying to help a decision-maker arrive at decisions about certain difficult issues where his criteria of choice or goals conflict. The decision theorist aims to discover the decision-maker's indifference curves with respect to those conflicting criteria or goals in order to help him to make the decision among the actual alternatives that places him on his highest indifference curve. To do this the decision theorist must depend on data provided by the decision-maker about what his preferences clearly are or would be in various cases which are easier for him to decide about than the case at issue is. These cases need not all involve feasible alternatives; some may be purely hypothetical. The exercise is one of extrapolating consistently from the set of settled preferences to a determination of the case at issue. Perhaps some of the settled preferences of the decision-maker are outliers and cannot be regarded as consistent with the rest within any theoretically acceptable representation of the decision-maker's preference space; such settled preferences may be disregarded as 'mistakes'. But it is of the nature of this exercise that there cannot be too many such mistakes. Settled preferences are here the data for which the decision theorist's representation of the decision-maker's preference space must account. Theories may tell us that some of the data they aim to account for are suspect or corrupt, and must be disregarded, but ultimately theories are supported by data. The basis for regarding some settled preferences as mistaken is their failure to cohere with the rest; thus

---

[25] Kress, op cit, at 400.

[26] At 398: '. . . since nothing in the argument has relied on the details of any coherence theory, it should be clear that ripple effects will occur in all coherence theories. . . .'. See also 371: 'The ripple effect will occur in any coherence theory with a principle of conservation. In adjudication, precedent provides the conservative element.' However, compare his concessions to the distinction between coherence theories in general and the legal doctrine of precedent in particular at the very end of the article, 401–2. It is possible that, despite the way Kress introduces his problem by reference to coherence theories in general, not just in law (369–70), the remarks quoted above should be interpreted as restricted to legal contexts, which involve the doctrine of precedent in particular. But my primary purpose is to address Kress's interesting problem on the merits, and the substantive issues I consider arise however Kress's remarks are interpreted.

there cannot be a basis for regarding too many of them as mistaken (though, of course, just what counts as 'too many' is difficult to specify).

The conservatism of this interpretative exercise is also attributed by a coherence account to legal reasoning: not too many settled cases can be regarded as mistakes, or the basis for regarding them as mistaken is itself undermined. However, these elements of conservatism do not entail that settled actual cases should be given more weight than settled hypothetical cases, and hence they are not sufficient to give rise to the problem of intervening cases. The mere fact that a decision-maker actually makes an intervening decision between the time at which certain events occur and the time at which he must face a further problematic decision about those events does not alter the set of settled cases with which his second problematic decision must cohere. (Of course a change of mind does alter the set of settled cases; but this is a different matter.) A settled case may be equally settled, whether actual or hypothetical. More generally, the set of settled cases does not coincide with the set of actual cases. Not all actual cases are settled (some are problematic), and not all settled cases are actual (some are hypothetical).[27]

If the stronger requirement of adherence to precedent were not imposed on legal reasoning in addition to the weaker elements of conservatism imposed by a coherence account and shared with decision theory, no problem of intervening cases would arise in law either. To see this, consider a revisionary conception of the law as equally responsible in principle to both settled actual and settled hypothetical cases, so that the change of a settled case's status from hypothetical to actual between occurrence of the events litigated and their adjudication cannot via precedent change the law about the later case. Such a revisionary conception of the law is compatible with a generally coherentist approach to practical reasoning, but it omits the distinctively legal doctrine of precedent. Now whether a case is settled or not does not depend on whether it has actually been decided; a settled case is equally settled whether its current status is actual or hypothetical, and retroactivity does not arise in the way Kress envisages.

Kress considers the possibility that the law does not change purely in consequence of legal decisions, but points out that this would be to purchase unchanging right answers at the cost of dispensing with the doctrine of precedent. He writes: 'Judicial decisions change the settled law' and: 'To deny that law and legal rights change at all in response to new decisions is to deny that legal rights are, at least in part, determined by settled law.'[28] While I think he is correct to regard the denial of any change of law in response to new actual decisions as giving up the doctrine of precedent, nevertheless, it is logically possible to hold that legal rights are, at least in part, determined by settled law, without holding that a change in a case's status from hypothetical to actual is *per se* a change from unsettled to settled. It is just this logical space that is occupied by the revisionary conception of law we are now

---

[27] Compare Kress on the analogy between legal and scientific theorizing, at 392n, and on the character of settled law, at 278. My use of the term 'settled' here does not coincide with his, but I believe that something like my use is essential to convey what is distinctive about coherentist views of practical reasoning, and of legal reasoning in so far as it is a species of practical reasoning.

[28] At 380, 393.

considering, which in effect does not incorporate the doctrine of precedent as we know it. Of course, new legal decisions may reflect extra-judicial changes in the settled law. But absent extra-judicial changes, under the revisionary conception new legal decisions would not change settled law, though they might change our awareness of it.

Kress further points out that, within Dworkin's theory at least, 'While at each point in time, there are right answers to all or nearly all legal issues, the right answer that is given may not be the same as that which would be given at another point in time, in consequence of changes in institutional history'. However, giving hypothetical and actual settled cases equal weight would *not* mean that the law cannot develop and change, but merely that such developments and changes, in *both* actual and hypothetical cases, would reflect *extra-judicial* developments and changes in institutional history, social practices, etc.[29] Cases that were unsettled might become settled as the law develops, in response to extra-judicial developments. But under the revisionary conception a case would not change from unsettled to settled *merely* by becoming the subject of a judicial decision and changing status from hypothetical to actual.

I emphasize that I have invoked this revisionary conception of law not in order to endorse it, of course, but merely to illustrate my claim that the problem of intervening cases does not arise from the coherentist character of legal reasoning *per se*, but rather from the further distinctive asymmetrical treatment of actual and hypothetical cases by the doctrine of precedent in particular. The point of the distinction between coherentist practical reasoning absent the doctrine of precedent and legal reasoning with the doctrine of precedent is not to suggest we should respond to Kress's problem by doing away with precedent, but rather to contribute to diagnosing the source of the problem. This distinction is important because it is the general character of consistency and conservatism with respect to hypothetical as well as actual cases in coherentist practical reasoning, which legal reasoning shares and which the doctrine of precedent does not eliminate but rather supplements, that supports the view I go on to assert in section 8 below, namely, that the special role of precedent in legal reasoning only makes a difference when the decided cases appealed to as precedent were not *ex ante* correct.

It may be objected that intervening case retroactivity would occur even under the revisionary conception of law, so long as the law is subject to change such that coherence with intervening, newly settled cases may be invoked to justify legal decisions about events that occurred before the change. Perhaps the objector will admit at this point that it would not matter whether the change in settled cases occurs within the category of actual or hypothetical cases; it need not be the result of a change in status from hypothetical to actual. But so long as the possibility of change in the set of settled cases is admitted, even though the initiation of change is distributed across actual and hypothetical cases, it may be claimed that the problem of intervening cases would remain.

---

[29] See and compare Kress, op cit, at 392–4.

Advocates of coherence accounts are not committed to denying that the law may change. However, they may wish, as Dworkin does, to deny that judges should initiate such changes, as opposed to trying to discover what the best theory of settled law requires. (There is nothing analogous to this division of labour between the judiciary and other, law-making, branches of government, in the ethical and decision-theoretic versions of the pursuit of coherence. In these latter cases, the deliberator plays the legislative as well as the judicial role; his decisions may reflect changes of mind that originate changes in the set of settled cases. At the same time, there is no problem of retroactivity, although if someone changes his mind about what he should have done after doing it, he may well regret having done it.) On the view that the judicial role is to discover the law, not to make it, changes in judicial perception of the content of settled cases, whether actual or hypothetical, *ought* to reflect extra-judicial legal developments, such as changes in social practices and customs with constitutive bearing on the law,[30] or in legislative or administrative background. Such extra-judicial developments put members of society on fair notice, and changes in legal theory which reflect such intervening changes should in principle be applied prospectively only.[31] However, legislative and administrative changes usually *are* applied prospectively only. Moreover, changes in social practices usually occur gradually enough that worry about such a change intervening between the time of the events litigated and their adjudication may often seem contrived and artificial. Perhaps there are occasionally abrupt, revolutionary changes in social practices, but they are surely unusual. Perhaps in these unusual cases changes in settled hypothetical cases which reflect the change in social practice should in theory be given effect prospectively only (although there may be practical difficulties in identifying such cases and the time of the change of social practice involved). Such exceptions would have a rationale in the extra-judicial source of the change, and could be admitted without threatening the normal judicial practice to the contrary. Thus, extra-judicial changes in law do not threaten my claim that the problem of intervening cases does not arise from the coherentist character of legal reasoning *per se*, but rather from the distinctive

---

[30] See Ronald Dworkin, *Taking Rights Seriously*, (London, Duckworth, 1977), at 40–2.

[31] An example would be given by a slight variation of the sequence of events in *California Federal Savings and Loan Association* v *Guerra*, 107 SCt 683 (1987). In *Cal Fed*, a pregnant worker's employer brought suit seeking a declaration that a California statute requiring employers to provide leave and reinstatement to employees disabled by pregnancy was preempted by the federal statute, Title VII, which prohibited sex discrimination. The court upheld the California statute, although in the 1976 case of *General Electric Co* v *Gilbert*, 429 US 125, 97 SCt 401, it had interpreted Title VII in a different manner, reasoning that discrimination against pregnant persons was not sex discrimination because many non-pregnant persons are female. In 1978 Congress expressed its disapproval of the *Gilbert* reasoning by amending Title VII to make clear that it intended sex discrimination to include discrimination against pregnant persons. The disputed events in the *Cal Fed* case occurred in 1982: the employee took a pregnancy leave, and when she informed her employer she was ready to return to work she was told her job had been filled and there was no available positions. She filed a complaint under the California statute, and her employer brought a suit seeking a declaration that the statute was preempted by Title VII's ban on sex discrimination. The case was decided in 1987.

Now suppose that between the *Gilbert* decision in 1976 and the 1978 amendment to Title VII events like those disputed in *Cal Fed* occurred, but only came to trial after the *Cal Fed* decision. Then *Cal Fed* would have the status of an intervening case. However, it would have been following an extra-judicial initiation of an addition to the settled law, namely, the amendment of Title VII in 1978. Under these circumstances it would seem that the legislative change should be given prospective effect only.

asymmetrical treatment of actual and hypothetical cases by the doctrine of precedent in particular.

In summary, the purely coherentist revisionary conception of law as lacking the stronger requirement, imposed by the doctrine of precedent, would support the following argument. Either cases intervening between the occurrence of events and their adjudication reflect intervening extra-judicial changes in settled law or they do not. If they do, the prospective-only application of the new legal hypotheses supported by the newly settled law is appropriate for the same reason that prospective-only application is appropriate for legislative decision-making, namely to avoid the unfairness of retroactivity. In such circumstances, we have judicial reflections of extra-judicial legal developments, not judicial law-making.[32] Cases that articulate such developments and incorporate them within a coherent legal theory may change what we believe the law to be, but they do not in themselves change the law, any more than an illuminating new scientific theory changes the truth about what the best theory is merely by changing our beliefs about what it is. On the other hand, if the intervening cases do not reflect extra-judicial changes, then either they are settled or they are not. The mere fact that they have been actually decided does not resolve this question. If an intervening case is not settled, the fact that it has been decided between the occurrence of events and their adjudication does not change the settled law. The fact that the case has been explicitly considered and decided *per se* does not make it a case that is clear to the relevant decision-makers. Moreover, it may have been a settled case before it was decided, if its resolution would have been clear had it been considered. That is, either the intervening case is not settled, despite being actual, or is settled, and was before it was decided. Either way, there is no retroactivity. Thus the coherentist character of the revisionary conception of law as merely requiring that like cases be treated alike and that hence not too many settled cases be regarded as mistaken is not sufficient to give rise to the problem of intervening cases; in addition, the doctrine of precedent is necessary.[33]

8. The Source of the Problem: Precedent vs Mistake or Underdetermination

There thus seems to be a—perhaps surprising—tension between the doctrine of precedent, on the one hand, and the requirements of fairness which make retroactivity objectionable, on the other. But perhaps the doctrine of precedent is not sufficient to give rise to the problem of intervening cases either, though necessary. It seems clear that the revisionary coherentist conception of law I sketched in the last section, under which no distinction of weight at all is drawn between settled actual and settled hypothetical cases, involves a substantial departure from the doctrine of precedent as we know it. Nevertheless, the doctrine of precedent as we know it is compatible with the significant influence of settled

[32] As in the variation on *Cal Fed*, ibid.
[33] Cf Kress, op cit, at 401–2.

hypothetical cases; it does not require that status as actual and status as settled coincide. Because of this, the argument that applied to the revisionary conception of law to show that intervening case retroactivity would not arise may be available, at least under certain circumstances, in a legal system that does incorporate the doctrine of precedent. I will briefly consider some cases to illustrate the point that status as actual and status as settled do not in fact coincide. I will then go on to try to sharpen the diagnosis of the intervening case retroactivity. I shall argue, largely following suggestions made by Dworkin, that only actual intervening decisions that are *ex ante mistaken*, or at least not uniquely correct (in cases of underdetermination), but which the doctrine of precedent nevertheless presumptively constitutes as judicially-initiated changes in the law, give rise to retroactivity.

Not all actually decided cases are settled; indeed, some actual cases, even some that are settled, may be mistaken,[34] in virtue of their failure to cohere with other settled, including actual, cases. Dependence on some actual cases, is avoided, even if they have not been explicitly overruled as mistaken, because they are highly controversial, and/or considered uncertain, dubious, or poor authority. Moreover, the doctrine of precedent may not treat actual cases of courts of other jurisdictions as settled. An example of an intervening actual case which was nevertheless not settled is that of *Brown* v *Porcher*.[35] In *Brown*, the US Court of Appeals held that the construal of a South Carolina statute to disqualify any claimant who voluntarily left her most recent employment because of pregnancy violated a federal statute providing that no person shall be denied unemployment compensation under state law solely on the basis of pregnancy. *Brown* was decided in 1981; the US Supreme Court denied certiorari in 1983. In 1980, however, events had already occurred which gave rise to the closely related case on the same issue of *Wimberly* v *Labor and Industrial Relations Commission*, which went up on appeal through the Missouri court system to the Missouri Supreme Court (in 1985), and eventually reached the US Supreme Court (in 1987).[36] The Missouri Court of Appeals had followed *Brown*, despite reservations concerning the soundness of its reasoning; but the Missouri Supreme Court reversed, declaring that it had never subscribed to the notion that Missouri state courts were bound to follow the decisions of lower federal courts in construing federal statutes.[37] The Missouri Supreme Court declined to follow *Brown*. 'We do not mean to suggest that a lower federal court's construction of a federal statute is wholly irrelevant. The courts of this state should "look respectfully to such opinions for such aid and guidance as may be found therein". . . . In some circumstances it may be appropriate for a state court to defer to long established and widely accepted federal court interpretations of federal statutes'. But it evidently felt that *Brown* was not a settled case in this sense. The US Supreme Court eventually resolved *Wimberly* in favour of the Missouri

---

[34] As Kress admits, at 378.
[35] 660 F2d 1001 (1981), cert denied, 459 US 1150, 103 SCt 796 (1983). Perhaps various abortion cases provide other current examples.
[36] 107 SCt 821 (1987).
[37] Justice Donnelly, concurring in the result, denied that US Supreme Court decisions interpreting the US Constitution are binding on the states.

view and against *Brown*. But the point to be made here is not that *Brown* was mistaken; perhaps it was correct. It is rather that *Brown*, the intervening case, did not change the settled law because it was not a settled case, from the perspective of the Missouri Supreme Court. Thus, whether or not *Brown* was correct, the best theory about settled law, which should determine the outcome in the similar case which comes to trial after *Brown*, was not altered by the intervening case. If the result in *Brown* were to have been upheld as the correct result, there would have nevertheless been no retroactive application of the decision in the intervening case, since, as the Missouri Supreme Court implied, it was not a settled case. Continuing uncertainty about the right answer is just that, not retroactivity.

Furthermore, there are many settled hypothetical cases which are more deeply entrenched and would be more difficult to justify regarding as mistaken than many actual cases: we are lucky that such cases have remained hypothetical rather than actual. They have not become actual, in some cases, because the flagrant violations of rights they would involve luckily have not occurred in our communities. But they are nonetheless clearly settled for being hypothetical. A good example is found in Justice Marshall's eloquent dissent in the recent case of *US* v *Salerno and Cafaro*. The majority had upheld a statute permitting the denial of bail altogether in certain cases against Due Process and Excessive Bail Clause challenges, on the grounds in part that the statute is a regulatory rather than a punitive measure. Justice Marshall writes:

> The ease with which the conclusion is reached suggests the worthlessness of the achievement. The major premise is that '[u]nless Congress expressly intended to impose punitive restrictions, the punitive/regulatory distinction turns on "whether an alternative purpose to which [the restriction] may rationally be connected is assignable for it, and whether it appears excessive in relation to the alternative purpose assigned [to it]."' The majority finds that 'Congress did not formulate the pretrial detention provisions as punishment for dangerous individuals', but instead was pursuing the 'legitimate regulatory goal' of 'preventing danger to the community'. . . . Concluding that pretrial detention is not an excessive solution to the problem of preventing danger to the community, the majority thus finds that no substantive element of the guarantee of due process invalidates the statute.

Justice Marshall produces a settled hypothetical case as a counter-example to the majority's hypothesis about the punitive/regulatory distinction. He goes on:

> This argument does not demonstrate the conclusion it purports to justify. Let us apply the majority's reasoning to a similar, hypothetical case. After investigation, Congress determines (not unrealistically) that a large proportion of violent crime is perpetrated by persons who are unemployed. It also determines, equally realistically, that much violent crime is committed at night. From amongst the panoply of 'potential solutions', Congress chooses a statute which permits, after judicial proceedings, the imposition of a dusk-to-dawn curfew on anyone who is unemployed. Since this is not a measure enacted for the purpose of punishing the unemployed, and since the majority finds that preventing danger to the community is a legitimate regulatory goal, the curfew statute would, accord-

ing to the majority's analysis, be a mere 'regulatory' detention statute, entirely compatible with the substantive components of the Due Process Clause.[38]

He regards the absurdity of this conclusion as a settled aspect of the law, and nonetheless settled for the fact that the case envisaged is merely hypothetical. Here is a settled hypothetical case that is more entrenched, and less likely to be regarded as mistaken by the best legal theory, than many actual cases.

We have considered two cases in which the dissenting opinions appeal persuasively to hypothetical cases to defeat hypotheses on which the majority opinion seems to turn, *Parham* and *Salerno*. Suppose for the sake of argument that these decisions were mistaken up to the time of the decision, or *ex ante mistaken*. Nevertheless, the doctrine of precedent tells us we cannot assume them to be *ex post mistaken*; we cannot infer an *ex post* mistake from an *ex ante* mistake because the fact of the actual decision may change the law. It is possible that an *ex ante* mistake is so serious that the enormity of the mistake outweighs its precedential force, and it remains a mistake even *ex post*; but the mere fact of the decision has loaded the balance against this possibility. A mistake must be more serious, must be more deeply incoherent with the settled law, including hypothetical as well as actual cases, to be an *ex post* mistake than to be an *ex ante* mistake; the difference is a matter of degree, a matter of how much must be uprooted to accommodate the law to the mistake.

We see then that the doctrine of precedent permits determinately *ex ante* mistaken decisions to change the law;[39] such decisions, as intervening cases, may give rise to retroactivity. Of course, the doctrine of precedent is not addressed to mistakes in particular; it does not perversely dignify *ex ante* mistaken actual decisions as opposed to *ex ante* correct actual decisions by presumptively constituting only the former as law henceforward. But precedential force is not needed to constitute an *ex ante* correct decision as correct *ex post*; in this respect it is redundant (though of course it may feature nonredundantly in the reasoning from previous precedents that makes the decision *ex ante* correct). No special method of transition between *ex ante* standing and *ex post* standing is needed in the case of correct decisions; precedent has no law-changing work to do in these cases. Since resolutions that are *ex ante* correct all things considered do not conflict with one another to begin with, increasing the weight of a correct settled case as it changes from hypothetical to actual makes no difference. Of course, courts may not *know* whether the actual cases they defer to as having precedential force were *ex ante* mistaken or not. Nevertheless, we may issue a challenge: how, on coherentist assumptions, could the precedential force of a decision, other than one reflecting extra-judicial legal developments, change the *law* itself, as opposed to our *beliefs* about it, if that decision were *ex ante* correct?

---

[38] *US* v *Salerno* 107 SCt 2095, 2107–2108 (1987).

[39] Compare Kress's claim at 394 that 'wholesale and final determination of the truth or falsity of all possible legal propositions leaves no room for the operation of the dominant notion of precedent'.

This in effect is Dworkin's response to the problem of intervening cases. He argues as follows.[40] He does consider that integrity requires us to give weight to the fact that a case was actually decided so, even if it was decided wrongly. Either an intervening case is wrongly or rightly decided. Suppose it is wrongly decided. Then it will indeed change the law retroactively, and for the worse, since it was wrongly decided. That is one reason it is so important for judges to reach the right answer! We can accept that there is objectionable retroactivity in this case, but that is not a consequence of the coherentist account of adjudication, or of the doctrine of precedent, but rather of the fact that the wrong answer was reached. Suppose, on the other hand, that the intervening case was rightly decided; then we are presented with a challenge. How could a correct decision in an intervening case make for retroactive change of the law?[41] How could the affirmation of a correct hypothesis itself change hypotheses in subsequent cases from right to wrong or vice versa? It might make the correct answers to later cases more evident or predictable, but this is not what Kress needs for his claim; retroactivity involves a change in the law, not merely a change in our beliefs about the law.

For the moment put aside the possibility, which I will return to, that the correct decision (not merely our beliefs about it) was *ex ante* underdetermined, rather than mistaken. To claim, following Dworkin, that precedent only makes a difference given an *ex ante* mistake does not amount to saying that precedent does not make any difference to the way people *should* reason about the law. One can hold that decided cases do and should make a difference to the way people should reason, via the doctrine of precedent, *though they are ex ante mistaken*, even if one also holds that they make a difference only when they are *ex ante* mistaken, since they must be either correct or mistaken, and if they are correct their actually being decided makes no difference. The argument for the latter qualification derives from the role of hypothetical cases in coherentist practical reasoning in general; precedent is an additional special feature of legal reasoning, but it does not eliminate the general

---

[40] In discussion.

[41] Kress gives an example, in which the force of precedent is conceived in a mechanical way to involve counting the number of steps required for privity of contract, which he claims is a paradigm case of coherentist reasoning. See 382–3. However, it can be dismissed as not an example of Dworkinian, or more generally, coherentist reasoning at all, since it does not involve consideration of the reasons or principles that support particular results.

Some implicit support is found in Supreme Court cases for Dworkin's view that a correct decision in an intervening case does not change the law. In the criminal procedure context, see in particular the dissents by Justice Harlan and Justice Fortas in *Desist*, op cit. Justice Harlan writes: '. . . If a "new" constitutional doctrine is truly right, we should not reverse lower courts which have accepted it; nor should we affirm those which have rejected the very arguments we have embraced. Anything else would belie the truism that it is the task of this Court, like that of any other, to do justice to each litigant on the merits of his own case. It is only if each of our decisions can be justified in terms of this fundamental premise that they may properly be considered the legitimate products of a court of law, rather than the commands of a super-legislature'. See also H. Schwartz, 'Retroactivity, Reliability, and Due Process', (1966) 33 *U Chi LR* 719 at 748–9. In *Hanover Shoe* v *United Shoe Machinery Corp*, an antitrust case, the US Supreme Court discussed the intervening case issue explicitly, writing: 'The theory of the Court of Appeals seems to have been that when a party has significantly relied upon a clear and established doctrine, and the retrospective application of a newly declared doctrine would upset that justifiable reliance to his substantial injury, considerations of justice and fairness require that the new rule apply prospectively only.' The Supreme Court, however, did not find before it a situation in which there was a clearly declared judicial doctrine upon which a party had relied and which was overruled in favour of a new rule. The intervening cases in question did not indicate that the issues they decided were novel, or that they involved a departure from an earlier line of cases or the need for innovative principles. 'Whatever development in antitrust law was brought about was based to a great extent on existing authorities and was an extension of doctrines which had been growing and developing over the years.' See *Hanover*, 392 US 481, at 496–9 (1968).

role of hypothetical cases in legal reasoning as a special case of practical reasoning. Precedent does and should make a difference to correct reasoning about what the law is, and this is why, in part, the problem of retroactivity does arise. Reasoning from an *ex ante* mistaken precedent is not itself mistaken simply because of the *ex ante* mistake.

The argument as to under what circumstances an intervening precedent can change the law may be elaborated as follows. Either the intervening decided case was *ex ante* correct or *ex ante* mistaken; moreover, either the corresponding hypothetical case was settled in the same way as the actual case was decided, or it was not so settled. Then there are four cases to consider. Suppose first that the decision was *ex ante* (but not *ex post*) mistaken in fact, but nevertheless settled, ie it was, or would have been, wrongly believed of the corresponding hypothetical case that the (in fact) mistaken decision would be the correct decision for such a case. False beliefs about the *ex ante* law have been replaced by true beliefs about the *ex post* law, made true because the law has changed, in virtue of an *ex ante* mistaken precedent that is good *ex post* law. The retroactivity problem arises with respect to what the law is (though not with respect to beliefs about the law), but that is due to the *ex ante* mistaken decision. Second, suppose that the decision was *ex ante* (but not *ex post*) mistaken, though not settled as a hypothetical case. In this case the law and beliefs about it may change as a result of the decision, but again retroactivity is associated with an *ex ante* mistaken decision. Third, suppose the decision was *ex ante* correct and settled. In this case there is change neither in the law nor beliefs about it, so no retroactivity problem can arise.

The fourth case is the interesting case: here the decision was *ex ante* correct, but the corresponding hypothetical case was not settled in accord with the correct decision. The truth about the law has not changed as a result of the correct decision, though what is believed about it *may* have changed (again, the change from hypothetical to actual does not *necessarily* entail a change from unsettled to settled, since a decided case may remain unsettled). If beliefs about the law do not change as a result of the correct decision, neither the law nor beliefs about it have changed, so it is hard to see how the correct decision in a subsequent case could change. If beliefs about the law do change, it may be in one of (at least) two ways. On the one hand, they may have been undetermined before, and may now be settled in accord with the correct decision. Could this change in belief, absent a change in the law, be sufficient to change what the law is in a subsequent case? Whatever considerations they were in virtue of which the intervening decision was correct still obtain, and, to the extent they ever applied to the subsequent case, apply equally after the intervening case is decided. How could the mere addition of true beliefs about these unchanged considerations change the correct decision in the subsequent case, as opposed to making it more evident? On the other hand, beliefs about the law may have been mistaken before the intervening case, and they may have changed to accord with the correct decision in the case. How could this change from false to true beliefs about the intervening case change the law, as opposed to beliefs about it, in the subsequent case? It does not help to point out that according to a coherence account not too many settled cases can be mistaken, because we are now supposing the prior beliefs were false; if they were true, we are back to case three above, and there is no retroactivity. Whatever considerations they were in virtue of which the prior beliefs about the hypothetical version of the intervening case were false would apply also to the subsequent case, to the extent relevant. If we continue to assume that the law in the subsequent case was either determinately one thing or another at each point, and no change of law with respect to the intervening case was brought about by its correct decision, the challenge on coherentist assumptions still stands: how could a decision in the subsequent case be changed from correct to mistaken or vice versa merely as a result of a change in beliefs about the law in the intervening case from false to true, given no change in the law itself with respect to that case? Note that it is incorrect to object here that the determinacy assumption leaves no room for the operation of precedent, since we have seen that it does leave room for it in cases of mistaken decisions. What is at issue is whether precedent can make a difference given correct intervening decisions.

At this point we should consider the consequences of suspending the assumption of determinacy. If we allow that prior to a decision the right answer (not merely beliefs about it) may be underdetermined, then precedent may make a difference not just as a result of *ex ante* mistake, but also as a result of resolving *ex ante* underdetermination. Dworkin, of course, would resist the possibility of under-determination in arguing for his right answer thesis, so it does not, in the absence of an independent argument against the right answer determinacy thesis, help Kress make a case against Dworkin in particular. But some coherentists might accept the possibility of underdetermination, so it is relevant to the general discussion with respect to coherentism.

Thus, from a theoretical point of view at least, intervening case retroactivity can be laid at the feet, not of coherentist legal reasoning, or even of the doctrine of precedent, but rather of mistaken decisions, and perhaps also of underdetermi-nation of the law, to the extent a given version of coherentism admits this possibility. That legal mistakes are unfair to people is hardly news; the theoretical novelty and interest of the problem of intervening cases thus looks to diminish to the extent mistakes are its source. Moreover, the use of the problem as a means of criticizing Dworkin's version of coherentism in particular is limited by his rejection of the possibility of underdetermination. The general shape of my response to Kress with respect to the problem of intervening cases has been to draw out the consequences of a coherentist view of practical reasoning in general for legal reasoning and the doctrine of precedent in particular, which consequences limit intervening case retroactivity. The argument has proceeded by presenting a challenge to show how, *given the role of hypothetical cases within coherentist views of practical reasoning*, a correct, as opposed to *ex ante* mistaken or indeterminate, intervening case could give rise to retroactivity. Of course we may reject coherentist views and their consequences with respect to the doctrine of precedent altogether, but then we depart from Kress's subject matter. Note that my aim has not been to dispute the interest of the retroactivity problem which Kress has high-lighted, but rather his conception of coherentism in general and Dworkin's version thereof in particular as the proper targets of the argument.

In pursuing my course of argument, however, I have at several points had to put considerable weight on the distinction between changes in the law and changes in our beliefs about the law in particular cases. Coherentism admits this theoretical distinction on a case by case basis, even though it ties right answers and beliefs about them together globally in the way indicated in section 7 above, in that not too many settled cases can be mistaken. However, perhaps from a more pragmatic point of view, one more concerned with matters of notice and predictability, which may be closer to that of litigants and potential litigants, this distinction has been strained even so. Perhaps it is from this more pragmatic point of view that a distinctive problem about intervening cases arises.

Legal Reasoning and Coherence Theories: Dworkin's Rights Thesis, Retroactivity, and the Linear Order of Decisions

Kenneth J. Kress†

Coherence and holistic theories of truth maintain that a proposition is true if it fits sufficiently well with other propositions held to be true. Philosophers developed coherence theories in an attempt to avoid inadequacies in foundationalist accounts of truth and justification offered by traditional empiricists. The empiricist program to construct a theory of knowledge that explains all truths as inferences from general first principles and particular experiences has proven to be difficult.[1] There are serious objections to all of the major attempts.[2]

Led by Professor W.V.O. Quine's powerful arguments,[3] coherence and holistic theories of knowledge and justification predominate in current Anglo-American philosophical circles, and foundational empiricist theories are on the wane.[4] Coherence theories are more easily charac-

    † Third-year law student and doctoral student, Jurisprudence and Social Policy Program, Boalt Hall School of Law, University of California, Berkeley. B.A. 1978, University of California, Los Angeles; M.A. (Jurisprudence and Social Policy) 1983, University of California, Berkeley. An early version of this Article was presented on April 12, 1980 under the title *The Right Answer but the Wrong Right* at the Stanford-Berkeley Student Philosophy Conference held at the University of California, Berkeley. I am grateful to the commentator on that occasion, Richard Galvin, for his comments. More recent versions were presented at Boalt Hall School of Law, University of California, Berkeley, in November 1983 and at the philosophy department of the University of Illinois, Urbana-Champaign in December 1983. I regret that I am unable to list all of the many persons in attendance at these presentations, and others, who have made thoughtful and helpful remarks on the subject of this Article. It is with pleasure that I explicitly thank Robert Cooter, Melvin Eisenberg, George Fletcher, David K. Lewis, Joseph Raz, Philip Selznick, Stuart Sobel, Jack Tweedie, and Richard Wasserstrom for thoughtful remarks. For perceptive comments on several drafts, I am especially indebted to Michael S. Moore, Phillippe Nonet, Gerald Postema, and Jan Vetter. A special thanks is due to Jules Coleman, whose comments on the very first draft helped me to see the full impact of ripple effect retroactivity on Dworkin's right answer thesis.

    1. *See, e.g.*, R. CARNAP, THE LOGICAL STRUCTURE OF THE WORLD (2d ed. 1967); N. GOODMAN, THE STRUCTURE OF APPEARANCE (3d rev. ed. 1977).
    2. G. HARMAN, THOUGHT (1973); M. WILLIAMS, GROUNDLESS BELIEF (rev. ed. 1977).
    3. W.V.O. QUINE, *Two Dogmas of Empiricism,* in FROM A LOGICAL POINT OF VIEW 20 (2d rev. ed. 1980) [hereinafter cited as W.V.O. QUINE, *Two Dogmas of Empiricism*]; W.V.O. QUINE, *On What There Is,* in FROM A LOGICAL POINT OF VIEW 1 (2d rev. ed. 1980); W.V.O. QUINE, WORD AND OBJECT (1960) [hereinafter cited as W.V.O. QUINE, WORD AND OBJECT].
    4. *See, e.g.*, G. HARMAN, *supra* note 2; M. WILLIAMS, *supra* note 2; Harman, *The Inference to the Best Explanation,* 74 PHIL. REV. 88 (1965). In this Article, I gloss over the distinctions

terized by their denial that knowledge has the linear structure that foundationalist theories assert, than by a full-blown positive doctrine, as unfortunately happens all too often in philosophical disputes. A complete and convincing coherence epistemology has also proven elusive. There is agreement that the relation of coherence among propositions is more strict than logical consistency, yet less strict than logical entailment. But it is unclear where coherence lies between the extremes of consistency and entailment.[5] Nevertheless, the force of the criticism of foundationalism, together with the suggestive and illuminating beginnings by coherence theorists, has caught the philosophical imagination. Coherence theories of knowledge,[6] justification,[7] perception,[8] truth,[9] and ethics,[10] to name a few, have been proposed or developed in recent years. Coherence theorists have been a powerful, and perhaps the predominant, force in modern philosophy.

Given this philosophical climate, and the significant role played in law and adjudication by the concepts of legal and factual knowledge, legal and factual justification, legal and factual truth, and ethical truth and justification, it would not be surprising if legal theorists and legal philosophers were to develop coherence theories. Indeed, since the notions of precedent and argument from analogy have been explained in ways that resemble, and in ways that can be characterized as, holistic and coherence theories, we should expect and welcome the development of implicit and explicit coherence theories by legal scholars.[11]

We have not been disappointed. For example, Professor Dworkin has argued that judges do and should determine the right answer in hard cases by deciding whether the proposition advocated by the plaintiff or by the defendant provides a better fit or coheres better with the best theory of settled law.[12] Professor Moore has also given a central

---

among foundationalist theories and the differences among theories of justification, knowledge, and truth.

5. For a recent attempt to develop the concept of coherence, see N. Rescher, The Coherence Theory of Truth (1973).

6. Harman, *supra* note 4.

7. *See supra* note 3.

8. Chisholm, *On the Nature of Empirical Evidence*, in Empirical Knowledge: Readings From Contemporary Sources 224 (R. Chisholm & R. Swartz eds. 1973).

9. *See generally* 2 B. Blanshard, The Nature of Thought 212-331 (1939); N. Rescher, *supra* note 5; Dauer, *In Defense of the Coherence Theory of Truth*, 71 J. Phil. 791 (1974).

10. J. Rawls, A Theory of Justice 46-53 (1971); Rawls, *Outline of a Decision Procedure for Ethics*, 60 Phil. Rev. 177 (1951); *see also* R. Dworkin, Taking Rights Seriously 159-60 (rev. ed. 1978). *But see id.* at 353 (denying that the reflective equilibrium coherence theory provides a satisfactory account of private moral reasoning).

11. The importance of precedent and the related requirement of treating like cases alike suggest that coherence theories are especially appropriate in theories of adjudication.

12. *See* R. Dworkin, *supra* note 10, at 283; *see also id.* at 44, 340-42, 360. *See generally id.* at 81-130; Dworkin, *"Natural" Law Revisited*, 34 U. Fla. L. Rev. 165 (1982) [hereinafter cited as

role to coherence in his theories of facts, morality,[13] law, and legal reasoning.[14]

There is much to be said in favor of coherence theories and about their particular appropriateness to theories of legal reasoning. Nevertheless, I shall argue that currently accepted, and arguably desirable and necessary, features of modern Anglo-American legal systems[15] and straightforward aspects of coherence theories will sometimes result in decisions that appear morally arbitrary.

This Article has two related purposes. First, I develop an internal criticism of Dworkin's theory of law and adjudication. Many writers have criticized Dworkin's theory externally, by denying one or more of his premises. I grant Dworkin's premises and then argue that the theory does not fulfill its own aims. Second, I generalize the criticisms of Dworkin, and apply them to other theories of adjudication.

Part I describes Dworkin's motivation for rejecting positivism and his detailed criticisms of it. Part II examines Dworkin's theory of legal reasoning and presents an argument I call the "ripple effect." That argument leads to the conclusion that Dworkin's criticism of Professor Hart's positivism applies as well to Dworkin's own theory, the rights thesis. Dworkin claims that the positivist doctrine of discretion is unacceptable because it requires judicial legislation that results in retroactive application of law. The ripple effect argument shows that Dworkin's rights thesis is itself subject to retroactivity. Retroactivity is a more serious defect for Dworkin than for Hart because of Dworkin's commitment to the enforcement of preexisting rights and his right answer thesis. Part III considers potential responses to the ripple effect argument. Part IV illustrates the generality of the ripple effect argument. The ripple effect will occur in any coherence theory with a principle of conservation. In adjudication, precedent provides the conservative element. This Part also argues that conservative coherence theories and, more generally, the doctrine of precedent lead to a mor-

---

Dworkin, *"Natural" Law*]; Dworkin, *No Right Answer?*, 53 N.Y.U. L. REV. 1, 28-29 (1978) [hereinafter cited as Dworkin, *No Right Answer?*].

    13.   Moore, *Moral Reality*, 1982 WIS. L. REV. 1061, 1106-10.

    14.   M. Moore, Law, Language and Ethics (tent. ed. 1981) (unpublished casebook on file with the *California Law Review*); M. Moore, A Natural Law Theory of Interpretation (Feb. 25, 1984) (originally presented at the University of Southern California *Interpretation Symposium*, forthcoming in volume 58 of the *Southern California Law Review*). *See generally* Moore, *The Semantics of Judging*, 54 S. CAL. L. REV. 151 (1981).

    15.   The restriction to Anglo-American legal systems should not be taken to imply that there are reasons for believing that the arguments presented in the text do not apply to other legal systems. Rather, they express the fact that the attempt to apply them to other legal systems has not yet been undertaken. Insofar as other legal systems embody the preconditions of the ripple effect argument presented below, *see infra* text accompanying notes 53-76, 112-24, these conclusions hold for other legal systems also. Hereafter, I will use the term "legal system" to refer to Anglo-American and relevantly similar systems.

ally troubling linear ordering problem: legal rights depend upon the temporal order in which cases are decided.

I
POSITIVISM AND THE RIGHTS THESIS

A. *Dworkin's Motivation for Rejecting Positivism*

Dworkin's dissatisfaction with Hart's positivism provides the setting for the development of his rights thesis.[16] Dworkin's claim that legal positivism is false provides major support for his rights thesis. The shortcomings Dworkin finds in positivism inform his attempt to develop an alternative theory that successfully avoids those defects. Thus, one must understand Dworkin's criticism of positivism to evaluate his theory of law.

Dworkin selects as his target H.L.A. Hart's important version of legal positivism in *The Concept of Law*.[17] Dworkin claims that positivism is committed to four central claims:[18]

(1) *Model of Rules*: A legal system is a set of rules.

(2) *Rule of Recognition and the Separation of Law and Morals*: Valid legal rules are distinguished from spurious legal rules and from moral rules and etiquette by a master rule, the rule of recognition.[19] The rule of recognition sets out specific noncontentful criteria for legality. Dworkin calls these criteria tests of "pedigree or the manner in which they were adopted or developed."[20]

(3) *Discretion*: The set of valid legal rules is all there is to "the law." If a case is not clearly covered by rules, whether due to vagueness, conflicting rules, or a gap, the case is not covered by "the law."

---

16. R. DWORKIN, *supra* note 10, at 81-130 (Dworkin's theory of adjudication); *id.* at 14-80 (criticism of positivism); H.L.A. HART, THE CONCEPT OF LAW (1961).

17. H.L.A. HART, *supra* note 16. Dworkin's criticism appears in R. DWORKIN, *supra* note 10, at 14-80. Dworkin attacks Hart's positivism, as Dworkin understands it, but he intends his criticism to apply generally to all positivist theories. *Id.* at 22.

18. R. DWORKIN, *supra* note 10, at 17. Dworkin's list has been reorganized and renumbered to better suit present purposes.

19. The rule of recognition is discussed in H.L.A. HART, *supra* note 16, at 92-107, and in R. DWORKIN, *supra* note 10, at 20-21. Oversimplifying greatly, the United States Constitution can be considered a rule of recognition insofar as it ultimately determines the validity of any purported law within its jurisdiction.

20. R. DWORKIN, *supra* note 10, at 17 (emphasis omitted). "Pedigree" has been used in many different senses in recent jurisprudential writings. The test of "pedigree" has sometimes been conceived of as: (1) a historical test; (2) a formal test; (3) a noncontentful test; (4) a nonmoral or morally neutral test; (5) a noncontroversial or easy to determine test; (6) a simple or noncomplicated test; or (7) a mechanical test. Dworkin generally uses the term "pedigree" to mean a historical or morally neutral test, and sometimes uses it to mean a noncontroversial test. However, it is likely that Hart at most needs a morally neutral notion of pedigree.

The judge must exercise his discretion, creating new law and applying it retroactively to the case at hand.

(4) *Legal Obligation*: Citizens have obligations and duties only when their cases are covered by valid rules. In hard cases, judges exercise discretion because there is no preexisting right to enforce.[21]

Dworkin's objections to positivism are motivated by the need to provide a principled justification for the state's use of coercion and force in enforcing judgments. Dworkin's early critique of positivism, *The Model of Rules I*, opens with the claim that we have a fragile understanding of the notion of a legal obligation:

> Even in clear cases (a bank robber or a wilful breach of contract), when we are confident that someone had a legal obligation and broke it, we are not able to give a satisfactory account of what that means, or why that entitles the state to punish or coerce him. We may feel confident that what we are doing is proper, but until we can identify the principles we are following we cannot be sure that they are sufficient, or whether we are applying them consistently. In less clear cases, when the issue of whether an obligation has been broken is for some reason controversial, the pitch of these nagging questions rises and our responsibility to find answers deepens.[22]

Dworkin's criticism of legal positivism is based on the claim that the retroactive applications of law resulting from the positivist doctrine of discretion make it difficult to justify the use of the state's coercive power.[23] Dworkin argues that Hart's doctrine of judicial discretion entails that judges legislate in hard cases, thereby creating new rights and then applying those rights retroactively to the case at hand.[24] Dworkin asserts that if this account of adjudication in hard cases were correct, the use of the coercive mechanism of the state to enforce those judgments would be not only unjustified but unjust: "We all agree that it would be wrong to sacrifice the rights of an innocent man in the name of some *new duty created after the event*."[25] Thus, Dworkin's criticism of legal positivism is grounded in the difficulty of justifying retroactive

---

21. The claim that judicial discretion is a consequence of other positivist positions—for example, the view that rules do not resolve all cases and the view that in hard cases there are no preexisting rights—and not an argument for those positions is first clearly suggested by Dworkin in his introduction to THE PHILOSOPHY OF LAW 6-7 (R. Dworkin ed. 1977) (explicitly stating that the positivist doctrine that controversial legal propositions cannot be true or false supports the doctrine of discretion and denying the reverse).

22. R. DWORKIN, *supra* note 10, at 15.

23. Dworkin also bases his objection to the positivist doctrine of discretion on the ground that it violates the democratic principle of separation of powers. *Id.* at 30-31, 84, & *passim*. In addition, Dworkin claims that positivists cannot satisfactorily explain and justify the phenomenon of overruling. For further discussion of these points, see *infra* note 97.

24. R. DWORKIN, *supra* note 10, at 17, 30-39.

25. *Id.* at 85 (emphasis added).

application of law. In discussing what he describes as the *"ex post facto"* application of judicial discretion, Dworkin admits that:

This may not shock many readers—the notion of judicial discretion has percolated through the legal community—but it does illustrate one of the most nettlesome of the puzzles that drive philosophers to worry about legal obligation. If taking property away in cases [not covered by rules] cannot be justified by appealing to an established obligation, another justification must be found, and *nothing satisfactory has yet been supplied.*[26]

Dworkin's theory of adjudication, the rights thesis, is designed to avoid retroactive application of law. Dworkin names his theory so that it wears its major claim on its face: judicial decisions enforce preexisting (political) rights.[27] The rights thesis is able to avoid retroactivity because it asserts the controversial right answer thesis: there are always legally authoritative standards (for example, principles) that recommend single right answers in hard cases.[28] This claim allows Dworkin to deny the positivist doctrine of discretion that leads to the charge of retroactivity, which itself leads to the further charge that enforcing judicial decisions in hard cases has not been justified. There is no need for, and no room for, the positivist doctrine of discretion in Dworkin's theory. Because Dworkin's theory does not require, or even allow, judicial discretion, it has been thought to avoid retroactive application of law.

B. Principles as Authoritative

In criticizing Hart, Dworkin attempts to establish four propositions that form the foundation of his theory of adjudication. First, rules are distinguishable from principles.[29] Second, judges use principles (in addition to rules).[30] Third, principles are part of the law.[31] Fourth, the positivists' master rule, the rule of recognition,[32] cannot validate principles as law.[33] For purposes of this Article we need not determine whether Dworkin establishes any of the above propositions.[34] Brief explanation of the distinction between rules and princi-

---

26. *Id.* at 30 (emphasis added).

27. *Id.* at 87.

28. *Id.* at 81, 279-90; Dworkin, *No Right Answer?, supra* note 12. Dworkin admits that it is theoretically possible that a case could have no right answer. He believes that in a "modern, developed, and complex" legal system, such occurrences "will be so rare as to be exotic." *Id.* at 30-31, 32; *see also* R. DWORKIN, *supra* note 10, at 334.

29. R. DWORKIN, *supra* note 10, at 24-28.

30. *Id.* at 23-24.

31. *Id.* at 29-39.

32. *See supra* note 19.

33. R. DWORKIN, *supra* note 10, at 39-44.

34. For discussion of these issues, see Coleman, *Negative and Positive Positivism*, 11 J. LEGAL

ples and the argument that principles are part of the law will enhance understanding of the ripple effect argument proposed in Part II.

Dworkin's criticism of positivism in *The Model of Rules I* begins with the claim that positivism underestimates the resources available in the law to settle hard cases.[35] Dworkin claims that positivism has neither the theory nor the analytical tools for deciding cases that are not covered by rules. What positivism misses is the role in adjudication of policy, principle and other standards.[36] In his article *Hard Cases*, Dworkin eschews policy (and other standards) as a basis for judicial decisionmaking and narrows his criticism to the claim that positivism misses the role of principles alone.[37] Thus, Dworkin's attack on Hart's positivism revolves around the claim that in addition to rules, law contains principles.[38]

According to Dworkin, principles function differently from rules in the arguments that lawyers make about legal rights and obligations, particularly in hard cases.[39] Dworkin tells us that there is a logical distinction between legal rules and legal principles. Rules apply in an all-or-nothing fashion.[40] They can be canonized as general statements of the form "whenever A, then B" where "A" states facts and "B" states a legal conclusion.[41] If the antecedent A holds, B must be accepted. If A does not hold, B does not follow and the rule contributes nothing to any legal argument. Rules may have exceptions, but the exceptions would be included in an accurate statement of the rule.[42] In particular, rules cannot conflict. If two rules conflict, at least one of them is wrong, that is, not really a rule. As examples of rules, Dworkin gives us "A will is not valid unless signed by three witnesses" and "The

---

STUD. 139 (1982) [hereinafter cited as Coleman, *Negative and Positive Positivism*]; Coleman, Book Review, 66 CALIF. L. REV. 885 (1978) (reviewing R. DWORKIN, TAKING RIGHTS SERIOUSLY (1977)) [hereinafter cited as Coleman, Book Review]; Lyons, *Principles, Positivism, and Legal Theory* (Book Review), 87 YALE L.J. 415 (1977) (reviewing R. DWORKIN, TAKING RIGHTS SERIOUSLY (1977)). Additional discussion of Dworkin's views can be found in RONALD DWORKIN AND CONTEMPORARY JURISPRUDENCE (M. Cohen ed. 1984); *Symposium: Taking Dworkin Seriously*, 5 SOC. THEORY & PRAC. 267 (1980), and in *Jurisprudence Symposium*, 11 GA. L. REV. 969 (1977).

35. R. DWORKIN, *supra* note 10, at 22.

36. *Id.*

37. *Id.* at 81-130. Arguably, in his reply to Professor Greenawalt, Dworkin uses the concept of an argument of principle in so expansive a way that it includes what would ordinarily be thought of as policy arguments. *Id.* at 294-330.

38. *Id.* at 22.

39. *Id.*

40. *Id.* at 24.

41. Actually, this claim needs refinement since there may be chains of legal inferences. For example, [if A, then B] and A, therefore B; but also [if B, then C], therefore C, and so on. Thus, A, B, and C may be mixed statements of fact and law; or they may be statements of fact relative to one rule yet statements of law relative to another.

42. R. DWORKIN, *supra* note 10, at 25.

maximum speed on the turnpike is sixty miles per hour."[43]

Principles, according to Dworkin, do not provide for legal consequences that follow whenever certain conditions are met. For example, the legal principle that no man shall profit from his own wrong is not refuted by the doctrine of adverse possession or the fact that a man who jumps bail to make a brilliant investment in another state will keep his profits (although he may be returned to jail).[44] Rather, Dworkin claims, principles have a dimension of weight or importance.[45] Principles state reasons for a particular decision, but may not require it. For there may be principles of greater weight that point to the opposite conclusion.

That a particular principle does not determine a decision to which it applies does not, according to Dworkin, mean that it is not part of "the law":

> [A] principle may not prevail but that does not mean that it is not a principle of our legal system, because in the next case, when these contravening considerations are absent or less weighty, the principle may be decisive. All that is meant, when we say that a particular principle is a principle of our law, is that the principle is one which officials must take into account, if it is relevant, as a consideration inclining in one direction or another.[46]

If principles are not part of the law, Dworkin argues, then we cannot escape the unjustified retroactivity that undermines positivism. Dworkin sets up an alleged dichotomy:[47] either

(a) principles function authoritatively within the law the same way rules do in the sense that they are binding as law. Thus, they must be taken into account by judges and lawyers who make decisions of legal obligation: principles are part of "the law"; or

(b) principles cannot[48] be binding. They are not part of the law but are rather available to judges to use in hard cases if they so choose.

Dworkin claims this distinction is more than just a verbal question of the application of the word "law":

> The choice between these two accounts has the greatest consequences for an analysis of legal obligation. . . . The choice between these ap-

---

43. *Id.* at 24.
44. *Id.* at 25.
45. *Id.* at 26.
46. *Id.*
47. *Id.* at 29. The dichotomy is not jointly exhaustive. It may be the case that some principles judges cite are part of the law while others that they cite are not. *See* Raz, *Legal Principles and the Limits of Law*, 81 YALE L.J. 823, 836 (1972).
48. Dworkin erroneously employs the modal term "cannot." The appropriate parallel to (a) would be: (b) principles *are* not binding.

proaches will affect, perhaps even determine, the answer we can give to the question whether the judge in a hard case . . . is attempting to *enforce pre-existing legal rights and obligations.* If we take the first tack [(a)], we are still free to argue that because such judges are applying binding legal standards they are enforcing legal rights and obligations. But if we take the second [(b)], we are out of court on that issue, and we must acknowledge that the [litigants in hard cases are] deprived of their property by an act of judicial discretion applied *ex post facto*.[49]

Thus, according to Dworkin, unless we acknowledge that principles are part of the law, we cannot avoid the unjustified enforcement of retroactively applied law. Where the positivist finds a gap in the law because rules do not provide guidance, Dworkin discovers preexisting legal rights supported by authoritative principles.

II
Dworkin's Theory of Legal Reasoning and the Ripple Effect Argument

Dworkin claims that the rights thesis avoids the unjustified retroactivity that besets positivism. A close examination of Dworkin's theory of legal reasoning reveals that Dworkin's rights thesis is vulnerable to the same criticism Dworkin makes of Hart's positivism. The rights thesis requires retroactivity as well.

A. *The Settled Law and the Determination of Authoritative Principles*

To understand the ripple effect argument it is necessary to explicate Dworkin's theory of legal reasoning. While the broad outlines of Dworkin's theory of law are clear, there remains room for debate on many of the details[50] and Dworkin's views will probably continue to evolve.[51] Fortunately, the variations that occur in Dworkin's expression of his theory and the respects in which the account below may elaborate upon or differ from Dworkin's current views will not affect the conclusions of this Article.[52]

The rights thesis maintains that even in a hard case, where rules do not provide definitive guidance, there is a single preexisting right answer. Guidance is provided, according to Dworkin, by authoritative principles. The judge's problem is to determine which principles are

---

49. R. Dworkin, *supra* note 10, at 29-30 (emphasis added).

50. *E.g.*, W. Wilcox, A Theory of Legal Theory 167 (August 1981) (unpublished doctoral dissertation on file with the *California Law Review*).

51. Dworkin's views have evolved in a number of articles published over the last twenty years. In some respects, the later essays elaborate upon earlier essays. In other respects, the later essays involve changes in doctrine. *See* Lyons, *supra* note 34, at 415; *see also infra* note 53.

52. For discussion of one respect in which my account may diverge from Dworkin's view, see *infra* text accompanying notes 109-11.

authoritative. Dworkin's answer is that a principle is part of the law and hence authoritative if it is part of the theory that provides the best explanation and justification of the settled law.

According to Dworkin,[53] when a judge confronts a legal question he should first determine the settled law in the jurisdiction. Settled law consists of the complete institutional history of the jurisdiction including constitution(s), enactment and repeal of statutes, judicial pronouncements, and perhaps administrative rulings. To simplify somewhat, settled law is the explicit, clear, black letter law.[54] Some aspects of the settled law may be disregarded as mistakes. Dworkin's theory for determining which prior decisions and other parts of institutional history may be considered mistakes is quite complicated.[55] Those parts of institutional history that are no longer persuasive to courts, legislatures, and the legal profession are particularly vulnerable to being labeled mistakes. So too are those parts that are unjust.[56] Adjusting the settled law by deleting mistakes is a subtle process that Dworkin has described as seeking a "reflective equilibrium" between the institutional facts and a coherent theoretical structure that could justify those

---

53. The account that follows is largely taken from Dworkin's inaugural lecture as Professor of Jurisprudence at Oxford, *Hard Cases*. R. DWORKIN, *supra* note 10, at 81-130. In his reply to critics, Dworkin amends the theory, giving a tentative account of the tradeoff between the dimension of fit (explanation of the settled law) and the dimension of moral appeal (justification of the settled law). Roughly put, the best theory of settled law is the most morally appealing theory of all those theories that exceed a set threshold of fit. *Id.* at 340-42, 360. In yet more recent writings, Dworkin suggests that the threshold of fit is not an absolute minimum, but only a rule of thumb. A theory that is sufficiently better on moral grounds than any theory that meets the threshold of fit may be the best theory of settled law even if it does not quite reach the threshold. *See, e.g.*, Dworkin, *"Natural" Law, supra* note 12, at 171-72.

The greater emphasis that Dworkin's writings since *Hard Cases* place on substantive moral considerations and consequent lesser role played by the notion of fit suggests that the new theory may not be a strict coherence theory. (Whether the new theory is a pure coherence theory will depend upon whether moral theory, and the full theory that combines or adjudicates between moral appeal and fit, are pure coherence theories.) In any event, the ripple effect argument presented in Part II, suitably modified, will apply to any version of the new theory.

Additionally, this interpretation of *Hard Cases* may be inaccurate if Dworkin intends his theory of legal truth to parallel those aspects of Quine's theory of evidence that reject the analytic/synthetic distinction in favor of a "continuum" of propositions from those at the center of our field of beliefs to those at the periphery. *See* W.V.O. QUINE, *Two Dogmas of Empiricism, supra* note 3, at 42-46. *But see* R. DWORKIN, *supra* note 10, at 164-65 (denying that Quine's theory is an accurate picture of the technique of reflective equilibrium that is analogous to common law adjudication and distinguishing the natural and constructive models of theorizing). However, the ripple effect argument that will be presented below applies, with the necessary changes, to a Quinean interpretation of Dworkin. For further discussion of this point, see *infra* text accompanying notes 110-11.

54. Dworkin's theory is more complex because it attempts to explain and justify not only currently operative law but, in addition, the enactment and repeal of a statute and a judicial decision and its later overruling. *See, e.g.*, R. DWORKIN, *supra* note 10, at 342, 360; Dworkin, *"Natural" Law, supra* note 12, at 165, 166, *passim*.

55. R. DWORKIN, *supra* note 10, at 118-23.

56. *Id.* at 122-23.

facts.[57] In the attempt to determine the best theory of the institutional facts, neither the judge's initial theory nor the judge's initial view of the settled law is immune from revision. Either may require revision in the attempt to obtain an equilibrium that best accommodates both. More likely, both will require revision. Put briefly, the judge should construct or determine that theory STL (the soundest theory of law) which best explains and justifies the settled law.

The soundest theory of law may be conceived as a set of basic principles P from which each of the propositions of settled law SL follow by deductive logic (or some slightly less strict form of theoretical consequence).[58] However, there are some propositions of law L which will remain open in the sense that neither the proposition nor its negation will follow deductively (or theoretically) from the basic principles P. The set of all such propositions L comprises the set N of nonconsequences. This set N of nonconsequences can be conceived as a set of ordered pairs of propositions and their contradictories. Since on Dworkin's theory there is always a single right answer, exactly one member of each pair of contradictories will be true. The class consisting of all the true members of these ordered pairs is the set of true but unsettled law, UC. (Intuitively, these are the implicitly true legal propositions, the coherence consequences.) The truth of a member of UC cannot consist in its following from P, the principles, by definition. Rather, Dworkin tells us, the members of UC are true by virtue of coherence. For example, if not-L, a member of the set N of nonconsequences is more coherent with STL than L is, not-L is true (and thus a member of UC), whereas L is false (and not a member of UC), and vice versa.

Thus, at any time, propositions of law that are not consequences of the basic principles P are true (or false) by virtue of their greater (or lesser) coherence with the soundest theory of law at the time. On the other hand, from the perspective of the theory, propositions of settled law may be said to be true by virtue of their following logically (or theoretically) from the basic principles P.[59]

---

57. *Id.* at 155, 159-68. The term "reflective equilibrium" derives from Rawls, who employed the concept in connection with moral theory and the theory of justice. J. RAWLS, *supra* note 10, at 46-53; Rawls, *supra* note 10.

58. The theoretical consequences that are not logical consequences contemplated in the text include analytic consequences, by which I mean consequences flowing from the meanings of words. Discussion and criticism of the concept of analyticity can be found in the writings of Quine. *See* sources cited *supra* note 3. The text leaves open the possibility that theoretical consequence also encompasses consequences even less strict than analytic but more strict than coherence. Nothing in this Article will depend upon the particulars of such more expansive forms of theoretical consequence.

59. This assertion may be misleading. The qualification "from the perspective of the theory" is significant because it signals one respect in which the strict separation of legal truths into settled law and coherence consequences is misleading. *See infra* text accompanying notes 109-11.

B.   *The Ripple Effect Argument:*
The Right Answer but the Wrong Right

Dworkin's theory of legal reasoning is built on the proposition that litigants are entitled to the enforcement of preexisting legal rights. One way in which the rights thesis expresses this major claim is by presupposing that litigants have a right to have decisions in civil cases determined by settled law.[60] In Dworkin's theory, settled law (together with moral theory) determines litigants' rights and litigants' rights determine the proper outcome. Thus, decisions are a function of, among other things, the settled law.

The argument I call the "ripple effect" relies upon these features of the rights thesis. In particular, the ripple effect argument depends upon legal rights being a function of settled law and upon the temporal gap between events being litigated and their eventual adjudication. Judicial decisions change the settled law. Often, if not always, the settled law will be changed between the occurrence of events being litigated and their eventual adjudication. In consequence, a litigant's rights will sometimes also be changed. If changes in the settled law change the dispositive legal right, a litigant who would have prevailed given the legal rights existing at the time of the occurrence will lose because he no longer has that right at the time of adjudication. The opposite is true of the opposing litigant.

This is retroactive application of law. The ripple effect argument suggests that the rights thesis sometimes enforces the wrong preexisting right. The rights thesis does not enforce the right that the prevailing party had when the events being litigated occurred, but rather the possibly different right existing at the time of adjudication.

1.   The Ripple Effect Argument

Dworkin's theory tells us that in a hard case, when a judge is called upon to decide a legal question Q that is not a logical (or theoretical) consequence of the principles P, he must do so by determining whether Q or not-Q coheres better with the soundest theory of law STL. Consider a case where Q coheres better with STL than not-Q does and the judge so holds. By virtue of that judical decision Q is no longer part of the true but unsettled law UC. It is now part of the settled law. This disturbs the theory STL and, as one would expect in a coherence theory, has *ripple effects*[61] on the rest of the system. More

---

60.   Coleman, Book Review, *supra* note 34, at 904.

61.   The terminology "ripple effect" was chosen to reflect the common metaphors of a coherence theory as a unified field of propositions, or as a spider's web with propositions at the intersections of the web's strands. Because of the many interconnections among the propositions (or points), any change in the location of any proposition within the field or web will occasion ripple

precisely, settled law now contains one more proposition, namely Q. Call the new settled law SL'. The new soundest theory of law STL' will, in general, differ from STL since it must explain and justify the additional data Q.[62] While STL' need not necessarily cohere with a different set of propositions than STL, in most cases STL' will so differ. With at most rare exceptions, STL' will cohere with a different set of propositions than STL did. That is, for some proposition X of the set of nonconsequences N, X cohered better with STL than not-X did, and was hence true and a member of UC with respect to STL before the decision. After the decision, not-X coheres better with STL' and is hence true and a member of UC' with respect to STL'. X was true but became false as a ripple effect of Q being settled by explicit judicial decision. Thus, while the judge discovered and did not create the truth of Q, the question at issue, he nonetheless created as an unintended consequence the truth of not-X. In a sense this should have been obvious: judicial decisions change the law.

Once it is admitted that judicial decisions can change the truth value of propositions of unsettled law by the ripple effect, it is easy to see how retroactive application of law can arise. Suppose that a lawsuit is pending in which X is dispositive. In the above example, if Q is settled after the events that gave rise to the lawsuit but before it comes to judgment, the law will change from X to not-X and a litigant will be subject to retroactive application of law.[63]

Note that the judge has inadvertently caused retroactive application of law, without exercising discretion. Q was the right answer, re-

---

effects on the rest of the propositions in the field or web. *See, e.g.*, W.V.O. QUINE & J. ULLIAN, THE WEB OF BELIEF (2d ed. 1978); W.V.O. QUINE, *Two Dogmas of Empiricism*, *supra* note 3, at 42-44.

62.   Since Q was part of the unsettled law, neither Q nor not-Q followed logically or theoretically from P.

63.   The argument is quite general. It requires only that legal truths sometimes change when settled law is enlarged by new decisions and that sometimes such changes occur in legal propositions that are dispositive of cases where the events occurred prior to the change and the adjudication occurs after the change.

The generality of the argument can be seen even more clearly in light of a set-theoretic characterization of coherence. Conceive of coherence as a mathematical function from sets of accepted data (or truths) to sets consisting of all true propositions including those true by virtue of coherence with accepted data. In Dworkin's theory, for example, the coherence function will take as argument (or input) institutional histories (or settled law) and will produce as value (or output) the complete set of legal truths given that institutional history. All that is required for ripple effects is that sometimes different inputs result in different outputs from the coherence function C. Put set theoretically, all that is required is that the coherence function C be nonconstant. In other words, a restriction of the image of C is a function. Given that minimal condition, ripple effects will occur. As noted above, retroactive application of law will occur if any such ripple effects change dispositive propositions of cases whose events occurred prior to the ripple effect and whose adjudication occurs after. For further discussion of the generality of this argument, see *infra* text accompanying notes 112-23.

quired by Dworkin's theory of adjudication, since Q cohered better with *STL* than not-Q did. Thus, we see that Dworkin's rights thesis requires that, *without exercising discretion*, judges sometimes retroactively apply law. Dworkin claims that the rights thesis is preferable to positivism because by avoiding judicial discretion it avoids retroactive application of law. That claim goes awry because it equates judicial discretion with judicial creation of law. In fact, it is the creation of new law, and not judicial discretion, that leads to the possibility of retroactivity. Once the concepts of law creation and judicial discretion are distinguished, it is possible to see how, *without exercising discretion*, applying law created (perhaps by other judges) after the events being litigated occurred can result in retroactive application of law. The acts of "law creation" by prior judges that result in the current judge's nondiscretionary yet retroactive application of law were themselves performed *without exercising judicial discretion*, according to Dworkin's own theory.[64]

A simplified example will illustrate the basic thrust of the ripple effect argument. Consider a hypothetical jurisdiction which is just developing the law of privity of contract. Suppose that in this jurisdiction, a case holds that direct contractual relations give rise to liability. For example, one may sue those from whom one purchases defective merchandise; liability exists at one step removed. However, another case holds that there is no liability six steps down the line. If consumer A buys from retailer B who bought from local distributor C, who bought from regional distributor D . . . who bought from manufacturer G, A may not recover from G even if the product is defective. Assume for the sake of illustration what is undoubtedly false, that each step in the chain of privity is of equal moral and legal "distance" in the relevant respects.[65]

The geometric model of the doctrine of precedent tells one, in a hard case, to split the legally relevant distance between the closest cases

---

64. The conflation of judicial discretion and judicial creation of law may result from the connection between discretion and legislation. By equating judicial discretion with judicial legislation, and legislation with creation of law, one might conclude that discretion entails creation of new law. In fact, discretion neither entails nor is required for creation of new law. First, discretion may exist but not result in legislation or creation of new law. A legal system could allow that in some areas where law is clear, judges may nonetheless be accorded discretion to change that law. Whenever the judge "exercises" discretion to retain the old law, discretion without legislation or creation of new law occurs. Second, as the text demonstrates, new law may be created without judicial discretion.

65. I have deliberately chosen an example where it is wildly implausible to suppose that the steps in question are of equal morally or legally relevant distance in order to focus on the general point. A more plausible example would draw attention to the details of the example, and whether the example's steps were of equal distance, thereby losing sight of the general point.

on point.[66] If a novel privity case were to come up in our jurisdiction at this point in time, the judge should find liability if the plaintiff is two or three steps removed since, by our assumption, two and three are closer to one than to six, and four and five are closer to six than to one. However, suppose that the next case decided is four steps removed and the judge correctly finds no liability. If a case three steps removed comes up at this point, the plaintiff will lose because three is closer to four, the closest no-liability case, than to one, the closest liability case. Although our imaginary plaintiff would have won had his case preceded the four-step case, he now loses. This situation creates a race to the courthouse that appears contrary to our notions of justice. If the three- and four-step cases are going up the appellate ladder simultaneously, an unfortunate situation results. If the four-step case reaches the top first, the defendants in the three- and the four-step cases win; if the three-step case reaches the top first, both plaintiffs win.

Of course, this is only a fanciful example. It assumes that precedent or argument by analogy is the whole of legal reasoning, while in any sophisticated legal system it will only play a part. In Dworkin's scheme, argument by analogy, coherence, or institutional fit (that the soundest theory of law must explain the settled law) competes with moral appeal (that the soundest theory of law must justify the settled law) in the account of legal reasoning.[67] Nonetheless, to the extent that precedent plays a part, the ripple effect will occur, bringing in its wake retroactive applications of law.[68] Precedent indeed plays a substantial role in Dworkin's theory. He tells us that the principle of fairness that like cases be treated alike requires that prior decisions have "gravitational force."[69]

2. The Right Answer but the Wrong Right

The ripple effect argument suggests that the right answer thesis is incorrect because it requires enforcement of the wrong right. As

---

66. The geometric model of precedent as splitting the legally relevant distance between the two closest cases, or lines of cases, on point is a paradigm example of a step-by-step coherence theory with a principle of conservation that leads to ripple effects. For a classic characterization of the geometric model, see E. LEVI, AN INTRODUCTION TO LEGAL REASONING 5 n.8 (1949). Dean Levi does not appear to endorse this geometric model.

67. R. DWORKIN, *supra* note 10, at 40-45, 60-65, 81-130, 342-44, 360.

68. Additionally, it must be admitted that theories of precedent that do not "split" the legally relevant distance are both possible and plausible. Such theories may maintain that when a new case "between" the two cases closest on point is decided, the borderline between plaintiffs' cases and defendants' cases does not move to half the distance between the new decision and the closest contrary case. Rather, these theories claim that precedent will result in the borderline moving a lesser amount in the direction of the closest contrary case. Such theories of precedent will allow fewer instances of ripple effect retroactivity, but will not totally avoid them.

69. R. DWORKIN, *supra* note 10, at 110-18.

Dworkin develops his theory in *Taking Rights Seriously*, it appears that judges are to enforce the rights that exist at the time of adjudication (adjudication rights).[70] The ripple effect argument establishes that the rights existing at the time of the event in issue (event rights) may differ from the adjudication rights. Unless event rights are enforced, the point of enforcing preexisting rights will be lost because law will be applied retroactively.[71]

Nowhere in Dworkin's writings does he explicitly discuss the question whether the right answer thesis applies to event rights or adjudication rights. The issue does not appear to have occurred to him. However, Dworkin's insistence on the injustice of "sacrific[ing] the rights of an innocent man in the name of some *new duty created after the event*"[72] is substantial evidence that he may believe that judges should enforce the rights existing at the time of the events. There are also strong arguments from the requirements of the rule of law that citizens be given notice of the laws to which they are subject and that their justified expectations not be upset, particularly when they have relied upon those expectations.[73] The arguments from the rule of law

---

70. R. DWORKIN, *supra* note 10, at 81-130.

71. *See infra* note 73 and accompanying text.

72. R. DWORKIN, *supra* note 10, at 85 (emphasis added).

73. Dworkin believes that the unfairness of retroactive application of law is not fully explained by the rule of law requirements to give prior notice, satisfy justified expectations, and the like. *Id.* at 335-38; *see also id.* at 85-86, 325. Dworkin must take this position because the controversial nature of right answers even when they exist means, as Dworkin admits, that right answers often cannot be demonstrated and therefore often are not known in advance. *Id.* at 81. Dworkin's objection to retroactivity appears to focus on the importance of giving a principled justification for enforcing judicial decisions. Dworkin's concern with retroactivity derives from the belief that creating and applying new rights at the time of adjudication cannot be given a principled justification. *See supra* text accompanying notes 22-26 & 49. Arguably, therefore, ripple effect retroactivity with its consequential disruption of expectations and failure to provide notice is not the kind of retroactivity that would concern Dworkin.

My response has three strands. First, even if the unfairness of retroactivity goes beyond the unfairness of upsetting expectations and failing to provide notice, surely expectation, notice and other rule of law virtues are at least part of the story. Dworkin's statements on this matter are not entirely clear, but he appears to agree that rule of law virtues are part, but not the entirety, of the point of enforcing preexisting rights. *Id.* at 336 ("An argument about legal rights, even in a hard case, is an argument about something relevant to fairness; if the court believes that the plaintiff has a right, then it believes, all things considered, *including the question of surprise*, that a decision against the plaintiff would be . . . unfair.") (emphasis added); *see also id.* at 325, 335-36. Thus, to the extent that the unfairness of retroactivity involves additional factors, those factors may well make ripple effect retroactivity more objectionable. They will not, however, diminish the objections provided by rule of law concerns. At most these fairness concerns, about which we may hope Dworkin will tell us more in the future, may sometimes outweigh the rule of law objections, justifying occasional episodes of ripple effect retroactivity.

Second, the moral force of the fairness of treating like cases alike, insofar as it extends beyond the demands of rationality resulting from the generality of reasons, is a difficult and elusive concept. It is yet more elusive when the cases that require like treatment occur after the events being litigated. For further discussion of this issue, see *infra* text accompanying notes 118-19 & 127-29.

Third, to the extent that the judge's decision depends upon events (decisions) after the events

virtues suggest *normative* grounds for enforcing the event rights. This is as we should expect, because the rule of law concerns are related to the desire to avoid retroactive application of law. Enforcing the event rights avoids the retroactivity engendered by the ripple effect argument.

Dworkin claims that the rights thesis has both prescriptive and descriptive aspects.[74] If Dworkin modifies his theory to enforce event rights, he may be able to save the prescriptive claim that this revised version of the rights thesis and right answer thesis is the theory of adjudication that judges should follow. However, in amending or further developing his theory in this way, Dworkin will be forced to give up the theory's descriptive aspect. The normative rule of law arguments and the related argument from the unfairness of retroactive application of law suggest that judges should decide cases on the basis of the law existing at the time of the events being litigated. This is not the current practice of courts, however. Judges in general enforce the rights and law that exist at the time of adjudication precisely because of our commitment to the Blackstonian declaratory theory that Dworkin defends.[75] Thus, the advocate of the rights thesis may adopt this position only at the expense of the claim that the theory is a correct description of judicial behavior.

It might be thought that the virtues of the revised theory justify giving up the descriptive claim. However, other factors militate against the proposed revision. First, the revision appears inconsistent with Dworkin's intention to distinguish adjudication from legislation.[76] Second, the theoretical and practical difficulties of implementing the revision are considerable and perhaps insuperable.

The proposed event right revision entails giving judicial decisions prospective effect only. To say that a judge is to decide a case on the basis of the law existing at the time of the events is to say that the judge is to give no precedential force to decisions after the events. From the perspective of the subsequent decisions, this means that the decisions

---

being litigated, the decision cannot be said to be an evaluation of the conduct of the litigants. When judges take into account post-event decisions, their judgments appear to reflect forward-looking considerations that are incompatible with the overall thrust of Dworkin's claim that adjudication looks backward to preexisting rights and duties.

74. R. DWORKIN, *supra* note 10, at 123. Although Dworkin is often thought to be giving both an account of how judges should decide cases and of how they do decide cases, *see, e.g.,* Lyons, *supra* note 34, at 415, he claims in his reply to Professor Soper that he is not making a conceptual or descriptive claim but rather defending a conception of the concept "law." R. DWORKIN, *supra* note 10, at 350-53. *See generally id.* at vii, 90, 123.

75. 1 W. BLACKSTONE, COMMENTARIES *69-70; Friedland, *Prospective and Retrospective Judicial Lawmaking*, 24 U. TORONTO L.J. 170, 170 (1974); Mishkin, *The Supreme Court, 1964 Term—Foreword: The High Court, The Great Writ and The Due Process of Time and Law*, 79 HARV. L. REV. 56, 58-72 (1965).

76. R. DWORKIN, *supra* note 10, at 82.

only apply to cases whose events occurred after the decision. But that is equivalent to saying that decisions have only prospective effect.[77]

Prospective decisionmaking is, however, inconsistent with the overall purpose of Dworkin's rights thesis. The rights thesis distinguishes arguments of principle, which are appropriate for the judiciary, from arguments of policy, which are appropriate for the legislature.[78] Dworkin's distinction between principle and policy, together with the claim that judicial decisions are to be justified by arguments of principle rather than policy, is intended to capture what is distinctive about adjudication.[79] But prospective overruling has been said to be particularly appropriate when the judge's decision appears legislative in character. The doctrine of prospective overruling is the legacy of legal realism, the doctrine that maintains that judges legislate.[80] For Dworkin to adopt that legacy of legal realism would indeed be ironic; it would undermine his thesis that judges are finding and declaring preexisting rights and not legislating new policy decisions.

Of course, this argument is merely suggestive and not conclusive. There may be grounds justifying prospective overruling that do not depend upon the view that judges legislate. The difficulty of implementing the revised event right theory suggests that we need not explore such grounds.

It is unlikely that the revised event right theory could be developed in detail, or utilized by judges if it could, for several reasons. First, the possibility of temporally extended events and transactions raises difficult problems in determining the date of the law to be applied. These problems are compounded if several related but separable transactions are being litigated and there are multiple issues. The prospect of ap-

---

77. Moreover, one must maintain an extreme view of prospective overruling. It would not be enough to simply adopt the common form of prospective overruling found in criminal procedure. *See, e.g.*, Linkletter v. Walker, 381 U.S. 618 (1965); Beytagh, *Ten Years of Non-Retroactivity: A Critique and a Proposal*, 61 VA. L. REV. 1557 (1975); Note, *Retroactivity and Prospectivity—Current Trends in the Law of Retroactive Decision-Making*, 7 WAKE FOREST L. REV. 500 (1971). This more common form of prospective decisionmaking will, by definition, affect those cases whose events occurred prior to the prospective decision but whose final adjudication did not. *See, e.g.*, *Linkletter*, 381 U.S. at 622-29; Molitor v. Kaneland Community Unit Dist. No. 302, 18 Ill. 2d 11, 27, 163 N.E.2d 89, 96-97 (1959). *See generally* Mishkin, *supra* note 75; Note, *Prospective Overruling and Retroactive Application in the Federal Courts*, 71 YALE L.J. 907 (1962) (Dean James O. Freedman's student note) [hereinafter cited as Note, *Prospective Overrulings*]. Because of its limited focus, this form of prospective overruling allows the possibility of the ripple effect, and its consequent retroactive application of law. This is not surprising since it is designed to allow for limited retroactivity. Thus, Dworkin would require an extreme version of prospective overruling to avoid the possibility of retroactivity resulting from the ripple effect.

78. R. DWORKIN, *supra* note 10, at 82-86, 90-94.

79. *Id.* at 82. *See generally id.* at 81-130.

80. *See, e.g.*, Friedland, *supra* note 75, at 170-71; Levy, *Realist Jurisprudence and Prospective Overruling*, 109 U. PA. L. REV. 1, 1-2, 6, 27-30 (1960); Note, *Prospective Overrulings*, *supra* note 77, at 910-11.

plying the law at different times to different but related aspects of a complicated transaction raises unappealing complexity. Further and perhaps insuperable complexity arises if it is possible to analyze the overall transaction in multiple ways into different temporal components. Unless we can be sure that one temporal analysis will be superior to all others, we will need rules to choose among the various analyses. More important, it is unclear what precedential effect should be given to a decision that applies law from many time periods, law that by definition[81] differs from the law that would be applied to an event that occurred at the time of adjudication if litigated at that time.

The problem of determining precedential effect is telling against the event right revision. It applies not only to cases involving temporally extended transactions, but to all cases. This point can be illustrated by the simple privity of contract example discussed above.[82] Suppose the history of the law in some jurisdiction is that as of year 1, there is liability at one step removed but not at six. In year 2, a three-step case is adjudicated and the court correctly finds liability. In year 4, a four-step case arising from events in year 1 comes to trial. Under the unrevised rights thesis, there is ripple effect retroactivity. The defendant, who would not have been liable had his trial preceded the three-step case, is now liable. Property would be redistributed due to new rights created after the events. The four-step defendant may even have relied upon his correct belief that when he acted in year 1 he was not liable.

Consider the result under the revised event right theory. Because the event rights imply no liability, the defendant prevails. The law after these cases would be that one- to three-step defendants are liable while four-step and "higher" defendants are not liable. Or is it? Suppose further four-step cases arise. In case A, the events occurred in year 3, after the decision in the three-step case and before the decision in the four-step case. It would be a mistake to think that since A is a four-step case, the year 4 four-step case is dispositive and the defendant prevails. Under the event rights in year 3, when case A arose, a four-step defendant would have been held liable, because four is closer to three than to six. So the defendant in case A loses. We now have two four-step cases; in one the defendant prevails, in the other the plaintiff prevails. What is the applicable law when case B, arising from events after A is adjudicated, comes to trial? Do we follow the result in case A and find the defendant liable? Or do we follow the year 4 four-step

---

81. The event right revision of the rights thesis will only make a difference when there would have been a ripple effect under the unrevised rights thesis. That is, only when the event rights differ from the adjudication rights.

82. *See supra* text accompanying notes 64-67.

case, and find the defendant not liable? A solution based upon the fact that *A* was decided later will not do, since we can change the hypothetical by replacing case *A* with case *A'* which arises from facts at the same time as *A*, but is decided simultaneously with the year 4 four-step case and correctly finds liability.

The example can be expanded endlessly, creating further difficulties in determining the force of precedent in the event right revision. The theoretically thorny problems that arise may be impossible to resolve.[83] Further, even if they could be resolved, the resolution would be too complicated for judges to utilize. This practical problem highlights a respect in which Dworkin's theory of adjudication may be incomplete.[84] A complete theory must include not only an account of what judges should do and in fact do, but also an explanation of how it is possible for them to adjudicate as they do and as they should. More generally, a complete theory must acknowledge and describe the limits of what is humanly possible in judicial decisionmaking.[85]

The attempt to avoid the ripple effect argument meets with insuperable difficulties. The resulting retroactivity cannot be avoided. Dworkin's theory offends the same rule of law and fairness prohibitions as Hart's positivism. Reappraisal of the rights thesis is in order.

III

RESPONSES TO THE RIPPLE EFFECT ARGUMENT

This section addresses two potential responses to the ripple effect's impact on Dworkin's jurisprudence. First, one could argue that retroactivity is a less serious problem for Dworkin's theory than for Hart's. Second, one could argue that the ripple effect argument is invalid. This latter objection could take two forms: the first form begins with the premise that principles never change; the second with the premise that the "right answer" never changes.

The first line of defense open to the rights theorist is to claim that there is far less retroactivity in the rights thesis than under Hart's positivist doctrine of discretion. Ripple effect retroactivity occurs only in those few hard cases where a ripple effect has changed a dispositive legal right. By contrast, on Hart's theory, all hard cases involve retroactive application of judicially created law. Thus, while the rights the-

---

83. A glimmer of the difficulties involved in constructing such a theory can be extracted from the discussion of a not totally dissimilar problem in Munzer, *Retroactive Law*, 6 J. LEGAL STUD. 373, 389 n.21 (1977). The theory would likely be at least as complicated as double-indexed tense logics. *See generally* N. RESCHER & A. URQUHART, TEMPORAL LOGIC (1971); A. PRIOR, PAST, PRESENT AND FUTURE (1967).

84. *See supra* note 74 and accompanying text.

85. Moore, *supra* note 14, at 154.

sis does not totally eliminate retroactivity, despite Dworkin's ambition, it allows very little retroactivity, and fares significantly better on this score than does positivism. The ripple effect may dent the rights theorist's armor, but does no real damage.[86]

The proposed defense cannot be accepted, for several reasons. First, it understates the pervasiveness of the prohibition against retroactivity in Dworkin's theory.[87] Second, although ripple effect retroactivity may occur less frequently than hard case retroactivity in Hart's positivism and is in this sense a less serious criticism of the rights thesis, in another sense, it is a deeper criticism.

Because Hart does not maintain the right answer thesis, he can claim that some propositions of law are undecided in the sense that they are neither true nor false. These are the dispositive propositions of future hard cases. Prior to the judge's decision, the proposition is neither true nor false. As a result of the decision, the proposition may be true thereafter. Nonetheless, the unsuccessful litigant cannot claim that the law has been *changed* on him. What was formerly an open question was decided against him, as he knew it might. The litigant has been subjected to retroactive application of *new* law, but not to retroactive application of a result opposite to that which would have been required, by law, at the time of the events.

By contrast, the right answer thesis denies that, in practice,[88] any propositions of law are neither true nor false. By definition,[89] ripple effects change legal propositions from true to false, and vice versa. If the right answer thesis is correct, ripple effects sometimes cause retroactive applications of the result opposite to that required by the law ex-

---

86. The claim that there are few instances of ripple effect retroactivity because retroactivity only occurs when ripple effects change dispositive legal rights is difficult to assess because our knowledge of the operation of precedent is abstract and general, as are Dworkin's expositions of the rights thesis. It cannot, however, be excluded *a priori* that law is a seamless web and that, in theory, every new decision affects, at least minimally, every legal proposition. Ripple effects could result from accumulation of minimal changes, in addition to dramatic changes, thereby increasing the potential for retroactivity.

Shifting focus from Dworkin's pure theory, at least two other sources of retroactivity may exist in practice. First, to the extent, if any, that judges' theories of rights are consequentialist, R. DWORKIN, *supra* note 10, at 294-301 & *passim*, rights may depend in part upon instrumental values. If circumstances change so that bestowing a right upon the litigant no longer results in the desired consequence, the right may no longer exist.

Second, Dworkin concedes that reasonable judges will often disagree about what the right answers are. In practice, therefore, judges will often decide cases differently than Dworkin's superhuman judge Hercules would have. These judicial "errors" will result in failure to enforce preexisting rights. Insofar as there is more disagreement about right answers in the rights thesis than about correct judicial behavior in positivism, the rights thesis will result in greater retroactivity from reasonable judicial mistakes.

87. *See supra* text accompanying notes 22-26.

88. *See supra* note 28 and accompanying text.

89. *See supra* text accompanying notes 61-63, 65-67.

isting at the time of the events in issue. In this sense, the litigant is subjected to retroactive application of law that "overrules" the previously required result. If the right answer thesis is correct, the frustration of the litigant's expectations appears to be more severe, and the unfairness of retroactive application of law greater, because the litigant's right is in some sense more vested, or tangible.

Because ripple effect retroactivity, when it occurs, constitutes a more serious defect for Dworkin's theory than the retroactivity engendered by hard cases does for Hart's, advocates of the rights thesis must meet the challenge of justifying ripple effect retroactivity. It is possible that their response will justify retroactivity in hard cases generally, thus casting a new light on Dworkin's criticism of positivism. Even if the response does not justify retroactivity in all hard cases, it may be the wedge that opens the door to a justification that does. We cannot fully assess Dworkin's jurisprudence, and his criticism of Hart, until more is known about the possible justifications for ripple effect retroactivity, and retroactivity in general.[90]

The impact of ripple effect retroactivity on the rights thesis and the debate between Hart and Dworkin should not be underestimated. But neither should it be overestimated. Dworkin's attack on positivism is rich and subtle, with many prongs.[91] If the rights thesis is not superior to positivism because it successfully avoids retroactive application of law, it may still be preferable for other reasons. For example, the rights theorist could deemphasize the undesirability of retroactivity and focus on Dworkin's related point that Hart's positivism requires, while the rights thesis does not permit, that most undemocratic of acts: the exercise of judicial discretion.[92] The initial attractiveness of this idea fades under the tension between the democratic separation of powers foundation for rejecting judicial discretion[93] and the pervasive undemocratic flavor of Dworkin's commitment to some form of natural law,[94] to the existence of best answers to moral and political questions,[95] and to the appropriateness of judges making moral and political decisions.[96] Even if the retreat from retroactivity to discretion does not seem promising, the general point is worth repeating: Dworkin's other arguments

---

90. One place to begin is with Professor Munzer's recent article *A Theory of Retroactive Legislation*, 61 TEX. L. REV. 425 (1982). Other valuable writings include Mishkin, *supra* note 75; Munzer, *supra* note 83; Note, *Prospective Overrulings*, *supra* note 77.

91. *See* R. DWORKIN, *supra* note 10, at 14-130.

92. *Id.* at 17, 31-39, 84, 279.

93. *See id.*

94. *See* Dworkin, *"Natural" Law*, *supra* note 12.

95. *See, e.g.*, R. DWORKIN, *supra* note 10, at 279-90; Dworkin, *Law as Interpretation*, 60 TEX. L. REV. 527, 546 (1982). *See generally* Dworkin, *No Right Answer?*, *supra* note 12.

96. R. DWORKIN, *supra* note 10, at 123-30.

against positivism, besides the argument that it leads to unjustified retroactivity, are quite forceful and may themselves be decisive.[97]

Rather than minimize the seriousness of ripple effect retroactivity for Dworkin, one might instead seek to rebut the ripple effect argument itself. One possible refutation can take either of two forms.[98] Neither form succeeds because each involves giving up the dominant notion of precedent: the view that prior decisions provide reasons that later deci-

---

97. The significance of the ripple effect for the dispute between Hart and Dworkin may be illustrated by reference to the controversy about the relationship between law and morals. Dworkin has developed two major (and several minor) criticisms of the positivist doctrine of the separation of law and morals. These criticisms may be labeled the argument from controversy and the argument from the possibility of overruling. It has generally been thought that the argument from controversy is the more forceful of the two major arguments. Dworkin, among others, has written more expansively and explicitly on it than on the argument from overruling. *See* R. DWORKIN, *supra* note 10 *passim*; *see also* sources cited *supra* note 34. The argument from controversy asserts that even in a hard case, where the result is controversial, there are preexisting legal rights. These legal rights cannot be fully supported simply by legal rules since, by definition, we are considering a hard case. Thus, there must be nonrule legal standards—call them principles— that support the rights.

The claim that there are preexisting legal rights in hard cases is in turn supported by two main arguments and several minor arguments. The minor arguments include the denial that judging in hard cases is a two-step process, as positivism apparently asserts, R. DWORKIN, *supra* note 10, at 86, 112, and the assertion that our linguistic practices presuppose that even in hard cases, legal arguments are arguments of entitlement. *Id.* at 81. We argue to the judge that the law is *P*, not that the law should be *P*.

In the main, however, the argument for the preexistence of rights in the face of controversy is supported by objections to retroactive application of law, *see supra* text accompanying notes 22- 26, and to the exercise of judicial discretion. The objections to judicial discretion derive in part from the doctrine of separation of powers and similar democratic concerns. R. DWORKIN, *supra* note 10, at 84.

The second major criticism of the doctrine of the separation of law and morals is the argument from the possibility of overruling. The best explanation of the practice of overruling of prior precedent and justification of decisions that overrule is that the substantive (legal/moral) principles recommending the new rule outweigh the substantive (legal/moral) principles favoring the old rule plus the conservative rule of law principles that disfavor change. *Id.* at 37, 44, 65-68. *See generally id.* at 110-23. Similarly, the justification of the decision to follow precedent must be that the principles supporting the old rule outweigh the principles recommending a change. *Id.* at 38.

The impact of ripple effect retroactivity on Dworkin's assertion of an essential connection between law and morality can be tentatively described as follows. Proponents of the doctrine of the separation of law and morals will view the ripple effect argument as a central part of the defense against Dworkin's attack. It significantly diminishes the force of Dworkin's central criticism, the argument from controversy, by deflating the objection to retroactivity, leaving that argument supported by the less persuasive separation of powers objection to judicial discretion and the minor arguments related above. From the perspective of the defender of an essential connection between law and morality, or of Dworkin's rights thesis, the ripple effect argument will suggest that the argument from overruling may be a more secure foundation than the currently more popular argument from controversy. The ripple effect argument therefore suggests that further development and analysis of the argument from overruling is warranted.

98. One or both of these forms of the objection have been advanced at nearly every presentation of this Article. These objections appear to derive from the intuition that the right answer thesis is straightforwardly inconsistent with the possibility that future decisions will change the law by the operation of the doctrine of precedent.

sions be decided in like ways, even if the prior case was decided incorrectly.

The first form of the objection starts from the premise that principles never change, thus preventing the ripple effect at its source. Since principles remain constant, the objection continues, so do litigants' rights. There are no ripple effects and resulting retroactive applications of law.

While a theory of legal reasoning that employs unchanging principles may be possible, it does not appear to be Dworkin's theory. For Dworkin, legal principles are those principles that provide the best explanation and justification of the settled law in the jurisdiction.[99] Which principles are authoritative depends upon two factors—institutional history and moral appeal. With at most occasional exceptions, the principles that best explain and justify two different sets of precedents will themselves differ.[100] To completely avoid the possibility of

---

99. *See supra* note 67.

100. If the two sets of precedents (and institutional facts) differ only in that the latter contains a decision logically deducible from the principles that best explain and justify the first set, it may well be that the latter set will be explained and justified by the same principles. If, however, the latter set of precedents contains an additional decision that is not logically deducible from the principles that explain and justify the first set of precedents, but merely coheres better with those principles than the opposite decision does, then most likely the principles that best explain and justify the later, enlarged set of precedents will differ. At the very least, the weight of the principles will differ because principles that recommend the additional decision will be accorded extra weight. For discussion of the concept of weight, see *supra* note 45 and accompanying text.

That different institutional histories will generate different principles can be seen by considering theory construction in science. In science, data or observations play the role of institutional history, while axioms or first principles play the role of authoritative principles. It cannot be seriously entertained that any two sets of data can be explained by precisely the same set of axioms or first principles. Nor could it plausibly be maintained that adding one additional piece of data (that is not deducible from the best theory of that data) would not sometimes require at least minor revision of the basic principles. Nor could one plausibly maintain that the addition of one piece of data would never require revision of the basic principles because only the addition of large sets of data could have that effect. The addition of large amounts of data can, and in general will, be achieved by successive additions of single pieces of data. Thus, large amounts of additional data can occasion a change in principles only if addition of individual pieces of data can.

The hypothesis that adding one piece of data would never occasion a change in the principles is false because it leads to absurd conclusions. The hypothesis entails that any two sets of data that overlap, even in the slightest degree, are best explained by the same principles. By the hypothesis, the data sets $\{a_1\}$, $\{a_1, a_2\}$, and $\{a_1, b_1\}$ are all best explained by the same set of principles since the latter two sets differ from the first set only by addition of one piece of data. Applying the hypothesis again, the data sets $\{a_1, a_2, a_3\}$ and $\{a_1, b_1, b_2\}$ are also best explained by the same principles. By repeated application of the hypothesis $\{a_1\}$, $\{a_1, a_2, a_3, \ldots an\}$ and $\{a_1, b_1, b_2, \ldots bn\}$ are best explained by the same principles, for any n. The hypothesis robs the notion of explanation of its content and must be rejected.

Admittedly, the relationship between authoritative principles and institutional history (including prior precedents) is in some ways more complex in Dworkin's theory of adjudication than the correlative relationship in science. Legal principles must not only explain, but must also *justify* the legal "data." The theory of mistakes allows the judge to discount a few pieces of legal data. Some precedents may be ignored if they would no longer command assent in the legal

ripple effect retroactivity, one would have to take the highly implausible position that principles never change no matter how extensively institutional history changes. Even if a new line of cases were to develop, or an old line were overruled, the objection would require that the old principles provide the best explanation of the new law.

It may be argued that any well-developed legal system, such as those in the present day United States and England, already contains all the principles that are likely ever to be authoritative.[101] Even if no new principles arise, however, an adequate explanation of the new precedents would require revision of the relative weights[102] of the legal principles. Moreover, even if the "grand rights" of political rhetoric[103] and the principles that describe them[104] do not change, more "concrete rights"[105] and principles will change in response to common law development, and that is all that is needed for the ripple effect. To deny that law and legal rights change at all in response to new decisions is to deny that legal rights are, at least in part, determined by settled law. It is thus not only to deny one of Dworkin's major theses, but more fundamentally to give up the dominant conception of precedent altogether.[106]

The second form of the objection begins from the premise that the right answer thesis must imply that the right answers are already present at the beginning of any period of common law development. In the

---

community. *See supra* notes 55-57 and accompanying text. *See generally* R. DWORKIN, *supra* note 10, at 159-68 (discussing the difference between natural (scientific) and constructive (legal) models of theory construction). Although these additional elements require complications in the argument rejecting the claim that legal principles do not change in consequence of new decisions, the basic thrust of the argument remains secure. To the extent that explanation plays a role, even if diminished, in the relationship between legal principles and legal data, changes in data will occasion changes in principles.

101.   Dworkin's remarks in a recent article about density of developed legal systems and the right answer thesis may be urged—probably incorrectly—in support of this claim. Dworkin, *No Right Answer?, supra* note 12, at 30 & *passim*.

102.   For a discussion of Dworkin's notion of the weight of principles, see *supra* note 45 and accompanying text.

103.   *See* R. DWORKIN, *supra* note 10, at 89.

104.   *Id.* at 90.

105.   *Id.* at 89, 93-94.

106.   I do not deny that the ripple effect argument can be circumvented by denying its meager premises. The ripple effect argument shows that legal systems embodying the dominant conception of precedent retroactively apply law. The ripple effect argument applies to coherence theories because they provide a particular explanation of how precedent operates. Legal systems that do not include the dominant notion of precedent are not subject to the ripple effect. But the argument does not pretend that they are. Of course, the Anglo-American legal systems and many others undoubtedly do include the authority conception of precedent. Some sections of the French Civil Code suggest that the doctrine of precedent does not apply in the French legal system. *See* CODE CIVIL § 5 (Fr. 1895) ("Judges are not allowed to decide cases submitted to them by way of general and settled decisions."). It is unlikely that § 5 has been strictly followed.

above example,[107] this form of the objection can be stated as follows. If after the judge explicitly decides that Q, the new best theory of settled law (STL') requires that not-X be true, it cannot be the case, as the example suggested, that the prior best theory of settled law (STL) required that X be true. Not-X always was and always will be the case, if the right answer thesis holds. This claim involves, once again, the abandonment of the dominant conception of precedent. It requires that the law never change in consequence of judicial decisions.

For the objection to be sustained, it must provide a means for deciding among possible complete coherent continuations of the settled legal truths. The pair Q and not-X is not the only possible coherent continuation. If X were to come up for decision before Q the judge should decide that X, thereby occasioning the truth of not-Q.[108] Thus, the pair X and not-Q is also a possible coherent continuation. If right answers never change, we must have a method for choosing whether the right answers include Q and not-X or, in the alternative, X and not-Q. Further, the method must determine the truth value not only for Q and X but also for all other possible legal propositions. But wholesale and final determination of the truth or falsity of all possible legal propositions leaves no room for the operation of the dominant notion of precedent. The objection purchases unchanging right answers and avoidance of the ripple effect at the cost of dispensing with the doctrine of precedent.

Further, this objection misunderstands the right answer thesis in Dworkin's theory. While at each point in time there are right answers to all or nearly all[109] legal issues, the right answer that is given may not be the same as that which would be given at another point in time, in consequence of changes in institutional history. Part of the point of rigidly separating legal truths into two classes, the settled law (SL) and the coherence consequences (UC), is to highlight the greater instability of legal truth when it results from better coherence with the best theory of settled law rather than from membership in the set of propositions comprising the settled law.

This is perhaps an appropriate place to mention one respect in which the rigid separation of legal truths into settled law and coherence consequences may be misleading. The rigid separation suggests that the positivist or formalist claim that the results in easy cases can be

---

107. *See supra* text accompanying notes 61-63.

108. This is premised on the plausible hypothesis that Q and X are incoherent. That incoherence best explains why the addition of Q occasions the falsity of X. It is possible that the addition of Q will occasion the falsity of X even though Q and X are not incoherent due to "accidental" aspects of the methodology of constructing the soundest theory of the law. The text considers an instance of the more likely case of at least partial incompatibility between Q and X.

109. *See supra* note 28 and accompanying text.

logically deduced[110] is accepted by the proponent of the rights thesis. The rigid separation further suggests that Dworkin criticizes positivism because it is incomplete: positivism's theory of easy cases must be supplemented by a further theory of hard cases, involving coherence rather than deduction, and it must be recognized that there are more hard cases than the positivist might lead us to believe. Yet Dworkin would resist these suggestions because his criticism of positivism is more radical. Dworkin believes that positivism's theory of easy cases—in the area of settled law—is incorrect, and not merely incomplete. Decisions in easy cases are justified not because they can be deduced from legal rules or settled law but because those decisions cohere or fit better with the soundest theory of law than the opposite decision. The positivist's deduction appears from this perspective as an easy case because it is a strong form of coherence. The difference between judicial decisions in the area of settled law and in the area of coherence consequences is one of degree and not kind.

That the difference is one of degree and not kind does not undercut the ripple effect argument. Even if the "boundary" between settled law and other legal propositions is vague or uncertain, it is still true that judicial decisions will affect the location of propositions decided by the court relative to that boundary, thereby occasioning ripple effects in the full universe of legal propositions. Put differently, judicial decisions will change the degree to which legal propositions are settled, thereby occasioning ripple effects.

IV
CONSERVATIVE THEORIES AND THE RIPPLE EFFECT

A.   *Legal Reasoning and the Ripple Effect*

The ripple effect argument causes particular problems for Dworkin because of his commitment to the enforcement of preexisting rights and the right answer thesis. However, the ripple effect will also occur in theories of adjudication not committed to these positions.

Imagine, for example, a coherence theory of legal reasoning that denies the right answer thesis. One such theory might hold that some hard cases have right answers but others do not.[111] The hard cases that have right answers are those where the prevailing litigant's position coheres significantly better with the best theory of settled law than the

---

110.   *See* Coleman, *Negative and Positive Positivism, supra* note 34, at 164 n.15; Moore, *supra* note 14, at 155-56.

111.   Some theorists have claimed that Dworkin holds this view. Galis, *The Real and Unrefuted Rights Thesis*, 42 PHIL. REV. 197, 218-21 (1983); *see also* Lyons, *Justification and Judicial Responsibility*, 72 CALIF. L. REV. 178, 180 n.3 (1984) (asserting that Dworkin only claims that sometimes there are right answers). *But see supra* note 28.

opponent's position does. If the litigants' positions are equally compatible with settled law, or one litigant's position provides only a slightly better fit with settled law, then the case has no single right answer.[112] Rather, the judge may exercise discretion and decide for either litigant.[113] This theory might be labeled the "ping-pong" theory of adjudication: a litigant must defeat his opponent by at least "two points" in order to have a right to a decision in his favor.

Legal propositions may be categorized as follows in the ping-pong coherence theory. First, there are the propositions of settled law. These roughly correspond to the prevailing parties' positions in easy cases, to those legal truths within Hart's core of settled meaning,[114] and to the formalists' heaven where judicial decisions can be deductively justified.[115] Correlative to this class of legal truths are the settled falsehoods, the contradictories of settled truths, the contentions of losing parties in easy cases. Second, there are those legal propositions that are true because they cohere sufficiently better with the settled law than their negations do. These are the implicit legal truths. Correlative to the class of implicit truths is the class of the implicit truths' contradictories, the implicit falsehoods that cohere significantly less well with settled law than do their negations. Finally, there is the class of open questions, consisting of propositions that fit the settled law to approximately the same degree as their negations.

It should be clear that ripple effects will occur in this ping-pong theory, just as they do in the rights thesis.[116] Some ripple effects will result in formerly open questions becoming either implicit coherence truths or implicit coherence falsehoods. When this happens, an adversely affected litigant cannot claim that the law has been "overruled,"[117] because by definition the dispositive legal proposition was previously open. The litigant is not subjected to a retroactive change that denies him a right to prevail that he previously possessed, as is the

---

112. For ease of exposition only, this Article sometimes discusses coherence (fit) with the settled law, and not with the best theory of the settled law, the best justification of the settled law, or the soundest theory of law. This abbreviated terminology is not intended to suggest a lesser role for justification. The arguments in this Section assume only that explanation plays a role in the coherence theory, and apply whatever the exact tradeoff between explanation and justification.

113. The theory may be filled out in ways that constrain the exercise of discretion by requiring that the judge consider only some kinds of additional standards, or by requiring that the additional standards used be principled, neutral, and the like. For present purposes, these refinements are irrelevant.

114. H.L.A. HART, *supra* note 16 at 120, 124-32; *see also* Hart, *Positivism and the Separation of Law and Morals*, 71 HARV. L. REV. 593, 607-10 (1958).

115. *See* Moore, *supra* note 14, at 155-56; *see also* Zane, *German Legal Philosophy*, 16 MICH. L. REV. 287, 338 (1918).

116. *See supra* text accompanying notes 61-63.

117. See the analogous discussion of hard case retroactivity in Hart's positivism, *supra* text accompanying notes 86-90.

case with ripple effects in a theory that maintains the right answer thesis. In this respect, this litigant is subjected to less unfairness than his counterpart in a jurisdiction adhering to the right answer thesis. Nor can the litigant fairly claim complete surprise, or justified reliance, because he should have known that the dispositive legal proposition could have been decided either way.

Nonetheless, something here is unfair, or at least arbitrary. Because legal decisions that cohere better with the opponent's position than with the litigant's have been decided after the conduct in issue, the litigant has lost the right to persuade the judge to exercise discretion in his favor.[118] Arbitrary historical facts compel a decision against him because they enlarge the standards that the judge is obligated to consult. The litigant has lost the right to have his rights determined by appeal to a particular limited class of standards.[119]

There is something morally unsettling about the contingencies that determine which new standards will be applied. Had cases cohering better with the litigant's position been decided after the events and prior to trial, they might have compelled a decision in his favor. Moreover, the litigant is being subjected to retroactive application of new law, although the unfairness of that retroactivity is mitigated because new law had to be created to answer what by definition was previously an open question.

However, the ripple effect argument's applicability to this ping-pong coherence theory extends beyond the attenuated unfairness resulting when ripple effects change open questions to implicit coherence legal truths and falsehoods, and vice versa. Some litigants will be subject to ripple effect "overrulings" that exactly parallel the ripple effects that occur in Dworkin's rights thesis.[120] The percentage of ripple effects that cause overrulings, rather than determinations of previously open questions, will depend upon the relative sizes of the class of implicit, coherence truths and the class of open questions.[121] In turn, the difference in the sizes of these classes will depend upon how much greater the fit with settled law must be in order for a proposition to be a coherence truth rather than an open question.[122]

---

118. This claim depends upon how, in this theory, open questions are decided and may require revision if judicial discretion is limited. *See supra* note 113.

119. Because of ripple effects, the case will be decided in part on the basis of the precedential force of cases decided after the conduct in issue. *But see supra* note 118.

120. *See supra* text accompanying notes 61-63, 65-67, 87-90.

121. There will also be occasional cases where settled legal truths become falsehoods and vice versa. This is unlikely to be a significant factor, however.

122. On one explication of the Quinean metaphor, it will also depend on the number and strength of connections between dispositive propositions and other legal truths. More generally, it will depend upon how the notion of coherence is developed.

Thus, the ripple effect argument applies, within the somewhat restricted class of nonopen legal propositions, with the same force that it does to Dworkin's rights thesis. The move to a theory that denies the right answer thesis merely restricts the most morally objectionable ripple effects to that portion of the law where there are right answers; it allows for less disturbing ripple effects in those areas of the law without right answers. Indeed, since nothing in the argument has relied on the details of any coherence theory, it should be clear that ripple effects will occur in all coherence theories, with or without the right answer thesis, with or without the ping-pong threshold explanation for denying the right answer thesis.

The only way to avoid the more objectionable ripple effect "overrulings" would be to deny that there are any right answers outside the area of settled law. It would be to assert that the right answers encompass only decisions deducible from settled legal rules. Besides being grossly implausible, this formalist position,[123] in effect, denies coherence any role in adjudication. It is thus the exception that proves the rule: coherence theories lead to ripple effect retroactivity and "overrulings."

B. The Impact of the Ripple Effect on Coherence Theories

Assuming that the ripple effect argument holds for all substantial coherence theories,[124] we should assess the resulting jurisprudential problems. The ripple effect argument challenges legal theorists to avoid or justify the resulting retroactivity. Ripple effect retroactivity results from the conservative element in legal reasoning: precedent. A linear ordering problem also arises from this conservative element. Legal theorists must also justify the moral arbitrariness resulting from this linear ordering problem.

1. Retroactivity

It has been argued that "overrulings," and not mere retroactive applications of newly created laws that fill the gaps, will occur in other coherence theories, as they will in the rights thesis. Nonetheless, it might be thought that the undesirability of retroactivity is overemphasized in Dworkin's jurisprudence, and is no more than minimally troubling once Dworkin's theoretical commitments are abandoned.

Consider, for example, a utilitarian legal theorist. The utilitarian will advocate the retroactive application of a new rule whenever the

---

123. The formalist claim that the legal propositions necessary for judicial decisions are deducible from legal rules and facts does not accurately express the formalist position. One needs to add that the contradictory of the proposition cannot also be deduced.

124. See *supra* text accompanying notes 112-23.

overall utility of that application exceeds the utility of applying the prior law, counting, among other things, the disutility of upsetting justified expectations, reliance, and the like. Retroactivity will be justified whenever its overall consequences are better than the consequences of avoiding retroactivity. Why should legal theorists who reject the rights thesis be concerned about retroactivity?

In part, retroactivity is troublesome because it conflicts with the rule of law virtues of satisfying justified expectations, providing citizens with notice of the law so that they may efficiently plan their affairs, and similar concerns. One could argue that these concerns are undercut by the litigant's awareness that her conduct will be adjudicated on the basis of the applicable law at the time of adjudication. Since the litigant realizes that her conduct may be judged under law differing from that in effect at the time she acted, any purported reliance upon the then existing law is arguably misplaced and thus unjustified.

This response has an air of circularity about it: the litigant's reliance is unreasonable only if legal practice is assumed to require enforcement of adjudication rights, and not event rights. In addition to being circular, the argument from the litigant's reasonable expectations overstates the degree to which the post-conduct law is written on a blank slate. Slow change in legal doctrine should be anticipated, but major or rapid changes may be unforeseeable. On balance, the argument from reasonable expectation of legal change dilutes, but does not totally eliminate, the force of the rule of law arguments for the unfairness of retroactive application of law.[125]

However, the objection to retroactivity goes beyond rule of law concerns. More fundamentally, retroactivity raises a conceptual puzzle that results in a moral quandary. It is conceptually impossible to "break" a law that did not exist when one acted. When judges create and retroactively apply "laws" as a consequence of the ripple effect, the justification for enforcing the judgment cannot be that the defendant *violated* the law. She may have acted contrary to a rule that later became the law, but that is another matter. Redistributing her property to the plaintiff cannot be justified on the ground that she violated the plaintiff's rights. Of course, redistributive acts are often justified on egalitarian or other fairness grounds. But social decisions to redistribute property are thought by many to be within the competence and authority of the legislature, not the judiciary. Nor is there any *a priori* reason to think that ripple effect redistributions would aid any particu-

---

125.　Professor Gary Schwartz has discussed some similar concerns in the context of tort law. *See* Schwartz, *New Products, Old Products, Evolving Law, Retroactive Law*, 58 N.Y.U. L. REV. 796, 817-18 & *passim* (1983).

lar economic or social group since ripple effects can help defendants as well as plaintiffs.

No theory of adjudication will be fully satisfactory unless it can justify the retroactive applications of judicially created "law" resulting from the ripple effect, or successfully avoid them. Thus, the ripple effect argument poses a challenge to legal theory generally, and especially to coherence theorists. Because Dworkin is acutely aware of this conceptual puzzle and related moral quandary,[126] he has committed the rights thesis to the enforcement of preexisting law and has made the attempt to avoid retroactivity a central part of that theory. Responding to that emphasis, my criticism of the rights thesis focused on the retroactivity resulting from ripple effects. In shifting focus from the rights thesis to coherence theories of legal reasoning more generally conceived, another morally troubling issue is raised: the linear ordering problem.

2. Precedent and the Linear Order of Decisions

The ripple effect will occur in any step-by-step technique for generating coherence sets that includes a principle of conservation. By a principle of conservation, I mean that the set's history of element inclusion is a factor in determining whether any current element is included. In other words, the order in which elements are considered determines what gets in the set because it determines what is already there to cohere (or fail to cohere) with. In adjudication, the doctrine of precedent supplies the conservative aspect: legal truths depend in part on prior legal decisions. The mere historical fact of a prior decision influences the decisions in later cases, and thus the law, because it enlarges the settled law with which later decisions must cohere. What the law is therefore depends on the linear order in which cases have been decided.[127] Precedent thus generates not only ripple effects but more generally, and perhaps more significantly, the linear ordering problem.

Ripple effects highlight one respect in which the dominant theory of precedent is morally arbitrary. According to that theory, prior decisions are to be accorded weight which may influence the outcomes in later cases merely by virtue of the fact that the decisions have occurred.

---

126. *See supra* quotes from Dworkin accompanying notes 25, 26; *see also* text accompanying notes 21-26, 47-49.

127. The linear ordering problem parallels, but is not identical to, results on agenda influence in recent literature on public choice. *See generally* Easterbrook, *Ways of Criticizing the Court*, 95 HARV. L. REV. 802 (1982); Levine & Plott, *Agenda Influence and Its Implications*, 63 VA. L. REV. 561 (1977); Spitzer, *Multicriteria Choice Processes: An Application of Public Choice Theory to Bakke, the FCC, and the Courts*, 88 YALE L.J. 717 (1979). The agenda influence public choice literature is a natural extension of K. ARROW, SOCIAL CHOICE AND INDIVIDUAL VALUES (2d ed. 1963).

The historical fact of the decision, even if it was required by prior law and could have been predicted with near certainty, increases its weight in later determinations of what the law is. Yet, from the perspective of a citizen whose conduct may later result in litigation, the historical fact of which cases are decided after his conduct but before his case is adjudicated appears to be morally arbitrary. To allow such historical facts to affect, or determine, the outcome of a case, as happens when there is a dispositive ripple effect, is therefore morally arbitrary.

Generalizing the point beyond ripple effects in dispositive legal issues currently being litigated highlights the moral dilemma ensuing from the linear ordering problem. Consider the simple privity of contract example once more.[128] When the cases find privity and liability at one step, but not at six, the implicit law is that there is liability in two- and three-step cases but not in four- and five-step cases. If at that time, a three-step case and a four-step case are simultaneously being litigated, the outcome in each case is determined by whether the other case has previously reached final adjudication. Which case is adjudicated first may depend upon morally arbitrary facts, including crowded court calendars, delaying tactics by opponents, and the like. The outcome, therefore, appears similarly morally arbitrary. As stated earlier,[129] if the three-step case is decided first, plaintiffs win in both the three- and four-step cases. If the four-step case is decided first, both defendants win.

The arbitrariness, however, extends beyond the unfairness to the losing litigants in the three- and four-step cases. The rights of parties litigating events that occurred after both the three-step and four-step cases also depend upon the order of the three- and four-step cases. While the unfairness to these later litigants is diminished by the notice provided by the earlier decisions, it is not completely eliminated. Adjudication of a series of legal issues in one order gives rise to law that may differ from the law that would exist had the same issues been decided in a different order. Legal rights depend not only upon which prior cases have been decided, but upon the order in which the cases have been decided.

This Article has shifted from the claim that coherence leads to ripple effects and to the linear ordering problem to the claim that the dominant conception of precedent does.[130] In fact, both claims are true because precedent serves as a principle of conservation in coherence theories of law.[131] Coherence theories are simply one particularly fa-

---

128. *See supra* text accompanying notes 65-67.
129. *See supra* text following note 66.
130. This shift occurred even earlier in this Article. *See supra* text accompanying notes 65-69.
131. The linear ordering problem and the associated ripple effect will occur in conservative

vored way of spelling out what has here been called the dominant conception of precedent. Because philosophers, including legal philosophers, have lately become enamored with coherence theories,[132] the ripple effect has been described in terms of coherence so that its connections to other coherence theories are more readily observable. Generalizing beyond coherence theories, we may conclude: the doctrine of precedent requires morally arbitrary decisions, and morally troubling retroactive application of law.

---

coherence theories outside the law. Many, if not most, coherence theories in modern epistemology include conservative principles that lead to the linear ordering problem and ripple effects. In Quine's epistemology, for example, the maxim of minimum mutilation recommends that one's beliefs be readjusted in the face of new information or evidence by changing one's overall network of beliefs as little as possible. W.V.O. QUINE, *Two Dogmas of Empiricism, supra* note 3, at 44. How new information is evaluated and accommodated depends upon one's prior beliefs. Those beliefs, in turn, depend upon the order in which prior evidence has been presented. Conservatives generally believe that history matters, and pragmatists who hold conservative coherence theories of evidence and truth are no exception. However, the ripple effect is less surprising, and therefore less troubling to pragmatists: they are likely to embrace the conclusion, given the skeptical tenor of their theories.

Although nonconservative coherence theories that avoid the ripple effect and the linear ordering problem could be constructed, they would not appeal to these pragmatists. Nonconservative coherence theories would require that observations, data, or evidence be determined and characterized independently of prevailing theory. Otherwise, each piece of data would depend upon the theory prevailing when the data was acquired, thereby reintroducing the ripple effect and linear ordering problem. Since pragmatists maintain that observations are dependent upon prevailing theory, they will reject nonconservative coherence theories. For example, these theorists claim that we perceive a stick in water as straight even though it appears bent because we know something about the consequences of the refractive properties of water and light. *See generally* Moore, *supra* note 13, at 1109-10 and the references cited therein.

In one respect, legal data is also dependent on prevailing theory. The issues that are raised by the participants in a lawsuit will depend upon their views of what the law is.

132. *See supra* notes 3-11.

THE
UNIVERSITY OF CHICAGO LAW REVIEW

VOLUME 32   SPRING 1965   NUMBER 3

THE NATURE OF JUDICIAL REASONING

Edward H. Levi†

I
N THIS PAPER I shall attempt to describe some attributes of judicial reasoning which give uniqueness to the process and concern to those who use it; to examine to some extent the process itself and the relationship between it and the articulation of neutral principles; and finally to examine once more the uncertainties of judicial reasoning in the light of the importance of time and place and changing function.

I.

The topic of judicial reasoning evokes the memory of countless after dinner talks given by members of the judiciary and a kind of entourage of lawyers and law professors. This is not all it evokes, of course. In any case many of the talks are good, and it would be churlish to mention this except to suggest one point and to ask a first question. The point is somewhat difficult to make. It involves questions of emphasis and degree and qualification to such an extent that I cannot help but have doubts about it. Yet to put it in the large it would be this: it would be difficult to think of another scholarly profession which speaks as little of the consequences of its acts or the discoveries it has made and as much about the circumstances of its own behavior. Surely these public expressions of wonderment at the difficulties and niceties of the judge's behavior are not to be dismissed simply as orgies of narcissism or flattery. I am not of course speaking of the judicial opinion, although there is a relationship between the

† Provost and Professor of Law, The University of Chicago. This article was presented as part of a series of papers delivered before the New York University Institute of Philosophy on May 10-11, 1963 and reproduced in LAW AND PHILOSOPHY (Hook ed. 1964). Republished with the permission of the New York University Press.

opinion and talks about how opinions get to be written. A facet to the point is that, as I believe, the literature about judging is an American, possibly an Anglo-American, phenomenon.

I have put the point which I am suggesting in terms of a concern with judging and a lack of inquiry into the effects of judging. This must be qualified. Inquiries into judicial behavior are related to inquiries into effect. A shift in constitutional interpretation can have obvious consequences, suggesting questions as to the relationship between judging and the justification for the shift. Perhaps it should be said that the effect of the shift so far as the judge or lawyer is concerned is primarily on the fabric of the law. The lawyer's or the judge's function may be sufficiently self-delimited so as to exclude from the realm of their professional competence the larger social consequences, for example, of the school desegregation decision or the recent reapportionment cases, even though the lawyer or judge will know or believe what others in that kind of segment of society will know or believe. For the judge or lawyer the relevant effects are upon the web of the law, the administration of law and respect for it. These are large items, and the priest who only keeps his temple in good repair is not to be condemned on that account. Yet with all these qualifications, and even with the difficulties which analogous illustrations suggest, the point though battered seems to me to persist. Is the analogy to be to the man of medicine who describes not what the virus does and how it is to be counteracted but rather emphasizes the difficulties and virtues of his diagnostic art? Is it to be to the scientist who cares less about his discovery and more about how he made it? Again it is to be recognized that perhaps the discovery is more the way and less the result. Perhaps the analogy should be to the novelist who thinks his reactions and growth are matters of importance to an understanding of the craft. I think the analogies on balance emphasize the point that there is indeed unusual concern with the decision-making processes of judges, and the question to be put is whether this unusual concern, if it does exist, points to a uniqueness in the judicial process itself.

The uniqueness does not appear to arise in any simple way from the importance of the items ruled upon by the judge. Much of what a judge decides, if you look at the situations with which he deals, is no more or less important than what a plumber does, to speak of the plumber as the symbol of the worker on every day items without whose skill matters could be uncomfortable, annoying, and at times catastrophic. Of course there is a difference, since the judge, even though the case before him may involve price-fixing on plumbing items, is dealing with rights and duties imposed or acknowledged by the state, and he is an instrument of government. But this is true also of the legislator, the policeman, and the prosecutor. Behavioral scientists do attempt to study the decision-making processes of these occupations. We know these groups do make important decisions, yet the literature of the wonderment and agony of the road to determination does not really pertain to them. A comparison between the judge and the legislator seems particularly suggestive, because even though we were traditionally told that the judge only applies old rules through specific determinations to cases brought before him, while the legislator changes the law, we know that to a considerable extent the judge and the legislator perform the same function. By this I mean that the legislator also must have points of reference to basic doctrines which justify the determinations of changes he makes. Yet the differences in the American practice between judge and legislator are there to be seen. First, there are many legislators, and while appellate judges are more than one, the comparison is not so much between individual judges and individual legislators as it is between a judge and the legislative body. The legislator is champion of a point of view. If all points of view are to be represented it is because the debate, if that is what it can be called, has brought them out and the legislator is but a participant, although a later voter, in that debate. On the contrary, the judge who writes an opinion has the task of reflecting the outlines of the debate, to show that he is aware of the different voices and that his thought processes have traveled through an inner debate prior to determination. In short, while this is honored in varying degrees, the judge, although he may feel strongly, does not appear as an advocate. Second, while we know that both judges and legislators change the law and both refer to immutable principles, the emphasis in the court in the American system is not only on the prior or stated rule but on its application in other cases, creating for the judge the problem of showing how an old equity can be preserved and better and new justice be done. Third, the assumption for the judge is that the process of determination is one of reason. There is almost a claim to infallibility if the system works properly. The result is not one of indifference or bias but follows from inner thought processes which bring the right result implicit in the rule. Judicial reasoning no doubt is like any other kind of reasoning which involves the use of a moving classification system. But here a moral judgment is frequently involved in the conclusions reached by the judge. Moreover, as I will indicate later, the integrity of the process in which the judge is engaged depends not only on distinctions which he may make reasonably, but also on his own belief in the legitimacy and decisiveness of these distinctions. Thus, there is an astonishing combination of compulsions on the Anglo-American judge: the duty of representing many voices, of justifying the new application in terms of a prior rule and the equality of other cases, the assumption that reason is a sufficient and necessary guide, the responsibility for moral judgment and the importance of sincerity—all these do tend to give uniqueness to the institution of judicial reasoning in our system and in our society.

II.

I come now to the second point which is that the technique of judicial reasoning is admirably adapted to a moving classification system and has a built-in device for the exploration and creation of ambiguities. At the same time the process tends to obscure the problem of the relationship between equality and change. Equality seems to be the moving principle which justifies, indeed compels, reference to the handling of similar cases once this material is readily available. I realize the reference to a similar specific instance could be considered solely as a means of supplying or clarifying a definition of a key concept in a rule. I do not mean to suggest either that the sole style of legal reasoning is from case to case to the creation of a rule. Styles change and the structure of the opinion at any given time and with a particular judge may appear to be from the general proposition downward. The problem of the determination of the application of the general proposition to the cluster of facts still remains, however. The adversary system, which is closely related to the idea of a fair hearing, creates a forum in which competing versions of the factual situation can be explored, and this is another way of saying that competing propositions are being advanced. And it is a little difficult even under the most static and simple view of law to see how competing versions of the same fact situation can be avoided. The briefs of counsel further the idea of the comparison of situations by their citation of cases. Yet it is true that the cases may be cited more for the statement of general propositions and less or not at all for any close scrutiny of similarity of factual situations. A judge with strong convictions and an authoritarian view as to good and bad cases and a well formed, logically held structure of the law in mind may cite only those good cases which reflect his view as to the appropriate and correct application of the right terms—much as it appears the early casebooks tended to do. One could then conceive of the process as laying down an understood logical structure of terms illustrated through cases which in their function with respect to the system are quite passive. Thus I would not want to say here that what is usually called reasoning by analogy is the sole judicial technique in opinion writing, nor even that it is the concealed starting point for the judge's own working out of the problem. But I do think that a closer look at how reasoning by analogy or example works in the judicial process reveals some interesting problems.

The Anglo-American legal system has as one of its comfort points the idea of dictum. The system is not very precise as to what dictum is. In some sense the idea undoubtedly is a necessary one since otherwise the judge could write a treatise as an opinion and accomplish an unacceptable codification of the law. So we say loosely that the judge's observations on matters not before him for decision, or which are perhaps not necessary for the conclusion which he reaches, are only dicta and not binding on future judges. At one extreme the doctrine suggests that the particular views of a given judge on propositions of law can be decisive on future cases, and indeed must be, if these views are given with cogent reference to the precise issues he had to decide. At the other extreme the doctrine contends that we need not permit the prior judge to overreach and establish law by his own exaggerated view of the issues or the relevance of what he feels called upon to say. At the same time, as we all know, in the web of the law one can find the compelling influence of repeated doctrine even though close scrutiny would show that for all the appellate cases which have discussed it the doctrine could be called only dictum. But the phrase "close scrutiny," while it may indicate diligence and the bringing to bear of an expert mind, does not disclose the rules of the game. I suggest as a starting point for inquiry the question of how pivotal the position taken by a prior judge is made to be by the inner discipline of the system. I believe a view of the system through the structure of reasoning by example is helpful in this connection.

From the standpoint of reasoning by example, the circumstances before the court are compared with a number of somewhat similar circumstances which have been classified in terms of opposing categories. These categories would result in opposite or at least different legal conclusions and different although presumably compatible rules of law. The fact cluster before the court could be included within either category. After enough successive fact clusters have been added, the probability is that it will be apparent that the original rule of law has changed its meaning and this may be reflected in a change in the name of the determining concept and therefore in the language of the rule. If it is correct that the fact cluster could be classified equally well under the categories of opposing concepts and rules, this must be because no authoritative definition has removed ambiguity. If reliance is to be on the authority of a prior case for the scope and effectiveness of an announced rule of law now to be applied, then the similarity and difference between the present fact cluster now up for decision and the fact cluster of the prior case are decisive. What power does the judge in the prior case have to establish for all time the compelling and, in the future, decisive aspects of the case before him, including (1) a determination of what is irrelevant and therefore would make no difference if present or absent, and (2) a determination of what cannot be done without? Thus, what is to be the result if the first judge forecasts similarity when the second and later judge finds a reasonable difference?

I think the answer in Anglo-American law, although some English writers have suggested this is only true of American and not English practice, is that the second judge, where only case law is involved, is free to make his own determination of decisive similarity or difference. This of course gives the law a great deal of flexibility and capacity for growth. I am not suggesting that the inner discipline of the system permits the later judge to create distinctions which he regards as irrelevant. If the judge reworks the system and has a new classification, he is under compulsion to supply reasons for reworked old cases in order to project a pattern which can guide later cases. The distinctions which he makes must appear reasonable to him. Under one view of the judge's restricted power the amount of change is limited by the judge's ability to encompass it within a logical structure which explains all prior cases, albeit the judges of the prior cases would have rejected the explanation. Under this view there is a sense in which the system is engaged not in change but in explication. At best this view of the constraint upon the judge is somewhat idealized. It is recognized that cases are discarded and are explained in terms of the now inoperative ideas of their time rather than in terms of any present pattern. Particularly in those areas of the law where reported cases are so numerous, the present judge is really not compelled to organize them all. Yet the compulsion upon him is real and effective even though it does not require him to make sense out of every case which has ever occurred and even though now and then he may recognize a shift in the law so that he is not required to take account of an older view. If the views of the prior judge and the distinctions he made were decisive, the system would be much more rigid and change more frequently would have to come about through legislation.

When English commentators describe their system as one in which the second and later judge is bound by the determinations of the first judge, they appear to have reference to cases in which the question is one of statutory interpretation. They thus do not distinguish between common law cases and cases where the issue is the meaning of legislation.

I believe that to a considerable degree it can be shown that in this country also the second and later judge finds himself much more bound by the prior court's views when the prior court is construing a statute. In such situations the prior court's views even when broadly stated as dictum frequently determine the direction of future statutory construction. I state the matter too simply of course, but I think there is this basic difference in the freedom of the judge in case law areas as contrasted with the case law-statutory interpretation fields. The explanation may be that dictum places a gloss upon the statute; it is a kind of communication to the legislature as to how its words will be interpreted, and since the legislature has manifested an interest in the area anyway, if the gloss is not to its liking it can change the statute. This line of argument is not fully satisfying since it can be said that court and legislature should be considered in a partnership even in the absence of legislation. It may be that subsequent court interpretations of legislation reveal less leeway for the second court for the very reason that interpretation must focus on specific language and its meaning, and there may be a natural inclination to assume that the document takes on and keeps the meaning assigned to it. One way the restriction of the second court in statutory matters manifests itself in our country is in the plea of a judge that he is free of the restraints of the previous case because this is a case involving basic or constitutional issues. The written constitution and the insistence that it and not its interpretations must prevail, in marked contrast to the situation when legislation is involved, make it possible in constitutional matters to change from the even flow of common law case law accretions or from the more rigid following down the path in statutory interpretation to an abrupt, although usually foreshadowed, change in direction.

I do not deny that there are difficulties in the way of the application of this analysis. For example, the United States Supreme Court in 1922 held that the antitrust laws did not apply to baseball since the exhibition, although made for money, was not to be called trade or commerce.[1] In subsequent years as a matter of constitutional interpretation the scope of the commerce power of the United States was greatly increased. In 1953 the Court was again asked to rule on the application of the Sherman Act to baseball.[2] Quite apart from the point that the Sherman Act is so vague it may be regarded less as legislation and more as common law, one can argue that if this is a matter of statutory interpretation, then the 1922 opinion, assuming the basic facts of baseball are the same, must be adhered to; if it is a

---

[1] Federal Baseball Club v. National League, 259 U.S. 200 (1922).
[2] Toolson v. New York Yankees, Inc., 346 U.S. 356 (1953).

matter of constitutional interpretation, then presumably the wider impact of federal power would be acknowledged to exist. As we know, the way the matter was handled compels us to distinguish between baseball on the one side and theatres and boxing on the other, leading to the interesting argument, which failed when football was considered, that football was a team sport like baseball and unlike boxing and therefore should be exempt also. The point is that the jurisprudential question of the leeway in the law for particular categories really decided these cases.

This analysis of judicial reasoning is rudimentary and could be made more elaborate, paying more attention to those cases where there is a mixture of legislation and case law interpretation, or cases where legislation is persuasive as indicating a shift in policy or perhaps is to be treated much as an analogous case for reasoning by example to work upon. It is surprising, however, that a judicial reasoning system which places such great store on the correct analysis of cases should have as little doctrine as ours does upon the crucial question of whether the judge's own explanation of the decisive features of the case, a successor judge's rationale or perhaps the underlying structure as seen by some commentator are all equally available methods for finding or justifying the law. To the extent that there is any general assumption about this I would suppose that it is that the first judge's language, when not dictum, is decisive—a view which is not only unclear but wrong. This in itself suggests that for the effective operations of the system it is not necessary to be either clear or correct about such matters.

The compatibility of judicial reasoning, which relies heavily on reasoning by example, with a moving classification system is, I think, clear. The movement in the system frequently will not be apparent. When it is apparent, it is often justified obliquely on the basis that this policy step was taken some time ago and is reflected in prior decisions. The system permits a foreshadowing of results and therefore has built into it the likelihood of a period of preparation so that future decisions appear as a belated finding and not a making of law. The joint exploration through competing examples to fill the ambiguities of one or many propositions has the advantage of permitting the use in the system of propositions or concepts saved from being contradictory because they are ambiguous, and on this account more acceptable as ideals or common-place truths; the advantage, also, of postponing difficult problems until they arise, and of providing an inner discipline for the system by forcing an analysis of general propositions in terms of concrete situations. The avoidance of explicit policy determinations by referring to prior and selected examples appears as a substitution of the idea of equality for a head-on examination of issues of policy. Undoubtedly some of the magic of the judicial process stems from this fact, and also some of the doubt which has given rise to the literature of self-examination.

III.

Against this background it seems to me that a third point is at least tenable and it is this: the caliber of a court's opinion even in a constitutional case is not to be made dependent on its announcement of a principle which is fully satisfying in reason and which will indicate for us how future cases are to be decided. I put the matter this way in reaction to Professor Wechsler's observations on neutral or articulated principles[3] and upon the basis that the caliber of an opinion is to be seen in terms of the governmental function it performs. What Professor Wechsler said was that the courts in exercising their duty to review the actions of the other branches of the government in the light of constitutional provisions, must act as courts of law and not as naked power organs. The determinations of the court, then, to have legal quality must be "entirely principled," and a "principled decision . . . is one that rests on reasons with respect to all the issues in the case, reasons that in their generality and their neutrality transcend any immediate result that is involved."[4] The emphasis throughout his superb essay is on "standards that transcend the case at hand" and upon "principled articulation." I have heard it suggested that the use of the "neutrality" concept is unfortunate since it seems to give the impression that the values about which the judge feels deeply may not be the appropriately articulated reasons for decision. And this has thrown the essay into a kind of maelstrom of discussion as to whether judges should be neutralists or umpires or social reformers. I would suppose that all would agree with the answer I think is suggested by Professor Wechsler's essay: namely, that a judge who makes changes in the law must take seriously the duty of reworking the pattern of the law. The distinctions which he makes must be genuine, articulated, and sufficiently acceptable. But granted the description of judicial reasoning as the working or reworking of a moving classification system, to what extent must the judge have worked out the full impact upon future cases of conflicting values and legal concepts? And to what extent is it appropriate or necessary for a judge to plot out in the written opinion, as contrasted with the inner process of decision, the future course of

[3] Wechsler, *Toward Neutral Principles of Constitutional Law*, 73 HARV. L. REV. 1 (1959).

[4] *Id.* at 19.

the law as to those instances and future distinctions which seem foreseeable to him?

Surely there are several meaningful ways in which the Constitution is something more than what a court says it is. In our country in any event the Constitution is a written document embracing basic and sometimes contradictory values and using both very broad and sometimes rather specific concepts. The freedom which the Court has to abandon its prior reading of the Constitution is a recognition of primacy of the document. Granted the right and duty of the Court to interpret the document, it has not been given the duty or the opportunity to rewrite the words. It can decide cases on the basis of its interpretation of the words, but if the analysis of reasoning by example means anything, it means that a later court can accept the results in those cases but justify them on a different theory. And the value of court action as opposed to action by a constitutional convention or a legislature is that the matter can be taken one step at a time. This does not mean that the steps can be taken without justification—the discipline requires a justification which will explain the way prior cases and this case have been handled, and may even be a justification which latches onto a shift in constitutional interpretation. But I do not think this is equivalent to demanding a fully satisfying theory which projects a line to the future and steers a safe course for future conflicts. Particularly where a constitution is involved, with its conflicting values, such a demand seems unobtainable. In addition to the point that it is one of the values of court action that it can deal with the case at hand and avoid the broad reach, there is the more central complexity that with conflicting values a political system has to decide some things on the basis of specific decisions approaching a dividing line which in fact may be a moving line and not one which can be grandly fixed through articulation. Because the Supreme Court has ventured into an enlarged circle where primaries are protected from racial discrimination does not, I think, require it or make it desirable for it to attempt to leap to a determination of whether under any and all circumstances political parties should be prevented from being organized on racial or religious grounds in the United States. An attempt to make a judicial pronouncement on this subject might be more fraught with mischief than a wrong decision crossing a line which it should not cross and resulting from the misapplication of a more standard principle that a governmental function must be carried on without that kind of clear discrimination. And so for the opinion of the Supreme Court in the segregated schools case,[5] I would not suppose it would be desirable for the Court to have

[5] Brown v. Board of Education, 347 U.S. 483 (1954).

attempted to articulate its adjudication upon the basis of a resolution of the conflict between the right of freedom of association and the right to not associate—a conflict which Professor Wechsler has suggested he would like to see come out on the side of association, but where he indicates there are certain difficulties, and, as he said, he has "not yet written the opinion."[6] It is because Professor Wechsler has not yet written the opinion that I am dubious that others can. But it does not follow that segregation in schools should be allowed to persist. It is possible that the *Brown* case should have been decided with the same result but with less of an immediate jump and on the partial basis of an old and accepted theory.

The recognition and preservation of future leeways in the law until the time for decision has been reached is of course not a new thought or a new value. The doctrine that constitutional matters should not be decided until their resolution is necessary to the case at hand is in part a reflection of that thought. Of course it is virtuous in terms of the legal process to be willing to deny the legitimacy of desired results which cannot be reached through appropriate reasoning. But the process of judicial reasoning is frequently, perhaps basically, retrospective, taking advantage of situations which have been met. This in itself involves some projection into the future as well, going beyond the case at hand, but it can also involve care not to foreclose the consideration of future distinctions and further relevance. This is in recognition that time has its advantages, that the constitutional or legal posture of later cases may be doctrinely different, that situations which seem the same now under a new light may appear otherwise, and that situations and doctrine may be more interrelated than is earlier realized.

Having said this much I hasten to add that I realized that a call for responsible articulated reasons does not mean that a judge must shoulder the responsibility for deciding all future cases. And probably the articulation of reasons in the opinion is of greater or at least different importance in constitutional cases to the extent that the Court's overriding authority has to be justified. The course of common law cases in which one can find inchoate theories, incomplete expressions of new views, and then finally the better expression of the theory is well known and includes the best judges as the writers of opinions. Shocking as it may be, even the case which has no articulated theory to support it but seems right and is treated as a kind of unique incident has a place in our jurisprudence. Perhaps one's point of view on the importance of the completed theory depends upon whether one sees the theory in some sense as prior to the determination of result or rather

---

6 Wechsler, *supra* note 3, at 34.

as arising out of the same process of seeing similarity and difference. If it is the latter, then the completed theory is less important than the description of the process of comparison (which of course includes a statement of what are the crucial points of comparison) for after all it is that process upon which we must rely. I trust that the category of articulated neutral principles is broad enough to permit this approach.

IV.

I have tried to describe some of the strains inherent in judicial reasoning which perhaps have contributed to the literature of self-examination, and to describe also the process of this reasoning which is adapted to a moving classification system. I have urged that the articulation of neutral principles be regarded in the light of a process of judging in which the direction of perceived standards and the comparison of situations both play a part but one in which it is not always possible or wise to anticipate the inevitable collision of important values too far beyond the case at hand. But of course the choice of the preferred way of judicial reasoning depends upon a judgment as to the functions which judicial reasoning is to perform. Clearly these functions are not always the same. They depend in part upon the needs of a society at a given time and the availability of other and possibly better ways of fulfilling these needs. The classic function for judging is to redress a wrong caused by a violation of a sufficiently understood legally authorized standard. The clearer the standard, and the more acceptable that standard is to elements within the community, the greater the moral judgment carried by the decision. Because rewards and punishment are involved and the relationship to moral judgment very close, judging is an important educational and changing factor. The interpreter of the standard becomes the creator of the standard. And the standard or law which is applied may become in varying degrees no more than, but as much as, the changing customs or value systems of the community as seen through a particular mechanism. As we know, there need not be an institutional separation of judging from executive or legislative authority. The functional lines between them can become exceedingly blurred in part because even naked power hardly ever is that simple. We can begin with a skeletonized view of the judicial process: the received standard, the adversary proceeding, the focusing on a single situation and the exemplification of the standard in similar actual or hypothetical cases. But these are the broad outlines and the working of the process will change as needs are felt differently.

It is perhaps relevant to remind ourselves that law as regulated by the judicial opinion operates within a literary tradition. One function of the opinion has been to map out the contours of the law, much as a text writer would do, and in this sense the reasoning of the judge as dictum has been quite important. But the view of the judge on the effects of laws or on the quantity and types of cases and issues which may arise within the legal system itself may be quite limited. I do not know whether it is worthwhile, but modern methods of research could tell us a great deal more about the operations of the legal system itself—that is, the frequency with which particular types of cases arise, the relationships among issues, the likelihood of recovery and similar questions, than can be handled appropriately in legal opinions. This limitation of judicial reasoning to an examination of the facts which arise in the particular case, an acceptance of enlightened or sound social views and an intense scrutiny of the intellectual issues thought to be involved in the case is no doubt regarded as a positive value by members of our craft. Judges are not behavioral scientists. The point is, however, that there was a time when no one else was, and the sphere of the judge as social philosopher was less limited or threatened. Today the organization by the bar of various instruments for mapping out the law and also for such collaborative research as can be done both on the operations within the legal system and the effect of laws on social problems—all these suggest a certain limitation on the need for formal judicial reasoning as words on high to fill these gaps. We still want to know what the judge thought was relevant in deciding the case but the thought that he might do some research on his own in matters economic or sociological fills us, no doubt correctly, with dread.

But we still think of the judge as appropriately law reformer and also as wise man or political scientist for the community. The meaning of the image of the judge as law reformer is clouded because in part it refers only to the restating and remaking of the case law as the pattern of the law. But the fact is that in our society the law court is a powerful instrument for effecting changes which the legislature will not enact or for preventing for some time at least the changes which legislatures do enact. And the defense of judicial action against the charge that its behavior is simply legislative, and therefore the assumption of naked power, is frequently but not always that where action is prevented, the matter is so great as to go to the essential spirit of institutions, and where change is effected, that the amount of change is so small that a comparison of other situations will show it has already occurred. It would be comforting to think that an analysis of proper judicial reasoning would show which actions were appropriate. I do not think an articulation of powerful reasons and serious concern is sufficient to separate proper judicial from improper judicial or essentially legislative behavior or wise from imprudent judicial behavior. It seems to be a question partly of time and place, the acceptability of what is done and the need for it. It can be plausibly argued that all great judges have recognized this, and that it is one of the tragedies of judging that, with this recognition and perhaps because of it, misconceptions of felt needs can make for unwise decisions. Of course a court which operates in areas where there are strong differences of views runs great risks, but in our system it is supposed to do so somewhat. The analysis of jurisprudence which makes much of the difference between the *is* and the *ought* does not seem to me to be helpful at this point. A judicial system which makes this distinction and echews the *ought* will have lost both the spirit and symbol of justice. In effect it will have made the *was* the *is*.

Yet it can be asked whether at a particular time and place it is valuable for a court to become the main forum for basic political debate. It is somewhat anomalous in a highly developed political society that lawyers in court and lawyers in robes should have to discuss matters of political power which certainly as appropriately come within the province of lawyers in the legislature, but which presumably are inadequately treated there. The fact of the anomaly is not necessarily a criticism of the Court's behavior. The fact is that in our society, although some may disapprove, the Court has advantages as a forum for the discussion of political-moral issues. In a broadly based, vocal and literate society, susceptible to the persuasion of many tongues and pens, and with inadequate structuring of relevant debate, the Court has a useful function not only in staying time for sober second thought but in focusing issues. It is sometimes the only forum in which issues can be sharply focused or appear to be so. It has the drama of views which are more opposing and less scattered because its procedures require a certain amount of relevance. It operates more within a structure of logical ideas, and yet one into which current views may be infused through new words which must find a relationship to the old and through new meanings. It has the drama of a limited number of personalities who are called upon to explain their views. It has the advantage of beginning with certain agreed upon premises to which all participants profess loyalty and thus can force concentration upon the partial clarification of ambiguities. It must reach a conclusion for the particular situation which has the force of a moral judgment. The Court operates from a base in which the identification of its members is explicitly to the higher ideals of the entire community. This freedom and responsibility minimizes that kind of double standard between public and private convictions which cannot so clearly be said to be inappropriate in other areas. This does not mean that the price for such participation by a court does not come high nor that there are not substantial weaknesses in its fulfillment of these functions. A basic insecurity in the foundation for a court's approach to such issues is that it must proceed with a standard of constitutionality, including problems of distribution of powers, or a rule of minimum fairness distorts the lesson. It makes for poor public education even though it may be the best available. Finally, without regard for the technical propriety of what the Court does, there is no doubt that the Court's influence as an acceptable objective force is diminished the greater the controversy. This easy and customary point, however, must be corrected by an awareness that it is the Court's appeal to our better selves, connoting some controversy, which is the source of its moral power and persuasion.

In this setting the function of articulated judicial reasoning is to help protect the Court's moral power by giving some assurance that private views are not masquerading behind public views. This might lead to the conclusion that the more controversial the issues the more the Court should endeavor to spell out the future rules of the road. But I doubt if this conclusion follows. I do not ignore the obligation of higher courts to give directions to trial and intermediate courts, the need greater in some areas than in others to guide private transactions, the special duty to enforce rules of fairness when court procedures are involved, and the requirement that law not be segmented but be a continuing pattern. But the existence of controversy on public issues may speak for a less decisive and far-reaching determination by a court which can have the advantage of taking the law a step at a time. The commentators' happy and useful lament that the reasoning is unclear and that ambiguities and uncertainties remain in itself is no cause for alarm; future courts can and will take advantage of such learning and hindsight as they take advantage of their own. What is needed in the judicial opinion is an indication of the points at issue, a narrowing of the determinative factors, and to some extent care not to take unnecessary steps until they can be taken in a sense retrospectively. This is not an argument for the thoughtless decision. It is rather an argument that the decision must bear witness that it was reached through the discipline of the pattern of the law, which provides both restrictions and leeway. It is indeed the recognition of the present and future leeway, as much as of the prior restrictions, which compels the thoughtful decision and makes of judicial reasoning something more than arrangements to be projected on a computer or predicted from the bias of a judge.

Ratio Juris. Vol. 6 No. 1 March 1993 (16–29)

Argumentation and Interpretation in Law

NEIL MacCORMICK

Abstract. The author proceeds from a brief elucidation of the concept "argumentation" through a more extended account of substantive reasons in pure practical argumentation and of institutional argumentation applying "authority reasons" as grounds for legal decisions to an initial account of the nature and place of legal interpretative reasoning. Then he explores the three main categories of interpretative arguments, linguistic arguments, systemic arguments and teleological/deontological arguments; and he examines the problem of conflicts of interpretation and their resolution. His conclusion is that legal argumentation is only partly autonomous since it has to be embedded within wider elements of practical argumentation.

This paper offers a challenge to theories of the autonomy of law, and thus by implication opposes the fashionable idea of law as "autopoietic system." Interpretation is, as everyone agrees, an omnipresent activity in law. But what is interpretation? According to the present view, it is a particular form of practical argumentation in law, in which one argues for a particular understanding of authoritative texts or materials as a special kind of (justifying) reason for legal decisions. Hence legal interpretation should be understood within the framework of an account of argumentation, in particular, of practical argumentation. In this framework, it turns out that interpretation can only be a part of legal argumentation, and can only be finally elucidated within a wider view of normative constitutional and political theory, which themselves belong within a broader view of practical argumentation.

I. Argumentation

Argumentation is the activity of putting arguments for or against something. This can be done in speculative or in practical contexts. In purely speculative matters, one adduces arguments for or against believing something about what is the case. In practical contexts, one adduces arguments which are either reasons for or against doing something, or reasons for or against holding an opinion about what ought to be or may be or can be done. In the present paper, I am concerned with practical argumentation and practical arguments.

II. Pure Practical Argumentation: Substantive Reasons

If we consider what might be called pure practical argumentation, outside of any particular institutional setting, can we say anything about basic kinds of arguments it would be possible to make? The answer is almost trivial, certainly trite. There are two widely acknowledged possibilities (though later, in Section V I shall add a third) and these two are teleological argumentation and deontological argumentation.

A reason given for acting or not acting in a certain way may be on account of what so acting or not acting will bring about. Such is teleological reasoning. All teleological reasoning presupposes some evaluation. That bringing about x is a good reason for doing a (which will bring about x) presupposes that x has some positive value. To the extent that judgments of value are themselves challengeable, it follows that we acknowledge some scope for axiological argumentation, giving reasons for the value ascribed to x. But some such arguments must be taken as ultimate, appealing to final values which cannot be further justified. Whether these final values are objectively or subjectively grounded, all axiological and thus also all teleological reasoning must stop at some x the value of which is just taken for granted or apprehended as self-evident.

Deontological reasoning appeals to principles of right and wrong, principles about what ought or ought not to be or be done, where these principles are themselves taken to be ultimate, not derived from some form of teleological reasoning. It is of course controversial at the deepest level in metaethics whether or not there are any such non-derivative principles of the right, or whether the right always depends on the good. And conversely, it can be disputed whether or not our sense of the good is (as Kant in effect argued) derived from our apprehension of what is right. But this does not have to be resolved here. For our concern is with the phenomenology of argumentation rather than its ultimate ontology, and it is clear enough that sometimes people argue for a course of action just because it is the right thing to do regardless of consequences, that is, argue deontologically; whereas there are other occasions on which they argue for a course of action because of the value they attach to the state of affairs that way of acting will bring about, that is, argue teleologically.

Robert Summers has proposed the term "reasons of substance" or "substantive reasons" as a name for those reasons that have practical weight independently of authority. And he divides what I here call teleological and deontological reasons into "goal reasons" and "rightness reasons." I shall follow him in the usage of the term "substantive reason," but shall retain the more traditional philosophical terminology of "teleology" and "deontology" where he speaks of "goals" and "rightness" (Summers 1978).

III. Institutional Argumentation: Authority Reasons

The above might be the only available types of pure practical argumentation, in abstraction from any institutional setting. But in fact most practical argumentation does proceed in an institutional setting. And in such a setting it is common to make use of a different kind of reason why things ought to be (or not be) done, one to which Summers (1978) has given the name an "authority reason." That an action of a certain kind is required according to some ruling or command or instruction issued by somebody in an appropriate setting can count as a reason for action in compliance with this requirement. Such a reason, which is supposed to hold good as a reason by virtue of the authority of its source, is an "authority reason." The law is one obvious and prominent setting in which such reasons are regularly put forward in argumentation. If a legislature has enacted a requirement that (say) automobile passengers must wear seat belts, or that no one may fish in coastal waters if not a citizen of the coastal state, then that constitutes from the juridical point of view a reason for wearing a seat belt, or a reason why certain people may not be permitted to fish in certain waters.

Sometimes one may be inclined to think that only authority reasons are acceptable reasons in legal decision-making. The doctrines of the rule of law and the separation of powers can be understood as combining to support the thesis that those who make legal decisions in litigation must only act on the basis of prior legislative decisions, and must not add anything of their own to the decisions made by the legislator.

According to most contemporary opinion, that view is too restrictive; nevertheless, some standard initial expansions of it do not greatly weaken the claim of authority reasons to be sole grounds for legal decisions. For one may expand the list of reasons operative in law to include precedent, doctrine, and custom; but it will remain the case that at any given moment of decision, the essential argument for (or against) the decision to be made is that it is required (or excluded) according to some such authoritative source.

Nevertheless it is fallacious — we could perhaps call this the "positivistic fallacy" — to hold that arguments from authority reasons, even in a wide sense, are the only acceptable arguments in law. As we shall see, this is not true. The truth lies with a significantly weaker proposition, namely that legal argumentation can never proceed acceptably without some basis in some argument from authority. Arguments from authority have everywhere a special place in law, though not an exclusive one. This is because it is in the very nature of law to constitute a common and authoritative set of norms for some community or group. One point of law is that, where it exists, it sets up a special sort of reasoning on practical matters. The special sort of reasoning is one which leaves aside any general and abstract deliberation on what in a given context it would be best or would be all things considered right to do or not do. Where law is appealed to, all things are not considered. Rather, the law's requirements (and, perhaps, enablements and permissions) are considered, and decision focuses on application of, or compliance with these requirements, or "norms" more generally.

This omnipresence of authority reasons in legal argumentation is not, however, independent of substantive reasons. That which has authority is that which has a right to be obeyed; where there is authority exercised legitimately, disobedience is *prima facie* wrong. Notwithstanding theories of autopoiesis and self-referentiality, the reasons on which authority claims are founded cannot all be themselves authority reasons. Ultimately, to make intelligible (not to say acceptable) any claim of authority, is to enter into either deontological reasoning or teleological reasoning, or both. Authority has to be grounded in some way on the rightness of observing norms posed or evolved in a certain way, or on the values (peace and good order, perhaps) secured by such recognition. And the justification of norms posed by authorities must presumably be in terms of their rightness (justice) or the good they bring about. Even where the rightness of using authority reasons (or the value secured by respecting them) is deemed to exclude any further appeal to substantive reasons, that in itself indicates the ultimate dependency of reasons of authority upon reasons of substance, and shows how institutional argumentation has to be anchored in pure practical argumentation. Still, the law is a forum of institutional argumentation to the extent that it gives, and necessarily gives, a central place to "authority reasons" in the form of statutes, precedents, doctrinal materials and the like.

IV. Interpretative Reasoning

This leads on to the second limb of my present topic. This paper is about argumentation and interpretation. The place of interpretation is an inevitable corollary of the place accorded to authority reasons in legal arguments. For the norm posed in an authoritative source of law has to be understood before it can be applied. Accordingly, in a wide sense of the term "interpretation," every application of an authority reason requires some act of interpretation, since one has to form an understanding of what the authoritative text requires in order to apply it, and any act of apprehension of meaning can be said to involve interpretation. If I see a "No Smoking" sign and put out my cigarette in response, I evince simple understanding of the sign, and compliance with it, without any element of doubt or resolution of doubt; I immediately apprehend what is required, and thus interpret the sign in this broad sense of "interpretation."

There is, however, a more restrictive conception of interpretation, according to which only a conscious attention to some element of doubt about meaning, followed by a resolution of that doubt, amounts to "interpretation" as such. This reflective elimination of doubt is to be distinguished from simple unmediated understanding of a text. For example, there might be a particular occasion when I see a "No Smoking" sign while wearing a formal dinner jacket (a "smoking," as they call it in French), and pause for a moment to ask myself whether the notice requires me to change into less formal attire, rather than to abstain from tobacco. To think over this doubtful point, and to resolve one's doubt by opting in a reasoned way for one rather than another view of what the text requires is to "interpret" it in this stricter sense of the term. By "interpretation in the stricter sense," I thus mean entertaining some doubt about the meaning of proper application of some information, and forming a judgment to resolve the doubt by deciding upon some meaning which seems most reasonable in the context. Henceforward, I shall be dealing only with interpretation so understood (see Wróblewski 1985; MacCormick and Summers 1991, chs. 2 and 8).

It will not have escaped attention that this kind of interpretation is omnipresent in law. For it is frequently the case that consideration of authority reasons in legal contexts, especially contexts of law-application and legal decision-making, raises difficulties or doubts about their meaning either abstractly or for a particular context of decision, and that a judgment has to be formed to resolve the difficulties or doubts. The legal process as an adversarial process can itself generate doubts, since in a situation of conflict of interests, each party to the conflict is anxious to find a reading of authoritative texts which supports its own favoured outcome.

This setting also makes it likely (and anyway it is always possible) that rival approaches to interpretation are themselves supported with arguments. Arguments can be, and may have to be, deployed to show reasons in favour of one's preferred interpretation, in a setting in which one's interpretative judgment is a necessary condition of the relevant applicability of a given authority reason to the decision to be taken. So not merely is interpretation relevant to argumentation, but argumentation may be relevant to interpretation. For among the arguments relevant to decision are those arguments which support or oppose a given interpretation of an authority reason deployed in support of a (possible) decision.

V. Categories of Interpretative Argument

The next logical stage of this paper is therefore to examine some of the kinds of arguments—interpretative arguments—that legal systems characteristically deploy in the justification of interpretations where these are themselves reasons for decisions. In recent work, some colleagues and I have suggested a typology and systematisation of the interpretational argumentation characteristic of a wide range of contemporary systems and traditions of law. According to this, there are three main categories of interpretative argument, and within reach of these several different types of interpretative argument (MacCormick and Summers 1991, chs. 12 and 13).

The categories of interpretative argument are, first, those that appeal to language itself as a source of reasons for favouring one interpretation or another ("linguistic" arguments); second, those that look at the legal system as the special context of the authoritative text to see how best to make sense of it in that context ("systemic" arguments); third, those that look to the end or point of the authoritative text to see how best to make sense of it given that end or point (here, for the sake of internal present consistency though departing a little from the usage in MacCormick and Summers 1991, ch. 2, I shall refer to these as "teleological/deontological" arguments). A further element in interpretational argument is the possibility of appeal to authorial intention as material to elucidating the meaning of the authoritative text; but this conceals a well-known ambiguity between objective and subjective conceptions of intention, and intention may be connected to narrowly linguistic elements of semantics or syntax, to all the multifarious elements of the systemic context of a legal text, or to the aims pursued or principles upheld by the legislature either as an historic body or as an ideally rational legislator; hence this rather indeterminate element of interpretative argumentation is best considered as one ranging across the three main categories. So we call it a "transcategorical" type of argument.

I shall now consider in the order stated some aspects of my three main categories to see what they add to the theory of argumentation.

1. Linguistic Arguments

Linguistic arguments divide into two types concerning either the ordinary meaning or the technical meaning of terms used in legal texts. For example, if a statutory provision has an obvious and intelligible meaning simply as a matter of what the interpreter takes to be the ordinary usage of the natural language employed, that is in itself a good reason for interpreting the text so as to give effect to this "ordinary meaning." On the other hand, if the text is dealing with some technical subject-matter with a specialized vocabulary of its own, terms which have a technical as well as an ordinary meaning are better understood in the technical sense. For example, the world "diligence" in "ordinary" English means praiseworthy and careful application by a person to a task. But in Scots law, it has a technical usage, meaning a legal process for enforcing judgments; and at one time, in the terminology of transport, it meant a particular kind of horse-drawn vehicle. So in Scottish legislation about legal procedures, it should be read in its technical legal sense, and in an ancient piece of English transport legislation, it should be read as signifying the relevant sort of carriage. But in the rules of a school or university offering students prizes for special diligence, the "ordinary" meaning should prevail.

Why do such arguments carry weight? It may be said that this is just a necessary part of respecting authority. If someone in authority issues a norm of some kind, using language to do so, one does not respect that authority unless one reads the norm-text in the language and register in which it was issued. To treat a linguistically formulated text as authoritative, one must also ascribe a kind of normative authority to the syntactic and semantic conventions of the language (whether "ordinary" or "technical" in which the text has been formulated). Not infrequently, appeals are made to "intention" in such a setting—the legislature "must be taken to have intended" the legislation to be understood in the light of its "plain meaning"—even if there might be other reasons for favouring some other outcome than that authorised by the legislative norm-text so understood.

Behind this can be detected, perhaps, an appeal to substantive reasons at the level of pure practical argumentation. The reception of linguistic arguments could be justified on an appeal to principle; for example, the principle that language ought to be used by the legislator and understood by the citizen in a straightforward and unambiguous way. Observing this principle will prevent legislative texts being in effect given new meanings retrospectively by judges to the disadvantage of citizens and hence will uphold a more fundamental principle of justice.

An alternative line of substantive argumentation would look to the cumulative effect of a practice of relying on linguistic arguments in interpretation. By upholding "ordinary" or respectively "technical" meanings in disputes about the meaning of legislation, even in cases in which this brings about non-ideal outcomes, one creates a situation in which legislatures (and their draftsmen) have to take care to draft statutes in ordinarily intelligible terms, and citizens can with confidence read them in terms of their plain meaning, hence the possibility of effective and trouble-free communication between legislature and citizen is maximised, and the trouble and expense of litigation about proper interpretation minimised.

In either event, it has to be recognised that behind what are often described somewhat disapprovingly as "formalistic" or "legalistic" approaches to interpretation there do lie substantive reasons of a perfectly respectable kind, whether these be interpreted deontologically or teleologically.

2. Systemic Arguments

These are a set of arguments which work towards an acceptable understanding of a legal text seen particularly in its context as part of a legal system. I shall mention particularly six:
(i) The argument from contextual harmonisation says that if a statutory provision belongs within a larger scheme, whether a single statute or a set

of related statutes, it ought to be interpreted in the light of the whole statute in which it appears, or more particularly in the light of closely related provisions of the statute or other statutes *in pari materia*, and that what is a more or less obvious "ordinary," or respectively "technical," meaning ought to be interpreted in that light.

(ii) The argument from precedent says that if a statutory provision has previously been subjected to judicial interpretation, it ought to be interpreted in conformity with the interpretation given to it by other courts. (Where there is a strict doctrine of precedent based on a hierarchy of courts, lower courts must conform; where particular weight is given to a *jurisprudence constante* of the higher courts, this would also affect the exact application of this form of argument in the system under view; in general, the argument has to be constructed appropriately to the doctrine of judicial precedent prevalent in the legal system under consideration.)

(iii) The argument from analogy says that if a statutory provision is significantly analogous with similar provisions of other statutes, or a code, or another part of the code in which it appears, then even if this involves a significant extension of or departure from ordinary meaning, it may properly be interpreted so as to secure similarity of sense with the analogous provisions *either* considered in themselves *or* considered in the light of prior judicial interpretations of them. (The argument from analogy appears to be stronger on the second hypothesis, where it incorporates a version of the argument from precedent.)

(iv) Logical-conceptual argument says that if any recognised and doctrinally elaborated general legal concept is used in the formulation of a statutory provision, it ought to be interpreted so as to maintain a consistent use of the concept throughout the system as a whole, or relevant branch or branches of it.

(v) The argument from general principles of law says that if any general principle or principles of law are applicable to the subject matter of a statutory provision, one ought to favour that interpretation of the statutory provision which is most in conformity with the general principle or principles, giving appropriate weight to the principle(s) in the light of their degree of importance both generally and in the field of law in question.

(vi) The argument from history says that if a statute or group of statutes has over time come to be interpreted in accordance with an historically evolved understanding of the point and purpose of the statute or group of statutes taken as a whole, or an historically evolved understanding of the conception of rightness it embodies, then any provision of the statute or group of statutes ought to be interpreted so that its application in concrete cases is compatible with this historically evolved understanding of point and purpose or of rightness.

All these arguments are well-known to lawyers and, I suppose, easily recognisable even without weighing the present essay down with illustrations and examples. What is of importance in the present context is to ask why such arguments carry the weight they obviously do in contemporary legal systems. A part of the answer simply relates back to the linguistic arguments. No linguistic communication is fully comprehensible save in a whole presupposed context of utterance. All legal materials are uttered in the context of the legal system in general, and in the light no doubt of a whole complex of concrete legal, political and factual circumstances. So interpretation cannot be satisfactorily carried through even in a purely linguistic sense unless the whole context is kept in mind.

But that is not the whole story, for it fails to say just why the legal context gives special appropriateness to arguments stressing the six features I have mentioned. As to that, I think it is necessary to draw attention to an ideal of overall *coherence* which governs our view of the legal system as a system and hence gives weight to the interpretative approach favoured by our various types of systemic argument. This is a theme which I have explored at some length elsewhere, and on which Ronald Dworkin has had much to say lately in commending an ideal of "integrity" in a legal system. The point is that legal systems do not contain single or isolated commitments of principle or determinations of policy. Rather, they comprise a multiplicity of interacting norms of many kinds, and these may be taken to express a plurality of principles and policy-choices. As such, they are capable of being handled in a way that tries to make as much sense as possible of the whole taken together and taken as a whole (MacCormick 1984; Dworkin 1986).

If one were to reject the attempt to view law holistically as a coherent system, each decision would presumably have to be considered as taken on its own merits with regard to any attractive interpretation of norms relevant to the instant case. In an extreme, the law would then approximate to the poet's wilderness of single instances. By contrast, a practice of construing the law so as to give it coherence in form and content is one which actually constructs and reconstructs law into an ordered scheme of intelligibly differentiated cases and situations.

In interpretative dilemmas, recourse to systemic argumentation exhibits a special regard for this overall quality of rational coherence and intelligibility in law. It involves superimposing a principle of rationality on the institutional actuality of law. As such, it adds a missing element to our two substantive arguments as elements of pure practical argumentation. The argument from coherence is a necessary supplement to teleological argument and deontological argument for any setting in which it is envisaged that there is good reason to have recourse to a plurality of norms all together, not just to isolated moment-by moment aims or principles.

3. Teleological/Deontological Arguments

These arguments contextually replicate what I have in this paper characterised as the two forms of substantive argumentation, the arguments which would be available in a context-free realm of pure practical argumentation. But of course in the legal context they remain in an important way institutional arguments, not free-floating arguments of pure practical reasonableness.

Teleological interpretative argument concerns the end or purpose imputed to a piece of legislation on the assumption of its having been enacted by a rational legislature in a given historical setting. Whether one expresses this in negative terms as a matter of the "mischief" or undesirable state of affairs the legislature was (or was presumptively) trying to remedy, or positively in terms of some supposedly good state of affairs imputed as the end and aim of the act of legislating, the idea is that of treating legislation as a teleological enterprise where the *telos* or aim is independent of the terms of the text enacted and hence can provide a guide to their interpretation: So interpret as to help realise the imputed purpose; do not so interpret as to defeat that purpose. For example, if a tax statute contains a section on penalties for non-disclosure of earnings, impute to the legislature the purpose of establishing a fair and rational scheme of disincentives to non-disclosure. Then interpret the penal provisions in the statute so as to bring about fairness and rationality, even at the expense of a literal reading of the terms of the act in their ordinary meaning. Do not read the act—even in its "ordinary meaning"—so as to defeat the presumed aim of its penal provisions (*Inland Revenue Commissioners v. Hinchy* [1959]. 2 Q.B. 357, Reversed, 1960, A.C. 748).

Deontological interpretative argument is argument in terms of principles of rectitude or justice which in the interpreter's view ought to be observed in respect of a given situation or subject matter. Intention to act justly can always be imputed to a legislature considered as an ideally rational law-making body, and particular concrete conceptions of justice are often reasonably imputable to actual historically situated legislatures. For example, the principles imputed to the Rome Treaties and associated acts foundational of the European Community allow for the "four freedoms" to be enjoyed throughout the Community by all citizens of all member states. Hence legislation by a member state which seeks to protect coastal fisheries by restricting fishing rights to its own nationals cannot be compatible with the treaties on any reasonable interpretation, nor should the quota provisions of the Common Fisheries Policy be interpreted as creating an exception to the fundamental principle of freedom of establishment (*R v. Secretary of State ex P. Factortame* [1991] 3 All E.R. 769; Court of Justice of the European Community, Case C-221/89).

The connection between such interpretative arguments and pure practical argumentation is obvious enough. For these are simply institutional applications of the two basic forms of practical argument. But they are restricted by the institutional setting. For the question must always be as to *telos* or principle in relation to the statute or other text as one finds it, and with some regard to its historical and systemic context. For any given problem situation, we can always differentiate the question "What would be the best aim to pursue here, or the best principle to apply?" from the question "What aim is it plausible to ascribe to the legal text before us, or the best principle to frame as expressing its underlying point?" The latter are the true questions of interpretation, whether or not legal decision makers are also entitled to have some regard to the former in the setting of adjudication. (And I am by no means sure that Ronald Dworkin (1986) does not conflate them in advancing his theory of "constructive intepretation," though that is another story.)

The institutional setting exerts other pressures here. Especially in the case of statutory texts recently enacted by a democratic legislature, the weight of the practical principles favouring linguistic interpretation will place limits on the propriety of effectively rewriting the law to match imputed purposes or commitments of principle only implicitly to be found in the text as enacted. And the principle of rationality noted above favours systemic coherence over momentary aim or isolated principle.

VI. Conflicting Arguments and Conflict-Resolution

From all the above, it is only too clear that interpretative argument in law presents considerable complexity, since there are many types of argument available, and each is capable of generating an interpretation of a given text at variance with that generated by some other possible argument. Indeed for any set of rival interpretations $I_1, I_2, \ldots I_n$, if these were seriously viable rivals at all, there would be some arguments of one or another of these types (or perhaps others similar) to support one or another of the rival interpretations. Nor is there any reason to suppose that arguments of different types within the same category must all tell in the same direction; of course not, for there can be intra-categorial conflicts of argument as well as conflicts between (or in some cases convergence of) arguments of different categories. Hence there must be a stage of argumentation which concerns the ranking of arguments or cumulative sets of arguments when there is conflict among the interpretations these generate.

As for this one can certainly suggest relatively simple models for ordering and ranking possible arguments. It is tempting to suggest that in all systems there is a tendency to start out with the linguistic arguments, then to proceed to systemic, and only to have recourse to teleological/deontological argumentation when arguments of the other sorts remain problematic. A relevant doctrine of positive law in this context is provided by what Scottish and English lawyers call "The Golden Rule." Here is a classical formulation:

We are to take the whole statute together and construe it altogether, giving the words their ordinary signification, unless when so applied they produce an inconsistency, or an absurdity, or inconvenience so great as to convince the court that the intention could not have been to use them in their ordinary signification, and to justify the court in putting on them some other signification which, though less proper, is one which the court thinks that the words will bear. (Lord Blackburn, in *Weger v. Commissioners Adamson*; [1874–78] All ER Rep. 1, at 12)

And here is a relatively more recent formulation:

One is to apply statutory words and phrases according to their natural and ordinary meaning without addition or subtraction, unless that meaning produces injustice, absurdity, anomaly, contradiction, in which case one may modify the natural and ordinary meaning so as to obviate such injustice etc. but no further. (Nowadays we should add to "natural and ordinary meaning" the words "in their context and according to the appropriate linguistic register.") (Lord Simon, in *Stock v. Frank Jones (Tipton)*; [1978] 1 All ER 948, at 952)

As these dicta suggest, if there is one interpretation that is clearly favoured by a reading of the text in the light of syntactic and semantic conventions of ordinary language (or special registers in special settings), and if this is confirmed by a reading of the text in its whole systemic context, there is no need for recourse to teleological/deontological arguments. But if there remains uncertainty in the light of all the linguistic and systemic arguments, further grounds of interpretation are required, or if there is an "absurdity" of some sort, that should be resolved. A valuable recent study by Dr. Yezhar Tal (1992) stresses, contrary to much that has been said in doctrinal literature, that both in practice and in authoritative rulings about interpretation "absurdity" for the purpose of the Golden Rule includes conflict either with justice or with other aspects of what is deemed the public good. The present paper owes much to Tal's work. It is in the relevant sense "absurd" to read a statute either in such a way as to generate injustice by reference to some legally recognised principle of justice or in such a way as to be self-defeating in terms of presumed objectives of public policy pursued through legislation. So it would not be correct to say that the category of teleological/deontological argument comes into play only if the other two categories fail to yield an unequivocal result. Consideration of arguments in that category may show up such an absurdity as will displace a *prima facie* binding conclusion about the meaning of the legislative words in their (fully contextualised) "ordinary signification."

Interesting and suggestive though the Golden Rule is, however, it is not really a "rule." It is better considered as a maxim of practical interpretative wisdom, indicating how the various types of argument may be handled in cases of real interpretative difficulty arising from conflicts among relevant arguments. It does not provide any simple binary directive about right and wrong interpretations in the difficult cases. It indicates an approach to the resolution of difficulty.

VII. Conclusion: Interpretation within Practical Argumentation

In understanding such difficulty and its resolution, we need to reflect further on the values and principles I have suggested as underlying each of the categories of argument. Behind linguistic interpretation lies an aim of preserving clarity and accuracy in legislative language and a principle of justice that forbids retrospective judicial rewriting of the legislature's chosen words; behind systemic interpretation lies a principle of rationality grounded in the value of coherence and integrity in a legal system; behind teleological/deontological interpretation lies respect for the demand of practical reason that human activity be guided either by some sense of values to be realised by action or by principles to be observed in it. But in the case of this last most fundamental level of practical argumentation, the perennial problem of the human situation is the interpersonal disputability of the values and principles that should guide us. As is commonly held, a strong justifying reason for the maintenance of legal and other common social institutions among humans is to diminish the scope for disputes about governing values and principles in the social arena. And this is what in turn justifies giving considerable weight to linguistic and systemic argumentation in law, and imposing rather heavy threshold constraints against too ready recourse to teleological/deontological argumentation to raise, and some-times to resolve, interpretative difficulties in law.

These remarks cannot be uncontroversial, since they themselves take a practically argumentative position about the right way to understand, to justify, and to use legal and related institutions in democratic societies. They show that one cannot confine argumentation about law to purely inter-pretative argumentation. Law may indeed be an "interpretive concept" (Dworkin 1986), but in forming a view about law and its interpretation, we must do more than interpret the concept of law and the texts that belong to what we conceptualise as law. We move in the end into a broader sphere of practical argumentation. Here, we must reflect on the values and principles appropriate to the institutions of the societies, the states and the supra-national and international communities which we inhabit. We need to think about the meaning of constitutionalism or *Rechtsstaatlichkeit*, democracy, the rule of law, the separation of powers, procedural justice, equality before and under law, human rights and the integrity of public offices. All these, and more besides, come into play when we seek a fully explained and justified view of the best approach to legal interpretation in trouble cases.

In short, the theory of interpretation as a topic intrinsic to the study of practical argumentation leads one necessarily on into the deepest waters of normative constitutional and political theory, that is, to quite free-ranging practical argumentation applied to basic legal and political institutions. In that light, it is not surprising if a short paper on argumentation and inter-pretation in law offers suggestions rather than conclusions about the best approach to the resolution of interpretative difficulties in law. But it does enable us to say that even if law can effectually regulate its own creation, it can never completely regulate its own interpretation.

University of Edinburgh
Faculty of Law
Old College, South Bridge
Edinburgh EH8 9YL
UK

References

Dworkin, Ronald. 1986. *Law's Empire*. London: Fontana.
MacCormick, Neil. 1984. Coherence in Legal Justification. In *Theorie der Normen. Festgabe für Ota Weinberger zum 65. Geburtstag*. Ed. W. Krawietz, H. Schlesky, G. Winkler, and A. Schramm. Berlin: Duncker & Humblot.
MacCormick, Neil, and Robert S. Summers, eds. 1991. *Interpreting Statutes. A Comparative Study*. Aldershot: Dartmouth.
Summers, Robert. 1978. Two Types of Substantive Reasons. The Core of a Theory of Common Law Justification. *Cornell Law Review* 63: 707–88.
Tal, Yezhar. 1992. *Statutory Interpretation and Expressed Reference to Justice. A Study of Cases in English Law and Implications for Interpretative Approaches*. Oxford: Ph.D. Thesis.
Wróblewski, Jerzy. 1985. Legal Language and Legal Interpretation. *Law and Philosophy* 4: 239–55.

Coherence in Legal Justification

By Neil MacCormick, Edinburgh

I. Introduction

That a piece of reasoning be coherent as a whole is one commonly accepted criterion of its soundness as reasoning. Our problem is to make intelligible the nature of the criterion so set, and to show its place within a canon of rational justification. This paper will suggest that, in legal justification, there are two distinct sorts of test for coherence: the first, which we may call the *'normative coherence'* test, has to do with the justification of legal rulings or normative propositions more generally in the context of a legal system conceived as a normative order; the second, which we may call the *'narrative coherence'* test, has to do with the justification of findings of fact and the drawing of reasonable inferences from evidence.

I shall not assume too quickly, if at all, that normative coherence and narrative coherence have much more than name and assonance in common. Yet perhaps even from the outset we may allow this as a common feature of the two cases; either in normative or in narrative contexts, a lack of coherence in what is said involves a failure to make sense. An incoherent set of norms might be such that each could be fulfilled without infringing any other, yet the whole seems to make no sense as constituting or mapping out a reasonable order of conduct — imagine a house within which all inhabitants are to make their rooms as untidy as possible on Mondays, Wednesdays and Fridays, then tidy them up to the highest perfection on Tuesdays, Thursdays and Saturdays, Sundays being strictly observed as a day of rest. To have, and to observe, such house rules is possible — but what sense does it make? Likewise an incoherent story, though it may contain no proposition which directly contradicts or logically entails a contradiction of any other proposition in the story, yet in some way fails to make sense. That a perfect stranger entered the house, that he therein committed a crime, and that the watch-dog failed to bark, is a story which contains no contradictions; but once Sherlock Holmes has drawn our attention to it, we see that it does not make sense — it does not 'hang together' — no more than our crazy house-rules hang together.

265

But what do we mean by 'make sense', 'hanging together', 'cohe-rence'? Is such 'sense' or 'intelligibility' the same in normative and narrative contexts, or substantially different? I shall explore these questions through illustrative examples respectively in the normative and in the narrative cases in the two main sections of the paper, before I proceed to essay some conclusions. In the meantime, one further introductory point may be apt.

Here as in previous writing[1], I have assumed that 'coherence' can usefully be distinguished from consistency. This is partly a matter of fidelity to the nuance of ordinary language but more a matter of prejudice in favour of letting different words serve different purposes. So I interpret consistency as being satisfied by non-contradiction. A set of propositions is mutually consistent if each can without contradiction be asserted in conjunction with every other and with their conjunction; for my part, I see no difficulty in using the term 'contradiction' as freely in the case of norms and normative propositions as in the case of narrative propositions, but in this case, those who are hesitant about such a usage may rephrase normative consistency as that property of a set of norms or normative propositions none of which 'controverts' or 'conflicts with' any other or the conjunction of all the others.

By contrast, coherence, as I said, is the property of a set of proposi-tions which, taken together, 'makes sense' in its entirety. What this elusive notion of 'making sense' implies has yet to be investigated. Even at the outset, let me say that I do not regard consistency as a necessary condition of coherence, since unlike consistency, coherence can be a matter of degree. A story can be coherent on the whole and as a whole, though it contains some internal inconsistencies — and in this case, the sense of the overall coherence of the story may be decisive for us in deciding which among pairs of inconsistent propositions to discard. Obviously enough, as earlier examples showed, the mere consistency of a set of propositions is no guarantee of their coherence as a story.

These preliminaries settled, I turn to consideration separately of normative and of narrative coherence.

---

[1] On normative coherence, chiefly *Legal Reasoning and Legal Theory* (Oxford, 1978) chapters 7 and 8; on narrative coherence, *id.* chapter 4, pp. 89 bis 92, and also 'The Coherence of a Case and the Reasonableness of Doubt', Liverpool Law Rev., 2 (1980) pp. 45 - 50.

II. Normative Coherence

(a) The Meaning of Coherence

Why is it that a set of legal norms might sometimes appear incoherent, even when as a set they are not inconsistent? An example of such a set which I previously suggested was if a statute laid down different speed limits for different cars according to the colour they were painted. Little did I realise when I figured that fanciful case that there was a real case rather like it. Now I am indebted to Mr Justice Ruggero Aldisert (Justice of the U. S. Court of Appeals, 3rd Circuit) for producing a real case more or less to the same effect. For some time ago the legislature in Italy determined that there should be differential speed limits for different types and makes of car[2].

Do such laws fail to make sense? And if they so fail, why do they so fail? My answer to that is that they fail to make sense if there is no common value which the enactment of such laws subserves. In our examples, is there no common value at issue? At least at first sight, it appears that there is not. Consider: there are three ends which statutes limiting driving speeds may promote, all of which we may suppose to be of serious social value: the safety of road users; economy in the use of fuel; and prevention of excessive wear and tear of road surfaces. If the colour of cars is purely a matter of taste, and many colours are available (as is true in Western Europe and North America at least), it seems doubtful whether any speed limit differential between differently coloured cars could possibly subserve effectively any such end as those envisaged above. Moreover, if people have bought cars prior to the colour-laws, it seems unfair that they should *ex post facto* be treated differently according to the colour choice they made. So without subserving any value special to road safety laws, the colour-laws would in fact conflict with or subvert another value of importance in a very general way to legal systems.

Of course, we can imagine circumstances in which the colour-laws *would be* coherent. If all cars had to be repainted according to their weight and fuel consumption, and if all inexperienced drivers had to acquire or drive only cars of a low-speed colour, we would begin to see that the colour-laws were part of a scheme which after all does rationally relate to the endeavour to minimise fuel consumption and damage to roads while tending to improve road safety.

---

[2] *Ruggero J. Aldisert,* book review of Legal Reasoning and Legal Theory, Duquesne Law Rev. 20 (1982), pp. 383 - 398 and, in general, cf. Aldisert J.'s opinion in *Pfeiffer* v. *Jones and Laughlin Steel Corp.* 678 F 2 d (1982) 453, esp. at 461.

Perhaps the Italian law was designed according to some such principles. Perhaps there was a legislative intent rationally to relate differential speed limits to such objectives as economy and safety. Aldisert J. reports, however, that the car-drivers of Italy did not see it that way[3]. They treated the differential speed limits as incoherent nonsense, and ignored them entirely. Desuetude overruled the act. May be the car-drivers judged wrongly. May be the lawmakers failed in persuasion rather than in coherent thought. But we need not go into that. Sufficient has been said to ground the suggestion, arising from these examples, that at least one aspect of normative coherence is a matter of the common subservience by a set of laws to a relevant value or values; and an absence of avoidable conflict with other relevant values (e. g. with justice, as in the above case).

Are there then other aspects of coherence? One candidate which comes to mind has to do with principles. We might say that a set of rules is coherent if they all satisfy or are instances of a single more general principle. If it is a principle that human life ought not to be unduly endangered by motor traffic on the roads, this will (help to) make sense of speed limit laws and many other parts of road traffic law taken together: but not of all possible speed-limit laws — judged by reference to that principle, car-colour differential speed limits will be arbitrary unless in some such expanded context as was imagined above.

The very fact that we can re-express in terms of common principles the coherence of a set of laws (road traffic laws) which we previously expressed in terms of common values poses the question whether appeal to 'values' is different in substance from appealing to principles, or only different in grammatical form. 'Safety on the roads' is a noun phrase; 'safety on the roads' conceived as a *value* is the state of affairs signified by the noun phrase conceived as being a state of affairs which is a good or worthy purpose of human endeavour. 'That human life ought not to be unduly endangered by motor traffic on the roads' is a normative sentence which in virtue of its very general scope can be considered as a possible principle. It is actually somebody's principle or a principle of some normative system if some person assents to it

---

[3] *Op. cit.*, p. 395 'A few years ago Italian officials could not agree upon a speed limit for Italy's superhighway, the *autostrada*. They compromised on regulations that set speed limits according to automobile engine size. Thus a small Fiat was limited to 80 k. p. h., a larger car to 100 k. p. h., and so on. Each car owner was required to post on the rear of his vehicle a decal showing the car's assigned speed limit. If the desired goal was road safety, the regulations seem absurd. Though internally consistent, they had no coherence. In practice no problems have resulted, however, because neither car owners nor police have paid any attention to the regulations.'

as a practical norm for his/her own and others' conduct or, respectively, if it is an accepted or acceptable justifying norm for more particular and specific norms ('rules') within that system.

In short, if 'values' are, as I suppose, not merely the *de facto* purposes, aims, goals or ends actually pursued from time to time by individual persons or institutional agencies, but rather actually pursued or possibly pursued states of being or of affairs which are conceived to be legitimate, desirable, worthy or even (the scale ascends by degrees) mandatory for pursuit as standing purposes, aims, goals or ends, then there appears to be an extensional equivalence as between 'values' and 'principles'. For any value V there is a principle according to which V either may be, or ought in the absence of countervailing considerations to be, or ought normally to be, or must in the absence of overriding considerations be, pursued or realised. Observance of principles is not an instrumental, but an intrinsic, means of realising values.

This conforms to a suggestion which I have recently put forward[4] that systems of practical reason necessarily require the framing of hierarchically related rules and principles of conduct exhibiting consistency over time and universalisability over cases, this being essential to the achievement of a rational order superimposed on what would otherwise be a chaos of particular purposes. Under such principles some actual recurring purposes can be generalised as standing aims legitimated (or made mandatory) by one's principles. So values are the product of a system of practical principles. This, if sound, accounts for the extensional equivalence of values and principles.

Nevertheless, the formulation of values (or virtues) like 'safety', 'health', 'considerateness', 'justice' or whatever may have a particular utility for the purposes of a critique of a system of rules or principles as hitherto (at any given time) formulated. By reflecting on what it is that we suppose to be, or are committed to treating as, good to bring about, we may be led to better or more general expressions of the principles of our practical systems or (yet more likely) to see new areas for their application. This perhaps accounts for the standing popularity of utilitarian and other consequentialist doctrines in ethics and legal and political philosophy.

I conclude that the coherence of norms is a matter of their 'making sense' by being rationally related as a set, instrumentally or intrinsic-

---

[4] In my paper 'The Limits of Rationality in Legal Reasoning', presented to the 11th World Congress of I. V. R., Helsinki, 1983; to be published in the proceedings of that Congress under the editorship of Aulis Aarnio; also, in a German version in *MacCormick* and *Weinberger*, Die Theorie der institutionalistischen Rechtspositivismus (Berlin. 1984, forthcoming).

ally, *either* to the realisation of some common value or values; *or* to the fulfilment of some common principle or principles. At the level of the highest-order principles or values there is a further requirement of coherence: that, after allowance for the fulfilment of priority rankings of principles and/or values we consider that in their totality they express a satisfactory form of life[5], and one which it would be possible for human beings, as human beings are, to live. In short, the coherence of a set of norms is a function of its justifiability under higher order principles or values, principles and values being extensionally equivalent; provided that the higher or highest-order principles and values seem acceptable as delineating a satisfactory form of life, when taken together.

(b) Coherence in justification: an example

A well known decision in English criminal law, that of *Sweet* v. *Parsley*[6] concerned the problem of interpreting a statute which provided:

'If a person — *(a)* being the occupier of any premises, permits those premises to be used for the purposes of smoking cannabis or cannabis resin or of dealing in cannabis or cannabis resin ...; or *(b)* is concerned in the management of any premises used for any such purpose as aforesaid; he shall be guilty of an offence against this Act.'
(Dangerous Drugs Act, 1965, section 5)

The particular problem in the case focussed on paragraph *(b)*, to be precise, whether the offence of 'being concerned in the management of any premises used for any such purpose' requires or does not require guilty knowledge or intention or participation in the 'purpose' in question. Miss Sweet, a schoolteacher in Oxford, was tenant of a farmhouse outside Oxford. She sub-let rooms in the house to other persons. After a certain time, her car broke down, and she had to take rooms in Oxford. Thereafter she kept only one room in the farmhouse as her own, and sub-let all the other rooms, with a kitchen etc. retained for common use. She was able to visit the house only occasionally to stay over a night, collect rent, and check that the house was in reasonable condition.

In due course, the police discovered that cannabis was being smoked by residents in the house. They charged Miss Sweet, who was indubitably managing the premises, with 'managing premises used for [the purpose of smoking cannabis]', contrary to section 5 *(b)* of the Act. The trial court found as a fact that 'she had no knowledge whatever

---

[5] Cf. *Aulis Aarnio*, On Legal Reasoning (Turku, 1977) pp. 126 - 9; I am almost tempted here to introduce a concept of 'Aarnio-optimality'.
[6] [1968] 2 All E. R. 337; [1969] 1 All E. R. 347 (H. L.).

that the house was being used for the purpose of smoking cannabis or cannabis resin'. Nevertheless, the court convicted her, being of the opinion that the Act was in terms which implied absolute liability, that is, liability without regard to a person's intention or knowledge as to the purpose in question, provided she or he were actually concerned in the management of the relevant premises. At the first level of appeal, this view was upheld: 'paragraph *(b)* in dealing with somebody concerned with the management of premises where cannabis is smoked contains an absolute liability; it does not depend on knowledge at all'[7], this being in contrast with paragraph *(a)*, under which 'permitting' necessarily involves knowledge of what is going on.

On the final appeal to the House of Lords, this interpretation of the Act was rejected. There can be discerned at least three elements in the reasoning in favour of allowing the appeal and quashing the conviction: first, there is ambiguity in the Act: 'Is the "purpose" the purpose of the smoker or the purpose of the management[8]?' Either possible answer to that question being *consistent* with the express terms of the Act, either answer is permissible in law, given the requirement that rulings in law and particular decisions must not contradict established rules of law. Secondly, however, the consequences ('consequences-as-implications') of holding that the smoker's purpose suffices are unacceptable:

'The implications are astonishing. Parliament would not only be indirectly imposing a duty* on persons concerned in the management of any premises requiring them to exercise complete supervision over all persons who enter the premises to ensure that no one of them should smoke cannabis, but Parliament would be enacting that the persons concerned in the management would be guilty of an offence if, unknown to them, someone by surreptitiously smoking cannabis eluded the most elaborately devised measures of supervision.'[9]

Such reasons — and many such points were taken by the five Law Lords — indicate the extreme undesirability, in their Lordships' view, of imputing to Parliament the intention that the word 'purpose' be read

---

[7] [1968] 2 All E. R. 337 at 339, per Lord Parker C. J.; the magistrates' finding of fact quoted above has the same source.

[8] [1969] 1 All E. R. 347 at 352, per Lord Reid.

* A duty which, as Lord Pearce pointed out, [1969] 1 All E. R. 356, would necessarily extend to 'the innocent hotel keeper, the lady who takes in paying guests, the manager of a cinema, the warden of a hostel, the matron of a hospital, the housemaster and matron of a boarding school' though 'the most that vigilance can attain is knowledge of their own guilt. If a smell of cannabis comes from a sitting room, they know that they have committed the offence. Should they then go at once to the police and confess their guilt in the hope that they will not be prosecuted?'

[9] *Id.* at 355, per Lord Morris of Berth-y-Gest. On 'consequences as implications', see *MacCormick*: On Legal Decisions and their Consequences, N. Y. U. Law Rev. 58 (1983) 239 - 258.

as referring to anything other than the purpose *of the person concerned in management*. What is said, of course, is that Parliament 'cannot' have intended so unjust a result. But the grounds for the imputation of intention are the evaluations of the implications of the rejected interpretation; no independent recourse is available to the otherwise mysterious concept of 'legislator's intention'[10].

Thirdly, and also apparently essential to the justification of the ruling in law is what I call the argument from 'coherence':

> 'A consideration of previous and analogous legislation removes any doubt that these words are intended to refer to such a special and limited class as I have described, one which quite clearly excludes such persons as the appellant. This legislation deals with other "anti-social" activities, such as the keeping of brothels, opium "dens" and gaming houses[11].'

Thus for example:

> 'The Dangerous Drugs Act, 1920 dealt with opium. The relevant sections are reproduced in the Act of 1965 (s. 8), and it is obvious that the provisions regarding cannabis are based on them. In dealing with the management of premises it seems clear enough that what is in mind is not the lessor of premises on which opium may come to be smoked, but a manager of what, if a noun is required, might be called "opium dens"[12].'

So, if a coherent view is to be taken of the legislation controlling such 'anti-social activities', it must be the view that none creates offences of strict or absolute liability. Reference was also made to the earlier decision of *Warner* v. *Metropolitan Police Commissioner*[13], from which, especially from the leading opinion of Lord Reid, there can be extracted a general principle as to the differentiation of offences of absolute liability from those requiring *mens rea*. As he re-stated that principle in *Sweet*'s case, it is to the effect that there is a class of 'quasi-criminal acts', acts which 'in the public interest are prohibited under a penalty'. Being penalised in such matters involves no real moral stigma. By contrast, in the case of 'acts of a truly criminal character', 'a stigma ... attaches to any person convicted ... and the more serious or more disgraceful the offence, the greater the stigma'. It has then to be asked whether 'in a case of this gravity, the public interest really requires that an innocent person should be prevented from proving his inno-

---

[10] But see *id.* at 351, per *Lord Reid*, ... 'Speaking from a rather long experience of membership of both Houses, I assert with confidence that no Parliament within my recollection would have agreed to make an offence of this kind an absolute offence if the matter had been fully aired before it.' Does the counterfactual at the end support or confute my suggestion in the text?

[11] *Id.* 359 per Lord Wilberforce.

[12] *Ibid.*

[13] [1968] 2 All E. R. 356 (H. L.).

cence in order that fewer guilty men may escape'. That is: where an offence is created to regulate in the public interest a potentially dangerous activity of a specialised kind, and where conviction does not carry moral stigma, liability may be strict or absolute; where offences properly carry some stigma, *mens rea* ought to be required. This Lord Reid took to be the best — though not a perfect — rationalisation of the previous decisions on the question of absolute liability versus *mens rea*. In the former class of cases, in his view, the value of public safety is promoted without grave injustice. In the latter class of cases the injustice of a stigmatising conviction of a morally innocent person is normally and properly taken to outweigh any competing public interest in general safety and good conduct[14].

These considerations, together with the principle of interpretation that 'if a penal provision is reasonably capable of two interpretations, that interpretation which is most favourable to the accused must be adopted[15], completed the justification of the decision.

I hope it is clear how this reading of the reasoning in *Sweet* v. *Parsley* conforms to and illustrates what I said earlier by way of explaining my conception of 'coherence'. So far as concerns the coherence argument, the task the judges undertake is a two-fold one. First, the inquiry is as to the principles or values which as far as possible make sense of a relevant set of legal norms — statutes and precedents dealing with similar subject matter in the same field of law. These are partly to be found in the existing materials, partly to be constructed so as to establish a coherent view of the branch of the law, by showing it to be compendiously justifiable by reference to some 'underlying' principle or value or coherent set of principles and values which can be conceived as justifying the rules and rulings (the norms) under consideration. These are then applied to the purpose of justifying the actual ruling in the present case, as an analogous application of the same principles or values, and thus as coherent with the pre-established body of law. Where, as in *Sweet* v. *Parsley* (and, I suppose, as is almost invariably the case in codified systems of law) the problem concerns the interpretation of a statutory text, the rhetoric of such justification is to pose it as the intention of the legislator to legislate coherently. But there is an air of pious fiction about such rhetoric. It is the theory that legislators ought to legislate for a coherent body of law which justifies the imputation of such intention to the legislator; it is not an actual, independently established fact of proven legislative preference for coherent law which constitutes (as under voluntarist theories of law) a duty

---

[14] See [1969] 1 All E. R. p. 350.
[15] *Ibid.*

of the judge so to interpret the law in subservience to this real will of
the real legislature.

(c) Why Coherence justifies

If we can only fictitiously treat a real legislative intention as that
which constitutes 'coherence' as a relevant justifying quality in legal
reasoning, we are left with the question why, and in what sense,
coherence does justify. Is the theory that legislators ought to legislate
for a coherent body of law a sound theory? More generally, is coherence
a quality which legal norms ought to exhibit, and, if so, why?

To sketch a few considerations in virtue of which 'coherence' may be
esteemed relevant to justification: first, it is agreeable to a certain conception of rationality in practical life, that which requires both universality and also the greatest possible degree of generality in practical
principles. There are also reasons (fair notice to subjects, relative
specificity in the law) why the law should be expounded at the level
of relatively detailed rules. But these relatively detailed rules will be
arbitrary if they are not also instances of more general principles,
fewer in number than the number of the detailed rules, and more
general in their terms. Further, since few people can know much of the
detail of the law, they are more likely to find it cognisable and predictable in substance if it does instantiate a reasonably small range of
general principles. This further point amounts to an element of justice
in the dealings between citizen and state. Finally, in so far as (to borrow from Professors Hintikka and von Wright)[16] a legal order is an
ideal order in the sense of a possible ordering of human affairs which
is taken to set a pattern at least for aspiration in the actual conduct of
affairs, it seems not enough that it should constitute merely an aggregate of non-contradictory propositions of a relatively detailed sort,
the whole having subjoined to it a single general norm that this order
is to be realised in social practice. Judged by the standards of extra-
legal practical reason, such an order could not be a satisfactory form of
'ideal order' for rational human agents.

All this implies a formalistic (formally rational) and relativistic sort
of justification. Whatever the actual content of a legal system may be,
the above considerations and their like imply that it is preferable that
the system be interpreted and applied so far as possible under the
supposition that its more detailed provisions can be conceptualised as

---

[16] G. H. von Wright, Opening Lecture 'Is and Ought', to 11th World Congress of I. V. R., Helsinki, 1983: 'In order to be rational to entertain, the ideal
must be a picture of a *possible world* which is, to use a phrase coined by
Jaakko Hintikka, *deontically perfect*.'

deriving from or instantiating (in the sense of being together justifiable under) some general principles; and also that the principles themselves as a set, making allowance for priorities and for different justificatory levels, are capable of being thought coherent in the ultimate sense suggested above at the end of II (a). Put in the alternative, the detailed provisions of the system ought to be interpretable as subserving a possible set of mutually compatible values. 'Coherence' can then be satisfied by a system which does subserve what those responsible for determining its content do suppose to be values (e. g. racial purity under various elements of National Socialist law), even although from another point of view — let us say bluntly a better one — these supposed values are truly evils.

On this ground, considerations of 'coherence' may be considered to be only weakly justifying considerations. To borrow a term from David Lyons's recent paper 'Justification and Easy Cases'[17] coherence concerns the *derivability* of a novel decision or ruling in law from the pre-existing body of law, not the ultimate *defensibility* of the decision or ruling from a moral point of view. Moreover, the constraint of coherence seems to be treated by lawyers as a relatively weak constraint, perhaps because it determines only what we might call the 'weak derivability' of a ruling or decision from the pre-existing law. This contrasts with 'strong derivability' where some ruling or decision is deductively derivable from binding rules of the system, in the sense that any other decision would be directly inconsistent with (or contradictory of) some such binding rule. (I do not say that, if the rules are themselves wicked rules, strong derivability entails defensibility. But in so far as the adjudicative role is a role determined by positive law, it is clear that the legal duty of the judge is to decide only in ways that are consisent with the established rules of law. The moral duty of the person who holds the judicial office can however over-ride the legal duty.)

The reason why coherence determines only weak derivability of ruling or decision from established law is dependent on the fact that coherence is a desirable ideal feature of a system of law. As such, however, it may compete with other ideal features of law, like substantive justice (judged by appropriate criteria) and so forth. Yet it imposes a real and important constraint on judges if we interpret it in a negative sense: unless, by the coherence test, some ruling or decision is at least 'weakly derivable' from existing law, it is not permissible for judges in their judicial capacity to make such a ruling or decision, however desirable on other grounds it may be.

---

[17] D. *Lyons,* Justification and Easy Cases, paper presented to 11th World Congress of I. V. R., Helsinki, 1983.

This finally enables me to contrast 'consequentialist' reasoning in the special sense alluded to above with coherence reasoning in law. For in the evaluation of the implications of rival rulings in a contested case judges and lawyers raise questions of justification in Lyons' sense of *defensibility*. Certainly, this is defensibility within narrow constraints posed on the one hand by the requirement of consistency and on the other hand by the negative requirement of coherence. The most 'defensible' decision may be one outside the legal power of judges — and there are sound principles of political morality under which judges should not except in extreme cases opt for the best purely moral decision of a case in defiance of their legal duty as officers of the (positive) legal system. Certainly, the values by which judges evaluate the defensibility of decisions and their consequences are in fact (and, I think, ought to be) noticeably legal values. Yet the value judgments made in the course of consequentialist reasoning in law are — and ought to be — value judgments of the kind engaging the genuine commitment of the judge. The question is: which decision seems genuinely best *among the legally admissible ones?* The judgment here is a judgment of substance, not a 'formal' one in the way that judgments of coherence are. The issue is: what is in principle the best way in which to decide the case in hand? It is not: what is the principle which best explains the law as heretofore established by those responsible for establishing it?

III. Narrative Coherence

'Narrative coherence' is my name for a test of truth or probability in questions of fact and evidence upon which direct proof by immediate observation is unavoidable. Since almost all legal disputes, trials and litigations concern past facts and events, and since no past facts or events are susceptible of direct proof by immediate observation, narrative coherence is a test of great, indeed central, importance in the justification of legal decisions. For most legal decisions require findings of fact as well as applications of, or rulings on and applications of, the law.

Detective fiction, none better than the Sherlock Holmes stories, gives ample illustration of the force of 'narrative coherence'. The case of the dog that did not bark in the night is a good illustration. The horse has been taken from the stable by night. The trainer has been found dead on the Downs nearby. A suspicious-looking stranger has been picked up by the police and held on a murder charge. But Sherlock Holmes elicits from reliable witnesses the information that they did not hear the dog barking by night. 'The dog did not bark' and 'a stranger took the horse' are not propositions which contradict each other. Yet if, as a generalisation, dogs bark at strangers, then, under this common-sense principle, the dog's not barking becomes incompatible with a stranger's taking the horse, unless there is some further explanation, or some relevant exception to the general common-sense principle.

Compare real decisions at law, especially where the main evidence is circumstantial. Take *Rex v. Smith*[18]. The short summary of the evidence in the case given in the headnote of the report is sufficient for our purpose:

> The appellant was indicted for the murder of M. who had been discovered dead in her bath after having gone through a ceremony of marriage with him. At the trial evidence was given that subsequently to the death of M. two other women had died in their baths in similar circumstances after having gone through marriage ceremonies with the appellant. Evidence was also given of a consultation between the appellant and a solicitor concerning, *inter alia*, the effect in law of a voluntary settlement made by M., and whether the trustees could buy an annuity without M's permission.

Not surprisingly, Smith's defence lawyers had objected at the trial to admission of evidence about the deaths of his two 'wives' subsequent to M. by the same misadventure as M. Not surprisingly, the defence had sought to exclude the solicitor's evidence. For reasons of no concern to us today, the Court of Criminal Appeal held that the evidence had been properly admissible, and therefore upheld the conviction.

But why was this evidence so damning? Why so vital to the defence to have it excluded? In a common-sense way, the answer is obvious. A man is to be pitied if he loses one wife by drowning in a bath, to be suspected if he loses two, and to be judged a murderer if he loses three. A man whose wife dies is to be pitied. A man whose wife dies shortly after he has checked to ensure that her death will benefit him financially is to be suspected as a possible murderer. All this because unlikely misadventures which befall a person once can well be sheer accidents, but unlikely misadventures which recur three times in materially similar circumstances are not usually misadventures at all but the product of design. A *fortiori* where there is not merely a possible motive (money) but where the motive has been checked out by the person whose possible motive it is. He had checked up to be sure about the money, so we can suppose this possible motive was an actual topic of interest to him, a matter actually before his mind.

(1) 'The first Mrs Smith died in her bath, and Smith was at home at the time.' (2) 'The second Mrs Smith died in her bath, and Mr Smith was at home at the time.' (3) 'The third Mrs Smith died in her bath and

---

[18] [1914 - 15] All E. R. Reprint 262.

Mr Smith was at home at the time.' (4) 'Before the first Mrs Smith died, Mr Smith checked up on the probability of his inheriting her money.'

These sentences (1) - (4) are not themselves contradictory of either (5) 'All the Mrs Smiths died by sheer accident.' or (6) 'Mr Smith wilfully killed all the Mrs Smiths in their baths.' Yet, in the absence of some further sentences disclosing weighty matters of exculpation, (6) coheres with (1) - (4) in a way that (5) does not. This justifies our concluding that we have less ground to doubt (6) than to doubt (5). Whether this puts (6) 'beyond reasonable doubt' so as to justify deeming it true for the purposes of the criminal law (or whether that calls for further evidence, such as was provided at Smith's trial) need not detain us.

Why is the story (1) - (4) plus (6) coherent in a way that (1) - (4) plus (5) is not? Why could that justify deciding to take (6) as being the fact of the matter?

The answer, I suggest, is that we treat the natural world as explicable in terms of explanatory principles ('laws') of a causal and probabilistic kind, and the world of human affairs as being explicable in terms of explanatory principles of a rational, intentional and motivational as well as a causal and probabilistic kind. Accidents which occur without human intervention have to be explained in a non-intentional and non-motivational causal or probabilistic way. The probability of the conjoint occurrence of the necessary causal conditions for any person's drowning in a bath is low. Even lower is the probability of these conditions recurring three times in the case of three persons successively enjoying the same relation-ship with a given fourth party. But the probability that a human agent can intentionally bring about the realisation of these necessary conditions is so high as to amount to certainty. And the probability that someone who has a strong motive to do this intentionally will do so is high. Given those explanatory principles, we can weakly derive (6) from the combination of (1) - (4) and the relevant explanatory principles. This is not a deductive derivation of (6) from the other set. Rather it is the case that (6) plus (1) to (4) belongs within a single rational scheme of explanation of events; whereas (5) plus (1) to (4) does not; not without the supposition of further facts and auxiliary hypotheses.

So far, then, I have tried to do compendiously for narrative coherence what I did for normative coherence in sections II (a) and II (b), namely to show what I understand by narrative coherence and to illustrate very sketchily its application as a test justifying a decision about the *probandum* of a given murder case: that Mr Smith wilfully killed his 'wife' M. in her bath.

I am left with my third question, why narrative coherence has justificatory force in making decisions about matters of fact. As to this, the idea of rationality again has a role to play. Our intellectual and our practical life is not a mere chaotic succession of Humean impressions and ideas. As both Hume and Kant recognized (though putting the point differently — perhaps less differently than is commonly supposed), we do not actually, nor should we if we esteem rationality a virtue, rest content with a more succession of ideas and impressions. We construct explanatory principles of at least the various sorts mentioned above. We make our world an intelligible world for us. One of the conditions of intelligibility is the supposition that what we perceive is real. Another is the supposition that whatever is real is rationally related under some explanatory principle to whatever else is real. Therefore, whatever propositions about unperceived events fit into our explanatory schema in rational relationships with true propositions about perceived events are, under the second supposition, true propositions about the reality of the unperceived events. The difficulty, however, is that the suppositions have to be tentative, for three reasons: one is the revisability of our explanatory schemes; the other is the incompleteness of the information derivable from perception — there could be other relevant things that we failed to perceive, that we 'did not notice'. (Nobody, till Holmes came on the scene, had noticed that the dog had not barked); the third is the known delusoriness of some of our perceptions.

This perhaps lets us see why the truth is indeed stranger than fiction. Fiction, historiography, and legal proofs all have narrative coherence in common. But in fiction the 'perceptions' are imaginary ones; and we can imagine as many as we want so 'the facts' of the story can always be as complete as the novelist wants them; and the novelist can decide in advance which perceptions by his characters to propound as delusory perceptions; in real life we decide only tentatively and *ex post* which must have been delusions, precisely because they do not fit our present tentatively held explanatory scheme. Finally, in science fiction at least, the novelist is allowed to present an imaginary world for which a perfect set of explanatory principles is available. Thus can the world of fiction be a more coherently understood universe than can the 'real world' ever be for those of us who inhabit it and try to make it intelligible to us. The price of this is that the world of fiction is at some remove from the real world.

In a similar way, superseded explanatory principles come to be reckoned as 'fictions' or 'superstitions' by those whose world view is shaped by new explanatory principles. Think of our view of the

Homeric Gods or the Ptolemaic spheres. We do not suppose there is no possible world or universe explicable in those terms (otherwise we would not understand how godly arbitrariness or Ptolemaic astronomy could count as an explanation at all). But we do suppose that no world or universe so explicable is our real one. It is our awareness that our successors will do for our explanations what we have done for our predecessors', and for the same good reasons as we have done so, that should encourage us to a proper tentativeness about our own explanations. But this tentativeness is not to be equated with scepticism.

Be that as it may. To sum up on narrative coherence: this provides a test as to the truth or probable truth of propositions about unperceived things and events. The test is of the explicability of the tested proposition within the same scheme of explanation as explains propositions considered true on the basis of perception. The relative probability of mutually inconsistent propositions relating to the same unperceived event (e. g. the drowning of a Mrs Smith) depends on the number of other events which have to be supposed to have occurred to allow of coherence and on the extent to which further auxiliary explanatory hypotheses have to be resorted to to achieve coherence. The most coherent story among mutually inconsistent stories is that which involves the lowest improbability by such a test. Few such stories allow of certainty as to the truth of the probandum in question. Such a test justifies beliefs, and thus justifies decisions about matters of past fact because (a) it is a necessary condition of the intelligibility of the phenomenal world; and because (b) rationality requires us to make the phenomenal world intelligible. This may involve and would not be inconsistent with a transcendental presupposition that there is a noumenal world which is so ordered as to be perfectly intelligible, and that the phenomenal world perfectly replicates the intelligible structure of that noumenal world. So the propositions which satisfy truth conditions set within our schemes of explanation could be true about the reality of things. But we could never be sure that they are.

IV. Conclusion

If the preceding sections have been rather more explicit on normative than on narrative coherence, that merely reflected their author's greater confidence about the former than the latter topic. I am very aware that in the latter field I have ventured into topics in which the patchiness of my reading exposes me to the reproach either of presumptuous naiveté (dressing up as new thoughts jejune rediscoveries of fragments out of long-recognized and far more refined theories) or of crass error (advancing opinions already fully exposed as untenable by prior but unread work in the field).

Under this confession of possible inadequacy of scholarship, I nevertheless feel entitled tentatively to reach a conclusion on my starting question, whether normative and narrative coherence have anything in common. If my suggestions in each case are in some degree sound ones, then there is a genuine parallelism between that 'coherence' which justifies normative conclusions (or contributes to their justification) and that 'coherence' which justifies factual conclusions. A rational normative order is one which comprises a mutually consistent set of principles and values such that these principles and values propose an ideal pattern of a satisfactory way of life, and such that all the more detailed practical rules and principles within the system are justifiable under (and thus explicable with reference to), though not deducible from, the highest-order principles and values. A rational world-view is one which comprises a mutually consistent set of explanatory principles such that these principles delineate an intelligible pattern of events in a possible world, and such that they make intelligible (because explicable with reference to the principle) the events which our perceptions disclose to us. We could not have a rational normative order without having also a rational world-view. But we should not need a rational world-view, and should certainly not need ways of *deciding* about the reality of things, if we were not also active subjects desirous of practical rationality in our actions.

Finally, however, although there are these parallels and connections between our two sorts of coherence, there remains an important difference. Narrative coherence has to do with the truth or probable truth of conclusions of fact. Coherence here justifies beliefs about a world whose existence is independent of our beliefs about it. But, as Ota Weinberger has so often and so convincingly shown, there is no analogous reason for believing in some sort of ultimate, objective, humanly-independent truth of the matter in the normative sphere. Coherence is always a matter of rationality, but not always a matter of truth.[19]

---

[19] A shorter version of this paper was presented at the Lund Symposium on Philosophy of Law and Philosophy of Science in December 1983, and will be published in the volume of proceedings of that symposium, edited by A. Peczenik and G. van Roermund, and published by Reidel. I am much indebted to David Lyons for criticisms of the paper in draft.

THE THEORY OF JUDICIAL DECISION

III

A Theory of Judicial Decision for Today [1]

I N a developed legal system when a judge decides a cause he seeks, first, to attain justice in that particular cause, and second, to attain it in accordance with law — that is, on grounds and by a process prescribed in or provided by law. One must admit that the strict theory of the last century denied the first proposition, conceiving the judicial function to begin and end in applying to an ascertained set of facts a rigidly defined legal formula definitively prescribed as such or exactly deduced from authoritatively prescribed premises. Happily, even in the height of the reign of that theory, we did not practise what we preached. Courts could not forget that they were administering justice, and the most that such a theory could do was to hamper the judicial instinct to seek a just result. The proceedings of our bar associations and the memoirs of our judges written by lawyers are full of proofs of the regard accorded by layman and lawyer alike to the strong judge who knew how to use the precepts of the law to advance justice in the concrete cause. Whenever the exigencies of legal theory did not interfere with expression of our real feeling, we honored the magistrate who administered justice according to law.

When justice in the cause in hand has been attained as near as may be and has been attained on grounds and in a manner prescribed by law, the duty of the judge under the civil law has been performed. But the Anglo-American judge must do more. At least if he is an appellate judge, and to some extent in any court of general jurisdiction, he must so decide that his decision will enter into the body of the law as a precedent. He must so decide that his decision or the grounds thereof will serve, first, as a measure or pattern of decision of like cases for the

---

[1] The third of three lectures delivered before the Bar Association of the City of New York on January 17 and January 23, 1923.

future, and, second, as a basis of analogical reasoning in the future for cases for which no exact precedents are at hand. In a very great proportion of the causes that come before the judge on the crowded judicial calendars of today this additional duty is relatively negligible. Happily, the bulk of these cases repeat or ring insignificant changes upon familiar states of fact. Yet in an appellate court, which has the power and hence the responsibility of laying down a binding precedent by its decision, the fact that each departure, however slight, from the states of fact to which settled legal precepts have attached defined legal consequences calls for consideration not merely of the relation of such departure to the just result in that case, but quite as much of the possible operation of the decision as a precedent or as furnishing an analogy for future cases — this responsibility adds to the burden of the tribunal. Indeed the necessity of weighing not merely the grounds of its decision, but the exact words in which those grounds are expressed with reference to their possible use in other cases and thus of foreseeing within limits the potential analogical applications thereof, is perhaps the gravest of the burdens involved in the crowded dockets of modern American appellate courts. If it were not for the need of scrupulously careful formulation of their decisions with reference to other cases in the future, our appellate courts could despatch the business that comes before them with less than half of the effort which our system of precedents requires. As it is, one or both of the aspects of the court's function must suffer. Having to decide so many cases and to write so many opinions, either consideration of the merits of the actual controversy must yield to the need of detailed formulation of a precedent that will not embarrass future decision, or careful formulation must give way to the demand for study of the merits of the case in hand. In the event, too often both these things happen and the case itself is not as well considered as the court could wish, while much is said in deciding it which must be re-examined as well as may be when cited to the court in other controversies.

In another respect these two sides of the judicial function in Anglo-American law, the function of deciding the controversy and the function of declaring the law for other controversies, have a reciprocal influence. On the one hand, as the saying is, hard cases make bad law. On the other hand, regard for the stability of the legal order inclines courts to be callous toward unfortunate results in particular cases. And if a compromise sometimes results, as like as not it neither gives a just decision between the parties nor a practicable instrument of justice for the future.

Our reports are full of illustrations of this reciprocal influence of the deciding and the declaring function. More than one general rule, more than one doctrine has been determined or has been directed into a certain course by the hard circumstances of the particular case that first called upon a common-law court to state it or to fix its limits. To put but two instances of arbitrary doctrines with which our case law has since waged a long struggle, consider *Winterbottom* v. *Wright*,[2] which seemed to establish that the general principle of liability for an active course of conduct, carried on without due care under the circumstances, did not apply to a manufacturer or dealer who negligently put upon the market an article containing an unknown hidden defect, whereby the ultimate purchaser was injured, or *Thorogood* v. *Bryan*,[3] which, for a time, set up an artificial conception of imputed negligence. In each case, when we look narrowly at the cause presented to the court which established the doctrine, we discover that there is an element moving behind the logical scene. In each case we struggled painfully for more than half a century to unshackle the law from these decisions and their consequences, and in more than one jurisdiction the process is far from achieved. On the other hand quite as many cases may be found where strong judges have said, in effect: The result is unfortunate in this particular case, but we must apply the appointed legal precept or the logical consequences of the applicable precedent, be the result what it may. When they reason thus often they not merely sacrifice the interests of the parties to the particular litigation, but they extend the potential application of the precept calling for such a result and threaten an ascending series of like sacrifices until the whole has to be overturned.

One cannot understand American case law without bearing in mind the disturbing influence of the facts of particular cases

---

[2] 10 M. & W. 109 (1842).   [3] 8 C. B. 115 (1849).

upon the general rule. Nor can he understand American judicial decision without bearing in mind the disturbing effect of the exigencies of our doctrine of precedents upon the disposition of particular cases. At one moment courts are tempted to modify a general rule with reference to appealing circumstances of one case. The next moment fear of impairing a settled rule or of unsettling it by analogy will tempt them to ignore appealing circumstances of another case. If we actually set as much store by single decisions as we purport to do in legal theory, the path of the law would lie in a labyrinth. In truth, our practice has learned to make large allowances for both of these features of decision which are inseparable from a judge-made customary law. The tables of cases distinguished and cases overruled tell a significant story. Out of the struggle to decide the particular cause justly and yet according to law, while at the same time furnishing, or contributing to furnish, a guide for judicial decision hereafter, in time there comes a logically sound and practically workable principle derived from judicial experience of many causes. In the meantime there has been sacrifice of particular litigants and sacrifice of certainty and order in the law, as decision has fluctuated between regard to the one or to the other of the two sides of the judge's duty.

It may be observed in passing that the foregoing considerations explain what American lawyers find so hard to understand, namely, how civil-law tribunals, which decide the particular case without settling or attempting to settle any general point of law, merely determining that controversy for those parties on general legal grounds found for that case, can act on such a theory consistently with the general security. In fact, their decisions are much more consistent and ours are much less consistent than they appear respectively in theory. Probably just about the same degree of certainty is attained in practice in each system, for if our results were as rigid or theirs as loose as the respective theories taken at their face value indicate, neither system would be tolerable under the conditions of today. Permanent judicial tribunals manned by trained lawyers are sure to follow their own decisions and the decisions of other like tribunals to the extent of being guided by experience and adhering to precepts that have approved themselves in experience. Tribunals set up to administer justice are no less sure to seek and to achieve just results between the parties despite theories that call upon them to subordinate such results to formulation of general rules on the basis of the facts of the cases before them.

Throughout the world and in all departments of intellectual activity there is a demand for individualization. Eighteenth-century natural law thought of the abstract individual man in a perfect state and of his ideal qualities and ideal conduct in such a state. Nineteenth-century metaphysical individualism thought of the rights of the abstract individual man and the deductions therefrom. It thought of " the individual," not of individuals, and in its desire to uphold the rights of the individual in the abstract, often sacrificed needlessly the claims of concrete individuals. Recognition of the social interest in the individual human life is making for a new attitude in the application of law. But this only goes along with a like movement in morals. The eighteenth century knew of universal natural moral principles for the abstract man. Later we had common sense theories of principles applicable to the statistical average man. Later still, under the influence of Darwin, we had theories of principles applicable to man as a species, with resultant belief that all human beings, without regard to race, sex, condition or age, must conform to some norm or standard. Today we recognize that the moral judgments pronounced on such bases were too often empty and that we have to deal not with " the individual " but with separate and distinct individual human souls.

Treatment of the individual human unit has become the quest in medicine also. At one time the physician treated the abstract disease. Aristotle speaks as if treatment of disease by written formulas prescribed in advance for each malady, and administration of justice by written formulas, laid down in advance for each species of wrong, were essentially like processes. Later the physician began to think in terms of organs — but again as if they were *in vacuo.* " Man seemed to the analytical pathologist of the last century," says Dr. Southard, " a heap of viscera in which systems, such as digestive, muscular, nervous, respiratory and excretory, were to be found." As they had treated rheumatism as an abstract entity, now they treated the heart or the liver or the kidneys " taken as separately subject to disorder."

Today in contrast they seek to treat the individual concrete man and recognize that abstract conceptions and analyses are but rationalizings and orderings of knowledge acquired by experience whereby that knowledge may be retained and developed and applied to the treatment of the concrete human being with all his individual peculiarities. The parallel of legal treatment and medical treatment is not complete because the judge must bear in mind the effect of his treatment of a particular cause upon judicial treatment of other causes, while the physician may treat each case as wholly unique. But there is none the less a significant parallel for our understanding of one side of the judicial function. It is no more possible to treat negligence in the abstract than rheumatism in the abstract. It is no more possible to isolate and standardize types of controversy out of their concrete setting and treat all controversies solely on this basis than it was to treat " the heart " or " the liver " or " the kidneys " apart from the actual man whose heart or liver or kidneys were not operating as they should. Analyses and abstract conceptions that serve us well in the legal securing of interests of substance, where cases are alike and the economic order admits of no individualization, are vain as anything more than organizings and rationalizings of experience when applied to the individual human life.

Insisting, then, that the decision of a case under the Anglo-American legal system involves both a process of achieving a just result between the parties to that case on grounds and by a process provided by law, and also a duty, peculiar to our system, of so deciding that the decision or the grounds on which it proceeds may be a ground of decision in future cases, let us look into the elements of the process and the nature and mode of performance of the duty as they are and as they may be.

Supposing the facts to have been ascertained, decision of a controversy according to law involves (1) selection of the legal material on which to ground the decision, or as we commonly say, finding the law; (2) development of the grounds of decision from the material selected, or interpretation in the stricter sense of that term; (3) application of the abstract grounds of decision to the facts of the case. The first may consist merely in laying hold of a prescribed text of code or statute, or of a definite, prescribed, traditional rule; in which case it remains only to determine the meaning of the legal precept, with reference to the state of facts in hand, and to apply it to those facts. It is the strength of judicial administration of justice today that in the general run of causes that have to do with our economic life this is all that is called for, or so nearly all, that the main course of judicial decision may be predicted with substantial accuracy. But it happens frequently that the first process involves choice among competing texts or choice from among competing analogies so that the texts or rules must be interpreted — that is, must be developed tentatively with reference to the facts before the court — in order that intelligent selection may be made. Often such interpretation shows that no existing rule is adequate to a just decision and it becomes necessary to formulate the ground of decision for the given facts for the first time. The proposition so formulated may, as with us, or may not, as with the civilian, become binding for like cases in the future. In any event this process has gone on and still goes on in all systems of law, no matter what their form, and no matter how completely in their juristic theory they limit the function of adjudication to mechanical application of authoritatively given precepts.

All three of the steps outlined above are commonly confused under the name of interpretation. This is partly because in primitive times, when the law was taken to be god-given and unchangeable, the most that might be permitted to human magistrates was to interpret the sacred text. Partly also it is because the Middle Ages received the Corpus Iuris as an authoritative text under the influence of an academic theory that gave it statutory binding force in Western Europe. It followed that jurists could do no more than interpret the text. Partly it is because in our stage of strict law we conceived of an immemorial common custom of England that could only be developed by logical discovery of and deduction from the principles which it presupposed. Chiefly, perhaps, it is due to the dogma of separation of powers, which refers lawmaking exclusively to the legislature and would limit the courts to interpretation and application. The analytical jurists first pointed out that finding a new rule and interpreting an existing rule were distinct processes, and Austin distinguished them as spurious interpretation and genuine interpretation respectively, since his belief in the possibility of a complete body of enacted rules, sufficient for every cause, led him to regard the former as out of place in modern law. Indeed he was quite right in insisting that spurious interpretation *as a fiction* was wholly out of place in legal systems of today. But experience has shown what reason ought to tell us, that this fiction grew up to cover a real need in the judicial administration of justice, and that the providing of a rule by which to decide the cause, or at least the reshaping of one which is inadequate in its given form, is a necessary element in the determination of all but the simplest controversies. More recently the growing insistence upon the importance of reasonable and just solution of the individual controversy has led jurists to distinguish application of legal precepts to particular cases from the more general problem of interpretation. Application of legal rules is regarded today as one of the chief problems of jurisprudence.

Dividing our process of decision, as apart from the duty of providing a well considered precedent, into the three steps, finding the law, interpreting the legal material selected, and applying the resulting legal precept to the cause, let us look into the first of these, the process of finding or selection, and ask what it involves, as the process actually goes on. It may .involve nothing more than a selection from among fixed precepts of determined content calling only for a mechanical ascertainment of whether the facts fit the rule. Such is the case when a tribunal looks to an instrument to see whether it contains the words of negotiability required by the Negotiable Instruments Law or by the law merchant, or when it looks to a conveyance to see whether it contains the formal covenant of warranty without which at common law one may not hold his grantor. Or it may involve selection from competing analogies, urged by the respective parties as the ground of decision. Here, as it were, there is to be an inductive selection. Or it may involve selection by logical development of conceptions or principles. Here, as it were, there is a deductive selection. If these fail, it calls for selection from outside of the legal system in whole or in part — from custom, from comparative law, from morals, or from economics.

How, in practice, do courts determine when to resort to the one of these and when to another and in what order? It is manifest that the general security requires that they should select the grounds of decision with reference to fixed precepts wherever possible, and that selection from outside of the legal system should be resorted to only when the others fail or at least when they clearly fail to give a just result. As things go it is apparent that courts proceed in the order of (1) selection with reference to fixed precepts, (2) inductive or deductive selection, and (3) selection from outside of the legal system. As between inductive selection and deductive selection the practice of courts and even of individual judges varies. There is no standard method of determining between them, although some judges habitually proceed in the one way and others as habitually proceed in the other. The mental bent of the particular judge or the availability of the result with reference to the particular case seem to be the decisive factors. Likewise there is no standard practice determining when to invoke custom, when comparative law, when current morals and when economics, in case selection must be made from outside of the legal system. In general, custom has been resorted to only in special types of case where a definite custom of popular action was at hand and was clearly applicable, as in Western mining law and water law and in the old decisions of controversies arising in the whaling industry. Comparative law was drawn upon largely in the formative era of our commercial law, but was drawn on rarely in the latter part of the last century. Current moral ideas are drawn upon continually, although seldom consciously. Usually they play their most important rôle in the process of interpretation. Yet one may see them as the basis of the formulated ground of decision in much recent decision in the law relating to labor, in much recent decision as to interference with advantageous business relations and in not a little decision on due process of law. Economic ideas are used as the ground of decision today chiefly in applying the Fourteenth Amendment; but also in labor cases, in cases on restraint of trade, and in connection with attempts to impose restrictions upon chattels binding upon those who acquire with notice. In these cases the economic proposition is sometimes formulated as a principle of natural law and sometimes assumed as a fact of external nature of which courts are required to take notice.

It was chiefly these cases, where courts have had to go outside of the given legal materials and find grounds of decision in economic ideas, that gave rise to so much criticism of judicial decision and excited projects for recall of decisions or recall of judges a decade ago. On the one hand, it was not appreciated that the process of selection of grounds of decision from outside of the strictly given legal materials was a legitimate and necessary one. On the other hand, courts afforded some basis for the agitation by assuming the economics of half a century before as something incontestibly applicable to urban industrial America of the twentieth century. There could not but be popular irritation, after legislative committees had investigated a situation elaborately and had formulated a statute in the light of the best economic knowledge of the day, when courts rejected the statute on the basis of judicial notice of economic ideas of a prior generation. It was not the method of falling back upon materials outside of the legal system that was at fault. It was the theory that led to a false picture of what was doing and why, and hence led to a blundering process of selection where, had the process been consciously carried on, the judges would not have been content with anything short of the best economic materials available.

In the second step in decision, namely, development of the grounds of decision from the material selected, the usual process is one of traditional legal reasoning, scholastic down to the seventeenth century, rationalist more and more in the seventeenth and eighteenth centuries, and tending to be deductive on a metaphysical basis in the nineteenth century. But in new and difficult cases this merges in, and in all cases is influenced by, current moral, political and social ideas, especially fixed pictures of the end of law and of an ideal legal and social order, by reference to which, consciously or subconsciously, the tribunal determines how far possible interpretations will yield a just result in the individual cause and judges of the intrinsic merit of the different developments of the legal materials potentially applicable which are urged by the contending parties. Along with these we must put an intuition of what will achieve justice in action and what

291

will not, expressing the experience of the magistrate both as lawyer and as judge. The traditional legal reasoning represents the experience of generations of judges in the past. It is in some sort a traditionally transmitted judicial intuition founded in experience. But it has been given shape by philosophy. In our stage of strict law it was cast in a mold of scholasticism which gave it permanent shape. Rationalism in the seventeenth and eighteenth centuries and the metaphysical jurisprudence of the nineteenth century affected its substance more than its form. It is at its best as a technique of developing the grounds of judicial decision from materials selected from reported judgments of the past. It is usually at its worst, except in simple cases, in developing the grounds of judicial decision on the basis of materials found in legislation. A theory of " the will of the lawmaker " taken over from the civilian who thought of a text of the Digest as the declared will of Justinian, and a traditional attitude toward legislation discussed in my first lecture, make judicial handling of statutes the least satisfactory part of the work of American tribunals.

Application of the abstract grounds of decision to the facts of the particular case may be purely mechanical. The court may have to do no more than ask, did title pass on a particular sale, was possession given in a particular gift of a chattel, did a particular possession comply with the requisites of acquiring title by adverse possession? Or application may be apparently mechanical but with a greater or less latent margin of something else. For example, consider the cases with respect to acquisition of an easement by adverse user. As one reads these cases he can but see how much beneath the surface depends on the judge's feelings as to what is right between the parties to the particular case and how this is covered up by a margin of choice between competing rules. Where it seems the better solution to hold that an easement was acquired, a court will speak only of adverse user. Where it seems a preferable solution to hold that an easement was not acquired, the court speaks of permissive user. As like as not in each case there was a known user not objected to or not prevented, which may be construed either way to meet the exigencies of justice between the parties.

But there is a more important form of application which is

of a wholly distinct type. Frequently application of the legal precept, as found and interpreted, is intuitive. This is conspicuous when a court of equity judges of the conduct of a fiduciary, or exercises its discretion in enforcing specific performance, or passes upon a hard bargain, or where a court sitting without a jury determines a question of negligence. However repugnant to our nineteenth century notions it may be to think of anything anywhere in the judicial administration of justice as proceeding otherwise than on rule and logic, we cannot conceal from ourselves that in at least three respects the trained intuition of the judge does play an important rôle in the judicial process. One is in the selection of grounds of decision — in finding the legal materials that may be made both to furnish a legal ground of decision and to achieve justice in the concrete case. It is an everyday experience of those who study judicial decisions that the results are usually sound, whether the reasoning from which the results purport to flow is sound or not. The trained intuition of the judge continually leads him to right results for which he is puzzled to give unimpeachable legal reasons. Another place where the judge's intuition comes into play is in development of the grounds of decision, or interpretation. This is especially marked when it becomes necessary to apply the criterion of the intrinsic merit of the possible interpretations. A third is in application of the developed grounds of decision to the facts.

Nor need we be ashamed to confess that much that goes on in the administration of justice is intuitive. Bergson tells us that intelligence, which frames and applies rules, is more adapted to the inorganic, while intuition is more adapted to life. In the same way rules of law and legal conceptions which are applied mechanically are more adapted to property and to business transactions; standards where application proceeds upon intuition are more adapted to human conduct and to the conduct of enterprises. Bergson tells us that what characterizes intelligence as opposed to instinct is " its power of grasping the general element in a situation and relating it to past situations." But, he points out, this power is acquired by loss of " that perfect mastery of a special situation in which instinct rules." Standards, applied intuitively by court or jury or administrative officer, are devised for situations in which we are compelled to take circumstances into account; for classes of cases in which each case is to a large degree unique. For such cases we must rely on the common sense of the common man as to common things and the trained common sense of the expert as to uncommon things. Nor may this common sense be put in the form of a syllogism. To make use once more of Bergson's discussion of intelligence and instinct, the machine works by repetition; "its use is mechanical and because it works by repetition there is no individuality in its products." The method of intelligence is admirably adapted to the law of property and to commercial law, where one fee simple is like every other and no individuality of judicial product is called for as between one promissory note and another. On the other hand, in the hand-wrought product the specialized skill of the workman, depending upon familiar acquaintance with particular objects, gives us something infinitely more subtle than can be expressed in rules. In the administration of justice some situations call for the product of hands not of machines. Where the call is for individuality in the product of the legal mill — i.e., where we are applying law to human conduct and to the conduct of enterprises — we resort to standards and to intuitive application. And the sacrifice of certainty in so doing is more theoretical than actual. The instinct of the experienced workman operates with assurance. Innumerable details and minute discriminations have entered into it, and it has been gained by long experience which has made the proper inclusions and exclusions by trial and error until the effective line of action has become a habit.

Turning now to the second phase of the office of the judge in Anglo-American law — the duty of so deciding the particular case that the grounds of decision will serve both for deciding other cases involving the same facts and for the basis of analogical reasoning in analogous cases in the future — it should be noted at the outset that this part of the judge's duty has a collateral importance as a check upon the deciding function, and, vice versa, the deciding function has no less collateral importance as a check upon the law-declaring function. For it is no mean advantage of our doctrine of precedents and judicial finding or making of law that the common law is always found and made with reference to actual controversies. It is not declared in the abstract except in relatively rare cases by legislation. For the greater part it is made under the pressure of actual human claims asserted in a pending litigation and to meet the needs of a satisfactory adjustment of these concrete claims. Thus, no matter how abstract and mechanical our legal theory for the time being, it can never develop that serene indifference to the facts of life that has sometimes marked the juristic speculation of the civilian. In the classical Roman law the juristic speculation of the jurisconsult was carried on in the same way with reference to the needs of opinions on actual controversies, so that Roman juristic writing was in truth a body of case law quite analogous to the law contained in our reports. But in the modern Roman-law world, the jurist is an academic writer, developing legal principles as such in a world of legal reasoning and as abstractions. Hence, if his reason is free to make notable theoretical forward steps, as it has done so often to the benefit of law throughout the world, it is also out of touch with the life which law is to govern and hence too often gives us mechanical constructions of a beautifully logical operation in which the alogical circumstances of real life are ignored.

Our chief agency of lawmaking is judicial empiricism — the judicial search for the workable legal precept, for the principle which is fruitful of good results in giving satisfactory grounds of decision of actual causes, for the legal conception into which the facts of actual controversies may be fitted with results that accord with justice between the parties to concrete litigation. It is a process of trial and error with all the advantages and disadvantages of such a process.

But what is to govern this judicial search for the law through trial and error? What is to hold down this judicial experimenting with tentative legal propositions in the endeavor to find the practicable precept and to define it by inclusion and exclusion through experience? What is to confine the process within limits compatible with the general security? In the past it has been governed and its path has been defined by ideals of the end of law and of the legal and social order, and it is submitted that such ideals must be our reliance today and tomorrow.

Only we must be conscious that these ideals are invoked, of the purpose for which they are invoked, and of the paramount importance of them as maintaining the general security against rash experimentation and wilful giving rein to personal inclinations. First of all our theory of judicial decision must recognize what actually takes place and why, and must endeavor to give a rational account of it. Next it must give a rational account of the check upon the process, upon which we must rely for safeguarding the general security, and enable us to make that check the most effective for that purpose and yet the least obstructive of legal growth and of individualization of decision that may be. To do this it must give us a picture of the end of law and of the legal and social order adequate to these demands.

On many other occasions I have urged that for the purposes of today our picture should be one, not of a god-given order laid down once for all on the lines of a society of the past, not of a reflection of the divine reason governing the whole universe and photographed once for all in the last century, not of a body of unchallengeable deductions from ultimate metaphysically-given data at which men arrived a century ago in seeking to rationalize the social phenomena of that time — that our picture should be none of these things but rather a picture of a process of social engineering. What we seek is a picture which will best enable us to understand what we are doing and to do it most effectively. Such a picture, I venture to think, would represent the social order as an organized human endeavor to satisfy a maximum of human wants with a minimum of sacrifice of other wants. It would represent the legal order as that part of the whole process which is or may be achieved by the force of politically organized society. It would picture elimination of friction and waste, economizing of social effort, conservation of social assets, and adjustment of the struggle of individual human beings to satisfy their overlapping individual claims in life in civilized society, so that if each may not get all that he demands, he may at least obtain all that is reasonably practicable in a wise social engineering.

For it is not difficult to show that the legal order has always been and is a system of compromises between conflicting and overlapping human claims or wants or desires in which the continual pressure of these claims and of the claims involved in civilized social life has compelled lawmakers and judges and administrators to seek to satisfy the most they might with the least sacrifice.

How may we generalize and rationalize the details of this process for the use of judge and jurist? Such a generalization and rationalization must hold fast to what actually takes place. It must seek to put what takes place as a rational process. It must endeavor to put it in an ideal form representing it at its best and thus enabling those who employ it to realize its highest possibilities. And we may actually see such a rationalization latent in judicial decision. For I submit that what courts do subconsciously, when they are at their best, is to generalize the claims of the parties as individual human claims, to subsume the claims so generalized under generalized claims involved in life in civilized society in the time and place, and endeavor to frame a precept or state a principle that will secure the most of these social interests that we may with the least sacrifice. As carried on by judges and jurists this process has suffered from a conception of the generalized individual claims as natural rights, as deductions from an idea of individual liberty, each to be given a complete logical development within its logically defined scope. It has suffered from a notion that if these natural rights were logically defined with exactness neither the rights nor their logical consequences could come into conflict. It has suffered from a setting off of the claims involved in life in civilized society in a distinct category as policies with a resulting suspicion of those claims, thus branded as on an inferior plane, and tendency to give too much effect to certain longer-recognized claims as against others newly pressing for recognition. For this nomenclature made it easy to argue that rights were sacrificing to expediency when the rights and the so-called considerations of expediency were each but claims, to be compromised and reconciled by some general principle that would give the greatest possible security to both.

In such a conception of judicial decision as part of a larger process of social engineering, in a sense legislation and judicial decision are put on the same basis. Each is or may be creative. Each is and should be governed by principles of social utility.

Each should be guided by a picture of the completest satisfaction of human claims or wants or desires that is compatible with the least sacrifice of the totality of such claims or wants or desires. But one of the chiefest of human claims in civilized society is the general security, and this paramount interest requires a distinction between judicial lawmaking through decisions in their capacity of precedents and legislative lawmaking. For legislative lawmaking, at least in its ideal form, prescribes a rule for the future to apply to the situations and transactions of the future. Judicial declaration of law, on the other hand, prescribes a rule with reference to and as a measure for a situation or transaction of the past and, as a precedent, is to be applied to past and future alike. Hence, if but his precept is otherwise good social engineering, it is quite immaterial what are the premises of the legislative lawmaker or how he develops them or whether he has any premises at all. On the other hand, no matter how wise the judicially-found and declared precept, as a precept for the future, it is usually consonant with the general security only in case it rests upon traditional premises and is developed therefrom by the traditional technique. We must urge upon judges that in their law-declaring function they are indeed lawmakers with the responsibilities for wise social engineering that rests upon all lawmakers. But we must urge upon them no less that their lawmaking function is subject to limitations that do not bind the legislative lawmaker, and that a compromise between the general security and social progress is likely to be involved in every important step that they take.

In such a picture as I have sketched an important item is partition of the field of the legal order between legislation and common law and also between judicial justice and administrative justice. Social engineering may not expect to meet all its problems with the same machinery. Its tasks are as varied as life and the complicated problems of a complex social order call for a complicated mechanism and a variety of legal implements. This is too large a subject for discussion in the present connection. Suffice it to say that conveyance of land, inheritance and succession, and commercial law have always proved susceptible of legislative statement, while no codification of the law of torts and no juristic or judicial defining of fraud or of fiduciary duties has ever maintained itself. In other words, the social interests in security of acquisitions and security of transactions — the economic side of human activity in civilized society — call for rule or conception authoritatively prescribed in advance and mechanically applied. These interests also call peculiarly for judicial justice. Titles to land and the effects of promissory notes or commercial contracts cannot be suffered to depend in any degree on the unique circumstances of the controversies in which they come in question. It is one of the grave faults of our present theory of judicial decision that, covering up all individualization, it sometimes allows individualized application to creep into those situations where it is anything but a wise social engineering. On the other hand, where we have to do with the social interest in the individual human life and with individual claims to free self-assertion subsumed thereunder, free judicial finding of the grounds of decision for the case in hand is the most effective way of bringing about a practicable compromise and has always gone on in fact no matter how rigidly in theory the tribunals have been tied down by the texts of codes or statutes. Likewise it is in these cases involving individual self-assertion, especially in affirmative courses of conduct and the conduct of enterprises, where there is never exact repetition of any former situation and each case is more or less unique, that administrative justice is tolerable and that judicial justice must always involve a large administrative element.

Our theories of decision have not recognized this partition of the field of the legal order. They have insisted upon one machine, set up with reference to the work to be done in one field, for all the work to be done in all fields. Our current theory of decision as a simple process of mechanical manipulation had its origin in the strict law which was a system of remedies only, before the system of rights, elaborated in the nineteenth century, had been conceived. Thus our ideas of judicial technique, our theory of that technique, are behind our actual practice, which although hampered by the theory, has yet been obliged to improve itself under the pressure of new claims and demands for recognition and better securing of new interests. Our theory of judicial technique belongs to a stage of legal development

that antedates the weapons of the judicial armory of today.   On
the whole, the judges have done their part better than the jurists
and the teachers.   They have pushed forward cautiously but
on the whole with reasonable speed along paths worked out by
judicial empiricism, while those who should have rationalized the
forward movement and furnished ideal plans of the forward
path have urged pseudo-scientific reasons why they should stand
fast, and have preached that progress would spontaneously
achieve itself.

   I repeat, on the whole the judges have been doing their part
well.   The real responsibility is upon our jurists and teachers
to rationalize the process of judicial decision for the purposes
of today and not rest content with the rationalizings for the
purposes of the past that have come down to them; to substitute
a larger and more varied picture of the end of law and a better
and more critically drawn idealization of the legal and social
order of the present for the simple picture of the past with its
broad lines and impressionistic details.   In this newer picture
which jurists must draw for the courts, the important items will
be: (1) to paint a process of legal social engineering as a part
of the whole process of social control; (2) to set off the part of
the field of the legal order appropriate to intelligence, involving
repetition, calling for rule or for logical development of principle,
from the part appropriate to intuition, involving unique situations, calling for standards and for individualized application;
(3) to portray a balance between decision of the actual cause
and elaboration of a precedent, in which, subsuming the claims of
the parties under generalized social claims, as much of the latter
will be given effect as is possible; and (4) to induce a consciousness of the rôle of ideal pictures of the social and legal order
both in decision and in declaring the law.   Indeed the last is
the item of most importance.   For we shall have done much if
we induce on the part of judges a searching examination of how
far these pictures that enter into their work so largely are
personal pictures and how far they are general pictures; if we
induce judges to inquire of themselves whence come the pictures
with reference whereto they decide causes and whence their
details are derived; if we induce the self-examination that will for
the most part show them how far they may act upon these ideal
pictures with assurance.

Socrates was not all wrong in holding that much which seems wrongdoing is but ignorant doing.   Much will be gained when courts have perceived what it is that they are doing, and are thus enabled to address themselves consciously to doing it the best that they may.

Roscoe Pound.

Harvard Law School.

VOLUME 72   NUMBER 2   MARCH 1992

BOSTON UNIVERSITY LAW REVIEW

THE RELEVANCE OF COHERENCE†

JOSEPH RAZ*

Coherence is in vogue. Coherence accounts of truth and of knowledge have been in contention for many years. Coherence explanations of morality and of law are a newer breed. I suspect that like so much else in practical philosophy[1] today they owe much of their popularity to John Rawls. His writings on reflective equilibrium,[2] while designed as part of a philosophical strategy which suspends inquiry into the fundamental questions of moral philosophy, had the opposite effect. They inspired much constructive reflection about these questions, largely veering toward coherence as the right interpretation both of reflective equilibrium and of moral philosophy. In legal philosophy, Ronald Dworkin's work contributed to an interest in coherence accounts of law and of judicial reasoning.[3]

---

† © 1992 Joseph Raz.

* Professor of the Philosophy of Law, Oxford University, and Fellow of Balliol College, Oxford. This Article is an expanded version of a lecture given in the Boston University School of Law Distinguished Lecturer Series in October, 1991. I am grateful to Brian Bix, Penelope Bulloch, Michael Harper, Robert Bone, Avishai Margalit, Sidney Morgenbesser and Kenneth Simons for comments on earlier drafts.

[Editor's Note: The footnotes in this Article appear in the form that the author requested. In many instances, they do not conform to the standards of the *Bluebook*.]

[1] Practical philosophy includes moral, legal, social and political philosophy, especially when they are conceived of as so many aspects of the general problem of rationality in action, emotion, attitudes, etc.

[2] *See* JOHN RAWLS, A THEORY OF JUSTICE (1971); John Rawls, *The Independence of Moral Theory*, 48 AM. PHIL. ASS'N PROC. & ADDRESSES 5 (1974-75). For a sympathetic discussion of Rawls, see Norman Daniels, *Wide Reflective Equilibrium and Theory Acceptance in Ethics*, 76 J. PHIL. 256 (1979). An incisive critique of Rawls's doctrine can be found in JAMES GRIFFIN, THE PROJECT OF ETHICS ch. 1 (forthcoming). I attempted some critical reflections in Joseph Raz, *The Claims of Reflective Equilibrium*, 25 INQUIRY 307 (1982).

[3] Interestingly, neither Rawls nor Ronald Dworkin (in his earlier writings) presents or discusses their work as coherence-based. For writers explaining Dworkin's as a coherence-based account, see Kenneth J. Kress, *Legal Reasoning and Coherence Theories: Dworkin's Rights Thesis, Retroactivity, and the Linear Order of Decision*, 72 CAL. L. REV. 369, 398-402 (1984); S.L. HURLEY, NATURAL REASONS 262 (1989); S.L. Hurley, *Coherence, Hypothetical Cases, and Precedent* 10 OXFORD J. LEGAL STUD. 231

There were, however, other important influences on the growing popularity of coherence accounts in law and morality. They came from the application of a Davidsonian approach to ethics by Wiggins and McDowell.[4] Their work points to the way coherence accounts chime in a vaguer, more pervasive way with the current philosophical climate. Coherence accounts fit well with the rejection of the Cartesian approach to philosophy. For one thing they seem a natural conclusion of the rejection of foundationalism, with its commitment to the view that all justified beliefs are justified by their relations to some incorrigible beliefs. Even those who accept that some beliefs are incorrigible would reject that. Moreover, under the impact of Quine's dual rejection of empiricism (with its belief in incorrigible foundations for all justified beliefs) and the analytic/synthetic distinction, many philosophers embraced holism, that is, the view that everything depends on everything. Coherence accounts, while not logically entailed by holism, seem to go well with it. If everything depends on everything, how is one to distinguish between truths and falsehoods if not by a test of coherence?

All this leads naturally to a frame of mind which, once one gets used to it, turns out to be oddly reassuring. We are all in mid-ocean on Neurath's ship.[5] We cannot disembark and make a fresh start with a sound vessel, accepting only safe beliefs. We must use what we have, repairing our ship from within, jettisoning that which, in the light of our current beliefs, corrigible and possibly mistaken as each one of them may be, seems mistaken. "What is reassuring here?" you may ask. Is that not a recipe for skepticism? Not if one is convinced by Wittgenstein, or alternatively by the very different and incompatible argument of Davidson, that such skepticism is incoherent. Davidson's, rather than Wittgenstein's, arguments show the way toward

---

(1990). The degree to which Dworkin's theory relies on considerations of coherence is examined in the Appendix.

[4] *See, e.g.*, DAVID WIGGINS, NEEDS, VALUES, TRUTH (Basil Blackwell rev. ed., 1991); John McDowell, *Are Moral Requirements Hypothetical Imperatives*, 52 THE ARISTOTELIAN SOC'Y 13 (supp. 1978); John McDowell, *Virtue and Reason*, 62 THE MONIST 331 (1979); John McDowell, *Aesthetic Value, Objectivity and the Fabric of the World*, *in* PLEASURE PREFERENCE AND VALUE 1 (Eva Scharer ed., 1983); John McDowell, *Values and Secondary Qualities*, *in* MORALITY AND OBJECTIVITY: A TRIBUTE TO J.L. MACKIE 110 (Ted Honderich ed., 1985). The influence of Wiggins and McDowell is evident in MARK PLATTS, WAYS OF MEANING (1979), and S.L. HURLEY, NATURAL REASONS (1989). The merging of more traditional epistemic considerations with Rawlsian influences is seen in DAVID BRINK, MORAL REASON AND THE FOUNDATIONS OF ETHICS ch. 5 (1989). A hankering after coherence in morality, differently understood, and deriving from independent sources, is also manifested in Germain Grisez et al., *Practical Principles, Moral Truth, and Ultimate Ends*, 32 AM. J. JURISPRUDENCE 99 (1987).

[5] "No tabula rasa exists. We are like sailors who must rebuild their ship on the open sea, never able to dismantle it in dry-dock and to reconstruct it there out of the best materials." Otto Neurath, *Protocol Sentences* (George Schick trans.), *in* LOGICAL POSITIVISM 199, 201 (Alfred J. Ayer ed., 1959).

coherence. Davidson concludes that it is incoherent to suppose that all or most of one's beliefs are false. Instead, he argues that to understand people presupposes accepting their beliefs as largely true. This confidence in the essential soundness of Neurath's ship seems to point to coherence as the inescapable solution to our puzzles.

I am not trying to describe a specific thesis here. My aim is to indicate some of the leading elements in the philosophical climate of opinion which make it congenial to coherence-based accounts—which make the air buzz with coherence. I will consider the merit and relevance of coherence in explaining the nature of law and of adjudication. In doing so, I will mention points derived from the writings of theorists who favor coherence. These borrowings notwithstanding, this is not an article about the work of any particular theorist. It is an exploration of the role and value of an idea, and of some of the different forms that it can take.

Herein lies a difficulty. How can one make sure that the main, the most promising and interesting uses of coherence have been examined? That is the claim I make for my discussion, but I know of no way to prove it. It is possible that there are other more interesting and promising uses of coherence in explanations of law and adjudication than those here considered. With that caveat let us begin.[6]

I. Against Epistemic Coherence Theory

Coherence explanations can feature in theories of knowledge. As such, they hold coherence to be the condition of justified belief. But coherence explanations are also advanced as explanations of what makes a judicial decision correct or what makes a legal proposition true. Because a justified belief can be false, epistemic and constitutive (as I shall call coherence accounts of what makes propositions true or decisions correct) coherence-based explanations do not coincide. Rather, they respond to different concerns. Because one can be justified in holding a belief or taking an action which is, in fact (though unknown to one), wrong or mistaken, epistemic theses appear more moderate than constitutive ones, and therefore perhaps more appealing. But it would be wrong to think of them as being on a scale of moderation. Appearances to the contrary notwithstanding, the epistemic theses are more straightforwardly flawed than their constitutive counterparts. For most of this Article, I will be concerned with constitutive coherence theories of law and adjudication, which claim that coherence makes legal propositions true or judicial decisions right. But to show constitutive coherence-based explanations to best advantage, and to clarify their differ-

---

[6] I have put forward some considerations relevant to this issue before. *See* JOSEPH RAZ, *The Rule of Law and Its Virtue, in* THE AUTHORITY OF LAW: ESSAYS ON LAW AND MORALITY (1979); Joseph Raz, *Authority, Law and Morality*, 68 THE MONIST 295 (1985).

ence from epistemic employment of coherence, I will begin with a consideration of the latter.

The first thing to note is that epistemic coherence-based explanations are
not specifically legal. They claim that one's belief is justified (or that one's
decision is justified) if it coheres better than any alternative with one's other
beliefs generally, legal and non-legal alike. The reason is simple. A decision
which coheres best with all legal propositions one believes may cohere less
well than some alternative with all of one's believed propositions.[7] Of
course, it is possible to argue either (1) that general coherence accounts
entail specifically legal coherence accounts of justified legal beliefs or legal
decisions because they regard local coherence (i.e., coherence among one's
beliefs about the law and adjudication) as in itself a strong constituent component of general coherence, strong enough to make the divergence impossible or at least very unlikely, or (2) that justification lies in coherence between
beliefs of a certain class only, that is, that only beliefs about the law matter
for the justification of legal decisions or of beliefs about the law. But those
who uphold the epistemic force of coherence must have a reason for the
exclusion of other beliefs, or for making coherence in a certain area the test
for overall coherence. That reason will inevitably show that considerations
other than coherence matter to justification, for only such considerations can
lead to a deviation from a uniform account of coherence. Such explanations
are only partially based on coherence. There is nothing objectionable in this,
but as I am not aware of any reason favoring such a limited view of epistemic coherence, I will abandon that possibility and consider only general
coherence-based epistemic explanations.

Their appeal derives not simply from the positive connotation of "coherence." Coherence conveys a specific good, the value of which is undeniable.
What is incoherent is unintelligible, because it is self-contradictory, frag-
mented, disjointed. What is coherent is intelligible, makes sense, is well-
expressed, with all its bits hanging together. Let us leave on one side the
question of the relative importance of coherence. (Does it make sense to say:
"I prefer him not to be so coherent, for only then does he succeed in expressing his free spirit which is his best aspect"?). Can any one doubt the value
of coherence itself?

One can if one is a philosopher. I do not mean that philosophers can be
expected to say any silly thing. I mean that philosophers, some philosophers, have taken "coherent" to mean not just "intelligible", but something
(some things) quite different. Nobody would think that a text ought to be
believed just because it is intelligible. But some philosophers think that it
ought to be believed just because it is coherent. So let us leave on one side
the undoubted value of coherence as intelligibility. We are after the philosophical notion of coherence. Realizing this is the first step in breaking the
enchantment with coherence theories. In denying them one is not denying

---

[7] Or, for that matter, it may cohere less well than some alternative with all known
propositions.

the undoubted, familiar value of coherence (=intelligibility). The argument is about a technical notion of coherence and its systematic use in some philosophical theories.

I should not exaggerate the point. The philosophical notion, while deviating from the ordinary significance of "coherence," is continuous with it. This is readily seen when we consider coherence-based epistemic theories of justified belief.[8] To say that a belief is justified is to say that it is epistemically permissible to hold it, that there is no epistemic defect in holding it. The notion is vague, perhaps even obscure. But we need do no more than use it intuitively to see the appeal of coherence theories of belief justification.

How so? Because in epistemic theories philosophers use "coherent" to mean something like "mutually supporting." Two beliefs cohere if each makes belief in the other more reasonable than its rejection. Opinions vary as to what relations must exist among beliefs in order for them to be mutually supporting. Let us say that if beliefs fit together they are mutually reinforcing, using "fit together" in place of whatever relation(s) between propositions makes them cohere, i.e., makes them mutually reinforcing.[9] I will return to this problem later on. At the moment all we need to do is to acknowledge the force of this idea. It recognizes a relation of justification which is not linear and asymmetrical, but is circular and symmetrical. This may appear puzzling. If A justifies B, surely A cannot be justified by B. Justification must be asymmetrical, must it not? But, in fact, the thought that justification is circular and symmetrical is deeply rooted in our ordinary understanding of justification.

Suppose I believe (1) that John was seen going into Emily's house. Suppose further that I believe (2) that John has long wanted to visit Emily. My belief about John's desire to visit Emily tends to reinforce my belief that the reported sighting of John is correct. At the same time, if someone questions John's desire to visit Emily, I am likely to rely on the reported sighting as

---

[8] Among the most instructive discussions of coherence theories of epistemic justification are: KEITH LEHRER, THEORY OF KNOWLEDGE chs. 5-7 (1990); GILBERT HARMAN, CHANGE IN VIEW (1986); JOHN L. POLLOCK, CONTEMPORARY THEORIES OF KNOWLEDGE (1986). For an attempt to justify epistemic coherence with special reference to moral beliefs see BRINK, supra note 4. Not all of these authors have the same aim. Some are interested in the notion of justified belief for its own sake. Others are concerned primarily with an explanation of knowledge in which "justified" belief features. Harman advances an account of rational belief change. The discussion is aimed at the employment of coherence in accounts of justified belief only, and does not affect Harman's explanations in Change in View.

[9] Should one not say that philosophers use "coherent" as meaning "fitting together," claiming what is coherent (=fits together) is mutually reinforcing as their substantive conclusion? I do not think so. The procedure seems to be the reverse. One starts by regarding coherence as a justificatory relation (i.e., as meaning mutually reinforcing) and proceeds to find what substantive relations make propositions or beliefs coherent in that sense. The main conclusion which defines the coherence theorist is that there is nothing to justification other than coherence.

confirmation. The two beliefs "fit together"—in this case because (2) explains (1), but we need not worry about what makes various beliefs "fit together" at the moment—and they are therefore mutually supporting or reinforcing. All this is common sense. But in this example "fitting together" is not an isolated and independent factor sufficient in itself to justify believing either proposition. I was told, by Jill, who is known to me to be trustworthy, that John was seen going into Emily's house, and I have reasons for holding that he has long since wanted to visit her. It is, one is inclined to say, only because of these further factors that I am justified in regarding the two beliefs as mutually reinforcing.

This seems sensible, but, as the advocate of the coherence theory of knowledge will point out, it does not show that there is anything more to justification than coherence. This point establishes only that coherence requires a larger circle to carry much weight. To justify my belief that it was John who was seen going into Emily's house, my belief about John's desire to visit her has itself to fit other of my beliefs (for example, about his general conduct toward Emily and his feelings about her). In order for my belief that John was seen going into her house to justify my view about his desire to visit Emily, it also must fit other of my beliefs (e.g., that the person who claims to have seen him knows him). It is all a matter of coherence, except that coherence works in larger, rather than smaller circles.

At this point things become problematic. Do we add nothing but further beliefs and further "fitting" relations to the two beliefs from which we started? Surely it matters that the reliable Jill told me that someone, call him Jim, saw John go into Emily's house. In other words, the fact that some beliefs were reliably acquired—that they are not tainted by superstition, prejudice, rashness, jumping to conclusions, or other epistemic defects in the way they were reached or in the way that they are held, as well as their "fitting together"—matters to the justification of holding them.

At this juncture the advocate of epistemic coherence theories may try his master argument. He may dismiss the objection on the ground that there is no escape from relying on the way one's beliefs relate to each other, for beliefs are all we have. What can one rely on in justifying one's beliefs other than further beliefs one has? Of course, he will concede that some of my beliefs may have been reliably reached, while others may not. But these facts cannot help me to justify my beliefs. In trying to justify my beliefs, all I have to go on are my own beliefs about the ways I arrived at them and their reliability. In asking when is a belief justified, we are asking when is it justified for a person to hold it.

How is one to judge between the coherence theorist and his opponent? At first blush it would appear that we are offered here two rival and coherent (=intelligible) ways of understanding "justified belief." The coherence theorist holds a belief to be justified if and only if something within the resources of the person who holds that belief provides better support for it than for other competing beliefs. The coherence theorist further holds that the resources of people which are relevant to the justification of their beliefs consist entirely of their other beliefs, including their beliefs about the ways they formed, the ways they hold their beliefs.

Against the coherence theorist is the view that there are epistemic defects in the ways beliefs are formed or held: for example, that they were formed through prejudice or superstition, or by people who are not competent to judge the matters concerned, which render beliefs infected by them unjustified, even when the person whose beliefs they are has no inkling that his beliefs are so affected. A belief is justified if the person who has it is not epistemically at fault, if he has done what can be expected of him, or something to that effect.[10]

Both accounts of justified belief allow that justified beliefs can be false. I think that both regard justification as person-relative, that is, dependent on the state of the believer. They differ, however, on the basic features of justification of beliefs. They each have ramified implications and presuppositions, examination of which helps settle the dispute. They feed into one's account of reasoning and deliberation, they affect one's view of the nature of knowledge, and they reflect familiar differences of opinion concerning the presuppositions of responsibility. It is on the last aspect of the problem that I will comment.

I proceed on the assumption that we are interested in explicating the notion of justified belief which is part of our common epistemic vocabulary. The first step in the clarification is to identify justified belief with belief that one is not epistemically at fault in holding, belief that one may properly hold. The coherence theorist proceeds from here to claim that if one's other beliefs support the belief in question better than any of its alternatives, the condition of epistemic blamelessness is satisfied. What else can one expect of a person?[11] His opponent replies that we also can expect that a person

---

[10] Notice that for a belief to be justified it is not necessary that the believer has a justification for it. It is merely neccessary that the believer is justified in holding it. I am wary of attributing such considerations to any particular theorist. Many treatises in epistemology are inexplicit about the way they understand the nature of their endeavors.

[11] Two comments on the wider aspect of the problem will help clarify the comments that follow. First, we need to distinguish between holistic views of epistemic justification and coherence accounts of justified belief. Holistic views of justification hold that any belief may (depending on what else one justifiably believes) bear on the justification of holding any other belief. Holism implies (1) that there are no incorrigible beliefs and (2) that beliefs cannot be compartmentalized (by subject-matter or otherwise) into mutually invulnerable sets of beliefs. Holism is logically independent of coherence accounts, that is, it neither implies them nor is it implied by them. Coherence accounts of justified belief imply that if a belief-set can be made more coherent by replacing one of its members by another which is inconsistent with it, this should be done. Holism does not sustain this conclusion.

My discussion here is aimed against coherence accounts, and has no bearing one way or another on holism. One may say, following Pollock, that its real target is the doxastic assumption, that is, the view that justification of a person's beliefs depends exclusively on that person's other beliefs. *See* POLLOCK, *supra* note 8. In other words, the discussion is

should not be rash, or gullible, or prejudiced, or superstitious. That is, he upholds (in addition to coherence) objective conditions of epistemic blamelessness. People are to blame—epistemically speaking—when they fail to meet these standards. In these cases their epistemic functioning is at fault. The coherence theorist will acknowledge that when we do not function epistemically well we are more likely to fall into error. But when we have no inkling that we suffer from such failings we are not, according to him, to blame, and when our beliefs are blameless they are justified even when they happen to be false.

When we think of justified beliefs in this light, that is, as turning on whether the believer is at fault, whether he is responsible for holding a false belief, several observations become evident. First, it is simply false that we hold as justified beliefs conceived in prejudice and superstition, or entertained because of gullibility, obstinacy, or similar cognitive defects of the believer. The racist's belief in the untrustworthiness of members of a certain race, bred of prejudice, is not justified even if it coheres best with all the racist's other (mostly racist) beliefs. Coherence theory may seem plausible when attention is focused on the believer alone. But it is seen to be plainly false to our entrenched understanding of justified belief when we consider our judgment on the beliefs of others. We agree that people's beliefs are justified even when false, when they hold them in a reasonable way, on adequate evidence, and so on, but we regard them as unjustified when their cognitive processes or capacities are at fault, when they should have known better.

Second, the prejudiced, gullible, obstinate, etc., can avoid their mistake. They can acknowledge that they are prejudiced, gullible, obstinate, etc.— many people are aware of possessing such faults—and can counteract the effects by double-checking their evidence, consulting others, refusing to come to any conclusions, etc. One suspects that coherence theories appeal in part because there seems no alternative. If a belief coheres best with one's other beliefs, there is nothing to alert one to its defects. This is true so far as it goes. But it does not follow that one could not have known, or could not have suspected that it is not safe. It is a non sequitur to conclude that because one did not question a belief, one could not have, or that one could not have known what one's other beliefs did not provide (sufficient) reason to suspect. Justification and absence of blame may follow from an impossi-

---

aimed as much against foundationalism as against coherence accounts. I avoid referring to foundationalism as a possible alternative to coherentism. I find, however, most discussions of the subject confused. Some versions of foundationalism are not committed to the doxastic assumption (here belong those who believe that perception is a source of knowledge, whereas hallucination, let us say, is not). Other accounts of foundationalism are firmly committed to the doxastic assumption. They understand the foundations to be beliefs identifiable by their form or content, rather than by their sources. While I hold no brief for either variant of foundationalism, the arguments advanced in the main text apply against the last variant only.

bility of knowing that one's belief is suspect. They do not follow where there was an epistemic fault which could have been avoided.[12]

Third, it seems likely, though no firm conclusion can be reached without examining closely what the "fitting" relation consists of, that coherence is not only insufficient for justification but that it is not necessary either. For example, you see your friend, John, out of your window. You believe, therefore, that he is in town. This contradicts your other belief that he is on holiday in Spain, and various other beliefs which you have about his actions and plans. As it happens, you momentarily forgot about his holiday and all the rest, and are not in the least surprised to see him out of your window. There is no doubt in my mind that your belief that John is in town today is justified. At least on superficial examination, however, that belief does not fit as well with your other beliefs as the belief that you are mistaken in thinking that you saw John in the street.[13] If so, then coherence theory leads to the erroneous conclusion that your belief that John is in town is unjustified. It seems to me, though I am not confident about this, that there is no way of explaining what counts as "fitting together" which will avoid the conclusion that the belief that he was in town did not fit best with one's other beliefs, though one will have to construct careful counterexamples to various possible articulations of that relation.

Fourth, another reason for rejecting coherence as necessary for justified belief becomes evident when we consider cases when one is justified in accepting or holding inconsistent beliefs. It is true that all true propositions are necessarily consistent. But it is false that any coherent set of propositions is closer to the truth than any incoherent set. It is not even the case that every consistent set of propositions is closer to the truth than any inconsistent one. This is so even when we confine ourselves to two sets which largely overlap in content, except that one is consistent and the other is inconsistent.[14] Even under these circumstances we have no reason to believe that the consistent set is necessarily closer to the truth. (Inconsistent though the Fregean articulation of the foundations of arithmetic was, it was closer to the truth than many of its consistent rivals.) Bear in mind here that because we are concerned with believed propositions and because people do not believe all that is entailed by their beliefs, I am referring to sets of propositions which are not closed under entailment, i.e., which do not include all that they entail.

---

[12] Notice that not all flaws in the way a belief is acquired or held render it unjustified. Sometimes, for example, the believer cannot avoid falling prey to a trick or being taken in by unusual circumstances.

[13] I believe that Burns wrote the *Waverly* novels. But last week when asked who their author was I could not remember. It does not follow that at that time I had lost my incorrect belief. My failure was of recall, of the ability to tap my memory, to activate it when the need arose.

[14] I am assuming that we can establish the overlap in content even though the set is inconsistent.

Given the possibility that a contradictory set is closer to the truth than a consistent alternative, the move to consistency can be a move in the wrong direction: the consistent set of beliefs replacing the inconsistent one may be both false and further away from the truth than the inconsistent one. Given that one knows that, it would hardly seem epistemically justified to move from the inconsistent to the consistent beliefs—at least not without further information, i.e., information which goes beyond indications of consistency to identify either which set is more likely to be true, or which of the propositions yielding the contradiction is in fact false. Again, it is possible, but seems to me unlikely, that an articulation of a relationship of "fitting together" can be found to avert this possibility.

Finally, the last two points depend on the following proposition: while coherence theory, to make sense at all, must relate to the totality of one's beliefs, and not merely to what one is thinking of at the time, many of one's beliefs are not accessible to one at will. Much of what we believe we do not remember and cannot recall at will. Furthermore, many of the implications of our remembered beliefs elude us. This brings out the inherent incoherence of coherence theories. Their appeal depends on rejecting, as irrelevant to the justification of belief, everything other than a person's beliefs, on the ground that those other factors are not available to him. But by the same reasoning most of his beliefs are to be discounted as well. On the other hand, as we saw, sometimes what is not available could have been available. In many cases one could have come to recognize the existence of various epistemic defects, such as biases, prejudices, or incompetence to judge the matter at hand, much more easily than one could have come to remember certain of the things one knows which bear on the matter, or to work out their implications. Indeed, a defect one may be able to realize one suffers from is precisely this difficulty in remembering information of a certain type, or in realizing its consequences when one is under stress, and so on. Hence, sometimes one can know that one cannot remember correctly more easily than one can remember. But this shows that coherence theories are guilty of greatly exaggerating one's voluntary control over one's beliefs, as well as of espousing excessively voluntaristic notions of responsibility and justification. It is this excessive voluntarism which renders coherence theories ultimately incoherent.

II. From Epistemic to Constitutive Coherence: Redefining Coherence

So far I have been concerned to refute the view that coherence provides the key to the justification of belief. You may, of course, say that all this is irrelevant because my topic is coherence and the law. Writers who have advanced coherence theories of law and justification did not offer them as epistemic accounts but as explanations of the nature of law and of correct adjudication. So why deviate from the view that coherence provides the key to the objective constitution of the law, to the view that it is the key to the justification of belief? There are three reasons for the detour. The first is rhetorical. Coherence enjoys such a good name that we should be on our guard: coherence may be the key to the solution of some problems, but it is not the solution to all the problems it is invoked to solve. This touches on the second reason for the detour. It is not always clearly understood that the jurisprudential theories of coherence are not epistemic, but constitutive. It is important to make clear that coherence is invoked in several distinct contexts, and that its success in some of them may well be logically independent of its success in others.

This brings us to the last reason for the detour. It may be thought, though I do not know of anyone actually making this claim, that the success of the coherence account of the law follows directly from the coherence theory of justification of belief. Roughly speaking, the claim would be that if justified beliefs form a coherent whole then so does the reality they represent. The subjective and the objective, the beliefs and the reality they are about must, when the beliefs are true, mirror each other. Whatever the independent problems with this argument, it can be put aside given the rejection of theories of epistemic coherence.[15]

I stated at the outset that constitutive coherence theories of law and adjudication are more plausible than coherence theories of justified belief. While by now my reasons for finding epistemic views suspect are clear, it may still be puzzling how constitutive theories can be taken seriously. Coherence may be a desirable feature of an intellectual system, the objector may say. We may prefer theories which display more coherence to those which display less. But this is all either a matter of intellectual satisfaction in one mode of presenting results rather than others, or a value judgment of some sort. Such judgments and preferences, the objector will continue, are irrelevant to an inquiry into the nature of law.[16] When we ask about the nature of law we aim to discover how things are independently of us. I do not mean that the law is as it is independently of human beings and their activities, only that what it is, is independent of my, or anyone else's, inquiry into its nature. Therefore, our preferences or value judgments are immaterial. Our account of the law should be faithful to the nature of legal phenomena. And while it is possible that some legal systems display considerable coherence, there surely cannot be a general reason to suppose that they all do. There is no reason to suppose that the law lives up to our preferences or values.

In the end, this objection may very well prove decisive. But things are not that simple. To begin with, we need to recharacterize the way coherence is understood when it is advanced as a constitutive thesis about the nature of law, or as a thesis about correct adjudication. The epistemic notion of

---

[15] It does not follow, of course, that because justification is not by coherence alone, reality or the law is not a coherent whole. They may be coherent wholes even if considerations about the coherence of one's beliefs are irrelevant to their justification.

[16] To simplify, I will concentrate on law, and will make no special mention of adjudication except when the arguments bear differently on law and on adjudication.

mutual support is inappropriate to the new context.[17] For one thing, we are now concerned not with coherence of beliefs but with the coherence of legal norms, rules, standards, doctrines, and principles.[18] Furthermore, epistemic coherence is relative to each person. The justification of each person's beliefs is relative to that person's totality of beliefs. This makes it possible for each of two people to be justified in holding beliefs that contradict those of the other. As justified beliefs may be false, there is no problem about that. A constitutive account of law cannot enjoy the same luxury. It cannot be person-relative. What is or is not the law in the United States today is one thing, and what people believe it to be is another. If two people hold contradictory views about American law, then at least one of them is wrong. So if coherence is to play a role in an account of the nature of law (or of correct adjudication), it cannot be understood in a person-relative way.

This draws attention to the fact that to make coherence play a role in an account of the law (or of justified belief) that account must consist of another consideration beside a preference for coherence. It must include a principle providing what I will call "a base," that is, something which is to be made coherent. Epistemic accounts take the base to be a person's belief set. Each of a person's beliefs is justified if and only if it stands in a certain relation to that person's belief set. Constitutive coherence accounts of the law cannot have the same base. They cannot take as their base each person's beliefs, nor that person's legal beliefs which correspond to (a potential) legal principle. That would make them person-relative and we have just seen that they cannot be person-relative. Their base must be, practically speaking, the same for all believers, so that the coherence imposed on it will yield one legal system per state, however much people may disagree about its content.[19]

The introduction of the base may sound like a betrayal of coherence in favor of a form of (a constitutive version of) foundationalism. Why should we not say that all legal propositions, let us say all the propositions starting with "according to law . . .," should be submitted to the test of coherence? On this view, the law is as stated by the most coherent subset of all legal propositions. Only in this way—you may say—can coherence be the sole

---

[17] I do not mean that it is logically impossible to apply the epistemic notion of mutual support here. I suggest only that we need a more abstract formulation of coherence, not committed from the outset to its epistemic understanding. That formulation, broadly of a system whose principles are unified, will leave open what form of unity is relevant. It may turn out that epistemic support provides the answer to this question.

[18] For every standard there is a corresponding belief. To the principle *pacta sunt servanda* corresponds the belief that they should be. But not every belief corresponds to a legal standard. Neither the belief that oaks blossom in the spring, nor the belief that Jenny made a valid contract with Jane correspond to any legal principle. Constitutive coherence is not even the coherence of all legal propositions, only of those which correspond to legal principles.

[19] In principle, if a transitory base is admitted, each person may have a different transitory base from which he or she is led, by considerations of coherence, to converge on everyone else's conclusions.

judge of truth in the law. And I agree. So the first lesson we learn is that, even according to coherence accounts, coherence is but one of at least two components in any theory of law. The other component provides the base to which the coherence account applies.

This is the first lesson we learn, for clearly the suggestion we just envisioned, namely that the coherence test be applied to all legal propositions, is a non-starter. Think of it: among possible legal propositions are the propositions, "According to law one should act to maximize the happiness of the greatest number," and "According to law one should always act in accordance with the categorical imperative." That is, if we take all possible legal propositions as the base, we may end up with a morally perfect set of propositions as allegedly being the law, but this moral perfection will be purchased at the cost of losing contact with reality. What will be baptized as law by the pure coherence account of the law will bear no relation to the law.

This first lesson has far-reaching ramifications. It suggests a division of labor between the two components of a theory of law. The base assures it contact with the concrete reality of the law; the coherence test provides the rationalizing element which enables us to view the law as a rational system governing the conduct of affairs in a country. This characterization is not precise, but its intuitive force is sound. It is strengthened by the second lesson which has already been pointed out above: the base cannot be subjective. It must be the same for all persons. In particular, theories of law cannot take as their base each person's beliefs, nor each person's legal beliefs. The law is not subjective in that way. It is not the case that there are many legal systems in the United States because different people have different beliefs about what American law is. Because the law is one, the base to which the coherence test must apply is one. Were the coherence test to apply to people's beliefs about the law, one would end with different legal systems for different believers. The need to find a common base to which the coherence test applies emphasizes the importance of that part of the theory and its connectedness to the concrete realities of the country concerned.

It is true that the base itself is not immune to coherence considerations. It provides the starting point, the material to which one applies the coherence test. In the process of applying the test, the base may be modified. Elements may be added while others are rejected. One possibility for a coherence theory is to have a transitory base, that is, one which provides a starting point on which some coherence-maximizing procedure is applied, leading eventually to a discarding of the base. Rawls's writings on reflective equilibrium illustrate the possibility of a base which can, in principle, be transitory. To achieve reflective equilibrium one starts a process of deliberation leading toward it from one's existing normative beliefs, against the background of all other beliefs. During the deliberation one is led to accept principles which increase the coherence of the totality of one's normative beliefs at the time (again, given the rest of one's beliefs). In this process one also may discard some of one's original beliefs or beliefs which one has reached at that stage. Deliberation continues until one is content with the beliefs one has at that time. While in practice one is likely to reach that point while continuing to hold many of one's original beliefs, in principle they all may have been replaced by other beliefs.[20]

While a transitory base is logically consistent with a coherence account of law and adjudication, we can dismiss that possibility from our deliberation. Nobody has ever suggested a view of law which allows for it. All coherence accounts of law admit an additional consideration, one which provides the base from which only modest deviation is allowed. Thus, all coherence accounts of the law are mixed accounts. In due course I will raise the question of what that additional consideration could be. For now, it is enough to understand coherence theories of law as those which take a certain base, say court decisions and legislative and regulatory acts, and hold the law to be the set of principles that makes the most coherent[21] sense of it. The more unified the set of principles, the more coherent it is. If all the principles follow from one of their number, then we have strong monistic coherence. If they all follow from a small group of principles which display a unified spirit or approach, they are less coherent but more so than if the principles derive from a plurality of distinct and irreducible principles which do not display a unified spirit or approach.[22] Similarly, if the law is derivable from a set of distinct principles which are completely ranked, then it is more coherent than if they are only partially ranked, and so on. Other forms of unity displaying coherence are possible as well. One can imagine unity through circular interdependency of a set of propositions such that giving up one principle requires the abandonment of all the others. If coherence takes this form, then no proposition enjoys priority over any other.

It is not possible to determine in advance precisely what coherence means, and how precisely different accounts of the law compare in the degree of coherence they show the law to have. These questions are among those which are at issue between competing accounts of the law and can only be determined concretely in the face of the competing accounts. Only the very broad characterization of coherence as the degree of unity in the legal system can be stated in advance. The more united the law is made to be the more coherent it is. The more pluralistic the law, the less coherent it is. Coher-

---

[20] *See* Raz, *The Claims of Reflective Equilibrium, supra* note 2. As is clear from this schematic and not very accurate description, reflective equilibrium need not be committed to coherence. But consideration of this point need not detain us here.

[21] But resist the natural inclination to understand "coherence" as "intelligible" in this sentence.

[22] I am assuming here that distinct principles can display a similar approach, or one spirit, without being derivable from one more abstract principle. Different jokes can evince the same attitude, or express the same outlook, without being derivable from a statement of that point or attitude. I am assuming that the same is true for moral, political, or legal principles.

ence theories claim that a greater degree of coherence is one of the considerations which make an account of the law true.[23]

III. Is There an Argument from Radical Interpretation?

The existence of law depends on social practices, and this makes coherence theories tempting. There are two arguments to be considered. The first
can be dismissed fairly quickly. The second, however, will occupy much of
the rest of this Article. The first argument suggests that law is dependent on
social practices, that is, dependent on human actions, desires, and beliefs. If
so, then to identify the law one needs to identify the relevant social practices,
and the actions, desires, and beliefs which constitute them. Familiar arguments establish that the attribution of actions, desires, and beliefs to people
is interdependent. What a person does depends on what he believes and
wants, what he wants depends on what he does and believes, what he
believes depends on what he wants and does. There is no need to rehearse
these arguments here.[24] An example will make their point clear: The Metropolitan Police in London used a photograph of Don McCullin in its drive
to recruit more minority police officers. In it a young black man is running,
followed by a white police officer. The caption read something as follows:
"Do you see a policeman chasing a black youth? If so you are prejudiced
not us." The photo is of a uniformed constable assisting a black plainclothes
police officer in pursuing a suspect. You see the point: While one knows
neither the beliefs nor the desires nor the goals of the agents, one cannot
know what actions to attribute to them. Once one knows their beliefs and
goals, one knows what they are doing. Conversely, once one knows the
agents' actions and desires, one can easily determine their beliefs. (The
agent wants to eat, he opens the cupboard, so he must believe that there is
food in the cupboard.) Similarly, once one knows their beliefs and actions
one knows what they want. (The agent takes a book off the shelf, believing it
to be a biography of Jean Rhys, so he wants to find out something about
Jean Rhys.)

These examples are simplified. They overlook the possibilities of alternative explanations and other nuances. They do illustrate, however, the general point we need: that we attribute beliefs, goals, and actions to people, not
singly but in interdependent clumps. This interdependence means nothing
other than a presumption of coherence. That is, the attributions determine
each other on an assumption that the agent has coherent sets of beliefs, goals
and actions; that the agent acts rationally as one would given that one has
these beliefs and goals; that one has the goals appropriate to someone with
these beliefs who performs these actions; that one has the beliefs appropriate

---

[23] The Appendix includes a discussion of some other ways in which "coherence" is
sometimes used.

[24] A crisp statement of them may be found in Anthony Kenny, The Metaphysics
of Mind (1989).

to someone who, having the goals one has, performs these actions. Given that actions, beliefs and goals are attributed on an assumption of coherence, and that the law depends on social practices, i.e., on actions, beliefs and goals that people have, does it not follow that the law forms a coherent whole?

Clearly, to conclude so would be to commit a gross non sequitur. The argument merely establishes that to have beliefs and goals and actions one must have clumps of coherent sets of the three. Cases in which the coherence fails do exist, but they are—must be—the exception rather than the rule. It is a far cry from here, however, to an assumption of global coherence in any agent's overall set of beliefs, goals, and actions. Conceding that local coherence is necessary for rational agency is consistent with recognizing that people are all too often quirky, inconsistent, wayward, and even incoherent overall. It is certainly consistent with thinking of them as having consistent but mutually independent sets of goals and desires, displaying very little unity.

Some philosophers, notably Davidson,[25] have generalized the argument in an attempt to establish that to understand any creature as a person, i.e., as an agent who has goals and beliefs, presupposes an assumption that for the most part his beliefs are true and his goals and beliefs cohere. That argument depends for its plausibility on the supposition that we understand our parents and closest friends, indeed that we understand ourselves, in the same way in which we might inquire whether a newly encountered creature of an unknown species on Mars is a person, and what beliefs and goals he has. The soundness of that argument need not detain us here. Even if it is sound, it does not establish that the law is coherent. What the law is is the result of the activities of a multitude of people, and the interactions among them, over many years, sometimes over centuries. One cannot infer, in a Davidsonian-style argument about radical interpretation, the coherence of the activities, beliefs, or goals of all those whose activities make the law what it is.

Given the previous remarks, I will proceed on the basis of two propositions. First, that the law is a function of human acts and social practices (though not necessarily exclusively so). Second, that one can identify the acts, beliefs, and goals of people without presupposing that they form, collectively, a coherent set. When discussing the law we are often concerned with the promulgation of statutes or statutory instruments, and with judicial decisions stating reasons for reaching a certain outcome to litigation. Such acts have a content: the statute, the judicial reasons. Coherence theories offer a solution to the problem of the relation between human action and the law.

To show how coherence theories deal with this relation, I will look at the two steps of another simple alternative—what I call the intention thesis. First, statutes and judicial decisions have the content that their makers

---

[25] For example, see DONALD DAVIDSON, *Radical Interpretation*, *in* INQUIRIES INTO TRUTH AND INTERPRETATION 125 (1984), and other of the essays in that volume.

intended them to have. Second, the law is the sum total of all the statutes and those judicial decisions which have the force of precedent. The intention view is widely ridiculed today. But it is not without its appeal. After all, legislators promulgate statutes with the content they intend to become law; courts advance those reasons which they intend to be understood as the justification of their decisions. If the intentions of legislators and judges are not made into law, it is not clear why they are chosen to legislate or adjudicate. This explains why we care so much who is elected or appointed to the legislature and to the courts. We know that those people will try to affect the content of our law, and given the power to legislate or decide cases they will do so. They will be able to translate their intentions into law. But for this, why do we care whether a Democrat or a Republican is elected to the Senate? Why care whether a pro-choice or an anti-abortion person is appointed to the Supreme Court? It is not enough to say that we care because the court and the legislature affect the law. If they do not affect it by translating their intentions into law, then there is no need to care about their intentions. So the intention thesis has a core of good sense. Many dismiss it because legislatures and courts consist of many people and no single person's intention can be decisive. The problem of institutional intention is a serious one, and not only for supporters of the intention thesis, but it cannot be discussed here. The burden of the earlier discussion is that we can identify intentions without presupposing any degree of collective coherence. So there is no way from the intention thesis to any coherence account of the law. Quite the opposite. It is unlikely that the intentions of all lawmakers cohere, and, therefore, one would not expect the law to display a high degree of coherence.

Given all that, can one resist the intention thesis? Is it not the inevitable consequence of the fact that the law is a function of human acts and social practices? Not at all. The answer depends on what sort of a function it is. We share a concept of law which assigns a special status to rules and other standards which stand in a certain relation to, are a certain function of, human activities. But what is this function? The intention thesis suggests that it is one of identity with all the principles representing the content of the intention with which lawmaking acts and court decisions are undertaken. This is but one possibility. Another might be that the law consists of the valid moral principles which are closest (i.e., most similar) to the propositions representing the intentions of lawmakers and courts. On this thesis, which we may call the moral approximation thesis, one acts as if each lawmaking act points to a valid moral principle. Sometimes it identifies the principle correctly. In these cases, the result of the moral approximation thesis is the same as that of the intention thesis. At other times, the lawmaker's or the court's intention, while aiming at a valid principle, misses it. The lawmaker or the court wants to identify correctly the principle of respect for freedom of contract, or of just, progressive taxation on income, but the rule they establish falls short of the morally sound rule. In this case the law is not as is stated by the intention thesis; rather, it is the valid principle nearest to the legislator's or court's intention.

I do not suggest that the moral approximation thesis be taken seriously. I mention it only because it shows how the law can be a function of legislative acts and judicial decisions without being as stated by the intention thesis. Moreover, the moral approximation thesis is sensitive to the intentions of the legislator. It therefore can claim to explain why it makes sense to care who the legislator is. It shows that the intention thesis is not the only one which can capture the basic sound sense which lies at its core. Nor is the moral approximation thesis the only alternative to it which is sensitive to the intentions of courts and legislators.

It all depends on the concept of law, by which I mean the way we conceive of the social institution known as the law.[26] The exploration of that understanding is a theoretical enterprise aimed at improving our understanding of human society. On the one hand, it must be true to the basic features of the institution, which in its basic elements and manifestations is known to all. On the other hand, it is not an attempt at an exhaustive description of the law. Rather, it is an attempt to highlight the law's most significant features, those which contribute most to our understanding of the functioning of the institution in our lives and its relations to other institutions and social practices. The intention thesis is one suggested partial answer to this theoretical quest. It captures some elements correctly, and any adequate explanation of the law will have to succeed in doing justice to these elements. The moral approximation and the coherence views of the law offer rival ways of understanding the law. It remains to be seen how successful coherence accounts are.

IV. THE EXTREME PARADIGM: LAW AS COHERENCE

Following my method so far, I will formulate a pure version of a coherence-based account of the nature of law:

The law of a certain country consists of the most coherent set of normative principles which, had they been accepted as valid by a perfectly rational and well-informed person would have led him, given the opportunity to do so, to promulgate all the legislation and render all the decisions which were in fact promulgated and rendered in that country.[27]

---

[26] I have discussed the methodology of the inquiry into the nature of law elsewhere. *See, e.g.*, Raz, *Authority, Law and Morality, supra* note 6; Joseph Raz, *The Problem About the Nature of Law*, 21 W. ONTARIO L. REV. 203, 210-12 (1983).

[27] Many accounts of law emphasize the importance of coherence. Many of them bear no resemblance to the thesis formulated here. An example of such an unrelated accounts is to be found in Ernest J. Weinrib, *Legal Formalism: On the Immanent Rationality of Law*, 97 YALE L.J. 949 (1988). I have discussed Weinrib's ideas in Joseph Raz, *Formalism and the Rule of Law, in* NATURAL LAW THEORY (Robert George ed., 1992). Other theorists who assign importance to coherence include: Rolf E. Sartorius, *The Justification of the Judicial Decision*, 78 ETHICS 171 (1968); ROLF E. SARTORIUS,

Before we consider the thesis, the examination of one possible objection to it will help clarify its nature. The thesis, one may say, presupposes that we know what legal decisions, legislative or judicial, are, but that we do not know their content without the coherence exercise. This, the objector concludes, is unwarranted. If we know what the decisions are, we also can know their content, and have no need for the coherence thesis. The objector claims that having to introduce a base to which the coherence test applies undermines coherence. The base provides all we need for a theory of law without help from coherence. But in this form the objector misunderstands the thesis. It is perfectly capable of accommodating the objection, by incorporating the very identification of the legal acts of promulgating legislation and rendering of judicial decisions within the coherence test itself. After all, the content of the law which the test identifies includes the rules establishing courts, their rules of jurisdiction, and their procedures, as well as rules for the constitution, election, appointment, and procedures of legislative institutions. The identification of the legal acts which the test uses to establish the law is itself secured by the law which the test identifies. This is a totally innocuous circularity. Of course, the thesis assumes some base. It assumes a rough identification of the relevant legal acts with which to start, an identification that can be confined to the totally uncontroversial acts of the legal institutions of the country concerned. But the thesis does not remain bound by this initial identification. It expands the range of legal activities assigned to its rational legislator-cum-court as the legal doctrine it identifies requires, and it may even, within limits, conflict with the initial consensus and delete certain institutions from its list if that seems necessary to improve the coherence of the main body of legal propositions.[28]

INDIVIDUAL CONDUCT AND SOCIAL NORMS 181-210 (1975); S.L. HURLEY, NATURAL REASONS, *supra* note 4; Robert Alexy & Aleksander Peczenik, *The Concept of Coherence and Its Significance for Discursive Rationality*, 3 RATIO JURIS 130 (1990). Ronald Dworkin's work also has affinities with coherence theses, and will be considered below. My aim here, however, is not to address any theorist's specific views, but rather to address a generic position. Given the difference in the understanding of the relations between the law and coherence, my arguments do not apply directly to all these coherence-oriented accounts. But they do bear on the general merits of coherence, and to that extent they have implications for all coherence-oriented accounts.

[28] A similar objection has been raised against H.L.A. Hart's doctrine of the Rule of Recognition. According to it the law of a legal system consists in those laws which the courts and other institutions of that country are under a customary duty to apply. This presupposes an independent way of identifying which are the relevant institutions, it has been objected. *See* NEIL MACCORMICK, H.L.A. HART (1981); *see also* MATHEW H. KRAMER, LEGAL THEORY AND POLITICAL THEORY AND DECONSTRUCTION 120 (1991). Not so. The Rule of Recognition itself identifies certain institutions as the relevant ones. Potential Rules of Recognition are represented by any proposition of the right form, for example, a proposition identifying certain bodies and imposing on them a duty to apply a set of doctrines and rules. That proposition is the Rule of Recognition of a country which meets the following two conditions: First, the institutions it refers to do

Think of this thesis what you like. It clearly offers various hostages to fortune, for example in its fictional would-be single legislator-cum-judge, acting on the basis of a set of principles, and outside the constraints of any political process. Nevertheless, two features stand out as potentially great advantages of the coherence over the intention thesis. First, it regards the law as contemporaneous, and as free from the dead hand of age-old intentions which shackles the intention thesis. Second, it presents the law as a rational meaningful whole, rather than as the higgledy-piggledy assemblage of the remains of contradictory past political ambitions and beliefs, as does the intention thesis.[29] I describe these as potential advantages because, as they stand, they are suspect of wishful thinking. It would be nice if the law were a coherent rational system, free from the dead hand of past intentions and from the debris of past political struggles. But we all know that this is not so, that the law suffers precisely from all these disadvantages, and that so long as it remains, as it must, the main vehicle of politics, it will remain so marred.

Are these suspicions justified? Defenders of the coherence thesis will protest that they are as aware as anyone of the vagaries of politics. The question, as we saw, is what is the relation between these facts and the law. It is common ground to most writers on the nature of law today that the law is meant to be taken as a standard for conduct and for judgment by its subjects, and that typically they do take it so. That fact must be at the center of any explanation of law. An explanation must show how the law can be taken as a standard for conduct and for judgment, and how it is typically so taken by its subjects. Further, the explanation must make these facts central to our understanding of the law.[30] The acceptance of the law as a standard is some-

---

exist. Second, they actually follow a rule whose content is that proposition, that is, they have a practice whose content is as stated by the proposition. Hart's Rule of Recognition escapes from the circularity even without assuming an external starting point, which seems necessary for coherence thesis. But if his theory is to be a theory of law, rather than of some other institutionalized normative system, Hart needs to rely on a similar device to identify the undoubted legal institutions as the starting point for the process.

[29] The coherence thesis also gets around the problem of attributing intentions to institutions. But, as I have indicated, there is no reason to take this problem too seriously, except as against rather silly versions of the intention thesis. The problem may be sufficient, however, to reject the views sometimes known as "originalist." Compare their discussion in MICHAEL J. PERRY, MORALITY, POLITICS, AND LAW (1988).

[30] This point has been more or less explicitly denied by O.W. Holmes in *The Common Law*, and implicitly by Marxist and economic theories of the law. *See* OLIVER WENDELL HOLMES, THE COMMON LAW (1881). It has been made central to his theory by H.L.A. Hart, in developing his thesis about the centrality of the internal point of view. *See* H.L.A. HART, THE CONCEPT OF LAW (1961). Among other works which further developed this idea (in ways which go beyond Hart's conception of it) are: R.A. Duff, *Legal Obligations and the Moral Nature of Law*, 25 JURID. REV. 61 (1980); JOSEPH RAZ, PRACTICAL REASON AND NORMS (2d ed. 1990); JOSEPH RAZ, THE AUTHORITY OF LAW: ESSAYS ON LAW AND MORALITY ch. 2 (1979); JOHN M. FINNIS, NATURAL LAW

times regarded as the reason for embracing the coherence thesis. The reason is plain to see. An outsider observing a foreign legal system can see it as a hodgepodge of norms derived from the conflicting ideologies and the pragmatic necessities which prevailed from time to time over the many years of its evolution. Someone who adopts the internal point of view cannot possibly do this. Adopting the internal point of view means that he regards the norms as valid for him, as guides for his behavior and judgment. It makes no sense to accept an assemblage of norms as one's own norms unless one regards them as valid and justified, and one cannot regard them as justified unless they form a coherent body.[31]

There are several decisive objections to this argument, but before I address them let me discard one failed objection. It is no objection that we do not always view the law from the internal point of view. True, most people have this attitude toward the law of their country only, and some do not share it even there. All people are perfectly capable of understanding that states have legal systems and of finding out what the law is. Therefore, the law must be comprehensible from the point of view of an observer. And it was acknowledged that, for an observer, it need not be coherent. All this is true, but none of it is an objection to the argument. Given the admitted priority of the participant's point of view, even the observer, in order to acquire a sound understanding of the law, must understand it as it would be seen by a participant. If it must be coherent to a participant then coherent it is.

The most fundamental objection to the argument I am considering amounts to a rejection of its premise that it is unintelligible for people to accept a less coherent body of principles over a more coherent alternative. The clearest counter-instance is the case of morality. Some moral theories enjoy great coherence, perhaps even the greatest coherence possible. Utilitarianism might be such an example, but any monistic morality, that is, one which derives all its precepts from one fundamental precept, is an illustration of a coherent moral system. All of them, however, are misguided. In fact, morality is not a system or a coherent body of principles. It contains, to be sure, pockets of coherence, and it is consistent. But it consists of a large number of principles which neither derive from a common source nor are capable of fitting into a uniform system or a system whose principles are mutually supportive and interdependent. Unfortunately, though sound and interesting, this objection cannot be pursued here, as this is not the occasion

---

AND NATURAL RIGHTS ch. 1 (1980); RONALD DWORKIN, LAW'S EMPIRE (1986) (hereinafter LAW'S EMPIRE) (the theme has, of course, been central to Dworkin's work from the beginning); PHILIP SOPER, A THEORY OF LAW (1984). On Hart's distinctive position, see H.L.A. HART, ESSAYS ON BENTHAM ch. 5 (1982). See my comments on it in Joseph Raz, *Hart on Moral Rights and Legal Duties*, 4 OXFORD J. LEGAL STUD. 123 (1984) (book review).

[31] This argument does not vindicate the coherence thesis as articulated above, nor any other specific coherence thesis. All it does, if anything, is argue for coherence as an element in any explanation of the nature of law.

to explore the nature of morality. Instead, we can resort to a second argument, of a more limited scope but pertinent to law. The argument for coherence we are considering proceeds from the assumption that, to be acceptable, a set of principles must be coherent. Let us assume that to be cogent and valid in themselves, directly, that is, due to considerations which are of the primary, most basic kind in establishing validity and cogency, principles must be coherent. This is consistent with the possibility that they are valid even though they do not form a coherent body of principles, for their validity may derive from indirect considerations. For example, if the set of principles one is considering represents the dictates of authority, they may fail to cohere and yet be valid because the authority is a legitimate one with power to bind its subjects.[32]

An authority may be justified, for example, because it is capable of achieving social coordination without which the level of personal security, social facilities, and economic prosperity enjoyed by the population would be much lower. Granting for the sake of argument that an ideal authority would have promulgated and sustained a coherent set of principles, an authority may be legitimate and its directives may be binding on its subjects, even if it is far from ideal and its directives a far from coherent body of rules. Even so, it is entirely possible that those rules secure the social cooperation necessary for the realization of goals which could not have been secured any other way, and whose importance is sufficient to overcome the shortcomings resulting from the fact that the authority is less than ideal.

To put the point more directly, it is possible, indeed I would argue that it is the case, that many existing governments and legal systems fit the description of the previous paragraph. That is, their law is the result of the rough and tumble of politics, which does not exclude the judiciary from its ambit, and reflects the vagaries of pragmatic compromises, of changing fortunes of political forces, and the like. Their law, therefore, does not form a coherent body of principle and doctrine. But it makes sense to accept it and regard it as binding. Sometimes citizens are duty-bound to do so because of the benefits of maintaining its authority in spite of all its defects. At other times, it may be morally wrong to acknowledge the legitimacy of legal authorities. Most of the time, however, it is intelligible that people take it to be binding, regardless of its degree of coherence. None of this assumes that the law is not necessarily coherent. I merely point out that sets of principles can be sensibly embraced even when not coherent. Therefore, the fact that the law is typically embraced by many of its subjects is no argument that it is necessarily coherent.

This second argument, the argument from authority, applies only to the special cases where principles are valid for indirect (content-independent)

---

[32] The comments on authority and the law which follow draw on my discussions of authority in Joseph Raz, *Authority, Law and Morality*, 68 THE MONIST 295 (1985) and JOSEPH RAZ, THE MORALITY OF FREEDOM pt. I (1986).

reasons.[33] But that the law is such a special case is not disputed. The coherence thesis takes as its base the activities of legal authorities. It regards the law as the most coherent set of principles which could lead one who believes in them to act as the legal authorities in the country concerned have acted. The existence of legal authorities is fundamental to the law: on this, coherence theorists agree with their opponents. Hence we come to the third argument against the coherence thesis, which establishes that it fails to make sense of the existence of legal authorities. The third argument is simple. This much is common ground: (1) the law is to be explained in a way that illuminates how those who are subject to it are meant to view it;[34] (2) those subject to the law are meant to take it as a set of valid standards for the guidance of their conduct and judgment; (3) those standards are, moreover, standards which emerge from the activities of authoritative institutions, and are to be taken as justified in the way which is appropriate to the justification of authority; (4) legal authorities are required to act with deliberation and for good reasons. Judicial authorities are often required to state their reasons, or some of them. Legislative bodies are not as commonly required to state their reasons, but they are subject to a requirement of acting with deliberation, in good faith, and for cogent reasons.

As we saw, the third point means that, if the law reflects the intentions of its makers, we need not expect a high degree of coherence in the law. Together with the fourth point it also means that we must assign considerable importance to the intentions of legal authorities and to their reasons for acting as they do when we interpret the law and establish its content. Otherwise, it would be a mystery why legal institutions are invested with authority in the first place, and why they are required to exercise it on the basis of reasons. If the way we determine the content of the law does not reflect the intentions and the reasons of legal authorities, then—barring the existence of a yet to be discovered invisible hand mechanism—nothing is gained by their acting for reasons rather than arbitrarily.

This point is so simple that I feel I ought to apologize for making it. My excuse is of course that it shows that the coherence thesis is wrong. It establishes that because the law is meant to be taken as a system based on authority its content is to be determined by reference to the intentions of legal authorities and their reasons, and, therefore, that given the vagaries of politics, including, let me repeat, judicial involvement in politics, there is no reason to expect the law to be coherent. By and large, one would expect it to be coherent in bits—in areas relatively unaffected by continuous political struggles—and incoherent in others. Perhaps coherent regarding the mental conditions of criminal liability, but not on the rights and wrongs of abortion.

---

[33] *See* RAZ, *supra* note 32, at ch. 2.

[34] I have here gone beyond the vaguer, more open formulation of the primacy of the internal point of view given above, in order to render it in the way which I believe is most appropriate. While this formulation will be disputed by some, most theorists agree on the primacy of the internal point of view, and that is all that is required here.

I suspect that one reason, perhaps the main reason, why this lesson is often overlooked is that people think that it drives them back into the bosom of the intention thesis, which we all know to be wrong. But it does not. It points to the importance of the intentions and reasons of legal authorities, not necessarily to those of the legislator. This is a large theme and cannot be fully addressed here. Briefly, the intention thesis errs in isolating each act of lawmaking and regarding the law made by it as determined by that episode in isolation, once and for all. This is an unsustainable view. What we need is a way of regarding the law as the function of the activities of legal authorities in general, that is, a way of seeing how its content is a function of various activities, and layers of activities, in continuous interaction, rather than as a function of a single act, fixed once and for all. This authority-based view of the law will avoid the pitfalls of the intention thesis, while preserving its ability to explain the institutional nature of the law, something the coherence thesis fails to do.[35]

The failure of the coherence thesis which I have been tracing can be viewed as a failure to take due notice of the base to which the coherence thesis applies. The coherence thesis seeks the most coherent set of principles which would have led to the promulgation of all the legislation and the rendering of all the judicial decisions which have been promulgated and ren-

---

[35] It may be of interest to reflect on the methodological assumption underlying this argument by comparing it with Ronald Dworkin's views on method, a subject to which he has contributed more than any other legal philosopher in recent years. Dworkin would regard the considerations raised here as legitimate (though not necessarily convincing), but would place them further down the deliberative process. For him, explaining the nature of law (the main task of jurisprudence) is one of many questions about American law. For example, can corporations be guilty of intentional crimes? It is a legal question like any other, except at a higher level of abstraction. As such, it is to be understood as an attempt to interpret the legal practices of the United States, an attempt which is subject to the fundamental principle of (constructive) interpretation: that interpretation is correct which shows the law to be the best item of its kind. The criteria for assessing which explanation of the nature of law is correct are essentially moral criteria. The conclusion that the law is to be understood as authority-based and, therefore, that its content is a function of the intentions and reasons of legal authorities, if correct, is to be regarded as based on the view that seeing the law in this way makes it morally better than alternative ways of seeing it.

By contrast, I am regarding the question of the nature of the law as different in kind from questions about the content of American law, different even, for example, from questions of the constitutional conditions of validity of legislation in the United States. In addition, while the argument, like Dworkin's, relies both on familiar and uncontroversial facts about the law and on evaluation, the evaluation involved is not a moral one, nor is it concerned with showing American law to best (moral) advantage. Rather, the evaluation concerns structural aspects of practical reasoning, and not its content (authority-related, content-independent justification of principles versus their direct, content-dependent justification). The evaluation is of what is important to our understanding of the processes shaping our social environment, for example, that the existence of social authorities is important, rather than of anything which shows them to be morally worthy.

dered in a country. But why pay such attention to these acts of legislation and adjudication? One reason is that one has to do so because we are concerned with the law, and whatever a coherence theory which has a different base may be a theory of, it is not a theory of law. Our common understanding of the law, that is, of "the law" when used in the relevant sense, is that it is intimately concerned with acts of legislation and adjudication. This is true, but it fails to answer the question. When I asked why we take these acts as the base, I did not mean to question that they are to be taken as the base. I asked about the significance of this fact. We take legislation as the base because of its centrality to the understanding of law and of the governance of human affairs by deliberate decisions of human institutions appointed to control and give direction to human conduct and to social change. An account of the law must explain the main features of the working of those institutions, for example, that they tend to generate a plurality of directives which cannot be readily fitted into a neat system. It must explain why they have these features. Coherence accounts take the base because it is too absurd to disregard it; then they strive to ignore it and to explain the law in a way which transcends the inherent limitations of the workings of human institutions, and by transcending them they misunderstand them.

V. Coherence in Adjudication

Some may feel that, so far, I have refrained from mentioning the most powerful case for coherence, that is, that courts have no alternative but to rely on coherence in deciding cases. The case is, one may say, a variant of the argument from the priority of the internal point of view. It says that even if ordinary citizens can have the internal point of view without seeing in the law a coherent whole, judges cannot do so. Their job requires them to apply a coherent body of principles. The argument about adjudication, however, cannot undermine our conclusions so far. I have argued not only that the advocates of the coherence thesis have failed to produce convincing arguments for their thesis, but also that it is false because it is inconsistent with the authority-based character of law. This argument establishes that the existence and content of statutes and binding precedents must be identified in relation to the intentions and reasons of legal institutions. The argument from adjudication must, and can, accommodate this conclusion. I will take the argument as advanced to support the Adjudicative Coherence thesis which claims:

> Given the law's settled rules and doctrines a court ought to adopt that solution to the case before it which is favored by the most coherent of the theories (i.e., set of propositions) which, were the settled rules of the system justified, would justify them.[36]

---

[36] It may have been simpler to say "statutes and binding precedents" instead of "settled rules and doctrines." But in order to accommodate legal systems which admit

The difference between the Adjudicative Coherence thesis and the extreme paradigm considered in the previous part is that the Adjudicative Coherence thesis assumes a way of establishing, free of coherence considerations, the content of the prima facie rights, duties, and powers created by law. Coherence comes into play at a later stage. Given that the law consists of many prima facie reasons, arising out of myriad pieces of legislation, rules and doctrines, including the common law and constitutional doctrines, the different prima facie legal reasons may, and often do, conflict. Coherence is invoked by the Adjudicative Coherence thesis to establish the relative ranking of the different prima facie reasons. By allowing for a coherence-independent identification of the settled law, the thesis is consistent with the argument from authority, which led to the rejection of the extreme paradigm. Considerations of authority are given their due in the first stage, in establishing what is the settled law. The resolution of the conflict among the prima facie reasons established by settled law is the province of coherence.

Some advocates of this thesis distinguish between a doctrine of law and a doctrine of adjudication. The law, they would say, consists of what I called the settled rules and doctrines.[37] The Adjudicative Coherence thesis is about how courts should decide cases. Its import is that they should follow the law where it applies, and should extend it according to its "spirit," as articulated by the most coherent theory which would justify the law were it justified. Others regard the thesis as being about the nature of law, on the ground, perhaps, that if it is true then courts never have discretion. They always are duty-bound to decide cases according to what the most coherent theory which justifies settled law requires. If the Adjudicative Coherence thesis is sound, then this latter view has much to recommend it. I will, however, refrain from engaging in this argument, as I suspect that the thesis is not sound.

How strong is the thesis meant to be? It can be read to state a necessary and sufficient condition for a judicial decision being correct. It can be seen as a comprehensive and complete theory of adjudication. Alternatively, it can be seen as advancing one desirable feature of judicial decisions only. It is possible to hold that while it is desirable that judicial decisions should accord with the most coherent theory, they are to be judged by other criteria as well. Given a multiplicity of criteria, it is possible that sometimes coherence has to be sacrificed for some other good. There is one powerful argument favoring the latter view. It appears that the relation "a more coherent theory than" is not connected, that is, various theories are neither more nor less coherent than each other. Various theories can equally account for the settled law without any of them being the most coherent one. If so, then it is

---

other sources of law, let us use the wider expression, understanding it to mean all those rules and doctrines to which the argument from authority applies.

[37] They include much more than what David Lyons called the explicit law. *See* David Lyons, *Moral Aspects of Legal Theory, in* 2 MIDWEST STUDIES IN PHILOSOPHY 223 (Peter A. French et al. eds., 1982).

reasonable to invoke other criteria for the guidance of courts, and to hold that coherence is but one of various considerations which make one outcome better or more correct, legally speaking, than any other. A natural suggestion is to add that of the theories among which coherence does not decide, that theory is to be preferred which is morally best.[38] But natural as this suggestion is, it is eminently resistible on reflection: Must moral merit be confined to being a tie breaker? It may be thought more plausible to make it another desired feature of the best theory of adjudication, so that one may prefer the morally better theory over the more coherent one, up to a limit. Given my doubts about the importance of coherence, I share the sympathies of those who prefer that option. Once this further step is taken the problem of underdetermination reappears, that is, there is no way of deciding which mix of coherence and other values is best.[39] I will consider the weaker of these interpretations of the Adjudicative Coherence thesis. That is, I will take it merely to indicate one desideratum in good judicial decisions. If this weaker theory is vindicated, one will have to consider the stronger thesis, giving it lexical priority over all other values, or even excluding all other values.

A number of arguments in support of this thesis can be culled from writings on coherence.[40] To consider them we have to understand clearly what it is they must show. The Adjudicative Coherence thesis applies to all judicial decisions. It applies to cases to which settled law provides a definite solution, and it instructs the court to adopt that solution. It also applies to cases

---

[38] It is possible that all the solutions recommended by all the theories which account for settled law and are not less coherent than any other theory which does so, are acceptable, and it is a toss up between them. But it is more plausible to expect that while quite possibly some cases may have various outcomes, all of which are acceptable with nothing to choose between them, some of the time there are other considerations which may break ties.

[39] For a criticism of Dworkin's theory which points out that it is caught in an analogous problem, see John M. Finnis, *On Reason and Authority in* Law's Empire, 6 LAW & PHIL. 357 (1987). Of course, the problem is not necessarily overwhelming for anyone who is willing to allow for underdetermination and for gaps in the law. But the matter requires further consideration which cannot be undertaken here, as we are not specifically concerned with problems of underdetermination.

[40] *See, e.g.*, NEIL MACCORMICK, LEGAL REASONING AND LEGAL THEORY chs. 7, 8 (H.L.A. Hart ed., 1978) (hereinafter LEGAL REASONING); Neil MacCormick, *Coherence in Legal Justification, in* THEORY OF LEGAL SCIENCE 235-51 (Aleksander Peczenik et al. eds., 1984); ROBERT ALEXY, A THEORY OF LEGAL ARGUMENTATION (Ruth Adler & Neil MacCormick trans., 1989); S.L. HURLEY, NATURAL REASONS, *supra* note 4, chs. 4, 10, 12; S.L. Hurley, *Coherence, Hypothetical Cases, and Precedent,* 10 OXFORD J. LEGAL STUD. 221, 222-26 (1990). As has been noted at the outset, the most influential writer on coherence in the law has been Ronald Dworkin who has developed a rich legal theory which is generally taken to be based on coherence. *See* DWORKIN, LAW'S EMPIRE, *supra* note 30. I will adapt some of his arguments in considering the Adjudicative Coherence thesis in this section and consider his own use of these arguments in the Appendix.

to which settled law fails to provide a definite answer. Plainly, the reason courts should follow settled law when it provides a definite solution has nothing to do with the merits of coherence. The Adjudicative Coherence thesis presupposes that settled law is to be followed, and extrapolates from this to other cases. The answer to the binding force of settled law derives from the doctrine of authority.[41] The Adjudicative Coherence thesis comes into its own where settled law does not provide a definite answer.[42] These are the cases on which we should concentrate.

Recall that we are assuming, for the sake of argument only, that sound moral and political principles form a strongly coherent theory. It follows that if the law is all that it should be, the Adjudicative Coherence thesis leads to the same results that the courts would reach if they were to disregard it and successfully follow sound moral and political principles, because those principles form a coherent set of which settled law is a part. Were we faced with such an ideal law, it would be difficult to determine whether the courts ought to decide according to the morally best outcome or to follow the Adjudicative Coherence thesis. Fortunately, no legal system is that perfect. Therefore, among other alternatives, the courts are faced with the question, "Should we adopt what would have been morally the best outcome had settled law not been imperfect, or should we follow the Adjudicative Coherence thesis, which may lead to an otherwise less than ideal solution in view of the imperfections of settled law?" The arguments I will canvass all support the second alternative.

A. The Argument from the Nature of Theory

THE ARGUMENT: No argument for the Adjudicative Coherence thesis is needed. It is simply an application to the law of the general maxim of rationality. Rational conflict resolution is simply the construction of the most coherent theory incorporating the settled cases.

REFUTATION: If anything hangs on the idea of constructing "a theory," then the argument begs the question. Perhaps the right way for courts to adjudicate does not involve any theory construction.[43] If the argument is that there is no method of rational reasoning other than maximizing coher-

---

[41] I have argued elsewhere that it is wrong to think that judges should always follow the law where its effect is definite. Their power may vary from one country to another, and their desirable power depends on complex factual issues such as the legal culture of the country concerned, the traditions of advocacy, and the qualifications of judges. But in all Common Law countries courts, both judges and juries, have a legally recognized discretion to refuse to enforce a clear law on grounds of equity, or because it violates fundamental constitutional doctrines. While this refutes the Adjudicative Coherence thesis, I will not pursue this matter here.

[42] Such cases are sometimes known as "hard cases," though they need not be hard at all. The best outcome in them may be evident to any right-minded person upon a moment's reflection.

[43] This indeed is my view.

ence, it begs the question in another way. It assumes that there is a general method of rational argument, or of rational thought. But there is no general method of rationality in the sciences or in daily reasoning. We use whole congeries of methods and rules of reasoning and inference, almost entirely unawares. Nor are they constant fixtures of rationality. We learn to discard some, and we acquire others. And so do science and other areas of human endeavor through their history. If, given the state of our knowledge, legal adjudication should be governed by the one method of Adjudicative Coherence, then there must be specific reasons to explain why this is so.

B. *The Argument from Analogy*

THE ARGUMENT: This is exactly what adjudication is like. It requires no argument, looking only at the facts. The facts are that courts always rely on analogies, and analogies are an informal way of describing the process of establishing coherence between previous decisions and the current one.

REFUTATION (or perhaps I should call it a deflection): The view of analogy presupposed in the argument is correct.[44] But the conclusion does not follow from the very reliance on analogy. First, while use of analogy is a common feature of common law jurisdictions, there is no evidence that it is universal, let alone necessary, in all legal systems. Second, reliance on analogy in common law countries is too unsystematic and unreliable in effect. The apparently random effects of resort to analogy have often been used as evidence that courts do what they like, and use arguments from analogy as a fig leaf, because one can use analogy of one kind or another to vindicate any possibly supportable conclusion.[45] None of this shows that reliance on analogy is humbug. But it does mean that the apparent facts do not speak for themselves. One needs an account of the rationale of argument by analogy. Although coherence accounts offer one such rationale, it is not the only one available.[46] Moreover, analogies are always partial and local. The Adjudicative Coherence thesis is global and speaks of coherence with the totality of settled law. No direct support for any such practice can be gleaned from simply noticing the facts of judicial practice. One needs a theoretical argument to support one understanding of them or another, and we are yet to find one leading to the Adjudicative Coherence thesis.

C. *The Argument from Fairness*

THE ARGUMENT: A principle of formal justice requires treating like cases alike and different cases differently. Treating certain people one way, under settled law, and others, in like situations, in some other way is unjust

---

[44] On the analysis of analogies, see MacCormick, Legal Reasoning, *supra* note 40, and Raz, The Authority of Law, *supra* note 6, ch. 10.

[45] *See, e.g.*, Julius Stone, Legal System and Lawyers' Reasoning (1964).

[46] I will discuss several alternatives below.

to them. The Adjudicative Coherence thesis establishes a baseline of similarity, so that treating people who are alike, in its terms, differently is unjust. REFUTATION: The weakness of the argument is evident. The question is why should the Adjudicative Coherence thesis provide the baseline for the application of the principle of formal justice (if there is such a principle). Surely there could be some other baseline, and what we need is a reason to prefer this one to others. That the argument does not provide. Instead, it betrays a misunderstanding of the nature of formal justice. Given that it can be satisfied by any baseline, and that the choice of the correct baseline requires independent justification, formal justice itself cannot help in justifying any principle of action. Its effect is confined to condemning arbitrary deviations from principles which are otherwise justified.[47]

D. The Argument from Authority

THE ARGUMENT: In a way, the duty to follow (an imperfect) settled law is itself an example of justified deviation from doing what would be right had settled law not been imperfect. Following the most coherent theory which leads to all the same decisions as settled law leads to is no more a deviation than that. It requires no more than following the spirit of the law, or the implicit law, just as the duty to follow settled law requires following the letter of the law, or explicit law. Both flow from the duty of obedience to legitimate authority.

REFUTATION: Could the argument be based on a misunderstanding of the nature of authority? Authoritative directives bind because they are actually promulgated by authority. A principle cannot be authoritatively binding because of abstract arguments. It must arise out of actual human or institutional actions. Of course, one can direct implicitly as well as explicitly. But one has to direct for there to be directives to obey. Because settled law includes all the law issued by authority, implicitly and explicitly, the Adjudicative Coherence thesis cannot apply outside settled law on grounds of obeying authority.

But there is another way of reading the argument. It can be seen as a denial that there is anything which falls outside settled law, if settled law is understood broadly to include implicit law. For it can be seen to argue that implicit law always includes all that is required by the Adjudicative Coherence thesis. The thesis is simply a way of working out the (implied) meaning of authoritative actions. But if so, then the argument is misguided. Different legal institutions at different times pursue different goals; the implications of their activities are as numerous, diverse, and lacking in coherence as their explicit directives. There is no spirit to the law, only different spirits to

---

[47] The argument from fairness is supported by MacCormick. Dworkin introduces it as an independent argument only to relegate it to a consequence of his argument from integrity, which will be considered below. See DWORKIN, LAW'S EMPIRE, *supra* note 30, at 165-67.

different laws or bodies of law. Working out the implications of the law on the assumption that all of it was promulgated in pursuit of one set of principles is to be false to the spirit of all of the bodies which enjoy legal authority, and cannot be justified as an obligation of obedience to their authority.

E. The Argument from Loyalty to the Community

THE ARGUMENT: Perhaps I should have called it the argument from integrity, for I have in mind Dworkin's argument.[48] But, as I am using it to support the Adjudicative Coherence thesis rather than Dworkin's own view of adjudication, it is best to give it a different name.[49] The demise of the argument from authority makes the justification of the Adjudicative Coherence thesis much more difficult. The problem we face is how the existence of a less than perfect settled law justifies deviating from what is otherwise morally best. The authority argument amounts to saying that we are not really deviating from the best that we can do. Rather, our limitations and the limitations of political practices make following the authority the best approximation of doing the best which is open to us.[50] Barring this justification, however, how can the existence of less than perfect settled law justify (even if prima facie only) doing less than the best in cases to which settled law provides no definite solution? The answer must be that such deviations from what would otherwise be best are justified, because they manifest a distinct virtue which is brought into play precisely by the existence of a less than perfect settled law.

This is precisely what Dworkin claims to have established. He argues that in all but degenerate legal systems, one has an obligation to obey the law. Legal systems, he implies, are constitutive elements of political communities. Therefore, membership in a political community entails an obligation to obey the law. Moreover, he argues that the features which make communities genuine political communities ensure them a character which makes membership in them intrinsically valuable. Those features entail the doctrine of law as integrity. Here, I am not concerned with all aspects of Dworkin's views on Law as Integrity. Instead, I will consider the claim that genuine political communities have a character which yields the Adjudicative Coherence thesis (a thesis which is, arguably, an aspect of the law as integrity doctrine). Naturally, this consideration cannot be regarded as an

---

[48] See DWORKIN, LAW'S EMPIRE, supra note 30, at chs. 6, 7.

[49] One may also doubt whether Dworkin's argument has anything to do with integrity. Dworkin's integrity comes into play when people or communities fall short of the requirements of justice and fairness. It is the virtue of sticking by principles which "justify" one's past actions, however misguided they were, even though such principles fall short in justice and fairness. See id. at 176-77. It is doubtful whether any of this is true of the virtue of personal or institutional integrity.

[50] For a detailed argument that authority is justified only when this is so, see RAZ, supra note 6.

examination of Dworkin's own views, though my conclusions may be transferable to a consideration of his writings.

"Political association, like family and friendship and other forms of association more local and intimate, is in itself pregnant of obligation."[51] Membership in a society is a good in itself, and the duty to obey the law is part and parcel of membership. There can be no doubt that membership in decent political communities is valuable, both instrumentally and intrinsically.[52] The question is what this tells us about the law. The argument from loyalty makes four claims: First, membership in a genuine political community carries with it an obligation to obey the law, because the law is the organized voice of the community. Second, this presupposes personifying the law, regarding it as a separate person, which means, of course, that the law does not speak for any of the institutions which create it and administer it, nor for the social groups which dominate and direct them; rather, the law speaks in its own voice, which differs from theirs. Third, this independent voice is an extrapolation from actual decisions. Fourth, this extrapolation is the one described by the Adjudicative Coherence thesis. All four stages are necessary to the argument, for it is people's relation with their community which explains the obligation to obey the law, and it is the fact that the law is an aspect of the community which forces one to accept its personification. The personification in turn leads to the need to disregard, to transcend, as one may say, the political vagaries reflected in the law. This is achieved, and here I turn Dworkin's argument away from its original target and toward ours, by embracing the Adjudicative Coherence thesis.

REFUTATION: The argument touches on more issues than can be adequately handled here. I will comment briefly on each of the points. First, we should beware of a tendency to over-intellectualize the implications of membership in national groups. It is primarily a matter of socialization, which is a major factor giving content to and setting the limits of one's options and capabilities on the one hand, and of one's imagination, affection, tastes and ambitions on the other hand. National groups vary in character.

---

[51] DWORKIN, LAW'S EMPIRE, *supra* note 30, at 206. At times Dworkin appears to say that the existence of such a duty as an element of membership in what he calls "political communities" is clear and beyond dispute. *See, e.g., id.* at 208. But as it is in fact very much disputed by philosophers and non-philosophers alike, and as he offers no arguments in support of his position, I will disregard these claims.

[52] On the notion of a decent society, see AVISHAI MARGALIT, THE DECENT SOCIETY (forthcoming). We need not consider here whether Dworkin's description of what makes a community a genuine moral one is adequate to what I called a decent society. More relevant to our purpose is the question whether only degenerate societies fail to be decent societies, or at least approximately decent ones. If, as some would argue, most human societies to date fail this test, if most of them are such that their members (ought to) feel shame in their societies and guilt by association for their character and actions, then there is little we can learn about the law in general from the notion of an approximately decent society. For law exists in all political societies, decent or otherwise, and those which fail the test of decency cannot be dismissed as occasional deviations from the norm.

Most of them are nonideological in the sense that membership in them does not require adherence to any religion or morality.[53] Some, however, are ideological. One cannot be a member of those (assuming membership to be morally permissible) without being bound by the duties their ideology imposes. It is less clear whether membership in other societies imposes any additional moral duties. To be sure, living in one's own country concretizes many universal duties in ways which direct one toward one's society: one should contribute to its services, to the support of its members (though not only to them) who require assistance, and so on. When one is visiting a different country, however, those duties are directed toward that society and its members.

Does membership impose duties which are not so contingent, that is, which are really essential to membership in national communities?[54] I believe that there are such duties. They appear to me to derive from one's own identification with certain groups and communities.[55] It does not follow, however, that membership in a community carries a special obligation to obey the law. Dworkin bases his claim to the contrary on his view that the law is a constitutive aspect of the community. This view is difficult to assess. Communities are constituted by social practices, and there is no reason to think that they are all constituted by similar practices. It is clear that the relations between the polity and the law vary from place to place and from time to time. Today, in many countries, we are used to associating the law with the state, though some believe, and many hope, that the development of supernational organizations portends a decline in that identification in the future. In Britain, for example, where there are several legal systems (notably the English and the Scottish) in one country, the association has never been very strong. Perhaps for the Scots, their law is an important aspect of their Scottish identity (though not of their British identity). For the English, things are very different. Many in the middle classes regard the Common Law and its judicial institutions as part of the English genius. Statutory law and Parliament, however, are a different matter. Moreover, working class English people have traditionally felt that the law is not theirs but that of the upper classes.

---

[53] For a more extensive discussion of membership, see Avishai Margalit & Joseph Raz, *National Self-Determination*, 87 J. PHIL. 439 (1990).

[54] The question is not whether such duties will or will not be universalizable. I take it for granted that they all are. The question is whether they are such as to be undetachable from membership in a national society, rather than those which are addressed toward one's national community simply because one happens to reside there at the time, or due to other contingencies which can change without change of membership.

[55] Identification does not mean willing endorsement. It means one's self-understanding of who one is. People can see themselves as Jews, or Moslems, or as academic types, and so on, while hating themselves and/or Judaism or Islam or academic types generally, and that hate may be fueled precisely because their identification with the group, or type, is hateful for them.

More generally, in many subcultures a fierce sense of national pride and loyalty (not always expressing itself in admirable forms: football hooligans tend to be fiercely nationalistic) accompanies a lack of any sense of obligation to obey the law, and often a high degree of lawlessness without guilt feelings. While these are empirical observations, the claim about what accompanies membership in certain communities should be regarded as subject to empirical examination.[56] As a general claim about political communities, however, it is mistaken.

The second limb of the argument, that the law should not be regarded as a simple function of the aims and actions of the people engaged in shaping it, is clearly true. It is true simply because the law is the product of such complex interactions between so many individuals that, as we were taught by students of collective action, it is idle to think that its content can correspond to the beliefs or goals of any of the people who contribute to its creation and administration. Notice, however, that this argument for the personification of law has nothing to do with any moral value that it, or the society of which it is the law, possesses. There is no moral argument for personification. Dworkin rests his claim to the contrary on the fact that integrity presupposes personification, and that there is a (partially moral) argument for integrity.[57] Before turning to this point, however, let me pause to agree with the third proposition in the argument from loyalty—that the independent voice is an extrapolation from previous decisions. As I argued in the previous part, the fact that the law claims authority requires regarding its content as a function of the activities, aims and beliefs of the legal institutions with authority to fashion it. The question is why should its content be extrapolated from their activities in accordance with the Adjudicative Coherence thesis?

The answer is that we recognize, as a distinct virtue of communities, that the government is required "to speak with one voice, to act in a principled and coherent manner toward all its citizens. . . ."[58] This involves two principles: "a legislative principle, which asks lawmakers to try to make the total set of laws morally coherent, and an adjudicative principle, which instructs that the law be seen as coherent in that way, so far as possible."[59] It is this second principle which is our concern, as it is the one which governs adjudication, and (partially) determines the content of the law (it determines the "grounds of law" as Dworkin says[60]).

---

[56] Dworkin regards it, I assume, as an interpretive claim. But that leaves it subject to the sort of empirical considerations I adduced.

[57] See DWORKIN, LAW'S EMPIRE, *supra* note 30, at 187-88 ("We must not say that integrity is a special virtue of politics because the state or community is a distinct entity, but that community should be seen as a distinct moral agent because the social and intellectual practices that treat community in this way should be protected.").

[58] *Id.* at 165.

[59] *Id.* at 176.

[60] *See id.* at 110.

The notion of "speaking with one voice" is taken by Dworkin to require coherence. But why should it? We can readily see that a person who is contradicting himself, saying and unsaying the same thing, is not "speaking with one voice." Is there anything more to "speaking with one voice" than consistency? It seems that one speaks with one voice if one is saying, or promulgating as law, what could be said or made into law by a single person who does not act randomly and who does not change his mind. "Speaking with one voice" can be understood as a metaphor for these two conditions. It can also be understood to include a third condition, the "no-compromise" condition. I speak or legislate with one voice if I say or enact what I think is in its content best, given the conditions of the society to which my legislation applies. I do not speak with one voice if, in order to secure a majority in the legislature, or to avoid a presidential veto, or to secure re-election, or for other similar reasons, I compromise what I say or enact in order to secure the agreement or lessen the opposition of people whose views I regard as mistaken. Unless otherwise indicated, I will use "speaking with one voice" to express all three conditions. Should adjudication be guided by the ideal of speaking with one voice, thus understood? And, if so, does this vindicate the requirement of coherence in adjudication?

This last question will be taken up in the Appendix. Let us now confront the first, more fundamental issue. Should adjudication be conducted on the assumption that the law speaks with one voice? Ideally, the law should speak with one voice. That much follows from the fact that it should be just and fair, and, in general, morally ideal. It cannot be morally ideal if it is random or reflects changes of mind or compromises with people whose views are wrong. This does not entail, of course, that speaking with one voice is something desirable in itself. It may be simply the by-product of what is correct and sound. But possibly being random is a distinctive way of going wrong. We need not adjudicate such questions here.[61] The problem is that we know that it is in fact unlikely, to engage in hyperbolic understatement, that the law is just and fair and morally correct in all respects. Given that the law falls short of the mark, should the courts decide cases as would be right were it up to the mark? Should they decide cases as if the law is morally correct, even though it is not? In the politics of this imperfect world we know that imposing one voice on the law can be achieved—if at all—only through the imposition of a regime with an inherent tendency to sacrifice justice and fairness, restrict civil rights, and curtail individual freedom. We therefore design constitutional processes to foster compromises in a way which we hope will approximate the ideal.

Compromises take various forms. On the one hand, we accept as normal the persistence of laws passed by the previous government, even when a new, more morally sound government comes into power. There is a strong body of opinion, both lay and academic, in Britain, for example, which regards it

---

[61] I suspect, however, that reaching a compromise with people with wrong views or changing one's mind are not in themselves distinctive ways of going wrong.

as highly objectionable for either Conservative or Labour governments to overturn all the principled legislative innovations introduced by their predecessors in government. Another way in which we regard compromise as acceptable is in passing legislation which does not answer to the principles of any particular section of the population, but meets various of them halfway. To give examples of a similar, yet not exactly the same, kind let me confess that I do not believe that mothers have a right to maternity leave. I believe that, aside from what is required by the pregnant woman/mother for health reasons, either parent (at their discretion) or both should have it. But I am willing to accept existing arrangements as the best that can be expected at present. I believe that the right to marry should not be confined to marrying a person of the opposite sex, and that gay men and lesbians should not be denied the opportunity to adopt and to foster children. Again, while I regard present arrangements as unsound in principle, I accept them as the best that can be hoped for for the time being.

In all these cases we accept the nearest approximation to morally sound solutions that we can obtain, even though by doing so we may reduce the coherence of the law. We make no concession to any alleged principle about speaking with one voice. Nobody who cannot have a whole loaf refuses, on principle, half of one.[62] This is precisely what the Adjudicative Coherence thesis asks one to do with respect to adjudication. I do not mean to suggest that courts should themselves engage in direct political compromises. The question cannot be answered in the abstract because the role of the judiciary varies from country to country, and from time to time. In general, I would simply say that courts should adopt the most morally sound outcome. The question remains, however, whether they should deviate from what is otherwise the morally preferable solution on the ground that, in the past, less than satisfactory rules have been adopted, even though those rules do not apply to the case before them. In other words, should they deviate from what is otherwise the best solution in order to make the law speak with one voice? We must bear in mind the following important point: so that the law might speak with one voice, the thesis requires a court, say the High Court in Britain, to extend a precedent which it regards as misguided in principle, but cannot overturn in the instant case (either because the precedent has the authority of the House of Lords, or because given the cause of action before it the court has no jurisdiction to overrule those principles to which it objects), even though the doctrine of precedent does not bind the court to follow the objectionable precedent. Of course, sometimes it would be unjust to treat some people worse than others are treated, even if those others do not deserve the relatively favorable treatment they receive. Hence, if an unsatisfactory rule benefits some people this may be a reason for extending the benefit to other people, even though neither group deserves it. Sometimes, therefore, such considerations will weigh against replacing the unsat-

---

[62] They may do so on tactical grounds, for example as a means of forcing the rest of the population to concede their full case.

isfactory rule with a better one. But this is so only where special circumstances exist. Such circumstances are unlikely to exist, for example, when specified individuals will have to suffer in order to secure a benefit to those not entitled to it.[63]

In sum, no principle of speaking with one voice has any validity as a general principle of law or of adjudication.[64] It is not necessary in order to regard the national society or membership in it as valuable, nor is it necessary in order to regard the national society as a distinct entity, not reducible to its members. Speaking with one voice is a by-product of an ideal situation. In an ideal world, because morality is properly applied and morality speaks with one voice, so does the law. But it is not an independent ideal with the moral force to lead us to endorse solutions less just than they need be. Without it we are left with no reason to support the Adjudicative Coherence thesis.

VI. The Relevance of Coherence

The critical character of the discussion so far should not be seen as a sign

---

[63] McLoughlin v. O'Brian, 1 App. Cas. 410 (1983) is a case in point. In this case, the defendants objected to the payment of compensation to a woman who suffered nervous shock. Those who object to compensation for nervous shock would be happy to leave an anomalous exception allowing compensation for a shock caused at the scene of accident at the time or immediately after it. Ideally, they would like to overturn that rule. But if they cannot they would not regard its existence as a reason for extending it further to shock caused away from the accident. To extend it you must believe in its soundness, rather than in the need for the law to speak with one voice.

[64] It could be argued that in some countries, given their constitutional arrangement, the best implementation of a separation of powers doctrine requires judges to act on the Adjudicative Coherence thesis. It could be said, for example, that in the conditions of that country courts will forfeit their legitimacy if they attempt to apply considerations of justice and fairness. Therefore, it will be suggested, they should follow coherence simply because doing so keeps them away from attempting to follow moral and political considerations.

While the structure of the argument is sound and the need to minimize reliance on moral and political considerations by the courts may be important in some countries, it seems to me unlikely to lead to coherence doctrines because coherence does not provide courts with determinate guidance, as this argument requires. Due to pervasive incommensurabilities among values, many incompatible lines of reasoning are equally coherent with the rest of the law. This makes coherence an unsatisfactory guide to courts if the problem is finding a determinate and value-free guide. For a discussion of this problem, see John M. Finnis, *Natural Law and Legal Reasoning*, 38 CLEV. ST. L. REV. 1, 7 (1990), and Finnis, *On Reason and Authority in* Law's Empire, *supra* note 39. On incommensurability in general, see RAZ, THE MORALITY OF FREEDOM, *supra* note 32, at ch. 13.

It is also worth noting that coherence is in fact very difficult to establish. It requires intellectual capacities, formal training, and a command of information about the law generally that is in excess of what is needed to reach decent decisions on most moral issues facing the courts.

that I do not see a role for coherence in the law. In conclusion I will mention three reasons for valuing coherence in the law. The coherence I will speak in favor of is local coherence: coherence of doctrine in specific fields.[65] The coherence-based explanations to which I objected are global coherence accounts. They impose coherence on the whole of the law. They seem to me to err in two important ways, and these considerations underlie the discussion in the preceding parts. First, and this point must remain in the background for it cannot be explored in this Article, global coherence accounts underestimate the degree and implications of value pluralism, the degree to which morality itself is not a system but a plurality of irreducibly independent principles. Second, and this has been the main lesson of the arguments above, they are attempts to idealize the law out of the concreteness of politics. The reality of politics leaves the law untidy. Coherence is an attempt to prettify it and minimize the effect of politics. But, in countries with decent constitutions, the untidiness of politics is morally sanctioned. It is sanctioned by the morality of authoritative institutions. There is no reason to minimize its effects, nor to impose on the courts duties which lead them to be less just than they can be.[66]

Where does coherence come in? The first point to bear in mind is that value pluralism does not mean incoherence. Sound moral principles are consistent, and should be consistently applied in the law. The coherence to which value pluralism is hostile is the felt need, to which moral philosophers seem to be professionally prone, to subsume the plurality of values under as few as possible supreme principles. While these attempts ought to be resisted, we must recognize that the application of each of the distinct values ought to be consistently pursued, and this generates pockets of coherence which exist, or should exist, where the law should reflect one overriding moral or evaluative concern. Two examples of such cases are the doctrines concerning the mental conditions of criminal responsibility and those which establish fault in private law, where fault is a condition of a duty of reparation. Morality recognizes mental conditions for responsible agency and also separates conditions which render the agent guilty from those which make him liable to a duty of reparation (in some circumstances I ought to apologize and help someone I hurt by accident, even though I am not guilty and do not deserve punishment). The law ought to incorporate these precepts in

---

[65] For an instructive account giving coherence a limited role in reasoning, see Barbara B. Levenbook, *The Role of Coherence in Legal Reasoning*, 3 LAW & PHIL. 355 (1984).

[66] While I am not advocating courts which are fully involved in political decisions on the same footing as legislatures, the nature of their task requires them to be somewhat political (in the wider meaning of the word). The form and manner of their political involvement, however, should be sensitive to the methods of recruitment to the courts, the qualifications and terms of tenure of judges, the nature of other political institutions, and—most importantly—the political culture of the country at the time. There is little of general principle that can be said. What was true of the United States in the mid-19th century is not true of the Unites States today.

its doctrines of criminal and civil liability, and we can expect it to develop a coherent body of doctrine deriving from the consistent application of the moral doctrines to the complex factual situations which confront the courts, taking into account the institutional setting of their application.

Three features distinguish this type of case from the other two to which coherence is also relevant and which are discussed below. First, coherence is not here an independent consideration, not something to be pursued for its own sake. It is a mere by-product of the consistent application of a sound moral doctrine. Second, I am tempted to say that the moral doctrine of responsibility is a pure one, that is, it does not reflect the outcome of a conflict of competing values and rival concerns. This may be an exaggeration, but it is true if qualified somewhat by saying "in the main" or "as applied under normal circumstances," or some other moderating qualification. In the main, the moral doctrines of the personal conditions of responsibility do not involve settling conflicts between competing values, or other legitimate concerns. This is a type of case to which value pluralism is largely irrelevant. Finally, this type of case illustrates coherence as applying equally to legislation and adjudication.

Perhaps in this last respect the contrast between my first type of case where coherence is relevant in the law and the others is only a matter of degree. In the first case, in common law countries, doctrines of responsibility are primarily developed by the courts, legislation having a subsidiary role. The other two cases also apply to legislation as well as to adjudication, differing only in their special pertinence in common law adjudication. Both, however, are cases in which coherence becomes an independent (though not ultimate) consideration, and is no mere by-product. Each of them arises out of one of the two types of value and moral pluralism: pluralism in the sense in which a society is pluralistic when there is wide divergence of views in it regarding value and moral issues (at most one of which is true or sound, the others being mistaken); and pluralism in the sense that morality is pluralistic if it (truly or correctly) asserts the validity of a plurality of irreducibly distinctive and competing values.

Social pluralism, that is, the existence of a plurality of inconsistent views on moral, religious, social and political issues in democratic (and in many other) societies, is likely to be reflected in a society's law. That is, it is likely to lead to legal rules and principles being in force reflecting the different outlooks of the people who fashioned them. This may lead the courts (and legislatures) to a dilemma. A court may be faced with a case in which it can, in principle, embrace a ruling which is morally best. Because the law on related matters was developed by people with misguided ideas, however, embracing the morally best rule may lead to bad consequences. That is, it may lead to the existence of different rules pushing in different directions, encouraging conflicting social and economic conditions. Thus, the actual consequences of embracing the (otherwise) morally best ruling may be far from ideal. Indeed, there may be a less than ideal alternative ruling which, if adopted, would have better social and economic consequences for as long as the other misguided rules remain in force.

When a problem of this kind faces the legislature it can simply revoke the bad rules, replacing them with better ones. The legislature can, in principle, opt for a comprehensive reform. The courts have fewer opportunities to do so. Given the cause of action in the instant case, for example protected tenancy, they may be unable to revise other laws (e.g. tax laws) which promote opposing social consequences. Even the legislature, empowered though it is to adopt comprehensive reform, may find it politically inexpedient to do so. In such cases, both courts and legislatures are faced by what I term "the dilemma of partial reform."[67] They have to decide whether compromising and choosing the morally second best rule which has better conse ,lences is best in the circumstances, or whether it is more important to let the law speak clearly and soundly on a moral issue, and hope that an occasion to extend the correct ruling to other cases will arise and be followed before long. This conflict is a conflict between coherence of purpose[68] and uncompromising pursuit of the morally correct line. Depending on the circumstances, it will be best to go one way on some occasions and the other way on others. In such circumstances we see pluralism[69] generating the dilemma of partial reform, and giving a local and limited value to coherence.

Finally, the third reason for local coherence. It derives from the way moral pluralism gives coherence (non-ultimate) value. Moral pluralism means that various irreducibly distinct and competing values are valid. It leads to conflict as a permanent moral state, arising not because of moral disagreement and mistakes but as an inescapable aspect of sound morality. Moral pluralism means that conflict is not a result of any imperfection, but is the normal state for human beings. Furthermore, most of the time, "the correct way of balancing the competing values" does not exist. More precisely, on many occasions there is a whole range of ways of mixing the different values, none of which is superior to the others.[70] In such situations there is no moral objection to adopting any of the mixes which are not ruled out as inferior. People simply do what they like, choosing in accordance with their personal taste. Where many people are involved, the ability to achieve any of the not-ruled-out possibilities may depend on social coordination, that is, on its adoption as a rule for this society. Hence the permanent state of conflict between opera lovers and sport lovers, puritans and hedonists, and so on, over collective decisions.

Legislatures may be required to strive toward some equitable resolution of such disputes, allowing those who share each taste opportunities to satisfy it.

---

[67] *See* RAZ, THE AUTHORITY OF LAW, *supra* note 6, at 200-01.

[68] *See id.* at 200-06.

[69] I highlight the role of social pluralism here, but the same problems can arise because of previous mistakes of like-minded judges or legislatures.

[70] *See* RAZ, THE MORALITY OF FREEDOM, *supra* note 32, at ch. 13; Joseph Raz, *Mixing Values*, 65 THE ARISTOTELIAN SOC'Y 83 (supp. 1991).

That means legislatures should give weight to numbers, and decide on equitable distribution, through zoning or other measures. Even after such considerations are exhausted, there still remain many mixes of values which are not inferior to any alternative. It comes down to choice. Courts may reach situations of choice even more quickly than legislatures, because their institutional ability to reach sensible judgments on equitable distributions and their jurisdiction to put them into effect are much more limited. Either way, moral pluralism leads to the permanence of conflict and to occasions in which social policies are adopted by choice rather than reason.[71] In these instances, it is important to adhere to a policy once it is chosen.[72] There are two reasons for this. First, adhering to the chosen solution is necessary for it to work in all cases where its benefits depend on social coordination. It is often also necessary for the efficient operation of bureaucratic institutions. Where a person can decide one way one day and the opposite way the following day (in matters in which there is no overriding reason to decide one way or the other), an institution may well be thrown into considerable confusion and chaos if it is allowed to do so. Second, ordinary rule of law considerations come into play. Only by adhering to one coherent policy can the law be made widely known and its application predictable.

Thus, this is another context in which coherence comes into its own, another context in which precedent acquires a natural force, where there is reason to follow it even in countries which do not have a formal doctrine of precedent.[73] Coherence, as we saw in the previous part, forces one to decide in a certain way because past decisions are of a certain character. Coherence gives weight to the actual past, to the concrete history of the law. The burden of the argument of the previous part is that there is no general reason of coherence which applies to the settlement of all cases. The consideration of moral pluralism shows, however, that local coherence is, because of moral pluralism, of great importance. I call it local coherence because there are many isolated decisions which amount to an unconstrained choice between

---

[71] This does not mean that these choices are either arbitrary or unreasoned. They are not unreasoned because they are taken for the reasons which support that policy. Reason only fails to provide sufficient argument to prefer this policy over all alternatives. That is where choice comes in. They are not arbitrary for it is only arbitrary to disregard reason. That is, where reason dominates one can be arbitrary; where there is none it is not arbitrary to choose in accordance with one's wish or taste (is it arbitrary to choose a peach rather than an apricot when offered one or the other?).

[72] I do not mean that it should never change, only that it should not be changed too frequently.

[73] Formal rules of precedent, like the English rule that all the courts (other than the House of Lords itself) are bound by the ratio decidendi of the House of Lords, give precedent a force similar to that of legislation, i.e. within the scope of the rule laid down in the ratio of the binding decision. The natural force of precedent which does not depend on any formal doctrine is not so limited. It works through considerations of coherence of purpose, and applies outside the scope of the rule enunciated in the precedent-setting decision, so long as coherence considerations require that.

different possible compromises between conflicting values. There is no reason to lump all these compromises together as one decision covering all cases, and I suspect that the very attempt is incoherent. Societies are faced with numerous discrete issues of conflict, and decide on solutions to them as they arise. Each solution gives rise to considerations of coherence within its scope, based on the need to secure coordination and on rule of law values.

In this schematic discussion it is impossible to analyze conflict cases in detail. It is important, however, to note in conclusion how pervasive they are. They include issues of the allocation of resources to public amenities; regulation of the character of the natural and human environment (noise as well as river pollution); constitutional rights adjudication, such as the balance between the interest of people in being able to express their views and being heard and the interest of the same or other people in being able not to listen and not being made to hear unless they want to; and the allocation of liability to risk and its imposition on others, as in rules which determine what forms of conduct are negligent and what standards of care people are required to observe. These are but a few examples of the pervasiveness of choice-demanding conflicts. Therefore, they are also examples of the pervasiveness of the force of localized coherence considerations.

Coherence, one might say, is everywhere. But it is local rather than global coherence, and it comes into its own mostly once questions of principle (including questions of resolving conflicts of value where they are resolvable by reason) are resolved on other grounds.

APPENDIX
SPEAKING WITH ONE VOICE:
ON DWORKINIAN INTEGRITY AND COHERENCE

It is impossible to miss the ambivalent interpretation of Ronald Dworkin's work in this Article. On the one hand, it is regarded as one of the main springs of the interest in coherence theories in the law, and the argument from integrity has been examined as the most promising argument for a coherence account of the law. On the other hand, I dissociated Dworkin from this use of the argument, and warned the reader not to assume too hastily that Dworkin does see coherence as important. My ambivalent attitude stems from Dworkin's less than clear discussion of these subjects. In this Appendix, I will examine his attitude toward coherence as revealed by the central chapters of *Law's Empire*. The interest in doing so is not merely an interest in understanding Dworkin. Part IV of this Article included a refutation of the suggestion that there is a distinct virtue of coherence through loyalty to the past which justifies deviating from the precepts of justice and fairness. I will suggest below that Dworkin's view of law as integrity is subject to the same criticism independently of whether it does favor coherence. This shows that the argument deployed in the text catches theories other than coherence theories. It applies to any idealizations of the law which diminish the importance of the doctrine of authority and the role of politics in its explanation. It is an objection of principle to any doctrine which requires the courts to adjudicate disputes on the assumption that the law speaks with one voice, regardless of whether this univocality expresses itself through a doctrine of coherence or in some other way.

For Dworkin, explaining the nature of law is offering an interpretation of the law. This is not the place to assess his view of the nature and role of interpretation. I merely want to discover the way it does or does not interact with considerations of coherence. The ambivalence begins at the beginning. At the most basic level, Dworkin explains interpretation as follows: "constructive interpretation [of which the interpretation of the law is an instance] is a matter of imposing purpose on an object or practice in order to make of it the best possible example of the form or genre to which it is taken to belong."[74] Here, interpretation is defined in terms of strong monistic coherence. Coherence, as we know, means close systematic interdependence of all the parts. Seemingly, Dworkinian interpretation is conceived from the start as committed to strong monism, for it is committed to finding *one* purpose which unites and dominates all the parts of the interpreted object or practice (dominates, for in the post-interpretive stage,[75] what the practice requires is adjusted to suit the imposed purpose).

But is it right to attribute to Dworkin this commitment (which is never justified even by a shadow of an argument) to strong coherence? Perhaps his

---

[74] DWORKIN, LAW'S EMPIRE, *supra* note 30, at 52.
[75] *See id.* at 66.

reference to one purpose is simply a *façon de parler*; perhaps Dworkin is willing to contemplate a plurality of unrelated purposes imposed by the interpretation, which shows whatever is interpreted as being the best of its kind. In the more detailed general description of interpretation, he writes of "some general justification" for the practice.[76] A general justification can be monistic, exhibiting a high degree of coherence, but it need not be. It may be of any degree of coherence down to pluralistic justifications by a plurality of unrelated elements. The evidence is ambiguous, tending on balance to support an unargued-for endorsement of monistic coherence when the interpretation of social practices is concerned.[77]

The tendency toward strong coherence seems to reappear when Dworkin introduces integrity:

> "It will be useful to divide the claims of integrity into two more practical principles. The first is the principle of integrity in legislation, which asks those who create law by legislation to keep that law coherent in principle. The second is the principle of integrity in adjudication: it asks those responsible for deciding what the law is to see and enforce it as coherent in that way."[78]

Dworkin's first principle is to guide legislators in making law. My concern is with the second principle, which determines both how cases are to be decided and what the law is, because, according to Dworkin, these two question are one and the same. How the courts should determine the law is far from clear from this statement. What stands out is the duty to see the law as coherent. But does the principle as stated really express an endorsement of coherence? It seems to do so because the word appears in its formulation. We know, however, that coherence is often used to indicate no more than the cogency or even the intelligibility of a principle or an idea. Which way does Dworkin mean to use it? Dworkin's earlier discussion of interpretation, which, to be any good, must be understood to lead to a strongly, monistically coherent view of interpretation, suggests that he means something similar here.

But does he? A few pages later he states (discussing integrity in legislation): "Integrity is flouted . . . whenever a community enacts and enforces different laws each of which is coherent in itself, but which cannot be defended together as expressing a coherent ranking of different principles of justice or fairness or procedural due process."[79] There is no trace of one point or purpose here. The degree of coherence is much less; it is merely that of ranking a plurality of irreducibly distinct principles of justice and fairness. This is still a commitment to a greater degree of coherence than

---

[76] *Id.*

[77] For several additional references to one purpose in *Law's Empire*, see *id.* at 67, 87, 94, 98. Other locutions, however, are more open to pluralistic justifications.

[78] *Id.* at 167.

[79] *Id.* at 184.

exists, given that, in fact, such principles are not rankable. My purpose is simply to point out the difficulty in attributing any definite view on coherence to Dworkin.

When Dworkin turns from integrity in legislation to his explanation of law as based on integrity, coherence simply drops, quietly and without comment, out of the picture: "According to law as integrity, propositions of law are true if they figure in or follow from the principles of justice, fairness, and procedural due process that provide the best constructive interpretation of the community's legal practice."[80] It is inconceivable that Dworkin would have allowed coherence to disappear without explanation had he been genuinely committed to it. It is especially important to remember that there is nothing in *Law's Empire* to suggest that the principles of justice are not themselves irreducibly plural, and the same is true of fairness and procedural due process.

I suggest, therefore, that his is not a coherence explanation of either law or integrity. His position is as explained in this quotation: The law consists of those principles of justice and fairness and procedural due process which provide the best (i.e., morally best) set of sound principles capable of explaining the legal decisions taken throughout the history of the polity in question. Whether or not such principles display any degree of coherence, in the sense of interdependence, is an open question. Thus, while coherence may be a by-product of the best theory of law, a preference for coherence is not part of the desiderata by which the best theory is determined. The reason for thinking that Dworkin is not at all committed to the desirability of coherence is that his text is ambivalent and that while Dworkin argues at length that interpretations are necessarily evaluative, and that they try to show their object as the best of its kind, and that the interpretation of the law is committed to integrity, he never provides any reason whatsoever to suggest that coherence is a desideratum in correct interpretations.

Three objections may be raised to the conclusion that Dworkin's theory of law contains no commitment to any degree of coherence. First, in the quotation above, while coherence is not specifically mentioned, it is implied in the reference to "constructive interpretation," for as we saw above interpretation must, according to Dworkin, be not only coherent but monistic. This would be a decisive argument but for the fact that Dworkin's commitment to a monistic view of interpretation must itself be questionable, partly on textual grounds, partly because it is so unlikely that he would have committed himself to such an initially implausible view without even a shadow of an argument to support it.

Second, it may be argued that while integrity (in adjudication) itself is not committed to coherence, this does not show that either the law or adjudication need not be based on a set of principles displaying tight coherence, because integrity is only one element in law and adjudication. This is a mat-

---

[80] *Id*. at 225.

ter of some delicacy. Clearly, integrity is not a conclusive ground for good legislation. While legislators should value integrity for its own sake, they may find that other considerations prevail and thus may compromise it.[81] The adjudicative principle of integrity has, however, a different status from that of the legislative principle. On the one hand, it is a principle about how courts should decide cases. On the other hand, it is a principle identifying the grounds of law[82] and, as such, is the touchstone distinguishing what is the law from what is not.[83] As a principle about how courts should decide cases it is merely prima facie,[84] and there may be cases in which the courts ought not to compromise justice and fairness for the sake of integrity. But in its second capacity it is definitive. Rules which do not pass the test of integrity are not part of the law.

The two aspects of the principle are consistent. It merely means that sometimes courts ought not to decide cases on the basis of the law, but that they should overturn it and lay down a different rule. Less clear, however, is whether this imperative—the requirement that judges go against the law when it calls for too great a sacrifice of justice for the sake of integrity—is a legal or a non-legal one. That is, does *Law's Empire* recognize a legal duty on the courts to decide cases on appropriate occasions by transcending the law, or does the book hold that legally the courts ought always to apply the law, but morally they sometimes should not do so. Most theorists agree that the latter is sometimes the case. Many legal theorists believe that the former is always the case, though not normally for the reasons indicated in *Law's Empire*. When courts are legally required to apply non-legal considerations they are commonly said to have discretion.[85] Dworkin has first distinguished himself as a legal theorist who denies that courts are ever legally required or permitted to do anything other than apply the law (to the facts). It therefore would seem that while he holds that courts always have and sometimes should exercise moral discretion to transcend the law, they are never legally allowed to do so. This position indicates a major development in Dworkin's views. In the past he had no independent theory of law. Unlike theorists like Hart, Kelsen and others who distinguish between (1) "what is the law?" and (2) "what considerations should guide courts in deciding cases?" and hold that the answer to the second includes more than the law, Dworkin has always identified the two questions. His theory of adjudication was his theory of law. The answer to the question what consid-

---

[81] *See id.* at 181, 217.

[82] *Id.* at 218.

[83] *Id.* at 225.

[84] *Id.* at 218.

[85] The term does not mean that they can do what they like. Its meaning in the debates in legal theory is that courts are entrusted with more than applying the law. Their task, their legally appointed task, includes power to revise and develop the law, which they do with guidance from legal standards which direct them to step beyond the bounds of the law and apply moral considerations.

erations should guide courts in deciding cases answers the question of what is the law. Given that assumption,[86] courts have no discretion and must always obey the law. In *Law's Empire*, a new position emerges. We have a concept of law which is totally independent of any reference to adjudication.[87] This leaves room for the possibility of discretion. As we saw, Dworkin allows that such discretion exists. He still seems to differ from other theorists, however, in thinking that in exercising discretion courts violate the law. But that is a moot point. First, he does not explicitly say this. Second, because according to *Law's Empire* the reasons to deviate from the law are open moral reasons which guide the action of the courts in appropriate circumstances, it is not clear why the law should not be understood to sanction them. Even writers like myself and others whose understanding of the law allows room for the role of extra-legal considerations in adjudication hold that the law recognizes the practice of resorting to them, a recognition which is expressed in the very fact that courts do so openly and without any legislation or directive to stop them. In the past, Dworkin suggested that there be no resort to extra-legal considerations in adjudication. There was never a strong argument to justify this and he does not repeat this claim in *Law's Empire*. It is now moot whether and why Dworkin does not accept judicial discretion as a legal practice. Be that as it may, given that the requirement to go against integrity is a requirement to go against the law, there is nothing we can learn from it about the degree of coherence in the law.

I have to admit that there are further unclarities in the position advocated in *Law's Empire*. In the course of Dworkin's extensive discussion of the *McLoughlin* case,[88] he says "but here . . . questions of fit surface again, because an interpretation is *pro tanto* more satisfactory if it shows less damage to integrity than its rival. [The judge] will therefore consider whether interpretation (5) fits the expanded legal record better than (6)."[89] This seems to imply that integrity is a matter of achieving the greatest possible fit with past legal record. We know from the general discussion that fit is but one of two dimensions which identify the law. The other is value. If so, then integrity is but one, and not—according to *Law's Empire*—a lexically prior

---

[86] I call it an assumption as Dworkin has never argued for it. It may seem that he has not realized, at least not at the beginning, that it is at this point that he disputes the work of Hart and others. That is, he may not have realized that once this assumption is granted the question whether courts enjoy discretion is settled. Of course, if everything they can take into account is the law, they do not have (so-called strong) discretion to go outside the law. *See* Joseph Raz, postscript to *Legal Principles and the Limits of Law, in* DWORKIN AND CONTEMPORARY JURISPRUDENCE (M. Cohen ed., 1984); Raz, *The Problem About the Nature of Law, supra* note 26.

[87] Dworkin states, "The law of a community . . . is the scheme of rights and responsibilities that meet that complex standard: they license coercion because they flow from past decisions of the right sort." DWORKIN, LAW'S EMPIRE, *supra* note 30, at 93.

[88] McLoughlin v. O'Brian, 1 App. Cas. 410 (1983).

[89] DWORKIN, LAW'S EMPIRE, *supra* note 30, at 246-47.

consideration in determining the content of the law and what the courts may legally be required to do. Hence, it may well be that Dworkin regards the law as much more coherent than his commitment to integrity would suggest, for it may be that the combination of the two dimensions will make it so. But this line of thinking gives undue weight to the one text in which Dworkin equates integrity with fit. It seems best to disregard it.

Third, the final objection to my earlier conclusion that *Law's Empire* assigns no importance to coherence in the law is that my arguments turn on close textual analysis. This, according to the objection, is the wrong attitude toward the understanding of a book which does not carefully formulate the views it advocates. The general feel of the book suggests that coherence is to be striven for. Perhaps it is impossible to say in advance what degree of coherence is to be achieved. But the drift of the argument suggests that coherence is a distinctive advantage, and that therefore one should strive to end up with a view of the law which regards it as coherent as possible, provided not too much violence is done to other values.

There is something to this point. The position it assigns to *Law's Empire* is explicitly advocated by Hurley,[90] who seems to think that she is following Dworkin with regard to the law. The difficulty is that Dworkin provides no argument to support that position, unless the suggestion is made that the arguments for integrity are also meant to be arguments for coherence.[91] If so, then they have been dealt with above. My feeling that Dworkin does not regard coherence, as understood in this Article, as a virtue at all is strengthened by his use of the term at times to convey other ideas, and by Dworkin's belief in the virtue of coherence when understood in some of those other ways. He believes that the law is coherent=intelligible, he believes that the law is coherent=holistic, and, more distinctively, he believes that the law speaks with one voice (on the strength of the argument canvassed in Part V). In Part V, I took that requirement to imply at least a preference for coherence=unity. But there is no sign that Dworkin does so, nor is there any reason to do so. Speaking with one voice may mean no more than that the law is not arbitrary nor reflects changes of mind or policy. For Dworkin, "speaking with one voice" means also that the law does not reflect compromises among people or factions. Whatever "speaking with one voice" means in Dworkin's writings, it can be represented as "coherence," and it is a way of employing "coherence" unrelated to the concerns explored in this Article. Finally, "coherence" is sometimes used by him to indicate fitting the historical record.[92] This again has nothing to do with coherence as explored here. None of this shows that Dworkin does not regard coherence as unity as desirable. The degree to which, and the reasons for which, *Law's Empire* is committed to coherence must remain moot.

But if I am right in the main conclusion above, namely that there is noth-

---

[90] See S.L. HURLEY, NATURAL REASONS, *supra* note 3, at 262.
[91] This is indeed Hurley's view. *Id.* at 262-63.
[92] See discussion *supra* note 89 and accompanying text.

ing in the book's advocacy of what Dworkin calls interpretation and integrity to require an endorsement of, or any presumption in favor of coherence, any tendency to favor coherence, does this not undermine my own criticism of the value of Dworkinian integrity offered above? Not so. My criticism of integrity is valid even if integrity is not taken to support coherence. It relies on one feature of integrity only: that it advocates acting on principles which may never have been considered nor approved, either explicitly or implicitly by any legal authority, and which are inferior to some alternatives in justice and fairness. The objections I raised were to this as groundless in morality and as deriving from a desire to see the law, and judicial activities, as based to a larger degree than they are in fact or should be in morality, on an inner legal logic which is separate from ordinary moral and political considerations of the kind that govern normal government, in all its branches.

Formalism

Frederick Schauer*

Legal decisions and theories are frequently condemned as formalistic, yet little discussion has occurred regarding exactly what the term "formalism" means. In this Article, Professor Schauer examines divergent uses of the term to elucidate its descriptive content. Conceptions of formalism, he argues, involve the notion that rules constrict the choice of the decisionmaker. Our aversion to formalism stems from denial that the language of rules either can or should constrict choice in this way. Yet Professor Schauer argues that this aversion to formalism should be rethought: At times language both can and should restrict decisionmakers. Consequently, the term "formalistic" should not be used as a blanket condemnation of a decisionmaking process; instead the debate regarding decision according to rules should be confronted on its own terms.

With accelerating frequency, legal decisions and theories are condemned as "formalist" or "formalistic." But what *is* formalism, and what is so bad about it? Even a cursory look at the literature reveals scant agreement on what it is for decisions in law, or perspectives on law, to be

* Professor of Law, University of Michigan. I am grateful to audiences at Brooklyn Law School, Cornell Law School, DePaul University College of Law, Duke University School of Law, Indiana University at Bloomington School of Law, New York University School of Law, and the American Political Science Association for helping me to clarify some of my good ideas and jettison some of my bad ones. I am also indebted to Alex Aleinikoff, Bruce Frier, Leo Katz, James Krier, William Miller, and Richard Pildes for commenting on earlier versions of this article with just the right blend of hostility and sympathy.

formalistic, except that whatever formalism is, it is not good.[1] Few judges or scholars would describe themselves as formalists, for a congratulatory use of the word "formal" seems almost a linguistic error. Indeed, the pejorative connotations of the word "formalism," in concert with the lack of agreement on the word's descriptive content, make it tempting to conclude that "formalist" is the adjective used to describe any judicial decision, style of legal thinking, or legal theory with which the user of the term disagrees.

Yet this temptation should be resisted. There *does* seem to be descriptive content in the notion of formalism, even if there are widely divergent uses of the term. At the heart of the word "formalism," in many of its numerous uses, lies the concept of decisionmaking according to *rule*. Formalism is the way in which rules achieve their "ruleness" precisely by doing what is supposed to be the failing of formalism: screening off from a decisionmaker factors that a sensitive decisionmaker would otherwise take into account. Moreover, it appears that this screening off takes place largely through the force of the language in which rules are written. Thus the tasks performed by rules are tasks for which the primary tool is the specific linguistic formulation of a rule. As a result, insofar as formalism is frequently condemned as excessive reliance on the language of a rule, it is the very idea of decisionmaking by rule that is being condemned, either as a description of how decisionmaking can take place or as a prescription for how decisionmaking should take place.

Once we disentangle and examine the various strands of formalism and recognize the way in which formalism, rules, and language are conceptually intertwined, it turns out that there is something, indeed much, to be said for decision according to rule—and therefore for formalism. I do not argue that formalism is always good or that legal systems ought often or

---

1. *See, e.g.,* H.L.A. HART, THE CONCEPT OF LAW 124-30 (1961) (formalism as refusal to acknowledge necessity of choice in penumbral area of rules); M. HORWITZ, THE TRANSFORMATION OF AMERICAN LAW 254 (1977) (formalism as refusal to recognize instrumental functions of law); K. LLEWELLYN, JURISPRUDENCE: REALISM IN THEORY AND PRACTICE 183-88 (1962) (formalism as excessive reliance on canonically written language of rules); R. UNGER, THE CRITICAL LEGAL STUDIES MOVEMENT 1-2 (1986) (formalism as constrained and comparatively apolitical decisionmaking); Kennedy, *Legal Formality,* 2 J. LEGAL STUD. 351, 355 (1973) (formalism as view that rule application is mechanical and that mechanical rule application is just); Strauss, *Formal and Functional Approaches to Separation-of-Powers Questions—A Foolish Inconsistency?,* 72 CORNELL L. REV. 488, 489 (1987) (formalism as refusal to acknowledge practical consequences of judicial decisions); Tushnet, *Anti-Formalism in Recent Constitutional Theory,* 83 MICH. L. REV. 1502, 1506-07 (1985) (formalism as artificial narrowing of range of interpretive choices).

One can avoid the confusion of multiple usage by simply stipulating a meaning for the term "formalism." *See, e.g.,* Posner, *Legal Formalism, Legal Realism, and the Interpretation of Statutes and the Constitution,* 37 CASE W. RES. L. REV. 179, 181-82 (1986). This tack, however, evades most of the interesting problems. Having stipulated that "formalism" means deductive logical reasoning, Judge Posner proceeds easily to the conclusion that formalist reasoning has no application to the interpretation of canonical texts. That conclusion, however, follows, if at all, only from the narrowness of the stipulated definition. By not stipulating a meaning in advance of the analysis, I intend to focus on a broader range of issues. In the process, I will explore the way in which deduction, even in Posner's sense, may be related to the interpretation of canonical texts. *See infra* note 48.

even ever be formalistic. Nevertheless, I do want to urge a rethinking of the contemporary aversion to formalism. For even if what can be said for formalism is not in the end persuasive, the issues should be before us for inspection, rather than blocked by a discourse of epithets.

I. FORMALISM AS THE DENIAL OF CHOICE

A. *Choice Within Norms*

Few decisions are charged with formalism as often as *Lochner v. New York*.[2] But what makes Justice Peckham's majority opinion in *Lochner* formalistic? Surely it is not just that the Court protected an unrestricted privilege of labor contracting against the first stirrings of the welfare state. For the Court to make such a political decision under the rubric of broad constitutional clauses like "liberty" is a far cry from what seems to be meant when decisions are criticized as being formal. To the extent that the charge of formalism suggests narrowness, *Lochner* is hardly a candidate. We criticize *Lochner* not for being narrow, but for being excessively broad.

Although *Lochner* is criticized for the length of its reach, a closer look reveals that it is not the result that is condemned as formalistic but rather the justification for that result. The formalism in *Lochner* inheres in its *denial* of the political, moral, social, and economic choices involved in the decision, and indeed in its denial that there was any choice at all. Justice Peckham simply announced that "[t]he general right to make a contract in relation to his business is part of the liberty of the individual protected by the Fourteenth Amendment"[3] and that "[t]he right to purchase or to sell labor is part of the liberty protected by this amendment."[4] To these pronouncements he added the confident statement that "[o]f course the liberty of contract relating to labor includes both parties to it."[5]

Justice Peckham's language suggests that he is explaining a precise statutory scheme rather than expounding on one word in the Constitution. It is precisely for this reason that his opinion draws criticism. We condemn *Lochner* as formalistic not because it involves a choice, but because

---

2. 198 U.S. 45 (1905). For condemnations of *Lochner* (and the era of which it is taken to be archetypal) as formalistic, see Gordon, *Critical Legal Histories*, 36 STAN. L. REV. 57, 99 (1984); Peller, *The Metaphysics of American Law*, 73 CALIF. L. REV. 1151, 1193, 1200–01 (1985); Seidman, *Public Principle and Private Choice: The Uneasy Case for a Boundary Maintenance Theory of Constitutional Law*, 96 YALE L.J. 1006, 1006–07 (1987); *Developments in the Law—Immigration Policy and the Rights of Aliens*, 96 HARV. L. REV. 1286, 1292 (1983); Note, *The Constitutionality of Rent Control Restrictions on Property Owners' Dominion Interests*, 100 HARV. L. REV. 1067, 1077 (1987); Note, *Formalism, Legal Realism, and Constitutionally Protected Privacy Under the Fourth and Fifth Amendments*, 90 HARV. L. REV. 945, 951 (1977); Powers, Book Review, 1985 DUKE L.J. 221, 232; Rotenberg, *Politics, Personality and Judging: The Lessons of Brandeis and Frankfurter on Judicial Restraint* (Book Review), 83 COLUM. L. REV. 1863, 1875 n.60 (1983).
3. 198 U.S. at 53.
4. *Id.*
5. *Id.* at 56.

it attempts to describe this choice as compulsion.[6] What strikes us clearly as a political or social or moral or economic choice is described in *Lochner* as definitionally incorporated within the *meaning* of a broad term. Thus, choice is masked by the language of linguistic inexorability.

When I say that pelicans are birds, the truth of the statement follows inexorably from the meaning of the term "bird." If someone disagrees, or points at a living, breathing, flying pelican and says "That is not a bird," she simply does not know what the word "bird" means.[7] We criticize *Lochner* as formalistic because it treats the word "liberty" (or the words "life, liberty, or property, without due process of law") as being like the word "bird" and the privilege of contracting as being like a pelican, i.e., subsumed in the broader category. According to the reasoning in *Lochner*, if you don't know that contracting for labor without governmental control is an example of liberty, then you just don't know what the word "liberty" means.

Lochner is condemned as formalistic precisely because the analogy between pelicans (as birds) and unrestricted contracting (as liberty) fails. One can understand much about the concept of liberty and about the word "liberty" and yet still deny that they include the privilege of unconstrained labor contracting.[8] Thus, a decisionmaker who knows or should

---

6. This was noted by Holmes in his now-famous observation, "General propositions do not decide concrete cases." *Id.* at 76 (Holmes, J., dissenting).

7. Of course when I use the term "inexorable," I do not mean that the world and our language could not have been otherwise; the word "bird" could have referred to frogs instead of pelicans, or to only puffins, robins, and sparrows, but not pelicans, ostriches, and condors. Definitions are contingent and subject to change, and therefore the word "bird" might yet come to be the word that speakers of English use to refer to frogs, or only to small and not to large birds. Yet although there remains a possibility that the word "bird" will come to mean these things, this is only a possible world—it is not *our* world. In our world, the exclusion of frogs and the inclusion of large birds is definitionally part of the meaning of the word "bird." As I argue below, *see infra* notes 56-57 and accompanying text, the contingency of definition hardly entails the view that it is within the province of any one actor, legal or otherwise, to change it. Neither you nor I have the power to make it proper to use the word "bird" to refer to a frog, even though the word "bird" could in another world be used to refer to frogs.

8. The extent to which this is true for morally and politically loaded words such as "liberty" is likely to vary with time, place, and culture. Take, for example, the transformation of the "honor codes" at various venerable universities. These codes were phrased in quite general terms at their inception in the 18th and 19th centuries because these schools contained homogeneous student bodies who shared a common conception of the type of conduct definitionally incorporated within the word "honor." If a person thought that purchasing a term paper from a professional term paper service was consistent with being honorable, then that person simply did not know what "honor" meant. As values have changed and as student bodies have become less homogeneous, however, shared definitions of terms such as "honor" have broken down. Some people now *do* think that buying a term paper can be honorable, and this breakdown in shared meaning has caused general references to "honor" to be displaced in such codes by more detailed rules. There may now be little shared agreement about what the precept "be honorable" requires, but there is considerable agreement about what the rule "do not purchase a term paper" requires.

Thus, the criticism of *Lochner* and its ilk as "formalistic" in the sense discussed in the text is ambiguous. The critic could mean that the term we *now* take to be susceptible to debate was not as debatable at the time of the relevant decision. But this would hardly explain the pejorative, unless we want to condemn an entire era and the conceptual and linguistic apparatus that reflected its understandings. The alternative is that the term "formalism" charges that there was *at the time* room for debate about the application of the general term to the particular case, but the relevant decisionmakers either did not recognize that fact (perhaps because they refused to look outside their own socioeco-

know that such a choice is open, but treats the choice as no more available than the choice to treat a pelican as other than a bird, is charged with formalism for treating as definitionally inexorable that which involves nondefinitional, substantive choices.[9]

Lochner is merely one example in which a false assertion of inexorability is decried as formalistic. Much contemporary criticism of Blackstone, Langdell, and others of their persuasion attacks their jurisprudence on similar grounds.[10] They stand accused of presenting contestable applications of general terms as definitionally incorporated within the meaning of the general term. It is important, however, to understand the relationship between the linguistic and the ontological questions for those of Blackstone's vision. Blackstone's view that certain abstract terms definitionally incorporate a wide range of specific results is tied intimately to his perception of a hard and suprahuman reality behind these general terms. If the word "property," for example, actually describes some underlying and noncontingent reality, then it follows easily that certain specific embodiments are necessarily part of that reality, just as pelicans are part of the underlying reality that is the universe of birds. These instantiations might still follow even if the general term is not a natural kind whose existence and demarcation is beyond the control of human actors. There is nothing natural or noncontingent about the term "basketball," but it is nevertheless an error in this culture at this time to apply that word to a group of people hitting small hard balls with one of a collection of fourteen different sticks. Still, linguistic clarity and rigidity are both facilitated insofar as the words track the natural kinds of the world. To the extent that Blackstone and others believed that categories like liberty, property, and contract were natural kinds rather than human artifacts, they were less likely to perceive the choices we would now not think to deny. When one believes that a general term reflects a deep reality beyond the power of human actors, the view that certain particulars are *necessarily* part of that reality follows with special ease.

Thus, one view of the vice of formalism takes that vice to be one of deception, either of oneself or of others. To disguise a choice in the lan-

---

nomic and political class) or intentionally chose to hide it.

9. Formalism may be more broadly viewed as extending to any justification that treats as inexorable a choice that is not. In this broader sense, the claimed inexorability might come from something other than rule formulations. To mask, for example, a political, moral, or social choice in the language of "original intent" when original intent in fact does *not* provide a uniquely correct answer to the issue might be considered formalistic in the same way that masking a political, moral, or social choice in the language of the meaning of a rule is considered formalistic when that language does not provide a uniquely correct answer. Similarly, masking choice in the language of mathematical economic derivation or in the language of a unique solution to some "balance" might be considered formalistic *if* these methods are in fact comparatively indeterminate.

10. *See, e.g.*, Grey, *Langdell's Orthodoxy*, 45 U. PITT. L. REV. 1 (1983); Hart, *Positivism and the Separation of Law and Morals*, 71 HARV. L. REV. 593, 610 (1958); Kennedy, *The Structure of Blackstone's Commentaries*, 28 BUFFALO L. REV. 205 (1979); Lyons, *Legal Formalism and Instrumentalism—A Pathological Study*, 66 CORNELL L. REV. 949, 950 (1981).

guage of definitional inexorability obscures that choice and thus obstructs questions of how it was made and whether it could have been made differently. Use of the word "formalism" in this sense hinges on the existence of a term (or phrase, sentence, or paragraph[11]) whose contested application generates the choice. Some terms, like "liberty" and "equality," are *pervasively indeterminate*. It is not that such terms have no content whatsoever; it is that *every* application, every concretization, every instantiation requires the addition of supplementary premises to apply the general term to specific cases.[12] Therefore, any application of that term that denies the choice made among various eligible supplementary premises is formalistic in this sense.[13]

More commonly, however, the indeterminacy to be filled by a decisionmaker's choice is not pervasive throughout the range of applications of a term. Instead, the indeterminacy is encountered only at the edges of a term's meaning. As H.L.A. Hart tells us, legal terms possess a core of settled meaning and a penumbra of debatable meaning.[14] For Hart, formalism derives from the denial of choice in the penumbra of meaning, where applying the term in question is optional. Thus, Hart conceives of formalism as the unwillingness to acknowledge in cases of doubtful application, such as the question of whether a bicycle is a vehicle for purposes of the prohibition on vehicles in the park, that choices must be made that go far beyond merely ascertaining the meaning of a word.

Hart's conception of formalism[15] is closely aligned with that undergirding those who criticize both Blackstone and *Lochner*.[16] Hart's formalist takes the penumbra to be as clear as the core, while the *Lochner* formalist takes the general term to be as determinate as the specific. Both deny the extent of actual indeterminacy, and thus neither admits that the application of the norm involves a choice not determined by the words of the norm alone.

---

11. *See infra* note 85.

12. For a discussion of the often-ignored necessity of relying on such supplementary premises in the application of the term "equality," see Westen, *The Empty Idea of Equality*, 95 HARV. L. REV. 537 (1982). I disagree, however, with Westen's argument that the necessity of adding those supplementary premises to give the primary term meaning renders the primary term superfluous. Because a term is not self-standing does not mean that it serves no purpose, even if it needs external assistance in order to serve that purpose.

13. On the choices necessitated (but often denied) by general terms, see Cohen, *Transcendental Nonsense and the Functional Approach*, 35 COLUM. L. REV. 809 (1935); Dewey, *Logical Method and Law*, 10 CORNELL L.Q. 17 (1924); Horwitz, Santa Clara *Revisited: The Development of Corporate Theory*, 88 W. VA. L. REV. 173, 175-76 (1985); Singer, *The Player and the Cards: Nihilism and Legal Theory*, 94 YALE L.J. 1, 9-25 (1984).

14. Hart, *supra* note 10, at 608-12; *see also* H.L.A. HART, *supra* note 1, at 121-50.

15. H.L.A. HART, *supra* note 1, at 121-50; Hart, *supra* note 10, at 608-12.

16. *See, e.g.*, Gordon, *supra* note 2; Grey, *supra* note 10; Peller, *supra* note 2.

B. Choice Among Norms

Implicit in Hart's conception of formalism is the view that in the core, unlike in the penumbra, legal answers are often tolerably determinate. Even if this is true, and I will examine this claim presently, the possibility remains that a decisionmaker has a choice of whether or not to follow a seemingly applicable norm even in its core of meaning. The question in this case is not whether a bus is a vehicle, or even whether the core of the rule excludes buses from the park, but whether the rule excluding vehicles must be applied in this case. At times a decisionmaker may have a choice whether to apply the clear and specifically applicable norm. In such cases we can imagine a decisionmaker having and making a choice but denying that a choice was in any way part of the process. Thus, a variant on the variety of formalism just discussed sees formalism as involving not denial of the existence of choices within norms, but denial that there are frequently choices about whether to apply even the clear norms.

As an example of this type of formalism, consider the unreported and widely unknown case of *Hunter v. Norman.*[17] Hunter, an incumbent state senator in Vermont seeking re-election, filed his nominating petition in the Windsor County Clerk's office on July 21, 1986 at 5:03 p.m. In doing so he missed by three minutes the petition deadline set by title 17, section 2356, of the Laws of Vermont.[18] The statute provides, in its entirety, that "Primary petitions shall be filed not later than 5:00 p.m. on the third Monday of July preceding the primary election prescribed by section 2351 of this title, and not later than 5:00 p.m. of the forty-second day prior to the day of a special primary election."[19] The Windsor County Clerk, Jane Norman, duly enforced the statute by refusing to accept Hunter's petition, observing that "I have no intention of breaking the law, not for Jesus Christ himself."[20] Hunter's name, consequently, was to be withheld from appearing on the September Democratic primary election ballot.

Hunter, not surprisingly, took his disappointment to the courthouse and filed an action in equity against Norman for extraordinary relief.[21] He asked that the court order her to accept his petition and to ensure that his name would appear on the primary ballot. At the hearing, Hunter alleged that he had called the clerk's office earlier on the date in question and been told that he was required to deliver the petition in person because of

---

17. No. S197-86-WrC (Vt. July 28, 1986). The following account of the case is drawn from Judge Cheever's brief opinion, the pleadings, news accounts in the *Rutland Herald* of July 22, 23, 24 and 26, 1986, and a conversation with Marilyn Signe Skoglund, Assistant Attorney General in the Office of the Attorney General, State of Vermont.

18. Vt. Stat. Ann. tit. 17, § 2356 (1982).

19. *Id.*

20. Rutland Herald, July 23, 1986, at 5, col. 4.

21. The petition is unclear as to whether Hunter was seeking the extraordinary legal remedy of mandamus or a mandatory injunction in equity.

the necessity of signing forms consenting to his nomination. In fact, these consent forms were not due until a later date. Hunter claimed that had he not been led to appear in person by receiving this erroneous advice, the petition would have been filed earlier in the day. He argued that in light of the erroneous information given to Hunter by the Clerk's office, the clerk (and the state) were estopped from relying on the statutory deadline. In support of this proposition, Hunter offered *Ryshpan v. Cashman*,[22] in which the Vermont Supreme Court, on similar facts, held that because "reliance on erroneous actions on behalf of the State has put . . . its citizens in inescapable conflict with the literal terms of one of the time requirements instituted by that same sovereignty . . . [t]he statutory time schedule must . . . as a matter of equity . . . yield."[23]

Ultimately, Hunter prevailed, and it appears that *Ryshpan v. Cashman* saved the day—or at least saved Hunter's day. *Ryshpan* therefore seems to have operated as an escape route from the rigors of the statute. Suppose, however, that everything in Hunter's case had been the same, including the existence of *Ryshpan*, but that the judge had ruled against Hunter solely on the basis of the statutory language. Had this hardly unrealistic alternative occurred, it would seem but a small step from the brand of formalism discussed above to a formalist characterization of this hypothetical decision. As long as *Ryshpan* exists, the judge has a choice whether to follow the letter of the statute or instead to employ the escape route. To make this choice and merely cite the statute as indicating the absence of choice would therefore deny the reality of the choice that was made. The crux of the matter is that this choice was present as long as *Ryshpan* existed, whether the judge followed that case or not. The charge of formalism in such a case would be but a variation of formalism as the concealment of choice: Instead of a choice within a norm, as with either pervasively indeterminate language or language containing penumbras of uncertainty surrounding a core of settled meaning, here the choice is between two different norms.

This variation on *Ryshpan* reveals the reasons we condemn the masking of choice. When the statute and *Ryshpan* coexist, neither determines which will prevail. Thus, the choice of the escape route represented by *Ryshpan* over the result indicated by the statute, or vice versa, necessarily would be made on the basis of factors external to both. These factors might include the moral, political, or physical attractiveness of the parties; the particular facts of the case; the judge's own views about deadlines; the judge's own views about statutes; the judge's own views about the Vermont Supreme Court; the judge's own views about clerks of courts; and so on. Yet were any of these factors to cause a particular judge to decide that

---

22. 132 Vt. 628, 326 A.2d 169 (1974).
23. *Id.* at 630–31, 326 A.2d at 171.

the statute should prevail, mere citation of the statute as inexorably dictating the result would conceal from the litigants and from society the actual determinative factors. Insofar as we expect the reasons for a decision to be open for inspection (and that, after all, is usually the reason judges write opinions),[24] failure to acknowledge that a choice was made can be criticized because knowing how the choice was made helps to make legitimate the products of the system.

C. *Is There Always a Choice?*

Ryshpan v. Cashman is a trifle obscure, but it is hardly unique. Consider the number of *Ryshpan* equivalents that allow decisionmakers to avoid the specific mandates of a particular rule. A decisionmaker may determine that the literal language of a rule does not serve that rule's original intent, as the Supreme Court has interpreted the Civil Rights Act of 1964,[25] the contracts clause of the Constitution,[26] and the Eleventh Amendment.[27] Or a decisionmaker may apply the "mischief rule" or its variants to determine that a literal application of the rule would not serve the rule's *purpose.*[28] Or a decisionmaker may apply a more general rule that denies relief to a claimant entitled to relief under the most locally applicable rule;[29] for example, she might apply the equitable principle of

---

24. Although it is generally accepted that judges should write opinions explaining their actual reasons for decision, *see, e.g.,* Shapiro, *In Defense of Judicial Candor,* 100 HARV. L. REV. 731 (1987), some scholars have suggested that there may be reasons to avoid a candid explanation of the reasoning process. *See* sources cited *id.* at 731 n.4. Thus an opinion might be equated with a statute, whose message legitimately may depart from a reflection of the process that generated it. While recognizing that reasons going to the symbolic, guiding, and persuasive function of opinions may urge against candid explanation of the decision process, I address here only opinions in which honesty is deemed appropriate.

25. *See, e.g.,* California Fed. Sav. & Loan Ass'n v. Guerra, 107 S. Ct. 683, 691 (1987); United Steelworkers v. Weber, 443 U.S. 193, 201 (1979).

26. *See, e.g.,* Keystone Bituminous Coal Ass'n v. DeBenedictis, 107 S. Ct. 1232, 1251 (1987).

27. *See, e.g.,* Monaco v. Mississippi, 292 U.S. 313, 329-30 (1934); Hans v. Louisiana, 134 U.S. 1, 10-11 (1890).

28. Heydon's Case, 76 Eng. Rep. 637 (Ex. 1584), phrases the rule as deriving from original legislative intent. *See infra* note 68. However, limitation of the purpose of a rule to the intent of the legislature that passed it unnecessarily restricts the meaning of the term "purpose." Purpose gleaned from the words of a rule itself should not be confused with the psychological intentions of the drafters. Consider a rule which specifically excludes from a park children, radios, musical instruments, dogs but not cats, and cars and trucks but not bicycles. One might conclude from reading this rule that its purpose is to prevent noise. Even if the drafters of the rule intended to promote safety rather than prevent noise, their psychological intentions would not negate this reading of purpose from the rule's words themselves, any more than a person, having said "stop," could deny the import of that phrase because she in fact meant "go."

29. *See* Singer, *supra* note 13, at 17-18. The most "locally" applicable rule (or statute) is that which most narrowly pertains to the situation at hand. "Dogs should be leashed" is, in a case involving a dog, more locally applicable than "animals should be restrained." Similarly, "beneficiaries named by the testator are to inherit according to the will" is more locally applicable than "no person should benefit by his own wrong." The idea of *local* applicability distinguishes the rules in each of these pairs, for in each pair both rules might apply to the same situation. Local applicability captures our intuition that a more specifically applicable rule is somehow *more* applicable than a less specifically applicable, but still applicable, rule.

unclean hands or laches,[30] the legal principle of *in pari delicto*,[31] or the civil law principle of abuse of right.[32] Any reader of this article could easily add to this list.[33]

Yet, what if none of these established routes were available in a particular case—would a judge then be forced to apply the specifically applicable rule? To answer this question, let us examine another variation on *Hunter v. Norman*. Suppose that *Ryshpan v. Cashman* did *not* exist, but that everything else about the facts and the applicable law in *Hunter* remained the same. What choices, if any, would be open to the judge? The judge could, of course, simply hold that the statute applied and rule against Hunter. But must he? Could the judge instead "create" *Ryshpan* by concluding that Hunter should win because he was misled by the clerk's office?

This option of creating *Ryshpan* does not seem inconsistent with the way the American legal system operates. Despite the lack of any specific statute or case authorizing such a result, allowing Hunter to win because he was misled would raise no eyebrows in American legal circles. No one would call for an investigation of the judge's competence, as someone might had the judge ruled for Hunter because Hunter was a Capricorn and Norman a Sagittarius. If the creation of such an escape route would be consistent with American judicial traditions, then the judge can be seen to have had a choice between deciding for Hunter and deciding for Norman even without *Ryshpan*. Thus a judge who ruled against Hunter on the basis of the statute would be denying the extent to which there was still a choice to create *Ryshpan* and thereby rule for Hunter.

Of course, a judge who decided to "create" *Ryshpan* would probably not simply assert that Hunter should win because he relied on erroneous information from a state official. Rather, the judge would justify this conclusion by reference to general principles that lurk in various corners of the legal system. For example, the judge might say that, as a general principle, parties are estopped from relying on laws whose contents they have

---

30. *See, e.g.*, Brenner v. Smullian, 84 So. 2d 44 (Fla. 1955) (unclean hands); Gorham v. Sayles, 23 R.I. 449, 50 A. 848 (1901) (laches).

31. *See, e.g.*, Rozell v. Vansyckle, 11 Wash. 79, 39 Pac. 270 (1895). Riggs v. Palmer, 115 N.Y. 506, 22 N.E. 188 (1889), made famous in R. DWORKIN, LAW'S EMPIRE 15-20 (1986) [hereinafter LAW'S EMPIRE] and R. DWORKIN, TAKING RIGHTS SERIOUSLY 23 (1977) [hereinafter TAKING RIGHTS SERIOUSLY], presents a similar issue. *Riggs* is significant because the most locally applicable legal rule, the relevant statute of wills, would allow the murdering heir to inherit. Only the imposition of the less locally applicable general principle that no person should profit from his own wrong allowed the court to avoid the result indicated by the most directly applicable legal norm. From the perspective dictated by the most immediately applicable legal rule, *Riggs* is not a hard case, but an easy one. Understanding Dworkin's enterprise requires an understanding of his attempt to explain the ways in which the result "easily" dictated by the most locally applicable rule frequently yields to less locally applicable legal and nonlegal norms. *See* Schauer, *The Jurisprudence of Reasons* (Book Review), 85 MICH. L. REV. 847 (1987).

32. *See generally* Gutteridge, *Abuse of Rights*, 5 CAMBRIDGE L.J. 22 (1935) (discussing possibility of incorporating principle forbidding exercise of legal rights for purposes of malevolence).

33. *See* Singer, *supra* note 13, at 17-18.

misstated to the disadvantage of another; a decision against the clerk would be merely a specific instance of the application of that general principle. Or, the judge might cite other particular principles, such as the principle of reliance in securities law, and analogize this case to those.[34] Under either analysis the judge would attempt to ground the new principle in some already existing principle.

On the basis of these variations, we can distinguish three possible models of escape route availability. Under one model, the existing escape routes in the system represent an incomplete list of principles to ameliorate the rigidity of rules, and the judge may add to this list where amelioration is indicated but no applicable ameliorative principle exists. In such instances, the judge might discuss justice or fairness or some other general value and explain why this value supports the creation of a principle like that in *Ryshpan v. Cashman*. The implicit ideal of this system is the availability of an ameliorative principle whenever the circumstances demand it. Thus the judge who creates a new ameliorative principle on an appropriate occasion furthers the goals of this system.

Alternatively, we could develop a model of a system in which there is already a more or less complete stock of ameliorative principles. In such a system, a judge would *always* have some escape route available if all the circumstances indicated that the applicable norm was not the best result to be reached in that case. If *Ryshpan* itself did not exist, the judge would be able to pick other extant ameliorative principles that would get Hunter's name on the ballot.

Both the first model, which resembles Dworkin's account of the law,[35] and the second, which borrows from Llewellyn's,[36] acknowledge the pervasiveness of judicial choice in their recognition of the judge's opportunity (or perhaps even obligation) to avoid the arguably unjust consequences of mechanical application of the most directly applicable legal rule. If either of these models is an accurate rendition of some legal system, then a decisionmaker within such a system who simply applies the most directly applicable legal rule without further thought or explanation either denies herself a choice that the system permitted or required, or denies to others an explanation of why she chose not to use the escape routes permitted by the system. This failure to explain the choice to apply the most locally applicable rule is simply a variation on the more egregious forms of formalism as denial of choice.[37]

---

34. Use of precedent is not as simple as I make it out to be here, but these subtleties of precedential reasoning need not detain us here. For a discussion of precedent, see Schauer, *Precedent*, 39 STAN. L. REV. 571 (1987).

35. See LAW'S EMPIRE, *supra* note 31; TAKING RIGHTS SERIOUSLY, *supra* note 31. *See also* discussion of Dworkin, *supra* note 31.

36. See especially Llewellyn, *Remarks on the Theory of Appellate Decision and the Rules or Canons About How Statutes Are To Be Construed*, 3 VAND. L. REV. 395 (1950).

37. Whether a system allows judges to create norms of rule avoidance where none exist, whether

These two models—one allowing the creation of rule-avoiding norms, and the other presenting a complete list of such norms for use[38]—must be contrasted with a third model. Under this third model, the stock of extant rule-avoiding norms is not temporarily incomplete but completable, as in the first model, nor is it complete, as in the second. Instead, it is both incomplete and closed. A decisionmaker will therefore be confronted with situations in which the immediately applicable rule generates a result the decisionmaker wishes to avoid but for which the system neither contains an escape route nor permits one to be created. Under this model, a judge who followed the rule—rather than the course she otherwise would have taken on the basis of *all* relevant factors—would not have acted formalistically in the sense now under discussion. Where there was no choice, a decisionmaker following the mandates of the most directly applicable norm could not be accused of having a choice but denying its existence.

If we can imagine a model in which a rule-avoiding norm is both non-existent and precluded in some instances, then we can also imagine a model in which no rule-avoiding norms exist at all. In such a system, a decisionmaker would be expected simply to decide according to the rule when there was a rule dealing specifically with the situation. Because there was no choice to be made, the decisionmaker could not be charged with masking a choice.

This third model presents the conceptual possibility of a different type of formalism than that which has been the focus of this section. In this third model, the charge of "formalism" would possess a different significance than in the other two models, for the decisionmaker accused of being formalistic might not be denying a choice made in the decisionmaking process, but might never have had a choice at all. To investigate the possibility of this type of formalism we must determine whether a system can truly foreclose choices from the decisionmaker. It is to this issue that I now turn.

II. FORMALISM AS THE LIMITATION OF CHOICE

A. *Can Language Constrain?*

Each of my variations on *Hunter v. Norman* presupposed that the judge reached a conclusion that was not influenced by the language of the

---

judges in fact create such norms, and whether a sufficient stock of rule-avoiding norms exists such that judges need only apply them are all unavoidably empirical questions. *See* Kennedy, *Toward a Critical Phenomenology of Judging*, 36 J. LEGAL EDUC. 518, 547-48, 562 (1986); *see also* Trubek, *Where the Action Is: Critical Legal Studies and Empiricism*, 36 STAN. L. REV. 575 (1984). There is no reason, of course, to presume that the answers to these empirical questions will remain consistent across all decisional domains within a legal system. For example, no logical necessity dictates that the stock of rule avoidance norms applicable to administrative determination of individual social security claims be identical to that applicable to Supreme Court adjudication of constitutional questions.

38. There need not be any conceptual inconsistency between the two models. The second can be conceived of as the end product of the first.

rule.[39] This rule-independent conclusion presents the possibility that the results required by the most locally applicable statute may diverge from the result the judge considers to be the optimal result for this case in light of a range of factors wider than that specifically mandated by the statute. In cases of such divergence between a judge's unconstrained judgment and the result indicated by the most locally applicable statute, a rigid requirement that the decision follow the statutory language would limit the choices open to the judge.[40]

Insofar as rigid adherence to the most locally applicable statute is required, either by the norms governing a decisional domain or by a judge's understanding of her role, a judge following that requirement would not be formalistic in the sense discussed in the previous section. Nevertheless, legal theorists condemn this type of decisionmaking as formalistic because it requires that a decisionmaker allow her best judgment about what should be done in *this* situation to yield to the dictates of a mere rule. In particular, it is the language of the rule that is perceived as binding the decisionmaker;[41] critics therefore condemn this decisionmaking process as formalistic because it appears to be a commitment to constraint by mere words on a printed page, words chosen and perpetuated without consideration of the exact situation now at hand. Formalism in this sense is not the denial of choice *by* the judge, as above, but the denial of choice *to* the judge. To be formalistic, it is said, is to be enslaved by mere marks on a printed page.[42]

---

39. I need not consider here which factors the judge actually used to reach a conclusion, for I am not trying to catalog the considerations comprising an ideal decisionmaker's totally particularized decisionmaking process. Instead, I seek merely to distinguish the concept of a complete array of factors that any particularizing decisionmaker would take into account, regardless of the source of the particularizing norms, from the more limited array of factors available to a decisionmaker inhibited by rules.

40. I assume here a distinction between internal and external constraint. A host of factors defining what I am and how I got that way constrain me from appearing unclothed in a football game at Michigan Stadium. Some of these are internal constraints—the factors that shape my very existence. These internal constraints may be psychological, ideological, or economic, but all shape what I *am* internally up to the moment of decision to appear clothed rather than naked at the football game. Even if I could overcome these internal constraints, however, external ones, such as social disapproval and a formal rule against such behavior, still might deter me from that action. Similarly, all sorts of internal factors influence the decision a judge might reach about the optimal result in this case. But these influences are distinguishable from external constraints, such as rules, that come from outside the judge's personal determination of what should be done.

Rules are only one possible example of external constraints. A decisionmaker also may believe herself to be externally constrained by statutory *purpose*. As I will demonstrate below, however, *see infra* text accompanying notes 77-79, statutory purpose is an external constraint when, and only when, it operates as a *rule* in the sense central to my argument. That is, purpose is an external constraint only when some *formulation* of that purpose, on paper or in the mind, operates in substantially the same way that a canonically formulated rule operates.

41. I explore this issue in depth below. *See infra* Section II-C.

42. For an example of this common use of the term "formalism," see Levinson, *What Do Lawyers Know (and What Do They Do with Their Knowledge)? Comments on Schauer and Moore*, 58 S. Cal. L. Rev. 441, 445 (1985) (erroneously concluding that Schauer "is much too sophisticated a theorist to endorse . . . linguistic formalism"). This usage of the term "formalism" parallels that of other disciplines. *See, e.g.,* Michaels, *Against Formalism: The Autonomous Text in Legal and Literary Inter-*

Formalism as the linguistic limitation of choice can be illustrated in a number of ways. Think of the judge who evicts the destitute widow and her family on Christmas Eve because "the law" permits no other result. Consider the classic, fictional case of *R. v. Ojibway*,[43] in which the judge determines that a pony with a down pillow on its back is a small bird because it literally fits a statutory definition of a small bird as a two-legged animal covered with feathers.[44] And recall Justice White's dissent in *Bowsher v. Synar*,[45] in which he accuses the majority of being "formalistic" for taking its narrow reading of article II to be more important than the practical consequences of striking down attempts to deal with the deficit problem.[46]

These cases exemplify a decisionmaking process that, by distinguishing the literal mandates of the most locally applicable legal norm from some arguably better result reachable by considering a wider range of factors, reinforces the systemic isolation, or closure, of the legal system.[47] Those who condemn such an outlook as formalistic criticize the perception of law as a closed system, within which judgments are mechanically deducible from the language of legal rules.[48] Note that this description of formalism

---

pretation, 1 POETICS TODAY 23 (1979).

43. Pomerantz & Breslin, *Judicial Humour—Construction of a Statute*, 8 CRIM. L.Q. 137 (1966).

44. Note, of course, that four-legged animals have two legs—and more. *Id.* at 138.

45. 478 U.S. 714, 106 S. Ct. 3181, 3205 (1986) (White, J., dissenting).

46. The plausibility of Justice White's dissent indicates that the majority opinion may also have been formalistic in the first sense considered in this article, *see supra* Section I, for it suggests that the majority had a choice. Yet by phrasing the opinion largely in terms of the clear mandate of the Constitution, the majority denied the existence of that choice and thus denied its audience the benefit of knowing how that choice was made. *See* Strauss, *supra* note 1.

47. On the relationship between the idea of systemic isolation and the more familiar terminology of legal positivism and its opponents, see *infra* note 81.

48. *See, e.g.*, M. HORWITZ, *supra* note 1, at 250–51. After defining formalism as syllogistic deduction, Judge Posner concludes that formalism is inapplicable to statutory rules (rules with a canonical embodiment) because the decision to take these rules literally is itself a choice. Posner, *supra* note 1. Posner stumbles, however, in taking this preliminary choice to distinguish rule interpretation from common law adjudication. He offers the following as an instance of a common law deduction: "So if an enforceable contract is a promise supported by consideration, and *A*'s promise to *B* was supported by consideration, the promise is a contract." *Id.* at 182. He then contrasts that example with the following requirement: "[O]ne must be at least thirty-five to be eligible [to be President], X is not thirty-five, therefore X is not eligible." *Id.* at 188. The latter case, says Posner, is not deductive, superficial appearances to the contrary, because interpreting the text to produce the premise is not deductive. According to Posner, the text could have been interpreted nonliterally; thus interpretation of the text to require that a President actually be at least thirty-five years old, rather than some less determinate measure of maturity, involves a nondeductive choice.

Posner's conclusion is correct, but only because of Posner's sleight of hand in drawing the preliminary distinction between statutory rule application and common law adjudication. Posner builds into the common law case a hardly noticeable "if." Thus, although the statutory case is not deductive because the generation of the major premise involves an interpretive *choice*, neither is the common law case deductive, because its major premise is also a choice. Note that although both are equally nondeductive, both can be equally deductive once the major premise is generated. We therefore can reformulate the issue this way: If we make the original determination that the language of a rule is to be interpreted literally, then the process of rule application is indeed deductive in any case in which a putative application is definitionally incorporated within the scope of the rule as set forth in its major premise.

conjoins two different elements: mechanical deducibility and the existence of a closed system. Neither element on its own necessarily implies the other, however. Mechanical deducibility need not entail closure. If we had a legal rule prohibiting all actions specifically condemned by the United Nations, for example, the coverage of the rule would be readily determinable, even if the answers were found outside the legal system (narrowly construed). Conversely, nonmechanical judgments can be made within the boundaries of a single system.[49] Consider the questions of whether there should be a three-point shot in basketball or a designated hitter in baseball. These are not easy questions (nor are they important ones), but their answers are *internal* to the games at issue; they involve a determination of whether the proposed change serves the goals of the game.[50] Although mechanical deducibility is thus analytically severable from systemic isolation, the two are commonly conjoined when critics deride legal decisions or theories as "formalistic," because both limit the domain of choices available to a decisionmaker.[51]

Having posited a model in which the decisionmaker's choice is limited by rules, we now must determine whether this model is descriptively accurate and normatively sound. The descriptive question, which I will take up first, is whether such limitation of choice by the words on a printed page is possible. To put it differently, and to distinguish this version of formalism from that considered in the previous section, the question is whether choice can be constricted by a canonical set of words on a printed page, or whether the choices open to a seemingly constrained decisionmaker are in fact virtually the same as those available to an unconstrained decisionmaker. This descriptive question in turn has both conceptual and psychological aspects. Even if it may be conceptually possible for language to constrain choice, it may still be beyond the psychological ca-

---

49. For an important defense of this variety of formalism, see Weinrib, *Legal Formalism*, 97 YALE L.J. (forthcoming 1988).

50. My point here parallels Dworkin's notion of "fit." As Dworkin illustrates the point, the determination whether the existence of a homosexual relationship between David and Steerforth best fits *David Copperfield* is by no means mechanical, but its resolution takes place largely within the boundaries of the novel. Dworkin, *No Right Answer?*, in LAW, MORALITY AND SOCIETY: ESSAYS IN HONOUR OF H.L.A. HART 58 (P. Hacker & J. Raz eds. 1977). A slightly different version of this article appears under the same title in 53 N.Y.U. L. REV. 1 (1978) and as *Is There Really No Right Answer in Hard Cases?*, in R. DWORKIN, A MATTER OF PRINCIPLE 119 (1985). In a later work, LAW'S EMPIRE, *supra* note 31, Dworkin broadens the systemic boundaries with which he is concerned to encompass those norms commonly understood as legal, political, and moral. The expansion of these boundaries is a separate issue, however; one could agree with Dworkin that it is possible to look for fit *within* a domain while disputing the size of the relevant domain.

51. The mechanical aspects of formalism are stressed in the important discussion in Kennedy, *supra* note 1. The concept of formalism as not necessarily mechanical but involving significant limitations on otherwise eligible results is the focus of Tushnet, *supra* note 1. *See also*, Grey, *The Constitution as Scripture*, 37 STAN. L. REV. 1, 4 n.8 (1984) (distinguishing between "operative" textual norms that guide decisions themselves and "non-operative" textual norms that tell decisionmakers to use decisive norms outside text).

pacity of those who make decisions to abide by these constraints. But let us turn first to the conceptual question.

Is it possible for written norms to limit the factors that a decisionmaker considers? At first glance, the answer to this question seems to be "no." Language is both artificial and contingent and therefore appears insufficiently rigid to limit the choices of the human actors who have created it. The word "cat," for example, could have been used to refer to canines, and the English language could have followed the language of the Eskimos in having several different words to describe the varieties of snow. Yet this answer confuses the long-term mobility of language with its short-term plasticity, and is a conclusion comparable to taking the ponderous progress of a glacier as indicating that it will move if we put our shoulders against it and push. Of course language is a human creation, and of course the rules of language are contingent, in the sense that they could have been different. It is also beyond controversy that the rules of language reflect a range of political, social, and cultural factors that are hardly *a priori*. But this artificiality and contingency does not deny the short-term, or even intermediate-term, noncontingency of meaning. If I go to a hardware store and request a hammer, the clerk who hands me a screwdriver has made a mistake, even though it is artificial, contingent, and possibly temporary that the word "hammer" represents hammers and not screwdrivers. Similarly, a rule requiring candidates to file nominating petitions at a certain place by a certain time on a certain day is violated by filing in the wrong place or after the specified time. Whatever the real judge *did* say in *Hunter v. Norman*, and whatever some judge might have said in any of my hypothetical variants, none of them would be that Hunter, in filing at 5:03 p.m., had filed at or before 5:00 p.m.

The questions about the possibility of linguistic constraint can be clarified by considering again the rule prohibiting vehicles in the park. But now let us turn from its peripheral applications to the central applications—whether cars and trucks are excluded. Hart assumed that, whatever else the rule did, it excluded cars and trucks. This was the rule's "core" of settled meaning and application.[52] Against this, Fuller offered the example of a statue of a truck erected as a war memorial by a group of patriotic citizens. According to Fuller, the example challenges the idea that a rule will have a settled core of meaning which can be applied without looking at the rule's purpose. Fuller argues that it cannot be determined whether the truck, which is a perfectly functional vehicle, falls into the rule's periphery or core unless one considers the purpose of the rule.[53] Fuller's challenge is ambiguous, however; there are three variant interpre-

---

52. Hart, *supra* note 10, at 607.
53. Fuller, *Positivism and Fidelity to Law -- A Reply to Professor Hart*, 71 HARV. L. REV. 630, 663 (1958).

tations of his challenge to the theory of linguistic constraint.[54] One interpretation of Fuller's challenge is that legal systems necessarily incorporate rule-avoiding norms such as those discussed earlier.[55] Legal systems must provide some escape route from the occasional absurdity generated by literal application because applying the literal meaning of a rule can at times produce a result which is plainly silly, clearly at odds with the purpose behind the regulation, or clearly inconsistent with any conception of wise policy. Insofar as a legal system offers its decisionmakers no legitimate escape from unreasonable consequences literally indicated by the system's norms, the system is much less a *legal* system, or is at least not a legal system worthy of that name. This argument, however, asserts a normative point about how legal systems should operate, rather than any necessary truth about how the norms themselves operate. Moreover, the argument itself admits the potential binding authority of rules: If rules require an escape route to avoid the consequences of literal application, then it must be that literal application can generate answers different from those which a decisionmaker would otherwise choose. Thus, this interpretation fails to challenge the possibility of linguistic constraint; it merely points out the undesirability of employing it too rigorously in certain domains.

Alternatively, Fuller might be arguing that legal systems necessarily require the interpretation of regulatory language in light of the purpose of the regulation. As with the first interpretation of the challenge, however, this interpretation focuses on whether a rule should bind, and it leaves the claims of linguistic determinacy untouched. We still can imagine a system in which decisionmakers do not interpret clear regulatory language according to its purpose if its purpose diverges from the regulatory language. The outcome in some instances might seem absurd, but it is question-begging to use the existence of the absurd result as an attack on the possibility of a core of literal meaning.

Finally, Fuller might be interpreted as making a point about language itself: He might be arguing that meaning cannot be severed from the speaker's purpose and that meaning must be a function of the specific context in which words are used. Fuller's argument that the idea of literal meaning is incoherent, an argument also made by other critics,[56] reveals a

---

54. Fuller's example and other illustrations of seemingly absurd results generated by applying a rule without attention to the circumstances of its creation figure prominently in criticism of formalism. *See, e.g.,* Moore, *A Natural Law Theory of Interpretation,* 58 S. CAL. L. REV. 277, 386–88 (1985); H. Hart & A. Sacks, The Legal Process: Basic Problems in the Making and Application of Law 1148–78 (tentative ed. 1958) (unpublished manuscript); *see also* Dworkin's use of *Riggs v. Palmer, supra* note 31.

55. This use of the term "necessarily" to describe the essential features of anything properly called a legal system would be consistent with the general tenor of Fuller's jurisprudence. *See* L. FULLER, THE MORALITY OF LAW (1964); R. SUMMERS, LON L. FULLER 27–31, 36–40 (1984).

56. *See, e.g.,* Boyle, *The Politics of Reason: Critical Legal Theory and Local Social Thought,* 133 U. PA. L. REV. 685, 708–13 (1985) [hereinafter *The Politics of Reason*] (arguing that words do not

mistaken view of the nature of language. Fuller and his followers fail to distinguish the possibility and existence of meaning from the *best* or *fullest* meaning that might be gleaned from a given communicative context. In conversation, I am assisted in determining what a speaker intends for me to understand by a number of contextual cues, including inflection, pitch, modulation, and body language, as well as by the circumstances surrounding the conversation. That such contextual cues assist my understanding, however, does not imply that the words, sentences, and paragraphs used by the speaker have *no* meaning without those cues. The "no vehicles in the park" rule clearly points to the exclusion of the statue from the park even if we believe that the exclusion is unnecessary from the point of view of the statute's purpose.

If I come across an Australian newspaper from 1827, I can read it because I understand, acontextually, the meaning of most of the words and sentences in that newspaper, even though with better historical understanding I might understand *more* of what was written by a colony of transported English convicts. This example does not demonstrate that language is unchanging, nor that language can be perfectly understood without attention to context, but rather that some number of linguistic conventions, or rules of language, are known and shared by all people having competence in the English language. Linguistic competence in a given language involves understanding some number of rules also understood by others who are linguistically competent in the same language. When individuals understand the same rules, they convey meaning by language conforming to those rules.[57] Members of the community of English speakers,

---

have essences or core meanings); Boyle, *Thomas Hobbes and the Invented Tradition of Positivism: Reflections on Language, Power, and Essentialism*, 135 U. PA. L. REV. 383, 408–19 (1987) (discussing Hobbes' rejection of notion of linguistic essences). In passing, I note my disagreement with those who describe as "post-Wittgensteinian" the view that meaning cannot be separated from the particular context of a particular utterance. *E.g.*, Boyle, *The Politics of Reason, supra*, at 708. A footnote in a law review article is hardly the place to debate interpretations of Wittgenstein, including whether Wittgenstein can even plausibly be interpreted to support a pragmatist/particularist theory of meaning. Yet I would briefly note that a fair reading of Wittgenstein reveals that he argued that the meaning of a word is a function of how that word is contingently used in an existing linguistic community, but emphatically not a function of how the word is used on a particular occasion by a particular member of that community.

It is crucial to recognize the seductive quality of phrases like "post-Wittgensteinian," which suggest that if the reader acknowledges Wittgenstein's genius, then she must agree with the point described in those terms. It is better to discuss the point at issue without attempting to lean on the argumentative props of associations with philosophers whose names are currently fashionable in legal circles. In light of the still-raging disputes about the most foundational questions in the philosophy of language, to substitute Wittgenstein's name for an argument is unwarranted even if the use of his name is accurate. When that use is mistaken or at the very least contested, the dangers of facile borrowing from other disciplines are compounded.

This criticism of the presentation of Boyle's argument has no bearing on its underlying validity, however. Although I disagree with much of what he and Fuller argue, those arguments raise central questions about the nature of law which I believe should be confronted directly. Boyle's useful perspectives are ill-served by clothing them in what appears to me to be an idiosyncratic misreading of Wittgenstein.

57.   For a particularly insightful and influential articulation of the view that meaning exists inde-

for example, possess shared understandings that enable them to talk to all
other members of the community.

Among the most remarkable features of language is its compositional
nature, i.e., the way in which we comprehend sentences we have never
heard before. We can do this because rules, unspecified and perhaps un-
specifiable, allow us to give meaning to certain marks and certain noises
without having to inspect the thought processes of the speaker or the full
context in which words appear. Words communicate meaning at least
partially independently of the speaker's intention. When the shells wash
up on the beach in the shape of C-A-T, I think of small house pets and

---

pendent of speaker's purpose or other related aspects of context, see J. SEARLE, SPEECH ACTS: AN
ESSAY IN THE PHILOSOPHY OF LANGUAGE 42–50 (1969). This view also seems to be the import of
paragraphs 489–512 of L. WITTGENSTEIN, PHILOSOPHICAL INVESTIGATIONS (G.E.M. Anscombe
trans. 3d ed. 1953). A similar interpretation of Wittgenstein, relying on different passages, is G.
BAKER & P. HACKER, WITTGENSTEIN: RULES, GRAMMAR AND NECESSITY 329–38 (1985). Indeed,
even those who are rightly concerned with the foundational rule-following questions posed by
Wittgenstein would not dispute that "communal language constitutes a network of determinate patterns." Wright, *Rule-Following, Objectivity and the Theory of Meaning*, in WITTGENSTEIN: TO
FOLLOW A RULE 99, 105 (S. Holtzman & C. Leich eds. 1981).

  Interpretations of Wittgenstein apart, acceptance of the possibility of literal meaning has passed
into the commonplace of contemporary analytical philosophy of language, even while philosophers
hotly dispute the source or explanation of that phenomenon. *See, e.g.*, W. ALSTON, PHILOSOPHY OF
LANGUAGE 74–75 (1964); M. BLACK, *Meaning and Intention*, in CAVEATS AND CRITIQUES: PHILO-
SOPHICAL ESSAYS IN LANGUAGE, LOGIC, AND ART 109 (1975); S. CAVELL, *Aesthetic Problems of
Modern Philosophy*, in MUST WE MEAN WHAT WE SAY? 73, 80–82 (1969); S. CAVELL, *Knowing
and Acknowledging, id.* at 238, 248–49; D. DAVIDSON, INQUIRIES INTO TRUTH AND INTERPRETA-
TION xix, 243–64 (1984); D. HOLDCROFT, WORDS AND DEEDS: PROBLEMS IN THE THEORY OF
SPEECH ACTS 122–23 (1978); R. MARTIN, THE MEANING OF LANGUAGE 217 (1987); M. PLATTS,
WAYS OF MEANING: AN INTRODUCTION TO A PHILOSOPHY OF LANGUAGE 130–32 (1979); I.
SCHEFFLER, BEYOND THE LETTER: A PHILOSOPHICAL INQUIRY INTO AMBIGUITY, VAGUENESS AND
METAPHOR IN LANGUAGE 81 (1979).

  In one philosopher's words:
    It is a platitude—something only a philosopher would dream of denying—that there are con-
  ventions of language, although we do not find it easy to say what those conventions are. If we
  look for the fundamental difference in verbal behavior between members of two linguistic communities, we can be sure of finding something which is arbitrary but perpetuates itself because
  of a common interest in coordination. In the case of conventions of language, that common
  interest derives from our common interest in taking advantage of, and in preserving, our ability
  to control others' beliefs and actions to some extent by means of sounds and marks. That
  interest in turn derives from many miscellaneous desires we have; to list them, list the ways
  you would be worse off in Babel.
D. LEWIS, *Languages and Language*, in 1 PHILOSOPHICAL PAPERS 163, 166 (1983).

  Obviously some tension exists between the way that language is discussed in analytic philosophy of
language and the way that it is discussed in other circles, including literary theory. Part of the difference between the terms of the debate in these two circles can be explained by the different extent to
which the two disciplines focus on "difficult" interpretations. This may also explain the extent to
which *some* branches of legal theory, with their focus on difficult interpretations in linguistically hard
cases, have been drawn to literary theory. Moreover, insofar as literature exists primarily to illuminate, inspire, and transform, its very existence encourages attempts to pierce literal meaning. The
relationship between the enterprise at issue and the view of literal meaning adopted suggests an important question: Might the purposes of the legal enterprise be so different from those of interpreting
literature that literal meaning is no longer an obstacle but instead a tool? I have no answer to this
question, nor do I intend to offer a few easy citations to suggest a familiarity I do not possess. Nevertheless, the very differences in focus between analytic philosophy of language and literary theory may
suggest that it is a bit too easy, for me or for those who draw on literary theory or other perspectives
on language, to assume that the applications of these perspectives to law cannot take place without
some theoretical slippage.

not of frogs or Oldsmobiles precisely because those marks, themselves, convey meaning independently of what might have been meant by any speaker. Of course there can never be *totally* acontextual meaning.[58] The community of speakers of the English language is itself a context. Yet meaning can be "acontextual" in the sense that that meaning draws on no other context besides those understandings shared among virtually all speakers of English.

Given that the meaning of words may be acontextually derived from our understandings of language, the central question becomes whether enough of these understandings exist to create the possibility of literal language. In other words, we must ask whether words have sufficient acontextual import so that communication can take place among speakers of English in such a way that at least a certain limited range of meaning, if not one and only one meaning, will be shared by all or almost all speakers of English. The answer to this question is clearly "yes." As with the shells that washed up on the beach in the shape of C-A-T, words strung together in sentences point us toward certain meanings on the basis of our shared understandings. At times these sentences may be descriptive, but at other times these comprehensible sentences may be general prescriptions—rules. Because we understand the rules of language, we understand the language of rules. Contextual understanding might be necessary to determine whether a given application does or does not serve the purposes of a rule's framers. Yet the rule itself communicates meaning as well, although that meaning might depart from the purposes behind the rule or from the richer understanding to be harvested from considering a wider range of factors than the rule's words. That we might learn more from considering additional factors or from more fully understanding a speaker's intentions does not mean that we learn nothing by consulting the language of rules themselves.

Of course, certain obvious, accessible, and by and large undisputable features of rules distinguish the meaning we cull from them from our interpretation of other types of communications. For example, when we interpret a rule of law, we understand that it is a law and that it is to be interpreted in light of surrounding language in the same law. In addition, ordinary "lawspeak" (habeas corpus, certiorari, party, appeal) can be viewed as a language for a subcommunity in the community of English speakers, capable of doing within the subcommunity what ordinary language does within the larger community of English speakers. Thus, although all those reading a statute come to that task with certain shared

---

58. *See* J. SEARLE, *Literal Meaning*, in EXPRESSION AND MEANING 117 (1979) (literal meaning exists albeit only against a set of background assumptions about contexts in which sentence could appropriately be uttered); Moore, *supra* note 54, at 304-07 (arguing that minimal context allows and is required for fixing references to singular terms).

assumptions, it is probable that almost all lawyers add to these an additional set of assumptions which are shared mainly by lawyers.[59]

Both those within the legal community and those within the larger linguistic community are capable of deriving the literal import of rules, even though the literal lawyer's meaning may occasionally diverge from the literal lay meaning of the same term. A law that limits membership in Parliament to those who take an oath "on the true faith of a Christian" literally excludes Jews by its language.[60] A statute requiring that the master of a vessel shall record in the log book "[e]very birth happening on board, with the sex of the infant, and the names of the parents,"[61] can be understood by virtually any speaker of English as requiring the master to take certain actions.[62] In these and countless other cases, statutes can be wrenched from most of the context of their enactment and application and still be read and understood.

---

59. Note that I am talking about language and about two different embellishments on the main theme of literal meaning. First, ordinary people within a given linguistic culture might share, as linguistic conventions, knowledge about how to interpret the language of rules, including conventions relating to the difference between normative and descriptive language and conventions telling them to interpret words in light of surrounding language in the same rule or statute. This suggests only that all competent speakers of the language in which the text is written have access to a certain minimal amount of noncontroversial information about what kind of text it is.

Second, literal meaning is not necessarily ordinary meaning, because linguistic conventions may exist within a technical or professional subcommunity of a larger community. For example, photographers may have a literal sense of the meaning of the term "burning in," physicians may have a literal sense of the meaning of the term "Cushing's Syndrome," and lawyers may have a literal sense of the meaning of the term "assumpsit," even though none of these are terms used at all or in the same way by ordinary English speakers. This second embellishment, however, must be sharply distinguished from other notions of "conventionalism" that build in much more than linguistic meaning. *See, e.g.,* S. Burton, An Introduction to Law and Legal Reasoning (1985); Fiss, *Conventionalism,* 58 S. Cal. L. Rev. 177 (1985); Fiss, *Objectivity and Interpretation,* 34 Stan. L. Rev. 739 (1982). The conventionalist legal literature talks merely about the conventions of permissible legal argument and does not confront the question of the relationship between the conventions of permissible legal argument and the conventions of literal meaning, whether ordinary or technical. Thus, legal conventionalists such as Fiss avoid questions regarding whether and why certain literal readings of legal rules are or are not permissible arguments within the legal interpretive community. It is these questions, in some sense more foundational, that concern me here, because my aim is to locate the particular permissible arguments in the legal interpretive community, rather than merely to assert the existence of permissible arguments.

60. Salomons v. Miller, 8 Ex. 778, 155 Eng. Rep. 1567 (1853); Miller v. Salomons, 7 Ex. 475, 155 Eng. Rep. 1036 (1852).

61. 46 U.S.C. § 201 (1958), *repealed by* Pub. L. No. 98-89, 97 Stat. 600 (1983).

62. "When you come tomorrow, bring my football boots. Also, if humanly possible, Irish water spaniel. Urgent. Regards. Tuppy."

"What do you make of that, Jeeves?"

"As I interpret the document, sir, Mr. Glossop wishes you, when you come tomorrow, to bring his football boots. Also, if humanly possible, an Irish water spaniel. He hints that the matter is urgent, and sends his regards."

"Yes, that's how I read it, too . . . ."

P.G. Woodehouse, *The Ordeal of Young Tuppy, quoted in* S. Blackburn, Spreading the Word: Groundings in the Philosophy of Language 3 (1984).

B. Does Language Constrain?

The conceptual question of whether literal meaning is possible can therefore be answered affirmatively. Rules may point to results that diverge from those that a decisionmaker would have reached apart from the literal meaning of the rule. When there is such divergence, however, the psychological question remains: Is it possible in such cases for decisionmakers to follow the literal meaning of the rule rather than their own judgment regarding how the case should be resolved?

The psychological challenge to formalism involves the claim that decisionmakers will usually take all factors they believe to be relevant into account, or at least that they will usually feel compelled to reach "reasonable" results whether or not the language of the rule points in that direction.[63] When expressed this way, it is obvious that the psychological question is an empirical one. Accordingly, it cannot be answered by mere argument. Yet despite legal scholarship's sorry failure to take the psychological challenge seriously,[64] the possibility that judges usually obey their own rule-independent judgment is, on its face, quite plausible. We can easily imagine a world in which decisionmakers consider everything that they feel relevant and ignore, or at least slight, any inconsistent external instructions in making their decisions. The question is whether that is the world of the law.

Certainly some legal decisionmakers conform to this model. Although one may dispute as excessive the generalizations of the more extreme Realists, it is difficult to deny the existence of decisionmakers who consult the rules only to create *post hoc* rationalizations. Indeed, to the extent that legal systems resemble the model in which a rule-avoiding norm is always available, such behavior is encouraged. Insofar as the view ever prevailed that there were few decisionmakers who rejected, ignored, or bent the plausibly determinate mandates of governing rule, it is important that that view be shown for the optimistic fantasy it is. Yet to accept that some judges arrive at decisions without considering rules does not imply that all or most decisionmakers act in such a way as either an inevitable feature of human nature or even as a contingent feature of judicial behavior.

Just as it is a mistake to assume that because some judges ignore rules most judges do so, it is also a mistake to assume that because rules sometimes constrain, they usually constrain. The truth, an empirical rather than a logical one, plainly lies between the extremes of always and never, or even between the lesser extremes of rarely and usually. Although this is not the place to examine the rudimentary empirical work that has been

---

63. *See* Aleinikoff, *Constitutional Law in the Age of Balancing*, 96 YALE L.J. 943, 985, 1004 (1987).

64. Noteworthy exceptions are J. FRANK, LAW AND THE MODERN MIND (1930), and Kennedy, *supra* note 37. However, legal scholarship still must systematically investigate the important issues that Frank, Kennedy, and others have raised in an impressionistic way.

done on the question, it is sufficient for my purposes to note that this research has, not surprisingly, yielded the result of "sometimes."[65] In some settings, decisionmakers sometimes apply instructions external to their own decisional process even if those instructions diverge in outcome from the results the decisionmakers otherwise would have reached. This conclusion should cause no surprise as long as we recognize that people often do what *others* think best. If privates in the army often follow orders instead of making autonomous choices, and if privates might behave in this way with respect to general orders in addition to particularized commands, we can imagine judges doing the same with respect to rules.[66]

We have seen that, as a descriptive and conceptual matter, rules can generate determinate outcomes; that those outcomes may diverge from what some decisionmakers think ought to be done; and that some decisionmakers will follow such external mandates rather than their own best particularistic judgment. The normative question of formalism now remains: To what extent *should* a system legitimate the avoidance of literal meaning when avoidance seems to be the optimal outcome to the decisionmaker? To put it simply, now that we have established that formalism—in the sense of following the literal mandate of the canonical formulation of a rule—is conceptually and psychologically possible, we must ask whether it is desirable. Before turning to that question, however, I want

---

65. *See* D. BLACK, THE BEHAVIOR OF LAW (1976); L. FRIEDMAN, THE LEGAL SYSTEM: A SOCIAL SCIENCE PERSPECTIVE (1975); Hogan & Henley, *Nomotics: The Science of Human Rule Systems*, 5 LAW & SOC'Y REV. 135 (1970); Johnson, *Law, Politics, and Judicial Decision Making: Lower Federal Court Uses of Supreme Court Decisions*, 21 LAW & SOC'Y REV. 325 (1987); Scandura, *New Directions for Theory and Research on Rule Learning*, 28 ACTA PSYCHOLOGICA 301 (1968).

66. There is something unrealistic about all of this, because it erroneously assumes that my paradigm "easy" cases are representative of the kinds of decisions that come before decisionmakers. They are not, at least when we take "decisionmaker" in a somewhat narrow sense to refer to formal decisionmakers such as judges sitting in courts of law. In most legal systems, various screening devices ensure that cases at the center of decisional determinacy will not enter the formal adjudicative process. The time and expense of litigation and the widespread inclination to avoid futile battles are such that decisions at the core of settled meaning seldom confront any formal decisionmaking process. *See* Priest, *Reexamining the Selection Hypothesis: Learning from Wittman's Mistakes*, 14 J. LEGAL STUD. 215 (1985) (develops selection hypothesis to determine which cases are settled and which are litigated); Priest and Klein, *The Selection of Disputes for Litigation*, 13 J. LEGAL STUD. 1 (1984) (presents model to predict whether litigation will be resolved by suit or settlement).

This, however, is but a contingent feature of modern legal systems. It is possible to imagine a legal system closer to a sporting event, where umpires call "safe" or "out" on every play, or where officials with red penalty flags patrol the social landscape, ready to throw the flag and call "tort," or "crime," or "breach of etiquette" whenever there is a transgression of the rules. Obvious logistical problems prevent such a system from being a reality, but it is a useful *Gedankenexperiment* for thinking about the innumerable instances in which rules are followed or clearly broken without coming to the attention of the judicial system.

Many legal systems, unlike those with "roving umpires," operate largely in the area of linguistic indeterminacy, generated either by vagueness of the governing norm or by open texture when previously clear norms confront the unexpected. And in some systems, such as that of the United States, the likelihood of success is sufficient to make it worth litigating cases in which linguistic determinacy produces a politically or morally uncomfortable result. But that is exactly our question, because the weight the system gives to literal meaning will determine the extent to which it is worth litigating against literal meaning.

to answer an important counterargument to the possibility of the type of formalism defined in this section.

C. *Language and Rules*

Until this point my argument may appear to create a false dichotomy. I have counterpoised the vision of decisionmakers who follow the literal language of a rule with that of decisionmakers who follow the dictates of their own externally unguided opinions. But are these the only alternatives? Although *rules* can and do constrain, is it not possible that these rules need not be equated with the literal meaning of the language in which they happen to be articulated? In other words, is portraying the vice of formalism as the vice of literalism actually confusing rules with the literal meanings of their explicit formulations?

The argument that rules can be distinguished from the language in which they are written has a distinguished lineage in Anglo-American legal thought. We see, for example, Ronald Dworkin urging interpreters to search for or to construct the "real" rule lying behind the mere words on a printed page.[67] Somewhat less explicitly, the "mischief rule" of the common law compels the literal language of a rule to yield to the purpose behind a rule when application of the literal language would frustrate the rule's purpose.[68] Indeed, the mischief rule and related principles urging the primacy of purpose over text are features of the thinking of Fuller, of Hart and Sacks, and also of Llewellyn's "Grand Style" of judging.[69] As a matter of fact, Llewellyn distinguished the Grand Style from the Formal Style because he believed that formalism, as the obeisance to the literal language of a rule, could frustrate the rule's purpose and lead to difficulties where the practical consequences of the decision would indicate a different result.

The language in which a rule is written and the purpose behind that rule can diverge precisely because that purpose is plastic in a way that literal language is not. Purpose cannot be reduced to any one canonical formulation, for when purpose is set down canonically, that canonical formulation of purpose may frustrate the purpose itself. It is because purpose is not reduced to a concrete set of words that it retains its sensitivity to novel cases, to bizarre applications, and to the complex unfolding of the human experience. Thus, for the recourse to purpose to "solve" the problem of formalism, the purpose must not be imprisoned in the rigidity of

---

67. LAW'S EMPIRE, *supra* note 31, at 16–17.

68. The standard references for this rule are Heydon's Case, 76 Eng. Rep. 637 (Ex. 1584), and Church of the Holy Trinity v. United States, 143 U.S. 457 (1892); see discussion *supra* note 28. *See also* J.G. SUTHERLAND, STATUTES AND STATUTORY CONSTRUCTION §§ 45.05, 45.09 (N. Singer rev. ed. 1984).

69. K. LLEWELLYN, *supra* note 1, *passim*; *see* W. TWINING, KARL LLEWELLYN AND THE REALIST MOVEMENT 210–11 (1973).

words. This unrigidified purpose can be explained, clarified, and enriched as new examples and applications come to our attention. The purpose behind the "No vehicles in the park" regulation is not embarrassed by the statue of the truck exactly because purpose can bend to the circumstances of the moment in a way that language, with its acontextual autonomy of meaning, cannot. In contrast, the term "vehicles," at least at the core, literally refers to vehicles;[70] if it turns out that the prohibition of some vehicles does not serve the purpose of the regulation, then the embarrassment is unavoidable.[71]

If adhering to concretized language causes this embarrassment, then why not adhere to the purpose of the rule rather than the words of the rule? To do so would conform with the models advocated by Fuller,[72] Hart and Sacks,[73] Dworkin,[74] and Llewellyn[75] and would match what can be called, with only negligible exaggeration, the current paradigm of American statutory interpretation.[76] Yet locating the idea and the force of a rule in its purpose rather than in its formulation poses the same problem posed by concretized rules, except at one remove. To illustrate the point, suppose the purpose of the "no vehicles in the park" regulation is the preservation of peace and quiet in the park. Suppose, as well, that this purpose derives from an even deeper purpose of maximizing the pleasure of the residents of the town. Now imagine that a town native who has just

---

70. Note that the "No vehicles in the park" example may be a flawed illustration of the problem Hart, Fuller, and I explore, because locomotive capacity may now be definitional of a "vehicle." Insofar as this is true, the statue is not a vehicle, and no conflict arises between literal meaning and purpose. This is a defect only in the example, however, rather than in the general formulation of the issue. I will therefore stipulate, for the purposes of this argument, that a statue of a vehicle *is* a vehicle, just as a lion in a cage is still a lion. Consider a rule prohibiting "live animals on the bus" and whether it would prohibit carrying on the bus three live goldfish in a sealed plastic bag.

71. My point about the plasticity of purpose should not be confused with claims, often correct, about the indeterminacy of purpose. *See, e.g.*, Easterbrook, *Foreword: The Court and the Economic System*, 98 HARV. L. REV. 4, 15-18 (1984); Easterbrook, *Statutes' Domains*, 50 U. CHI. L. REV. 533, 537-38 (1983); Kennedy, *supra* note 1; Posner, *Statutory Interpretation—In the Classroom and in the Courtroom*, 50 U. CHI. L. REV. 800, 819-820 (1983). Insofar as purpose becomes both concrete and determinate, as when everyone agrees what the purpose is, the argument that "ruleness" resides in purpose becomes more plausible. But when some conception of purpose is determinate, noncanonical purpose itself can operate formalistically. Conversely, if purpose is comparatively indeterminate, then it looks especially odd to say that the rule exists not in the specific rule-formulation, but in the quite different and nonspecific purpose. Thus, those who argue for the indeterminacy of purpose make claims consistent with mine.

72. L. FULLER, *supra* note 55, at 81-91; Fuller, *supra* note 53; Fuller, *The Speluncean Explorers*, 62 HARV. L. REV. 616, 620-26 (1949) ("opinion" of Foster, J.).

73. H. Hart & A. Sacks, *supra* note 54.

74. LAW'S EMPIRE, *supra* note 31.

75. K. LLEWELLYN, *supra* note 1.

76. *See* Wellman, *Dworkin and the Legal Process Tradition: The Legacy of Hart & Sacks*, 29 ARIZ. L. REV. 413 (1987); Note, *Intent, Clear Statements, and the Common Law: Statutory Construction in the Supreme Court*, 95 HARV. L. REV. 892 (1982). Recent manifestations of this paradigm include G. CALABRESI, A COMMON LAW FOR THE AGE OF STATUTES (1982); Eskridge, *Dynamic Statutory Interpretation*, 135 U. PA. L. REV. 1479 (1987); Langevoort, *Statutory Obsolescence and the Judicial Process: The Revisionist Role of the Courts in Federal Banking Regulation*, 85 MICH. L. REV. 672 (1987). *But see, e.g.*, United States v. Locke, 471 U.S. 84 (1985) (failure to file timely claim deprives petitioner of right, irrespective of statutory purpose).

won six gold medals in the Olympic Games is returning to this park, the scene of her youth, along with a widely popular President of the United States. Suppose as well that the park with the "no vehicles in the park" regulation is the only suitable place for the motorcade, which must be a motorcade because the President is disabled and cannot walk. Under these circumstances, the purpose behind the "no vehicles in the park" rule would be served by excluding the motorcade, but the purpose behind *that* purpose would be frustrated. Thus the same logic that requires the formulation of a rule to be defeasible in the service of its purpose would also require that purpose to be defeasible in the service of the purpose behind *it*.

As the example reveals, the potential tension between the general goal and its concretized instantiation exists at every level. At one level, the tension is between language and purpose; at the next, it is between that purpose and the deep purpose lying behind it; at the next, between the deep purpose and an even deeper purpose; and so on. When we decide that purpose must not be frustrated by its instantiation, we embark upon a potentially infinite regress in which all forms of concretization are defeasible.

The view that rules should be interpreted to allow their purposes to trump their language in fact collapses the distinction between a rule and a reason, and thus loses the very concept of a rule.[77] Rules are by definition general. They gather numerous known and unknown particulars under headings such as "vehicles," "punishment," "dogs," and "every person who is directly or indirectly the beneficial owner of more than 10 per centum of any class of any [registered] equity security (other than an exempted security)." After identifying a category of items or events to which the rule applies, in the *protasis*, rules then prescribe what shall be done with these particulars in the *apodosis*.[78] Occasionally, however, not all of the particulars comprising the rule's category of coverage are suitable for the prescribed treatment; the generalizations that are a necessary part of any rule treat all members of the class in a manner that may be appropriate only for *most* members of the class. What, then, is to happen when a case arises in which the generalization does not apply to this particular? When a rule's prescribed treatment is unsuitable, if the decisionmaker

---

77. Note, however, that this claim is not inconsistent with the view that rules should be interpreted to further their purposes when several interpretations of the rule are possible *and all are supported by the language of the rule.* In such cases, it is not only possible but positively desirable to choose the interpretation that will serve the rule's purpose. *See* H.L.A. HART, *Introduction*, in ESSAYS IN JURISPRUDENCE AND PHILOSOPHY 1, 8 (1983).

78. On this terminology for the structure of rules, which distinguishes the part of the rule specifying its operative facts from the part describing the consequences flowing from the existence of those facts, see W. TWINING & D. MIERS, HOW TO DO THINGS WITH RULES 136–40 (2d ed. 1982). *See also* Friedman, *Legal Rules and the Process of Social Change*, 19 STAN. L. REV. 786, 786–87 (1967) (same distinction with different labels); Schlag, *Rules and Standards*, 33 UCLA L. REV. 379, 381–83 (1985) (same).

were to ignore the rule, the rule would not be a real rule providing a reason for decision but would be a mere rule of thumb, defeasible when the purposes behind the rule would not be served. If every application that would not serve the reason behind the rule were jettisoned from the coverage of the rule, then the decision procedure would be identical to one applying reasons directly to individual cases, without the mediation of rules. Under such a model, rules are superfluous except as predictive guides, for they lack any normative power of their own. By contrast, if in cases in which the particular application would not serve the reasons behind the rule, the rule nevertheless provides its own reason for deciding the case according to the rule, the rule itself has a normative force that provides a reason for action or decision.

In summary, it is exactly a rule's rigidity, even in the face of applications that would ill serve its purpose, that renders it a rule.[79] This rigidity derives from the language of the rule's formulation, which prevents the contemplation of every fact and principle relevant to a particular application of the rule. To be formalistic in Llewellyn's sense is to be governed by the rigidity of a rule's formulation; yet, this governance by rigidity is central to the constraint of regulative rules. Formalism in this sense is therefore indistinguishable from "rulism," for what makes a regulative rule a rule, and what distinguishes it from a reason, is precisely the unwillingness to pierce the generalization even in cases in which the generalization appears to the decisionmaker to be inapposite. A rule's acontextual rigidity is what makes it a rule.

D. The Idea of a Closed System

We now are in a position to reconsider the charge that formalism embodies the erroneous view that law (or any other decisional domain) is a closed system. We have seen that rules can generate answers or exclude otherwise eligible answers from consideration. We also have seen that there are rules, such as one prohibiting the shooting of pelicans, whose application throughout much of their range requires recourse only to the rule and to uncontroversial judgments of meaning and identification of discrete particulars. There can therefore be systems whose operations require recourse only to the norms of the system and to accepted linguistic and observational skills.

Such a system would be closed, but it would not necessarily be complete. Closedness and completeness are different properties. Closedness refers to the capacity of a system to decide cases within the confines of that

---

79. This is not to say that rules are always or even ever good things to have. My aim now is to distinguish a form of decisionmaking in which generalizations have independent normative power from a form of decisionmaking in which the full richness of the particular event always is open to consideration. The questions of whether rules should be employed, in which domains, and to what extent, are addressed below. *See infra* Section III.

system, while completeness refers to the extent to which a system deals with those cases at all. A mathematical system is closed insofar as the rules of mathematics provide an answer to the question "What is the sum of 97 and 53?" But that same system is incomplete insofar as it provides no answer to the question "What should the United States do about the problem of poverty?" The dimension of completeness, although perhaps unimportant for mathematics, is important for law precisely because most modern legal systems claim the ability to deal with a wide range of issues. Insofar as the human experience is especially complex and fluid, the legal system is likely to be frustrated by its incompleteness, its frequent inability to answer the questions it wants to answer. Commonly, we plan for these frustrations by rendering the norms of the law less determinate and thereby using vagueness as the tool by which we plan for the open texture of experience.[80] As a result, legal systems, to avoid the consequences of widespread incompleteness, often employ norms sufficiently indeterminate to accommodate much that is important in the world at large, and in doing so sacrifice the occasional virtues of closedness. Such systems are more open even at the expense of being less predictable and less constraining of their decisionmakers.

Thus, legal systems often reject closedness because they must deal with a large array of problems presented by a complex and fluid world. But this is to say that comparatively closed systems may sometimes be undesirable, not that they are not possible. The importance of drawing this distinction is to stress that the degree of closedness may vary, and that closedness is a tool that might be usable in some domains even if, in untempered form, it is not the *only* tool we would want to use for an entire system of social control.

When applied to individual norms rather than to entire systems, closedness is merely another word for ruleness. By limiting access to the reasons behind the rule, rules truncate the array of considerations available to a decisionmaker.[81] Rules get in the way. They exclude from consideration factors that a decisionmaker unconstrained by those rules would take into

---

80. *See* Schauer, *Authority and Indeterminacy*, in AUTHORITY REVISITED: NOMOS XXIX 28 (1987).

81. The closed system/open system dispute merely recasts the debate about legal positivism in different terminology. Any version of legal positivism is premised on what Ronald Dworkin, no positivist, has felicitously referred to as "pedigree." TAKING RIGHTS SERIOUSLY, *supra* note 31, at 17. Positivism posits that *legal* norms are identified by reference to some other norm, rule, or standard that distinguishes legal from non-legal norms. Hart's "rule of recognition" serves this purpose, H.L.A. HART, *supra* note 1, as does the "next higher norm" for Kelsen. H. KELSEN, THE PURE THEORY OF LAW 193–278 (M. Knight trans. 1967). The positivist conceives of the set of norms so pedigreed as constituting some sort of a closed system, although that system will not necessarily decide all or even most cases that come before the courts. Kelsen, for example, sees every law-applying act as only partially determined by law. *Id.* at 233–36, 244–45. By contrast, the opponents of positivism, most notably Dworkin, attack the pedigreeability thesis by arguing that in no case is the distinction between pedigreed and nonpedigreed norms dispositive and consequently the characterization of law in terms of pedigreed norms is descriptively inaccurate.

account. Understanding the way in which rules truncate the range of reasons available to a decisionmaker helps us to appreciate the distinction between formalism and functionalism, or instrumentalism.[82] Functionalism focuses on outcomes and particularly on the outcome the decisionmaker deems optimal. Rules get in the way of this process, and thus functionalism can be perceived as a view of decisionmaking that seeks to minimize the space between what a particular decisionmaker concludes, all things considered, should be done and what some rule says should be done. Rules *block* consideration of the full array of reasons that bear upon a particular decision in two different ways. First, they exclude from consideration reasons that might have been available had the decisionmaker not been constrained by a rule. Second, the rule itself becomes a reason for action, or a reason for decision.

The notion of a rule as a reason for decision requires further exploration. What makes formalism formal is this very feature: the fact that taking rules seriously involves taking their mandates as reasons for decision independent of the reasons for decision lying *behind* the rule.[83] If it were otherwise, the set of reasons considered by a decisionmaker would be congruent with the set of reasons behind the rule, and the rule would add nothing to the calculus. Rules therefore supply reasons for action *qua* rules. When the reason supplied by a rule tracks the reasons behind the rule, then the rule is in a different way superfluous in the particular case. Rules become interesting when they point toward a different result than do the reasons behind the rule—when they indicate, for example, that statues of vehicles ought to be excluded even though the reasons behind the rule indicate that the statues ought not to be excluded. To take these occasionally perverse reasons as always relevant and therefore sometimes dispositive is condemned as "formalistic" because it abstracts the mandates of a rule from the reasons behind it. Yet that is what rules do. Refusal to abstract the rule from its reasons is not to have rules. This refusal reduces rules to rules of thumb, useful but intrinsically unweighty indicators of the results likely to be reached by direct application of reasons.

Thus, the essential equivalency of formalism and "ruleness" is before us. Viewing formalism as merely rule-governed decisionmaking does not make it desirable. Yet recognizing the way in which formalism is merely a way of describing the process of taking rules seriously allows us to escape

---

82. *See, e.g.*, R. SUMMERS, INSTRUMENTALISM AND AMERICAN LEGAL THEORY 136-75 (1982); Aleinikoff, *supra* note 63, at 985; Summers, *Professor Fuller's Jurisprudence and America's Dominant Philosophy of Law*, 92 HARV. L. REV. 433 (1978).

83. Insofar as a system permits recourse to the purpose behind a rule's formulation but does not permit departure from *that* purpose when adhering to it will produce unfortunate results or will frustrate the even deeper purpose behind it, that system will still be formal in the sense I am now using that term. It will also be rule-bound, because the less than totally plastic purpose (although more plastic than the rule-formulation) will operate as a rule vis-a-vis the higher order reasons that generated that particular purpose.

the epithetical mode and to confront the critical question of formalism: What, if anything, is good about the unwillingness to go beneath the rule and apply its purpose, or the purposes behind that purpose, directly to the case before the decisionmaker?

III. Should Choice Be Restricted?

Let me recapitulate. One conception takes the vice of formalism to consist of a decisionmaker's denial, couched in the language of obedience to clear rules, of having made any choice at all. Yet rules, if followed, may not leave a decisionmaker free choice. Rules *can* limit decisional choice, and decisionmakers *can* abide by those limitations. Those limitations come in most cases from the literal language of a rule's formulation, for to take a rule as anything other than the rule's formulation, or at least the meaning of the rule's formulation,[84] is ultimately to deny the idea of a rule.

Thus, formalism merges into ruleness, and both are inextricably intertwined with literalism,[85] i.e., the willingness to make decisions according to the literal meaning of words or phrases or sentences or paragraphs on a printed page, even if the consequences of that decision seem either to frustrate the purpose behind those words or to diverge significantly from what the decisionmaker thinks—the rule aside—should be done. But does dem-

---

84. In a trivial sense, rules differ from their formulations. *See, e.g.*, G. BAKER & P. HACKER, *supra* note 57, at 41–52; M. BLACK, *The Analysis of Rules*, in MODELS AND METAPHORS: STUDIES IN LANGUAGE AND PHILOSOPHY 95 (1962); D. SHWAYDER, THE STRATIFICATION OF BEHAVIOUR 241 (1965); G. vonWRIGHT, PRACTICAL REASON 68 (1983). "Do not walk on the grass," "Walking on the grass is prohibited," and "No walking on the grass" constitute one and not three rules. Referring to these three formulations as formulations of only one rule, however, presupposes that all have the same meaning, that the differences are syntactical and not semantic. Thus, the distinction between a rule and its formulation is like the distinction between a proposition and a sentence. When I discuss a rule and equate it with its formulation, I therefore mean that a rule is that set of semantically equivalent rule formulations.

85. My references to "literalism" are slightly metaphorical. As noted above, *see supra* note 59, literalism includes those aspects of context, such as the appearance of words in a statute rather than in a poem, that are accessible to all or most readers. Moreover, although I often use single words as examples, statutes are not read word by word, but instead by sentences, paragraphs, and larger units of text. This is not to deny, however, that the ability to assign meanings to individual words is what enables us to understand a sentence we have never seen before. *See* D. DAVIDSON, *Truth and Meaning*, in INQUIRIES INTO TRUTH AND INTERPRETATION 17 (1984). This assertion, however, superficially in conflict with Frege's assertion that only in the context of a sentence does a word have any meaning, *see* G. FREGE, THE FOUNDATIONS OF ARITHMETIC (J.L. Austin trans. 1959), is not without its detractors and complexities. *See, e.g.*, Wallace, *Only in the Context of a Sentence Do Words Have Any Meaning*, in CONTEMPORARY PERSPECTIVES IN THE PHILOSOPHY OF LANGUAGE 305 (P. French, T. Uehling, Jr., & H. Wettstein eds. 1979).

Still, *pace* Fuller, *supra* note 53, at 662–63, sentences and paragraphs can have literal and even acontextual meaning insofar as an entire sentence or paragraph may supply enough context to make its meaning comparatively clear. As texts become lengthier and richer it is often *more* possible to understand those texts without departing from them and thus *more* possible for them to have acontextual meaning.

Moreover, literal meaning need not always be ordinary meaning. Where some aspect of the minimal and uncontested context makes it plain that a settled specialized or technical meaning of a term or phrase applies, that technical meaning, rather than the ordinary usage of the man on the Clapham omnibus, is controlling.

onstrating that formalism is ruleness rescue formalism? Restated, what is so good about decision according to rules?

The simple answer to this question, and perhaps also the correct one, is "nothing." Little about decision constrained by the rigidity of rules seems intrinsically valuable. Once we understand that rules get in the way, that they gain their ruleness by cutting off access to factors that might lead to the best resolution in a particular case, we see that rules function as impediments to optimally sensitive decisionmaking. Rules doom decisionmaking to mediocrity by mandating the inaccessibility of excellence.

Nor is there anything essentially *just* about a system of rules. We have scarce reason to believe that rule-based adjudication is more likely to be just than are systems in which rules do not block a decisionmaker, especially a just decisionmaker, from considering every reason that would assist her in reaching the best decision. Insofar as factors screened from consideration by a rule might in a particular case turn out to be those necessary to reach a just result, rules stand in the way of justice in those cases and thus impede optimal justice in the long term. We equate Solomon's wisdom with justice not because Solomon followed the rules in solving the dispute over the baby but because Solomon came up with exactly the right solution for that case. We frequently laud not history's rule followers, but those whose abilities at particularized decisionmaking transcend the inherent limitations of rules.

Still, that rules may be in one sense unjust, or even that they may be inappropriate in much of what we call a legal system, does not mean there is nothing to be said for rules. One of the things that can be said for rules is the value variously expressed as predictability or certainty. But if we pursue the predictability theme, we see that what most arguments for ruleness share is a focus on disabling certain classes of decisionmakers from making certain kinds of decisions.[86] Predictability follows from the decision to treat all instances falling within some accessible category in the same way. It is a function of the way in which rules decide ahead of time how *all* cases within a class will be determined.

Predictability is fostered to the extent that four different requirements are satisfied. The first of the factors contributing to predictability is the capacity on the part of those relying on a rule to identify certain particulars as instances of a given category (for example, that pelicans are birds). When there is a more or less uniform and uncontroversial ability to say

---

86. *See generally* A. KOCOUREK, AN INTRODUCTION TO THE SCIENCE OF LAW 165–85 (1930); R. WASSERSTROM, THE JUDICIAL DECISION: TOWARD A THEORY OF LEGAL JUSTIFICATION 60–66 (1961); Marsh, *Principle and Discretion in the Judicial Process,* 68 LAW Q. REV. 226 (1952). Along with Wasserstrom, *supra,* at 61, I object to the use of the word "certainty" in this context because, unlike the term "predictability," it suggests that no doubt is involved. I can predict that it will snow in Vermont this winter and rely on that prediction in making winter plans, yet still not be *certain* that it will snow. Although one usage of "certain" does recognize variability, I prefer the term "predictability" because its common usage implies such variability.

that some item is a member of some category, little in the way of potentially variable judgment clouds the prediction of whether the rule will apply to this particular item. This relates to the second factor: that the decisionmakers in the system will perceive those particulars as being members of the same category perceived by the addressees and will be seen as so perceiving by those affected. That is, people perceive pelicans as birds; decisionmakers perceive pelicans as birds; and people know that decisionmakers will perceive pelicans as birds. Third, the rule must speak in terms of an accessible category. Predictability requires that a rule cover a category whose denotation is substantially noncontroversial among the class of addressees of the rule and common to the addressees of the rule and those who apply it. Finally, the rule must treat all members of a category in the same way. Only if the consequences specified in the apodosis of the rule are as accessible and noncontroversial as the coverage specified in the protasis can a rule produce significant predictability of application. Thus, predictability comes from the knowledge that if this is a bird a certain result will follow, and from the confidence that what I now perceive to be a bird will be considered a bird by the ultimate decisionmaker.

This predictability comes only at a price.[87] Situations may arise in which putting this particular into that category seems just too crude—something about this particular makes us desire to treat it specially. *This* vehicle is merely a statue, emits no fumes, makes no noise, and endangers no lives; it ought to be treated differently from those vehicles whose characteristics mesh with the purpose behind the rule. Serving the goal of predictability, however, requires that we ignore this difference, because to acknowledge this difference is also to create the power—the *jurisdiction*—to determine whether this vehicle or that vehicle actually serves the purpose of the "no vehicles in the park" rule. It is the jurisdiction to determine that only some vehicles fit the purpose of the rule that undermines the confidence that *all* vehicles will be prohibited. No longer is it the case that anything that is a *vehicle*, a moderately accessible category, is excluded. Instead, the category is now that of *vehicles whose prohibition will serve the purposes of the "no vehicles in the park" rule*, a potentially far more controversial category.

Thus, the key to understanding the relationship of ruleness to predictability is the idea of decisional jurisdiction.[88] The issue is not whether the statue serves the purpose of the "no vehicles in the park" rule. It is whether giving some decisionmaker jurisdiction to determine what the

---

87. *See, e.g.*, H.L.A. HART, *supra* note 1, at 121-32.
88. On jurisdiction in this sense, see Schauer, *Slippery Slopes*, 99 HARV. L. REV. 361, 367-68 (1985). *See also* Fried, *Two Concepts of Interests: Some Reflections on the Supreme Court's Balancing Test*, 76 HARV. L. REV. 755, 759-65, 771 (1963) (noting that courts define their competencies in the process of making substantive decisions); Rawls, *Two Concepts of Rules*, 64 PHIL. REV. 3, 10 (1955).

rule's purpose is (as well as jurisdiction to determine whether some item fits that purpose) injects a possibility of variance substantially greater than that involved in giving a decisionmaker jurisdiction solely to determine whether some particular is or is not a vehicle. Note also that the jurisdictional question has a double aspect. When we grant jurisdiction we are first concerned with the range of equally correct decisions that might be made in the exercise of that jurisdiction. If there is no authoritative statement of the purpose behind the "no vehicles in the park" rule, granting jurisdiction to determine that purpose would allow a decisionmaker to decide whether the purpose is to preserve quiet, to prevent air pollution, or to prevent accidents, and each of these determinations would be equally correct. In addition to increasing the range of correct decisions, however, certain grants of jurisdiction increase the likelihood of erroneous determinations. Compare "No vehicles in the park" with "The park is closed to vehicles whose greatest horizontal perimeter dimension, when added to their greatest vertical perimeter dimension, exceeds the lesser of (a) sixty-eight feet, six inches and (b) the greatest horizontal perimeter dimension, added to the greatest vertical perimeter dimension, of the average of the largest passenger automobile manufactured in the United States by the three largest automobile manufacturers in the preceding year." The second adds no inherent variability, but it certainly compounds the possibility of decisionmaker error. Creating the jurisdiction to determine whether the purposes of a rule are served undermines predictability by allowing the determination of any of several possible purposes; in addition, the creation of that jurisdiction engenders the possibility that those who exercise it might just get it wrong.

Grants of decisional jurisdiction not only increase permissible variance and the possibility of "computational" error, they also involve decisionmakers in determinations that a system may prefer to have made by someone else. We may believe that courts are less competent to make certain decisions than other bodies; for example, we may feel that certain kinds of fact-finding are better done by legislatures. There may also be moral or political reasons to restrict the judge's discretion, for decision-making implicates profound questions of just who in a given domain may legitimately make certain decisions. It is, for example, a plausible position that the public rather than the University of Michigan philosophy department should make the moral determinations involved in governing the United States, even if the University of Michigan philosophy department would make better choices.

Although decreasing the possibility of variance and error by the decisionmaker contributes to the ability of addressees of rules to predict the consequences of application of those rules, limited variance can serve other values as well. If decisionmakers are denied jurisdiction to determine whether a particular instance actually justifies its inclusion in a larger generalization or are denied jurisdiction to determine the best result on the basis of all germane factors, the part of the system inhabited by those decisionmakers becomes more stable. Treating a large group of different particulars in the same way—the inevitable byproduct of the generalization of rules—dampens the range of variance in result by suppressing consideration of a wide range of potentially relevant differences. Thus, stability, not as a necessary condition for predictability but as a value in its own right, is fostered by truncating the decisionmaking authority.

Because rule-bound decisionmaking is inherently stabilizing, it is inherently conservative, in the nonpolitical sense of the word.[89] By limiting the ability of decisionmakers to consider every factor relevant to an event, rules make it more difficult to adapt to a changing future. Rules force the future into the categories of the past. Note the important asymmetry here, the way in which rules operate not to enable but only to disable. A decisionmaker can never exceed the optimal result based on all relevant factors. Thus, a rule-bound decisionmaker, precluded from taking into account certain features of the present case, can never do better but can do worse than a decisionmaker seeking the optimal result for a case through a rule-free decision.

Yet this conservatism, suboptimization, and inflexibility in the face of a changing future need not be universally condemned. Rules stabilize by inflating the importance of the classifications of yesterday. We achieve stability, valuable in its place, by relinquishing some part of our ability to improve on yesterday. Again the issue is jurisdiction, for those who have jurisdiction to improve on yesterday also have jurisdiction to make things worse.[90] To stabilize, to operate in an inherently conservative mode, is to give up some of the possibility of improvement in exchange for guarding against some of the possibility of disaster. Whether, when, and where the game is worth the candle, however, cannot be determined acontextually.[91]

---

89. *See* Horwitz, *The Rule of Law: An Unqualified Human Good?* (Book Review), 86 YALE L.J. 561 (1977). I use the term "conservatism" to refer to the desire to hold onto the past or present in the face of pressures to change. This usage bears only a contingent connection to the range of political views now labeled "conservative." Left-wing conservatism is not oxymoronic, because one can imagine left-wing systems adopting preservational (conservative) strategies or systems to prevent movement away to the right.

90. This is not a logical truth. Grants of jurisdiction can incorporate substantive requirements. Dworkin, *Non-Neutral Principles*, in READING RAWLS: CRITICAL STUDIES OF A THEORY OF JUSTICE 124 (N. Daniels ed. 1975). Insofar as some grants of jurisdiction aim to increase the ability of decisionmakers to adapt to an unknown future, however, they will be comparatively open-ended. It is this open-endedness, whether couched in substantive (do good) or less substantive (determine the purpose) terms, that creates the possibility of unintended and uncontrollable variance.

91. I therefore disagree with Kennedy, *Form and Substance in Private Law Adjudication*, 89 HARV. L. REV. 1685 (1976), insofar as he argues that ruleness is acontextually individualistic and particularization is acontextually altruistic. Even if there is truth in Kennedy's acontextuality, it still is not clear that his analysis of the acontextual tendencies promoted by ruleness is correct. It is quite plausible that the inherently stabilizing tendencies of rule-bound adjudication will dampen individual differences, stifle claims to special treatment as an individual, and encourage decisional modesty rather than decisional arrogance. It could be argued quite sensibly that all these tendencies foster rather than impede altruism.

In sum, it is clearly true that rules get in the way, but this need not always be considered a bad thing. It may be a liability to get in the way of wise decisionmakers who sensitively consider all of the relevant factors as they accurately pursue the good. However, it may be an asset to restrict misguided, incompetent, wicked, power-hungry, or simply mistaken decisionmakers whose own sense of the good might diverge from that of the system they serve. The problem, of course, is the difficulty in determining which characterization will fit decisionmakers; we must therefore decide the extent to which we are willing to disable good decisionmakers in order simultaneously to disable bad ones.

With these considerations in mind, let us approach formalism in a new light. Consider some of the famous marchers in formalism's parade of horribles, examples such as *R. v. Ojibway*, Fuller's statue of the truck in the park, and the poor Bolognese surgeon who, having opened the vein of a patient in the course of performing an emergency operation outdoors, was prosecuted for violating the law prohibiting "drawing blood in the streets."[92] Each of these examples reminds us that cases may arise in which application of the literal meaning of words produces an absurd result. But now we can recast the question, for we must consider not only whether the result was absurd in these cases but also whether a particular decisionmaker should be empowered to determine absurdity. Even in cases as extreme as these, formalism is only superficially about rigidity and absurdity. More fundamentally, it is about power and its allocation.

Formalism is about power, but is also about its converse—modesty. To be formalistic as a decisionmaker is to say that something is not my concern, no matter how compelling it may seem. When this attitude is applied to the budget crisis or to eviction of the starving, it seems objectionable. But when the same attitude of formalism requires judges to ignore the moral squalor of the Nazis or the Ku Klux Klan in First Amendment cases, or the guilt of the defendant in Fourth Amendment cases, or the wealth of the plaintiff who seeks to recover for medical expenses occasioned by the defendant's negligence, it is no longer clear that refusal to take all factors into account is condemnable.

Modesty, of course, has its darker side. To be modest is at times good, but avoiding authority is also avoiding responsibility. In some circumstances we want our decisionmakers to take charge and accept the consequences of their actions.[93] But it is by no means clear that just because it is good for some people to take charge some of the time, that taking charge, even accompanied by acceptance of responsibility, is a universal

---

92. The last example, from 1 S. PUFENDORF, DE JURE NATURAE ET GENTIUM LIBRI OCTO (1672), comes to us through United States v. Kirby, 74 U.S. (7 Wall.) 482, 487 (1868).

93. For a recent articulation of this view, see Michelman, *Foreword: Traces of Self-Government*, 100 HARV L. REV. 4 (1986). A useful contrast is Christie, *An Essay on Discretion*, 1986 DUKE L.J. 747.

good. "I'm in charge here" has a long but not always distinguished history. Part of what formalism is about is its inculcation of the view that sometimes it is appropriate for decisionmakers to recognize their lack of jurisdiction and to defer even when they are convinced that their own judgment is best. The opposite of modesty is arrogance, not just responsibility. True, modesty itself carries responsibility, because an actor behaving modestly is participating and thus assisting in the legitimacy of the grant of authority to someone else. But this is a responsibility of a different and limited kind. That one accepts partial responsibility for the decisions of others does not entail the obligation to substitute one's judgment for that of others.

The distinctive feature of rules, therefore, lies in their ability to be formal, to exclude from consideration in the particular case factors whose exclusion was determined without reference to the particular case at hand. This formalism of rules is not only conceptually sound and psychologically possible, but it also, as I have tried to show, is on occasion normatively desirable. Insofar as formalism disables some decisionmakers from considering some factors that may appear important to them, it allocates power to some decisionmakers and away from others. Formalism therefore achieves its value when it is thought desirable to narrow the decisional opportunities and the decisional range of a certain class of decisionmakers.

I stress that all of this is compatible with agnosticism about how rule-bound decisionmaking applies to legal systems in general, to particular legal systems, or to particular parts of legal systems. It is far from a necessary truth that legal systems must be exclusively or even largely operated as rule-governed institutions. Judgments about when to employ formalism are contextual and not inexorable, political and not logical, psychological and economic rather than conceptual. It would blunt my point about the simultaneously plausible and contingent nature of decision according to rule to offer in this acontextual setting my recommendations about what if any parts of the American or any other legal system should operate in such a fashion. My goal is only to rescue formalism from conceptual banishment. But having been readmitted to the community of respectable ideas, formalism, or decisionmaking according to rule in any strong sense, still has the burden of showing that it is appropriately used in a particular decisional domain.

IV. THE DEGREES OF RESTRICTION

I have thus far presented formalism and maximally contextual particularism as mutually exclusive opposites, incapable of coexisting within the same decisional domain. It may therefore appear that the advantages of formalism can be attained only within a system willing to accept some proportion of preposterous results and only within a system willing to have its decisionmakers ignore the novelty of the situations that come before them. Accommodation between these two forms of decisionmaking might be possible, however.

Let us contrast two cases, both arising out of the "No vehicles in the park" rule. The first involves the statue of the truck erected by the veterans' organization. The second involves an electric golf cart, as quiet as a bicycle, incapable of proceeding at greater than ten miles an hour, and emitting no noxious fumes. Can these cases be distinguished? In both cases, exclusion of the object under consideration would not seem to serve any of the purposes behind the rule, regardless of whether the purpose was the suppression of noise, the reduction of noxious odors, the limitation of high speeds, or the restriction of forms of conveyance likely to be dangerous to pedestrians. Yet despite their similarity, there appears to be a difference between the cases. The statue seems to lie *more* outside the purpose behind the rule than the golf cart. If we assume that something like twenty miles per hour is dangerous, a totally immobile vehicle is further away from the danger point than one that can go ten miles per hour. Similarly, a vehicle with a totally inoperative engine makes less noise and emits no more noxious fumes than even an electric motor.

If the difference between the cases is a matter of degree, is there some way of empowering a decisionmaker to draw the distinction without at the same time discarding all of the formalist-inspired virtues from the decisionmaking process? That is, can we empower the decisionmaker to override the rule when its application would be totally preposterous, but not when its application, still outside the purpose of the rule, would fall short of the preposterous?

The question is the same one that arises in discussions regarding higher court scrutiny of lower court decisions, and lower court scrutiny of administrative decisions and state laws. Can a decisionmaker distinguish those state interests that are "compelling" from those that are "important" from those that are merely "rational"? Can a decisionmaker distinguish "proof beyond a reasonable doubt" from "clear and convincing evidence" from "a preponderance of the evidence"? Can decisionmakers distinguish "de novo" review from review only for "abuse of discretion"? The question raised by all of these standards and others is the same: Can we admit the possibility of overriding some judgment while at the same time not opening the door to unconstrained substitution of judgment?

It is debatable whether some form of deferential but genuine review is possible. It might be argued that deferential but not toothless review is an illusion. Once the reviewing decisionmaker has the authority to look at the decision below with at least the possibility of overturning it, deference becomes largely illusory. This hypothesis equates the review process with Pandora's box: Once the record below is opened, the review is in reality de novo, and the language of abuse of discretion—or compelling interest or whatever—is used merely as a tag line when the decisionmaker wishes to reach a conclusion different from that reached below.

An alternative hypothesis posits some ground between no review and unfettered intrusiveness. There might be cases in which the presumption in favor of the result below would cause the decision to stand. Under this hypothesis, we can have rebuttable presumptions—cases in which the presumption might be overcome in particularly exigent circumstances but nevertheless controls in many or even most cases.

If this latter hypothesis is correct, it is correct as a contingent empirical matter and not as a necessary truth. My instincts are that it is *sometimes* correct—that at some times in some domains presumptions can matter without being irrebuttable. This conclusion is based on my also instinctive view that presumptions create attitudes, and that attitudes can matter. I believe, for example, that I am more likely to admire an item of clothing if I discover it myself than if my mother tells me she saw it in a shop and it would look very nice on me. But I might be wrong. Even if I am right about clothing and mothers, those attitudes might not carry over to real decisions by real decisionmakers, and even if it does, it might be empirically false more often than it is empirically true.

Moreover, even if attitudes can be changed, it may be that linguistic instructions are not particularly effective in accomplishing those changes. The observation that linguistic instructions to adopt a certain attitude are in fact potent is not universally proved by the observation that such instructions are sometimes potent, any more than the observation that such instructions are sometimes impotent proves that they are never potent. Given all of this, let me satisfy myself here with the unproved empirical conclusion that linguistic instructions are sometimes potent.

If such instructions sometimes create presumptions, and if those presumptions sometimes work, then what does this say about the possibility of what we might call a *presumptive formalism*? In order to construct such a model, we would want to equate the literal mandate of the most locally applicable written rule with the judgment of the court below. The court below can be taken to have determined, for example, that in one case operable and operating automobiles are excluded from the park, in another case golf carts are excluded from the park, and in a third case immobile statues of trucks are excluded from the park. We can then equate the reviewing court with a determination of the correct result from the perspective of the reasons behind the rule rather than the literal language of the rule itself. We might conclude that in the first case even a de novo application of the reasons would generate the same result as generated by the formalistic reading, and therefore the formal mandate would prevail uncontroversially. In the second, a de novo application of reasons would generate a different result than that generated by the rule, but the result generated by the rule remains "in the ballpark" and therefore is upheld despite its divergence from the result that would be reached by direct application of the reasons. In the third, however, a de novo application of the reasons indicates that the result generated by the rule is so far out of bounds, so absurd, so preposterous that it is analogous to an abuse of discretion and would therefore be reversed—the rule would not be applied in this case.

Under such a theory of presumptive formalism there would be a presumption in favor of the result generated by the literal and largely acontextual interpretation of the most locally applicable rule. Yet that result would be presumptive only, subject to defeasibility when less locally applicable norms, including the purpose behind the particular norm, and including norms both within and without the decisional domain at issue, offered especially exigent reasons for avoiding the result generated by the presumptively applicable norm.

Such a system would bring the advantages of predictability, stability, and constraint of decisionmakers commonly associated with decision according to rule, but would temper the occasional unpleasant consequences of such a system with an escape route that allowed some results to be avoided when their consequences would be especially outrageous. Such a system would not be without cost. First of all, the escape route would necessarily decrease the amount of predictability, stability, and decisionmaker restraint. In short, it would diminish the amount of ruleness by placing more final authority in the decisionmaker than in the rule. Second, the presumptive force attached to the formalist reading of the applicable norms would still result in some odd or suboptimal results. In this sense, such a system would fail to honor all of the goals either of unrestrained particularism or unrestrained formalism. Finally, such a system would risk collapse into one in which the presumptions were for all practical purposes either absolute or nonexistent.

Even on the assumption that such a system might be desirable in some decisional domains, this does not mean that all or part of what we commonly call the legal system might be one of those domains. It might be that formalism, even only presumptively, is a good idea, but that the goals of the legal system, in light of the decisions we ask it to make, are such that it ought not to be designed along such a model. More likely, formalism ought to be seen as a tool to be used in some parts of the legal system and not in others. Determining which parts, if any, would be susceptible to such treatment is not my agenda here, for what I have attempted to offer is only an argument that formal systems are not necessarily to be condemned. That is not to say they are universally or even largely to be applauded, nor that they are to be pervasive or even frequent within that segment of society we call the legal system. To answer this last question we must ask what the legal system, in whole or in part, is supposed to do, for only when we answer that question can we determine what kinds of tools it needs to accomplish that task.

V. Conclusion

I have concluded this analysis by venturing no more than a prolegomenon to a theory of presumptive formalism, which, to avoid the pejorative (or at least to select a slightly less pejorative pejorative) might be called a theory of *presumptive positivism*. As I have said, to urge the potential advantages of such a view in some domains is to say little if anything about whether the domain of decisions of judges or the domain of decisions of the political state backed by force is amenable to presumptively positivistic decisionmaking. But even if we put aside the question of concrete applications, the presumptiveness that is central to this model may illuminate one final usage of the word "formalistic" in its pejorative guise. It may be that, in practice, to condemn an outlook as formalistic is to condemn neither the rule-based orientation of a decisional structure nor even the inevitable over- and under-inclusiveness of any rule-based system. It may be to condemn such a system only when it is taken to be absolute rather than presumptive, when it contains no escape routes no matter how extreme the circumstances. Such a usage of "formalism" is of course much narrower than is commonly seen these days. But with that narrower usage we see that formalism is no longer something to be roundly condemned, but rather, like the relation of fanaticism to enthusiasm, or bullheadedness to integrity, merely the extreme and therefore unfortunate manifestation of a fundamentally desirable characteristic. If we recognize that, we may ultimately cease to use the epithetical deployment of "formalistic" as a substitute for argument and turn instead to the central questions involved in determining what, if anything, lies at the heart of the idea of law.

Acknowledgments

Brink, David O. "Legal Theory, Legal Interpretation, and Judicial Review." *Philosophy and Public Affairs* 17 (1988): 105–48. Copyright 1988 by Princeton University Press. Reprinted by permission of Princeton University Press.

Cohen, Felix. "The Ethical Basis of Legal Criticism." *Yale Law Journal* 41 (1931): 201–20. Reprinted by permission of the Yale Law Journal Company and Fred B. Rothman and Company.

Dworkin, Ronald. "Law as Interpretation." *Texas Law Review* 60 (1982): 527–50. Copyright 1982 by the Texas Law Review Association. Reprinted by permission.

Finnis, John. "Natural Law and Legal Reasoning." *Cleveland State Law Review* 38 (1990): 1–13. Copyright by Cleveland State University.

Golding, M.P. "Principled Decision-Making and the Supreme Court." *Columbia Law Review* 63 (1963): 35–58. Reprinted with permission.

Greenawalt, Kent. "The Enduring Significance of Neutral Principles" *Columbia Law Review* 78 (1978): 982–1021. Reprinted with permission.

Hurley, S.L. "Coherence, Hypothetical Cases, and Precedent." *Oxford Journal of Legal Studies* 10 (1990): 221–51. Reprinted with the permission of Oxford University Press.

Kress, Kenneth J. "Legal Reasoning and Coherence Theories: Dworkin's Rights Thesis, Retroactivity, and the Linear Order of Decisions." *California Law Review* 72 (1984): 369–402. Reprinted with permission. Copyright 1984 by the California Law Review, Inc.

Levi, Edward H. "The Nature of Judicial Reasoning." *University of Chicago Law Review* 32 (1965): 395–409. Reprinted with the permission of the University of Chicago Law School.

MacCormick, Neil. "Argumentation and Interpretation in Law." *Ratio Juris* 6 (1993): 16–29. Reprinted with the permission of Basil Blackwell Ltd.

MacCormick, Neil. "Coherence in Legal Justification." In *Festgabe für Ota Weinberger zum 65. Geburtstag* (Berlin: Duncker & Humblot, 1984): 37–53. Reprinted with the permission of Duncker & Humblot.

Pound, Roscoe. "The Theory of Judicial Decision—III." *Harvard Law Review* 36 (1923): 940–59. Copyright 1923 by the Harvard Law Review Association.

Raz, Joseph. "The Relevance of Coherence." *Boston University Law Review* 72 (1992): 273–321. Reprinted with the permission of *Boston University Law Review*. Copyright by the *Boston University Law Review*. The publisher bears no responsibility for any errors which have occurred in reprinting, translation or editing.

Schauer, Frederick. "Formalism." *Yale Law Journal* 97 (1988): 509–48. Reprinted by permission of the Yale Law Journal Company and Fred B. Rothman and Company.